Ray Eden
1991

ADLAI
STEVENSON

ADLAI STEVENSON

His Life and Legacy

Porter McKeever

QUILL
WILLIAM MORROW
NEW YORK

Library of Congress Cataloging-in-Publication Data

McKeever, Porter.
   Adlai Stevenson: his life and legacy / Porter McKeever.
      p.   cm.
   Bibliography: p.
   ISBN 0-688-10387-1
   1. Stevenson, Adlai E. (Adlai Ewing), 1900–1965. 2. Statesmen—
United States—Biography. 3. United States—Politics and
government—1945–   . I. Title.
E748.S84M4   1989
973.921'092'4—dc19
   [B]   89-30055
                                                                      CIP

Printed in the United States of America

First Quill Edition

1 2 3 4 5 6 7 8 9 10

BOOK DESIGN BY NICOLA MAZZELLA

For Susan
And for
Jim, Bill, Karen, and Cho-Liang

Acknowledgments

ANYONE WRITING ABOUT ADLAI STEVENSON quickly accumulates a debt of gratitude to four who have gone before: John Bartlow Martin, Kenneth S. Davis, and Walter Johnson with Carol Evans.

John Bartlow Martin's *Adlai Stevenson of Illinois,* published in 1976, and *Adlai Stevenson and the World,* published a year later, both by Doubleday, are the product of prodigious research, extensive interviews, and meticulous writing which will always be a valued resource.

Kenneth S. Davis brought to his two books, *A Prophet in His Own Country,* published by Doubleday in 1957, and *The Politics of Honor,* a revised and updated version of the earlier book published by Putnam's in 1967, not only the talents of a fine writer and historian, but the advantage of having previously written a biography of General Dwight D. Eisenhower, and most of all, extensive interviews with Adlai himself.

Walter Johnson as editor and Carol Evans as assistant editor of *The Papers of Adlai Stevenson,* published in eight volumes by Little, Brown between 1972 and 1979, produced a model of scholarship and insight.

Special thanks are due to Adlai's three sons, most especially Adlai Stevenson III and his wife, Nancy, and Adlai's sister, Mrs. Ernest Ives. Every request for assistance was met promptly, generously, and without any request in return for an opportunity to review or comment on the manuscript. More wholehearted and trusting cooperation could not be imagined.

One concrete result of Adlai III's help was access to the legal proceedings in which the sons, joined by Mrs. John Carpenter, Ellen Stevenson's mother, undertook to have a conservator appointed to assume control over Mrs. Stevenson's finances. Their attorney, Mr. Lowell E. Sachnoff of Sachnoff, Weaver and Rubenstein, was particularly helpful in guiding me through the long record of suits and countersuits that marked this sad chapter in the lives of all concerned.

All the contacts with the Stevenson family were generously assisted and augmented by Phyllis Gustafson, secretary to Adlai III, who had served his father in a similar capacity.

From the beginning, Carol Evans was an invaluable guide to material and to people who could provide information and insights.

Requests for interviews received ready and warm responses. Judge Carl McGowan, although terminally ill, talked with characteristic acuity far longer than was good for him. George Ball, Bill Blair, John Brademas, Harlan Cleveland, Mr. and Mrs. Edison Dick, Ben Heineman, Philip Klutznick, Newton Minow, Dawn Clark Netsch, John B. Oakes, David Oskandy, James B. Reston, John L. Steele, Marietta Tree, Harriet Welling, and Willard Wirtz were especially generous in the time they gave to my requests.

Others who deserve special thanks are Alice Arlen, Charlotte Brenneis, Frances FitzGerald, Dorothy Fosdick, Stanley A. Frankel, Richard N. Gardner, John McT. Kahin, Daisy Kwoh, Eric Sevareid, Christiana Walford, Franklin Hall Williams, Thomas H. Wright, and Wilson W. Wyatt.

The counsel, encouragement, and assistance of Hedley Donovan, Thomas Morgan, and Arthur Schlesinger, Jr., require grateful acknowledgment.

Garry Trudeau's 1984 *Doonesbury* cartoon dramatized the inspiration that still lingers from the Stevenson career for a generation of Americans and I appreciate his permission to reproduce it.

The Stevenson papers in the Seeley G. Mudd Manuscript Library at Princeton University, which also includes material from John Bartlow Martin's awesome research work, is a treasure for any biographer. There is added good fortune in the stewardship of Mrs. Nancy Bressler, curator of public papers at the Princeton University Library. Her knowledge of the collection and her spirit of helpfulness often enable her to anticipate a researcher's needs and have the documents ready for examination immediately upon request. I was fortunate, too, that material the State Department had refused to release to Walter Johnson for *The Papers of Adlai Stevenson* has since been declassified and was made available to me.

The Oral History Collection at Columbia University proved to be an especially valuable source, thanks to a special project undertaken not long after Adlai's death that resulted in over five thousand pages of interviews with seventy-one people. In taking advantage of this storehouse, the help of Ronald J. Grele and Andor Skotnes, director and assistant director, respectively, of the Oral History Office, and their colleagues was uninstinting. I am grateful, too, to Megan Floyd Desnoyers, supervisory archivist at the John F. Kennedy Library, for access to interviews in its Oral History Collection. The Library of the Century Association and its librarian, Rodger Friedman, also provided much-appreciated assistance.

My former secretary of nearly twenty years, Barbara Eddy McLanahan, was quick to answer my numerous calls for help with such cheer and efficiency it would be easy to take them for granted.

I hope that Ralph G. Martin and Herbert Mitgang will not be too unhappy that they gave me the courage to undertake this work.

Carol Rinzler's talents as a lawyer are joined to exceptional skill as an editor. I was fortunate to have the benefit of both throughout the planning and writing of this book.

Finally, two expressions of very special appreciation are merited. Lisa Drew, senior editor and vice president of William Morrow, has provided inspiring support from the outset of this effort. Her understanding, knowledge, and wisdom, added to a sharp editorial eye, created a rewarding experience for me and, for the reader, most certainly a better book. If medals were awarded for patience and tolerance, my wife, Susan, would have earned the highest orders during her husband's obsessive preoccupation. In addition, she offered insights and suggestions that have improved what I earnestly hope will be an enriching time with a man unique in our political history.

Pelham, New York

Contents

Acknowledgments 9

1. Merging Streams 15
2. In the Wake of Tragedy 32
3. From Bloomington to Moscow to Marriage 48
4. Onto the World Stage 72
5. "Combat" Politics Begins 107
6. The Guv 128
7. Idealism with Muscle 149
8. Reluctant Candidate 173
9. "Let's Talk Sense" 199
10. C(2)K(1) 224
11. "Mistimed but Not Miscast" 247
12. "A Funny Thing Happened . . ." 265
13. "Chronic Stamina" Encounters McCarthy 278
14. Titular Leader 311
15. Eager Candidate 340
16. "This Will Lose You Votes" 362
17. Fulfilled Prophecies 391
18. Courting the Lightning 414
19. Disappointed Hopes 437

20. The Biggest Disappointment   465
21. From Crisis to Crisis with Kennedy   481
22. More Crises—and Tragedy   508
23. "Blinded by the Sunset and Groping for the Path Down"   540
24. "A Strange Animal"   566

    Bibliography   573
    Index   577

CHAPTER ONE
Merging Streams

"THE STEVENSONS MUST HAVE Chinese blood; they worship their ancestors so much."

Ellen Borden Stevenson's comment, made shortly before suing Adlai for divorce, was not intended to be either accurate or friendly; but it did contain a strong strain of truth. The Stevenson family and American history were intricately intertwined. Adlai Stevenson was endlessly fascinated and deeply influenced by both.

The first Stevenson in America, William, arrived in Pennsylvania from northern Ireland in 1748. He married there and in 1763 moved to what is now Statesville, North Carolina. A Presbyterian convert, his stentorian oratory and short stature led to his becoming widely known as Little Gabriel—foreshadowing in religion the impact of his descendant's eloquence in politics.

James, the fifth of William's twelve children, married Nancy Brevard, daughter of Colonel Hugh Brevard, a hero of the Revolution. Her uncle, Ephraim, was the author of the Mecklenburg Declaration in which the North Carolina county declared its independence from king and Parliament more than a year before Thomas Jefferson more elegantly and decisively wrote a similar declaration in Philadelphia. Adlai was always immensely proud of the family tie to the birth of American freedom.

James and Nancy crossed the mountains through the Cumberland Gap and settled in Christian County, Kentucky, where the Presbyterian church and a school went up along with the new log cabin homes. Jefferson Davis lived nearby. Not far away, Abraham Lincoln was born. John

Turner Stevenson, the sixth of their nine children, became the father of Adlai Ewing Stevenson, Vice President of the United States in Grover Cleveland's second term. Thus, the unusual name of Adlai was introduced into American political life.

Adlai I, as he became known in the family, was responsible for merging another historic stream into the Stevenson family. But the course of true love did not run smoothly for him. When he was sixteen, his father lost his tobacco crop to frost. Setting free the few slaves he owned, he moved in 1852 to Bloomington, Illinois, where he set up a small sawmill. Adlai I worked with his father and taught school to earn money for college. He and cousin James Ewing sought out Centre College in Danville, Kentucky, a citadel of Presbyterianism presided over by the Reverend Lewis Warner Green. Adlai I promptly fell in love with his daughter Letitia, and, after long delays caused by deaths and hardships in both families, they eventually married. Thus the Stevensons were united with one of the most distinguished families of early Virginia.

Among the Green family's ancestors was Oxford-educated Colonel Joshua Fry, professor of mathematics at William and Mary College who collaborated with Peter Jefferson, father of Thomas, in preparing the first accurate map of the "Inhabited Parts of Virginia." Facsimiles of this historic map were proudly shown to visitors to the governor's mansion in Springfield and Adlai's home in Libertyville. In the French and Indian War, Joshua had been given command of the Virginia militia, and on the march to take Fort Duquesne from the French, he was thrown from his horse and killed. His twenty-two-year-old aide and kinsman, Lieutenant Colonel George Washington, assumed command and carved into a large oak tree near Mills Creek, Maryland, "Under this tree lies the body of the good, the just and noble Fry." Another ancestor, Dr. Thomas Walker, a physician, surveyor, engineer and explorer, named the Cumberland Gap.

After Dr. Green's death, Letitia and her mother moved to Chenoa, Illinois, not far from Bloomington, to live with Letitia's older sister, Julia, and her husband, Mr. Matthew Scott, formerly of Lexington, Kentucky. The courtship that had been interrupted nine years earlier by the death of Adlai I's father now resumed in rnest. Mrs. Green was not pleased, even though by now Adlai I was prosecuting attorney of Metamora and was becoming well-known in political circles. To her, the Stevensons were far beneath the Greens and the Scotts. Letitia, however, was as determined as her suitor, and the wedding finally took place at the Scott home, now carefully restored by Adlai's sister, Elizabeth "Buffie" Ives.

Tiny Letitia Green Stevenson, eight years younger than her six-foot-tall husband, unremittingly looked up at him with love and respect. His adoration fully matched hers. They always addressed each other as "Mrs. Stevenson" and "Mr. Stevenson." Strangely, this formality only seemed to underscore the profound nature of their relationship that stretched un-broken until their deaths only five months apart in 1914. Of their four children, one daughter died young, two other girls became belles of Washington society when their father was Vice President, and a son, Lewis, became the father of Adlai.

Metamora held little promise for the practice of law, so in 1869, after his term as prosecuting attorney ended, Adlai I moved to Bloomington and formed a partnership with Cousin James. They were Democrats in a predominantly Republican region but their practice prospered, with Ewing concentrating on the law and Stevenson pursuing his already active political career.

Adlai I was a warm, generous, outgoing, buoyant personality, a great storyteller, well liked even by those who opposed him politically. In 1874 he ran for Congress in a strong Republican district. Grant was President, Republicans controlled the Congress by large majorities, and Reconstruction had built walls of bitter emotion. Republican papers attacked him as a "vile secessionist," but it was a former Union Army officer who wrote the newspapers refuting the charges. Despite the odds, he won.

He won again in 1878 running on both Democratic and Greenback party tickets. Personal popularity and constant speaking appearances around his district, however, could not sustain a congressional career in such a staunchly Republican territory.

When Grover Cleveland captured the White House for the Democrats in 1884 for the first time since the Civil War, he appointed the Bloomington Democrat first assistant postmaster general. The long Republican reign left the Democrats hungry for jobs, and Stevenson soon gained both fame and notoriety, depending on the political viewpoint, by replacing forty thousand Republican postmasters with patronage-seeking Democrats. For this he became known as the Headsman. When Cleveland then appointed Stevenson to a federal judgeship, vengeful Republicans blocked it. Grateful Democrats, however, nominated him as Cleveland's running mate in 1892. They won by a plurality of 372,736. They carried Illinois, but without much help from McLean County. Stevenson said it was immigrants and workingmen who voted for him and not his successful and socialite friends; a comment that could well have been made later by his grandson.

In 1900, the year Adlai was born, Grandfather Stevenson was again nominated for Vice President by the Democratic party. This time, William Jennings Bryan was his running mate. The country was properous and weary of idealism. They lost decisively. (One is reminded of 1952 and 1956). His final try for public office came eight years later in a race for governor. But once again it was a Republican year. William Howard Taft carried Illinois by a margin of 179,122 votes. Stevenson lost by only 23,164 votes, and retired to enjoy well-won prestige in Bloomington.

Their years in Washington demonstrated how important Letitia was to her husband's career. She was a keen observer and judge of people, and a charming hostess. Her strong character and dignified demeanor cloaked suffering from migraine headaches and severe rheumatism that often required her to wear leg braces, especially when standing for receptions. But she did not let these handicaps restrict her activities.

She worked hard to establish the Daughters of the American Revolution, thinking it might help heal the breach between the North and South, and she succeeded the former first lady, Mrs. Benjamin Harrison, to become its second president general. She was also an early leader in the National Congress of Mothers, which later became the National Congress of Parents and Teachers. She advocated that "all nursing mothers should read *Robert's Rules of Order.*"

Letitia's Washington friendship with Mrs. Phoebe Apperson Hearst of California, wealthy widow of Senator George R. Hearst, had far-reaching consequences. Her son, William Randolph, turned the wealth his father had made in western copper and gold mines to the building of a newspaper empire. The Stevenson son, Lewis, later worked for both mother and son, as a result of which California would become the birthplace of the future governor of Illinois.

The Stevensons epitomized one of the streams of migration that built the Midwest. They had come up the Cumberland Gap through Kentucky and the Carolinas and were largely Presbyterian and Democratic.

But there was another stream—flowing through Pennsylvania from New England and New York, strongly Quaker and Republican. It was these streams that merged in central and southern Illinois and produced Adlai Stevenson. It was the latter stream, the maternal side of Adlai's family, that first arrived in Bloomington. Adlai's favorite ancestor was his maternal grandfather, Jesse Fell, to whom Lincoln was indebted for a large part of his political progress.

Fell was born in Chester County, Pennsylvania, in 1808. He worked his way through boarding school and in 1828 headed west on foot. He sold books, worked for an abolitionist newspaper, and then "paused for two years" (a phrase Adlai loved), to work in a Steubenville, Ohio, law office, study law, and pass the bar examination there in October 1832. A month later he began going from town to town in eastern Illinois seeking the location for a career that proved to be one of extraordinary usefulness. In Springfield he called on John T. Stuart, who later became Lincoln's law partner, and who advised Fell to go to Bloomington, which had just been designated county seat of the new McLean County and as yet had no lawyer.

Fell's arrival in Bloomington in 1832, six years after its founding, increased its population to ninety-eight. Although his law practice later prospered as people kept arriving to take up land, it was buying and selling land himself that gave him his start. He often rode eighty miles a day on horseback looking for good, fertile land. In his saddlebags two shabby volumes of Shakespeare bounced along with him. His meager roadside meals were seasoned with sonnets or scenes and speeches from his favorite, *Richard III.*

In the winter of 1834–35 he felt obliged to go to Vandalia, then the state capital, to fight against a bill in the General Assembly to reduce the size of McLean County. At his boardinghouse he met and began a fateful friendship with a young member of the General Assembly, Abraham Lincoln.

Like his grandson, Fell's interest kept reaching beyond the law. He started Bloomington's first newspaper, the *Bloomington Observer and McLean County Advocate,* which lasted for only twenty issues. His tireless boosterism then found other channels. He fought hard in the 1830s and 1840s to bring railroad lines through Bloomington and personally secured the right-of-way for the first railroad. He helped found the towns of Clinton, El Paso, Leroy, Lexington, Pontiac, and Towanda. Another town he started, in 1854, was called North Bloomington; but Fell soon was engaged in a campaign to have the first teachers college west of the Alleghenies established there, so the name was changed to Normal. He donated land for the campus and led the drive to raise the $141,000 needed to outbid Peoria for the college. Abraham Lincoln drew up the bond to which eighty prominent Bloomingtonians subscribed to underwrite the pledge. The three-mile road that then connected the two towns is today appropriately named Fell Avenue. Its trees are another of Fell's legacies. In Normal alone he planted more than ten thousand. The treeless prairies of Illinois became dotted with green oases of trees he provided by the scores of thousands from his own nursery. He was unquestionably the greatest tree planter in the Midwest.

After a second unsuccessful try at newspaper publishing, he tried again in 1851 with a paper he soon called *The Pantagraph,* derived from the Greek words *pan* and *graph* signifying "write all things." Fell used this forum to campaign for public education, Prohibition, sidewalks, fire-fighting equipment, sewers, pavement—and Republicans. As the Whig party began to fall apart, he became a major figure in establishing the Republican party in Illinois. The paper prospered and remains to this day one of the most reputable and influential newspapers in central Illinois.

It was natural, then, that when Stephen Douglas came to Bloomington to make a speech, he would call on Jesse Fell. It was also natural for the latter to suggest that Douglas share the platform with Fell's friend, Lincoln. The Lincoln-Douglas debates did not help Lincoln win the Senate seat he sought, but they did move him onto the national political scene.

Like Adlai in early 1952, Lincoln was little known outside the Midwest, and Fell urged him to write a short autobiography to use for campaign purposes. Lincoln called the idea "foolish" and refused; but Fell persisted. Finally, Lincoln handed him a three-page sketch that he quickly sent to a friend, Joseph L. Lewis, in West Chester, Pennsylvania. This use of it played an important part in winning the crucial support of the Pennsylvania delegation for Lincoln's candidacy. Fell kept busy circulating this and other campaign material throughout the country while his brother became Lincoln's floor manager at the convention. The biography written for Fell, the only one in the subject's own handwriting, is one of the most precious items of Lincolniana in existence.

The Fell/Lincoln legacy also included an event that helped shape Adlai's attitude toward civil liberties and civil rights in the heated debates on McCarthyism and on school segregation in the 1950s.

Lincoln's assassination was a profound shock to his many friends in Bloomington and no one was more grief-stricken than Jesse Fell. He presided over a mass meeting in the town square the day after Lincoln's death and spoke of his old friend "with singular eloquence." So it was not surprising that furor swept the Free Congregational Church on Sunday, April 23 when the fervently abolitionist pastor, the Reverend Charles Ellis, delivered a sermon holding Lincoln morally responsible for his own assassination!

The minister argued that before God, John Wilkes Booth was less to blame for Lincoln's death than were the Founding Fathers who had permitted slavery to be woven into the Constitution. Lincoln, he added, had supported the "slave" Constitution until events forced him to issue the Emancipation Proclamation. "He had not the moral courage," Dr. Ellis cried, "to step forth like a strong man in his might and do what his better nature told him was his highest duty."

The angry uproar almost prevented the completion of the sermon, and a few days later a full meeting of the members of the church was held for the specific purpose of demanding the pastor's resignation.

Jesse Fell could only have been appalled by this attack on his friend in the church that, having earlier forsaken his Quaker piety, he had helped to establish. Yet, instead, he submitted a substitute resolution that opposed the demand for resignation, asserted the right of any man to express his views in the church, and reproved the "mob" that had caused the disturbance in the church on Sunday. It must have been a singularly effective appeal because it even persuaded those who were being reproved to vote for it, almost unanimously. Although publicly vindicated, the Reverend Ellis decided his usefulness in Bloomington was at an end and a few days later left town.

This was but one of many incidents that Fell's grandson would recount in unbounded admiration of the man's character and career. He saw Fell as the kind of man he himself would most like to be; the "best sort of citizen," a man who could be moderate, pacific, and yet an effective leader; a man who would persist patiently and stubbornly when principle was involved; a fearless visionary who was also shrewd, practical, and useful.

One of Fell's farseeing and practical moves was to reach back to his old Quaker community and persuade a former neighbor, William Osborne Davis, to come to Bloomington. Davis arrived shortly before his twentieth birthday in the fall of 1859, leaving behind a tradition of six generations of successful farming in Chester County. But William Osborne disliked farming and showed a distinct preference for intellectual pursuits.

That first winter in Illinois, he taught in a school Fell had set up in his home. The next spring he set out with some thirty-five others from Bloomington to look for gold in Colorado. The gold eluded them but they profited from the sale of their supplies. Returning to Illinois, he did guard duty in Springfield the first year of the Civil War. When President Lincoln appointed Fell Army paymaster, he took Davis with him to Louisville as his clerk. Letters from Louisville were addressed to "My dearest little Eliza," Fell's daughter, whom he married on June 17, 1863. By then he had been appointed a clerk in the federal Internal Revenue Service and he and his bride moved to Washington, which he found "full of interest." He also found that his health "would not stand the confinement of office work" and within a few months the young couple returned home to farm.

Soon, however, they moved into town and Davis assumed active management of *The Pantagraph*. It is the only survivor of 140 papers that have been started in that area, which is largely due to the dedication and business acumen of W. O. Davis. By 1871 he had acquired full control, and for nearly forty years directed its operations in almost every detail until it had the largest circulation in downstate Illinois.

Much of Adlai's feeling for Jesse Fell came to him through Grandfather Davis. He resolutely refused to talk about himself but delighted in talk about his father-in-law who, in many ways, served him as his model. Like him, he was shrewd, conscientious, and very capable; deeply committed to the public weal. He was also almost obsessively concerned with neatness and with health. He also possessed skills, later noted in his grandson, for drawing out other people, for being a good listener, and for being able to talk wittily on many subjects.

Another trait Adlai inherited was that of being close with money. Davis carried a pocket notebook in which he jotted down every expenditure; through practice and preachment he promoted thrift at every opportunity.

By the end of the 1880s, Davis was one of Bloomington's most prominent citizens. In his photos his face looks kind and confident. The Davis home was ornately and splendidly Victorian; the life-style within it comfortable though unostentatious. Summers were spent at the northern Michigan resort of Charlevoix. By then the family included a son and two daughters. The second child, Helen, became the unusually influential mother of Adlai Stevenson.

From their earliest childhood it was assumed that the son of the Democratic Vice President and the daughter of the Republican publisher would be married. Lewis and Helen also took it for granted. The wedding in 1893 was one of the most brilliant social events Bloomington had ever known. Governor John Peter Altgeld attended and the secretary of the navy came from Washington. The newspapers called it "a triumph of love over politics." The marriage, though, was not a happy one; fluctuating between loving family scenes and bitter, wounding quarrels, punctuated by long separations. The consequences clouded their lives and those of their children.

The early years had seemed idyllic. They had walked to school together; were in and out of each other's homes; sharing happy summers with their families at Charlevoix. When Lewis was at Exeter, they corresponded frequently, and in August 1891 they became secretly engaged. A year later Helen chose to let the engagement become known by wearing openly a gift from Lewis instead of making a formal announcement. She then went to Europe with her sister Jessie and returned to be married the following year, after Adlai I had been inaugurated as Vice President. She had chosen to be out of the country while her fiancé was working for his father's election. Her divorcement from her husband-to-be's political activities was echoed in her son's sad marriage.

The European honeymoon, though, was gay and eventful. Thanks to Grandfather Stevenson's prominence and letters from other prominent Americans to important people in Europe, they were handsomely entertained, everywhere but in Monte Carlo. Lewis decided he wanted to take his distinguished-looking bride to the gambling casino. The doorman bowed Helen in but stopped Lewis. "He probably thought she was royalty incognito," Lewis would recount gleefully. "But he said I was too young to gamble. He wouldn't even let me inside."

Gaiety, however, could quickly be replaced by bitter quarrels. Both were sensitive, high-strung, willful, and plagued by health problems that turned their gifts for articulation into cutting weapons. They could also be loving, charming, witty, and wonderful company. Dinner parties could be sparkling affairs with stories passing back and forth in mutual appreciation and enjoyment. To bright conversation could be added Helen's lovely contralto voice, Lewis's magic tricks, and the skill of both of them as mimics.

Handsome, blue-eyed, balding, Lewis made friends everywhere, except perhaps in Bloomington, toward which he and Helen both felt a bit superior. He also seemed to be ridden with fears. He kept a gun under the bed and once when someone rang the doorbell late at night, he opened the window and fired. At the same time, he was at ease in the company of the famous, but he was also haunted by a sense of inadequacy and torn by migraine headaches and pain from a youthful hunting accident.

When he was fourteen Lewis had gone hunting on a Sunday with some other boys, violating a stricture from his father against such activities on the Lord's Day. Lifting his gun for a quick shot, he failed to pull it tightly to his shoulder and the recoil sent him reeling. By the time he reached home his badly bruised shoulder was black, hot, and swollen. But he said nothing and weeks of pain passed before the injury was finally exposed. Doctors quickly operated, scraped the bone, but too much time had passed and a chronic infection had developed that they could neither diagnose nor cure. The result was a slight crippling of the right arm and an almost constant pain ranging from dull to acute that people seldom discerned except when he shook hands. Then, he would shove his right shoulder forward, brace his elbow slightly against his side—and smile. This infection could well have been the reason he spent much of his life in the quest for health.

After Philips Exeter Academy in New Hampshire Lewis attended Illinois State Normal University, and there developed a close friendship with Major John Wesley Powell, a founder both of the National Geographic Society and the U.S. Geological Survey, of which he became the head. Powell had been his father's friend for nearly forty years so it was not difficult for Lewis to ask for a place on a Geological Survey party into the Southwest. Lewis loved the desert and believed that its climate improved his health. The kinship was further encouraged by the fact that Powell had lost part of his right arm in the fierce Civil War battle of Shiloh.

Lewis took his new bride to Washington where he worked as private secretary for his father. When the term ended, his mother's friend, Mrs. Phoebe Hearst, employed him to help manage her mining properties in Arizona and New Mexico. This fitted in with his desire to return to the West for health reasons, but he also proved to be an effective manager of the enterprises. Additional responsibilities for the Hearst estates prompted him to move to Los Angeles in 1899. Not long after his arrival, his father's nomination as Vice President on the William Jennings Bryan ticket stimulated someone to write a long feature story on him in the city's leading newspaper. He quickly became well-known in southern California, especially among Democrats, and his name appeared frequently in political news stories.

The publicity, and Phoebe Hearst's strong endorsement of his work for the Hearst properties, commended him to her son, William Randolph, who was a Democratic member of Congress from New York with far-reaching political ambitions. In 1904, Hearst was looking for an assistant general manager of his newly purchased *Los Angeles Examiner*. Lewis had enjoyed a brief plunge into journalism a few years earlier as the result of a journey to Japan and China, without Helen. He had written articles on the Sino-Japanese conflict and had been introduced to the empress of China. He quickly accepted Hearst's offer.

When the great San Francisco earthquake struck on April 18, 1906, the *Examiner* organized the first relief train to reach the devastated city. Lewis Stevenson was in charge. Many grateful parents whose babies were born in relief tents named them for Lewis.

A clear path toward a successful public career in California was opening, but that very year he abandoned the West and returned to Bloomington. Helen had never felt at home in the West and took frequent trips back to Bloomington. Lewis, too, felt the pull of the prairies and of the family interests that centered there. Their parents urgings also were persuasive. Indeed, Helen's widowed father had given the young couple the home at 1316 East Washington Avenue where Adlai's sister still lives. But it was Lewis's Aunt Julia, Mrs. Matthew Scott, who tipped the scales. She had been a widow since 1901 with the responsibility for land holdings that, in forty-nine farms, stretched over more than twelve thousand acres. She asked Lewis to become her farm manager at a generous salary, and he agreed.

Their home on East Washington Street was a two-story, ten-room, gray stucco Victorian gingerbread building, bordered on two sides by a wide piazza. It was topped with a high Gothic gable—an attic that was almost an additional story. It is set well back from the broad tree-arched street and now, as then, is half concealed by trees and bushes. In those days the backyard, almost an acre in expanse, sloped down to a cow pasture and a small stream bridged by two shaky planks from which Adlai would catch crayfish and sail home-made boats.

Inside, the entrance hallway's walls were covered with mementoes of Lewis's travels in the Far East and Europe. The drawing room also contained similarly expensive artifacts. Family history was marked by a plain walnut table, the work of a Quaker ancestor during the Colonial period. Children were barred from this room except on special occasions.

Family life centered in the well-stocked library, brightened by three large bay windows and warmed by another fireplace. A facsimile of the Lincoln autobiography hung near bookshelves lined with volumes ancestors had bequeathed to them. Here Helen read aloud to her children and presided with a strength of personality that was pervasive.

Before settling in Bloomington, Lewis went to Europe to consult a "famous" neurologist he had heard about regarding his severe, recurring headaches. Helen, with Adlai and Buffie, went to Winter Park, Florida, with Grandfather Davis to treat Helen's lingering and debilitating cough. Failure to improve caused her to enter a sanatorium, but unhappiness with its rigid regimen prompted Grandfather Stevenson to send her with a nurse to a relative in Augusta, Georgia. Grandfather Davis reported to Lewis that she was improving but was "nervously weak from the excitement of her destructive illness." This pattern of separate quests for treatment of illnesses, with increasing emphasis on Helen's case of "nerves," was repeated in various forms throughout both their lives.

Helen was thirty-eight when they returned to Bloomington; a tall, slender, almost regal, and almost beautiful woman. Her long oval face, pale in complexion, was topped by a mass of dark hair brushed back from her high forehead to a soft bun. Her personality radiated strength even though her body was slight and frail. Actually, she had nearly died from pneumonia in Berkeley three years earlier and ever after health was a major, and finally obsessive, concern.

A decade earlier she had come home from New Mexico to have her first child, Elizabeth Ewing Stevenson, called Buffie, at the Davis home. Her second pregnancy, however, was a difficult one and she dared not travel; a condition made more painful by the fact that her mother was dying. On February 5, 1900, in Los Angeles, an anxious delivery produced a large boy weighing eleven pounds and eight ounces. Long before, it had been decided that he would be named for his grandfather.

The name Adlai appears only once in the Bible in the first book of the Chronicles of Israel, which tells how King David called into Jerusalem all the appointed officials of his realm to tell them of the Temple that would be built by Solomon. In the lengthy naming of these officials it was set forth that "over the herds that were in the valley was Shaphat the son of Adlai." The Reverend Richard Paul Graebel, minister of the First Presbyterian Church in Springfield, who became a close friend of Adlai's, stated that the meaning of the name in ancient Hebrew was "my witness; my ornament."

He was adored by parents and especially grandparents. At his birth, Grandfather Davis wrote Helen congratulating her on "the successful launching of this little Presidential craft." Unusually intense affection also was evident from his sister who early forsook sibling rivalry for a protective, almost motherly role. Buffie has written fondly, for example, of Sunday noon dinners presided over by Grandfather Stevenson in a Prince Albert coat at which Aunt Letitia always sneaked an extra helping of ice cream with chocolate sauce to Adlai but not to her. After dinner Grandfather Stevenson would select a volume from the library and read in a deep-voiced, dramatic manner such awesome items as Marc Antony's speech over the body of Caesar, Robert Ingersoll's funeral oration for his brother, the legend of Ichabod Crane, or dark and bloody sections of *Hamlet* or *Macbeth*. The children would listen in both horror and adoration. Adlai believed that it was his grandfather who aroused in him such an interest in American history that before he reached high school he had read all thirteen volumes of Markham's *The Real America in Romance*.

It was Helen who dominated family life. She had studied voice in Germany and in Paris and would lead the children in song fests that included such favorites as "The Bicycle Built for Two," "Can She Bake a

Cherry Pie, Billy Boy?" and sad Civil War songs, but also went on to German lieder, French art songs, and operatic arias. Most of all, she read to them. In fact, learning by listening became the principal means by which, throughout his life, her son accumulated his massive store of information.

The books she read to them, Buffie recalls, were "a magnificent variety" of classic novels and, of course, much poetry. Their favorite was *The Family Album of Poetry and Song,* a collection from "the best poets, English, Scottish, Irish and American," edited by William Cullen Bryant. Their mother's carefully cultivated reading instilled in Buffie a love for the theater and in Adlai a lifelong love affair with words as the conveyor of ideas and feelings. When Lewis was not traveling, he would sit by contentedly reading the newspapers and magazines that he preferred to "literature."

Too often, though, these idyllic scenes were torn by slashes of sharp-tongued tempers. Buffie has written that her father's outbursts could "come as unexpectedly as a summer storm." Many of their quarrels came from the clash of Lewis's impulsive generosity with Helen's inherited dislike of wasteful expenditure. She was horrified when she learned that before their marriage he had used his savings to buy a diamond ring to be buried with his sister, Mary. She was even more exasperated at Lewis's explanation that he had done it because "Mary always wanted to have a diamond."

During one of these storms, Lewis snapped, "Well, you took me for better or worse." To which Helen shot back, "Well, you are worse than I took you for!" This repartee shocked them into laughter. More often the ending was marked by Lewis storming out of the house, or Helen retreating to her bedroom, or both. Early in their married life, they began to live in separate rooms.

Difficulties extending beyond quick tempers and cutting tongues are evident in the letters that marked their intermittent separations. One from Helen to Lewis as early as 1899, six years after their marriage, was loving but sad. "Your birthday letter was written in a tone I don't quite understand. . . . I regret indeed, my love, if you are feeling old and dissatisfied [he was thirty-one] . . . I wish my love could compensate somewhat for all you feel you have lost in life. . . . Please do not grieve or resent the years already gone." When he was in Europe in 1906, he reported he was leaving a German sanatorium for treatment in Lausanne to "keep all unpleasant thought of you out of my mind." Before returning home, he wrote: "Your last letter pleased me greatly. It was really the first evidence of affection you have shown in a long time and made me very happy. It's all been so strange, so unnatural and untimely. We can never go through such an ordeal again. . . . I love you my Helen with all my heart . . . I'll be home soon. We will then begin anew." As late as 1917, Lewis was writing to Helen: "I counted for little as your thought seemed to be to repulse me rather than encourage our trying to get closer together, which I have always longed for. Possibly it will be different in the future. I hope so." It was a vain hope.

There were happy times for father and son, however. Adlai traveled with Lewis to the farms he supervised and they tramped together through the fields. Lewis was an early and enthusiastic "scientific" farmer, introducing new crop rotations, new fertilizer treatments, new methods of cultivation, and was a pioneer in introducing soybeans as a cash crop. Lewis bought one of the first automobiles seen in Bloomington and he and Adlai would take off in all kinds of weather over the unsurfaced roads. They would unload their tent, spirit stove, and folding beds in farmyard or pasture, eat and sleep outdoors, and swim in streams along the way; even when it was so cold, according to Adlai, that the cows looked on in astonishment. Adlai also spent hours lying under the car, happily tinkering, with oil dripping down onto his face.

Lewis taught Adlai the price of corn before he knew how to spell. The fact is that Adlai never did learn how to spell. But he never lost the love for the land that was instilled in him on these journeys.

Despite these happy interludes, letters from the period suggest the mother and two children saw themselves in a secret alliance against their father and his temper. He had to be handled; to be humored; his orders were not to be taken too seriously as they might, suddenly and reproachfully, be changed. At one point, Buffie wrote in her journal that she hated her father and blamed him for her mother's poor health.

Certainly, health was an unceasing concern. The cold baths indulged in on field trips became a daily regimen at home. When sleeping porches were recommended, Helen promptly built one and required Buffie and Adlai to sleep there even on bitterly cold nights. Health fads were quickly adopted. When deep breathing before open windows was prescribed, no one breathed more deeply than the Stevensons; health foods from Battle Creek, and orange juice and milk by the gallons were consumed; onion soup was adopted as a relief for headaches; each mouthful of food was to be chewed a prescribed, and large, number of times. These and more nostrums were avidly pursued.

In a setting where protective mothers were the norm, Helen stood out. If she was near the school at the end of the day, she would pick up Adlai in her electric car to "rescue" him from his "rowdy" companions. This tendency was so embarrassing that he resorted to various subterfuges, once hiding under the bearskin robe on the floor of another student's car so that he could ride home with his friends. Habits of both play and work were cultivated toward moral ends. Advice on attitude, conduct, social responsibility, schoolwork, flowed in a constant stream along with unabashed expressions of love and affection.

At Charlevoix he played tennis, went boating and swimming, and joined older boys in the strictly forbidden pleasure of diving from a high trestle into the channel through which freight boats came. He would re-call "many fights at school," in one of which his nose was broken. He engaged in all the standard Halloween tricks such as overturning out-houses and hoisting wagons up on roofs. He indulged his legendary love for tomatoes by raids into neighbors' gardens. His appetite then, as later, was prodigious. He was always on the go, exhibiting the virtually inex-haustible store of energy that marked his whole life. He was interested in everything, and seemed to want to do something with every interest.

His powers of observation had been sharpened by Grandfather Davis who, on their train trips, forbade reading so that the world passing by the window could be observed and lessons learned from it. "Observation walks" with his mother and sister in Charlevoix left him with a lifelong interest in conservation and what one biographer, Kenneth S. Davis, de-scribed as a "deep, lyric and knowledgeable love of nature and landscape beauty." Helen was taken aback one day when her customary question about what he and his friend Dave Merwin had been observing out in the field was answered with a stammering, "We were watching snakes do s-s-sex."

Trains fascinated him from as early as he could remember. He was so often at the station where the Chicago trains came in every morning that he became a favorite with the conductors, engineers, and firemen. From the stationmaster he collected baggage tags stamped with the names of different railway lines and faraway places and hung them on the walls of his bedroom.

He loved sports, but was never a star. His education had been inter-rupted by parental moves and he showed no signs of scholarship, or artis-tic or literary ability. Indeed, in his preteen years he seemed to lag behind his contempories. None of them have been able to recall anything remarkable about him, any outstanding capacity that signaled a distin-guished future.

Buffie would remember the stirrings of interest in girls. Two doors from them lived the Coolidge family. Mrs. Coolidge was the sister of Sidney Smith, a Bloomington boy who was the creator of the famous comic strip, *Andy Gump*. Her daughter, Betty, became an obvious favor-ite of Adlai's. Buffie noticed that the few times Adlai was willing to break off from play with the boys to participate in one of the plays she was continually producing would be when Betty had a part. Older people were impressed by his "good manners" and felt that they were the prod-uct not only of parental guidance but also of genuine concern for other people and for "principles of right conduct."

He was, from the very beginning, almost excessively conscientious. This stern conscience was something innate and not the product of pun-ishment. A mild slap of the hands was the most severe corporal repri-mand ever given. Once when he pulled some glasses and silver from a table set for dinner, he received this maximum punishment. Frantic parents later found him curled up beside his dog in the kennel outside, his dirty face streaked with tears. He never outgrew the sense that to hurt another through an act of aggression was morally unacceptable.

In 1912 the family took a European grand tour. With the death of Grandfather Davis, Helen had inherited a share in *The Pantagraph* and other valuable property. Even so, when they sailed on the *Lusitania* from New York in December 1911, Helen frugally took an inside cabin. Characteristically, she also had brought with them a Bloomington schoolteacher, Miss Lucy Youngman, to keep the children from falling too far behind in their schoolwork.

In Paris, Adlai suddenly developed what proved to be a lasting passion for stamp collecting, and was constantly dashing away to buy stamps in kiosks "with what, for him was spendthrift abandon," according to Buffie. Efforts to interest him in the old masters in Florence were frustrating. In Rome, Miss Youngman took Buffie and Adlai to the graves of Keats and Shelley to read aloud to them from the works of these poets. Hopes raised by the success of this tactic were dashed the next day at the Colosseum where she attempted to give a Latin lesson but found interest only in how lions were turned loose on the Christians.

She gave up and returned home; but she need not have despaired. A stamp with the head of Czar Nicholas aroused his interest in Russia, which he was later to pursue in an enterprising journalistic foray into revolutionary Russia. Thanks to stamps, he spent hours poring over maps and books of geography, travel, and history. A continuing fascination with the Middle Ages also was aroused. The romances of Sir Walter Scott, the legends of King Arthur, the tales of Robin Hood that his mother had read to him, now came vividly alive. The castles and cathedrals in France and Italy inspired an awe he never entirely lost.

"It seemed wonderful to me that men, so long ago, could build such vast structures on hills," he said long afterward. "It still does. All through my early teens I reveled in historical novels about the Crusades, the Hundred Years' War, and in histories of Joan of Arc and the whole medieval period." The 1912 trip had a lot to do with that.

That happy summer of 1912 the family stayed for a few weeks at a hotel in Spring Lake, New Jersey, near Sea Girt where the governor, Woodrow Wilson, the Democratic candidate for President, had his summer home. Wilson had vigorously attacked the fiscal policies of William Jennings Bryan, Grandfather Stevenson's running mate, and he was opposed by Lewis's former employer, William Randolph Hearst, but Lewis was an enthusiastic Wilson supporter. He took his son to meet the man who became one of Adlai's great heroes and a strong influence on his political thought. This meeting and the 1912 campaign marked the beginning of Adlai's political consciousness.

Politics had always been a part of the environment at Grandfather Stevenson's house, with politicians great and small coming and going; but that summer his own excitement was aroused by the parades and crowds, and the heated discussion of issues. The passionate commitment to Wilson in Grandfather Stevenson's household assumed a polite tone when dealing with the equally ardent Republican Davis household. Grandfather Davis was such a wonderful man it was clear to Adlai that Republicans could not be wicked; only mistaken.

One of the most lasting memories, though, was of the extra telephone that was installed in Grandfather Stevenson's house to receive election returns; one that did not have a crank and sat on a table rather than screwed to the wall. Adlai was there when *The Pantagraph* called about ten o'clock on election night to report that Wilson had won. Grandfather Stevenson promptly wired a message of congratulations to the President-elect and the next day the family was gratified by a response that said, "Your congratulations came to me like a benediction."

It was a joyous autumn. To Wilson's victory had been added the election of the first Democratic governor in Illinois since 1892, Edward Fitzgerald Dunne, longtime political friend of both father and grandfather Stevenson. Lewis justifiably assumed he would be offered a position that would advance his growing political ambitions, and a few weeks later he was asked to become chairman of the Illinois State Board of Pardons.

The Christmas season was a lively round of gay parties and family feasts. Buffie was given permission to have a supper party the evening of December 30 for her friend from Charlevoix summers, Margery McClelland, who had come for a holiday visit. Adlai was considered "too young," so he was given his dinner early after which he went up to his room. As Buffie and her friends gathered in the drawing room, Lewis and Helen went out to pay a neighborhood call. One of the boys lamented that he did not have a gun with which to demonstrate the manual of arms he had learned at military school. Buffie called upstairs to Adlai and asked him to go to the attic and look for an old .22 rifle she thought was there. Adlai ran down with it and handed it to Bob Whitmer who examined it to make sure there were no bullets in it, proudly explaining that such checking was always required at school. To the applause of the group, he smartly executed the manual, then handed the gun back to Adlai to be returned to the attic. As Adlai excitedly imitated the older boy's movements the gun went off. One of the girls, Ruth Merwin, dropped to the floor, dead.

She had become a close friend of Buffie's at University High and was a cousin of cousins.

In the echo of the blast, Lewis and Helen walked in the door. Adlai turned to his father and exclaimed, "I did it." Then he ran upstairs to his mother's room and threw himself on her bed, gasping moans that could be heard through the closed door.

Later examination revealed that the ejecting mechanism of the gun had a rusty spring that probably had prevented the emergence of the single bullet. No one ever doubted that the discharge was entirely accidental.

Ruth's mother, Mrs. Clarence Merwin, arrived and faced the situation with a courage the family ever after gratefully acknowledged. She told Adlai he must not blame himself. In her own grief she sensed that the experience would be devastating to a sensitive and exceedingly conscientious boy. Only Lewis and Buffie attended the funeral. Helen had taken Adlai, Dave Merwin, Margery McClelland, and the new French maid to the Chicago home of Aunt Julia Hardin, whose husband was the pastor of the city's Third Presbyterian Church. When they returned home, the tragedy was not referred to; not then, or ever again.

Forty years later, William Glasgow of *Time* magazine, in researching for a projected cover story, found the report of the event in *The Pantagraph* and somewhat hesitantly asked Adlai about it. After a painful silence, Adlai said, "You know, you are the first person who has ever asked me about that since it happened—and this is the first time I have ever spoken of it to anyone." Then, Glasgow reported, he "told me the whole story in a quiet matter-of-fact way."

No one can say with precision what impact the tragedy had on the man Adlai Stevenson became; but it can be said with certainty that the effect was profound. Does it account, at least in part, for his repeated self-deprecation, for the expressions of self-doubt and unworthiness, for making himself the butt of many of his jokes? Does it account for his incredibly calm acceptance of such wounding blows as his divorce and crushing defeats in two elections? Does it account for his intense concern with the careers of young people, both individually and collectively; for his visit to the bedside of the son of a UN staff member dying of leukemia even though he did not know either father or son? A definitive clue to the mysteries embedded in these questions can be found in a letter he wrote in 1955 to a woman he did not know, whose son had been involved in a similar accident.

"Tell him," Adlai wrote, "that he must live for two."

CHAPTER TWO
In the Wake of Tragedy

IN THE TRAUMATIC WAKE of tragedy, there was a quiet interlude before change began to make profound intrusions into the comfortable life of the Stevenson household.

Through the winter, it appears, every effort was made to ignore what had happened. In the spring, Lewis and Helen, together this time, took the children to a resort in Summerville, South Carolina. When they returned to Bloomington, the children were taken on weekly trips to Chicago to have their teeth straightened, and to attend matinees that intensified Buffie's interest in the theater. When they returned to Bloomington, the unruffled surface gave little hint of the recent tragedy or forthcoming change.

Adlai and Buffie enrolled in private schools on Normal's college campus along with many of Bloomington's elite. Adlai's academic and athletic efforts were extensive and utterly undistinguished. The poor spelling that plagued him throughout his life was evident in letters to his mother, visiting in the East, in such phrases as "an old fasianed [sic] school house," "2 dozen bottels [sic] of pop," "terrable [sic] conceptions," "mencioned [sic] in your letter," and "deprived of that pleasur [sic]". The long hours of listening to the readings of his mother and doting grandparents left him with an acute sense of the meaning and sound of words but not their spelling. The letters that autumn also revealed the beginnings of rebellion against his mother's domination. Parental opposition to his playing football aroused such persistent protest that they finally relented. However, their fears of injury and his hopes of gridiron glory both went unfulfilled.

Christmas of 1913 was darkened by the death of Letitia Green Stevenson, the wife of the former Vice President. The depth of their partnership was dramatized by his death only five months later. The funeral would remain the biggest in Bloomington's history until that of his grandson.

Lewis's work as chairman of the Board of Pardons had brought him favorable attention, thanks to improvements he had introduced in the administration of the parole laws. When the office of secretary of state of Illinois became vacant in October 1914, Governor Dunne promptly appointed Lewis to fill the unexpired term. The family stayed behind in Bloomington to finish the school term as Lewis moved to Springfield and into the spotlight in a long, bitter battle over the election of the speaker of the House. Lewis, as secretary of state, was the presiding officer of the House while the debate raged through five weeks and sixty-seven indecisive ballots. He presided with such skill and fairness that when, at last, the speaker was chosen, there was a unanimous vote of appreciation for the way he had discharged his responsibilities.

Meanwhile, Adlai and his mother moved to Springfield and Adlai was enrolled in the Springfield high school. Buffie already had been sent to the University School for Girls in Chicago, which she disliked so much that she was allowed to come home in the spring.

The ties to Bloomington would never be severed, but the move to Springfield marked the beginning of significant shifts in environment. Bloomington's influence would always be pervasive. Beyond the relatives and friends and the continuing involvement with *The Pantagraph,* there was Bloomington itself.

In the years of Adlai's boyhood, Bloomington was home to about twenty-five thousand people, and only a slightly smaller number lived in adjoining Normal. Waves of Germans, Irish, Swedes, and Hungarians had come to work in the now declining railroad shops and abandoned coal mines, the buggy factory and similar smaller industries, in much of which the Stevensons and the Scotts had extensive ownership. But the basic wealth came from the rich farmland; topsoil fifteen-feet deep made McLean County one of the most fertile and successful farm counties in the country.

For a town its size in the midst of the Illinois prairies, Bloomington possessed an unusual degree of sophistication. Illinois Wesleyan and, next door, State Normal College provided intellectual centers. Bloomington already was producing well-known figures other than Vice President Stevenson: the popular writers Frank Crane and Elbert Hubbard; the playwright Rachel Crothers; Clark Griffith, baseball; Sidney Smith, cartoonist. Its Grand Opera House seldom presented opera, but when it did Helen was there with Buffie and Adlai. Lewis would take them to the Majestic to see minstrel shows, and especially the Flying Wards World-

Famous Trapeze Act. The Wards as youngsters had first practiced their act in a local barn and were one of Bloomington's claims to fame.

Perhaps it was the Lincoln legacy and the many families associated with him that caused the town to be suffused with history; but whatever the reason, virtually every President was represented by a street or an avenue. And, of course, there were streets and parks named after Fells and Davises; there was even a section known as Stevensontown. It was definitely not as fashionable as the broad, tree-arched street named after George Washington in the best part of town where the Stevensons lived. In such a setting, it would have been impossible for Adlai to grow up and not have a sense of being rooted in America's history, of having a relationship to people and events that helped shape American progress. He summed up Bloomington's impact on him on the eve of entering presidential politics in these words:

> I have Bloomington to thank for the most important lesson I have learned: that in quiet places, reason abounds, that in quiet people there is vision and purpose, that many things are revealed to the humble that are hidden from the great. . . . The spirit of Bloomington is the midland concept of Americanism, progress coupled with order, liberty without license, tolerance without laxness, thrift without meanness. . . . My home town has taught me that good government and good citizenship are one and the same. . . . I learned that good government is good politics and that public office should double the responsibility that a man feels for his own home, his own neighborhood, his home town. I hope and pray I can remember the great truths that seem so obvious in Bloomington but so obscure in other places.

In Springfield, the pace of life and the centers of interest were different; even old interests had a new intensity. Lincoln's presence not only was felt, but in the person of the poet Vachel Lindsay, he came alive. Lindsay would come to dine with the Stevensons, read his poetry, and talk with passion about Lincoln. Buffie confesses she found him boring after a while but Adlai would sit through long evenings and listen in quiet absorption. Although politics was a constant interest in Bloomington, it became the center of nearly all activity in Springfield, thanks to the importance of Lewis's role as secretary of state. Although he was working very hard, his son remembered this period as one of the best in his relations with his father. He was a fascinated observer in the gallery of the State Assembly at the night sessions over which Lewis presided.

The fifteen-year-old's interest in girls also increased in Springfield. The shy attendance upon Betty Coolidge at Buffie's theatricals in Bloomington was transmuted into lively interest in "dates" and "the manily [sic] sport of dancing," including, according to Buffie, "such new-fangled steps as the Lulu Fado and the Vernon Castle Walk." One of his favorites was Mary Douglas Hay. Time with her was enhanced by the fact that her father, Logan Hay, a prominent attorney, was one of the nation's foremost Lincoln scholars, and a cousin of John Hay, Lincoln's secretary and biographer. The happy winter included not only other "dates," but also some improvement in his lackluster academic record.

That summer, Adlai was sent to Lake Pleasant Camp near Oxford, Maine. Buffie was at another Maine camp, and Helen stayed at an inn to be near them. The proximity, however, did not eliminate the necessity for frequent reports that show the beginnings of a continuing effort to escape from mother's domination. In one letter, he couldn't conceal a note of triumph that her letter urging him not to go on a White Mountain hike had arrived after he had returned. He reported at length on a rigorous experience, but he left out significant details that he later confided to Buffie. He and three other boys had slipped away from the camp counselor and instead of sleeping "in a railroad shop," as he had written, they had climbed into an empty boxcar. When they woke in the middle of the night, it was moving. Getting back extended their hike two more days as they lived "off the country."

His vigorous pursuit of athletics also alarmed his father who wrote, "I must urge you not to go in for so much athletics. I want you to stop right away. The purpose of your being there and my spending so much money to keep you there, is not for you to take long hikes and overdo yourself in athletics, but to get in good physical condition so you can have your tonsils removed without any harm."

The contents of Adlai's subsequent letters seemed to change more than his conduct. He won the camp's singles championship in tennis, he climbed Mount Washington, swam the two-mile lake in 1:16:21, and, in fact, returned to Bloomington in glowing health, fully prepared for the removal of his tonsils. Until then, his winters had been plagued by recurring attacks of bronchitis; but from then on his exceptionally vigorous habits were accompanied by health so excellent it almost seemed to chide the constant ailments that afflicted the lives of his parents.

That autumn, Buffie was sent off, protesting, to Miss Wright's School for Young Ladies in Bryn Mawr, Pennsylvania, and Helen returned with Adlai to Bloomington where he was enrolled for a final year at University High. Actually, she planned to spend time in the East, and in preparation she hired as a housekeeper nineteen-year-old Alverta Duff. Alverta's father was the son of a Mississippi slave who had come to Bloomington after the Civil War at the age of fourteen and looked up Jesse Fell because he had heard of his abolitionist activities. Fell took him in and gave him odd jobs "on condition that he go to school." By the early twentieth century, the Duffs were a respected family in Bloomington. Alverta's mother feared she was too young to take on the job offered her, but she quickly became an indispensable member of the Stevenson household.

She was also Adlai's good friend, and her youngest brother who played football at Normal was one of Adlai's high school heroes. Adlai was, she said, "a wonderful boy—so kind and considerate, and sweet tempered always . . . Adlai always phoned me ahead from school if he wanted to ask some of his friends home for dinner. He was just naturally thoughtful." Alverta also is the authority for the claim that at school that winter he studied long and hard.

His grades improved. In the spring semester he averaged 86 in English, 83 in geometry, 93 in history, and 83 in Latin. He wrote Buffie he was "working extremely hard in school," but his letters also dealt at greater length with a number of other activities: travels to high school football and basketball games, plays, dancing classes, and dances. In one he told her he "just wrote the 'old man' asking for fifty seeds [dollars]. I am expecting a hot reply." Gradually, he was beginning to assert himself.

Despite the confidentiality of his frequent correspondence with Buffie, he did not report, either to her or his parents, what he regarded as the most important event of the winter. A beautiful blond, dimpled girl with a radiant personality named Josephine Sanders had every boy in the school mooning over her. She would later, under the stage name of Irene Delroy, become a famous musical comedy star. But that winter it was Adlai whom she drove to music, if not distraction. For her he learned to play, with some proficiency, the mandolin, and to sing, with more ardor than musicality, such songs as George M. Cohan's "I'm Awfully Strong for You" and "Every Little Movement Has a Meaning All Its Own." The notes they exchanged in class were signed, with more youthful sentiment than Latin accuracy, "ETA" for *ego te amo*. In the spring, for the all-important senior prom, she chose Adlai. Decades later, his classmates would recall Adlai's triumph with envy.

Adlai was quickly brought down to earth by disastrous failure at college entrance examinations. His parents had their hearts set on Princeton. Ancestors had gone there and their political hero, Woodrow Wilson, had been its president. Adlai took the entrance examination three times and later said he did not believe the combined scores would have added up to the admission requirements. Lewis's quick hot temper shot up to white heat and stayed there. He did realize that the frequent changes of schools, and reliance on tutors whenever travel had interfered with attendance at school, might have had something to do with it, and he sought admission for Adlai at the Choate School in Wallingford, Connecticut, where Davis Merwin was enrolled. But Choate declined to take him because he was deficient in French.

"You'll just have to make it up this summer," Lewis told Adlai. "I'll arrange for a tutor, and you *will* study! You will study hard!"

With characteristic inconsistency, in June he wired both Adlai and Buffie telling them to join him in Chicago to attend the Republican National Convention. It was time, he said, "to learn about such things first hand." It was also exciting. Adlai wanted to go with his father to the Democratic convention that followed in St. Louis two days after the closing of the Republican convention, but Lewis now insisted that preparation for the Choate examinations had priority.

Nonetheless, politics intruded on summer studies. Josephus Daniels, Wilson's secretary of the navy, came to Bloomington to speak to a big rally and stayed at the Stevenson home. Lewis could not be there as he was engaged in a rough campaign of his own seeking election as secretary of state. His record had brought him widespread support, including even the *Chicago Tribune*. But, strangely, he was opposed by the powerful Democratic boss of Cook County, Roger Sullivan. Unknown men with names closely similar to Lewis's filed for the nomination in competition. It was a dirty and expensive campaign, but he not only won the primary by a big majority, he even carried Cook County, much to the displeasure of Boss Sullivan.

Lewis relented somewhat and allowed Adlai to forgo his studies and accompany him on campaign trips. Exultantly, Adlai drove the new Hudson Super Six he had persuaded his father to buy, going through the countryside tacking placards on telephone poles, and passing out cards at rallies. In September the news came that the examinations were satisfactory and he had been admitted to Choate.

Preparations for his departure were hurried; nevertheless, he left with dozens of bottles of medicines packed into his suitcase by his mother, and numbing torrents of her advice, admonitions, and exhortations.

The war in Europe seemed far away, but politics was close at hand. When Adlai arrived at Choate he found himself one of three Democrats in the student body of two hundred. Wilson seemed to be losing, and in Illinois Lewis was swimming hard against a Republican tide. He was alone. Helen had decided to stay in New Jersey, near Buffie. At Choate, a roommate, Harry Stearns, later told Buffie, "We used to argue politics by the hour, but I never saw Ad lose his temper or act bitter."

Nonetheless, Lewis's defeat was a bitter blow. He ran sixty thousand votes ahead of Wilson and thirty thousand ahead of everyone else on the state Democratic ticket, but it was a death blow to his political ambitions. His disappointment, however, was not evident in the cheerful letters he wrote his family and his plans to take them all to the Army-Navy football game at Thanksgiving as guests of the secretary of the navy. There was some consolation, too, in Wilson's narrow national victory and Democratic control of both houses of the Congress. As he closed out his office in Springfield, Lewis assigned low automobile license numbers to his friends. The number he gave himself, Adlai kept throughout his life. He also retained the lesson of his father's dignified acceptance of defeat.

His grades that first year ranged from 56 in Latin to 76 in French, with a barely passing average for the year of 70. The understanding headmaster, Dr. George St. John, wrote Helen that "examinations never do the boy justice," adding that Adlai had far more knowledge and intelligence than the tests indicated. Another teacher later said, "There was never any question he had the intelligence, but he was interested in so many things his studies often ran second or third." Certainly, his achievements in extracurricular activities were impressive, especially for a boy entering in the sophomore year. He was active in St. Andrew's, the school's religious society, the dramatics club, football, the tennis team, and most especially the school newspaper, *The News.*

That summer, accompanied by an unwelcome tutor of French, he headed for the H F Bar Ranch at Buffalo, Wyoming. Despite the tutor, it was a glorious summer with friends from Charlevoix days, including Hermon Dunlop "Dutch" Smith, who was to be one of his most intimate lifelong friends. Adlai's letters to his mother were ecstatic. He loved the mountains; he loved western life. He bought a pair of bearskin chaps and spent hours riding, even taking part in the cattle roundup. On "Frontier Day" he won a prize spearing potatoes while riding at full speed; he learned to be skillful fly casting in the rushing mountain streams; he went mountain climbing. His special friend that summer was a boy from Cleveland, Ralph Goodwin, with whom he began discussing the possibility of ranching. He had gone west with journalism as his vague career goal, but he left at the end of the summer with his heart set on becoming a rancher.

Journalism took over as soon as he arrived back at Choate and he entered a stiff competition for the board of *The News.* Buffie thinks his caution in making campaign promises was born that fall. Getting ads was a part of the competition and Adlai persuaded the reluctant Italian proprietor of the newly opened Papa's Candy Kitchen that an ad would bring students rushing to his store. When Adlai came back later to collect, the angry Papa grabbed a huge iron ladle and chased Adlai shouting, "Nobody come buy. I don't pay." Despite this frightening failure, he made the board and in the spring was elected editor in chief; an achievement whose only rival in his life up to then was the senior prom with Josephine Sanders. There were also other achievements. He was elected secretary-treasurer of his class, associate editor of *The Literary Magazine,* board member of the school Friendship Fund, and he made the tennis team.

Letters to his mother, and to his father who by now had been appointed by Secretary of the Navy Daniels chief special investigator to enforce contracts, to speed deliveries, and to prevent fraud, are enthusiastic and full of reports of school activities and, increasingly, about social engagements and plans.

Christmas and spring vacations in Washington were so socially active Adlai's letters home afterward complained about the difficulty of getting back to work. He had been placed on the "sub-deb" social register list and he and Buffie were included in a round of parties with the capital's elite. Adlai's letters now also began to show increasing concern about his mother's health. The previous year had been more difficult than usual for his parents. Helen had taken the management of her farms out of Lewis's hands. In offering to resume responsibility, he had written her. "I'll do anything and everything I can for you if you will only let me."

Except for the death of a cousin, Lewis E. Davis, in a plane crash while training in Texas, the war figured little in their letters. Adlai was scheduled to be a "big man on campus" his senior year as editor of *The News,* vice president of his class, president of St. Andrews, secretary of the Athletic Association, and captain of the football team. But, instead, he elected to take advantage of the opportunity of enlisting in the Navy as an apprentice seaman and being stationed as a student at Princeton, providing he passed his college entrance examinations. He left Choate reluctantly. They had been good years, as he recounted at a Choate function in 1936 in these words:

"My debt to Choate is formidable. Starting with something very fresh from the prairie and somewhat deficient in everything except appetite, the magic alchemy of Choate produced an accomplished actor, a promising writer, and a passable athlete with revivalist tendencies who sailed into college—on the wings of war—all in two years! All these things they did for me—and I enjoyed every minute of the operation."

Adlai probably did not know it, but the headmaster had been bombarded steadily by both Helen and Lewis with inquiries, injunctions, and advice on how to educate their son. These often detailed and urgent messages contained such phrases as "Will you please look into this matter at once and relieve our anxiety" and "Unless his appearance is better when he comes home for Xmas I shall feel obliged to take him out of school."

Despite his genuine interest in Adlai and the boy's steady development, Choate's headmaster, understandably, must have breathed a sigh of relief as his charge headed toward Princeton.

Adlai was proud to be at Princeton; and a little nervous. The entrance examinations had been such a grueling experience he couldn't help worrying about the Navy's physical examination. His weight of 137 pounds was a little less than normal for his age and height, but all else was normal, and he was in. Actually, he was "in" almost from the very beginning. Perhaps it was an interest in Buffie that caused his lieutenant commander, John Harlan, an older student and campus leader, to take him under his wing. In any event, Harlan, who later was to become a justice of the United States Supreme Court, was very helpful to the eager student-recruit. Helpful, too, was the presence of old friends and acquaintances from Charlevoix and Choate, and his good friend from H F Bar Ranch, Ralph Goodwin.

He was enrolled in advanced French, Spanish, chemistry, American history, naval discipline, and administration. The Navy commitment dominated those early months with hours of drills, marches to meals and to chapel on Sunday, rowing instruction in whaleboats on Lake Carnegie. Like most of his classmates, Adlai spurned the government-issue uniform for a tailor-made one. "I am one hot looking little 'Jack,'" he wrote his mother, "and you will just about split when you see me." He dutifully reported that it cost thirty-five dollars.

In November, this make-believe militarism came to an abrupt end with the signing of the armistice. By January he was a Princeton man in earnest. T. S. Matthews, an early friend who became editor of *Time* magazine, described him as "a slight, dark, nervously lively boy with a quick, lemony laugh; his ready mockery had a tentative air and was never wounding because it somehow included himself." He had reached his full height of five feet nine inches, but seemed taller because he was so slender. He had a deeply cleft chin, but by far the most notable aspect of his appearance was large blue eyes that had sparkle as well as depth.

He fitted comfortably into the Princeton that had successfully eluded most of Wilson's efforts to infuse its country club atmosphere with a greater emphasis on academics. The 1918–22 years were a period of raccoon coats and flapper skirts, postwar disillusion, and withdrawal. Academic excellence was frowned upon; it was much more acceptable to be mediocre. This came easily to Adlai as his academic record at Princeton was no better than at Choate. Princeton ranked students by grades into seven groups. Starting in the fifth group his first year, he made it to the third by the last year. At graduation, he ranked 105 in a class of 250.

"My greatest preoccupation," Adlai later wrote, "was with extracurricular activities and I think I was content with what we generally called 'a gentleman's third group.' Certainly I was never threatened with Phi Beta Kappa, nor, I fear, even tempted. . . . But, oh," he added, "what a Daily Princetonian was produced under my mothering eye."

He quickly acquired the nickname Rabbit, for which at least three reasons have been advanced. One was a fondness for carrots and for salads eaten with the enthusiasm of a rabbit. Another was his constant dashing from place to place at a half trot. Still another had it that he was sexually promiscuous. This last was surely a canard. At a time when kissing and "petting" were looked upon as signaling a "breakdown of moral values," he could not have departed so far from his consistent pattern of conscientious rectitude. Later in life he confided to one of his most intimate and reliable friends that not until he was married did he have sexual intercourse. As time went on, only his roommates would cling to Rabbit; generally he was known as Ad.

He promptly became a member of Whig Hall, which met every Friday for debates and at other times for "fireside talks" by faculty members. He enjoyed speaking and listening to speeches; instead of the usual freshman English course he took an English course in oratory and argument. He concentrated on tennis and golf; especially tennis. To his surprise, he was elected secretary and treasurer of the Choate Club of Princeton. He had vaguely hoped to get into the Ivy Club, considered top-ranking; but instead he made it into Quadrangle, again in the middle, but with men having some literary interests.

Not surprisingly, in view of the happy experience on the paper at Choate and the family tie to *The Pantagraph,* it was *The Princetonian* that became, from the earliest months, the object of his ambitions. By January he was reporting home that *"The Prince"* had printed two of his pieces. He had decided to "heel" for a regular position, which involved writing an article a day and competing with thirty-seven others for the two places on the board. John Harlan, who became chairman of *The Princetonian,* twice president of his class, chairman of the prestigious Senior Council, and Adlai's greatest hero of those days, gave him strong encouragement. He produced an exceptional quantity of high-quality copy and by the end of his freshman year, was one of the two winners of the competition and on his way to becoming managing editor in his senior year.

During the summer at H F Bar Ranch in Wyoming, Adlai received the alarming news that his mother had decided to rent a house in Princeton for the sophomore year.

Buffie wrote later that her brother "did his tactful best to discourage our coming, but he was too tactful—or probably Mother was too determined. I remember his saying he'd be too busy to see us often. . . . It wasn't until recently that he told me how apprehensive he had been. He said, 'I thought it was the cruelest thing a parent could do—coming to live at a son's school.'" This sentiment was echoed by a close friend in almost identical words.

Although some of Adlai's friends recalled his mother as a "charming hostess," others added that she was "overzealous" in her affection, that she was "overprotective," and that "she embarrassed him often." An occasion for that was her weekly foray into his dormitory room to gather up his dirty clothes for the laundry.

There were compensations, though. Helen had brought with her the Hudson Super Six that Adlai had selected earlier. It was great for attracting dates and schoolmates on trips to games, parties, and excursions into the country. Also, the Tudor mansion she had rented in Library Place became something of a social center. The big living room with its huge fireplace blazing on winter evenings was easily adapted to the open house that Helen maintained for Buffie, Adlai, and their friends. As a consequence, Adlai later admitted the arrangement was "not so bad." One of the high points was Christmas, when Lewis came from Bloomington to spend the holidays with them. Buffie remembered it fondly as a period in which "there was not a single row."

Lewis was full of enthusiasm for his latest enterprise; the establishment of an air service between New York and Chicago using German zeppelins. In Washington he had become interested in lighter-than-air craft and was convinced they might become as important to the travel of the future as the railroads were. Although he had returned to farm management, he had acquired American rights to basic patents for the German aircraft and had lined up an impressive list of American investors that included such people as Marshall Field, R. B. Mellon, Franklin D. Roosevelt, William Wrigley, Jr., and Owen D. Young.

The holidays were full of exciting talk about this venture and earnest, less effervescent, talk about politics. Wilson's illness and the rejection of the Treaty of Versailles cast gloomy clouds over the idealism and party loyalty Lewis felt deeply. He planned to attend the Democratic National Convention in June and then go to Europe for business and pleasure. Would Adlai join him? His mother's presence in Princeton intensified Adlai's increasing determination to assert his independence and he politely declined in favor of a European trip with college friends.

That summer he was on his own as never before. The amazing energy and insatiable curiosity that throughout his life left traveling companions gasping by the wayside quickly made itself evident.

On arrival in London, Adlai wanted to take off almost immediately for the British Museum, while Tom Matthews argued for exploration of pubs. This tug-of-war between places of historic interest and places to quench thirst intensified by Prohibition at home was waged throughout the summer. Judging from the accounts of walking trips through the English countryside, castles explored, and places where they "staid," Adlai must have scored an impressive number of victories. Despite the abiding affection for England that was born that summer, the highlight was the trip to Paris "by *airplane*!" He described in excited detail the ten-passenger plane "with windows, wicker chairs . . . even a lavatory."

Four days later he was writing his mother from Coblenz en route to Berlin, but much of the letter was devoted to an evocative description of the moonlit trip through the battlefields of Château-Thierry with its "great field of neat white crosses." Three days later, a letter reported on Berlin, a trip on the Rhine and to Frankfurt, with detailed accounting of costs for food and lodging reflecting his lifelong preoccupation with expenditures. After Potsdam and its gardens (which he loved), and Cologne, the main objective was Rheims and the Chemin des Dames battlefield where "the severest fighting of the entire war occurred," and the ground was "practically paved with iron."

Paris was a welcome change, "the most fascinating city I have ever been in" with "a charm & beauty that is absolutely unique." And there he had a surprise encounter with his father. He reported to his mother that the night of his return "about 12 of us had a big party and in the course of the evening we found ourselves at the Folie[s] Bergère. Imagine my astonishment to see Father walk in all of a sudden. Of course he said he was just looking for me but it certainly looked as though he had started out on a little party of his own and I had accidentally interrupted it." He went on to say he met "father and Buff the next day for lunch and hung around with them most of the time for the next few days until we started for Switzerland."

But there was more to the story than that, as he confided to a close friend years later. Earlier at the Folies Bergère his friends had decided to go off with some prostitutes and Adlai had gone with them. But in the room, as the girl undressed, Adlai became conscience-stricken, placed the agreed-upon fee on the table, and fled back to the nightclub where he then encountered his father.

Lewis reported "two glorious days with the Brute," as he often referred to Adlai. Buffie wrote her mother, "Adlai is the easiest and most delightful companion. We will never have a happier time together."

Helen had written Adlai warning him that mountain climbing might strain his heart and back. Fortunately, her letter arrived after he had returned from climbing the Breithorn. Lewis recognized the beauty of Adlai's description and urged Helen to have it published in *The Pantagraph*. But he also had another purpose. "I am anxious that it be known in Bloomington that I was successful in Berlin & I wish you would add the enclosed to Adlai's letter. It is about the only way I can see of getting it published, & it will be of value to me. Do it please, & send me a copy." Lewis had added to Adlai's letter, without his knowledge, a description of meetings with important people in Berlin. In his deep insecurity and broad ambitions, Lewis often resorted to using people; this time, even his son.

That fall at Princeton, Adlai plunged into work on *The Princetonian*, and also the Cox-Roosevelt campaign. He was one of the organizers of Princeton's Cox-Roosevelt Club and a member of the committee that brought James M. Cox to Princeton to speak. For Adlai, the central issue was the necessity of United States membership in the League of Nations. *The Princetonian* endorsed the League and Cox.

Buffie, meanwhile, was writing him from Switzerland, where she had remained to study psychoanalysis with Carl Jung, chiding him for his social and extracurricular activities and urging greater attention to studies. He was, indeed, very active. On February 1, he had been elected managing editor of *"The Prince"* and the March 1 issue for the first time carried his name on the masthead with that title. He had achieved one of his fondest ambitions. But it also led to another crisis with his father who had hastened to inform *The Pantagraph* and the *Chicago Tribune,* saying, inaccurately, that "the position . . . is the highest on the paper and the most sought after honor in Princeton literary life." Adlai was furious as he made clear in an uncharacteristically blunt letter:

Dear Father:

Once more my [may] I protest (as usual in vain I suppose) against your assumption of the duties of my publicity manager. As in the past, when I have strenuously objected, you have never- theless gone ahead and, with the apparent intent of pleasing a mere child, put things in papers which were altogether wrong in point of fact & most embarrassing to me. And now again; as- sailed from all sides with clippings from the Chi. Trib. to the effect that I am head of the Princetonian & as a matter of fact am only second. Consequently many stories about how it got in, can't understand it, etc. Please desist & do me a real favor.

Adlai.

"The Prince" was not the only triumph. He was elected secretary of the board of trustees of Quad, and was one of the twelve "most promi- nent" juniors to be nominated to serve on the Senior Council the next year. So it was a lighthearted young man who joined three others for another summer in Europe, heading first for Spain where John Harlan was studying at the University of Madrid, and then to Switzerland to join his mother who had arrived several months earlier to be with Buffie. It was a more leisurely and less programmed summer, and he was prepared to return to Princeton for the last, busiest, and probably the happiest of his years there.

The main cloud was his mother's determination to be in residence once again for his last semester. He argued vigorously; but lost. He did delay in finding a house, which resulted in an angry reprimand from his father. As late as 1963, Adlai would comment that taking the house was a dreadful thing to do to a son in his last semester at college. Nor was it the social base it had been in the sophomore year.

Classwork was heavier than it had ever been; he joined vigorously in the work of the Senior Council; participated in the Intercollegiate Disar- mament Conference, and at commencement, was a member of the Class Day Committee. But it was *The Princetonian* around which his life re- volved. For the rest of his life he would recall fondly the struggles of nights at the printers.

In the class voting toward the end of the school year, he placed third in the estimation of his classmates as "Biggest Politician," with 8 votes, against the 124 received by the winner (who then devoted his life to the stock and bond business). Only two of his classmates thought he would be "Most Likely to Succeed," and none included him among "The Wit- tiest." All would agree, though, that he had fulfilled Wilson's standard for a university graduate as one "who should be a man of his nation, as well as a man of his time."

Reluctantly, under prodding from his father, he had applied and had been admitted to Harvard Law School. But that summer he and Ralph Goodwin, working again on the Wyoming ranch, turned their previous wishful thinking into a decision to go into ranching together. When Adlai asked his father for some financial assistance, Lewis exploded. He warned his son that if he were not back in time for law school, he would come to Wyoming and bring him back.

If Lewis and Helen had held a controlling interest in *The Pantagraph,* he might have been willing to let Adlai return to Bloomington and a career in journalism. As it was, both Jesse Fell and Adlai I had been lawyers, and Lewis always regretted he had not followed in his father's footsteps. He was determined his son would make up for it. Walter Johnson, the editor of the Stevenson papers, has written: "Near the end of his life Governor Stevenson wondered what his life would have been like if he had lived it his own way. He commented that he felt that he had been pushed into things and asked: 'What if I had become a rancher, for instance?'" His son, John Fell, has achieved that ambition.

Adlai never liked the Harvard Law School, and, indeed, he never really liked the law. Harriet Cowles, a Charlevoix friend, was nearby, which was some compensation, and he developed a number of close friendships, most notably that with Francis T. P. Plimpton who much later became his deputy at the United Nations. Along with Charles Denby and William McIlvaine, two friends from Princeton, he was "taken into Lincoln's Inn—the best of the law school eating clubs." Through such associations as these he began a pattern of spending weekends at country houses of friends. After Christmas at home, he went to Lake Placid to join Princeton friends for skiing, hiking, and sleigh rides with girls including "one of the best ex-debs of NY's 400. . . . If there is heaven on earth, I've found it at last," he exulted.

As the year went on, he did discover that "parts of the law are quite interesting," but his textbooks continued to show few markings or other signs of having been read. He finished his first year with 58 in Civil Procedure, 70 in Contracts, 65 in Criminal Law, 65 in Property, 62 in Torts, an average equivalent to a C.

When he returned to Harvard in the fall, a favorite port of call became the Belmont home of Lorna Underwood, whose parents, Mr. and Mrs. Loring Underwood, were "apparently not tremendously wealthy, but very aristocratic, refined and cultured." Francis Plimpton said Adlai "pursued her hard but she never caught fire though I'm sure he did." That spring Harriet Cowles declared her intention to marry someone else, and only weeks later was he able to tell his mother that the "crumbling of the air castles is about over" and that he was moving away from his "self-imposed role of the martyred lover." She responded with a reference to God's will and then: "Are you looking after that old head, putting in lots of tonic and oil and occasionally washing well and rinsing well? Be careful not to take cold. The instant you have any stoppage, take care of it at once—rest, sleep and lots of drinking water—eight glasses a day." It was a strangely inappropriate response to a romantic crisis. The advice would have been more timely at prep school than at law school; but she wrote similar letters then as well.

One of her letters accused him and his roommates of drinking heavily. Actually, the drinker was the cousin who carried the tale to her, and Adlai replied angrily. Until the last few years of his life he drank little and, in fact, was repelled by heavy drinking. This is not to deny that his letters at this time dealt more with social activities than with the law. Moreover, some were marred by anti-Semitic comments that seemed to be the mark of his class and time. He described a man met on a weekend trip to New York as "loquacious like most of his race"; a shopping expedition on which "we Jewed them down from $35 to $25"; and in reporting a visit by his father to a class he said "he seemed very impressed with the display of erudition not to mention the thirsty intellects of the semitic element." Such references soon faded out and never reappeared.

More typical were the enthusiastic and sometimes somewhat awed descriptions of homes and people encountered on weekends; such as the "ancestral manor of the Plimptons, filled with pre-Revolutionary family relics, autographs of George Washington, and other celebrities." Another weekend that started with Princeton football and visits to the Quadrangle Club and Ivy ended in New York at the home of Norman P. Davis, financial adviser to President Wilson at the Paris Peace Conference and undersecretary of state in 1920–21. "I sat up & listened to Mr. Davis talk about democracy etc. until about 12:30—as you can imagine he is quite fascinating & has a tremendous fund of information."

His preference for socializing over the law took its toll. Despite frantic, late-hour cramming, he failed two courses; Agency and Evidence, with grades of 51 in each. His grades in other subjects, although better, added up to an average of only 58, a D. He had flunked out. While he was not eligible to return in September, he could have come back in 1925 and been readmitted on passing examinations. But there is little evidence that this option was seriously considered. For the most part, his letters report happy times with Lorna Underwood, weekend parties, including one on a yacht, and a return to the Norman Davis home to dine with the Democratic whip of the House, Finis J. Garrett, and Senator Key Pittman before plunging energetically into the famous "long" Democratic National Convention at Madison Square Garden where his father had arranged for him, Francis Plimpton, Norman Davis, and Robert Finley to be assistant sergeants at arms.

Lewis had been working hard to promote the candidacy of David F.

Houston, secretary of agriculture in President Wilson's Cabinet, and he placed his name in nomination at the convention. Franklin D. Roosevelt hobbled on crutches to the podium to nominate Al Smith. But Adlai, with some support from others, thought his father's speech nominating Houston was the better speech. He was very proud of his father and of the fact that some of the delegates were talking about him as a possible vice presidential candidate.

Regardless of the merits of the nominating speeches, the convention soon became deadlocked over the rival candidacies of Alfred E. Smith of New York and William G. McAdoo of California. After 103 ballots, the nomination went to John W. Davis. Added to this disappointment was dismay over the platform committee's equivocal endorsement of the League of Nations. Newton D. Baker, Wilson's secretary of war, presented a minority report together with a plea for an unqualified endorsement of Woodrow Wilson's ideals that Adlai later recalled as "the most moving speech I think I ever heard."

After the convention, Adlai returned to Bloomington to assume the main burden of the Stevenson family struggle for control of *The Pantagraph.*

CHAPTER THREE

From Bloomington to Moscow
to Marriage

THE PANTAGRAPH IN 1924 was an influential property—and a valuable
one. It also faced tough competition plus a divisive family dispute for
control.

When W. O. Davis incorporated the paper in 1907, the value of its
800 shares was $200,000. In 1929, net profit alone was $169,933. At the
conservative estimate of value at ten times net earnings, the paper would
be valued at nearly $2 million. In any event, it was a possession of impor-
tance.

An unlikely series of deaths, and a lack of precision in Grandfather
Davis's will, now set the stage for a battle that left enduring wounds in
the family. His will passed ownership to his two daughters, Helen Stevenson and Jessie Merwin, and to his son, Bert, who ran the paper. After
them, ownership was to be passed on to the children of these three.
Bert's two sons, however, died early. Bert's own health was not good,
and the paper declined under his leadership while a Democratic evening
paper, *The Bulletin,* began to gain on it. By 1922 he was spending most of
his time in California for his health, leaving the running of the paper to
Jessie Merwin's elder son, David.

On Bert's death in the spring of 1924, the question arose as to how
the estate of 800 shares, less 10 that had been bequeathed to a longtime
employee of the paper, was to be divided between the two families. By
the reading that the Stevensons favored, the 790 shares would be divided

equally between Helen Stevenson and Jessie Merwin. The Merwins favored a reading that would divide the shares in proportion to the grandchildren in each family, so that each grandchild would have the same number of shares. That meant that the Merwins would receive 474 shares—or 60 percent—and the Stevensons 316 shares—or 40 percent. Long and increasingly heated family meetings aggravated rather than solved the disagreement. Finally, it was agreed that a not-so-friendly "friendly suit" would be initiated to settle it.

Meanwhile, David was rebuilding the paper. Within five years he had it turned around and had persuaded the owner of *The Bulletin* to sell out. He was an intelligent and exceptionally hardworking executive, but he also had a quick temper and abrasive mannerisms that were ill suited to the family tensions and the sometimes acrimonious disputes that had set in after Bert's death. The feuding families were able to agree on buying and dividing equally between them shares that one of Bert's sons had left to his own widow. But about the only other thing they could agree on was that Adlai and his boyhood friend and cousin, Davis Merwin, should go to work on the paper while the lawsuit moved slowly through the courts.

In 1926 the circuit court ruled for the Merwins. The Stevensons appealed and in October 1927 the appellate court reversed the ruling and held for the Stevensons. But by then the ruling was irrelevant. The Merwins had managed to purchase the ten shares bequeathed to the elderly long-term employee, and this gave them control. The purchase had been made without informing the Stevensons. The resulting hard feelings lurked near the surface forever after and on occasion erupted unpleasantly. For Adlai, it was a fateful development.

When he began work in the newsroom of *The Pantagraph* in July 1924, a future in journalism rather than the law was an attractive prospect. Moreover, his two years in the newsroom with his cousin Dave in the business office were happy years. His title was managing editor and he supervised reporters, made assignments, and helped make up the paper. But it was his own articles and editorials that attracted attention.

In the summer of 1925 the country was gripped by the famous Scopes "Monkey" trial in Dayton, Tennessee, in which the young teacher indicted for teaching evolution in violation of Tennessee law was almost overlooked in the titanic clash of William Jennings Bryan for the prosecution and Clarence Darrow for the defense. For Adlai the trial was a test of a commitment to civil liberties that came into conflict with a family involvement. His grandfather had been Bryan's running mate in 1900, the year Adlai was born. They had remained close friends; Bryan had been a guest in the Stevenson home, and he was one of youthful Adlai's heroes. But in a series of five editorials he came down firmly on the side of Scopes and against Bryan. The convictions that later found vigorous expression in the courageous campaign against McCarthyism were already forming in the mind of the twenty-five-year-old who wrote:

"If our mental processes as a nation have become so devitalized that we must be blindfolded and led by the hand, then it is high time for those champions of democracy who seize each patriotic occasion to reaffirm their belief in the infallibility of the great public mind, view with alarm our latter-day degradation."

One of the events he assigned to himself produced a series of eyewitness accounts of the suffering and devastation left behind by a tornado that hit southern Illinois in the spring of 1925, killing over eight hundred people and injuring three thousand. In beautifully sensitive reporting, he caught the tragedy that struck so suddenly, and depicted the instinctively generous support the survivors extended to their neighbors. Lloyd Lewis, *Chicago Daily News* editor, author, and close friend of later years, regarded Adlai as "the best natural-born reporter he had ever known." The 1925–26 period provides ample evidence that he would have had a distinguished career in journalism. But it was not to be. He and Dave Merwin did not have an easy relationship, and the ten shares that gave the Merwin's control of *The Pantagraph* turned Adlai back to the law.

Lewis had persisted in urging his son to complete his law degree, but it was a trip to Washington for the wedding of his classmate Charles Denby that reduced his resistance. Denby was law clerk for Supreme Court justice Oliver Wendell Holmes and Adlai had what he recalled as an unforgettable afternoon with Mr. Justice Holmes talking about the law, legal education, history, and most especially the Civil War. The interest thus aroused was given further stimulation by the dean of the Northwestern Law School, John Henry Wigmore, and in the autumn of 1925 he registered at Northwestern, spending weekdays at the school in Chicago and weekends working on *The Pantagraph* in Bloomington. Apparently he thrived on this double duty as he graduated in June 1926 with five A's and nine B's, doing his best work in International Law, Professional Ethics, Constitutional Law, and Labor Law. The bar examination and admission to the Illinois bar followed swiftly, after which he took off on an eventful trip to Fascist Italy and Communist Russia for what he called "one last fling" at journalism.

In the meantime, he had suffered another romantic setback. During a Charlevoix vacation in the summer of 1923 he had met Claire Birge of Greenwich, Connecticut. He began writing her almost immediately at the end of the summer. The eighty letters she saved reveal an eloquent courtship nourished by occasional visits to Greenwich as well as by mail, culminating in a proposal of marriage by twenty-five-year-old Adlai to nineteen-year-old Claire in December 1925. Although she declined, a correspondence of remarkable affection and tenderness continued through 1928, when he told her of plans to marry Ellen Borden and urged her to meet them at the boat on which they were sailing on a honeymoon trip to Europe.

It was a wedding party, also, that sparked the idea of a trip to Russia. Adlai got into a discussion of Russia with George Norton and Bob Page in which all expressed eagerness to see what was going on. The Soviet government barred foreigners and the State Department refused passport protection to Americans wishing to go there. Adlai suggested they might get around all of this by getting credentials as newspaper correspondents. Aided by his father, Adlai was able to get credentials from the *Chicago Herald-American* and Hearst's International News Service. George Norton obtained credentials from his hometown paper, the *Louisville Courier Journal*. Bob Page did not have any such connections, but he decided to go along anyway.

Helen was sailing for Italy at the end of July and she wanted Adlai and Buffie to accompany her. She was worried about Buffie and disapproving of her efforts to become an actress. Buffie was playing in Rochester, New York, in Gilbert Miller's stock company with Ilka Chase and Louis Calhern, and Adlai was persuaded to stop off there en route to New York to convince Buffie that she should come with them to Europe. Subsequent events made her forever grateful that Adlai succeeded in his mission.

It was exciting from the very beginning. General Umberto Nobile, who had just flown over the North Pole in a dirigible and was the reigning hero of the hour on both sides of the Atlantic, was returning home aboard the *Conte Biancamano*. Buffie quickly became a favorite and he asked her to be at his side as he made a triumphant entry into the Naples harbor. The biggest excitement, however, came later that summer in Switzerland where she met Ernest Ives, handsome first secretary at the American embassy in Constantinople who was on vacation leave. Within three days he had proposed, she had accepted, and they were planning a honeymoon in Egypt where he had served as consul in Alexandria. Helen's caution, and Lewis's fury when he learned about it, resulted in the wedding being postponed until February 4, 1927, in Naples, followed by the deferred Egyptian honeymoon. Adlai's role was to mollify Lewis's vehement opposition, much of which had to be attempted by letter during his own hectic travels. On the boat en route to her wedding, Buffie wrote him:

> *You can't imagine what an effect your splendid letter had on Father. He has done everything possible to help me and not fret me, and I do appreciate your tact and understanding. . . . You should hear old papa tell me he thinks you have a "master mind, and altho' a boy, one of the great men he has ever known." He has utter awe of you, as I have love and confidence.*

Politics rather than romance was Adlai's main focus that summer. He sent two long articles about Fascist Italy back to *The Pantagraph*. The vivid reporting mixed admiration at Mussolini's achievements with revulsion over authoritarian excesses, as indicated by this excerpt:

> It is evident that order has come out of chaos and that Italy has witnessed the sunrise of a day of prosperity. But the "beneficent tyrant" who prefers "five thousand rifles to fifty thousand votes" has conferred these benefits by locking the lazy quarrelsome boy in a straight-jacket, stuffing a handkerchief in his mouth and then hypnotizing him with juggling feats performed with sticks of dynamite. . . . One wonders how much liberty you can take away before you begin to tyrannize.

With this question on his mind, he went on to Vienna to meet Bob Page and George Norton. The three of them had applied for Russian visas in New York and were hoping to pick them up in Vienna. After a week of frustrating encounters with Soviet officials who said they were awaiting word from Moscow, Bob Page gave up and left. Adlai and Norton were given a promise that if the visas arrived they would be forwarded to them in Budapest. They had decided to go there hoping that a friend of Adlai's in the American legation there might be of help. While they were pursuing this ultimately unsuccessful effort, Norton reported he had learned of a group of southern Baptists who were going to the Soviet Union via Poland and suggested they try to gain entry with them.

Adlai had his heart set on gaining an interview with Georgi Vasilievich Chicherin, the Soviet foreign minister who was then at the center of American curiosity about the Russian Revolution. He was thought to be the key figure in seeking compensation for repudiated czarist debts and for confiscated property that had been owned by Americans. So Adlai stuck to his determination to enter the Soviet Union as a foreign correspondent and went on alone to Belgrade. When no visa appeared there, he proceeded to Bucharest, then Sofia, and finally Constantinople. There he conspicuously planted himself in the office of the Soviet consulate for two stubborn days. Discouraged, he spent the next two days sightseeing and then somewhat hopelessly returned to the consulate. He was reprimanded for his absence—and handed his visa.

He talked his way onto a small Italian freighter about to sail up the Black Sea to the Russian port of Batum. There, hostile port officials confiscated his French-Russian dictionary, a copy of Sir Bernard Pares's *History of Russia,* and all his other papers. Without a dictionary, faced with an unfamiliar alphabet, and among people who knew not a word of English, he managed to travel to Tiflis, the capital of Georgia, then to Baku on the Caspian, and there find a train for Moscow. For five days he was locked in a compartment with a very dirty, long-bearded Russian who spoke not a word. Years later he told Kenneth S. Davis that he had never felt more "utterly isolated, nor more miserable physically." He emerged from the railroad station in Moscow to encounter "wolf-children"—homeless orphans of the civil war—scraping from the cobblestones the remains of a jar of jam someone had dropped, licking their fingers ravenously, and fighting like animals for bits and pieces.

He had the address of two kindly ladies who ran for the Friends Service Committee a house for stranded foreigners. All of his life he would remember with warmth a Miss Graves of Baltimore and a Miss Higgens from England who rescued him from his hunger, filth, and sense of isolation. Their hospitality extended to providing meals for the American correspondents in Moscow and there Adlai met almost daily such famous journalists as Walter Duranty of *The New York Times,* William Henry Chamberlain of the *Christian Science Monitor,* and H. R. Knickerbocker of Hearst's International News Service. These veterans were bemused by the young man's audacity in seeking an interview with Chicherin. Nevertheless, they undertook to help him, mainly by giving him the advantage of what they had learned of the crisis through which the Soviet Union was passing in the bitter struggle for succession between Stalin and Trotsky following the death of Lenin two years earlier.

Every afternoon he called at the Foreign Office trying to persuade the press secretary that an interview would be in the interest of "both of our countries." After every polite hearing, smilingly he would be told to return the next day. This went on for a month. With money running low, he decided the effort would be fruitless and decided to see Leningrad and some of Sweden before sailing from Gothenburg.

But the time had not been wasted. In Chicago, Adlai had met Prince Nicholas Galitzine, whose sister later became Mrs. Lester Armour. He had asked Adlai to look up his aunt, Countess Anastasia Galitzine, who had been a lady-in-waiting to the czarina. He found her in a fifth-floor room of a run-down tenement sharing a bathroom with about twenty others. Despite the danger entailed by the foreigner's visit, she received him warmly, apologizing in English for her costume, a court dress dating from the Edwardian era. "Please excuse these rags," she said. "I am getting to the bottom of my trunk."

Even more helpful was the Countess Sophia Tolstoy. As the daughter of the great writer and curator of the Tolstoy Museum, she was tolerated by the Bolsheviks. She helped him find and communicate with others whose names had been given to him by refugee relatives in the United States. They provided him with an exceptional insight into the aftermath of the Russian Revolution.

"The atmosphere of fear was palpable," he told Kenneth Davis in the 1950s,

> as palpable as the abject poverty of the masses. I never knew whether or not I was being followed, but I did know that people were afraid to be seen talking to me. . . . I have always been

very thankful for that trip. After what I saw there, I could never believe, as so many did in the early 1930's, that Soviet Russia's way was a good way for any state to go. Some men, from the highest humanitarian motives, became Communists or fellow travellers during the Depression, but I felt that I had seen at first hand what Communism really meant, in terms of terror and brutality. All that terror and brutality breed are more terror and brutality, and so it was in the Russia I saw.

These sentiments are a far cry from the accusations Senator Joseph McCarthy, Vice President Richard Nixon, and others were to hurl at him.

Back home in October 1926, it was time to get started on a career, which he did with minimum enthusiasm. He had been offered a job as a law clerk in one of Chicago's oldest and most prestigious law firms, then known as Cutting, Moore and Sidley. It had a penchant for Princeton men, but Adlai's family ties also helped. Vice President Stevenson had been a close friend of the firm's founder, and the firm of Stevenson and Ewing had handled cases for Sidley. His salary the first year was $1,450, about average for that place and time, and it augmented income in interest and dividends, most of it from *The Pantagraph,* that brought his total income for the year to $6,414.

His approach to the practice of law, which he never completely lost, is revealed in a letter written to a friend at that time:

> *I must confess, heretical and un-American as it may seem, that I view the prospect without the least eagerness. . . . I know perfectly well that if I am to make a "success," sooner or later I must "sell out"—I mean chuck most of my ideas and my acute sympathy for the less fortunate. A stony and obedient loyalty to class and vested interests seems to be the necessary adjunct of a life time of hard and imaginationless work.*

Whether or not the work was imaginationless, he did work hard at it. That was his nature. It was also his nature to socialize, and the setting was favorable for that. Some of the stately mansions built by wealthy and powerful Chicagoans along Lake Michigan in the area known as the Gold Coast were being converted to apartments for aspiring young professionals. Adlai was welcomed into one of those and into the opulent social life offered to favored young bachelors. Almost immediately he found himself on "Miss Campbell's list." Miss Eliza Campbell was the social secretary employed by upper-crust mothers to provide suitable names for the big debutante parties at which their daughters were launched into society's shallow waters.

His living room windows looked out on the lake where the waterfront offered facilities for exercise he needed to absorb the energies left over after long hours at the law firm. He was welcomed at the homes and galas of Chicago's top society. Gold Coast winters were followed by Lake Forest summers where cottages on the vast estates were made available to young bachelors with connections such as his. Moreover, he was not exempt from conscious social climbing. A friend from those days has said, "VIP-itis, both Ad and Buffie had it." But what were remembered most were his good manners, his quiet gaiety, his ease and pleasure in the company of pretty women, enthusiasm for sports, his even-tempered, open-minded approach to all situations, his zest for conversation, and a casual, almost debonair air that averted attention from the fact that in appearance he was neither distinguished nor handsome.

Through his grandfather, father, Princeton, Harvard, summers at Charlevoix and in Wyoming, he had acquired friends and acquaintances that led him to be welcomed at the homes of Chicago's elite, and most especially, at the John Paul Wellings, the Edison Dicks, and the Hermon Dunlop "Dutch" Smiths.

Harriet Welling was largely responsible for Adlai's introduction to the leadership of the Council on Foreign Relations that launched his public career. Edison Dick succeeded to the leadership of the A. B. Dick Company, and Jane Dick's father was the head of one of the country's largest wholesale grocery firms. Dutch Smith was then with the Northern Trust Company and later became the head of the insurance brokerage firm of Marsh and McLennan. Smith's wife, Ellen, was the daughter of the president of Montgomery Ward and Company. These three became lifelong and intimate friends.

He was soon a member of important clubs: in Lake Forest, the swank Onwentsia Club; and in the city, the Harvard-Yale-Princeton Club; The Wayfarers, made up of a small group of men with unusual experiences, usually related to travel, in their background; the Commonwealth Club, consisting of the younger business and professional men; before long, the Commercial Club, for business leaders interested in public service; and, most important, the Chicago Council on Foreign Relations.

Less typically, he involved himself in various social service organizations, such as Hull House and the Lower North Side Community Council. These involvements increased with the onset of the Great Depression. His personal situation was affected very little, but he was significantly more sensitive than most of his peers to the problems economic disaster had inflicted on others.

He was rapidly becoming his own person and began to move out from the shadows of his family. In Chicago, increasingly, he developed new facets of his personality, new interests, new friends, and, most important of all, new confidence in himself.

Until the 1929 crash, the Jazz Age fully engaged the energies of the bulk of Chicago's elite. Jane Dick, recalling those "glorious days," has said: "He was delightful and charming and always courteous. He made you feel you were the person he was interested in." Jane Dick particularly remembers a time when she sat out a dance to discuss politics with him. When she expressed impatience with political leaders who did not deliver "a few clear-cut ultimatums," Adlai responded with a discourse on compromise being the essence of democracy.

Harriet Welling recalls a debutante lunch she gave in the late 1920s at which the girls "argued hotly as to whom was first with Adlai." One of the group, Ruth Winter, remembers that he "was more interested in older women with experience in the world. That made him all the more desirable." But three relationships were ascendant. Jane Warner Dick was a close friend who remained so all his life. Alicia Patterson was the one many said he should have married; indeed, after his divorce he made such a comment himself. She was the daughter of Captain Joe Patterson, coeditor of the *Chicago Tribune* with his cousin, Colonel Robert R. McCormick, and also the founder of the *New York Daily News*. Six years younger than Adlai, she was more handsome than beautiful, outspoken, and strong-willed like her father who was then a major figure in Chicago. Adlai was fascinated by her, but also, apparently, a little frightened of her. There is some evidence that she suggested marriage to him, but that he declined. In any event, after his divorce, she became a central figure in his private life and remained so until her death.

The girl he chose, however, was Ellen Borden.

The tragedy that blighted both their lives was inconceivable that joyous Saturday afternoon, December 1, 1928, when eighteen-year-old Ellen Borden married twenty-eight-year-old Adlai E. Stevenson.

Friends and society reporters alike referred to Ellen as beautiful, vivid, charming, glamorous, gay. She was described as having "dark-blond" hair, wide hazel eyes, heart-shaped lips, and a plump-cheeked round face with an open childlike expression. Other words often applied to her were fey, birdlike, perky, fluttery, flighty. One friend said she was "like a butterfly coming out of a cocoon. Everything was a delight. Everything was new. She had been so protected. She had no relationship with the world."

In their world, though, her parents were outstanding. Her mother, the former Ellen Waller, and Mrs. Potter Palmer, were Chicago's "queens of society"; she was a member of an old and distinguished Chicago family and a leading patroness of the arts, particularly music. Her father's sister, Mary Borden, was a famous novelist who became Lady Spears as the wife of the famous soldier, diplomat and author, Brigadier General Edward Louis Spears, knight of the British Empire.

John Borden had inherited a fortune made in mining, and greatly enhanced it through daring speculations that finally led to his downfall.

At the time of the wedding his fortunes were at their height and included association with John Hertz in the Yellow Cab Company and oil leases throughout the Southwest. On a huge estate, Glenwild Plantation, in Mississippi, he raised prize-winning purebred cattle and hogs. In addition, he had so distinguished himself as an Arctic explorer that this is how he was identified in *Who's Who*. In 1925, after eighteen years of marriage, he sought a divorce and barely three months later married the second of his three wives.

Although her mother later happily remarried the composer, John Alden Carpenter, the divorce was a severe shock to Ellen and to her younger sister, Betty, that was unrelieved by the palacelike mansion they received in her mother's divorce settlement. The turreted sixteenth-century-style French château built by her grandfather, at 1020 Lake Shore Drive, was just across the street from the equally imposing but uglier mansion of Edith Rockefeller McCormick. Their mother, to whom Ellen felt very close, had the right to live there as long as she wished.

Ellen had been sent to an exclusive finishing school in Maryland, with an unlimited expense account, and then on to another in Florence, Italy. She had her debut in December 1926 and quickly became one of the most popular debutantes of the season. At her coming-out party at the Blackstone Hotel, Ethel Waters did the latest dance, called the Black Bottom. In the spring of 1928 she was presented at the Court of St. James.

Meanwhile, though, she had virtually decided that her choice among her various suitors was Adlai Stevenson. He had become her most frequent escort to the many parties and his instinctive trait of listening with keen concentration had convinced her he was interested in her as a person and not as an heiress. She enjoyed his lively conversation, his dancing ability, and his charming manners. Later she was to say that she never really loved him but married him because she believed that life with him would never be boring.

At the time, their friends saw them as being wholly and delightedly in love. She was captivating in her effervescent happiness. For his part, Adlai wrote glowing letters to his mother about Ellen and zestfully fought to overcome what he correctly sensed was his parents' disapproval of the match. He was proud of her artistic sensibilities and most especially of her literary talent. When one of her verses was printed by the *Chicago Tribune*, he bought a quantity of copies to send relatives and friends, including one for the family album in Bloomington. It is worth reprinting here as a harbinger of the confusion between shadow and reality that was to haunt their lives.

It Must Be Mad
I watch my shadow slide about
And O, I know without a doubt
It must be mad!

I watch it pick up things with care,
When I can see there's nothing there.

I watch it raise its fists and know
There's no one there to take the blow.
I see it going out the door
And wonder what it's going for:
It must be mad!

More than courtship filled that summer of 1928. Lewis had become an important contender for the vice presidential nomination as running mate with Alfred E. Smith. As the July convention in Houston approached, he was actively promoted as one who could attract the farmers' votes to the ticket of the urban Al Smith. At the convention, after the first-ballot nomination, Smith threw his support to the liberal Arkansas senator Joseph T. Robinson, who was duly nominated. Lewis, meanwhile, had a major hand in shaping the farm plank in the platform with which the Democrats confronted Herbert Hoover and Senator Charles Curtis of Kansas.

Buffie had returned with Ernest to the United States earlier in the year for the birth of their son, Timothy Read, and she was with Lewis in Houston. Adlai, however, was commuting between the law office and Lake Geneva, Illinois, where Ellen and her mother had taken a luxurious estate, Ceylon Court, for the summer. It was there on Saturday, July 28, that the engagement was agreed upon, with a formal announcement to be made in September. Three days later, he called with considerable trepidation on Ellen's father for an interview that he told his mother "turned out most pleasantly." John Borden was generous with advice on where and how they should live, and with information on Ellen's inheritance.

Adlai had barely caught his breath from this encounter when he was summoned to the office of Mr. McPherson, the senior partner of Cutting, Moore and Sidley. Adlai reported home that with "quaking knees I responded, but, wonder of wonders, instead of firing me he raised my salary beginning August 1 to $200 per mo." The good fortune gave him the courage to tell Mr. McPherson he was going to get married and would like to take a month or six-week vacation. "To the month he acquiesced eagerly—to the 6 weeks he hesitated on the ground of example to the other young men but said he would take it up with his partners. Hereafter, August 2 will always be my lucky day."

The autumn was filled with hectic, happy days and nights and party-packed weekends. Their excited, optimistic mood was duplicated in the stock market to such an extent that even Adlai forsook his prudence and bought stocks.

At four-thirty on Saturday afternoon, December 1, 1928, Dr. John Timothy Stone married Ellen Borden and Adlai Stevenson in the tiny chapel of the fashionable Fourth Presbyterian Church on Upper Michigan Avenue. The wedding party then moved to the mansion at 1020 Lake Shore Drive where Ellen's mother was the hostess at a large reception. On Tuesday, December 5, Mr. and Mrs. Adlai Ewing Stevenson II sailed from New York for a honeymoon lasting the six weeks that Adlai had requested and that included motor trips through Tunisia, Algeria, and Morocco.

Few couples ever could have seemed more happy than the Stevensons who moved in mid-January 1929 into a remodeled brownstone house at 76 Walton Place on the Gold Coast. Only a year later they moved up to a larger, more luxurious apartment on Lake Shore Drive. Adlai plunged into long hours at work, but his abundant energy also flowed into an exceptionally active social life. They were regarded as one of Chicago's most attractive young couples. Adlai amused, Ellen sparkled; Adlai glowed with pride on the edge of the spotlight that centered on Ellen in nearly every social gathering.

This too-good-to-be-true existence was interrupted on March 26 by Lewis. Sitting alone and lonely at a little desk in the Bloomington Club, he was writing a loving letter to Buffie. It was an oblique apology for one written a few weeks earlier in which he had chastised her for not using a thousand-dollar gift he had sent her, as he had requested, for her health; and had urged her to make her husband quit smoking. He added, "Observe your mother & me and our unhappy lives as examples to be avoided." Suddenly, he was hit with the excruciating pain of a severe heart attack. He was not a stranger to pain, but he knew this was different, and called a young cousin, Dr. E. M. Stevenson, for help. Dr. Ed's diagnosis quickly established the imminent possibility of death. He was struck, too, by the extent to which pain had ravaged the body of this active, witty man who had seemed younger than his sixty-one years, but whose body now seemed to be that of a man in his late seventies.

Adlai and Ellen immediately came down from Chicago. Helen, as so often in their married life, was away; this time in the south of France. Adlai later recounted to biographer Kenneth S. Davis a poignant and prescient incident when he was alone in the room with Lewis. In great pain, and barely able to whisper, he looked intently at Adlai and gasped that "politics is a hazardous life, full of ingratitudes." It seemed to Adlai that his father was trying to warn him against a political career. This mystified him because, except for a very brief consideration of a suggestion from Jane Dick's father that he run for the legislature, he had not considered entering politics. Adlai could not remember precisely what his father's words were. But he did clearly remember that his father murmured something about an "obligation" and "doing what you must" along with his warning. And he became convinced that his father had hoped and believed that Adlai, with his heritage, background, and convictions, was destined (or "doomed" as Adlai would sometimes say) to have a career in politics.

When it appeared that his father might survive, at least for a time, Adlai and Ellen had returned to Chicago, but on Friday, April 5, they boarded a one o'clock train to return to Lewis's bedside. At about the same time, Lewis, with his sister Julia, Mrs. Martin D. Hardin, beside him, dropped off to sleep. At five minutes before two he suddenly awoke and asked, "Is everything all right?" "Yes," she replied. "Everything's fine." He closed his eyes, sighed, and quietly died. Helen was in mid-Atlantic. The separation carried over even in the detailed instructions he had left for his funeral. "I want to be buried next to my father. Your mother should be buried in her father's lot." Immediately after the funeral, Adlai went to New York to meet her as she disembarked from the S.S. *Homeric.*

Six months later the great Wall Street crash of October 1929 punctuated, but inflicted no serious hardships on, the personal lives of Adlai and Ellen. Her fortune and her mother's shrank in proportion to the decline in values, and her father's losses were so severe he never recovered his position in the financial world. Lewis had not left a large estate, but his substantial interest in *The Pantagraph,* of which he was a director and vice president, would go to Adlai and his sister upon the death of their mother.

Work at the law firm actually increased as it helped its clients piece back together the financial structures torn apart by Wall Street's collapse. But Adlai was not wholly isolated from the human toll of the Depression. The men sleeping on the benches of Grant and Lincoln parks, the breadlines, the ragged, hungry men begging for food or nickles and dimes or selling apples even on fashionable Michigan Avenue, stabbed the conscience of people far less sensitive than he was.

He added to the fifty-hour-plus weeks at the law firm, work at the Lower North Side Community Council, at Hull House, where he was soon on the board of directors, the Immigrants' Protective League, and the Illinois Children's Home and Aid Society.

On October 10, 1930, Adlai Ewing Stevenson III arrived. Two more boys followed: Borden in July 1932, and John Fell in February 1936. Ellen delighted in being a mother and both were inordinately proud of the boys. They entertained less but went out a great deal. Their disagreements seemed to be confined mainly to Adlai's reluctance to spend money. His parsimony and her extravagance created situations that Adlai would try to handle, not always successfully, with a teasing joke. But it was only in hindsight that friends saw blotches on what seemed to be charmed and charming lives filled with weekend parties at Lake Forest and other fashionable places, plus such "extras" as fox hunts at the Onwentsia Club, ski trips to Michigan, and even vacations abroad, notably a tour of Scandinavia where Ernest and Buffie were stationed in Copenhagen.

Ruth Winter, in her recollections of this period, has said of Adlai and Ellen: "She was gay, she'd laugh a great deal. He was proud of her beauty—oh, she was pretty. She had a kind of inward grace. She'd come into a room rather quietly, with poise and would be charming. She was a very good hostess." Others had slightly different recollections. One has said that "Ellen was a little bit, oh, high-hatted." Another, that on entering a room, she "made an entrance," and dominated the gathering. There is no doubt that as Adlai gained in prominence and became the center of attention, her behavior became more quixotic and was even described as being, on occasion, "nasty." In the presence of Ed Austin, the senior partner of his law firm, and a colleague, James Oates, Ellen once maintained that "no gentlemen should work." Austin recalled the incident as throwing "a little light for me upon what he was up against at home." Visits to Bloomington seemed to be especially difficult. Adlai's friends and relatives there felt that she looked down on them.

John Bartlow Martin has observed that "the most striking thing" about this period in their lives was the parallel between Adlai's mother and his wife.

> His mother tended to dominate social gatherings by being stagy and "always on," as an actress is; so did Ellen. His mother pretended to considerable taste and ability in the arts but actually was neither very talented nor interested in intellectual things; so with Ellen. His mother was a snob; so was Ellen. His mother could make things difficult for her husband; so could Ellen. . . . Both his wife and mother were, if not real beauties, close to it. Both dressed beautifully—when they chose to—and were conscious of it. Both dominated, or tried to dominate, their husbands.

With the approach of the 1932 presidential election, Adlai became active politically. Democrats who lived on the Gold Coast and worked on LaSalle Street were rare indeed. So he quickly came to the attention of one other, Colonel A. A. Sprague, chairman of Sprague, Warner and Company and a director of the Continental Illinois Bank, who had been the Democratic candidate for the United States Senate in 1924. Thanks to him, Adlai was soon introduced to Alderman Dorsey R. Crowe and Ward Committeeman William "Botchy" Conners, both of whom were to become legendary figures in the Chicago "machine," or organization, that dominated Illinois Democratic politics for as long as Adlai lived. Out of these contacts, plus his father's long relationship with United States Senator J. Hamilton Lewis, came the suggestion that he run for the state

Senate. Adlai declined, but he was clearly beginning to test the political waters.

He went to the Democratic National Convention hoping to get a press badge, but did not succeed. He became a western treasurer for the Roosevelt presidential campaign and threw himself into the race for governor by Probate Judge Henry Horner, whom he had come to know professionally, and who later became a good personal friend. Horner, a Jew and a respected Lincoln scholar, was regarded as a "blue-ribbon candidate" rather than a party hack. To combat prejudiced attitudes that combined anti-Semitism with downstate mistrust of Chicago candidates, Adlai urged Horner to have "some one write a series of articles about your non-political activities, largely Lincoln and the Probate Court. To be saturated with Lincoln is to be saturated with Illinois, and I am confident that the story of your intimate acquaintance with the historical panorama of the whole state would help."

When Roosevelt's campaign train came to Chicago, Judge Horner took Adlai with him to meet the candidate. Roosevelt immediately recalled that his father and Vice President Stevenson had been good friends and that he himself had worked with Adlai's father in the Navy Department during the war. This encounter left him "stammering, surprised and devoted." He carried on a spirited debate with Dave Merwin about *The Pantagraph*'s political position and finally succeeded in getting an endorsement for Horner, but not for Roosevelt.

Ellen and Adlai went to Washington for the Inauguration, staying, characteristically, with Republican Chicago friends, Mr. and Mrs. James Douglas. He had been President Hoover's assistant secretary of the treasury. Efforts to call on Senator Lewis were unsuccessful but, he wrote his mother, he had "a very pleasant interview" with his father's friend, Harold Ickes, President Roosevelt's secretary of the interior, who "seemed very much interested in my vague suggestion that I might be interested in government employment."

The New Deal was attracting many young men to Washington, and Adlai responded quickly in July to an offer to become a special attorney and assistant to Jerome Frank, general counsel of the Agricultural Adjustment Administration. He owed the offer to his father. In the 1920s, Lewis had worked on farm problems with George Peek who was now head of the AAA. When Adlai's name was mentioned to him he exclaimed, "Why, that is Louie Stevenson's boy. . . . Let's get him if we can."

Ellen and the two boys remained at home through the summer. After a short stay in a hotel, he moved in with friends; as he nearly always did—partly to save money, and partly because he always wanted people around him. His letters to Ellen recounted long hours and hard work. Hers to him were warm, witty, and loving. She wrote him frequently, sometimes more than once a day. They looked forward eagerly to being reunited, as they were in late August when she and the boys came to a house he had rented in Georgetown. The happy accounts of this period are in stark contrast to her later aversion to Washington life.

At work, Adlai admired the intellect and intensity of Frank who had surrounded himself with top students from leading law schools; from Yale, Thurman Arnold and Abe Fortas; from Harvard, John Abt, Lee Pressman, Nathan Witt—and Alger Hiss. Arthur Schlesinger, Jr., in *The Coming of the New Deal,* reported that old agricultural specialists like Peek resented these young urban types. "There were too many Ivy League men, too many intellectuals, too many radicals, too many Jews." Adlai's letters to Ellen reflected some of these tensions that led to Peek's departure in December. This also may have been a factor in Adlai's decision in January to become chief attorney of the Federal Alcohol Control Administration that was set up following repeal of the Eighteenth Amendment, and where he remained until returning to Chicago in the fall. His experience in drafting farm marketing agreements in the first job, and pricing and distribution regulations in the second, he described in a paper he gave to the Legal Club in Chicago not long after his return.

He had gone to Washington, he said, "to solve the farm problem and ended up in alcohol." He went on:

> My first job was a marketing agreement for the fresh California deciduous tree fruit industry. The delegation from California was only a little upset when I asked what "deciduous" meant! . . . During the six months I was there, I negotiated with producers, processors or handlers of everything from Atlantic oysters to California oranges, and from Oregon apples to Florida strawberries. Walnut and asparagus growers from California, rice millers from Louisiana, lettuce shippers from Arizona, shade grown tobacco handlers from Connecticut, potato merchants from Maine, candy manufacturers from Pennsylvania, chicken hatchers from everywhere, date and grape shippers and olive canners from California, pea canners from Wisconsin, peanut processors from Virginia and the Carolinas—all these and dozens more came to confess their sins and beg for help. We laughed a little when the wintergreen trust appeared, and more at the pimento magnates who wanted an embargo on Spanish pimentos. The mayonnaise people won an endurance contest with the cotton seed crushers with three continuous months on the doorstep, and the Boston mackerel fishermen arrived in the Potomac in a Gloucester schooner. But the big laugh came the morning a Georgia delegation led by a Senator and a couple of Congressmen arrived and calmly announced that the Pa[c]kaged Bees Industry was going to hell!

Turning serious, he referred to a report by the secretary of agriculture that thirteen marketing agreements increased returns to growers more than thirty million dollars, "so I take some pride in the fact that of those thirteen agreements, I wrote ten."

He described the "ominous situation" arising from the lack of any regulatory legislation regarding alcohol following the repeal of Prohibition, stressing that "social welfare is the first consideration of the alcohol Codes" in contrast to industry welfare that marked codes under the National Industrial Recovery Act. His most serious comments he reserved for the end, and the call to public service he sounded was to be echoed again and again in the speeches made after he had become a national figure.

> Government is no longer as Aristotle and Livy said, an empire of laws. Government is ultimately a government of men and the alchemy of administration converts the abstraction of the state into the concrete. . . . I can look forward mistily to the time when government service will be one of the highest aspirations of educated men. . . . I have detected a growing consciousness in statecraft that bad government is bad politics and that good government means good men.

Much of the rest of his life revolved around those four sentences.

Returning to Chicago, Adlai took up the role that was to propel him into public prominence—the presidency of the Chicago Council on Foreign Relations. Actually, he had been elected president in April 1933, the youngest president since the founding of the council in 1922. But he had left almost immediately for Washington. They were glad to have him back, as some of its leaders, most notably Harriet Welling, had already discerned the qualities that helped him make the Chicago Council one of the most influential foreign policy platforms in the country.

Chicago was the capital of midwestern isolationism and Colonel McCormick's *Tribune* was its thunderous voice. The Council on Foreign Relations had been founded by League of Nations partisans and soon became the principal counter to the *Tribune*'s stridently narrow nationalism. Chicago's elite formed the council's leadership and flocked to its meetings. The large Saturday luncheons at the Palmer House became "in" social events, and the brilliant young executive director, Clifton Utley, made certain they exposed the audience to some of the best thinking on issues of foreign policy then available. But George W. Ball has written that "the attraction for many—the more cynical of us suspected—was hardly the wisdom of the speakers so much as Adlai's wise and scintillating introductions."

In delivery, they seemed spontaneous, off-the-cuff, but were in fact carefully constructed with serious argument lightened by witticisms, often directed at himself and a use of the language that sent people away admiring the "Stevenson style." However urbane and casual they seemed, they were the products of labor that cut deeply into his work at the law firm. His friend and partner there, Ed McDougal has said that "the law took second place in his interests to the Council." Adlai later told inquirers for the *Quarterly Journal of Speech* in 1956 that "I was scared to death when I spoke [at the Council]. I still am for that matter"; adding that it was the experience at the council that improved his ability as a public speaker, along with "hard work and deliberate and diligent discipline."

The Council on Foreign Relations did more for him. It brought him into active contact with people who later would be his strong supporters. Even people like Clay Judson, a leading lawyer and a leader of the more thoughtful isolationists wrote him: "It should be on your conscience that you are not serving your country by going into politics." The Council also made him a public figure. He was leading a movement for a more world-minded approach to foreign policy. He was reaching out to important figures here and abroad to bring them to Chicago to help in the movement, and they would remember him. Perhaps more important was the knowledge and understanding he was adding to his interest in foreign affairs.

The *Chicago Daily News* in those days maintained a brilliant staff of foreign correspondents, and invariably they would be invited to speak at the council when they returned from abroad, and Adlai would engage them in long private discussions. Carroll Binder and, especially, Lloyd Lewis became close personal friends. This broadening of contacts reached into the academic community as well, particularly at the University of Chicago, which was graced by Russian history professor Samuel Harper, international relations professor Quincy Wright, and economics professor Jacob Viner, as well as its president, Dr. Robert M. Hutchins, all of whom became personal friends.

The Council on Foreign Relations may have impinged on his law practice, but, happily, it did not do so on his marriage. Ellen enjoyed bringing her friends to the luncheons, where she could display the man she had married. At this time they were clearly very much in love, despite her later denials. Occasional eruptions were regarded as the jealous reaction of a spoiled child of privilege. The personality disorder that so tragically affected their later lives only gradually manifested itself as the spotlight shifted from her toward him.

Incidents that went from petulant to bizarre to nasty generally have been described without placing them in the context of the progression of increasingly serious mental illness. It was an illness that those closest to her—including Adlai for long after the divorce—were slow and reluctant to recognize. Hindsight, legal proceedings, and psychiatric testimony now make understandable the behavior that baffled and saddened her family.

It was his mother's mental and physical condition rather than Ellen's that commanded Adlai's attention in this period. Shortly before they had left Washington, Helen had suffered what Adlai described as a "severe nervous breakdown" while visiting Buffie and the John Alden Carpenters in Manchester, Massachusetts. He and Ellen hurried back from Hawaii and found her under the care of Lydiard Horton, who had counseled both Lewis and Helen decades earlier. Adlai had a low opinion of Horton and his "bio-psychic" theories and arranged to send Helen to the Battle Creek Sanitarium in Michigan. She became his prime concern, as she moved from doctor to doctor and institution to institution. Each move involved numerous family conferences, visits, consultations with doctors, and a steady flow of letters. She had spent much of her life traveling to places for "rest cures," but now the doctors Adlai was consulting were prescribing psychiatric diagnosis and treatment.

By year's end he had gained admission for her to the highly reputable institution of Dr. Austen Riggs in Stockbridge, Massachusetts, and with great difficulty persuaded her to go. She was not happy there and Dr. Riggs recommended Craig House in Beacon, New York. Although the diagnosis and treatment were the best she had ever received, when Adlai visited her in June, she was so "homesick and dissatisfied," he took her home to Bloomington.

By August she was in the Milwaukee Sanitarium in Wauwatosa, Wisconsin, and the pattern established at Riggs and at Craig House set in all over again. On November 7, the sanatorium told Adlai that she had developed a low-grade fever and a nose and throat specialist had been called in but found nothing. On November 13, Adlai went to see her and told the doctor he found her failure to improve "disconcerting," and the possibility of dental work was discussed. The sanatorium reported that she "seemed to react fairly well" to his visit and he proposed to come again on Sunday. On November 15, they told him she had suddenly developed a high fever and the dental work had been postponed. An internist examined her and found nothing to explain the fever. The next morning she was dead. The cause was said to be "fever of unknown origin perhaps acute endocarditis" with "manic depressive depression" a contributory factor. Her restless, troubled life was over.

In the midst of all this, Adlai was involved in changes at *The Pantagraph,* admission to partnership in the law firm on January 1, 1936, and the purchase of land, where he and Ellen would build the first of the two homes that became, along with his sons, the anchor of his life.

Dave Merwin accepted an offer from John and Gardner Cowles, Jr., to become publisher of their recently purchased *Minneapolis Star.* His brother Bud took his place. Before leaving, Merwin had begun the construction of a new building for the paper and Adlai involved himself in the details of the planning—mostly with the object of saving money. His relations with Bud were much more relaxed than with Dave even though they occasionally had disagreements—usually over expenditures that he watched closely and over editorial policy that rarely strayed from Republican orthodoxy.

Adlai had been admitted to partnership in the law firm after nine years, including the one year in Washington. This was close to the customary testing period for law associates. However, his partners were torn between the time that outside affairs, especially the Council on Foreign Relations, took from his practice and their pride in his steadily growing reputation. They nonetheless gave him a load of cases that kept him working late into most nights, and often on Saturdays. His income from the firm went from $5,655 in 1935 to $9,838 the next year, the first as a partner. But even in that year, there were tentative feelers that indicated the public-service "bug" was still there. A sense of discontent might have become a problem except that he and Ellen had at last found the place where they wanted to build their home.

In the aftermath of the Depression, the Libertyville estate of Samuel Insull had come on the market. The Stevensons bought forty acres, to which they later added another thirty, that was bordered by a small, pretty stream rather grandly called the Des Plaines River. When they bought it, the property could be reached only by canoe up the river, or by horseback. St. Mary's Road was built later. It was gentle, rolling farmland that rose from a low, slightly swampy area in the east to a knoll where they built their house, and then sloped down to the river. The acres to the north frequently were planted in soybeans, corn, and vegetables. Closer to the house, there were great maples and oaks amid the grassland that Adlai frugally kept mowed with a flock of roaming goats. Their voracious presence sometimes astonished distinguished visitors.

Originally they thought they would use the house only in the summer, but it turned out to be the place where Adlai lived longer than any other except for his early years in Bloomington. It was the place he kept coming back to, or dreamed of coming back to, during the long interludes away: the war years in Washington, the years in Springfield as governor, and the years in New York at the United Nations. It was, in the fullest sense, home.

Ellen's talents were in full and effective use in its design and decoration. Sadly, the house burned down after barely two years, destroying many of the family treasures and memorabilia Adlai had brought from Bloomington. But they quickly set about to rebuild it.

The house was low and white, and its rather modest appearance, as one came up the long lane, disguised a spacious, comfortable house with numerous rooms of generous size. Indeed, it was one place where spending money gave him pleasure. Guests felt at home in the large living room whose spaciousness was enhanced by French doors opening onto a porch that overlooked land sloping down to the river. But Adlai's favorite was the study; more accurately, a working library. One wall and most of two others were covered by books. There were three shelves of books on Lincoln, and others filled with family-related writings—campaign biographies of President Grover Cleveland and Vice President Stevenson; Grandfather Stevenson's book, *Something of Men I Have Known,* and a brief history of the Daughters of the American Revolution he had written in tribute to his wife; *The Life of Jesse W. Fell; A Life of L. W. Green;* and other family memorabilia. Friend and neighbor Lloyd Lewis had been able to save some of them from the fire that occurred in the Stevensons' absence. The books close to his desk were ones used in writing: an encyclopedia, a dictionary, a Bible, an anthology of quotations. The desk in later years was simply a long narrow table with a brown leather swivel chair. From it he could look out the corner windows to woods and rolling grassland.

Upstairs, the master bedroom occupied the entire south half of the second floor. It was large and looked even larger. Doors opened to a sun deck and porch with outside stairs, where hours were spent watching sunsets and the changes that came with the seasons, or falling asleep in the sun.

Nearby was the farmer's house and a garage-stable with three horse stalls where he, Ellen, and John Fell lived when the house was being rebuilt, with Adlai III and Borden sleeping in an adjacent tent. "It has been surprisingly comfortable," Adlai wrote. "I have even enjoyed sharing my wash basin with my horse!" For the duration of the building, however, the horses were exiled to the white-fenced corral behind the barn. There was a tennis court adjacent to the porch, where friends and neighbors would gather on weekends for fairly vigorous tennis and much relaxed conversation.

Adlai loved everything about the place. When he would come back, he would roam the woods, picking up broken limbs, carefully assessing the maples that were special favorites, running the dogs, checking on the vegetables growing in the garden, and occasionally climbing onto the tractor. He liked feeling close to the soil, particularly in Illinois.

He would go riding with the boys, fishing with them in the river, and, undoubtedly goaded by memories of his own childhood experience with a gun, teaching them how to shoot and handle firearms. Borden remembers when a gun he was carrying on a hunting expedition went off between him and his father, blowing a hole in the roof of a recently purchased car. To his amazement, his father did not get angry; he simply took great pains to point out quietly what had been done wrong and to practice procedures that would prevent a recurrence.

Not all the memories were idyllic. Adlai III, in an interview with John Bartlow Martin, spoke in these terms:

I remember the river—skating on the Des Plaines river. Taking the horse and the sleigh out on the river, which Dad liked to do. I did a lot of riding with him. I started early hunting pheasants and rabbits. Dad went along occasionally. He never was a compulsive hunter—he thought of it as an opportunity to be with the boys and to get outdoors. He loved to ride, especially a big horse named Jeb, named after Jeb Stuart of Civil War fame.

My memories of my mother are not all pleasant. I don't know when it all started—and I suppose a certain amount is normal with boys—she had all sorts of notions how to raise children—strict diets, eating regularly, cold showers every morning before breakfast. We were not allowed to read the newspapers because we might be infected by the evil in the world. Radio and comics were strictly out. She was very strict about taking risks with the family safety. There was no flying in airplanes unless all five of us were together. Borden bore the brunt of her discipline. [Other accounts refer to frequent face-slappings.] Dad rarely got involved in it. I can remember only once being spanked by him. We were rarely if ever permitted to go to the movies. There was a time when only French was spoken around the house. We usually had French governesses in Libertyville.

We didn't have a great deal of contact with Dad. He was a compulsive worker. We'd see him in the morning when he took us to school. Evenings he'd read to us before we went to bed or they went out. . . . They went out often. Then nights, if they were home, I remember the light burning in that library. I remember Sunday lunches—that was always a big meal, a family occasion. Weekends we saw the most of him, skating, riding, trap shooting, and lots of tennis at the house. . . . He encouraged the social life of the kids—having parties, having friends over.

I have a vague memory of quarrels, bitter quarrels. I guess we weren't very happy as children. There was the terrible discipline, few friends, living on the farm which we loved but which made us isolated. All these constraints started breaking down as Borden and John Fell came along. We were always closer to Dad and sympathized with him. We didn't like to see him hurt all the time.

In many ways she was a great mother. She worked hard. She had servants, but she drove us to town and worked in the house and gardened. The diets, the cold showers, and so on, must have been, although misguided, out of concern for her children.

It would be years before the possibility of mental illness occurred to anyone.

In the late 1930s, Ellen's name and picture appeared frequently in the society pages of Chicago's newspapers, and Adlai's name appeared almost as frequently as a result of his civic activities. To his leadership of the Council on Foreign Relations, vice presidency of the Illinois Children's Home and Aid Society, membership on the boards of the Immigrants' Protective League of Chicago and Hull House, he added board membership of International House at the University of Chicago, chairmanship of the Civil Rights Committee of the Chicago Bar Association, and the presidency of the Legislative Voters League, which carefully watched the work of the Illinois legislature and graded the legislators on their performance. The *Chicago Daily News* commented that "Mr. Stevenson accepted leadership under the compelling conviction that the opportunity for a necessary service constituted a civic obligation."

He had also become a director of the Personal Loan and Savings Bank, and was persuaded to become the general chairman of the 1937 President's Birthday Ball in Chicago. Earlier, in the 1936 presidential campaign, he had served as finance director of the Democratic National Committee and state chairman of the National Council of Roosevelt Electors. Repeatedly there were inquiries from Washington about his availability for various jobs. In May 1937, for example, Secretary of Labor Frances Perkins asked him to become commissioner-general of immigration and naturalization.

In 1936 and 1937, Adlai was also heavily involved in attempts to rescue from the wreckage of many of John Borden's enterprises as much as possible for the benefit of Ellen and her sister Betty. It is little wonder the boys remembered the lights burning late in the library.

Work at the law firm was intense. The financing of a gas company sent him and George Ball to Omaha, where they worked in oppressive heat for a month, after which Adlai proceeded to New York. Ball recalled that Adlai called him saying "I've just spent a magnificent morning with the bankers. The greed ran down their faces like sweat." He was hardworking, conscientious—and able. His colleagues kept telling him he had an outstanding future in the law, if he would concentrate his attention on it. But that is what he could not do. He knew he did not want to spend his life as a lawyer. His difficulty was that he could not decide what he wanted to spend his life doing. He just knew it had to involve larger issues, possibly government-related, but whether through appointive or elective office was not clear. His searching and discontent were evident, but his objective was not.

University of Chicago president Robert M. Hutchins has written: "Once long ago when he told me, as he often did, how much he disliked the practice of law and I replied, as I always did, by proposing he join the University of Chicago, he said: 'I'll tell you what I'm going to do: I'm going to stay in this infernal law firm until I make $25,000. Then I'm going to the chairman of the Democratic National Committee and say, Here's $25,000; I want to be an ambassador.'" Hutchins added that even though the remark was a joke, it reflected a deep desire.

In March of 1957, Adlai wrote biographer Kenneth S. Davis: "My fascination with public affairs—at home and abroad—must date from infancy, or almost! And in a curious inverted sort of way, have never found my own affairs quite as absorbing. Law, business, profit, *making* money, have never interested me as much as impersonal public affairs."

George Ball recalled: "He was always saying even then that so-and-so was talking to him about running for something. I didn't take it seriously. I thought it was fantasy."

CHAPTER FOUR
Onto the World Stage

GERMANY'S DECLARATION OF WAR on Poland on September 1, 1939, the entry of Britain and France a few days later, and President Roosevelt's declaration of a state of limited emergency on September 8 all led to increased attendance at the meetings of the Council on Foreign Relations. It was Hitler's stunning victories in the spring of 1940 that began to shove Adlai onto the scene as a distinctive political personality.

Earlier, William Allen White, the famous editor of the *Emporia Kansas Gazette,* backed by Clark Eichelberger, director of the League of Nations Association, had set up a national Non-Partisan Committee for Peace Through Revision of the Neutrality Law, known as the White Committee. In Chicago, they had been supported by Colonel Frank Knox, owner of the *Chicago Daily News* since the 1930s, and Alf Landon's running mate in the 1936 presidential election. The committee had played a helpful role in the repeal of the arms embargo, but then languished until Germany smashed into Norway, Denmark, Belgium, and the Netherlands, and drove British forces to the beaches at Dunkirk, followed by the surrender of France.

Shocked by these events, the Non-Partisan Committee transformed itself into the Committee to Defend America by Aiding the Allies and began recruiting support from all over the country. They focused on Chicago because the strident voice of the *Chicago Tribune* had made the city the symbolic if not the actual national capital of isolationism. Professor Quincy Wright, Professor (later Senator) Paul Douglas, then also on the city council, and Clifton Utley, executive director of the Council on Foreign Relations and radio commentator, all responded favorably to White's invitation to join and urged him to ask Adlai to become chairman of the Chicago committee. After discussing White's approach with his partners, Adlai agreed, and for the first time entered on a campaign that sharply divided families, friends and old loyalties, as it also divided city, state, and nation. He expected it to be a bruising experience. It was.

The organizing task was formidable. Money had to be raised, subchapters set up throughout the city and suburbs, rallies and public demonstrations arranged, speakers persuaded, newspaper and radio campaigns pushed to counter the *Tribune*'s attacks. Moreover, it was an election year and extraordinary agility was required to keep the committee and its positions out of partisan politics.

A significant contributor to this bridge building was William McCormick Blair, Jr., a young cousin of the *Tribune*'s publisher, who was to play an increasingly important role in Adlai's career. Fresh from Stanford University with an undergraduate degree, he walked into the White Committee offices and volunteered his services. His help was both symbolic and real. The presence of the scion of a prominent Republican family closely related to "the Colonel," sent an anti-*Tribune* message throughout the whole country, and it encouraged many wavering Republicans to lend their support. Moreover, he quickly exhibited the talent for organization, liaison, and general troubleshooting that later was to prove so invaluable to Adlai.

Partisan wrangling became especially acute in June when President Roosevelt responded to the collapse of France and the entry of Italy into the war by appointing two leading Republicans, former Secretary of State Henry L. Stimson and Colonel Knox as secretary of war and secretary of the navy. Outraged old-guard Republicans sought to delay their confirmation. Tension relaxed a little after the Republican convention nominated Wendell Willkie and the Democratic convention voted the unprecedented third-term nomination for President Roosevelt. Both candidates, however, carefully juggled the question of American intervention and pledged that American boys would not be sent to fight in foreign wars. The debates leading up to the conventions had been bitter, and Adlai, in his appearance before the Democratic Platform Committee, had followed the President's line in saying "Our soldiers shall fight only for our defense and not in Europe," while also maintaining that "it is in our manifest national interest to extend to Great Britain in this hour of peril to her democracy and to ours all possible material aid and comfort."

From this somewhat equivocal position, he returned home to fight more specifically for the plan to exchange old-age destroyers for British naval bases and for enactment of the Lend-Lease bill.

The national importance of the local debate took on new dimensions in September 1940 with the formation of America First, with the chief executive of Sears, Roebuck, General Robert E. Wood, as chairman.

Friends such as University of Chicago president Robert M. Hutchins, the bulk of the LaSalle Street lawyers, most of the wealthy businessmen, and Lake Forest neighbors became active America Firsters. It hurt, but he forged ahead building a coalition with important support from labor, the colleges, and some business and civic leaders.

He engaged in a remarkable series of debates with fellow lawyer Clay Judson before various civic groups. Though they disagreed vigorously, they remained good friends even as the arguments raging around them grew more personal and vindictive. Clifton Utley lost sponsors for his radio broadcasts. Important clients brought pressure on Adlai's law firm and some of them withdrew their business in repeated efforts to persuade the partners to restrain Adlai. The damage inflicted on the firm bothered him, as it did a few of the partners, but they stood behind him and refused his offer to have his share of the profits reduced.

The White Committee was excoriated as a front for Jews, a "mass murder committee," "warmongers," "cookie pushers," and "professional bleeding hearts," and Adlai himself was the object of running personal attacks in the *Tribune*. Supporters of the White Committee, for their part, indulged in similar invective, calling General Wood, for example, "Hitler's front man." Even Adlai, at a giant and wildly successful public meeting at the Coliseum—one of the largest ever held in Chicago up to that time—referred to "Chicago's active minority, well intentioned and otherwise, of appeasers, defeatists, and foes of aid to Britain."

"It was an exciting time," he later told biographer Kenneth S. Davis. "It was a knock-down-drag-out fight, really. The *Tribune* used to send photographers to photograph all empty seats, if any, in the halls where we presented programs—and the *News* photographers photographed all the full ones. I'd be a dirty dog in the *Tribune* in the morning, and a shining hero in the *News* at night." What he remembered with pain, however, were personal friends who made such comments as "Adlai's trying to kill our sons." "I was trying to save their sons," he protested. "I was convinced that aid to Britain was the only means, the only chance of our keeping out of the war."

He was concerned not only by the descending level of the debate, but even more so by the changes taking place in his own thinking. In two of their later debates, Clay Judson had posed a question that haunted him. "Is this our war? If it is our war, then we should be in it without delay."

Adlai could not escape asking himself, "Is this our war?" and moving toward the conclusion, as Britain's position became more precarious, that it was. His internal debate was decided by a "Letter to the Editor" read on the commuter train on the way home arguing that there was no tenable "middle ground" between isolationism and outright intervention; that one had to choose. He looked out on the speeding landscape and faced the fact that he had already chosen. This meant that as soon as he could do so without hurting his colleagues on the White Committee, he must resign as chairman. It was the honorable thing to do.

The decision also tipped the scales against continuing work in the law firm. He began making discreet inquiries about places of possible usefulness, although the answer had begun taking shape even earlier. Every time Knox had come home to Chicago, he had talked to Adlai about coming to Washington. The veteran of Teddy Roosevelt's Rough Riders and of World War I was a staunch, New Deal-hating Republican, but the outstanding staff of foreign correspondents working for the *News,* he said, had "educated" him. Therefore, he was willing to put aside his feelings about Roosevelt's domestic policies, endure the cruel attacks of his fellow Republicans, and become navy secretary. He had watched Adlai's leadership of the Council on Foreign Relations and of the White Committee with admiration. Finally, in early June 1941, he telephoned, and as Adlai recalled the conversation, said:

"I go to all these meetings. Every day, important meetings with important people. There sit [Sidney] Hillman, and [William] Knudsen, and [Henry L.] Stimson, and others—every one of them has his own personal lawyer. Even Jim Forrestal [Knox's undersecretary] has his own lawyer—and I don't have one. Why don't you plan to come down here and be my lawyer, so I won't feel so defenseless? When are you going to be in Washington?" Adlai replied that he had no plans to be in Washington. "Well, you'd better plan to come as soon as you can. Bring a big suitcase and plan to stay."

Jobs at higher pay were offered him by the Office of Production Management and at the Office of Emergency Management, but on June 30, he wrote Knox that his partners had agreed to a leave of absence for three months, "at which time we can look the situation over again," adding that "they were as much surprised and flattered as I was—and doubtless somewhat shocked by your doubtful judgement." Knox replied, "You tell your partners that I have no doubt whatsoever about my judgement on this particular matter." On July 6, two weeks after German armies had invaded Russia, the Navy Department announced the appointment of Adlai Stevenson as "Principal Attorney" in the Office of the Secretary of the Navy, and special assistant to the secretary, at a salary of $5,000 per year.

"I wish I could tell you what my job is," he wrote Dave Merwin at *The Pantagraph,* "but at the end of the first week I have not found out myself—perhaps legal maid servant to Frank Knox would be accurate. At all events, it is interesting if not important."

But it was important, and became more so. Archibald MacLeish, based on his experience in wartime Washington, has observed that "Adlai was doing far more responsible war work than was generally recognized. . . . The best way to get action in some places in the Navy Department was through Adlai." Carl McGowan, who had been called to

Washington by Adlai to work in the Bureau of Ships, has stated that "the confidence Knox had in Stevenson—and his respect for Stevenson's advice—meant that Stevenson influenced many major political-military decisions."

There was another aspect of his service that reflected a central element in his character and conviction. George Ball, in an *Atlantic Monthly* article in 1966, wrote of it in these terms:

> From the moment he arrived in the Navy Department, Adlai became a one-man recruiting office for the United States government, exhibiting an unflagging zeal for helping even casual acquaintances find appropriate assignments in the public service. . . . It sprang from his deeply held conviction that the government needed and deserved the best talents the nation could produce.

A specific test of his capabilities came very early. In late July, when Adlai arrived at the Navy Department, a strike appeared to be imminent at the huge shipyard of the Federal Shipbuilding and Drydock Corporation at Kearny, New Jersey, where some sixteen thousand workers were building fighting ships for the Navy and merchant ships for the Maritime Commission. The CIO Industrial Union of Marine and Shipbuilding Workers was insisting that a maintenance of membership clause must be in the contract under negotiation in return for a no-strike pledge during the emergency. As stalemate in the negotiations brought closer a crisis in the emergency shipbuilding program, Adlai was assigned to represent Knox and the Navy Department at meetings with the Defense Mediation Board, the Maritime Commission, and the Office of Production Management. It was quickly recognized that if a strike occurred the government must be prepared to take over and operate the shipyard. Adlai was asked to devise the legal machinery to implement the decision. It presented unprecedented problems: This would be the first seizure by the government of a great private plant engaged in national defense work, and, among other things, it required an executive order to be signed by the President. Days and nights of ground-breaking work produced plans and documents that all the above-mentioned agencies, plus the Justice Department, found satisfactory.

As feared, the union struck on August 7. Eleven anxious days of negotiation with the union and management at the Mediation Board followed with Adlai sitting at Knox's side or representing him. The board's recommendation was rejected by management. There was general consensus that continuation of the shutdown was intolerable and that there was no alternative but seizure. The difficulty was that the President was not available to sign the necessary executive order. The historic secret meeting off Newfoundland between the President, who had traveled aboard the U.S.S. *Augusta,* and Prime Minister Winston Churchill, on H.M.S. *Prince of Wales,* had begun on August 9. From it was to emerge the Atlantic Charter and its pronouncement of the Four Freedoms as the basis for future peace; but at that moment the attention of Washington, and of the country, was focused far more urgently on the resumption of shipbuilding. It was decided that Adlai must fly out to brief the President, and obtain his signature on the executive order. He was to fly up to Quonset Point, Rhode Island, where a Navy seaplane would be waiting to fly him out to the *Augusta.* Just as he was about to leave, he was summoned to Knox's office, where he found both Knox and Admiral Chester Nimitz with unusually solemn expressions on their faces.

"The Admiral has a message he wants you to take to the President and deliver to him in person," the secretary said. "Go ahead, Admiral."

"You are to deliver this message to the President and *to no one else,*" the admiral said sternly. "Tell him I have learned today, from a heretofore reliable source, that Stalin has opened negotiations with Hitler." Adlai says he gulped, realizing that this would nullify all the plans that had been based on the assumption that Russia for months to come would be absorbing much of Germany's offensive strength. This meant that Hitler would be free to turn westward again and perhaps be in a position to invade Britain in the autumn before American aid could be delivered in adequate measure to be effective.

Adlai says he repeated the message aloud to make certain he was stating it correctly. Again he was warned that only the President was to receive it, and as quickly as possible. The import of the message alone was enough to intensify his sense of urgency.

But when he got to Quonset Point, it seemed as if a Hollywood scriptwriter had taken over. Bad weather had all planes grounded. Despite Adlai's pleas about the vital nature of his mission, the admiral in charge refused to let a plane take off to search for a cruiser at sea in such weather. Finally, he agreed that in spite of the risk he would authorize a small plane to take Adlai to Rockland, Maine, on the assumption he could get there by the time the *Augusta* docked. As they circled Rockland, they saw the ship at the dock and a huge crowd around a train alongside. Adlai persuaded the pilot to put the plane down in a grass field, flagged down a car driven by a frightened elderly lady, and urged her to speed into the town. Six blocks from the station, they were stopped by a traffic jam. Adlai jumped out and started running toward the train only to see it pulling out. Swinging around, he hitchhiked back to the field and asked the pilot to take him to Portland, which was the train's next scheduled stop.

It was a roundabout trip for the train, and the plane arrived hours ahead of it. Adlai, restless and anxious, decided to sit out the time in a movie theater. But when he arrived at the Portland station, he discovered the crowd was many times larger than that at Rockland and every approach was blocked. Portland policemen were unimpressed by his insistence that he had a message of vital importance for the President. Suddenly he spotted Senator Claude Pepper, whom he knew only slightly, headed for the train accompanied by two policemen and two other men who turned out to be the mayor and a former governor. He explained to Senator Pepper that he had Kearny shipyard papers that required the President's signature immediately. The senator promised to see what he could do and took Adlai with him to the platform as the train pulled in, leaving him there when the Secret Service men would not allow him to come aboard with them. Fifteen agonizing minutes later, the President's aide, General "Pa" Watson, emerged and in a friendly fashion explained that the President was at dinner and asked Adlai to hand over the papers. Adlai insisted he had to see the President personally, and finally, Watson withdrew leaving Adlai red-faced with embarrassment and the crowd around him eyeing him derisively. After what seemed an eternity, Watson returned and said the President would see him.

When he entered the car, the President was still at dinner with Mrs. Roosevelt, Marvin McIntyre, Harry Hopkins, and Grace Tully.

"Well, Adlai," the President said, smiling, "I'm glad to see you again. Glad to hear you are working for Frank Knox."

Taken aback by such a warm personal greeting, Adlai could never remember what his reply was other than to say he had emergency papers for the President's signature.

"Let's have a look at them," the President said.

At this point, we turn to Adlai's own written account of what happened.

> I opened up my brief case clumsily and fished out the Kearny shipyard papers. I explained the intricate situation as best I could, as the President's dinner got colder and the others more restive, and pointed out where he was supposed to sign the order. He looked it over a minute and then said:
>
> "Well, now, Adlai, you just leave all those papers in your folder with me, and I'll read them over tonight. We'll have a meeting at the White House in the morning. You fly back to Washington and arrange it. Tell Secretary Knox I'd also like to see him and Myron Taylor and the Attorney General at nine o'clock—and you be there, too."
>
> "But, Mr. President," I said, "these are supposed to be signed right now!"
>
> "I think it will work out all right this way," said the President.
>
> "Well," I said, "if you say so I guess it will be O.K.!" I marvel that I could have talked like such a fool but I was so nervous I hardly knew what I was saying—mostly, I suppose,

because I hadn't yet said the really important thing—the message—and I didn't know how to deliver it with all those people sitting around. I could see he was waiting for me to leave, and I had to come out with something. The talk went about like this:

"I have something else to tell you, Mr. President."

"Do you, Adlai? What is it?"

"Well, Mr. President, it's a message from Admiral Nimitz. He said to tell you . . . alone."

"Oh, I think you can tell me here, Adlai."

"No sir, I can't." I had a feeling everyone was doing his best to keep from laughing! I had an idea, just in time. "Can I write it down, sir?"

"Why, certainly."

I took the menu and wrote on the back of it, "Admiral Nimitz has heard from a heretofore reliable source today that Stalin has started negotiations with Hitler."

Then I gave him back the menu. He read it carefully and then looked up at me.

"Adlai," he said, "do you believe this?"

That was too much! I didn't know what I thought. "Why, I don't know, Mr. President," I stammered.

"I don't believe it," said F.D.R. "I'm not worried at all. Are you worried, Adlai?"

I said I guessed I wasn't so much worried after all. Then, mission completed, after a fashion, I took my departure, and in my embarrassed confusion, I wheeled around and crashed right into a closed door, thus bending my crooked nose some more. I flew back to Washington, woke Secretary Knox to tell him about the meeting at the White House, and we all went over there at nine o'clock. My crowning mortification was that the President hadn't even opened the envelope containing my precious Kearny shipyard papers. He pulled them out and settled the whole business in fifteen minutes and signed the Executive Order. As for negotiations between Stalin and Hitler, the President was, of course, right, and the Admiral's source was unreliable this time.

Despite the self-denigrating nature of this account, the fact is that his handling of the Kearny shipyard matter prompted the President to express his satisfaction to Secretary Knox, further solidifying Adlai's relationship with Knox and establishing his reputation widely in wartime officialdom. He was named Secretary Knox's alternate on the Economic Defense Board headed by Vice President Henry A. Wallace, and he worked closely with such people as Undersecretaries James Forrestal and Robert P. Patterson, Assistant Secretaries John J. McCloy and Robert A.

Lovett in the War Department, Lend-Lease Administrator Edward R. Stettinius, Jr., and Librarian of Congress Archibald MacLeish, who had also been made head of the recently established Office of Facts and Figures to provide information on the Defense program.

Back home Adlai's reputation was growing as well, and talk about his running for the United States Senate became more widespread. Arthur Goldberg, then a Chicago labor lawyer and later Adlai's successor at the United Nations, introduced him to Illinois labor leaders. His friend and neighbor in Libertyville, Lloyd Lewis of the *Chicago Daily News,* wrote him that Democratic leaders in East St. Louis and Peoria had discussed him as a possible alternative to Cook County State's Attorney Thomas J. Courtney, who was believed to be the organization favorite. Barry Bingham of the *Louisville Courier-Journal* wrote him he would "start agitating for you." Both Mayor Kelly and Barney Hodes from the Cook County organization wrote Adlai asking him to drop in to see them when next in Chicago, which he did. Secretary Knox told Paul Douglas, who had called on him, that Adlai was interested in running for the Senate but was concerned about his lack of experience. Douglas, upon returning to Illinois, declared his own candidacy for the nomination. The party was scheduled to decide on its slate in late December. Adlai's interests in the nomination came to an abrupt end on December 7.

Old friends, Mr. and Mrs. Hermon Dunlop Smith, had come to Washington to spend the weekend with the Stevensons. Ellen and the boys had come in late September and they had rented a house at 1904 R Street, N.W. On Friday, December 5, she was an exceptionally charming hostess at a dinner party in honor of the Smiths that included such people as Ted Weeks of *The Atlantic Monthly* and J. P. Morgan's son, Henry. A picnic was planned for the next day at a favorite spot of the Stevensons along the old Chesapeake and Ohio canal beside the Potomac, but Adlai was caught at the office and they picnicked without him. The next morning, December 7, Adlai and Ellen drove the Smiths to Union Station. In the backseat, Ellen suddenly began to express her intense dislike of Washington and a feeling that life there was coming between her and Adlai. In the front seat, Adlai and Dutch Smith were engaged in a discussion of Illinois politics, which would be utterly changed by the end of that day.

On the way back from the station, they decided to pick up the boys and go for the family picnic they had missed the day before. It was a glorious day. They had lunch on a high rock overlooking the river, went canoeing, ran along the canal, played games beside the Potomac falls, leaving only when long shadows began to hide the view. At home, the telephone was ringing insistently and messages the maid had taken were stacked beside it. Adlai told Ellen they were undoubtedly about the Kearny matter that had kept him at the office the day before and he would call back after taking a shower. Another call while he was showering was from a newspaperman who insisted to Ellen that he had to speak to Adlai even if he was in the shower. Dripping, he took the call to confront an immediate demand for a statement.

"About what?" Adlai asked.

The astonished newspaperman told him as much as was then available about the Japanese attack at Pearl Harbor. Adlai put down the phone and rushed to the Navy Department. It was their last happy day together for a long time.

They had planned to spend the Christmas holidays with Buffie, Ernest, and Tim Ives at Southern Pines, North Carolina. There seemed little prospect of Adlai making it, but Ellen and the boys went anyway. He managed to get a night train on Christmas Eve that got him there for the day, and then he took a night train back to Washington. Even though Buffie had never been a confidante, Ellen told her as she had told Ellen Smith that she was unhappy in Washington where everyone was so self-important. Everything had to be planned, and that spoiled the fun of surprise. Ellen soon began leaving for visits to Libertyville and to her mother's house in Beverly, Massachusetts. She told Harriet Welling that she "couldn't stand those terrible people in Washington," naming such people as the Walter Lippmanns. Their friend, Ruth Winter, later recalled:

> When he went with Knox, that's when things started to fall apart. Something happened to her. She felt that she was responsible for everything that he was and that he didn't appreciate it. . . . She told me he was thoughtless and inconsiderate. Possibly the fact that he was getting a lot of attention in Washington and . . . she was entertaining not for herself but for him, because it was part of his business—she resented it and lost her taste for doing for him. Adlai must have seen this happening too and it must have been hard on him. She seemed to lose her identity, which was very important to her. She was trying to write poetry but not writing it as well as she thought she should have because of all this going on and so she took it out on him and blamed him for interfering with her poetry.

Adlai III, in retrospect, also sees the breakup beginning during this Washington period. Generally, Adlai III recalls, his father would handle disagreements by acquiescing in Ellen's wishes, particularly her ideas about raising children. He can remember only two specific incidents. One was what he called an episode outside the house when he was shocked by what Ellen said to his father even though he cannot remember what it was about. His memory of the other incident is far more vivid:

My father came in while I was in bed to say he was flying with the Secretary of the Navy the next day to see a football game and would I like to come along. Of course, I was so excited I couldn't sleep most of the night. When I did wake up I was sure I had dreamed the whole thing. Then Dad came in and quietly explained out of my mother's presence that she had vetoed it because airplanes were unsafe. She would not have any of her children flying in an airplane.

The situation finally led Adlai to consult a psychiatrist and as a result he and Ellen started seeing him together. Ellen would go only if he went, too. But after missed appointments, at least partly because of his travels, the effort failed. So would many similar efforts over the years, by the children as well as by Adlai.

During one of her absences in Libertyville, he wrote her a letter—one of many—that is particularly revealing:

Darling—

I am back at the old stand on R Street, and despite the usual frenzied day and a bulging brief case, my heart is still surging after that glorious weekend. I can still see you on the [railroad] platform—all three smiling and waving me good bye. I don't know why I am so immoderately sentimental but I almost cried as the train pulled out—until I got engrossed in the Daily News!

I am so glad we had those nice long quiet talks. I feel immeasurably better and I guess they were long overdue. I do hope you will write me . . . that you are having a thorough check-up, including a basic metabolism. Please don't feel that you must *come down here soon if you feel strongly that staying there next winter is best. . . .*

I have implicit confidence in your judgement and I know what ever you decide about next winter will be best for all of us. My heart is so full I am in danger of verbosity!—but I am sure you know how thankful I am for the tolerant, uncomplaining and forgiving way you talked to me and explained everything—how it wasn't what I have done but what had happened within you, etc.! I see everything much more clearly and I pray that somehow I can prove worthy of you. We are getting older now and the fever of youth is subsiding—so don't be alarmed by it & please don't feel that I can't understand your anxiety to find yourself and peace and the feeling of urgency. Your happiness is as important to me as my own, for they are the same, they are inextricably intermingled. . . .

On election night in Illinois, Paul Douglas reacted to his defeat by telling his wife he was going to enlist in the Marines the very next day.

He tried, but men his age were not welcomed into the Marine Corps, even in wartime. He asked Adlai to help him get the age limitation waived. Adlai immediately wrote a memo to Undersecretary Forrestal identifying Douglas as a "very distinguished professor," an alderman, and a friend of Secretary Knox. "He will be 50 on March 26 and is desperately eager to get into the service as an ordinary sailor or soldier," Adlai wrote. "Assuming he can pass the physical examination, do you know of anything that can be done with an over-age destroyer like this?" He suggested that Forrestal send a note to Knox since "special dispensation" was not easy. Knox responded with a letter to the commandant of the Marine Corps; Douglas was inducted, rose from private to lieutenant colonel, and returned a wounded war hero to run successfully for the Senate alongside Adlai's even more successful race for governor. However fateful, this was a fleeting incident in a problem-packed, travel-dotted, and generally lonely existence.

Adlai was writing speeches for Secretary Knox that Knox liked even when they did not sound like him, as they usually did not. And Adlai was making some on his own that were attracting favorable attention and giving him a new sense of the power of well-crafted, well-delivered words. A rousing speech to the Council on Foreign Relations caused the *Chicago Sun* to comment, "The talk that Adlai Stevenson gave . . . was sufficient to make him one of the most celebrated men of our times."

With the outbreak of the war, Archibald MacLeish had set up a committee on war information with representatives from the White House and the Departments of State, War, Navy, and Justice. Stevenson represented the Navy and was credited by MacLeish with making major contributions to the coordination of information policies that greatly increased the flow of news. In the Navy, he encouraged Knox to appear before congressional committees and report on problems as well as progress. He proposed that top members of the department identify the congressmen and senators they knew and make regular calls on them, and that the unfamiliar ones be earmarked for the attention of one of them. His list included fifteen congressmen and ten senators. He also became a favorite source for guidance on Navy policy and war strategy for such writers as Walter Lippmann and Arthur Krock.

In three years he traveled some two hundred thousand miles with the secretary, or on his behalf, on various missions around the United States, the Caribbean, Europe, North Africa, and the Pacific theater. On each one, he made detailed notes that led after every trip to a string of suggestions. The first one, to naval stations in the southern states, called attention to the important work being done by women workers and suggested that more be done to recruit them. On each trip he would carefully take the names of the sons and daughters of friends and acquaintances encountered along the way, and on his return to Washington he would call or write their parents. He took on personal problems such as arranging a trip home for the son of Henry Crown, a wealthy Chicago industrialist, and a Republican, whose mother was dying. He noted difficulties newspaper correspondents were having covering the war to see what could be done about them. In this, as in his sharp observations, his bent toward journalism was repeatedly evident. The last trip, in January 1943, was the longest and probably the most hazardous.

As they took off from Pearl Harbor in the predawn twilight, one of the engines on the big four-engine flying boat quit when they were only seventy feet over the water. The pilot managed to avoid a crash, but one wing went under the water with an impact that shook them all and cut Admiral Nimitz's scalp. At Midway Island, their plane smashed a pontoon on landing, and the delay gave them ample opportunity to see how severely the area had been battered during the Battle of Midway. At Espíritu Santo Island, while they slept on the deck of a Navy ship, a lone bomber slipped through to drop bombs, fortunately missing its target.

A different kind of hazard was waiting in Washington. The naval oil reserve at Elk Hills, California, had been a major element in the scandals of the Harding presidency. Of the forty-three-thousand-acre reserve, Standard Oil owned nine thousand acres; by operating those acres independently of government control, it could drain off oil that Congress had sought to preserve. Given the pressure to fill huge war orders for oil, Knox had entered into a contract with Standard Oil for operation of the entire pool under Navy supervision. Rumors that graft and corruption were involved and that the contract was illegal appeared in the press. There were people in the Justice Department advocating immediate condemnation of Standard's nine thousand acres, and holding the threat of scandal over Knox's head.

Knox handed the problem to Adlai. Adlai's main concern was to make sure the fifteen thousand barrels of Elk Hills oil required daily by the war effort not be interrupted. It appeared to him that only Standard could do the job. With Carl McGowan working with him, amendments to the Naval Reserve Act of 1938 were drafted for presentation to Congress. He recommended that, pending congressional action, a temporary operating agreement with Standard be executed to continue oil production. Knox accepted the plan, and it won the approval of the attorney general and the President. A House subcommittee headed by Representative Lyndon B. Johnson, who was later to attack Adlai as unfriendly to the oil industry, issued a report criticizing him for being too easy on Standard Oil. But the legislation was approved; the Navy's needs and Knox's reputation both were safeguarded.

Part of his troubleshooting involved dealing with the Russians and their naval supply requirements under the Lend-Lease agreement. For years he would gleefully tell of one encounter when a Russian colonel came to complain about delayed deliveries. Adlai had prepared himself, and when the Russian had completed his protest, Adlai replied:

"Yes, we are behind. But may I point out to you the specifications you are behind on delivering that are largely responsible for the delay?" and proceeded to point out that "you are behind on this, and you are behind on this, and on this . . ."

The Russian interrupted him. "Meester Stevenson! I did not come here to talk about MY behind! I came here to talk about YOUR behind!" He then stalked from the room.

In retrospect, his most difficult but satisfying experience of this period was the fight to break down the Navy's long established barriers against Negro officers. He discussed the issue with Admiral Nimitz during their Pacific tour, but the admiral had other other pressures to deal with. Finally, on September 29, 1943, he sent a memorandum to Secretary Knox saying:

> I feel very emphatically that we should commission a few negroes. We now have more than 60,000 already in the Navy and are accepting 12,000 per month. Obviously, this can not go on indefinitely without making some officers or trying to explain why we don't. . . . Ultimately there will be negro officers in the Navy. It seems to me wise to do something about it now. . . .
>
> I specifically recommend the following: (1) Commission 10 or 12 negroes selected from top notch civilians just as we procure white officers, and a few from the ranks. . . . (2) Review the rating groups from which negroes are excluded. Perhaps additional classes of service could profitably be made available to them.
>
> I don't believe we can or should postpone commissioning some negroes much longer. If and when it is done it should not be accompanied by any special publicity but rather treated as a matter of course. The news will get out soon enough.

The internal battle now was joined. It proceeded undramatically but persistently, gathering support, and, finally, was won.

A significant interlude took him away from the Navy Department in December 1943 and January 1944. Italy's surrender in September and the death of Mussolini had ushered in a long, bloody struggle with the Germans. In early October, Allied forces entered Naples to find a city in ruins, a harbor blocked by wrecks, and people dying from typhus and starvation. The human and material wreckage mounted as the fighting moved slowly north and came to a halt at Monte Cassino. President Roosevelt, in November, authorized the Foreign Economic Administration to send a mission to Sicily and that part of Italy under Allied control to see what relief and rehabilitation efforts could be initiated. On November 22, FEA Administrator Leo T. Crowley wrote Secretary Knox, "The man we should like very much to head this mission is Mr. Adlai Stevenson, if you felt you could spare his services to us for a period of about six weeks." Knox quickly agreed with the fatherly proviso that Adlai "takes the necessary innoculations [sic]. I do not want him to go without taking them."

Armed with letters of introduction to generals and admirals, including one to General Dwight D. Eisenhower, Adlai departed on December 7, accompanied by David D. Lloyd from the Office of Price Administration, Hugh Calkins from the Department of Agriculture, and Nils K. G. Tholand, an industrial engineer. He took with him also renewed determination to keep a diary that he had begun on the tour of the Pacific and then had let lapse. There are gaps; cryptic notes and comments; wet, muddy, and sometimes almost illegible pages, and he stopped before the end of the mission, but from this diary emerge a vivid description of battlefield destruction, poignant insights into conditions faced both by the Italians and our soldiers, and a keen recognition of the difficulties of putting back together a society torn by dictatorship and war.

They arrived at Dakar, North Africa, the day after President Roosevelt had stopped there on his way home from the meeting with Stalin and Churchill in Teheran; they found the city spruced up for the visit but the people exhausted from the strain of it. The flight from there to Oran was the most fearful of his life.

> The pilot was lost. The coast is dangerous flying—mountains and valleys. He had to pull her nose up sharp several times and almost turned me inside out & all the while the big plane was shaking like a leaf & the wind was howling as I've never heard it. It was raining torrents and the ceiling was 0. They put up a smoke screen on the ground that finally gave the pilot a fix & at last we landed.

He was on many dangerous flights later, but this is the one he always recalled.

In Oran, despite letters of introduction, including one from President Roosevelt, he did not get to see General Eisenhower, but he recorded that General Walter Bedell Smith was most helpful. Neither did the letters get him better than fourth-class accommodations: "no sheets, no hot water, tiny cell, dirty." Indeed, throughout the trip, he found the Army indifferent, if not actually hostile, to the mission of a group of civilians bent on bringing about some coordination of the work of both military and civilian agencies. It was the Navy, where he was well-known as the secretary's confidential assistant, that came to the rescue a number of times with transportation, shelter, and rations.

On December 18, he arrived in Palermo, Sicily, where he found most public buildings and 40 percent of the houses in ruins, the harbor being patched by Army engineers, and hunger intensified by hoarding and black-marketeering. Naples and the southern Italian countryside were far worse. In Naples he encountered General Eisenhower in a hallway and had a brief and pleasant chat. They were not to meet again until political warfare brought them together.

The group returned on January 15, 1944, and Adlai submitted his single-spaced 122-page report on February 5. Professor John Norman of Fairfield University, who specialized in studies of postwar Italy, has written: "The Stevenson report presented a masterly summary of the disruption in the collection, distribution, and marketing of food and other farm products. It listed deficiencies and shortages. But it did more! It analyzed the cause of all these pressing problems so that immediate corrective action could be taken." Another scholar, Professor Stuart Gerry Brown of Syracuse University, wrote that the report "became a model that was studied in connection with reconstruction and foreign aid for many nations."

The report took on another dimension when Senator Joseph McCarthy, during the 1952 presidential campaign, charged that Adlai had "connived" to get Communists into the Italian government. The report then was declassified and revealed how maliciously incorrect the charge was. It clearly recognized the dangers of a Communist Italy and the need to act against the spread of Soviet influence in the Mediterranean. Beyond that, he broadened the mission's study of the Italian economy to a consideration of the reconstruction of society; a task that had to go beyond Italy to all of Europe to build the foundations of an "enduring peace." In this sense, it was a forerunner of the Marshall Plan. It also influenced his vision of the postwar world, and of his own role in it.

A month after his return, in a speech to a group of Chicago lawyers, he forecast his later concern with the "revolution of rising expectations," with this closing paragraph:

> I've travelled during this war in the Pacific, the Caribbean, South America, West Africa and the Mediterranean, and . . . no one has enough food, enough clothing, enough anything—except in the United States of America. And now all these people—black, brown, yellow, white—have seen our forces move thru [sic]; have seen our healthy boys, their clothes, their food, and their equipment. It makes you wonder about tomorrow. Are they envious; is more and worse trouble in the making, or is there a great opportunity to improve their lot and ours at the same time? The demand is there; is the wisdom here?

For himself, whatever doubts he might have had about his own role were left behind in Italy. He told Joe Alex Morris that

> while I was in Italy I saw a public-opinion poll in which seven out of ten Americans said they didn't want their boys to enter

public life. Think of it! Boys could die in battle, but parents did not want their children to give their living efforts toward a better America and a better world. I decided then that if I ever had a chance I'd go into public life.

To another journalist, he said, "It seems to me sad that 'politics' and 'politician' are so often epithets and words of disrespect and contempt, and not without justification, in the land of Jefferson and in a government by the governed."

He had, of course, been toying with the idea of some kind of public service most of his adult life. But from then on, it was no longer a question of whether, but how.

On Sunday, April 23, Frank Knox, who had been warned that he was working too unremittingly for a man of seventy, had a heart attack when attending the funeral of an old friend in New Hampshire. He shrugged it off, returned to Washington on Monday, and was at his desk Tuesday morning intending to hold his regular press conference. He became too ill and was forced to go home and to bed. There, on Friday afternoon, he died. Adlai was devastated.

"I loved that man," he told biographer Kenneth S. Davis years later. "He was brave, and honest. And he made a very great contribution to his country in her hour of greatest need. It cost him a lot. I'm sure it shortened his life. He was no intellectual, God knows, but he was highly intelligent—which a lot of 'intellectuals' aren't. . . . He and I saw eye to eye on foreign policy. On domestic policy we often disagreed pretty radically. But he never held that against me. . . . Although he continued to regard himself as violently anti-New Deal, of course, he liked to call me *his* New Dealer. He used to say, 'I have to have a New Dealer next to me to protect me from the New Dealers around here.' And he'd turn to me and say, 'Adlai, you're not letting any of them creep in here, are you?' Yet I can't recall that he ever vetoed an appointment I wanted made or ever asked me more than perfunctory questions about it."

Undersecretary James Forrestal was named quickly to replace Knox. He and Adlai had worked together without friction, but they were not compatible people; indeed, George Ball has said that "Forrestal really hated Stevenson." They were completely different temperaments. Forrestal made almost a fetish out of being "tough-minded"—the kind of thing Adlai abhorred. Carl McGowan has added: "It turned out that Stevenson was an infinitely tougher guy than Forrestal. Forrestal cracked after a few months. Stevenson never did, even after the most terrible disappointments." In any event, when President Roosevelt expressed a desire to appoint Adlai undersecretary or assistant secretary, Forrestal objected and the President acceded to Forrestal's choice of associates.

Other jobs were offered. The report on Italy had brought proposals to become general counsel to the French Supply Mission, and to represent the State Department on economic operations in China. An approach from the Securities and Exchange Commission was quickly discouraged, but he responded with interest to a discussion with Archibald MacLeish and Raymond Gram Swing about the problem of educating the American people on the need for the United Nations. Later in the year, with President Roosevelt's approval, Leo Crowley asked him to head a new office "to assure the proper disposition of surplus property abroad and the settlement of claims in other countries." The Office of War Information asked him to head all of its overseas operations. But with the determination he reached in Italy probably in mind, as well as Ellen's aversion to living in Washington, Adlai submitted his resignation and went home to Illinois.

Politics and journalism competed for Adlai's commitment on his return to Illinois. Politics had a head start.

As early as June 1943 speculation about Stevenson for governor had begun to appear in the press. The influential Barney Hodes told him he thought the Democrats had a chance to unseat Republican Dwight Green in 1944 providing "the proper ticket" could be put together. "If you are interested, I do not think that you have too much time to lose although it might seem a little early." Paul Douglas wrote from the Pacific that he was "glad you are thinking of running for office. The state and the party need men like you." The reply Douglas got expressed a decision "to coast along without saying anything definitely and see what transpires." Among the many other letters stimulated by the speculation was one from Buffie, who wanted him to run for the Senate instead of governor; adding bluntly that whatever he did he needed Ellen's help and that he did not have it.

The death of Frank Knox abruptly shifted priorities. Following his funeral, a group of the key people on the *Chicago Daily News* told Adlai they wanted him to head the formation of a syndicate that would enable them, with others, to purchase the paper from Knox's widow, and to become publisher of the paper. It was the most exciting career opportunity that had come to him in his forty-four years. As a result of his service on the Council on Foreign Relations, he had come to know most of the men who constituted one of the most distinguished corps of foreign correspondents in the world. Close friends like Lloyd Lewis, Paul Scott Mowrer, and Carroll Binder were editors. Together they dreamed of making the *Daily News* one of the great newspapers in the world. They and four other executives formalized their ambition in a letter to Adlai eloquently recounting the paper's tradition and their concern for its future, a concern heightened by the bitter battle then being waged between the *Tribune* and the liberal Democratic *Sun*, owned by Marshall Field.

Knox had left his entire estate, including the paper, to his widow,

Annie Reid Knox, who was one of three executors along with Holman D. Pettibone, president of the Chicago Title and Trust Company, and Laird Bell, Knox's attorney. They had broad powers of discretion; they could sell to whomever they desired at whatever price they thought best, although the will did ask them to seek continuity in the personnel and policies of the paper. Knox had often stated that he hoped the paper would become employee-owned when he died.

So, it was with high hopes that Adlai began to put together a syndicate to which *Daily News* employees would subscribe $235,000, others from $25,000 to $100,000 each, and Adlai $250,000, most of it borrowed from Marshall Field, who offered to provide more if needed. The largest subscription, $400,000, however, came from Lessing Rosenwald, who, as a leader of America First, had vigorously opposed Adlai's position prior to Pearl Harbor, but was nonetheless an admirer. Early in the long negotiation, Jesse Jones, a Texas millionaire who had become an admirer of Adlai during his work in Washington, offered his financial backing. At one point, when it appeared that he and Jones, both active Democrats, would become the major figures in the deal, he wrote Bell to assure him "that partisanship is the antithesis of my view of a newspaper's responsibility for public enlightenment."

John Cowles was asked for his opinion of the paper's value. He replied that as a purely business proposition there were other papers that might be better investments, but that the *Daily News* had the intangible advantage of prestige similar to that of the *Times* and the *Herald Tribune* in New York, the *Post* and the *Star* in Washington. He added; "If you want, more than anything else, to be head of the Chicago *Daily News,* I would advise you as a friend to go ahead, and buy it if you can, on the theory that you might get deeper satisfaction from heading the *Daily News* than you could in any other way."

Adlai took the advice seriously. He virtually ignored President Roosevelt's campaign for a fourth term and Illinois races. All summer long and into the fall, he traveled, wrote letters, held meetings, raised money, sought advice, and made careful computations on the basis of elaborate professional appraisals. His first calculation was that $1,800,000 was all that could be justified and he submitted a bid of $12 per share for the 149,941 shares held by the Knox estate. Higher bids had been submitted by others, one of whom approached him with an offer to make him publisher at a handsome salary if Adlai would join him in seeking acquisition of the property. Adlai promptly declined. He raised his syndicate's bid to $13 per share, or $1,935,000. On October 1, Bell told him that there were higher bids and that a decision was imminent. Adlai believed the executors, who were not bound to accept the highest bid, would prefer to sell the paper to someone who lived in Chicago and would preserve its independent character. Although his backers had authorized him to go higher, he did not feel justified in doing so, and John Knight's bid of $15 per share was accepted.

In a letter to Jesse Jones, Adlai said, "Mrs. Knox insisted on the full amount she could get elsewhere. Using other people's money, I did not feel disposed to go further." Years later, Jones told him he should have submitted a higher bid. Whether or not Adlai agreed, he often expressed disappointment that the effort had not succeeded.

Three weeks later, George Ball telephoned him from Washington saying he was going to recently liberated Paris on a government mission and he wanted Adlai to join him. He explained that two months earlier President Roosevelt had established the U.S. Strategic Bombing Survey to assess the air offensives in Europe in their economic, political, and social as well as military aspects. Ball was to organize evaluation offices in London and Paris, and he wanted Adlai to head the Paris office as his alter ego. Adlai agreed promptly, providing he could be home by Christmas.

Once again, Adlai attempted to keep a diary. His first entry reported a "dreadful last minute scramble to get off. . . . Hard to say goodbye in spite of all the practice I've had." There was a day's delay in Washington, but the party of ten arrived in England on November 5. His diary is filled with the names of people he met and interviewed, including a chance street encounter with his cousin Bud Merwin, whom he had helped to get a commission in the Navy. Bud had just returned from a dangerous landing on the Dutch coast, so *The Pantagraph* was not the subject of discussion, although Adlai made a note to inform the paper about the citation Bud had received.

There was a more amusing encounter in Paris. The diary reported that en route home with George Ball in early-morning hours they came upon American military policemen raiding an off-limits house of prostitution, appropriately located, Adlai observed, on rue Casanova. "Out emerged fine assortment of Am. officers all very angry and irritable and one Britisher, quite philosophical and good humored about it all. Very entertaining performance." But Ball's account reveals that it became almost too entertaining.

> Adlai and I, although civilians, were in uniform (we each had the assimilated rank of colonel) and hence were indistinguishable from the culprits. This created a situation of some hazard, for Adlai was enchanted with the spectacle of so many chagrined and choleric officers "whose expectations and consummations," as he said, had been abruptly interrupted. He insisted on seeing the show, and at least twice his curiosity led him so far into the crowd that he found himself shoved into the paddy wagon. It took all the advocacy my colleague and I could muster to establish Stevenson as a noncombatant.

Status as a noncombatant, however, did not keep him away from the battle areas. He toured the Ardennes Forest where the Battle of the

Bulge was raging. A few days later he was in another area to confer with General Terry Allen, who was attacking from his forward command post in the basement of a bank. He encountered General George S. Patton, Jr., "pearl-handled pistols and all," met with General Omar Bradley and others on his staff and found them "very, very impressive." He toured radar installations and watched an experiment in blind bombing by automatic radar release. He studied engineering and transport problems encountered in the Battle of France.

"As always when he faced a new problem, he talked to everyone who might have information on the subject and filled dozens of yellow pages with his carefully handwritten notes," George Ball later reported. "His notes, gathered during his work in Paris and amplified and confirmed by expert advice and eyewitness accounts he collected at the front, provided an invaluable addition to the store of information needed for the work of the Evaluation Board."

The survey was highly regarded at the time, but apparently was largely forgotten. Certainly, few of its findings seemed to have been heeded during the war in Vietnam. But it was Ball's experience with the survey that was a central element in his becoming, when under secretary of state in the 1960s, almost the only one to argue with President Johnson that strategic bombing of North Vietnam would not cause Hanoi to surrender.

Ball kept his promise to get Adlai home for Christmas; he arrived back in Libertyville on Christmas Eve.

As he entered 1945, Adlai was torn between his desire to desert the law for public service, and Ellen's opposition, particularly if it involved living in Washington. Much of what later appeared to be indecision grew out of his struggle to reconcile his interests with Ellen's opposition and his own sense of responsibility to the family. The issue kept injecting itself into their lives. He had made a good record, and had made many friends and admirers who knew of his affinity for public service, appointive or elective; and they did not hesitate to try to entice him back.

Adlai later made a list of the job offers he received during 1945. They included: chief, Economic Mission to Italy with rank of minister and membership on the Allied Commission; chief, Economic Mission to the United Kingdom with rank of minister; chief, Office of War Information, London, with rank of minister; general counsel, Surplus Property Board; member, Securities and Exchange Commission; deputy director general, United Nations Relief and Rehabilitation Administration, London, in charge of all operations on the continent; assistant attorney general, Lands Division or Criminal Division; member, Federal Communications Commission; and in the State Department, proposals came from Assistant Secretaries Archibald MacLeish and Dean Acheson, as well as Secretary Stettinius.

The State Department efforts began January 16 with a long letter from MacLeish, then assistant secretary of state for public and cultural affairs. He began by saying that "I have felt since the days of the Committee on War Information that you were one of the most valuable men in this Government. . . . I felt at the time your resignation from the Government was a disaster. I feel the same thing now." He went on to explain that President Roosevelt and Secretary Stettinius were determined to improve communications between the State Department and the American people, and that this created a

> *job tailored to measure for you. The job is, first, to give the people of this country the information about public affairs they need to have in order to form a foreign policy which will produce the peace which alone will justify this war—and which alone will preserve us from another war to follow; second, to create, in a world in which communication has been interrupted and suppressed and blanketed by the war and by the conquests of our enemies, the kind of communication between peoples which is essential to the understanding on which, and on which alone, a true peace can be built. . . . I need the assistance and the counsel and the collaboration and the advice of a man who believes what you believe, who sees the problems as you see them, and who has had your experience, both of this country and of this Government.*

This letter was followed a few days later by one from Secretary Stettinius saying, "If there is any possible way you can arrange your affairs to join us in the Department, move Heaven and earth to do so."

On January 25, Adlai responded: "Dear Archie. This is the hardest letter I've ever written! The answer is no." He cited his decision "to come home and discharge some of my obligations to my family—and incidentally make a living again . . . It is hard enough to dedicate one's overvalued life to corporate sterilities in this tormented world without having estimable people weaving distracting spells; even poking a torpid conscience!" At the end of two more paragraphs in which he seemed to be arguing with himself as much as MacLeish, he attached a postscript: "Reading this over leaves me as confused as you will be. In short, I want to come but don't feel I should."

Whether or not the letter was calculated to intensify the campaign to get him to Washington, that is what it did, including a letter from the secretary of state to the head of Adlai's law firm asking for his release. There is no record of Ellen's reaction to these efforts, but in the third week of February, he arrived in Washington without her for duty, first as special assistant to Assistant Secretary MacLeish, then special assistant to the secretary, and finally deputy to Mr. Stettinius. He told Chicago friends he was simply taking a "temporary emergency job in the State Department." It was extreme understatement.

From February 4 to 11, Roosevelt, Churchill, and Stalin had met at Yalta and authorized the convening of a conference at San Francisco on April 25 to consider the proposals for a world organization that representatives of the three countries had been working on for months at the Washington estate known as Dumbarton Oaks. MacLeish and Stevenson promptly launched a public relations campaign to rally support for the Dumbarton Oaks proposals. Within six weeks, letters to the State Department on the subject of international organization jumped from five hundred a day to over five thousand. On April 12, the head of the *Daily News* Washington bureau, Edwin A. Lahey, reported that "MacLeish, with the valuable assistance of Adlai Stevenson of Chicago, is making the people of this country State Department conscious." A different kind of tribute came from Senator Robert A. Taft, who complained of "super-propaganda . . . aimed at Congress."

On the April 12 that Lahey reported the MacLeish/Stevenson educational campaign for the United Nations, the American Ninth Army reached the Elbe River in Germany, American air bases began functioning on Okinawa only 325 miles from Japan—and President Roosevelt died of a massive cerebral hemorrhage at Warm Springs, Georgia.

The American delegation that arrived in San Francisco for the opening of the conference on April 25 was packed with prima donnas, two of whom were prospective presidential candidates. Under any circumstances, Stettinius's position as chairman would have been difficult, but it was made almost impossible by the general knowledge that President Truman intended to appoint Senator James F. Byrnes as secretary of state as soon as the conference ended. It included Senators Tom Connally and Arthur Vandenberg, respectively chairman and ranking Republican on the Senate Foreign Relations Committee; Representatives Sol Bloom and Charles A. Eaton, respectively chairman and ranking Republican on the House Foreign Affairs Committee; former Governor Harold E. Stassen and Barnard College dean Virginia Gildersleeve. There were, in addition, four more members of Congress; seventeen advisers from other departments and agencies, including the secretary of agriculture, the undersecretary of the interior and the assistant secretaries of treasury and of war; three assistant secretaries from the State Department plus fourteen political and liaison officers, and five "principal" advisers, including John Foster Dulles. The secretary general was Alger Hiss; Dorothy Fosdick was his special assistant.

Adlai was not at the opening; he had been held behind to handle public relations problems dealing with the imminent surrender of Germany. The delegation's public relations, however, became so bad that it seemed a minor war might erupt in San Francisco. At one point people had to intervene to prevent a brawl between Secretary Stettinius and

Washington Post publisher Eugene Meyer in the corridors of the Fairmont Hotel. There was an enormous press and radio corps covering the conference—over twenty-five hundred—and the demand for information was incessant. The difficulty was that the publicity-jealous members of the delegation could not agree on what information should be provided and who would provide it. Senator Vandenburg had led the effort to deny Stettinius authority to speak to the press on behalf of the delegation. As a consequence, knowledgeable reporters developed sources in other delegations, and the vast bulk of them milled about in frustration and anger.

Finally, Arthur Krock and James Reston of *The New York Times* told Stettinius that someone had to be appointed to brief reporters, even if it was only an unofficial spokesman the delegation could repudiate, as long as it was someone the reporters trusted. They suggested Adlai and Thomas K. Finletter, later secretary of the air force. Stettinius assigned the task to Adlai on May 10. Finletter and Edward Miller, who were representing private groups affiliated with the American delegation, as consultants, filled in until his arrival. Shortly after arriving, he encountered Louise (Mrs. Quincy) Wright. She was there also for an interested organization and she asked, "What are you doing here, exactly?"

"Haven't you heard," he whispered. "I'm the official leak!"

That is, exactly, what he was.

He attended the delegation's meetings and went with Stettinius to meetings with the heads of the British, Russian, French, and Chinese delegations. He then used his judgment about what to say to the fifty to seventy-five selected reporters who called daily at the "leak" office established in room 576 of the Fairmont. Once when attending a meeting of the Big Five that was locked in disagreement, Lord Halifax sympathetically noted, "We are asking Mr. Stevenson to make bricks without straw, you know." On another occasion, however, the American position was published in *The New York Times* before the delegation had even acted.

At times like this, "there was always hell to pay in the Delegation meeting," Adlai later told the Commonwealth Club in Chicago.

The Secretary and the senators would get apopletic *[sic]* with rage and make speeches about the flannel mouth staff or look at one another suspiciously or threatened to call the President, while I cowered in my corner in abject terror, timidly proclaiming my innocence. But as they filed out of the room after the meeting I always had an approving wink from Vandenburg and Stassen. And it became standard operating procedure for Stettinius once a week to read me a burning lecture somewhere on the essential importance of absolute secrecy about delegation and Big Five meetings in the famous penthouse on top of the Fairmont. But these admonitions were always reserved for the presence of certain U.S. delegates and afterward we went into his bedroom for a drink and a review of "Operation Titanic" as it was called—whether I needed more help, what such and such a section of the press was saying and could I get out a little more in this direction or that.

In the opinion of James Reston: "This was one of the few conferences where the press was handled really well."

His assignment was over, but Adlai agreed to go back to Washington to help promote Senate ratification of the UN Charter. On July 7, in a ceremony at the Navy Department, he was awarded the Distinguished Civilian Service Award, the Navy's highest award for a civilian. Four days earlier, Byrnes had replaced Stettinius and Adlai told the new secretary of state it was his intention to resign and return to Chicago where the possibility of establishing a new law firm with Ed McDougal, James Oates, and Stephen A. Mitchell was under serious consideration. But in departing on leave without pay rather than resigning, he left behind his Libertyville telephone number should Secretary Byrnes wish to reach him. He did.

Calls from both Byrnes and Stettinius followed him to Michigan's Huron Mountains where the Laird Bells had loaned their cottage for the first vacation he and Ellen and the boys had taken together since 1940. The San Francisco conference had provided for a Preparatory Commission to meet in London to plan the first session of the UN's General Assembly, arrange for the transfer of assets from the League of Nations, organize the permanent Secretariat, establish relationships between the UN and its various specialized agencies, and determine the location of the permanent headquarters. Because of concern with possible reaction at home and among his law colleagues, Adlai avoided overt expressions of interest but the fact was that he wanted very much to be a member of the American delegation to the Preparatory Commission. So he hesitated no longer than appropriate when Byrnes urged him to be Stettinius's alternate and "first deputy." On September 4, President Truman appointed him deputy United States representative on the Preparatory Commission with the personal rank of minister.

This time he felt obliged to resign as a partner in the law firm. "You can be sure that when I return to Chicago for keeps, the office will be the first place I will go," he wrote his partners. "If there is then no position for me, I will be neither surprised nor hurt. . . . So please consider this a mutual release." The senior partner, William Sidley, replied that he thought "you did the right thing in accepting this London assignment," adding: "Much as I would like to have you return here for a full time partnership, I am even more interested in your making the right decision in your own interest. . . . You will always find a warm welcome in this office, whether you come as a permanent resident or a transient guest."

Before hurriedly getting to New York for the sailing of the *Queen Elizabeth* on September 4, he arranged for Ellen, Adlai III, and Borden to follow him to London on September 15, and for Buffie and Ernest to stay at Libertyville and take care of John Fell who was deemed too young for the journey. He told Jim Oates he had made their presence with him a condition of his accepting the appointment, adding that with a salary of $9,800 a year and a $25 per diem "taking the family won't be too disastrous."

It was a convivial crossing. Secretary Byrnes and his group were headed to London for the first of the meetings of the Council of Foreign Ministers. The group going to the UN Preparatory Commission was made up largely of veterans from the San Francisco conference, such as John Foster Dulles, Ralph Bunche, and Dorothy Fosdick. Adlai shared a cabin with Charles E. "Chip" Bohlen, a leading Russian expert in the State Department who later was ambassador to the Soviet Union and to France. Among the journalists aboard were friends who included Anne O'Hare McCormick of *The New York Times* and Robert Kintner, then vice president of the American Broadcasting Company.

He and Byrnes established a warm rapport; Byrnes's attitude toward the Russians, he thought, was "emphatic and firm." Byrnes also was knowledgeable and deeply interested in Illinois politics; he advised Adlai to think seriously about returning and becoming politically active when the work of the Preparatory Commission was done.

Arriving in London, he found Stettinius a sick man. The work fell increasingly on Adlai, and by the time Ellen and the boys arrived at the end of September the illness had been diagnosed as gallstones. Stettinius resigned to return to the United States for surgery and Adlai became the head of the United States delegation. Thus began what he later assessed as "the most exacting, interesting and in many ways the most important interval of my life." At home, the *Tribune* remarked that American interests were in the hands of "the boy orator from Bloomington." The *Daily News,* on the other hand, observed that "this step brings an able man to a bigger job than he had previously held . . . He has not been much in the public eye. Henceforth, he may be." He certainly moved onto center stage in London.

While Byrnes and V. M. Molotov were squaring off at the Council of Foreign Ministers, Andrey Gromyko was at the forefront of steadily mounting difficulties in the Executive Committee of the Preparatory Commission, the group of fourteen nations elected at San Francisco to prepare a working plan for the meeting of the full commission. Basic disagreement with the Russians arose at the outset over the relationship among the Security Council, the General Assembly, and the Secretariat of the United Nations. The Soviet Union regarded the Security Council as the only truly important organ and argued that all really important powers should be held by this body, each of whose five permanent members could exercise the veto. They saw the General Assembly, the Secretariat, the Economic and Social Council, and the Trusteeship Council as secondary or less. This led them to argue for a separate secretariat for each of the major organs—the Security Council, the Economic and Social Council, the Trusteeship Council, and the General Assembly—all nominally under the secretary general. The non-Eastern European members, headed by the United States, wanted to see the Secretary General at the head of a Secretariat that was organized by functions—economics, social problems, trusteeship, legal issues, personnel management, and so on.

Deep differences also arose from the Soviets' firm concept of the world as one divided into three interests—Russian, British, and American. This led them to insist that on every UN body, the Soviet Union and its allies should have one third of the total representation. Around these completely different approaches, Andrey Gromyko waged an unrelenting struggle over nearly every detail of organization.

As chairman, Adlai generally sought to avoid showdown votes that pitted three Russian votes against eleven from all the others because, he observed, such open defeats only made the Russians even more stubborn. Through patient personal negotiation day after day, by argument, and with good humor that occasionally coaxed a smile even from the dour Gromyko, he searched for common ground. He was the only delegate who achieved a first-name relationship with Gromyko, but he also demonstrated he could be as stubborn as the Russian when that was necessary.

Correspondents from the major American newspapers unanimously praised Adlai's performance. One said, "I never saw a man handle the Russians like he did." One commentator observed that while the world was falling apart at Lancaster House where the Council of Foreign Ministers was meeting, it was being put back together again at Church House, where the Preparatory Commission was meeting, largely through Adlai's efforts.

When the fifty-one nations comprising the full commission met on November 23, the work done in the Executive Committee and in detailed planning for the meeting paid off. It elected officers, organized itself, and started work on the agenda in two days with a minimum of disagreement.

Location of the permanent headquarters for the United Nations was a major item. Geneva, the headquarters of the League of Nations, was a major contender. Other countries also nursed ambitions. The leading prospect was the United States, but the British delegation in particular was strongly backing the Geneva site. The official American position of avoiding any appearance of seeking the headquarters was hardly necessary as twenty-two cities, including Chicago, sent missions to London to present arguments as to why theirs was the best location. Nevertheless, the issue became a tense one and one vote to place the headquarters in Europe was defeated by a margin of only 25 to 23 with 2 abstentions. Fortunately, a two-thirds vote was necessary for a decision.

Many agreed with the Philippine delegate, Pedro Lopez, who argued that the danger of isolationism in the United States was "as great today as ever," and that "the best way to keep the United States in the United Nations is to put UNO's feet in the United States."

At the height of the debate, Adlai issued a statement pointing out that while his country was not seeking the headquarters it would welcome a decision by the Permanent Commission to make the home of the UN in the United States. He said the deputations from American cities were composed of private citizens who had come to London on their own initiative and their arguments should be considered on the merits rather than as an expression of official American views.

This statement of the American position was greeted by the *Chicago Tribune* with an editorial headlining, MR. STEVENSON VOTES FOR EUROPE. "It is easy to understand why he does not want the international capital in America. He and his kind profess an interest in foreign affairs only because they wish to get away from America and associate with foreigners, to whom they pay fawning obeisance."

Finally, on December 18, 1945, in a British Broadcasting Corporation interview, Adlai hailed the commission's decision to place the UN headquarters in the United States, in these words: "It is America's destiny to take a leading part in the world of tomorrow and I hope and believe that the permanent headquarters in the United States will serve to increase the understanding of the American people in the objectives and problems of the United Nations. And with that understanding will come, I believe, a better informed public opinion, which will mean so much to the support of the Organization in the future." Public opinion, he said, "is the sovereign of us all."

In concluding its work on December 23, the Preparatory Commission voted to call the first meeting of the UN General Assembly in London on January 10. Adlai had long ago given up hope of being in Libertyville for Christmas and he had prevailed on Ellen to stay on with the boys until after the holidays. Actually, she had been enjoying London enormously. Work and pleasure had been happily mixed during weekends at Clivedon, the Astor estate, and Dytchley, Sir Ronald Tree's estate.

She and the boys were especially happy at "Ronnie's." He had been born in England of American parents; his mother was the daughter of Marshall Field I, and his grandfather had been involved in Democratic politics, once running on the same ticket as Adlai's grandfather. He had been a member of Parliament and was in Churchill's junior cabinet during the war. He was not yet married to Marietta, his second wife, who later became one of Adlai's most intimate friends.

There was a constant round of luncheons, receptions, and dinners at which Ellen shone, and she helped Adlai enormously as a charming hostess at dinners she gave in the small, bomb-damaged house she had fixed up at 2 Mount Row, just off Grosvenor Square. The boys were placed in school at Harrow, where they adjusted quickly. It was a happy time for them all. At home, John Fell was not having such an easy period. Stuttering marked his sense of rejection at being left behind. Letters home reflected anxiety and complicated the decision to remain in London for Christmas. Ellen left immediately thereafter to return Adlai III to Milton Academy and Borden to school at home and then sailed back to London to be with Adlai for the first session of the UN General Assembly. Her return, though, was marred by tragic family news. Her brother-in-law, Robert S. Pirie, manager of the New York office of Carson, Pirie, Scott and Company, was killed in a crash of a United Airlines plane in Wyoming, leaving her younger sister, Betty, to whom she was devoted, with two small children. It was a heavy blow to fragile emotional structures and Betty ultimately took her own life.

Adlai also was having a problem. His success with the Preparatory Commission fueled his desire to be a United States delegate to the first session of the General Assembly; so much so that he departed from his customary indirection and informed Secretary Byrnes of his ambition. President Truman and Secretary Byrnes, however, decided that bipartisan political support should be the first priority in selecting the delegation. Of the five positions, Secretary Byrnes and Stettinius, who had been named the United States ambassador to the UN to make way for Byrnes, were virtually mandated. President Truman had enlisted Mrs. Eleanor Roosevelt, and he felt it important that the remaining two places be held by the Democratic and Republican leaders of the Senate Foreign Relations Committee. Similar political considerations went into the selection of the five alternates. Adlai was deeply disappointed, but he accepted gracefully Secretary Byrnes's request that he become the delegation's "senior advisor."

Of his service at the London session, historian Walter Johnson, editor of *The Papers of Adlai Stevenson,* has given this account:

> Foreign correspondent William H. Stoneman wrote: "Foreign diplomats were slightly surprised when Stevenson was made senior advisor to the American delegation to the assembly, instead of being made a full delegate or an alternate. Americans who had watched his work during earlier meetings were not only surprised, they were slightly disgusted." Stoneman observed that the forty-six-year-old lawyer from Chicago "has become conspicuous for his skill and tact in getting the big boys to agree." While diplomats and politicians made speeches, Stevenson was the only one "who actually does much of the leg work and no small part of the brainwork. . . ." Stoneman added that during the Preparatory Commission meetings, "time and again he broke impasses between the powers when agreement seemed impossible. In the process he earned the full respect of large and

small powers alike, including that of the Russians, who are particular about their friends."

Byrnes left Stevenson in charge of the political negotiations for the United States with the other delegations on the selection of the president of the General Assembly, the vice presidents, the chairmen of the various committees, and the representatives on the UN agencies. . . .

The following day Saville R. Davis wrote in the *Christian Science Monitor* that the important posts had been filled. "Taken as a whole, it was a remarkable achievement." The "hero of the elections," he stated, "is Mr. Adlai Stevenson." Davis remarked that when Stevenson was being congratulated, he said with a laugh, "I guess I'm just a ward politician at heart." "This modesty wholly misrepresented his talents," Davis observed. "He drafted with great patience and skill a list which represented not what the United States wanted, but, nearly as possible, what all delegations and groups wanted. The result was a phenomenal electoral success."

The session adjourned in late February, to be resumed in New York in September. Adlai and Ellen sailed home on the *Queen Mary* to a spring and summer of indecision and discontent for him and increasing tensions for them both.

On arriving in New York, Ellen proceeded immediately to Libertyville. Adlai went up to Milton Academy to see Adlai III and then to Washington where Secretary Byrnes asked him to accept an appointment as ambassador to either Brazil or to Argentina. He declined, saying he would be available for short-term assignments but that he felt obliged to return to attend to affairs at home and resume his law practice. There was uncertainty, though, about what law practice.

He had been carrying on an intermittent correspondence with Edward D. McDougal, Jr., about setting up their own law firm; in the end he decided to go back to his old firm, now known as Sidley, Austin, Burgess and Harper. He worked hard and conscientiously, but not happily. Like many others returning from wartime experiences, it was difficult settling into former routines, but his discontent was intensified with his basic dissatisfaction with a career as a lawyer.

Not all the unhappiness was rooted in the office. Disagreements over help at home, over the raising of the boys, and over unimportant things were becoming more frequent. Ellen had come back from London with a renewed desire to become active in the arts. Her search, which she focused on home and Chicago, was in conflict with his pull toward public service that meant absence from these bases where she felt secure.

For him, temptations to leave Chicago and the law kept arising. In the spring of 1946, he rejected the chairmanship of the Securities and Exchange Commission as well as offers to become president both of the Foreign Policy Association and of the Carnegie Endowment for International Peace. The latter offer came from John Foster Dulles, its chairman, who subsequently offered the position to Alger Hiss, who accepted.

His foreign policy interest he kept alive by accepting numerous speaking invitations from many different groups in various parts of the state. In explaining his mixed religious background to a Jewish group, he recounted overhearing an argument between his Unitarian grandmother and Presbyterian grandfather that his grandmother ended abruptly, charging, "Yes, you Presbyterians do keep the Ten Commandments— and everything else you can get your hands on!"

Honorary degrees from Northwestern University and Illinois Wesleyan University in Bloomington were gratefully accepted. To the students in Bloomington, he sounded a theme that he would repeat over and over again:

> The United Nations is only a spade; it won't work by itself. . . . The weeds that smothered the League of Nations will smother it if the garden is neglected. You are the gardeners. We are all the gardeners, we who know that science has outdistanced philosophy, that there will be no victors in another war, that jealously, suspicion and intolerance are at last armed with weapons which in one burst of universal fury can fulfill Kant's grim prophecy that "the world will be the graveyard of the human race." This is a time for thinking, for discipline selfimposed by free men, for vision, for purpose, for example. It's a threshold—a threshold to something very bright or very dark. It's morning. It's exciting. It's a good time to be alive—and awake!

He hoped and expected to be appointed an alternate delegate to the resumed session of the General Assembly in New York in September; so he took advantage of the interregnum for a vacation with Ellen and John Fell in the Pacific Northwest with Mr. and Mrs. Richard L. Neuberger, both later to be United States senators. At Neuberger's invitation, he wrote a guest editorial for the *Portland Journal* extolling the beauty of the area but also expressing shock at the "jungles of stumps left by indiscriminate logging operations which clear-cut the land and left no seed trees."

Neuberger recorded his most vivid memory of the experience in an article he wrote during the 1952 campaign:

> We were looking down a steep white apron of icy snow on the ramparts of Mount St. Helens. At the bottom of this chute,

ugly boulders waited with sabre-toothed fangs. The forest ranger and I hesitated so that we could get our bearings. Was there some safer way around the shoulder of that 10,000-foot mountain? Adlai Stevenson plodded out onto the slippery gables of St. Helens and began kicking out footsteps for his wavering companions. "Come on, Neuberger," he scoffed. "Do you want to live forever?"

President Truman's announcement of Adlai's appointment as an alternate delegate to the UN General Assembly was made as he returned from vacation. The head of the delegation was to be Warren R. Austin, the Republican whip of the Senate, who had been named to succeed Stettinius as permanent United States representative to the UN. Senators Tom Connally and Arthur Vandenberg and Mrs. Roosevelt were to continue. Representative Sol Bloom, chairman of the House Foreign Affairs Committee, was the fifth delegate. The alternates were Representative Charles A. Eaton, ranking Republican on the House Committee; Representative Helen Gahagan Douglas; John Foster Dulles; and Adlai E. Stevenson.

When assignments were handed out, Adlai expressed concern to his friends that the work load was so heavy he wouldn't do a good job, but secretly he was delighted. Senator Vandenberg had insisted that Adlai have primary responsibility for all agenda items referred to Committee 2, which dealt with economic issues. He was to represent Ambassador Austin on the committee of the whole to recommend the site for the permanent headquarters, which meant playing a decisive role, and he was also to assist Ambassador Austin in all liaison work with other delegations. It was a fully packed portfolio.

In Committee 2 he became involved in a vigorous debate with New York's colorful Mayor Fiorello H. La Guardia, who as head of the United Nations Relief and Rehabilitation Agency, was advocating the agency's transition to a permanent organization with an initial funding of $400 million. Adlai was not wholly comfortable with the official United States position that basically meant transferring postwar emergency relief from international organization to national efforts. La Guardia's proposal presented a number of difficulties, but the main—and unspoken—one was that the key congressional representatives were firm in maintaining that the best hope of getting needed money was for a United States administered program. At one point, La Guardia reached across the table, shaking his finger in Adlai's face, and charged that the United States with the backing of the British "was making a political football out of food." After some compromising, Adlai won support for the American position, which he felt was the most practical one but was never certain it was the right one.

It was during this session that the friendship begun with Mrs. Roosevelt in London solidified to become one of the most important relationships in his life. On October 24, he noted he had driven back from the session at Lake Success with her: "Discussed politics, languages, and education. Everything confirms conviction she is one of the few really great people I have known." The next March, in introducing her at the Chicago Council on Foreign Relations, he described her with the phrase that was to resound around the world when he used it at the memorial service for her: "It is better to light candles than to curse darkness." But before that, he told the audience about the world traveler and professional lecturer who deplored his frequent misfortune in having people in his audience who knew more about the place he was talking about than he did. "My luck is so bad," the speaker said, "that if I talked about the Llamasaries of Tibet, Marco Polo would be in the audience—or Mrs. Roosevelt."

General Assembly agenda items were handled with skill and dispatch. But personal questions arose that, as usual, were more difficult for him to resolve. When he returned to New York from Christmas at home on January 6, 1947, Secretary General Trygve Lie asked him to become assistant secretary general for administration and finance, but in fact to function as deputy to Lie without a title that would stimulate Soviet opposition. That night, he noted in his diary: "Contacted a lot of people and arranged for Wilson Wyatt, Julius Holmes and Milton Eisenhower to see Lie. Tempted myself, but I must stay at home now and get family situation straightened out. Also might as well try the political situation there."

Over the next weeks he submitted over twenty names to Lie, pushing hardest for Milton Eisenhower, then president of Kansas State University, and Julius Holmes, career foreign service officer who had been General Eisenhower's deputy chief of staff for civil affairs. He was also having second thoughts about himself. On January 20, the following appears in his diary:

Have been worrying about declining that job at the UN—equivalent to $75,000 salary before taxes. Why don't I do what I want to do and like to do and is worthwhile doing?" And on February 5:

Am 47 today—still restless; dissatisfied with myself. What's the matter? Have everything. Wife, children, money, success—but not in the law profession. Too much ambition for public recognition; too scattered in interests; how can I reconcile life in Chicago as lawyer with consuming interest in foreign affairs—public affairs and desire for recognition and position in that field? Prospect of Senate nomination sustains & at the same time troubles, even frightens me. Wish I could at least get tranquil & make Ellen happy & do go[od] humble job at law.

After adjournment of the General Assembly, he repeated the pattern of the previous summer, speaking on foreign affairs to groups all over Illinois; but this time adding a political dimension. He had made some speeches downstate for congressional candidates the previous summer, talking mainly on foreign policy; this time there was more directed involvement as he supported the successful mayoral campaign of Martin H. Kennelly, a Chicago businessman untainted by the machine but supported by it, and accepted such political engagements as the Jefferson-Jackson Day Dinner at Pontiac, Illinois.

The midterm election in 1946, however, had been a disaster for the Democrats both nationally and in Illinois. The Republicans took control of the Senate and the House. This was the Eightieth Congress that President Truman campaigned against in 1948. Of the twenty-six congressmen elected from Illinois, only six had been Democrats. Even the Chicago machine had been battered. Most of the Cook County ticket had been defeated, including Richard J. Daley, who suffered his only defeat at the polls running that year for Cook County sheriff. The outlook would have been grim had it not been for the rise of Colonel Jacob M. Arvey to the leadership of the machine and his recognition that drastic change was necessary to avert irreparable wreckage.

Thus the Democratic debacle of 1946 paved the way for the Stevenson victory of 1948; but the road ahead was a rough one. Adlai cautiously watched developments and happily accepted President Truman's appointment as an alternate delegate to the General Assembly session meeting in New York in September. On July 29, a letter from Senator Vandenberg indicated that his credentials were stronger with this Republican leader than they were with the Democratic leaders at home.

"I want you to know—as a matter of record—that when I was asked for recommendations in connection with the United States Delegation, I put your name down as a 'must,'" Vandenberg wrote him. "I wish you were devoting all of your time to our foreign affairs at a high level in the State Department."

Stopping in Washington en route to the General Assembly in September, he was asked by Secretary of State George C. Marshall to succeed William Benton as assistant secretary of state for public affairs. Benton had urged him on both President Truman and Secretary Marshall. Sadly, he told Secretary Marshall he had to decline as his wife would divorce him if he took another job in Washington. He wrote a short note to Jane Dick about an unspecified offer that "leaves me a little full in the throat." Three days later he sent a more formal answer to Secretary Marshall saying, "I must decline, not alone with thanks, but with profound regret. . . . I hope you won't write me off altogether when other situations turn up where I might be of service because someday my situation may abruptly change. For the present I feel I can not make a major readjustment." The next week during a meeting of the delegation, Secretary Marshall sent a note down the table to Adlai saying how much he regretted the decision.

Midway during the session, Secretary Marshall flew to Chicago with Adlai to address the Chicago Council on Foreign Relations. In a later interview with Forrest C. Pogue, Marshall's biographer, Adlai recalled that they discussed politics and rumors that General Marshall might be the Democratic candidate for President in 1948.

"I told him," Adlai reported,

> that while at that time I had never been in politics, I was fascinated about it and extremely interested, of course. I had never been in "combat" politics. He unburdened himself in a most interesting way. He in the first place dismissed, as precisely and as finally and as conclusively and as briefly as one could possibly do it, any possibility of himself being considered. . . . And then we got on the subject of General Eisenhower and he explained . . . how he had counseled him to forsake any interest in politics or political preferment as inconsistent with the career of a professional soldier.

At the General Assembly, he had been assigned to Committee 5, handling administrative and budgetary matters, where one of the more controversial items related to Senator Vandenberg's determination to place a ceiling on United States contributions to the UN budget; but the most tricky issue was that of admission of new members, which was argued in Committee 1. The United States had taken a position opposing the admission of Albania, Mongolia, Hungary, Rumania, and Bulgaria, and the Soviet Union had taken stands against countries supported by the West. Finally, a "package deal" was worked out admitting a total of sixteen states: the foregoing, plus Austria, Ireland, Finland, Italy, Portugal, Spain, Jordan, Libya, Cambodia, Ceylon, Laos, and Nepal. Much of his time was devoted to working with Ambassador Austin in handling the responses to bitter attacks on the United States by U.S.S.R. foreign minister V. M. Molotov that set the cold climate for the whole session.

When the General Assembly adjourned on December 16, whatever regrets he might have had about the proffered jobs as assistant secretary general of the UN, or assistant secretary of state for public affairs, Adlai knew he was going back home to test the political waters.

CHAPTER FIVE
"Combat" Politics Begins

ADLAI'S STATEMENT TO GENERAL Marshall that he was interested in "combat" politics had been preceded by progressively deeper probes into the battlefield during much of 1947. Although hidden from him, shifting forces in the Cook County machine were providing openings that would have been inconceivable a few years earlier, and the consequences of which, many years later, still challenge credibility. It is a fascinating chapter in American politics.

Corruption was no stranger to either party in Illinois; indeed, much of the chicanery the Democrats practiced after Mayor Anton Cermak and Franklin Roosevelt led them to victory in 1932 had been learned during the notorious Republican regime of Mayor "Big Bill" Thompson, whose place in history was earned by offering to "bust the nose" of the king of England. Mounting layers of infamy stuck to the Kelly/Nash machine, and after the rout of the Democrats in the 1946 election, the all-important contest for mayor in 1947 loomed as a lost cause. It might well have been except for Colonel Jacob M. Arvey.

"Jack" Arvey had risen to leadership from what had been known as "the poor Jew ward," the twenty-fourth. His parents had immigrated from Poland; he worked in his teens as a delivery boy for a tailoring firm. He won his law degree by going to John Marshall Law School at night and working as a law clerk in the firm of John McInerary, who was associated with Pat Nash and Ed Kelly before they gained their grip on Chicago. He had become ward committeeman in 1922 and regularly delivered the vote for the machine.

He succeeded even in 1936 when the machine opposed Governor Henry Horner, a coreligionist and a personal friend. Nor did his control weaken when the ward shifted from being almost entirely Jewish to almost entirely black. Regardless of the candidate, the vote always came in close to twenty-four thousand for the machine candidate and three thousand for the opponent. By 1947 he was the Democratic leader of Cook County, having at least as much power but none of the crudity of such "bosses" as Hague of Jersey City, Pendergast of Kansas City, or Crump of Memphis. He was shrewd, imaginative, energetic, flexible, immensely likable, and was said to have undergone a conversion to clean politics while serving as Judge Advocate of the 33rd Division in the Pacific during World War II. He made no such claim; saying merely:

"When I was in the Army I was determined that if I went back into politics it would be on my terms—with good candidates. . . . The precinct captains have a better line to sell when they've got a good man on the ticket."

Subsequent events suggest conversion was at least a part of his practical politics. In any event, in 1947 he was convinced that if the machine was to be saved, he had to offer something new and different. That meant persuading Mayor Kelly to step down. He enlisted Spike Hennessey, a man who had gained Kelly's trust during many years of working as a Democratic press agent at City Hall, to conduct a poll based on the ward poll lists. Kelly was stunned by the results, but he accepted them, saying, "If I can't win . . . then no man close to me can." Kelly suggested as a possibility Martin H. Kennelly, a successful businessman with a reputation for being honest and civic-minded. He had actively opposed the machine in its campaign against Governor Horner, so his credentials as a Democrat but not an organization Democrat had been established.

The victory of "Honest Martin" Kennelly put Arvey in a strong position for pursuing a similar tactic in the 1948 election. As early as 1946 he had quietly made up his mind that Paul Douglas was the man who could defeat Senator C. Wayland "Curly" Brooks, a *Tribune* favorite.

"In 1946 Douglas came to a mass meeting in uniform," Arvey told John Bartlow Martin. "He did not make a speech but he waved a greeting to the crowd. I saw his withered hand [wounded in the war]. Brooks never made a speech without saying 'I got shrapnel in my back at Château-Thierry and I learned what it means to serve our country.' I knew the shattered hand would dispose of that."

The difficulty was that Douglas wanted to run for governor, and early in 1947 a modest but growing campaign had begun for Stevenson as senator. If the war had made a convert to clean politics out of Arvey, it had made a zealot for that cause out of Louis A. Kohn, then a thirty-nine-year-old attorney who all through the war remembered Adlai's speeches at the Council on Foreign Relations and the Bar Association. He returned determined that Adlai should replace Brooks; and he pursued his determination relentlessly. When Adlai began receiving letters, newspaper clippings, and telephone calls urging the Senate race, he could barely recall having met Kohn. He finally called Dutch Smith. "Lou Kohn is driving me crazy," he said. "He's determined that I run for the Senate. You talk to him." Dutch did, and while they agreed Adlai should be in the Senate, they also recognized that neither of them had any political connections.

They decided to enlist the help of Stephen A. Mitchell, a Chicago attorney they mistakenly thought was plugged into the Chicago machine. Actually, Mitchell was unpopular with Arvey and company, who felt he had tried to run around them in seeking appointment as United States attorney, a job that Arvey made sure went to someone else.

It was this unlikely trio—a Republican financier from Lake Forest, a Jewish lawyer whose connections outside the legal profession were mainly with journalists, and a lawyer close to the Catholic Church but in trouble with the Democratic machine—that lunched together in the late spring of 1947 and decided to launch a Stevenson-for-senator movement. They began a letter-writing campaign seeking support. They asked Loring C. "Bud" Merwin, now back at *The Pantagraph* as publisher, to write downstate publishers about a possible Stevenson candidacy. The letter gave biographical material and asked how well Adlai was known and whether he would draw Republican and independent votes. Most of the editors replied he was not well-known but none had negative reactions.

One of the trio's most overt actions, arranged by Dutch Smith, was a meeting between Adlai and Mayor Kennelly, who then, and later, declined to make a commitment. Thanks largely to Kohn's awesomely indefatigable efforts, publicity kept appearing that made the campaign seem more important than it really was. Kohn's pockets were always bulging with news clippings that he would urge on nearly everyone within reach to suggest that people all over the state were climbing on the nonexistent Stevenson bandwagon.

The most important event, however, was happening without their knowledge or participation. In late July, while Arvey was in Washington talking to Senator Scott W. Lucas about patronage, the secretary of the Senate, Leslie Biffle, arranged a luncheon that included former Secretary of State Byrnes. He overheard them discussing Ilinois politics and interjected, "Why don't you grab this fellow Stevenson—he's a gold nugget. I have had many dealings with him. He is an ideal man for you." Such an endorsement from such an experienced politician was one that Arvey knew he had to consider seriously, especially in view of his determination to fashion a ticket that did not carry the taint of the machine.

Adlai, in New York for the General Assembly, was bombarded with bulletins from Kohn, more quiet missiles from Dutch Smith, and a slowly building number of letters from people who had heard him speak or had read about him. The first week of November, Smith reported a long conversation with Milburn P. Akers, influential political and editorial writer for the *Chicago Sun,* who thought Adlai's chances of being nominated for the Senate were "quite favorable," but that he "certainly" could be nominated for governor. He said there was a feeling among Democratic leaders that Douglas, with his war record, would be a better candidate against Brooks; moreover, as a "reformist" alderman on the City Council he had created many enemies among the ward committeemen who would not want to see him in the governorship with its control of some thirty thousand patronage jobs. Akers speculated that the strongest ticket would be Douglas against Brooks and Stevenson against Dwight H. Green, the incumbent governor.

This was the first suggestion from a knowledgeable and influential political observer that Adlai should seriously consider the governorship. Smith did not know it, but Akers was reflecting Arvey's judgment. In responding to Smith's report, Adlai said, "I have never felt that [the governorship] was my 'dish' and still don't. However, perhaps I shouldn't be too emphatic and I won't be for the present."

All of this was leading up to a crucial meeting on November 15 between Arvey and Adlai's backers: Smith, Kohn, and Mitchell, joined by Laird Bell, another LaSalle Street lawyer, all amateurs in politics. Arvey's habitual courtesy was as untypical of his tough political heritage as their unaccustomed political activity was to them. Dutch Smith recalls that after they had presented their case, Arvey replied, "I would agree that Stevenson would make a very good Senator but you've got to get elected. Douglas has been working—'campaigning'—all summer downstate. He is much better known and I feel he would make a better candidate." Even though it was on his mind, he did not mention the governorship, and the quartet left somewhat deflated. Arvey then followed up with a call to Smith suggesting he bring Adlai to lunch with him and Senator Lucas. It was then that Arvey proposed the gubernatorial race. Adlai's reply was: "It's not my field. All my experience has been at the UN and in the State Department. I've never given it a thought. I don't think I'd be interested."

With this, Arvey began to look for another candidate, but continued quietly to check with a variety of people to obtain their assessment of Adlai.

Adlai was back in Chicago on December 1, and it was agreed that a formal announcement of the Stevenson for Senator Committee would be made and a letter seeking support would go out to a list of eight thousand people. The list of those signing the letter was notable for the absence of leaders of labor, blacks or other ethnic groups, or people other than LaSalle Street lawyers and financial men, Lake Forest suburbanites, college friends, and members of the Council on Foreign Relations, many of them Republicans. Nevertheless, this first solicitation of support for Adlai for any political office produced the excellent return of nearly one thousand endorsements. Though encouraged, the core group knew that with the machine's slate-making meeting scheduled for the end of that same month, there was little chance of success if Arvey persisted in his support of Douglas.

At this point, on a trip to New York, Dutch Smith encountered Arvey in the club car of the Twentieth Century Limited. Smith recalled:

> I'd seen him only that one time. But I went over and sat down beside him and recalled myself to him and said, "I'd like to talk to you a little more about him." I made it sound casual. We had been breaking our necks trying to get five minutes alone with Arvey. He invited me to go ahead, and I did. Colonel Arvey said, "Well, I don't know—a fellow was telling me the other day I'd better lay off Stevenson, that he went to Oxford."

Smith said he did not think that was the case, but he would ask to be certain; he knew that any charge as horrendous as that would be in Illinois had to be put to rest definitively. Arvey learned that Smith was returning to Chicago on the same day that he was and suggested they have dinner together then to discuss Stevenson further. Smith promptly wired Adlai, and when he boarded the train on Thursday he had Adlai's telegram: "Never went to Oxford, not even to Eton."

Arvey lamented that he had two good candidates for senator, but none for governor, adding that he wanted a "Kennelly type," a Democratic businessman not closely identified with the Democratic organization. Smith told him there was such a man on the train, James Knowlson, the president of a manufacturing company, and that if Arvey wished he would ask him. So Smith went to Knowlson and asked, "Do you want to be Governor of Illinois? Arvey is looking for a candidate." Knowlson replied he was voting Republican this year: "We need a change." Arvey's response to Smith's report was, "That's the trouble," and he proceeded to ask more questions about Adlai and also about his wife. Smith suggested that Arvey come to lunch the next Sunday at their estate fronting on Lake Michigan to meet Ellen and to talk to Adlai. Arvey accepted, and years later recalled the event in these words:

> I got lost on the way. Stevenson was playing tennis when I got there so I sat and talked to Ellen. I said, "Mrs. Stevenson, this is an opportunity for public service. What difference does it make which office it is? What matters is that he has an opportunity for public service and this will put him into the political picture, project him into the limelight. As far as the Governor's office being a dead end goes, it's just the opposite. More governors have gone to the presidency than senators. Senators have to vote on issues. The Governor is an administrator and doesn't

have to get tangled up in these controversial issues. He can run a clean slate government and an efficient one. He can do a good job and attract national attention." I had no more idea of Stevenson being President at that time than I have of that (pointing to an object on his desk) jumping up and turning a somersault by itself. But I used it with Mrs. Stevenson.

He came in from playing and asked me, he said, "Jack, I'm a little worried about this Governor thing. What's expected of me? Everybody says you don't trust Douglas on patronage." I said, "I will tell you the same thing I told Kennelly in 1947. The only thing I ask of you is that you help the Democratic Party as much as you can in a decent way. We want the patronage when a Democrat can fill the job. I am not talking about cabinet appointments or your own personal appointments. Get the best men you can for those. We want you to get the best. That's the way you can help the party the most. You're our showcase. If you do well, then we'll look good. All I ask is that you be loyal to the party—don't make an alliance with the Republicans."

Arvey recalled it as a pleasant conversation that ended with Adlai saying he wanted to think it over.

One of those Adlai consulted was Adlai III, who was home from Milton for Christmas. "It was on one of these walks along the river. I asked some silly questions such as was he sure he'd be nominated in the primary. He was terribly calm and man-to-man about it, sounding a little reluctant and weighing both sides." The son later told another interviewer, "He made a great point of consulting his family and particularly his sons about his political plans. He wanted always to feel that the family was behind him, that he was not doing something the family disapproved of, or that would be a hardship on the family." In addition, he respected the young man's judgment and probably felt he could get a more reliable reading of the family's reaction from him than he could from Ellen's changing attitudes.

The day after Christmas, Arvey told Smith that the slate for the 1948 election was going to be decided at the meeting of the thirty-man Democratic State Committee to be held at the Morrison hotel the next week. Douglas would then be named the candidate for the Senate. Did Adlai want the nomination for governor? Smith doubted he would take it but suggested that Arvey put the question to him directly. The three men met the next morning in Smith's office. Adlai's reaction was negative. He protested that his experience had been with the federal government, that he knew "Congress like a book," that he was qualified for and interested only in the Senate while he knew Douglas preferred to be governor. Why did the slate have to be the other way around? Arvey responded that there were practical political reasons for the lineup and that, in any event, the matter was no longer open for debate; Douglas was going to be nominated for the Senate, and if he wanted it, Adlai would be nominated for governor.

"What about my appointments, if I am elected?" Adlai asked, returning to the question he had raised at Smith's lunch. "Will I be entirely free on my appointments?"

"On your major appointments I wouldn't make a suggestion if you asked me to," Arvey told him. "On minor appointments—there would be scores of them—you'd need help. Even there I wouldn't suggest names unless you asked me to. My bet is that you'd ask me, as a practical matter, but it would be your free choice."

When Adlai said he wanted to think it over for a few days, Arvey reminded him that the final slate-making session was early the next week. With that, they parted. When he had received no word by Monday, Arvey called Smith and asked if Mrs. Stevenson was opposed to Adlai's acceptance. Smith said he didn't think so but would try to find out. Unable to reach Adlai, he talked directly to Ellen. She said merely that she preferred Springfield to Washington. When Smith reported back to Arvey that evening, Arvey finally expressed impatience, saying Adlai had only until noon the next day to make up his mind; by then the slate had to be completed.

Smith hadn't told Arvey, but the reason he couldn't reach Adlai was that Adlai was attending the Princeton Triangle Club show, and he was fearful of Arvey's reaction if he revealed that at such a time Adlai was engaged in attending a collegiate musical comedy. Nevertheless, he got to Adlai, who arrived at the Morrison's "smoke-filled rooms" at midnight, only to repeat what he had told Arvey on Saturday; that his experience had been "largely in the federal field" he had "never thought of anything else than the post of senator," and that he needed more time to "reflect."

Smith was at Adlai's office at nine the next morning, telling him bluntly that it was "now or never" so far as a political career was concerned. "They need you this year. If you say no when they need you, they won't take you when they don't need you." Smith recalled that Adlai paced the floor saying over and over, "I'm bothered. I'm bothered." Finally, he said that if he was going to do it he would have to have Kennelly's backing. Smith argued that once Adlai became the candidate, Kennelly would have no place to go. Adlai said he had to have Kennelly's active support, that what slim chance he had to be elected would be destroyed if Kennelly chose to sit out the campaign (which was largely what Kennelly did). Smith tried to reach Kennelly, but he was in a City Council meeting that would not adjourn until after Arvey's deadline had passed. As the clock moved toward noon, Adlai, with a tone of resignation, told Smith:

"Well, I guess you are right. It's now or never. I'll do it."

The episode is recounted in detail not alone for the fact that it marked the beginning of Adlai's career in "combat politics," but because of its relevance to his image as an indecisive man that later became so widespread. Those involved at the time argued that his apparent indecisiveness was more the product of his wanting to involve as many as possible of those close to him in the decision and to make sure he was giving it balanced consideration; it was also part of a hardheaded effort to move the slate-makers to accept Douglas's preference for the gubernatorial slot and his own desire to be senator. Arvey, on whom fell the burden of Adlai's delay, later wrote:

"I am greatly amused at the stories that Adlai Stevenson was indecisive. He was not a superficial man. He insisted on knowing everything about his subject. He did not do things impulsively. He did not make impulsive decisions, but wanted to know every facet of a problem before he decided upon action." To an interviewer he added, "Indecision means that you don't know how to implement a decision; you are unsure how to put it into effect. He was not indecisive at all once he had made up his mind; in fact, he was damned stubborn."

Another possible element in the hesitation was suggested the evening of his nomination. Lloyd Lewis and his wife Kathryn joined Adlai for a joyous train ride home. Gleefully, they read the newspapers Lewis had gathered reporting the nomination, and fellow commuters showered him with congratulations. Ellen was not waiting at the station as they had agreed and finally, after waiting for a while, Adlai accepted the Lewises offer to drive him home, suggesting they come in and celebrate. At the door, John Fell grabbed the newspapers and ran to show them to the cook. Adlai called upstairs to Ellen to announce the Lewises' presence for a celebration, and went to get ice for drinks. When, after some delay, she came down, she said nothing about the nomination but read to the Lewises a poem she had just written. After Lewis had expressed a favorable opinion, conversation drooped as she avoided the subject they had begun to celebrate before her appearance. "It was so awkward we finally left," Kathryn Lewis said.

On January 7, 1948, Adlai joined Arvey and other Chicago Democrats on the train en route to a meeting of the Democratic State Central Committee in Springfield. When Arvey told him he was expected to speak, Adlai asked if Spike Hennessey, the Cook County organization's publicity man would "dash off" something for him since he had never made a political speech. Arvey suggested that Adlai do a draft that Hennessey could edit. Adlai retreated to the club car and began writing in longhand on telegram blanks. When he returned about an hour later, Arvey has written, "Hennessey and I read it over and then looked at each other. 'Don't let anyone change a word of it,' I said to him. We knew then that this was a new style in political speaking and it was bound to make an impression upon all those who heard him."

"I want to win," he told the professional Democrats,

because I believe that we must and that we can give this state better, wiser, thriftier government. . . . I believe with all my heart and mind that as citizens of the Republic, not as Democrats, but as citizens of the richest, strongest, healthiest Republic on earth, we must restore popular esteem and confidence in the democratic system at all levels—municipal, state and national.

How else can we insure the survival of our free institutions when the winds begin to blow? If the people are cynical, suspicious and abused, if their confidence in their heritage is undermined by corruption, greed, excessive partisanship, we can not be sure that they will withstand or even identify the demagogues and false prophets of a better way who always march in the forefront of the reaction, be it of the right or left, be it fascist or communist, that will surely threaten us when the winds blow, and blow they surely will if we stumble headlong much further down this path of inflation, rising prices and corrosive, insensitive materialism. . . .

I say simply that our system is on trial; that our example in the years immediately ahead of us will determine the shape of things to come; that unless we continue healthy, strong and free we will not win many converts; that unless we can lift the hearts of men, unless we can reawaken the hopes of men, the faith of men, in the free way of life, we will be alone and isolated in a hostile world. . . .

I believe the people are wise and just; they are very tolerant, very forgiving. But once aroused by prolonged abuse they are merciless to their betrayers. It will not be enough to arouse them, it will not be enough to win the election. You have to deserve, you have to earn the people's confidence, not once, but constantly. . . . We will keep the people's confidence not by our words but by our works.

Arvey was right. The veterans of Illinois's grimy political battlefields had not heard talk like this. It contained elements of the message that would galvanize a large part of the nation four years later. That night it left the slightly stunned and somewhat skeptical Democratic leaders with a mixture of astonishment and enthusiasm. "We can go with him," one of the ward committeemen told Arvey. "He's got class."

The campaign seemed like a lost cause to virtually everyone but Adlai and Arvey. The latter believed he had winners in Douglas and Stevenson—provided Truman did not carry them down with him. Arvey's first effort was to advocate General Eisenhower for the Democratic nomination in place of Truman. He joined Mayor William O'Dwyer in New York, "Boss" Hague in New Jersey, the Americans for Democratic Action, Franklin D. Roosevelt, Jr., and others in arguing that Truman's unpopularity, plus the votes lost through the third-party candidacy of Henry A. Wallace, meant disaster for the Democratic ticket. Although Douglas supported Arvey's advocacy of Eisenhower, Adlai did not. Eisenhower was noncommittal when called upon by an emissary from Arvey's group. Shortly thereafter, however, he removed himself from consideration, leaving Arvey and his colleagues scrambling to get back on the Truman team.

As the Stevenson for Senator Committee converted itself to the Stevenson for Governor Committee and sent out its first mailing on January 8, the odds-makers were offering ten to one that Adlai would be defeated. Not until the final days of the campaign would the polls suggest that the race might even be close. Many of Arvey's committeemen believed that since there was no chance of winning, the candidate had been chosen just to make the party look good. One of them, with a sly wink, told Arvey they understood what he was up to.

"Where the hell did you get this guy Add-lay?" another asked. "He'll get his ears beat back."

Adlai, however, ignored the ten-to-one handicap as fund-raising efforts began, a staff started to assemble, and plans were made for an official launching of the campaign in Bloomington and Springfield in late February. At the same time, he was winding up legal work at the law firm. On February 4, one day before his forty-eighth birthday, he resigned, never, as it turned out, to return. The regard in which he was held was indicated by the anxious inquiries of two of his former partners. William Sidley approached Arvey, asking, "Jack, you're not hurting my boy too much are you?"

"What do you mean?" Arvey replied.

"He won't be beaten so badly he'll be disgraced, will he?" Sidley persisted.

Arvey's answer was "He's going to win." Sidley was not convinced.

Nor was Kenneth F. Burgess, who sought out Henry Crown and said, "You know a lot of Democrats—will they agree to reward Stevenson's yeoman service to the party with a judgeship?" Crown had already registered his estimate of Adlai's chances by telling his son, "Stevenson doesn't have a chance in hell of being elected but let's show our appreciation," and sending him to Adlai with one of the few checks that came trickling in during the early months. Sidley, a Republican, also was one of the early contributors.

The overwhelming conviction was that this was to be a Republican year; contributions to Democrats would be going to a futile cause. Even labor was split. The AFL was committed to Governor Green, and CIO support of Adlai contained significant fissures. Joe Germano, a powerful figure in the CIO, came with the offer of a contribution provided that Adlai would appoint their man, Frank Annunzio, director of labor. Arvey happened to be there at the same time and he reported what transpired:

> "I need your support," Adlai said frankly. "But I haven't made any promises about appointments and I'm not making any. I may or I may not pick a man from your union. Jack, here, hasn't asked me for such commitments. If he doesn't, why should you?"
> I went back to Germano and told him, "You think he is honest and fair and decent, don't you? Then why don't you take his word that he will do the honest and fair and decent thing?" Well, Germano sulked through the whole campaign. Nevertheless, Stevenson did not hesitate to appoint Annunzio. And a few years later when Annunzio got into trouble, Stevenson did not hesitate to fire him either.

Headquarters were opened at 7 South Dearborn Street on February 17 in a large, bare, poorly lit room, with temporary partitions providing cubbyhole offices. Its chief virtue, Adlai acknowledged, was that it was cheap. That, to him, was an important virtue even when money was not so scarce. The staff contained many of the faces and characteristics that were to mark much of the rest of his career.

The first was Carol Evans, daughter of a small-town minister, who had left Nebraska in the fall of 1936 to attend the University of Chicago. Before she could register, her hard-won savings were stolen; so instead of enrolling, she went job hunting. For two years she worked as a secretary in the Sidley law firm while going to night classes at the university. Her memory of Adlai, however, dates from the day in the fall of 1939 when, having saved enough money to enroll full-time at the university, she was leaving the firm.

"I knew who he was, but I had no idea he was even aware of me," she recalls.

> Much to my surprise, he stopped me in the hall and told me he was on the Board of Trustees of International House at the University and if I would like to live there he would try to arrange it for me. I had already made other arrangements, but I was quite overwhelmed by his thoughtfulness. Later I was to learn he did this sort of thing for many people. I was not in touch with him after that but when he asked the personnel manager of the firm to find him a secretary, I wanted very much to work for him. The only problem was money. He paid me out of his personal funds and did not have very much to spend. I had

to have a certain amount to live on, but we struck a bargain and I went to work on February 1, 1948.

She remained until he went to the United Nations as ambassador: fast, efficient, inexhaustible, with an unperturbability concealing a sense of humor that enabled her to write perceptive and amusing little notes to hundreds of correspondents, only the most knowledgeable of whom could discern they had not been composed and signed by Adlai himself.

James Mulroy, who functioned as campaign manager, was a large, ruddy, enthusiastic Irishman who had won the Pulitzer Prize for his reporting on the famous Loeb-Leopold kidnap-murder case. He had become managing editor of Marshall Field's *Chicago Sun,* but was caught in its merger with the Chicago *Times* in early 1948 and energetically moved into the Stevenson campaign headquarters. During the early months, at least, Marshall Field paid his salary. Mulroy loved the political battles, fought them with energy, devotion, and effectiveness throughout the campaign and through most of the Springfield years, when an innocent but unwise investment led to his resignation and, possibly, to his death.

Mulroy enlisted the help of a fellow Irishman, William I. Flanagan, who had left reporting to work for a public relations firm. Flanagan worked nights and weekends without pay for much of the time and started receiving a regular paycheck only in the final weeks of the campaign, after which he became the governor's press secretary. He combined ability with almost excessive zeal.

The other key members, all volunteers, were Lloyd Lewis, who wrote speech drafts; Walter V. Schaefer, a Northwestern University law professor who had worked in the Illinois Legislative Reference Bureau and later became an outstanding chief justice of the Illinois Supreme Court; Dutch Smith, Lou Kohn, Stephen Mitchell, and Jane Dick. At the outset, a number of suburban socialite friends were attracted to the headquarters, but dwindled away as the novelty wore off. Another trend quickly set in that became a hallmark of the Stevenson public career: Young people from all over Chicago began appearing, drawn by the attractive "new look" in politics.

Among them was Daniel Rostenkowski, who went on to become a member of Congress and chairman of the powerful House Ways and Means Committee; William R. Rivkin, lawyer and lecturer at Northwestern, who was President Kennedy's ambassador to Luxembourg; Bill Blair from the William Allen White Committee days who became Kennedy's ambassador to Denmark, Johnson's ambassador to the Philippines, and general director of the John F. Kennedy Center for the Performing Arts in Washington, D.C. By mid-campaign, eager young novices such as these, many of whom were Republicans, comprised the bulk of the fifty-odd volunteers who reported for work on a regular basis.

"We were all new and enthusiastic," Lou Kohn recalled. "We had some good issues. We had a bad administration to defeat. It was an ideal campaign." It was also to become a rough one.

The necessity of running in the primary election in April, although unopposed, was seized as an opportunity to become better known. The kickoff speeches at the Jefferson-Jackson Day Dinner in Springfield and a homecoming rally in Bloomington—one partisan and the other nostalgic—were successful. The editor of the *Springfield Register*, V. Y. Dallman, wrote him, "Your triumphs . . . gripped the imagination of central Illinois." John Dreiske, political editor of the *Sun-Times,* wrote: "He was a smash hit. There once were those who gloomily opined he should not travel in the same caravan with Paul H. Douglas because of the danger he would be eclipsed by that brilliant orator. Put away your handkerchiefs. Don't cry for Stevie." *Time* magazine, taking unusual notice of a state primary campaign, commented that the machine politicians, with their fears that "their gentlemanly candidate" would not do well, "needn't have been so nervous."

On March 1, Adlai and Douglas set out on a three-week statewide tour in which they would speak in 125 towns, splitting up for daytime meetings and each night appearing together at a rally. The relationship of the two men, however, was never an easy one and there were few joint appearances after this initial foray. Nevertheless, a momentum developed that kept building slowly. By mid-March, Governor Green, who had gone off to Florida on vacation announcing he would not bother to conduct a primary campaign, felt it necessary to return and enter the race with an attack on his opponent as "a man on leave from the striped-pants brigade of the Roosevelt-Truman State Department." Green and the *Tribune* kept repeating the striped-pants description until the *Daily News* found a photograph of the governor in striped pants and cutaway and printed it saying they had been unable to find a similar photograph of Adlai. Green and the *Tribune* joined in heaping scorn on the United Nations and Adlai's role in its founding. Adlai's response was, "How can any thinking man in the world today be anything but an internationalist?"

The primary election was good news for the Republicans. Green received some 200,000 more votes statewide than Adlai. Despite the power of the Cook County machine, Adlai had received only 113,500 more votes than Green out of 740,000 cast; to win a statewide election a Democrat had to do much better than that in Cook County. His running mate, Paul Douglas, received nearly 20,000 more votes than he did statewide. It was not a good start; nonetheless, he wrote Adlai III, "We did well in the primary . . . I am very optimistic."

Dwight Green had come into office in 1940 as a good-government reformer, riding the wave of an image of the vigorous and fearless young prosecutor who had sent Al Capone to prison. He had initially made some improvements, but by this third-term campaign his administration had become notorious for inefficiency and corruption. He had hopes of winning the vice presidential nomination at the Republican convention to be held in Philadelphia in June and had arranged to be the keynote speaker. It was such a vociferous attack on the liberal wing of the party headed by Governor Thomas E. Dewey that with the latter's nomination his hopes were dashed and his position diminished.

At the Democratic National Convention in mid-July, Adlai had better luck. Although he had barely mentioned Truman's name in the primary campaign, he had not joined Arvey's "Draft Eisenhower" movement and thus could be helpful to Arvey as well as to Truman in swinging Illinois's sixty delegate votes behind the President and his first-ballot nomination.

The big battle centered on civil rights. The specific issue was the seating of the Mississippi delegation, which had refused to pledge its support to Truman or to a candidate supporting his civil rights program. Within the Illinois delegation and in the convention, Adlai joined actively in the fight for the civil rights pledge led by Hubert Humphrey and the northern liberals that finally was won and that precipitated walkouts by Mississippi and Alabama. Although he had clashed with the presiding officer, Senator Alben Barkley, a distant relative, during the platform debate, he happily gave a seconding speech for Barkley's nomination for Vice President. He came away from the convention with strengthened credentials as a Democrat, as a politician, and as a civil rights advocate.

As the round of county fairs began, Green was the five-to-one favorite in an increasingly bitter and hard-hitting campaign. Talk that Adlai was "too gentlemanly" silenced as Adlai campaigned against the "Greed" administration and characterized his opponent as Governor Greed and Payroll Pete in the light of evidence of payroll padding. The candidate's pants also kept claiming attention. At one point, Adlai declared that if the laws were enforced "Green and his pals might each get a pair of striped pants, but the stripes would be running the other way."

The corruption at which this rhetoric was aimed became the central issue of the campaign, fueled by two dramatic events. On March 25, 1947, an explosion in mine number 5 at Centralia, Illinois, had killed 111 coal miners. A year later, an intensively researched article by John Bartlow Martin appearing in *Harper's* magazine revealed a shocking neglect of mine safety laws and an equally appalling laxity in inspection and enforcement. Despite repeated complaints and appeals from the miners pointing out the unsafe conditions, their warnings had been ignored by both operators and inspectors. Martin detailed the close relations between the owners and the inspectors and the extent to which the latter had solicited and obtained campaign contributions from the former. The damning account had been reprinted widely in the state and had prompted angry editorials that persisted in the face of inaction. Adlai returned to the issue again and again.

In late August, the *St. Louis Post-Dispatch* sent its expert investigative reporter, Theodore C. Link, to Peoria to look into a gang murder. On September 1, an article by Link reported, "Gamblers, slot machine operators and punch-board distributors in at least six counties were 'shaken down' for nearly $100,000 for Gov. Dwight H. Green's 1944 political campaign." Shortly thereafter, Link was arrested and criminally indicted by Green machine politicians. In the uproar that followed, it was revealed that scores of downstate newspaper editors were on the payroll of the state, put there by Green cohorts to keep them quiet while the gamblers were being shaken down; and that many had formed working alliances with all kinds of grafters, profiting richly from kickbacks, payroll padding, and fraudulent buying and selling of state materials. Papers that theretofore had ignored such stories now felt obliged not only to report them but to develop their own investigations.

The streets of Illinois's towns "danced in the heat," Adlai wrote Jane Dick as he began a grueling schedule that was to last until Election Day. Beginning early in the morning and going far into the night, dashing from place to place, eating irregularly and sleeping little, Adlai expressed a zest and appreciation of the experience in the numerous personal notes scribbled quickly to friends along the way. "I've come to wonder," he wrote Jane Dick from a downstate motel, "how anyone can presume to talk about 'America' until he has done some political campaigning."

"We drove in the heat until we were exhausted; that is, everyone except Stevenson," wrote campaign aide Jack O. Brown.

The man has the strongest self-control, both mentally and physically that I have ever witnessed. In my car he would sit by the hour with a fat brief case propped up on his lap, while he would draft his next speech, or a few press releases. . . . He never missed a chance to acquire more facts and he was always exploring possible information by asking questions of everyone who was near him.

Adlai III and Tim Ives, and occasionally Borden, traveled with him. Ellen never did. The use of travel time for speech writing that marked— some say, scarred—his presidential campaigns began in backseats on Illinois highways. As later, he kept bombarding friends for drafts and memos, but the speeches nearly always were his own. And, as later, he felt compelled to produce a separate speech for nearly every occasion. He did develop a "county fair" speech, but it too was revised as the car sped along on a schedule that generally tried to cover four counties a day. In a postelection story, *Newsweek* commented, "The friendly, earnest candidate visited almost every lunch wagon and curbstone from Little Egypt in Southern Illinois to the North Shore along Lake Michigan, making as many as a dozen speeches in a single night."

Adlai's preoccupation with speeches never extended to his appearance. His well-worn clothes were invariably rumpled. Jim Mulroy thought Adlai's hat was disgracefully disreputable and once stealthily dropped it out the car window. But before the wind could whip it across the prairies, Adlai stopped the car and retrieved it. It was an antecedent to the later Pulitzer Prize-winning photo of his shoe with a hole in the sole. Indeed, Lou Kohn assigned himself the task of surreptitiously slipping off the lunch counter the quarter tip Adlai would leave and substituting the dollar that not only was more appropriate but was expected of a candidate.

The backseat scribbling on yellow pads produced eloquent statements that gradually improved in delivery and gained in attention from growing audiences and mounting newspaper support.

"Surveys four years ago when you were fighting to preserve our political system disclosed that your elders—that seven out of ten adult Americans—thought so little of politics that they were definitely opposed to a son of theirs making a career of it," he told the Young Democrats. "Fight for it, yes; but work at it, no! . . . If this is to be the century of American leadership, then the leadership of Americans must be the honorable calling the founders of a government by the governed meant it to be."

Some of his talks were almost brutally blunt and direct. At Farmer City, Illinois, in August, he told his farm audience:

> After Roosevelt and the Democrats had given you farmers a fair break with a parity price support, soil conservation, rural electrification, benefit payments, farm loans, the reciprocal trade agreements act and farm prices had gone up and up, you voted for the Republicans who had never given you anything but Hoover's ill-fated Farm Board! I don't understand why people vote against their best friends.

During the campaign he also became one of the early advocates of equal pay for equal work for women, for a Fair Employment Practices Commission, for a constitutional convention to revise the state constitution adopted in 1870, for a long-term road-building program, and for a drastic overhaul of the state welfare system and in particular the state's mental hospitals that had degenerated "into unspeakable horrors of sadism, inefficiency, and corruption."

The corruption theme received dramatic emphasis as the campaign moved toward its climax.

After midnight, on October 7, a member of Green's State Industrial Commission, William John Granata, was killed, apparently with an ax, on the sidewalk in the heart of Chicago's Loop. The killing dramatized the corruption issue at a critical time, and Adlai used it as another example of the "sordid leadership" of Governor Green.

"Granata started his political career by stealing a ballot box in a class election at Urbana [the state university]," Adlai said.

He advanced rapidly. He was Republican ward committeeman and on Governor Green's payroll. His chauffeur, an ex-convict, also was on the Green payroll. His brother Pete is Republican leader in the legislature and distinguished himself in the last session by helping to kill the Crime Commission bills. Another brother was bookkeeper for the late gang chieftain, Frank Nitti [who was regarded as Capone's successor until he, too, was murdered].

A few days after this speech, the press reported that the FBI was investigating letters threatening Adlai and his son, John Fell, with death by strangulation.

Other members of the family, however, were the objects of Adlai's concerns in the midst of the campaign. Borden had been failing in school at Lake Forest and Adlai was writing the headmaster at Choate seeking his admission there. He finally agreed, provided that Borden went to summer school. Adlai III had graduated from Milton Academy and Adlai embarked on a determined campaign to get him into Princeton. The admissions officer was willing only to put him on a waiting list, and in a stream of letters to him, the Milton Academy headmaster, and influential Princeton alumni, Adlai sought more favorable action. Not only was he devoted to his son, but he thought Princeton was acting arbitrarily. Despite his efforts, the admissions officer was stubborn and they finally had to settle for Harvard.

Ellen's reaction to the campaign was confusing to him, but less so to their friends. At the outset, she accompanied him to an occasional local rally. At a meeting in a black ward of Chicago, she was enticed to the piano and happily led a brief songfest. The next morning, Adlai glowingly described the scene to the headquarters staff and said he hoped she would do it more often. She never did it again.

Early in the campaign, Ernest Ives, the most discreet of men, had written a long letter to Ellen's mother, Mrs. Carpenter:

"I have always tried to steer clear of family entanglements," he began,

> but the situation seems to me so serious that I am appealing to you to ask you to give a helping hand to Ellen and Adlai. . . . Adlai's speech last evening was delivered in a very tired and seemingly discouraged vein. His winning smile was even lacking and while he had had a tiring day I know that the principal reason was the discouraging attitude evinced by Ellen and [her] complete

lack of interest and cooperation here at the reception and at the dinner.

He went on to say that her "attitude seems to take all the fire and vim out of him" and that he had "endeavored to encourage Ellen to be helpful to Adlai, not to belittle his efforts and his aspirations but to play her role."

A few other close friends detected the growing rift. Clifton Utley's wife, Frayn, has said:

> I went through a hell of a summer with Ellen Stevenson. She would come over to the house all the time. Dutch Smith and I tried to tell her to go see a psychiatrist. So did others. She simply could not tolerate Adlai's achieving anything on his own. . . . She came over to my house six or eight times in the summer of 1948 and said she was going to divorce Adlai. She said he couldn't do anything without her help. She had started him. Her contacts made everything possible.

The elements of paranoia described by Mrs. Utley were obscured by Ellen's beauty, charm, talent, and intelligence. Even though Adlai had sought the help of a psychiatrist in their Washington days, he was among the most reluctant to recognize her illness. Jane Dick recalls that even though he knew the campaign was increasing their difficulties, he was shocked to learn of her intention to seek a divorce. "One day either in September or October Adlai came into the office where our headquarters were and his face as absolutely ashen. He said, 'She is going to divorce me!'"

Mrs. Dick and others undertook to persuade her not to go ahead with the divorce, or at least to postpone it. She did not emphasize the disastrous impact her action would have on the campaign because she suspected that Ellen's state of mind would welcome timing that would inflict the most damage.

Adlai was having his own emotional problems. In New York in the fall of 1947 while he was at the UN General Assembly, he again met Alicia Patterson in whom he had been deeply interested before he married Ellen. She was now married to her third husband, Harry F. Guggenheim, who used a portion of his copper-based fortune to found with her in 1940 the *Long Island Newsday*. It is evident that a serious love affair developed rapidly. Jane Dick has a letter written in April of 1949 in which he refers to "this mysterious dream that's enveloped me for a year and a half."

The first letter with a definite date among those Alicia later returned to him was one dated May 10, 1948, written after midnight from a hotel in Urbana, Illinois. In it he said, "I wonder what the hell I'm doing and

why—and then I think of you and that you think it's good and worth-
while and wouldn't love me if I didn't behave this way—and then I get up
and go at it again," and ended with "I love you—A."

Also, that spring after the primaries when he took a brief vacation at
Buffie's North Carolina home, he visited Alicia at her plantation in
Georgia, after which he wrote:

Alicia dear
  You asked for a bread and butter letter—instead you'll get
the disordered reveries of a drowsy, contented man high in the
clouds. There is something fitting about coming to you on the
wings of wind and floating away from you in the clouds. . . . I
enjoyed my little walk hand in hand down tobacco road—and I'm
still there. Indeed, I'm afraid I will be there for days to come—
even after this bird plunges down thru [sic] the white wool and
sets me gently on earth again. I'll see you striding in that solid
straight legged way along the bank and thru the pines, all white in
sunlight, looking quizzically here and there—half sinking, half
panting—but I'll be very circumspect, very casual, very
courteous, very banal. I'll resist the awful temptation to sweep
you up into a soft white ball, that, magically, unfolds a sharp,
savage little tigress. That is, I'll resist until I'm very much alone
and it's very late and very still. Then the cocoon will unfold in the
moonlight—very soft, very tender, and my heart will stop— . . . I
hope you will come out to Libertyville after this summer. I want
you to know the boys. I want them to grow to love you like their
father—well not just like their father. And I want you to know
Ellen better. You can probably help me a lot in that direction—
not that you are good, but because you are wise. . . ."

There were more letters during that summer and an occasional fleeting meeting. "Four counties a day is fine education," he wrote her in
September, "but I don't recommend it for human beings."

As the campaign ripened along with the rich fields of Illinois, paper
after paper endorsed the Stevenson-Douglas ticket until only the *Tribune*
and Hearst's *American* were supporting Green and Brooks. Their vitriolic
attacks prompted Adlai on occasion to respond in kind. "Where were the
McCormicks, Brooks, and Green when the Nazis were murdering Poland?" he asked at a Polish-American banquet. "I'll tell you where they
were. They were against aid to the Allies."

Although the odds were improving slowly, money problems continued to plague the campaign. Adlai's insistence on avoiding money that
might have strings attached did not help, especially after the encounter
with Germano became known. At critical moments, Adlai would give his

fund raisers the names of suburban neighbors who had over the years pledged their support, and they were always too embarrassed to tell him of their refusals. The meager cash flow and Adlai's aversion to deficit financing resulted in one of the least expensive campaigns ever recorded for a major office in a major state.

The audit of the Stevenson for Governor Committee books that Adlai insisted on showed a total expenditure of $154,215.44 (including $3,319.51 for the inauguration). Contributions totaled $172,840.10. Much of it came in the final weeks when victory became an increasing possibility; a substantial amount came in only after the election. Accusations were made that the machine had held back. This was unfair. Arvey, some of his colleagues, and the machine did contribute. It also exempted the Stevenson campaign from the large contribution that routinely was levied against each candidate to be spent on behalf of the entire ticket. The machine's support was behind the $2,500 each donated by the United Auto Workers and the United Steel Workers; and the $2,000 by the Amalgamated Clothing Workers. Charges that ward committeemen sat on their hands were met with demonstrable evidence that once baseball's World Series was over in October they were energetic in arousing the support of their constituents.

In mid-October, *Newsweek* reported that the Democrats had given up hope of electing Douglas "although they continued to claim that Stevenson had an outside chance." On October 31, *The New York Times* stated that "the GOP is expected to retain the Senate seat and the Governorship."

William Benton recalls that two weeks before the election, Edward Eagle Brown, the president of Chicago's First National Bank, said to him, "Your friend Adlai has as much chance to be governor of Illinois as I have to be Pope!"

On Election Day, Adlai and Ellen cast their ballots at a country school at Half Day, a small town near Libertyville, too late for their pictures to make the afternoon papers. Adlai was confident. So was Arvey, who had bet $3,000 at three-to-one odds. Dutch Smith was convinced they had lost; indeed, the most optimistic of Adlai's close associates thought they would come close to winning but doubted they would make it.

The size of the victory was stunning. Since the Civil War, only three Democrats had been elected governor in Illinois. Adlai won by the largest plurality any governor had ever received—572,067 votes out of a little less than 4 million cast. Douglas had defeated Brooks by 407,728 votes, a plurality of nearly 165,000 less than Adlai's. Truman carried the state by only 33,612. Clearly, Adlai had carried the President in with him. It also meant that more than half a million people had split their tickets, voting Republican for President and Democratic for governor and senator. His plurality in Cook County was 546,424, but, most astonishing of all, he carried mostly Republican downstate Illinois; something no one had thought possible. Bloomington's McLean County made a rare appearance in the Democrat's victory column. Libertyville's Lake County, however, maintained its fierce Republican allegiance.

The magnitude of the victory automatically thrust him onto the national scene. On November 19, Arthur Krock wrote in his *New York Times* column that Adlai was being seriously looked at as a candidate for President in 1952. He returned to the idea on December 14, describing Adlai's role in the formation of the United Nations and his "unblemished reputation."

Adlai wrote him: "I read the oracle of Washington's piece of December 14 with fear and trembling. Is anyone really looking me over? If so, the speculation will soon end!"

To which Krock replied,

"It is all right for you to be as modest as all that, but I did not dream up the piece, as you eventually will discover."

CHAPTER SIX
The Guv

WOULD ADLAI STEVENSON HAVE made a good President of the United States? The best clues are to be found in the record of his four years as governor of Illinois.

Immediately after the election, at a meeting to thank the ward leaders for their efforts in the campaign, he added that he regretted he would be leaving behind so many loyal friends when he moved to Springfield.

"Don't you worry, Adlai," came a voice from the crowd, "we will all be there." Many were, and many more tried to be. There were, after all, thirty thousand jobs to be filled.

Adlai believed, as he later told his son, that the test of any administrator was his ability to get good people to help him. That was the first task he set for himself in the hectic two months before the inauguration. The most important slots to be filled, he felt, were the top jobs in the Departments of Finance, Revenue, and Welfare. An immediate obstacle was salaries. His own was $12,000, compared to $25,000 paid to the governors of New York and California, and $20,000 for the governors of New Jersey and Massachusetts. After that ceiling, the top salary for his cabinet and department heads was $8,000. With that restriction, he set out to entice into government men who were earning much more. A related problem was the negative image attached to working in such a scandal-riddled environment.

Aided mainly by Smith, Kohn, Mitchell, and Walter Schaefer, he began an intensive search for people, telling them there were three ways to choose key staff—to appoint those recommended by the party, to pick the best of the people actively seeking a job, and to "go out and try to find your own men." He made it clear he preferred the third way, yet he spent hours on all three. Day after day, his calendar showed appointments every half hour and often every fifteen minutes. Twice in December, Arvey approached him on behalf of the most powerful members of the Cook County machine to urge the appointment of William Milota of the twenty-third ward either as member or secretary of the Liquor Control Commission. It was a sensitive position; Milota did not get the appointment. For one vacancy on the Court of Claims there were 107 applicants. After aides or friends had checked out applicants, he would interview them personally, and was always suspicious of those who seemed to have organized support. He offered the directorship of one department to nine men before one took it. Three of the first ten major appointments went to Republicans.

For director of finance, responsible for budget, purchasing, printing, and accounting controls, he persuaded George Mitchell, a nationally recognized tax expert and professor of economics, to take leave from the Federal Reserve Bank of Chicago. When he had to return to the bank, he helped Adlai persuade Joseph Pois, treasurer and board member of a major steel company in Chicago and consultant on budgetary problems in Michigan and Kentucky, to replace him.

Fred Hoehler resigned as director of the Chicago Community Fund to head the Department of Welfare with its budget of more than $100 million, more than ten thousand employees, and a scandalous record of corruption and neglect of the state's children's hospitals, mental hospitals, correctional institutions, sanatoriums, and schools for the deaf and blind that, supposedly, cared for some fifty thousand people. Hoehler's outstanding record in the welfare field had led to his election as president of the American Public Welfare Association and the National Council of Social Work. For him, a cut in salary from $18,000 a year to $8,000 catastrophic. At first he reluctantly declined Adlai's offer, but Adlai persuaded him to take the job for three months while he looked for a permanent director. Hoehler stayed the full term and established an historically notable record in public administration.

The most important "political" appointment was that of Richard J. Daley, the future mayor of Chicago, as director of revenue. He came from a ward near Chicago's stockyards, and three times had been minority leader of the Illinois State Senate. He also had a long record as comptroller of Cook County. When his appointment was announced, the *Sun-Times* commented, "If Adlai Stevenson can induce a few more men of Daley's unique qualifications—ability, political experience, and integrity—to associate themselves with him for the next four years he will do much to assure the success of his administration." Whatever one thinks of Daley's later career, his record in the Stevenson administration merited praise.

Another key post was the chairmanship of the Commerce Commission, which regulated utilities and common carriers and which had become a major focus of scorn in the Green administration. After repeated rejections, Adlai learned that Walter T. Fisher, a leading LaSalle Street lawyer who had long been interested in problems of public utility regulation, might be willing to take the job. The fact that he was a Republican made no difference to Adlai.

Another graft-riddled job, that of state purchasing agent, was the object of eager anticipation by many politicians. Adlai began seeking help from business acquaintances, including his bitter opponent from the prewar debates, the head of the America First Committee and chairman of Sears, Roebuck and Company, General Robert E. Wood. Wood told Adlai that Sears's purchasing agent, Carl Kresl, was retiring and might be interested. Adlai's successful persuasion undoubtedly saved the state millions of dollars.

Amid pressure from the Cook County machine to obtain a position in the three-man State Liquor Commission, where the issuance and revocation of liquor licenses provided a well-utilized opportunity for graft, Adlai sought for weeks to find someone he knew he could trust. Carl McGowan, while attending a dinner party at the home of his Northwestern University law faculty colleague, Willard Wirtz, talked about the problems they were having in finding good people for state jobs. Jokingly, Wirtz interjected, "Maybe that's because you don't ask."

Wirtz, born in DeKalb, Illinois, thirty-eight years earlier, had graduated from Harvard Law School and taught at the University of Iowa law school before joining the faculty at Northwestern, where he and McGowan had become close friends. A week after the dinner party, McGowan called him and asked if he would come meet the new governor. Without ceremony, Adlai asked him if he would accept appointment to the Liquor Commission.

"But I don't know anything about liquor control," Wirtz replied.

"What we need and find hard to get is somebody who'll just keep his hands out of other people's pockets," Adlai told him. "That is the chief qualification."

"If that's so, I'm not likely to deny I'm qualified," Wirtz told him with a grin and promptly accepted the $6,000-a-year-job. When Adlai then discovered that the law required the commission to be bipartisan, he called Wirtz and asked if he was a Democrat.

"Is it necessary that your appointee be a Democrat?" Wirtz asked. "It is."

"Then I'm a Democrat, as of now." Wirtz said, initiating a relationship that resulted in a law partnership with Adlai between presidential campaigns and service in the cabinets of both Presidents Kennedy and Johnson as secretary of labor.

Another function frequently corrupted by pressures from organized crime was the Parole and Pardon Board. He persuaded probably the best man in the country, the world-famous sociologist specializing in criminology, Joseph D. Lohman, to take the job.

Women rarely were even considered for top appointments in those days. Years earlier, Adlai had had a long discussion on the problems of the Women and Children's Division of the State Labor Department with Mrs. Stanley Pargellis, a leader in the League of Women Voters. He sought her out to ask for recommendations of women, particularly in the Labor Department. She recommended Martha Ziegler from the federal Department of Labor to head the division and Florence Klever as her deputy. They were appointed and introduced far-reaching reforms. Sadly, many reforms, like a number of Fred Hoehler's, did not survive the next change of administration. Adlai's inquiries also identified Maude Meyers, an outstanding career public servant who happened to be a registered Republican. He appointed her, over the protest of his fellow Democrats, to the Civil Service Commission, where she was both able and courageous in the battle to substitute a merit system for political patronage.

The immediate staff was small, the atmosphere relaxed, the weekly meetings punctuated by laughter. The tendency to address "the Governor" was soon shortened to "the Guv." As early as February 15, letters to close friends began to be signed, "The Guv," in place of the customary "AES." Carol Evans was joined by Mrs. Margaret Munn, a Springfield native, to handle secretarial work. Jim Mulroy became executive secretary with Bill Flanagan, working with him on public relations. Louis Kohn took a short leave of absence from his law firm to function as appointments secretary. Walter Schaefer extended his leave from the Northwestern law faculty to serve as counselor and help prepare the legislative program for the first session of the State Assembly. He was joined by J. Edward Day, a young lawyer whose father-in-law, Kenneth Burgess, was a principal in Adlai's former firm. Lawrence Irvin, then thirty-eight, came from Bloomington to handle the flood of patronage requests. Irvin had been a Red Cross field director and business manager of Illinois State Normal University, had many friends, and was remarkably skillful in discerning talent, or the lack of it, and soothing disappointments.

Completing this initial group was T. Don Hyndman, a holdover from Governor Green's staff whose background as a newspaperman had been most useful in drafting proclamations, statements, and speeches. He and Mrs. Anne Risse, who had served five previous governors, were valued aides throughout the Stevenson years. Similarly, all the stenographic and clerical help in the governor's office in the Capitol Building who had been given their jobs by Governor Green and were not Civil Service employees were asked to continue if they wished, and they did.

By Sunday evening, January 9, every place in Springfield that would accept guests was jammed and cots lined the corridors of the Springfield hotels and motels. Adlai, Ellen, Adlai III, and John Fell (Borden was away at school) stayed at the Abraham Lincoln Hotel, taken there from the train station in Governor Green's state limousine; in fact, the courtesy of the governor throughout eased the transition following the bitter campaign. On Monday, Inauguration Day, they moved through chilly, gray, drizzle-slick, and crowded streets to the Armory Building, where, in a joint session of the State Assembly, Adlai took the oath as the thirty-first governor of Illinois, and only the fourth Democrat since the Civil War.

The inaugural address was not one of his better efforts, but it did set forth an ambitious program: increased aid to local governments, especially for schools; a convention to revise the state constitution; higher pay for top state officials plus payroll disclosure to discourage patronage abuses and expansion of the merit system; increased aid to old-age pensioners and the blind; reorganization of the public welfare system with emphasis on the mental health system; improvements in workmen's compensation and employment services; creation of a Fair Employment Practices Commission; highway construction; a speedup in slum clearance and housing; reorganization of the Department of Mines and Minerals with emphasis on better mine safety; creation of a nonpolitical commission to deal with conservation; and a merit system for state police.

Most of the proposals were only in broad outline; he was still uncertain of his relations with the lawmakers. To begin with, the Republicans had a majority of fourteen in the Senate and the Democrats had a majority of nine in the House. Partisan struggles, however intense, took second place to nonpartisan struggles for more directly material and self-serving rewards. The new Democratic speaker of the House, Paul Powell, for example, complained that it had cost him a lot to be elected speaker and that Stevenson had thwarted his expectation of getting it back the first year. After he died in 1970, $800,000 was found in shoeboxes, envelopes, and a bowling bag in his Springfield hotel closet and office safe.

After the speech, the Stevensons, the Greens, and about seventy friends went to the mansion for lunch. A Bloomington friend, Mrs. John S. Miller, remembers that "Ellen went upstairs and refused to come down. We stood around in the receiving line downstairs waiting for her. Finally Buffie said, 'Let's go to lunch.' Poor Adlai just stood and stood. Finally, she did appear." But that night, at the Inaugural Ball, Ellen looked radiant; her dress received ecstatic notice from the society reporters. The packed floor pulled back to let her and Adlai dance the first dance alone.

The next morning he didn't arrive at his statehouse office until after eleven. He apologized to the waiting newsmen and laughingly explained the "major crisis" that had detained him. Carl Sandburg, the revered poet and Lincoln biographer, had spent the night at the mansion. Awed by his presence, John Fell and the eleven-year-old son of the Edison Dicks had slipped up to his bedroom to look at him in his sleep. When he stirred, they retreated in panic to the automatic elevator and pressed so many buttons it had become stuck between floors. It took more than an hour to extricate them.

On this informal note, the newspapermen began a prolonged honeymoon with "this strange new Governor" that for many weeks included even the *Tribune*. John P. Akers of the *Sun-Times* exclaimed, "A Governor who tries to keep his campaign pledges; imagine that, this day and year in Illinois!" Moreover, as they studied the speech they realized that it encompassed the most ambitious program any Illinois governor had ever presented to a single session.

J. Edward Day has described another of Adlai's first acts as governor in these words:

> From time immemorial it had been customary in Illinois for every state appointee, high and low, to have a picture of the current governor prominently displayed on the wall of his office. . . . When Adlai Stevenson took office he promptly passed the word that he preferred not to see his face on display in every state office he entered. In part this was modesty; in part it was his deeply ingrained aversion to the trite and the stereotyped. But most of all it was a symbol of his devotion to forthrightness—of his revulsion against the gimmicks and claptrap which are supposed to be standard operating procedure in the world of politics.

The burdens of office intruded instantly. The state penitentiary at Pontiac was reported on the brink of revolt as the result of overcrowding and maladministration by the Green-appointed warden, Arthur A. Bennett. The day after his inauguration, Adlai acted on the recommendation of the state public service director, T. P. Sullivan, another Green holdover, that Bennett be dismissed. Informed of the action, Bennett vigorously denied an unmade accusation that he had collected campaign contributions for Green at the prison. Twenty-four hours later, he was dead of a heart attack.

Adlai established his main office in the basement of the governor's mansion, a large, white, southern-style house set amid a broad, sloping, tree-shaded lawn. Ignoring warnings of danger, he worked with his back to the ground-floor window, beginning after a quick breakfast at about seven and continuing, after a break for dinner, usually till past midnight. Lunch normally was brought to the desk on a tray. Mulroy, Flanagan, and Irwin made their base in the governor's capitol offices, while Schaefer, Day, and later McGowan and Blair, joined Evans and Munn in the mansion basement, which actually, owing to the slope of the landscape, was the ground floor on that side. During most of his stay, Schaefer also lived in the mansion, as did McGowan until his wife was able to move to Springfield, and then Blair. All of them would remember the period as one of unremitting work, made light by the fun and sense of purpose that surrounded Adlai.

The state budget for the two years beginning July 1, had to be ready for presentation to the legislature by early April, and while he worked intensively on it with Schaefer and Day, other measures were placed before the suspicious if not hostile legislature—the increase in old-age pensions and aid to the blind, the convening of a constitutional convention, civil service reform, a series of anticrime bills prepared by an already established Crime Commission, the promised FEPC bill, and a bill establishing, almost unbelievably, the state's first reformatory for youthful offenders. The legislature had no intention of making life easy for the new governor and began passing bills of its own.

One of them, pushed for years by bird lovers concerned over dangers posed by cats, finally passed. Adlai's veto message attracted far more attention than most of the serious business conducted in that session.

"I can not agree that it should be the declared public policy of Illinois that a cat visiting a neighbor's yard or crossing the highway is a public nuisance," he wrote.

> It is the nature of cats to do a certain amount of unescorted roaming. . . . The problem of cat versus bird is as old as time. If we attempt to solve it by legislation who knows but what we may be called upon to take sides as well in the age old problems of dog versus cat, bird versus bird, or even bird versus worm. In my opinion, the State of Illinois and its local governing bodies already have enough to do without trying to control feline delinquency. For these reasons, and not because I love birds the less or cats the more, I veto and withhold my approval from Senate Bill No. 93.

By March it was clear his program was in trouble. He had begun the session by depriving the legislators of one of their most convenient perks. Traditionally, the state police had functioned as taxi drivers for the legislators, taking them wherever they wanted to go, waiting for them, doing errands for them. Adlai stopped that. He brought in the FBI and other experts to provide training and develop standards. Even worse, he ended the practice of having every job on the force subject to political patronage.

Arvey has reported he was "stunned and distressed" when Adlai told him he proposed to withhold hundreds of job appointments from the organization and install a merit system for the state police.

"To accomplish this," Arvey said,

> he planned to ask both the Republican and Democratic organi-

zations to share equally the initial appointments, which meant the Republicans would retain about three hundred men, who by custom would have been ousted. His program provided that once men put on the uniform of highway patrolman they would renounce all political identification and promise not to participate thereafter in politics. This stunned me, because every Republican Governor who had succeeded a Democrat discharged all the Democrats and put Republicans in their place. I not only argued but pleaded with him, and asked him why we should suffer patronage-wise because of his political victory. . . . All my cajolery went for nought. He was decisive and he was courageous as well. This was his idea, this was his conviction; and I finally found myself pleading with the legislature to enact Stevenson's program, the removal of politics from the state police system.

Others were not as understanding as Arvey. Resentment grew as accustomed largesse was cut off. Fred Hoehler's housecleaning included the firing of a state central committeeman and also a Chicago precinct captain. The superintendent of one institution involving alcoholics, under pressure from local politicians, had allowed inmates to buy drinks in town on credit. That stopped.

Such incidents multiplied as new administrators found their governor backing them up even as the thunder roared ever more loudly around the governor's mansion. The more sophisticated stifled their anger and turned their considerable ingenuity to devising deals and trades for the votes the governor needed to get his program adopted. Whether byzantine or brutal, the nefarious plans encountered an opponent who was stubborn, patient, but often discouraged. Mrs. Smith recalls that midway through the session he came to visit them in Lake Forest.

"He sat down at the edge of the lake and just stared at it. I asked him what was the matter. He said, 'I'm discouraged. I sometimes wonder if I can do it if I keep turning down deals. Now I'll probably lose both the Crime bills and Con-Con.'"

His heart was set on Con-Con, as the constitutional convention bill had come to be known. Twice, he took the case to the people in an unusual statewide radio hookup, initiating occasional "fireside chats" that he continued throughout his administration. Richard Daley, aided by Arvey, effectively waged the lobbying battles. As the vote, which required a two-thirds margin of 102 votes for passage, approached, all knew it would be close. At that point, the West Side bloc, generally believed to have stronger ties to the mob than to any party, offered its 5 votes if Adlai would drop his support for three of the anticrime bills that were pending. Those 5 would undoubtedly bring others with them. Adlai refused to deal. Then the 5 suggested that their votes could be had by

Adlai's dropping support of a bill to extend the length of grand jury sessions in Cook County. No deal. Finally, support was promised if he would agree not to veto pending legislation permitting dog racing. Again, he refused.

The vote on April 13 was just 5 short of the two thirds needed. An adroit maneuver by one of Arvey's men, a motion to postpone consideration, saved the bill for another try. The *Tribune*'s tribute to the achievement of "the gallant band" of five infuriated Adlai as few other attacks had, possibly because he recognized the opposition was gaining.

Important to their gains was a Republican-sponsored alternative called the Gateway Amendment, which provided that three amendments to the constitution could be submitted to the voters simultaneously instead of only one as stipulated in the 1870 constitution. Adlai had considered it earlier, but had chosen the more ambitious course. When the second vote on Con-Con failed on May 2, he promptly came out in favor of "Gateway." Since the first such amendment had been introduced in 1892, it had failed five times, but now it finally passed and was approved by the voters in a 1950 referendum. It began the process of constitutional change. The idea of a full-fledged constitutional convention persisted, and in 1969, four years after his death, the goal was achieved. It was perhaps his most important achievement as governor, but with the long lapse of time, few associate his pioneering effort with the final result.

In the 1952 campaign for the presidency, he was sharply criticized for failure to enact a Fair Employment Practices Act. He could have had it; the bill failed by two votes in the Senate and three in the House—which were for sale. His refusal to deal led to charges that he didn't know how to handle legislators and the legislative process.

"I tried to do for Stevenson something I tried with Kennelly—but Kennelly wasn't smart enough to let me do it," Arvey recalled later. "The Governor was. I tried to be a buffer between him and certain men in our organization that I am not very proud of. He turned to me when he had to deal with them. Kennelly would talk to them himself and he would lie to them. You can't lie in politics. It's different from business. In politics your word is your bond."

Arvey not only worked the telephone in building support, but made at least weekly trips to Springfield to make it evident that his support and that of the organization were behind Adlai. Little by little, the understanding grew that a different way of doing business was firmly in place in Springfield and, finally, in late June, as adjournment approached, victories began to outrun defeats.

In a statewide radio hookup after adjournment, Adlai summarized the results. Of the 44 major bills he had pushed, 21 had passed.

In all, a total of 833 bills had been passed, the most in modern times. He signed 751, allowed 16 to become law without his signature, vetoed sections of 5 and vetoed 61 completely. Some were vetoed because they were unnecessary or duplicated other legislation, some because they were unconstitutional or of doubtful constitutionality, and some to balance the budget. At the same time, he was working on other ways to balance the budget through orders to department heads to analyze personnel needs and eliminate every job possible and to hold operating expenses at 10 percent under the budgets.

The losses of Con-Con and FEPC were the big disappointments, but the defeat of bills to increase aid to the cities; to reorganize government departments in the interest of efficiency and elimination of duplication; to increase truck-licensing fees, broaden the gasoline tax, tax the capital stock of out-of-state corporations doing business in Illinois; and to adopt anticrime proposals all were important losses.

"On the positive side," he told the radio audience, "I think our major achievement has been in legislation pointing the way to better schools," providing more money than ever before and more effective nonpolitical ways for distributing it. Other victories were the removal of state police from political patronage and the introduction of a merit system; the reorganization of the Commerce Commission; the creation of county superintendents of assessments for all but Cook and St. Clair counties; an increase in fire protection; improvement of mine safety and removal of mine inspectors from politics; cost-of-living increases for old-age pensioners and the blind; increased unemployment compensation from $20 to $25 per week and extending coverage to pregnant women; increases in salaries for state employees; strengthened civil service; codification of public assistance laws; construction of a state reformatory; and establishment of a "Little Hoover" Commission to study reorganization of state government.

Adlai claimed that he had obtained nearly two thirds of the legislation "I particularly recommended," adding, that "maybe we tried to do too much all at once. Probably we did, but I think campaign talk should be more than sweet, deceitful words."

The Republicans had passed a large number of "Christmas tree bills," that at best were budget-busting, involving millions of dollars of local projects for which no revenue had been provided. Stevenson vetoes were expected, but the embarrassment was not intended to stop there. The powerful leader of the Republican-controlled Senate proposed that instead of adjourning sine die, that is, indefinitely, on June 30, as was customary, adjournment would be only until July 18. This would be after the ten days allotted to the governor to sign or veto bills, and would thus provide an opportunity to override the expected vetoes. This proposal was adopted by the Senate on the very last day of the session and sent to the House. All official clocks had been stopped to enable the Assembly to work into the morning of July 1.

Adlai and his staff had moved into his office on the second floor of the statehouse. As they listened to the wrangling over the microphones,

Adlai had a faint memory that in 1863, the famed Civil War governor, Richard Yates, faced with a similar situation, had successfully used a power buried in the Illinois constitution, but which had never again been used. The provision stated that if the two houses could not agree on adjournment, the governor had the power to prorogue the legislature— end the session by executive order "until such time as he thinks proper." Past midnight, with the clocks stopped, the House voted not to concur in the Senate resolution and to adjourn sine die. The Senate refused to accept this resolution; whereupon the House voted at 5:30 A.M. to certify that the two houses were in disagreement on adjournment. Walter Schaefer handed Speaker Paul Powell the governor's proclamation declaring the legislature adjourned. Lieutenant Governor Sherwood Dixon, presiding officer of the Senate, was standing in the House chamber with the Senate Republican majority leader, Senator Walter Thompson, as the proclamation was being read. Dixon grabbed the governor's proroging proclamation and raced Thompson back to the Senate chamber. Thompson tried to get the floor to move adjournment until the following Friday morning, thus killing the House action, but Dixon banged the gavel and declared the Senate—and the Assembly—adjourned, leaving Thompson at his desk "still hollering" long after it was all over.

The session had been a grueling experience.

"I was amazed at the way he worked—night after night after night he worked," Walter Schaefer recalled. "If there were guests, we'd go up for cocktails and dinner and then he would excuse himself and he and I would go back down to work." He almost never spent a full evening with anyone. In April he wrote Alicia Patterson, "Yesterday I was at it for 17 consecutive hours—today 16, and 26 legislators coming for dinner."

Exercise was sacrified, but his sense of humor was not. Midway during the session he had made a remarkably candid, off-the-record speech to the Commercial Club in Chicago in which, in addition to his efforts with the legislature he told of how he was seeking to establish better relations between the governor's office and local officials. A flood in downstate Illinois had prompted him to call mayors in the affected area, but on one of the calls, the operator mistakenly connected him with the mayor of Murraysville rather than Murphysville. Here is his report of the ensuing conversation:

"How do you do, Mayor. This is Governor Stevenson in Springfield."

"How do you do, Governor. I never had a governor call me before."

"I've been alarmed by your condition down there. How are you?"

"Oh, fine, Governor. I was never better. How are you?"

"I've been wondering, Mayor, how is your water?"

"My water is fine. How's yours?"

"Are you holding it back all right?"

"That's none of your damned business!" the mayor shouted, slamming down the receiver. Whether or not it ever happened, and Adlai told it in several versions, it was the kind of story he loved to tell on himself.

A sense of humor was much needed that spring. On April 23, Lloyd Lewis, his neighbor and probably his most intimate male friend, died suddenly and unexpectedly. He declined the invitation to speak at the simple Quaker service held two days later saying that his emotions were too deeply involved. Instead, Marc Connolly, the author-playwright, gave the eulogy. Fortunately, Mrs. Quincy Wright had arranged for the service to be recorded for Mrs. Lewis's sister who could not be there, and we have what is perhaps the most moving statement Adlai ever made, an impromptu statement prompted by Connolly's eloquence.

> It is April now and all life is being renewed on the bank of this river that he loved so well. I think we will all be happy that it happened on this day, here by the river with the spring sky so clear, and the west wind so warm and fresh. I think we will all be better for this day and this meeting together. . . .
> I think Mr. Connolly was right when he said he was the most successful man he ever knew. I don't know much about the riches of life, and I suspect few of you have found the last definition. But I do know that friendship is the greatest enrichment that I have found.
> Everyone loved this man. He enriched others and was enriched. Everyone was his friend—everyone who knew him or read him. Why was that? Why is he the most successful man that many of us will ever know? Our answers will differ. For me it was his humility, gentleness, wisdom and wit, all in one. And most of all a great compassionate friendliness.
> I think it will always be April in our memory of him. It will always be a bright, fresh day full of infinite variety and the promise of new life. Perhaps nothing has gone at all—perhaps only the embodiment of the thing—tender, precious to all of us—a friendship that is immortal and doesn't pass along. It will be renewed for me, much as I know it will for all of you, each spring.

His tribute was a cry of the heart—a heart that was being severely tugged at that spring. The morning after the Inaugural Ball, Ellen returned to Libertyville, explaining she had to return John Fell to school. After that she came to Springfield only occasionally, and only for official functions. Her erratic behavior made even these visits politically risky. At one dinner for legislators, Carl McGowan has reported, she charmed the guests, but "the next time she sulked," and some said her treatment of them was "insulting." Adlai would spend weekends in Libertyville, but the deterioration of the relationship became a subject of quiet gossip. They had gone to Truman's inauguration on the train with Illinois's leading Democrats. Arvey took advantage of the opportunity to bring Chicago's ward leaders into their car to meet the governor.

"It went well," he reported, "until suddenly Mrs. Stevenson said, 'I'm going to get out of here and go to bed,'" and left abruptly. Later that night, Mrs. Arvey told her husband, "That marriage won't last."

Although Ellen had been dissuaded from seeking a divorce during the political campaign, the shift from being a center of attention in Chicago society to merely the governor's wife was too much for her to bear.

"Many of us did not understand why she had encouraged him to run for governor and set Springfield as the place she wanted to bring up the boys, and then reversed herself when he won the election," Jane Dick has recalled.

> She would give one reason one day and another reason the next day; one reason to one person and a different reason to another person. . . . She was more mentally unbalanced than anybody recognized and certainly more than Adlai did. He was tremendously loyal to her. Later, he was very frank about her condition because it absolved her of responsibility. He was able finally to get over the strong personal attachment, and he tried hard to keep the boys loyal to her and to understand her illness so they would not condemn her.

Buffie Ives confided to Jane that during the early months in Springfield when she was filling in as a hostess for Ellen, she made a critical comment. "Adlai turned to me and said, 'Ellen is my wife. I never want to hear you say one word against her as long as I live.' And I never did because I wouldn't have dared."

Adlai seemed to be denying even to himself what was happening. He would report political opinions she had ventured. He clearly was trying desperately to involve her in his new life. He frequently expressed pride in her literary talents. One day he circulated around the office a dialogue in verse whose characters were Plato, Aquinas, Bacon, Voltaire, Freud—and Modern Woman.

Finally, on the weekend of June 4, Adlai met in Chicago with his old friend, Richard Bentley, and asked him to confer with William C. Boyden, Ellen's lawyer, about a divorce. He made a note to himself to check on securities held by the boys and by Ellen, and on her possessions in their safety deposit box, and on Monday he asked Brown Brothers Harriman to prepare an inventory of his securities.

Although Adlai had worried greatly about the impact on the boys, the divorce did not come as a surprise to them. "It was not an emotional thing for me because I knew it was coming," Adlai III said. "I'd over-heard enough. I thought it was overdue. There hadn't been a good rela-tionship for a long time. I remember her as the unreasonable one, not only with Dad, but with us and with servants. I was embarrassed by her peremptory way with servants."

The principal problem arose over Ellen's proposal for joint custody. Adlai was reluctant, but on the urging of young Adlai, agreed. Despite her substantial inheritance, there were endless complications about money. Finally, it was agreed he would pay her $32,000 for her interest in the Libertyville house; he would turn over to her a life insurance policy on Mrs. Carpenter's life. Although custody of the children would be joint, he would assume responsibility for their education. Then there was a drearily detailed list of personal possessions and household items that were to be divided between them.

The attorneys had gone to great lengths to keep the negotiations secret, avoiding the use of names in the exchange of documents, but on September 30 the story broke in the *Chicago Herald-American* and the *Tribune*. Adlai had learned in the middle of the night that the story was coming and he hastily wired Borden at the Choate School: "Mother has been unhappy and feels that we must be divorced. The story came out prematurely in today's papers. You boys will divide your vacations with mother and me and I will keep the farm. Please do not worry. Everything is all right. Love and best luck. Dad." The telegram was delivered to Borden by school officials and upset him greatly. Adlai III arranged for John Fell to come from Milton Academy and meet him at their Aunt Lucy's house in Cambridge where he gave him the news.

Carl McGowan recalls the morning the story broke.

I went to Libertyville to go down to Springfield with him. As my wife and I drove in, Adlai and Ellen were walking across the field. We exchanged greetings and left. Adlai said nothing on the plane. We went to the office and worked until 1 A.M. I decided to walk up to the bat, so I went into his office and said, "I just wanted to tell you, Governor, how sorry I am about what I read in the paper." He said, "Well, I don't know what the trouble is. She apparently feels her life is overshadowed, or con-stricted, or that she can't express herself in the way she wants to do in this relationship since I have become Governor. I don't understand it very well, but that is the way she feels." This is the only exchange I ever had with him about his wife. I never heard him say a word critical of her. He handled it with great dignity and charity. My wife and I always said we never thought he would marry again, that he had been so completely devoted to Ellen that he would never take another wife. And he didn't.

Earlier that day after arriving in Springfield, Adlai had issued a statement: "I am deeply distressed that due to the incompatibility of our lives, Mrs. Stevenson feels that a separation is necessary. Although I don't believe in divorce I will not contest it. We have separated with the highest mutual regard."

Ellen went to Las Vegas, Nevada, to take advantage of divorce laws less stringent than Illinois's and from there continued to write notes that alternately were friendly and bitter. The decree became final on December 12 and received far less attention in Illinois than it did subsequently during the presidential campaign in 1952.

No suggestion of scandal ever arose, although close friends knew that Ellen had fixed her attention on several other men. One of these was Robert H. Hutchins, the president of the University of Chicago, who was also going through a divorce. She told friends that she would sit in the back row of his lectures and they would communicate ardently over the heads of his audience. It was generally agreed that her other relationships were similarly fanciful.

Adlai's relationship with Alicia Patterson, however, had assumed a far more substantial character as the difficulties and tensions with Ellen had increased. By the time of the divorce, his correspondence with her had become intimate and occasionally passionate. Jane Dick, Marietta Tree, Ruth Field, and others all expressed the belief that Alicia was the one he most deeply loved and should have married. She was brilliant, vivacious, strong-willed, and hard-driving. By this time, she had built the *Long Island Newsday,* with the help of Colonel Guggenheim's fortune, in addition to her own wealth, into a respected daily with a circulation of more than a hundred thousand.

They had managed to see each other occasionally, in Chicago, in Washington, in Springfield. But in February she had written him saying that they should end their relationship. He responded with a long, rambling letter that began:

Dear "Friend"
 I have averaged less than 6 hours of sleep a night with lunch on a tray for all but two days since you were here. . . . Maybe we are cut of different cloths, as you say. I'm not resentful—I'm deeply grateful for even a few months of what was to be forever. And don't worry about me. Work has been my refuge for many years—now it will be for many more. . . .
 Don't be angry—don't be hurtful or prideful. If there's love, there's forgiveness—and I thought there was much, much love. Perhaps I've transgressed by not writing as I would rather do than anything else—as you well know—but there's only so much time,

only so much strength—and now that's running out all over the floor. . . .

This letter apparently crossed another from her because five days later he wrote to her at even greater length than before. This second letter concluded:

> *I loved every moment of your visit—it gave me a forgotten suppressed excitement feeling for days before you came and a wonderful foolish sort of exultation while you were here. . . .*
> *Do I love you? It seems a strange question and it embarrasses me a little to say I do, because it makes me feel that you might think that I've been a hypocrit [sic] all this time—that with all that's happened you're still in doubt. I can hardly believe the line between love and play could be so obscure. I'm going to sleep—I don't know what I'm saying or writing and it's 1 A.M. and it's been a hideous day. I wish I didn't feel so alone & with nothing but this little blue envelope and this precious scrap of paper and this splendid cut of a lovely bright eyed bird by the microphone. In a moment I'll be asleep and then I won't be alone—and I'll whisper to you in the dark and there will be no doubt.*

A barrage of letters, revealing his loneliness, also kept her informed of the divorce negotiations. As they came to a conclusion, he wrote her:

> *Why did it end in Greek ghastliness? I don't know in spite of harried hours of prayer and search. Am I mad? Is she? I don't know—but nothing's left & the eyes are dry, and I am staggering on & on in this fantastic routine without the faintest idea where I'm going or why? Come when you can.*

And then he signed it with his initial "A." upside down, apparently to signify his confused emotions.

After the story broke, he wrote her:

> *You must not grieve for me. . . . I was long reconciled to it as I told you. There's much I don't understand about life and human relationships, but there was little left for us, except the children, I know—whatever the reasons or the justice or the injustice. I feel no resentment or bitterness or pain and as for the bewilderment, I've surrendered to the inscrutable. But I am troubled about Ellen and her future.*

In the midst of all this occurred an event that was given little importance at the time; Adlai didn't even mention it in the account of the day he wrote to Alicia Patterson that night. It was his deposition on the reputation, as he knew it, of Alger Hiss—the deposition that Senator Joseph McCarthy, Richard Nixon, and others later would distort in their efforts to inflame public opinion and attack Adlai.

Hiss had resigned from the State Department and become president of the Carnegie Endowment for International Peace in December 1946, after Adlai had declined the offer of the post from John Foster Dulles. Dulles then participated in the decision to appoint Hiss. General Eisenhower was elected a member of the board at the same meeting at which Hiss was reelected president and Dulles, chairman. In the spring of 1949, Hiss was being tried in the federal district court in New York on a charge of perjury growing out of accusations of espionage made by Whittaker Chambers and subsequent congressional hearings. Hiss's attorneys assembled an impressive array of character witnesses that included two Supreme Court justices; a former Democratic presidential candidate, John W. Davis; and a number of other public figures. Hiss had become one of the brightest and best-known stars among the young intellectuals who had come to Washington during the Roosevelt administration. Adlai declined a request to come to New York but agreed to submit to interrogation in Springfield.

In the sworn statement, taken on June 2, just two days before his divorce arrangements were to be initiated, he described in detail the extent of his association with Hiss. They had first met when they both worked in the Agricultural Adjustment Administration in 1933. They had worked on different commodities, so the encounters, although frequent, were casual. They met again in late February or early March 1945, when Adlai went to the State Department and Hiss was in charge of arrangements for the San Francisco United Nations conference. They saw little of each other at San Francisco except at a few official social functions since Hiss was secretary general of the conference and Adlai was attached to the United States delegation. Back in Washington during July, they conferred several times on preparations for presentation of the United Nations Charter to the Senate for ratification.

After Adlai's return to Chicago in August 1945, they did not meet again until Hiss arrived in London in January 1946 with the United States delegation to the first UN General Assembly. During that session they had offices near each other and met frequently at delegation meetings and staff conferences. After returning to the United States in March 1946, they had not met again until Adlai was in New York for the 1947 session of the General Assembly. By that time, Hiss had become president of the Carnegie Endowment and he came to the delegation headquarters to discuss the UN budget, which had been assigned to Adlai as one of his responsibilities of the American delegation. They had not seen each other since. After this came the key portion of the "Direct Interrogatories in Behalf of Defendant Alger Hiss," and the ensuing cross interrogatory:

Q. No. 7 Have you known other persons who have known Mr. Alger Hiss?

A. No. 7 Yes.

Q. No. 8 From the speech of these persons, can you state what the reputation of Alger Hiss is for integrity, loyalty and veracity?

A. No. 8 Yes.

Q. No. 9 (a) Specify whether his reputation for integrity is good or bad?

A. No. 9 (a) Good.

Q. No. 9 (b) Specify whether his reputation for loyalty is good or bad?

A. No. 9 (b) Good.

Q. No. 9 (c) Specify whether his reputation for veracity is good or bad?

A. No. 9 (c) Good.

Cross Interrogatories in Behalf of the United States of America, Complainant in Said Case

Q. No. 1 Were you ever a guest in the home of defendant Alger Hiss at any time in 1935, to and including 1938?

A. No. 1 No, I have never been a guest in Mr. Hiss' home.

Q. No. 2 Did you, prior to 1948, hear that the defendant Alger Hiss during the years 1937 and 1938 removed confidential and secret documents from the State Department and made such documents available to persons not authorized to see or receive them?

A. No. 2 No.

Q. No. 3 Did you, prior to 1948, hear reports that the defendant Alger Hiss was a Communist?

A. No. 3 No.

Q. No. 4 Did you, prior to 1948, hear reports that the defendant Alger Hiss was a Communist sympathizer?

A. No. 5 No.

This is the deposition that later was the basis for the charge that he was soft on communism and a defender of traitors. Senator Nixon, in one of his gentler comments, said the statement reflected such "poor judgment" that serious doubt was cast on Adlai's capacity to govern. Only a short time before the deposition, John Foster Dulles had responded to a letter from a Detroit lawyer warning that Hiss had a "provable" Communist record, in these terms:

> I have heard the report which you refer to, but I have confidence that there is no reason to doubt Mr. Hiss' complete loyalty to our American institutions. I have been thrown into intimate contact with him at San Francisco, London and Washington. . . . Under these circumstances I feel a little skeptical about information which seems inconsistent with all I personally know and what is the judgement of reliable friends and associates in Washington.

Although many later chose to remain silent, Adlai was one of the very few to emerge from this sad episode with honesty and integrity intact.

With adjournment of the legislature, Adlai turned to rounding out his staff.

Richard J. Nelson, who had been an outstanding student of Walter Schaefer's at Northwestern, joined to help on political liaison. Tall, handsome, hardworking, he was not long in Springfield before he was also elected national president of the Young Democrats. After Adlai's term he became a vice president of the Inland Steel Corporation and, in 1971, president of Northern Illinois University.

The two who were to become his closest associates joined him during that summer.

Adlai had come to know Carl McGowan as a young law professor at Northwestern, introduced to him by Francis J. Plimpton, in whose law firm McGowan worked briefly after graduating from Harvard, and they had worked together in Washington during the war. His commitments had made it necessary to remain at Northwestern at the beginning of Adlai's term, but now with Walter Schaefer's return to the faculty, McGowan was able to take his place in Springfield and swiftly became the most important member of the governor's inner circle. Born in Paris, Illinois, he loved the law and its intellectual discipline. His rock-solid integrity, and his impatience with mediocrity and the tendency of politicians to dissemble, caused casual acquaintances to see him as cold, distant, even disagreeable. Those closer to him found boundless warmth and compassion, generosity of spirit, and a shy sense of humor. He came to be looked upon as "Stevenson's conscience"; certainly their values and the workings of their minds were in harmony; he was in every sense the fulfillment of his title of counsel. His performance in Springfield clearly forecast his future distinguished service on the court regarded as the one closest to the Supreme Court, the U.S. Court of Appeals for the District of Columbia.

In contrast to McGowan in almost everything but ability and dedication was William McCormick "Bill" Blair, Jr. After his work with Adlai and the White Committee in 1940, he had returned to the University of Virginia Law School, but enlisted in the Army immediately after Pearl Harbor. He spent most of the war in the China-Burma-India theater as an intelligence officer, returning to Virginia after V-J Day to finish his law degree. His family position rather than his excellent law school record probably caused him to be snapped up by one of Chicago's leading law firms. But like Adlai, he found the law, as well as the social life that was part of his heritage, a bore. By early 1950 he had decided that law firm life was not for him, resigned, and embarked on what was intended to be a long trip through Latin America. In Mexico, he received a wire asking him if he would head the Chicago office of the Hoover Commission studying government reorganization. That sounded more interesting and he returned to accept it. He had been in the office barely an hour when Adlai called saying he needed an administrative assistant and would Bill be interested. He was.

The job had opened up because Ed Day, despite his youth, had performed so impressively during the Assembly session that he was being appointed to head the Department of Insurance. Its head was going to the Illinois Supreme Court.

Relaxed, urbane, sophisticated, Blair's easygoing charm hid his seriousness of purpose. He became appointments secretary, general facilitator, buffer, and almost constant travel companion. Anyone who got to know either the governor or the presidential candidate came to appreciate Blair's seemingly diffident but constant devotion, his sharp and sometimes biting sense of humor, but above all, the acute and courageous way in which he handled the governor's schedule, making decisions Adlai would sometimes angrily protest but invariably accepted.

Staff duties were only vaguely defined. Though frictions occasionally developed, the arrangement worked; largely because of the open informal style maintained by the governor and the weekly staff meetings rigidly insisted upon by McGowan. These "skull practice" sessions were described as swift and searching reviews of all manner of current state problems and of underlying policies. They were marked by gaiety, wit, idealistic purpose, and youthful zest for the job at hand.

Mulroy, McGowan, Blair, Day, Nelson, Flanagan, and Hyndman, with McGowan and Blair first among equals, continued functioning as the inner circle throughout the administration, except, sadly, for Mulroy.

During the struggles of the legislative session, more than any of the others Mulroy had been in the thick of the political horse trading and had been a significant factor in the victories won. Late in the spring of 1951, House Majority Leader Paul Powell asked him if he would like to "take a flier" in the stock of Chicago Downs, a horse-racing association that had been legalized a few weeks before. Chicago Downs races took place at

Sportsman's Park, located in Al Capone's old hometown of Cicero on Chicago's West Side, and were generally regarded as an operation of the Syndicate, which had a working alliance with local politicians. Shares were selling at $0.10 apiece and Mulroy bought a thousand—$100 worth. A few months later a dividend of $1.65 a share gave him a profit of $1,550 on his investment.

In the summer of 1951, the Chicago Downs operation became the focus of Senator Estes Kefauver's Senate Crime Committee and it was revealed that close associates of members of the old Capone gang were major stockholders, that several legislators were on the payroll, and that a very select list of politicians and state employees had been offered the $0.10 stock. Mulroy insisted that the offer had been made after the legalizing bill had passed and that it could not have been an effort to buy his influence. Moreover, the bill had passed by wide margins; unanimously in the Senate. Those wise in the ways of Springfield, however, were certain that Powell was hoping to have a friend at the mansion if, later, something went wrong with this highly speculative stock.

Adlai was convinced that, whatever intent was behind the offer, Mulroy was guilty only of thoughtlessness, or at worst, imprudence. In Mulroy's case, the financial burden imposed by his low salary had been added to by hospital bills resulting from intermittent illness he had incurred since coming to Springfield. As criticism increased and even his own staff members insisted that Mulroy be fired, Adlai stood by him. Even the friendly *Sun-Times* editorialized that "racetrack operators don't cut people into their profits without a reason," and "if Mulroy doesn't understand that he's not smart enough to be assistant to the governor." Adlai also found out that Mulroy had bought a house from a man who was a big contractor with the state, and though it appeared to be legitimate, it did make Mulroy vulnerable to further attack. Finally, in October, he sadly told a mutual friend of his and Mulroy's, "Jim will have to go." He had a long session with Mulroy that he described as heartrending. Mulroy resigned and sank into a period of deep depression. Six months later he died of a heart attack that his widow and friends firmly believed was the direct result of his sense of public disgrace. Adlai's own sadness was deepened by the understandable bitterness of Mulroy's widow. In concluding an account of the affair to Alicia Patterson, he exclaimed, "What a job!"

CHAPTER SEVEN
Idealism with Muscle

ADLAI'S BELIEF THAT GOOD administration was based on getting good people was accompanied by an even more instinctive belief that good governance was based on better and broader public understanding.

At the beginning of 1950, over a statewide radio network, he quoted Socrates as saying that an unexamined life is not worth living, adding that "we who believe in democracy may just as truly say that the unexamined government is not worth having." He was determined to arouse public interest in state government. The answer to concentration of power in Washington, he said, "is effective, responsive, well-operated state and local governments. Too many of the problems of state's rights have been created by state's wrongs."

"I sometimes think my biggest job is preaching, and my biggest problem is to find time to write, and travel and talk about state government," he told the Illinois League of Women Voters later that year. "Unless citizen interest is a continuing process, the government reforms we institute today will degenerate into bureaucratic habits of tomorrow."

In the effort, he made over a hundred speeches throughout the state during 1950. His semiannual radio reports to the people sometimes became quarterly reports; indeed, he used the radio far more than any previous governor. He insisted that fancy state-produced brochures that had enriched the pockets of the printers rather than the minds of the public be simplified and that at least part of the savings be invested in wider distribution. He cultivated his relationships with newspapermen, wrote letters to the editor, encouraged others to write, and little by little, state affairs began to get more coverage. He sought out opinion leaders and influential volunteer groups; he filled the loneliness of the executive mansion not only with friends but with people who could help him explain his proposals. Over and over again, he kept developing the theme: "We *can* get better government. We *can* do away with graft and corruption."

"He believed if people understood they would support him regardless of political affiliation," historian Walter Johnson has written. "He tried earnestly to inform, to interest, to educate, the citizens of Illinois."

Gradually, the investment of effort and conviction began to yield dividends.

"When I went to Springfield in 1949, in the bars around Springfield I'd hear five or ten people saying, 'Of course, he's an accident, a one-termer,'" Carl McGowan has recalled. "By the next summer, you never heard this. . . . This means they recognized the fact of his political power. It was due to his own hard work, his radio speeches, his appearances. All this began to affect people."

A source of his political power, as well as a deadly challenge to it, was the graft and corruption that were pervasive in Illinois; stretching from back streets through country clubs, city halls, into the state capital and the executive mansion itself. When he took office, it was generally assumed that every state contract included a 10-percent payoff for the governor. One high state official in the pre-Stevenson period complacently described good government as one in which only fifty cents of the taxpayer's dollar went into politicians' pockets. The corruption issue helped elect him, but the public's expectation of real change was not high. When people began to perceive he intended more than cosmetic interest, cynicism began turning into support. The support was needed to encounter the entrenched resistance.

Organized crime and corrupt politicians and policemen had been a hallmark of Chicago since Prohibition days. The crude activities of the Capone era gradually had been supplemented by more sophisticated infiltration into labor unions and legitimate businesses whose customers were "encouraged" to remain loyal to their suppliers by threats and burly enforcers. In the early 1940s, the lucrative gambling network was extended throughout the state through an alliance with a gang in East St. Louis. A collision of the Chicago/East St. Louis alliance with the Shelton gang, previously dominant in downstate gambling, produced the Peoria murder at the height of the 1948 campaign that helped elect Adlai.

The support of the Cook County organization, with its presumed link to the Syndicate, raised doubts that the new governor would, or could, do anything about organized crime. A signal of his intention came quickly. The Lake Club, just outside Springfield, had become notorious during the Green administration for wide-open gambling, with the frequent patronage of legislators. With the help of the county prosecutor, it was closed down.

Adlai and his attorney general, Ivan Elliott, did not find many local law enforcement officials so willing to cooperate. Their quiet pressure throughout 1949 produced marginal results, and even where gambling was stopped, it had often been allowed to resume when it was assumed attention was diverted. Now, in the spring of 1950, with the state police taken out of politics, Adlai began to move. State police made gambling raids in the East St. Louis area, and in other counties where local officials had been recalcitrant either through fear or bribery. Even those in the Cook County organization who had become his supporters brought pressure on him to stop. The only doubt Adlai had was about the appropriateness of state officials doing what local officials ought to do.

"For the state to take over local police powers seems to me a dangerous acknowledgement of the failure of local government," he told the statewide radio audience. "But commercialized gambling with its attendant corruption and corroding disrespect for law is even more dangerous." Within a few months the state police raided three hundred gambling places in seventy-five towns. He also served notice that he would "deal mercilessly with any state employee under my control who has any tainted association with commercialized gambling."

He was striking not only at gambling itself but at the network of criminal activity related to it. He was also fully aware that the problem had even broader ramifications—and he was prepared for at least some of the repercussions. All the slot machine manufacturers in the country were located in Chicago and their connections were powerful. Of the twenty-seven hundred gambling machines registered in Illinois, less than one third were in gambling places; nineteen hundred were in such places as country clubs, veterans clubs, military clubs, and fraternal organizations.

At a highly respectable country club a child handed him a card to autograph. When he turned it over, he read a statement worded so that, if he had signed it, it would have, in effect, declared, "The slot machines in this club are for members only and meet with my approval. Adlai E. Stevenson."

Many American Legion posts depended for a substantial part of their operating income on their "take" from their slot machines. Many of them were outraged at the demand for their removal. In an action foreshadowing his attack on McCarthyism at the National American Legion Convention in 1952, he went before the state convention of the American Legion to talk about the double-standard morality of those who denounced corruption but defended slot machines in their clubs. In his speech, his answer to his own question about what could be done to improve law enforcement included: securing better personnel; divorcing crime and politics; severing police forces from partisan political control. Policemen must be trained as professionals and paid adequate salaries. Governors should be empowered to remove any local law enforcement officer failing to do his duty. The Bar Association should disbar any lawyer who, holding a public law enforcement position, failed to do his duty. Congress should bar slot machines and racing information from interstate commerce.

Senator Estes Kefauver, who had embarked on his Senate investigation of organized crime, published the speech in the *Congressional Record;* it was reprinted in the Bar Association *Journal,* and reprints were circulated widely. He accepted Kefauver's invitation to testify before his committee, described what he was doing, and recommended federal legislation in line with his speech. The raids continued. And so did the pressures from local politicians whose support he would need in the forthcoming legislature and in the election. Efforts at coercion simply increased his determination. As public and press support increased, so did his confidence in what he was doing.

The young editor and publisher of the *Troy Tribune* in Madison County, the scene of the earliest raids, wrote to encourage him. He was Paul Simon, later to be senator and also a presidential candidate. A few months later, Simon received the following:

> *Dear Mr. Simon:*
>
> *I hear today from Carl McGowan that you are shortly to be inducted into the Army. I find myself of two minds: I am delighted on the one hand that you are going to be serving in the armed forces, and disappointed on the other that your emphatic and clear voice is going to be stilled hereabouts for awhile. I hope it will not be long before you can resume your very important and helpful contribution to the revival of interest in law enforcement in Illinois.*
>
> *With all good wishes and my regards, I am*
>
> *Sincerely yours,*
> *Adlai E. Stevenson.*

In making the letter available years later, Senator Simon commented: "I was 22 years old when he sent this [letter]. Rather a remarkable thing for a governor to take this much interest in a 22-year-old." The remarkable thing is that, for Adlai, it was not remarkable but almost a routine part of his effort to encourage the involvement of young people in public affairs.

Eric Sevareid came to Springfield for a CBS network report on Adlai's "exposed, dangerous and exhaustingly difficult" campaign against crime. "But his ultimate record," Sevareid concluded, "will be of consequence not only to this hitherto graft-ridden state, but perhaps to other Midwest states struggling to clean their political stables. Every governor in the land, like every crook in Illinois, is watching Stevenson."

The political reporter for the Associated Press in Springfield, Roger Lane, wrote the editor of *The Atlantic,* enclosing a speech Adlai had given to the Sangamon County Bar Association, and suggesting that they invite the governor to write an article on citizen responsibility and government corruption. The article based on the speech appeared in the magazine under the title "Who Runs the Gambling Machines?"

The battle went on relentlessly throughout his governorship, with victories, setbacks, and some heartbreaks. In the hearings of the Kefauver Crime Commission held in Chicago, the efforts coming from the governor's mansion were favorably noted even as the spotlight was focused on "evidence of gangsters muscling into legitimate business and of political ties between gangsters and politicians of both parties." Although Kefauver did not hurt him, one of his own appointees did. The "horsemeat" scandal reverberated throughout the rest of the administration and into the presidential campaign.

In the summer of 1951, the director of agriculture, Roy E. Young, reported to the governor rumors that beef for use in hamburgers was adulterated with horsemeat, even though it had been inspected by state inspectors. Also, he had asked Charles W. Wray, the superintendent of foods and dairies, to investigate. Adlai had personally picked Wray for the job, which was known to be a center of corruption. Savings from the use of inferior substitute preservatives for cherries in premixed cocktails were sufficient to justify a substantial bribe to a state food inspector. The use of horsemeat in hamburgers was infinitely more lucrative; indeed, McGowan said, the profits exceeded those from prostitution and gambling. There had been pressure to put another man in the job, but Adlai had resisted simply because of the potential for bribery. Instead, he selected Wray, who lived near Libertyville, had been recommended by local farmers and businessmen, had been honored as head of a "typical farm family of Illinois," and whom he had met occasionally as a fellow commuter into Chicago.

Wray reported that the rumors of adulterated beef were unfounded. The rumors persisted, and in the fall, inspectors from the federal Office of Price Stabilization gave them strong, but inconclusive, support. Adlai was sufficiently troubled to have a series of meetings with Young and Wray, beginning in late July; but feeling frustrated, in early January he discussed the situation with the FBI man in Springfield, Ross Randolph. This was followed by a summoning of all inspectors, along with Wray, to a meeting in Springfield where questioning went on throughout the weekend. Gradually, Wray himself came under deepening suspicion. In a meeting with McGowan, Wray asked if he could telephone his lawyer. "Sure," McGowan told him, "but the minute you pick up the telephone we'll all leave the room, and you'll have crossed the line, you'll no longer be in the family."

McGowan said that what followed was "a very difficult thing. He paced the room. He wept. It was most painful." But he signed a statement and was fired forthwith. Having done so, he was in fear of his life and McGowan sent him home under police protection. The statement was turned over to the Lake County state's attorney. Wray was indicted on charges of bribery, but subsequently acquitted. The case against Wray was never proved, but the involvement of organized crime was clearly established. Murders were blamed on the horse racketeers. The Chicago Syndicate had set up a slush fund of $600,000 for payoffs. One of the mob, when told the amount of his bail, exclaimed, "Thirty thousand! They must think I ground up Man o' War."

The *Tribune* gleefully coined the term, "Adlaiburgers" and a favorite inquiry of housewives at the meat market became, "How do you want your hamburger—win, place, or show?" It was not funny to Adlai, although on one television show he assessed the damage by saying "It looks like I'll be on a steady diet of horsemeat from now until November." Privately, McGowan attested, he was deeply disturbed. "My God," he said to McGowan, "if Wray goes sour, I don't know, what can you depend on?" His practical reaction, however, was to persuade Randolph to resign from the FBI and become his administrative assistant. From then on, whenever a complaint was received involving a state official, he turned it over to Randolph rather than to the head of the department concerned.

A final scandal had an ironic twist. It was a victory that backfired. The millions earned from horsemeat were dwarfed by the income from the counterfeiting of state cigarette stamps. Illinois was not the only state where organized crime was profiting from every package of cigarettes sold; indeed, on one of his trips east he had quietly met with Governors Dewey in New York and Driscoll in New Jersey to discuss what might be done. Whatever the content of these discussions, it was the governor of Illinois who acted.

The three-cent-per-pack tax was collected largely through the use of meters that were manufactured by the Pitney Bowes Company in Connecticut. A wholesaler would go to the state revenue office and pay in advance for the number of stamps that would be printed on the bottom of each package of cigarettes by the meter he would then receive. When the assigned number was printed, the meter stopped, and the wholesaler returned it to the Revenue Department and paid for the next round. In late 1950, two things happened. Some wholesalers began complaining that their competitors were cutting prices to such a degree it suggested they were not paying the tax. Also, cigarette tax income started dropping even though cigarette consumption was increasing.

A young Chicago lawyer well-known to Schaefer, McGowan, and to a lesser extent, to Adlai, Ben W. Heineman, was called in and quietly made a special assistant attorney general. He was authorized to hire a firm of private detectives, and he sent them to Pitney Bowes for training in the recognition of counterfeit stamps. They soon found that about three out of every ten packs sold in the Chicago area bore counterfeit stamps. They finally discovered that in 1949 four of the tax meters had been stolen and that new dies and plates had been made from them by the counterfeiters who affixed to their new plates numbers that already had been assigned to legitimate wholesalers. Within six months of the initiation of the investigation, and without notifying the Chicago police or anyone else, fifty state policemen raided the suspected wholesalers, collected samples of their stocks, and had them examined by a Pitney Bowes expert. In all cases but one the stamps had been counterfeited. Several wholesalers were indicted and one was sent to the penitentiary. The head of the Chicago office of the cigarette tax collecting division and two inspectors were fired; a third resigned. The counterfeiting stopped.

Ironically, there was a backlash to this major coup. In the widespread publicity and comment on Heineman's success, the tendency was to lump the Mulroy resignation, the horsemeat scandal, and cigarette stamp counterfeiting all together as "Stevenson administration scandals." Adlai was proud of the fact that "we got on top of that one quickly and decisively." But, as McGowan later observed:

> Stevenson was the victim of the fact that he was the one state Governor who did something about it [cigarette stamp counterfeiting]. This made it look like he was the only one that had a scandal. The Governors of New York and Pennsylvania and New Jersey knew for sure that the same thing had been going on there for a long time. . . . This was one area where Stevenson got the unfair burden of seeming to have a scandal. I thought it was one of the best things he did.

McGowan put major blame on the *Tribune* for implanting the word "scandals" in the public mind, believing firmly that the correct word should have been "achievements."

"He was always a careful man about money," McGowan has observed, "but stealing the people's money was something he found especially repugnant."

Behind the more public assault on crime were quietly persistent demonstrations that the state's chief executive was determined to break the chain of corruption. The present writer remembers vividly a weekend visit to Springfield during which the Guv disappeared into the basement office shortly after dinner. About midnight he went downstairs, where the only light was in the governor's office, to suggest that bedtime had arrived.

"I can't quit yet," the governor responded. "I just know there's graft in this contract and I won't go to bed until I find it."

The assumption was immediately made that a very large project must be involved in the papers spread across the desk, so more information was asked for. The contract was for insulation on the heating pipes of a state mental hospital.

"Governor, why in the world are you spending so much of your time on something as small as that?" he was asked.

"When they realize I am looking for graft in something as small as this," he replied, "they will be a lot less likely to try to get away with big ones. It's important for the Governor to set an example on little things as well as big things." As the visitor climbed the darkened stairs the desk light spotlighted a lone figure bent over the spread of papers.

At breakfast Sunday morning the governor was asked if he had found any padding in the figures. He had. Another contractor had lost the state's business and state purchasing agents were on notice that the governor was watching.

The message spread and resulted in a level of rectitude alien to Illinois politics. Stephen Mitchell, who been a leader in the gubernatorial campaign, sent his law firm's audited annual statements to the governor to make it clear the firm had not profited from the relationship. Similar examples abounded. Just before leaving Springfield at the end of his term, Adlai asked Don Forsyth, a member of the Illinois Veterans Commission, who had been downstate chairman of his first gubernatorial campaign and was to have been his personal campaign manager in 1952, how he evaluated the four years.

"You are my most expensive friend," Forsyth told him. "For four years as an insurance man I made only $30 on commissions for state business. This is the greatest compliment I can pay you. You brought integrity to government."

Integrity had its price in resentful political bosses and legislators, but by the time the 1951 session of the General Assembly convened, public and editorial support were so strong that politicians saw that in opposing the governor they were facing increasing risks. Strangely, it also helped that both houses now were controlled by the Republican opposition. It was no longer possible to pass the buck from one house to the other, from one party to the other; legislative responsibility now clearly rested with the Republicans. And Adlai did not let them forget it.

The program he presented to a joint session of the Sixty-seventh General Assembly on January 3, 1951, contained little that was new but much that was controversial. Much of the controversy swirled around highway reconstruction and the means of paying for it.

Illinois had been one of the first to build a state highway system, but during the 1940s this had begun to fall apart. At the 1949 session, Adlai had proposed a ten-year building program to cost $100 million, and to be paid for by increasing the gasoline tax from three to five cents a gallon and license fees for trucks and buses. In 1951 as in 1949, swarms of lobbyists rushed to Springfield to prevent the increases. But, unlike in 1949, they found that the campaign of public education Adlai had pushed steadily had built up public and press support the legislators could not ignore. Faced with this situation, the lobbyists adopted divide-and-conquer tactics centered on the distribution of the increased funds—for example, pitting Chicago and its desire for arterial highways against downstate residents who wanted township roads, and special interest group against special interest group.

The tactics almost succeeded. The truck license bill was debated in a House committee for five legislative weeks. The Senate refused to act on the gas tax while the truck bill was stalled. On May 31, Adlai again took his case to the people over a statewide radio network. "I am obliged to say," he concluded after describing the situation, "that unless the will of the people is made clear now, unless the legislators know you want and expect action, there is real and present danger that Senate Bill 96 will be emasculated or defeated. Thank you for listening to me. It is *your* money and they are *your* roads." The fan mail poured into his office and that of the legislators. The continuing education effort had prepared the public to respond to this urgent call. Friendly legislators in both houses called for an investigation of the lobbyists. On April 4, Adlai called a meeting in his office at the mansion of all the key legislators, starting at 8:30 P.M. He kept them there until after 2:00 A.M. when they finally reached an agreement.

"I kept the warring wolves here in the Mansion 6 hours and 20 minutes straight," he wrote Alicia Patterson.

Exhaustion overtook them & they began to crack. We had arranged to have the press—15 of them—on hand and they stood by all night. Before anyone could leave I called them in and announced the terms of the agreement before any of the conferees could reverse himself! The exhaustion technique I learned from the Russians and it seems to work as well in Springfield as in London.

He added that he regarded it as "the major triumph of the session."

The wrangling went on, but both bills passed; the gas tax at the very end of the session. When Adlai thanked Democratic Speaker of the House Paul Powell, the reply was, "I'm mighty glad to have your thanks, Governor, because it cost me $50,000."

Not all the efforts were as successful. The Fair Employment Practices bill again went down to defeat. So did three of the Crime Commission bills, but the most important one—extending the life of grand juries in Cook County—which the West Side bloc had defeated in 1949, was passed.

The Commission to Study State Government, which Adlai had established after the 1949 General Assembly under the chairmanship of Walter

Schaefer, produced recommendations that were embodied in 166 bills. Of these, 78 were passed, plus about a dozen others that grew out of the commission's findings, but some of the most important recommendations went down to defeat.

With the onset of the Korean War, Adlai had ordered stringent restraints on spending, and continuing close control made it possible for him to submit a budget containing only a 3-percent increase in general fund appropriations in spite of a 10-percent inflation rate. Consequently, unlike what was happening in other large states, no new or increased general-purpose taxes were required. By far the largest expenditure increase went for education—$35.4 million out of the total increase of $85.6 million. A raise in the minimum wage for teachers was also particularly gratifying. "That we have almost doubled state aid for schools during my administration will be an everlasting source of satisfaction to me and I hope to all who made it possible," he said in his radio report at the end of the session, which he described as "unquestionably one of the most productive sessions in the history of Illinois.

"The new laws enacted to rebuild our highways, to reorganize some of the agencies of state government, to improve our schools and the administration of our welfare institutions, to modernize municipal government, and the initial steps taken in the direction of constitutional reform all were notable accomplishments."

The defeats included a proposal to establish a legislative commission on constitutional amendments, to consolidate agencies involved in higher education, to integrate employment services, and to broaden the minimum-wage law.

Out of more than a 1,000 bills passed, he vetoed 134, vetoed a few others in part, and allowed some others to become law without his signature. Hard work, plus a willingness to work out face-saving compromises, strongly supported a favorable judgment on the accomplishments of the session. He lightheartedly stated his belief in compromise with the comment that "if it's true that politics is the art of compromise, I've had a good start," and then pointed out: "My mother was a Republican and a Unitarian; my father was a Democrat and a Presbyterian. I ended up in his party and her church."

"The idea that he was a fish out of water among politicians is a myth," Carl McGowan has declared. "He did wear Brooks Brothers suits. He did wear button down collars. He did have friends in the upper social levels. But he did like politicians, and they liked him, and he had a strong sense of party loyalty. He and Mayor Daley were always close friends. He listened to the organization people and he was ready to give them the things that were justifiable. We would go to those big fund-raising dinners of the organization. I can remember him pausing outside the hall and saying, 'Ah, the deep rich smell of democracy of Cook County!' and then plunge into it and have the time of his life. He loved it and they responded to him. He handled the legislators, the farmers, the small town lawyers remarkably well. They never talked about his Brooks Brothers suits or called him a Hamlet. In fact, some of them thought he was a little too decisive."

Since the ability of a governor or a President to win support for his program from the legislature is a key measure of effectiveness as a governmental leader, the assessment of biographer John Bartlow Martin is worthy of note:

> He had begun to understand his own political power. He was making bold to go directly to the people. He was focusing hard on the key issues. . . . He was, in a few words, exercising powerful political leadership. . . . He was operating more effectively in quieter ways. He talked to more legislators. He held meetings that included both his legislative leaders and his own staff. . . . He had his picture taken time and again with legislators, Democrats and Republicans alike, when he signed bills they had sponsored—pictures that helped them in their home districts. . . . He had strong staff work and used it well. He involved himself directly in legislative battles. . . . He established priorities—decided which bills were most important and which should be dropped. He held back some bills until difficult related bills were passed.

There was bipartisan agreement with Adlai's own assessment that "we are on our way to something better in Illinois."

One of Adlai's vetoes was to become famous and join the Hiss deposition as a major weapon in the Nixon-McCarthy attacks in the 1952 presidential campaign. For years, Senator Paul Broyles, with the encouragement of the American Legion, had been advancing various legislative proposals designed, as Carl McGowan has written, "to set up machinery to flush out the Communists assertedly hiding behind every barn and silo on the prairie." Finally, amid the emotions aroused by Senator McCarthy, the General Assembly had passed by large margins in both houses, Broyles's bill, S.102, making it a felony to belong to any subversive group and requiring a loyalty oath of public employees and candidates for office.

McGowan has reported that the bill was "anathema" to Adlai on many grounds, but to make certain his bias was not blocking an unperceived public interest, he quietly went to Washington to consult the Federal Bureau of Investigation. There he was told that while the FBI could not say so publicly, such state antisubversive bills actually got in the way and that sometimes state officials were arresting FBI agents who had infiltrated subversive organizations. Thus satisfied, he came back to Springfield to write the veto message that he knew would stir a storm of protest from the American Legion, the *Tribune,* and Hearst's *Herald-American,* all swept along on the hot winds of McCarthy's charges.

"That the Communist party—and all it stands for—is a danger to our Republic, as real as it is sinister, is clear to all who have the slightest understanding of our democracy," the veto message began.

> No one attached to the principles of our society will debate this premise or quarrel with the objectives of this bill.
>
> Agreed upon ends, our concern is with means. . . . The issue with respect to means raised by this bill has two aspects. One is the question of the need for it in relation to existing weapons for the control of subversives. The other is whether this addition to our arsenal may not be a two-edged sword, more dangerous to ourselves than to our foes.

He then reviewed existing federal and state legislation and enforcement activities dealing with treason and subversion, and asserted that not only was no new legislation needed but that harm could come from increasing legal confusion.

It was the enforcement provisions, however, that he found "most objectionable." These required the state attorney general to appoint a special assistant attorney general "who must assemble and deliver to the State's Attorney of each county all information relating to subversive activities within such county." The latter was then required to present all information "however inconclusive or insignificant" to the grand jury. The special assistant in Springfield was to maintain complete records of such information, which might, with the permission of the attorney general, be made public.

"I know of no precedent of any such interference with the normal discretion accorded to a public prosecutor," he continued, and "I can see nothing but grave peril to the reputations of innocent people in this perpetuation of rumors and hearsay."

He objected to the provisions requiring special loyalty oaths of public employees and ordering all governmental agencies to "establish procedures to ascertain that there are no reasonable grounds to believe that any applicant for employment is committed, by act or teaching, to the overthrow of the government by force or is a member of an organization dedicated to that purpose." Thus the burden of proving their loyalty would be shifted to all current employees and to all job applicants.

> By such provisions as these, irreparable injury to the reputation of innocent persons is more than a possibility, it is a likelihood. If this bill becomes law, it would be only human for employees to play safe and shirk duties which might bring upon

them resentment or criticism. Public service requires independent and courageous action on matters which effect countless private interests. We cannot afford to make public employees vulnerable to malicious charges of disloyalty. . . .

Does anyone seriously think that a real traitor will hesitate to sign a loyalty oath? Of course not. Really dangerous subversives and saboteurs will be caught by careful, constant, professional investigation, not by pieces of paper. The whole notion of loyalty inquisitions is a natural characteristic of the police state, not of democracy. . . .

I know full well this veto will be distorted and misunderstood, even as telling the truth of what I knew about the reputation of Alger Hiss was distorted and misunderstood. I know that to veto this bill in this period of grave anxiety will be unpopular with many. But I must, in good conscience, protest against any unnecessary suppression of our ancient rights as free men. Moreover, we will win the contest of ideas that afflicts the world not by suppressing those rights, but by their triumph. We must not burn down the house to kill the rats.

The Republicans in the Senate, where the bill had passed 35 to 15, undertook to override the veto. His hard-won popularity and his arguments sustained him as even Republican senators voted to uphold the veto. Nevertheless, the uproar he expected came quickly—and it continued.

Unexpectedly, there was also a flood of praise from opponents of McCarthyism who had found few public figures willing to confront the issues so directly and eloquently. In the prevailing climate, it had been a courageous act. Even McGowan confessed he was "full of foreboding and nervousness. It didn't faze Stevenson. We never sat around and debated the veto. He just did it."

The zest and clarity of purpose in his legislative battles was lacking on the personal front. The divorce was behind him, but it left a large void in the life of such a warm-hearted and gregarious man.

Archibald MacLeish has told about a visit to Springfield during the session of the legislature:

It was cold. I arrived late for dinner. The Mansion was locked. A state policeman let me in and an aged Negro butler took me through dark empty halls. I found Adlai at the end of a big reception room with obviously political types who were haranguing him. Adlai was looking forlorn and lost and miserable. We had dinner, then I went to the frozen train. The whole evening left me with an impression of forlornness and misery. I had a dreadful feeling that even more than resentment of Ellen he felt a longing for her—he still loved her. If ever a man needed a wife, Adlai did.

Buffie remembers going down to his office one night during that first year to plead with him to go to bed as he had been working past midnight the entire week. He had shaken his head stubbornly and wearily replied:

"I've failed as a husband. I've failed as a father. I *will* succeed as governor!"

MacLeish's impression, however, was only partly true. Carol Evans has reported that

> after the first year or eighteen months following the divorce, life at the Mansion became very gay. People would come to visit. There were many parties, parties for the children and for the staff. We had what he called a White Elephant Christmas for two years and some of the things that were done were very funny. Mrs. Ives was a wonderful actress and very, very funny and entertaining. The boys usually had a big dance. People came from all over the state. Every room and every cot was used. Sometimes the Governor had to sleep in the servants' room.

The inclusion of staff members and their families in his own social life was an important element in the intense personal loyalty of the people around him, according to Carl McGowan. "His thoughtfulness made you feel you were truly an important part of his life, both personal and official."

Buffie was tremendously helpful in fulfilling the role of hostess and in taking charge of the mansion; decorating it, giving it a warm and homey atmosphere, and endowing it with the sense of history inspired by Lincoln's presence in Springfield. She could also be sharp-tongued, quick-tempered, and difficult, and her devotion to Adlai contained strong elements of maternalism and jealousy. Tensions often were dispelled by Ernest, whose soft, southern manners, added to diplomatic instincts as well as training, smoothed over many rough spots. His self-effacing devotion to Adlai concealed countless thoughtful courtesies to staff and to visitors. In addition, he was a relaxing companion who sensitively filled many of the lonely hours.

The boys were present at every opportunity that did not risk offending Ellen. Once, he exultantly wrote Alicia that the boys had come without his having to beg for them. In the summer of 1951, the three of them and Adlai had a vacation together at Jackson Hole, Wyoming, which he described as one of the happiest times of his life. Their visits clearly were highlights in what sometimes seemed almost frenetic comings and goings.

In addition to Chicago and Lake Forest friends, prominent people from all over the country and from abroad would visit. Writers such as

Carl Sandburg, John Gunther, Bernard De Voto, John Mason Brown; historians such as Allen Nevins, Arthur Schlesinger, Jr., Benjamin P. Thomas, and many other Lincoln scholars; reporters such as Edward R. Murrow, James B. Reston, Walter Lippmann, Raymond Gram Swing, Doris Fleeson, and Helen Kirkpatrick; UN figures such as Ralph Bunche, Lord Gore-Booth; the consuls of foreign governments stationed in Chicago; Bob Hope, Arthur Rubinstein, and many others.

"We had all the benefits of small-town life, with the attractions of seeing big people from all over the world," Carl McGowan remembered.

Lord Gore-Booth summarized in his memoirs the 1950 trip he and his wife made to Springfield in these words: "To stay with this lonely, thoughtful, sensitive man in the executive mansion of Abraham Lincoln was a moving experience and a denial for all time of the myth that Americans have no history." Lincoln, of course, never lived there, but the mansion was so filled with reminders of his stay in Springfield that visitors felt his presence, even when Adlai did not talk about him.

The mansion itself had a welcoming atmosphere, thanks largely to Buffie's care and taste. There were twenty-eight rooms in it. Above the modest offices that occupied the "basement"—really the ground floor—was a tall-ceilinged floor that managed to be both stately and inviting. Much of it was occupied by "official" rooms that were used not only for the governor's formal entertaining, but also by the women's clubs and service groups in Springfield for teas and similar special events. Two front parlors with long windows reaching to the floor, mirrors that rose to the ceilings above the mantels of the fireplaces, large crystal chandeliers, and white shaggy rugs made them seem larger than they were. Adjoining each parlor was a long room with a bay window; one the living room and the other the music room, behind which was the white-paneled state dining room.

The family dining room was behind the living room and off of it was a sunroom that originally had been a side porch. It was here that Adlai, Buffie, and Ernest, or the visiting guests, would gather before dinner and where informal times were spent.

Buffie successfully met the challenge of creating a pleasant atmosphere, mindful that it was a house of history and tradition, and especially of Adlai's insistence on frugality. This point was forcefully made soon after their arrival when she and Ernest persuaded the governor to go for an evening walk. As they returned, the mansion was ablaze with light from a number of empty rooms.

"I never want to see that again," he told Buffie sternly. "I keep preaching economy in government—and it's up to us to set an example." On another occasion when he found Jane Dick's son asleep in one of the upstairs rooms with all the lights on, he wrote the parents a note suggesting they remind him such a practice was wasteful. Adlai was also accused of opening the refrigerator door to make sure the light was out. The more likely explanation was his affection for late-night snacks.

The spirit of Lincoln filled Springfield more than at any time since he had left for Washington nearly a century before. Adlai promptly established a direct and active relationship with state historian Jay Monaghan, an authority and author of a number of books on Lincoln. With his help, books on Lincoln and Illinois history were placed on prominent shelves in the mansion along with oil portraits by Illinois artists for the walls.

Traveling the length and breadth of Lincoln's state gave him some of his most gratifying times. One or more of the boys and their cousin, the Ives's son, Tim, often traveled with him, adding to the joys of discovering more things to love about the state.

In deference to Ellen's fear of flying, he never took the boys with him on the aging twin-engined Beechcraft belonging to the National Guard; besides, his pilot's hair-raising stories about Adlai's insistence on flying when nearly all else was grounded became too well known for people to welcome invitations to fly with him except in good weather. Most of the travel, though, took place in a rolling advertisement of his frugality—a 1940 state-owned Cadillac sedan that already had traveled more than 300,000 miles.

By the end of the four years, it is doubtful if there was a section untraveled or a state institution unvisited. He gleefully reported how, just before arriving at the gate of a state mental hospital, the car had broken down. Thinking that his schoolboy tinkering back in Bloomington might help, he crawled under the car. A suspicious state trooper drove up and asked his companions what they were doing there. They replied they were on their way to the hospital with the governor.

"Oh, yeah," the skeptical trooper responded. "Just where is the governor?" He knew his suspicions were well founded when they pointed to the feet sticking out from under the car. Adlai had to be pulled out and recognized to save them all from being escorted forcibly into the institution.

Bill Blair reports that on one of their visits to a large mental institution, Adlai insisted on participating in a patients' social hour. One of the patients who believed she was the widow of Abraham Lincoln asked him to dance, and as they waltzed away, she was heard to say, "My husband spoke of you so often."

The exuberant confidence that now marked his public life was not duplicated in his personal life. The relationship with Alicia Patterson that had grown in the withering of his marriage now was joined by another.

Dorothy Fosdick, the daughter of Harry Emerson Fosdick, the great preacher for whom John D. Rockefeller, Jr., had built Riverside Church in New York, had been a helpful colleague at the San Francisco UN conference. She had been one of the small group that had gathered at

Dumbarton Oaks in Washington in the latter days of the war to begin shaping what became the UN Charter. They had worked together in London and again at the UN sessions in New York. Quick, bright, attractive, with a ready sense of humor, she was one of several of his UN friends who heeded his pleas for ideas and material for use in speeches and articles.

But in the weeks following the final divorce decree, the correspondence, and the meetings, assumed a more affectionate tone. After she made her first visit to Springfield in June of 1950, the relationship became a serious one. Long letters on foreign affairs, especially the war in Korea, were interspersed with advice on personal affairs and expressions of affection. She returned to Springfield in July and again in August and October. Although their shared interest in foreign policy events and issues was never absent, expressions of love now dominated the correspondence.

At the same time, he was also writing and occasionally meeting Alicia Patterson. From his Wyoming vacation with the boys, he wrote both of them. He was somewhat taken aback when, in November, Alicia asked him about Dorothy. He wrote a dissembling reply about how they had worked together at the UN.

Ideas and suggestions of Dorothy's were now appearing in the speeches he was making and his letters to her assumed the intimate tone that previously had been the special mark of his letters to Alicia. They were managing to see each other almost once a month into the early part of 1951. In March she joined him, Borden, and John Fell for four days at Southern Pines, North Carolina. His desire for the boys to get to know her was an indication of the seriousness of the relationship. He met her family and wrote engaging letters to her sister's children. There is good reason to believe that marriage was in his mind, and it certainly was in hers.

In the midst of this, Alicia Patterson informed him that she intended to seek a divorce from Harry Guggenheim. Whereas a year or two earlier, he had hoped this might happen so they could be married, he was now dismayed at the prospect. He wrote a curious, confused letter advising her not to act impetuously. He showed Jane Dick the letter and asked for her advice. She was fully aware of their long relationship, but she also reminded him that Alicia was "temperamentally unstable, self-centered and demanding," concluding with "Beware and be firm." She also observed that "the smartest most brilliant men are the most naive and gullible about women." Alicia apparently abandoned her intention.

Buffie had long ago accepted the relationship with Alicia, but she was, for some reason, intensely opposed to Miss Fosdick. In late 1951 she even went to the length of writing Adlai that he should forget about running for reelection if he married Dorothy Fosdick. She might be acceptable if his future were to be in her field which was diplomacy, but she would not be a help to him in politics. She described Dorothy as being too aggressive and too careerist for a political life. She also found other ways to make her disapproval known. Not long after this remarkable letter, one from Adlai to Alicia said, "I'm glad you're having Buffie to dinner. . . . She's a difficult person for me—little actual knowledge, very possessive and self confident about what's right and wrong for me, but irrationally loyal and loving, and sensitive about me. Besides, I love her very much! And you, too, my beloved."

Throughout 1951 and into 1952, Dorothy kept providing drafts of speeches, particularly in relation to the war in Korea, and offering comments on material submitted by others, along with expressions of love and caring. Her writings and her judgments were greatly respected and her advice often followed. They enjoyed each other's company, were stimulated by the views they exchanged and by the values they shared.

His heart definitely was divided. During the 1952 presidential campaign, Drew Pearson wrote in his column that Adlai was "reported to be in love with Dorothy Fosdick." He then went on to state that no divorced man had ever occupied the White House and that while Catholic voters might tolerate a divorced man, they would not tolerate one who remarried, "especially if his new wife was the daughter of Harry Emerson Fosdick, the outstanding Protestant cleric." Adlai responded in a statement saying:

"The newspapers have married me to three ladies in the last three months. I guess they think the plural of spouse is spice. And now Mr. Pearson has added still another. It is all very flattering to me—if not to the ladies! I apologize to them for any embarrassment the writers may have caused them."

In any event, in the aftermath of the presidential campaign, the letters and meetings with Dorothy slowly dwindled and those with Alicia resumed their previous pattern. A quieter period may have produced a happier result than a deeply hurt Dorothy Fosdick and an unresolved relationship with Alicia Patterson.

The mosaic of any public figure's life is made up of many pieces, and that was especially true of this one. The main patterns were intermittently darkened and illuminated by other, often fleeting but sometimes revealing events.

Jane Dick has recounted one that occurred in the early months in Springfield.

There was the night that Adlai, my husband and I sat alone in his office on the first floor of the Mansion waiting for the clock to strike midnight, at which time a condemned Illinois prisoner was to die in the electric chair. Adlai was personally opposed to capital punishment, but the law of the state provided for it, and this man had been convicted of a particularly heinous crime, and had exhausted his last appeal—except to the Governor. The telephone kept ringing wildly in all of the offices, and the Governor's administrative assistants talked to priests, relatives, drunks in bars, and emotionally wrought-up citizens, all making desperate last-minute pleas for the prisoner. Despite his aides' urging that he go to bed and not subject himself to the ordeal—for he had spent hours over the record and had concluded that justice had indeed been done and must now take its course—Adlai insisted on talking to the prisoner's hysterical mother himself, hoping, I believe, that somehow something new might be developed that would enable him to stay the execution. But the heartbreaking conversation was useless. Finally the calls stopped. A deathly silence invaded the dimly lit offices, when at long last the old grandfather clock on the Mansion stairs started tolling out its twelve interminable strokes. I glanced at Adlai, and then had to look away because I know he was sitting in that electric chair himself that night. When it was over, we all went up to bed without speaking.

It is a stark story of compassion, of moral courage, of meticulous concern for justice, of the acceptance of duty and responsibility, of placing personal convictions aside to maintain fidelity to the law.

On February 22, 1950, approximately ten thousand coal miners belonging to the Progressive Mine Workers of Illinois went on strike for higher wages and additional fringe benefits. Some nineteen thousand members of the United Mine Workers already had been on strike for several weeks. The combined strikes reduced the state's supply of coal to such an extent that many schools were forced to close, hospitals and other institutions were on the verge of having to operate without heat, and the Commonwealth Edison Company ordered a dimout of downtown Chicago.

The day the strike began, the governor, without fanfare, met with the leaders of the Progressive Union and the operators' association and persuaded them to resume negotiations. While the negotiations proceeded he maintained silence even though the press was sharply criticizing him for doing nothing. On March 1, he was able to announce an agreement under which the Progressive Miners, joined by some six thousand United Mine Workers, went back to work under terms of the old agreement while new terms were being agreed upon. Illinois led the other states in achieving settlements in the mines.

Few people realize that downstate Illinois is, in many respects, a southern state. Not until 1987, for example, did Springfield, Lincoln's hometown, revise the districting laws that prevented blacks from being elected to the City Council, and it was done only then under pressure from the courts. Consequently, little notice was given outside of Illinois to the governor's executive order on May 24, 1950, that all leases for concessions in Illinois state parks contain the following paragraph:

"The concessionaire agrees that no person shall be denied or rejected full and equal use of accommodations or facilities on account of race, color or religion."

This was not the first time he had used his executive powers in the service of desegregation. On July 30, 1949, as commander in chief of the state's military and naval forces, he had desegregated the Illinois National Guard.

In July 1951, a black family attempted to move into a white neighborhood in the industrial Chicago suburb of Cicero. As a large crowd gathered in front of the building in protest, the Harvey Clark family fled. A part of the mob entered their apartment, threw their furniture into the street, where it was burned. The Cicero police stood by and called on the Cook County sheriff for help. Some police were sent, but the disorder continued, whereupon the governor called out the National Guard with instructions to preserve order and prevent further mob violence. Among those congratulating him for the prompt action were Secretary of Interior Harold L. Ickes and UN Undersecretary General Ralph Bunche.

While voting down the FEPC bill, the legislature extended the governor a crumb in the form of extending the responsibilities of the Illinois Interracial Commission and renaming it the Commission on Human Relations. In the wake of the Cicero riot, the crumb provided a bit more nourishment to the struggle for equal rights than the legislators intended. At its first meeting on October 11, 1951, the governor emphasized the problem that remains, in the closing years of the twentieth century, at the forefront of the nation's social agenda.

"Deep beneath the Cicero disorders and the breakdown of local law enforcement," he said,

> lie the fears, the alarms, the pressures, and tensions of the continuously critical housing shortage. . . . Large numbers of the low income groups, and among them large numbers of the so-called minority groups, are inadequately housed, rigidly segregated and confined to slums and deteriorated residential areas. The demoralizing effects of overcrowding, of substandard housing, inadequate sanitation, illegal building conversions, and a host of resultant social evils, are placing a severe strain upon the whole range of state and municipal welfare services.
>
> This is the root of the Cicero affair—the grim reality underlying the tension and violence that accompany the efforts of minority group members to break through the iron curtain which confines so many of our fellow citizens.

It is difficult to avoid speculating what the social condition might be today if Adlai had won the opportunity to act upon this vision.

Another vision that he expressed ahead of his time has been acted upon. In October 1950, he announced his support of a proposal to lower the voting age to eighteen. It was a concrete way to express the interest and confidence in young people that marked his whole career.

In March 1951, Adlai made what years later he called his most lasting contribution to the welfare of Illinois—the appointment of Walter Schaefer to the Illinois Supreme Court. Death had unexpectedly created a vacancy, and Adlai, knowing that the organization would exert pressure to have one of its own appointed, immediately appointed Schaefer and insisted that the organization slate him to run for the full nine-year term in the June election. "He really put the hammer on the organization to slate him," McGowan recalled. Schaefer's opinions and his national reputation as a "judge's judge" brought renown to the Illinois court that lasted until his death in 1987.

Tragedy shadowed the beginning of the fateful year 1952, and later ironically gave a boost to the movement to nominate Adlai for the presidency. On December 21, 1951, the New Orient mine number 2 at West Frankfort blew up, killing 119 coal miners. Adlai flew to the scene the next morning for what he described as "about the most distressing experience in war and peace." The dead men had left 100 widows and 162 children under eighteen. Apart from the human toll, the question of responsibility immediately became a central political issue, particularly since the explosion at Centralia four years earlier had been a major point of attack against the Green administration.

Serious efforts had been made to get a revised mining code through the legislature earlier that year, but neither the unions, the operators, nor the members from the coal mining districts were interested. The proposal then had been abandoned in the hope that by the next session the necessary support could be organized.

The governor promptly ordered an investigation to be headed by the director of mines and minerals, Walter Eadie. He asked Professor Harold Walker of the University of Illinois to work with the investigators "on my personal behalf." And full cooperation was to be given to the federal investigation that began. Nevertheless, these various investigations were unable to determine precisely what had caused the explosion. But the vigor of Adlai's reaction to the tragedy, in sharp contrast to the Centralia disaster during the Green administration, muted criticism and even added to the perception of strong, honest leadership.

Pressure on Adlai to announce for reelection grew in the late months of 1951, but he held back. Later it was said he was already maneuvering for the presidential nomination. Others cited the delay as evidence of his indecisiveness. Neither was true. What he was doing was using the party's need for him to pressure the machine into leaving the Cook County state's attorney, John Boyle, off the ticket.

The Kefauver committee had established that, after his election, Boyle had done legal work for a racing service with gangster connections, and other disclosures focused on a man Boyle had hired as his chief investigator. Even worse, another of Boyle's investigators, Mike Moretti, had killed two men during an off-duty drinking spree. The *Sun-Times* had demanded an investigation of the failure of the grand jury to indict, and consequently, Moretti was brought to trial and, after special prosecutors had been brought in over Boyle's head, had been convicted. Also, Adlai believed that Boyle had mishandled the indictments returned in the Cicero riot that the court had dismissed.

On October 16, he wrote an especially revealing letter to Alicia Patterson that not only disclosed his immediate tactic, but said much about his long-term goals. After discussing at some length the relative strengths of Eisenhower and Taft in a race against Truman, he went on to say:

> *I don't want any national business, nor do I intend to run for reelection* unless *I can be sure that the Democratic organization in Illinois and Chicago will give me a really good candidate for state's attorney of Cook County, and some more things I will have to insist upon to make 4 more years of this hell endurable. I believe you will agree that I should use the large bargaining power I now have to the utmost to accomplish some of the less conspicuous and more important long range objectives I have— i.e. better people in this business to make it a better business. I've done it in the administrative branch, with great difficulty, and before I get out I would like to help the party save itself and the system, at least in a small way.*

It would be difficult to find a more succinct statement of his tactics, his hopes, and his achievements as governor. Moreover, the tactic worked. The machine finally dumped Boyle and slated Judge John Gutnecht, a man of probity and good reputation, but somewhat ineffective as a campaigner. Heartened by this vulnerability, Boyle ran against him in the primary, attacking Adlai in the process as a man "who will not turn his back on Alger Hiss but will on the State's Attorney of Cook County." Boyle lost badly.

Having won his contest of wills with the organization, Adlai promptly announced for reelection on January 5, 1952. In his statement, he said:

"I take great satisfaction in the progress we have made since 1949. But I have learned that the road is long and we have far to go before any of us, myself included, can in good conscience stop and rest."

Abner Mikva, from Chicago's South Side, was serving as a law clerk to Supreme Court Justice Sherman Minton in the third year of Adlai's term as governor and had been planning to join the federal government. Like Newton Minow, who had been law clerk to Chief Justice Fred M. Vinson, he was excited by what was happening in his home state and decided instead to return to Illinois and work for the governor. Arriving late, he could look at the record with more objectivity than most. Later, after service in Congress, he joined Carl McGowan on the U.S. Court of Appeals for the District of Columbia. From that vantage point he gave John Bartlow Martin this assessment:

> To this day you can't turn anywhere in Illinois without seeing his mark. For example, in the police. In gambling, after Stevenson there was always the threat of the state police coming in. So all the gambling became sneak stuff. For another example, the Department of Finance. Joe Pois made it the Governor's internal audit and fiscal agent of Illinois—and it still is. For example, the budgeting process—it is still terrible but it's better than most states. There are other examples of how he pushed things—FEPC, Con-Con, reapportionment. He was ahead of his time. These were all basic things, and they were all first pushed by Stevenson. And Stevenson was the first governor with a concept of civil liberties. His reforms in mental health did not stick—but later in 1960 it became the issue that elected Kerner. It's hard to think that he was only Governor for four years. He had a profound influence.

Time magazine, in its January 28, 1952, cover story that spurred his presidential nomination, said:

"The keys to Stevenson's success have been neither gold nor silver, but steelier and less flashy—patient persistence, hard work, diplomacy, good public relations and able assistance."

All close observers agree that recruitment of able people was the most distinguishing hallmark of his administration.

"In recruiting people he was prepared to spend long hours at the job," Carl McGowan has said.

> The kind of people he wanted were busy, capable people and he knew the best chances of getting them was to do the selling job himself. He appreciated the value of bringing young people in. In the last couple of years he made a special effort to recruit young people, often of limited experience, who might otherwise go to Washington. One of the fertile fields was the Supreme

Court and those who were completing their clerkships with Supreme Court Justices.

We would send them into various departments and give them a chance to show what they could do. He was prepared to delegate responsibility to those in whom he had confidence. He kept in touch with what was going on. He had a concept of individual responsibility that brought out the best in the performance of people. It was part of the whole aura he created in Illinois—making service to the state an exciting, appealing, attractive thing to do.

McGowan added years later:

If there is any criticism to be made of his governorship, it was that he thought too much about keeping expenditures down. He did increase expenditures for education and mental health, but they needed more. Perhaps *the* limiting factor of a Stevenson presidency would have been staying away from new programs that cost a lot of money.

In his assessment, John Bartlow Martin concluded:

While Stevenson was Governor, Springfield and the Statehouse seemed somehow cleaner and brighter than before or since. A fresh wind was blowing. If it did not work permanent change in many areas, if it did not cleanse every dark corner of the moldy Capitol, at least for a time it brought new promise to a capital that too often forgets that Abraham Lincoln is more than a tourist attraction.

Perhaps Willard Wirtz summed it up most succinctly in saying: "He brought into government idealism with muscle."

CHAPTER EIGHT
Reluctant Candidate

BEING DRAFTED FOR HIGH public office is said to be the politician's dream and the publicist's myth. The very idea is the object of the cynic's scorn. But it did happen in the presidential nomination of 1952—and twice before that: to Republicans, in 1880 and in 1916.

The Republican "bosses" of New York, Pennsylvania, and Illinois were determined in 1880 to renominate President Ulysses S. Grant for an unprecedented third term. Allied against them were the rival candidacies of James G. Blaine of Maine and John Sherman of Ohio. The convention remained deadlocked through thirty-three ballots. On the thirty-fourth, seventeen votes were cast for the recent senator and former speaker of the House, James A. Garfield, who was not a candidate. On the thirty-sixth ballot, he was nominated.

Charles Evans Hughes had gone to the Supreme Court from a highly successful term as governor of New York and in 1912 had rejected pleas that he become a candidate for the presidency against Woodrow Wilson. Nevertheless, four years later, when the Republican convention nominated him, he resigned from the Court to lose a close race against Wilson's bid for a second term.

Adlai's case was significantly different. No one was in control of the 1952 convention; the bosses were in the position of trying to discover if he would climb aboard a bandwagon no one was driving, then trying to hop aboard before it passed them by.

His overwhelming victory in 1948, with a plurality of 572,067 votes in contrast to Truman's 33,612, labeled him almost instantly as a presidential possibility for 1952. *New York Times* columnist Arthur Krock, in surveying the election results, wrote, "Quite naturally, after such a triumph in the vital state of Illinois, Mr. Stevenson is being surveyed as a possible Presidential candidate of the Democrats in 1952." He followed this with a private note saying, "I meant it most seriously, Adlai, and shall nudge the ball along from time to time." In its year-end review, *U.S. News & World Report* speculated that, in the event Truman did not seek reelection, the Democratic candidate might be either Chief Justice Fred M. Vinson, General Dwight D. Eisenhower, or Governor Adlai E. Stevenson.

In his *Memoirs,* President Truman says he decided right after his inauguration in 1949 not to run for reelection. That may explain the "summons" Adlai received to call on the President when he went to Washington on May 21 to attend the Gridiron Dinner. Adlai told the press that they discussed the legislative situation in Illinois, the economy, and international affairs. There is no evidence that presidential politics was mentioned; and indeed, the Truman *Memoirs* state that as late as the fall of 1951, the President was trying to persuade Chief Justice Vinson to become the candidate.

Adlai, for his part, concentrated on being governor, declining speaking invitations from outside Illinois; breaking the rule only once in 1949 to speak on "The Kind of Democrat I Am" at the *New York Herald Tribune* Forum in October 1949. A ready excuse for this departure was his desire to participate in President Truman's laying of the cornerstone of the United Nations headquarters building since he had played a central role in its location. Also, it gave him a chance to visit Borden at Choate. He worked hard on the speech because he knew that it would be scrutinized as his first national political speech, and it elicited favorable editorial comment.

Not until January 28, 1951, did he interrupt his concentration on Illinois affairs, and even then, he concentrated on Illinois audiences. At Northwestern University's Founders' Day convocation celebrating the hundredth anniversary of the university, he was asked to speak on world affairs in general terms and set the framework for speeches on specific subjects to be given by diplomat-scholar, George F. Kennan, and theologian Reinhold Niebuhr. The national atmosphere was charged. Barely two months earlier, Chinese armies had crossed the Yalu River in force and driven United Nations forces back beyond Seoul; Senate and House Republicans had called for the dismissal of Secretary of State Dean Acheson, and the debate led by Senator Robert A. Taft was approaching white heat.

The speech, a vigorous attack on isolationism, produced the largest flow of fan mail he had ever received, and the letters came from far beyond Illinois. In rapid succession, he spoke to the University of Chicago Round Table on national security and individual freedom; to the Chicago chapter of the American Association for the United Nations denouncing a resolution pending in the Illinois legislature urging withdrawal from the United Nations; to the Chicago World Trade Conference, on the Korean War and on American contributions to European recovery; at a Veterans' Hospital Day in Danville on Korea; and even at the Jefferson-Jackson Day Dinner in Springfield, where his talk about the Democratic record was fused with discussion of current foreign policy. His commencement address at the University of Illinois professional schools on June 15 in Chicago managed to deal not only with damage to the highways from overweight trucks, gambling, crime, and corruption, but also with McCarthyism and the search for solutions to "war, inflation, revolution, communism, imperialism, hunger, fear and all the diseases of a world in convulsive transition."

He had begun to think about running for President—in 1956. The present writer is confident of that assertion. In the summer of 1950, Adlai had inquired if I would be interested in leaving my post at the United States Mission to the UN and help on "writing chores" in Springfield. At that time, we agreed that the pressures of the Korean war made a move out of the U.S. Mission inadvisable, but the correspondence and conversation continued. I expressed concern that despite my South Dakota origins, someone arriving in Springfield from New York and the United Nations would be too tempting a target for the *Chicago Tribune* and inevitably would raise questions about the governor's objectives. I illustrated my concern by reporting a conversation with Chesley Manly, the *Tribune*'s Washington correspondent, who had unexpectedly appeared to open an office at the United Nations. In answer to my inquiry as to why the *Tribune*, with its attitude toward the UN, would send one of its leading correspondents to New York, Manly explained he had received his assignment from Colonel McCormick in these terms:
    "Ches, I've been thinking a lot about the UN lately, and I have come to the conclusion that Joe Stalin is about ready to plunge his knife right into the back of the UN. Now, Ches, I want you to go to New York—and beat him to it!" For Adlai's sake, I didn't want to give the Colonel a chance to use me as a weapon.
    Finally, in March of 1951, I suggested that until he decided to run for national office it would be better to forgo a position on his staff and to rely on informal efforts by friends such as Dorothy Fosdick and myself to feed his insatiable appetite for ideas and material on current foreign policy issues. To this, he agreed. It then developed that Mrs. Quincy Wright wanted to resign as executive director of the Chicago Council on Foreign Relations to head the Chicago office of the Institute for International Education. While I was in Paris for a session of the UN General Assembly, it was worked out that I would succeed her at the council, acquire Illinois citizenship, and sometime during his second term as governor move down to Springfield. It was never explicitly stated, but it was clear

that the only reason for my coming then would be to work on a buildup for the presidential nomination in 1956. My wife, two small sons, and I arrived in Chicago in late spring 1952 to begin work at the council, as planned. The rest of the plan was derailed at the Democratic convention but it left no doubt that Adlai was hoping for two terms as governor and for the presidential nomination in 1956. The interesting story is his losing struggle, unique in our history, to avoid the nomination.

When Chief Justice Vinson finally convinced President Truman that on grounds of health and Mrs. Vinson's opposition, he would not be a candidate, Truman says, he "began to canvass the situation from one end of the country to the other." He wrote in his memoirs that while "no one stood out at this time as the 'natural' choice" his search "for the best all-around candidate led to my consideration of Adlai E. Stevenson." Jack Arvey reported that on several occasions in 1951 the President asked him, "How's your Governor doing?"

The rumors of presidential interest fed the typewriters of the growing number of journalists impressed by Adlai and by the influence of such key figures as Krock, Reston, Lippmann, Alsop, and Childs who repeatedly wrote of his presidential caliber. They were fed, too, by William I. Flanagan, on Adlai's staff, who despite stern and repeated injunctions, kept circulating material to advance his ambition for Adlai's nomination. He assembled a background packet that became known as "Flanagan's twenty-pound packet," and a mimeographed collection of Stevenson wit. Knowing of Adlai's friendship since college days with T. S. Matthews, managing editor of *Time,* he began promoting the idea of a cover story.

As 1952 began, Adlai's old friend in Washington, George Ball, began to receive visits from two assistants to Charles Murphy, special counsel to the President, James Loeb, Jr., and David Lloyd (the latter had accompanied Adlai on the postwar economic survey of Italy). At first they said the approaches were with the knowledge of Murphy but not the authorization of the President. But soon he was told that the President wished to talk with Adlai, and was asked if he could arrange for Adlai to visit Washington.

In his memoirs, *The Past Has Another Pattern,* Ball wrote:

> I found Adlai stonily resistant. He had just announced his candidacy for a second term as Governor of Illinois. What did I think he was—"the garden variety of opportunistic pol who charged off looking for better pasture whenever he heard a distant bell"? During his first four years, he had, he said, started many projects and he intended to finish them; to walk out now would be "bad faith" to his supporters. There was much more of the same—scornful rejection poured out in exasperated phrases.

But a number of streams were rushing toward the floodplain. It was not necessary to be a cynic to believe that such a set of coincidences had to be contrived. They were not.

Concerned at the extent to which racial discrimination in the United States undermined our position at the United Nations, I had suggested to my friend, Frank Montero, at the Urban League, that they consider asking Adlai to talk about the issue at their annual dinner in January. While I was in Paris for the General Assembly, the invitation was extended, and accepted; Adlai welcomed the opportunity to link what had happened in Cicero to a broad perspective of racial issues.

Flanagan's promotion of the *Time* cover story had succeeded and the magazine was looking for a news peg for its release. The Urban League speech in New York seemed like a good opportunity, so Adlai prepared his speech knowing of the probable link to a big story in *Time*. Another coincidence was the appearance on the newsstands that week of the article on corruption that he had prepared weeks before for *The Atlantic Monthly*.

The tragic explosion at the West Frankfort mine on December 22 had made it urgent for Adlai to meet with Secretary of Interior Oscar Chapman and John L. Lewis, leader of the United Mine Workers, to discuss mine safety regulations and legislation. The New York trip provided an opportunity to slip down to Washington to see them without, he hoped, any publicity. He realized, in the light of the word from Ball, he would also have to call on the President to discuss a subject he wanted to avoid; in fact, Ball had told him that the President would be offended if he came to Washington without calling on him. He also hoped that, should his presence in Washington be discovered, the meeting with Secretary Chapman and Lewis would provide adequate explanation and help keep out of the papers what it was agreed would be a secret meeting with the President.

Again, only the first part of the plan worked. The Urban League speech was a great success, but from then on things did not go as planned. The next morning, bad weather had grounded most planes and one seeking to land at Newark crashed, killing everyone on board including former Secretary of War Robert Patterson. With no weather improvement in sight, Adlai and Bill Blair took the noon train to Washington. After seeing John L. Lewis, Adlai arrived late at George Ball's home for dinner and a discussion of what he was to say to the President later that evening. Ball's memoirs provide the most vivid and authoritative account of what happened.

Just before he arrived, Carlton Kent of the Chicago *Sun-Times*'s Washington bureau called me. He knew Adlai would be dining with me that night and wanted him to return the call. When Adlai finally arrived, breathless and complaining, he was upset at the message from Kent. "Why can't I do anything without some damn fool leaking it?" [In addition, Marquis Childs and *Time* had heard about the meeting. The leaks later were traced to Loeb at the White House and to Flanagan in Springfield.]

During dinner, Adlai rehearsed the coming interview. How could he explain to President Truman, without showing disrespect for the office of the Presidency, that he wished to remain Governor of Illinois? How could he make it clear to Truman that he was not going to run? To seek the Presidency now would be to break faith with the people of Illinois. He had been elected Governor by Republicans as well as Democrats and he would not turn his back on his friends. . . .

I tried to get him to promise that if Truman asked him to run, he would not flatly reject the idea. The United States was in a critical period. Taft might well be the Republican nominee, and we desperately needed a President with a broad view of the world who could carry on the grand enterprises begun in the postwar years. I continued on this theme as I drove him to Blair House but with a sinking feeling I was losing the struggle.

At another point, Ball reports that on the drive to Blair House, Adlai declared:

"I'll be damned if I want to be a caretaker for the party. If Eisenhower runs, nobody can beat him. And anyway, wouldn't Eisenhower make a pretty good President? There's a hell of a lot of truth in the need for a change."

The Ball memoirs continue:

When we reached the barricades on Pennsylvania Avenue, the Secret Service blocked the way. Who was this small, dumpy man who arrived in my old Chevrolet? Only after telephoning back and forth did they grudgingly open the barricade.

I told Ruth when I reached home that the interview then in progress would prove disastrous. Truman—brusque and decisive—would never understand Stevenson's subtle rendition of Prince Hamlet. My prediction seemed confirmed when Adlai called me the next morning to say he had "made a hash" of the meeting, but, in any event, "had put a stop to all the nonsense." He had, he said, told the President "very bluntly" that he did not wish to run. He knew Truman could not understand his reluctance and would think he was afraid to take on a hard fight. At one point, Truman had made a comment that I found particularly endearing: "Adlai, if a knucklehead like me can be President and not do too badly, think what a really educated smart guy like you could do in the job." Stevenson continued in a mood of lamentation. He repeated he had "made a hash" of the talk and that the President probably thought him an idiot. Truman, he felt sure, had written him off as hopeless; the only advantage was that the interview had definitely put an end to the question of his Presidential candidacy.

President Truman, in his *Memoirs,* quotes from notes he made after the meeting:

> We talked for an hour or more. I told him I would not run for President again and that it was my opinion he was best-fitted for the place. His grandfather was Vice President with Grover Cleveland in the campaign and the election of 1892. The grandfather had been on the ticket with Winfield Scott Hancock in 1880. He had served in Congress. Adlai's father had been connected with the government of the State of Illinois. Adlai had served the country in the State Department and the United Nations. He had made an excellent Governor of Illinois.
>
> When I talked with him, I told him what I thought the Presidency is, how it has grown into the most powerful and the greatest office in the history of the world. I asked him to take it and told him that if he would agree he could be nominated. I told him that a President in the White House always controlled the National Convention. Called his attention to Jackson, Van Buren and Polk. Talked about Taft in 1912. Wilson in 1920. Coolidge and Mellon in 1928. Roosevelt in 1936, 1940, 1944. But he said: No! He apparently was flabbergasted.

The two accounts reveal the deep chasm of misunderstanding that opened between the two men from the outset. Stevenson, always determined to be his own man, could only have been repelled by the offer to hand him the nomination on a platter in a convention controlled by the White House. Moreover, his political instincts told him that in the atmosphere of discontent that had intensified since the "Truman miracle" of 1948, running as the President's hand-picked man was akin to political suicide. Besides, he deeply desired a second term as governor. For his part, the President, with his profound feeling about the presidency, simply was not capable of understanding how any rational person could decline the nomination that was being offered.

Adlai's belief that the interview had ended the matter for him was proved wrong the very next day. The White House itself had released word about the meeting, and it coincided with the appearance of the

Time cover story on the newstands. Moreover, *Time* had taken advantage of the advance leak to change the focus from the Urban League speech to the Blair House meeting and rumors that the President wanted Adlai to succeed him. "In a cold season for the Democrats," the *Time* story concluded, "Adlai Stevenson is officially hot, and Harry Truman feels the need of a little warmth."

Unsuccessfully trying to avoid reporters and photographers, Adlai nevertheless managed to have breakfast with Senator Paul Douglas, and meet with Secretary Chapman and John L. Lewis on the mine safety issue. Late that evening he called James B. "Scotty" Reston of *The New York Times* to give vent to his frustration.

"He said Truman wanted him to run for President," Reston recalled. "He was very upset. I asked if he was going to do it. He said, 'What are you trying to tell me? That it's my duty to save Western civilization from Ike Eisenhower?'" Reston added that Truman was "furious." Truman felt that "anointing" Stevenson "should be enough," but that "instead of being grateful, he was getting brushed off."

Before leaving the next morning, Adlai had breakfast with Chief Justice Vinson's young law clerk, Newton Minow, in a successful effort to persuade him to come to work in Springfield rather than remain in Washington. Even the trip back to Chicago involved coincidence: The presence on the plane of John Foster Dulles aroused further speculation that mounted steadily in the weeks that followed. Reporters, columnists, photographers, even two authors commissioned to write biographies, flocked to Springfield, as exasperation competed with courtesy in Adlai's response to it all.

George Ball saw his job during this period as "trying to keep Stevenson from foreclosing the future," and staying in touch with Charles Murphy and David Lloyd at the White House, who advised him of the President's growing impatience. As a consequence, Ball told Adlai he owed the President a further talk and, finally, Adlai asked him to set up a secret meeting, which was scheduled for March 4.

The political pot, meanwhile, boiled and bubbled with increasing intensity. The day after the Blair House meeting, Senator Kefauver announced his candidacy. Shortly thereafter, Senator Robert S. Kerr of Oklahoma and Senator Richard B. Russell of Georgia announced their candidacies, and Averell Harriman prepared to do so. In New Hampshire, Eisenhower, Taft, and Harold Stassen were entered in the primary election to be held March 11. In Washington, Ball had raised a few thousand dollars and set up a "Stevenson information center" in his law office, which collected information on Adlai and encouraged articles in *The New Republic, Harper's,* and other magazines. In Illinois, on February 21, a Stevenson for President Committee was launched with a full-page ad in the *Sun-Times,* bearing the names of personal friends and people prominently identified with the Independent Voters of Illinois, an organization formed in 1943 to promote better candidates for office regardless of party affiliation but, in the event, mostly Democrats. It later became the Illinois affiliate of the Americans for Democratic Action.

Adlai knew in advance about the ad and did nothing to stop it, although he later sent word he disapproved of it. Ball also kept him informed of the activities of the Washington information operation and he did nothing to stop that either, although he did complain a few times about excessive activity. These operations by friends, plus his responsiveness to the journalists and broadcasters, caused many to conclude that he was secretly angling for the nomination; forgetting that such publicity was helpful to his announced candidacy for governor and unaware that he saw it as helpful to his unannounced desire to seek the presidency in 1956.

Seeking secrecy for the trip, he flew from Springfield the morning of March 4, using Bill Blair's name. During the stopover in Louisville, Kentucky, he met with Barry Bingham, publisher of the *Courier-Journal,* one of the many friends with whom he discussed what was to him the dilemma of avoiding the nomination without being disrespectful of either the office or the President.

"I argued, with as much force as the brief time allowed, my conviction that he should not fight against a fate which seemed to have settled upon him," Bingham recalled. ". . . As we parted, he laughed and said: 'Well, you certainly haven't been much help to me.'"

Of the meeting, which this time did not leak, President Truman reports in his *Memoirs:*

> On March 4 Governor Stevenson came to see me again, this time at his request, to tell me he had made a commitment to run for re-election in Illinois and that he did not think he could go back on that commitment honorably. I appreciated his viewpoint, and I honored him for it. He said he would not want to have people believe that he was announcing for re-election in his great state just as a stepping-stone to the White House.
>
> But I felt that in Stevenson I had found the man to whom I could safely turn over the responsibilities of party leadership. Here was the kind of man the Democratic party needed and, while I would not pressure him, I felt certain that he would see it as his duty to seek the nomination.

In the New Hampshire primary on March 11, Kefauver defeated Truman and Eisenhower defeated Taft. Adlai was in Washington for a meeting of the Governors' Conference committee with the House Ways and Means Committee and then went up to New York and Boston to see young Adlai and Borden and to pick up John Fell, who was just starting his spring vacation. Flying from Boston to New York with John Fell, he wrote Alicia a letter that revealed for the first time that, if it came, he would accept a draft.

"I just don't want to go out for it; I wouldn't be honest with myself if I did and I attach importance to the inconsistency of being a candidate for Gov. of Ill. and publicly or even privately running for Pres." He closed saying that he would return to Illinois "with my resolve hardened, I hope, that I will keep out of this thing and concentrate on *being* and *running* for Gov. unless the Democratic convention should nominate me which would seem very unlikely."

Adlai had been planning to fly directly to Florida with John Fell, but George Ball had reached him in Cambridge with word that the President had asked Charles Murphy and Jim Loeb to have another discussion with him and urged him to stop in Washington en route to Florida. Adlai protested at length, but finally agreed. Traveling again under an assumed name, he and John Fell went directly to Ball's home to spend the night.

"It was a dismal evening," Ball reports in his memoirs. "Stevenson was more obdurate than ever, insisting that he did not want to run and even going out of his way to attack Truman's liberal policies, as though wishing not only to distance himself from the President but also to compel Truman to write him off on ideological grounds." Ball states that Adlai criticized virtually every aspect of Truman's domestic policy and was positive only in the area of foreign policy. "I sat through the long, grim evening with increasing hopelessness, while Charles Murphy, a dedicated Fair Dealer deeply committed to Truman, cringed at Adlai's blasphemies."

Adlai realized that in trying to pull himself out of consideration he had exaggerated his opposition to Truman policies and three days later, from his Florida vacation spot, he wrote a letter to Murphy who was with the President at Key West. It summed up his reasons for not wanting the nomination so fully that it is worth repeating much of it here.

> *I have been thinking about our confused talk the other night at George Ball's house. . . . Let me try to summarize it as I see it.*
>
> *1. I do not want to be a candidate for the nomination; I do not want to run for President, and I do not want to be President at this time. I have been in "politics" only three years and while I have learned a great deal, I have a great deal more to learn. My ambitious program in Illinois is well under way but there is still much to be done. . . .*
>
> *2. I am the unopposed candidate for re-election and loathe to abandon an objective I do want to work for, for one which I do not honestly want. Even if I did want to run for President in these extraordinary circumstances, I would find it difficult to carry*

water on both shoulders and run for the nomination while osten-
sibly running for Governor. . . .

To the foregoing I could *add misgivings about my strength,*
wisdom and humility to point the way to coexistence with a
ruthless, inscrutable and equal *power in the world. That I am the*
best available man, aside from President Truman, to assume this
monstrous task, seems to me *grotesque. But I will quickly con-*
cede that that decision is for the President, and the many others
who have written and talked to me and share his view.

To the foregoing I must *add, however, that my children seem*
to me to be altogether too young and undeveloped to subject to
the pitiless exposure of a national campaign, let alone the presi-
dency. Nor do they have the advantage of a strong and stable
family life. . . .

Another four years as Governor of my beloved Illinois, and
many of these obstacles will have vanished. As a more seasoned
politician, with my work in Illinois behind me, creditably, pray
God, I might well be ready and even eager to seek the presidency,
if I then had anything desirable to offer.

Our talk Friday perplexed me a little because I was under the
distinct impression from my last visit with the President that,
given my Illinois situation, he was quite reconciled to run again
himself. If I misunderstood him, or that is no longer the case and
the question is whether I would accept the nomination at Chicago
and then do my level best to win the election, I should like to
know it. In that event, about the only solution I can see, in sin-
cerity and good conscience, would be for me to say publicly, and
I would like to say it before he announces his intention not to run,
if such is his decision, that all I want is to carry on my work in
Illinois, that I have no other ambition, desire or purpose; that I
do not want and will not seek the nomination; that if my party
should nominate me anyway I would accept proudly and prayer-
fully, of course, as should any American in good health with con-
victions about this tormented world.

This is the position Adlai maintained right up to the nomination in
Chicago. It is difficult to read this as the record of an indecisive man,
although that was the label the President, with notable success, took the
lead in attaching to him. He knew what he wanted to do. He stated it
firmly. And he acknowledged that if the nomination came to him in spite
of his desires, he could not reject it. Carl McGowan thought that was his
mistake; that he should have bluntly, and if necessary, brutally, said he
would not accept the nomination under any circumstances. But such a
course ran counter to his sense of public duty; probably a more important

consideration for him than the adverse impact such a stand might have had on any effort to obtain the nomination in 1956.

Most writers dismiss Adlai's concern about the possible impact of the nomination on his sons. This writer does not. It arose in several conversations in the weeks before the convention, and it was on his mind in the final hours before the nomination became official and he had turned without jubilation to the writing of an acceptance speech he knew he would have to deliver. His feelings for his sons were intense and he worried about the strains imposed on them by Ellen's progressive illness and by his public life. As with other deep emotions, this one was stated rarely, and then guardedly, but it was profound.

His letter to Murphy evoked an immediate reply:

> *I received your letter this morning and have talked with the President about it. He was much impressed by what you had to say—impressed in the sense that it confirmed and strengthened the high regard he already had for you. I do think it helped a great deal to clarify your situation in his mind. He said he would like to think the matter over for a few days, and would then talk to me about it again. Until he does, there is little I can add about his views. . . .*
>
> *The reasons you give for not wishing to seek the nomination are very compelling. I honestly wish I could say that you ought to be left alone. But the more I think about it, the more I am driven to the conclusion that if the President "propositions" you, on the basis indicated in your letter, you should accept. The reasons for this are more than compelling. They are overwhelming. . . .*
>
> *If the President's final decision is not to run, it will be because he thinks such a decision is in the best interest of the country. . . . And in such a case, you are just "it". . . . It will be a matter of duty, as I see it.*

On the day this was written, March 18, Minnesota was holding its primary election. As a favorite son, Senator Hubert H. Humphrey got 98,704 votes and all twenty-six delegates. But the write-in votes provided the big news: Kefauver received 19,783; Truman, 3,602—and Eisenhower, more than 100,000!

For the next ten days, until Adlai left Springfield for the March 29 Jefferson-Jackson Day Dinner in Washington and an appearance the next day on *Meet the Press,* the pressure kept building through letters, calls, news stories, and commentaries until he told a few friends that he felt "the noose" tightening around his neck. Democrats from all over the country, gathered in the huge armory, were stunned when President Truman, at the end of his speech, announced, "I shall not accept a renomination." After the shouts of "No!" died down, but almost before the

President finished speaking, the reporters and photographers all converged on Stevenson. He fended them off and escaped with Averell Harriman and Arthur Schlesinger to the Metropolitan Club, where George Ball was waiting to discuss the next day's appearance on *Meet the Press.* All three report that they argued vigorously with Adlai that he had no choice but to run, and little was said about the television program on which all the curiosity aroused by the President's announcement now was focused. Arvey called Mayor David L. Lawrence of Pittsburgh to tell him to be sure to watch, but most political figures didn't need such encouragement.

Adlai had never seen *Meet the Press;* indeed, he had seen very little television. There was no set in the mansion. On the few occasions when he wanted to watch a football or baseball game, he would go to Bill Flanagan's home. For a man who was about to become a central figure in the first presidential campaign conducted mainly on television, he was uncharacteristically unprepared. He had been warned that the moderator, Lawrence Spivak, conducted the program in a confrontational style and sought journalists for his panel who shared this approach.

Roscoe Drummond of the *Christian Science Monitor* and Richard Wilson of the *Des Moines Register and Tribune* were relatively mild, asking general questions about what he saw as the major issues and bipartisanship in foreign policy. Ed Lahey of the *Chicago Daily News* turned up the heat in pressing him on his attitude toward the nomination, asking, "Wouldn't your grandfather, Vice President Stevenson, twirl in his grave if he saw you running away from a chance to be the Democratic nominee in 1952?" To which Adlai replied, "I think we have to leave Grandfather lie." It was Spivak and Mae Craig of the *Portland* (Maine) *Press-Herald* who sought to provoke: Spivak with more pointed questions on his reluctance to be a candidate and on labor laws, the Taft-Hartley Act, civil rights, and a compulsory FEPC; and Craig, first with questions on corruption, then on the need for a change, and then Alger Hiss. The answer was the high point of the program.

> Pursuant to an order of the court, some questions, interrogatories as they are called, were sent out to me in Springfield . . . and the question in effect was: From what you have heard from others, that is, from what others have told you, what was Mr. Hiss' reputation for loyalty, integrity, honesty, as of that time, in 1948? My answer was that it was good. . . . I'm a lawyer. I think that one of the most fundamental responsibilities, not only of every citizen, but particularly of lawyers, is to give testimony in a court of law, to give it honestly and willingly, and it will be a very unhappy day for Anglo-Saxon justice when a man, even a man in public life, is too timid to state what he knows and what he has heard about a defendant in a criminal

trial for fear that defendant might later be convicted. That would to me be the ultimate timidity.

Pressed further, Adlai was asked his view of the efforts to form a committee under Senator Pat McCarran "to find out how deep the roots of Communism go." "I don't condemn that," he answered. "I do very much condemn the danger of very broad accusation, unsubstantiated charges, which not only endanger the reputation of an individual, but they actually do an injustice to the Republic, because we can't let hysteria, in our anxiety to prevent any injury to the Bill of Rights, destroy the Bill of Rights itself."

Repeated applause in the studio prompted Spivak to ask, "Doesn't this large studio audience give you an indication how some of the people of the country feel about that [his declaration that he must run for governor]?"

"It's very flattering, indeed," Adlai replied, "and I suppose flattery hurts no one—that is, if he doesn't inhale it."

The favorable reaction of both public and politicians to this performance pushed him further down the road to the nomination. In the chorus of praise that followed, only Walter Lippmann, at dinner that night at George Ball's, urged him not to run on the ground that Eisenhower would be the Republican nominee and was unbeatable.

The weekend had been a fateful one. Within days, the Independent Voters of Illinois group reorganized as a National Draft Stevenson Committee. Similar groups were organized in Iowa and Indiana, and moves in that direction began in several other states. More important were the signs of consensus developing among the professional politicians. Kefauver was opposed by party leaders; Truman referred to him derisively as "Cowfever." Chief Justice Vinson had removed himself; Humphrey was too liberal; Harriman had not held public office and was little known outside of Washington and New York; Barkley was too old; Russell was opposed by Negroes and pro-civil rights leaders, especially in the North; Kerr was regarded as the servant of oil and gas interests. Adlai was the only Democrat all the factions of the party could support. So, among party leaders, interest in Adlai quietly grew amid uncertainty whether he would accept a nomination while a more public campaign was being waged by the amateurs who chose to ignore the question.

Adlai, meanwhile, was trying to turn aside discussion of national politics and concentrate on his race for governor. In the primary on April 8, running unopposed, he received 708,275 votes, 8,000 less than the winner of the Republican primary, William G. Stratton, but he also received 54,336 write-in votes in the presidential vote where Kefauver was the only candidate. Now, with the official designation as the Democratic candidate for governor, he made a determined effort to take himself out of the presidential race with the release, on April 16, of the following statement:

> I have been urged to announce my candidacy for the Democratic nomination for President, but I am a candidate for Governor of Illinois and I cannot run for two offices at the same time. Moreover, my duties as Governor do not presently afford the time to campaign for the nomination even if I wanted it.
>
> Others have asked me merely to say that I would accept a nomination which I did not seek. To state my position now on a prospect so remote in time and probability seems to me a little presumptuous. But I would rather presume than embarrass or mislead.
>
> In these somber years the hopes of mankind dwell on the President of the United States. From such dread responsibility one does not shrink in fear, self-interest or humility. But great political parties, like great nations, have no indispensable man, and last January, before I was ever considered for the Presidency, I announced that I would seek re-election as Governor of Illinois. . . . No one should lightly aspire to it or lightly abandon the quest once begun.
>
> Hence, I have repeatedly said that I was a candidate for Governor of Illinois and have no other ambition. To this I must now add that in view of my prior commitment to run for Governor and my desire and the desire of many who have given me their help and confidence in our unfinished work in Illinois, I could not accept the nomination for any other office this summer. . . .
>
> I cannot hope that my situation will be universally understood or my conclusions unanimously approved.
>
> I can hope that friends with larger ambitions for me will not think ill of me. They have paid me the greatest compliment within their gift, and they have my utmost gratitude.

He hoped the statement would close the matter. He sent a copy of it to President Truman, among others, who wrote back that he appreciated the letter but not the "attached statement which I didn't appreciate so much." A *New York Times* editorial observed that he seemed "effectively to have closed the door to his nomination."

Although General Eisenhower had succeeded in taking himself out of the race in 1948 by saying he "could not" accept a nomination; now, when Adlai said "could not accept" instead of "would not accept," it was seized upon very quickly as indicating he would accept a draft. The record, and his precision with language, gives support to this conclusion. The first draft prepared by Carl McGowan stated, "I cannot and will not accept the nomination." When he got it back from Adlai, the phrase had been changed to "cannot, in good conscience, accept." McGowan thereupon concluded that Adlai would accept the nomination, and suggested that the phrase "in good conscience" might as well be dropped. Moreover, it had become increasingly clear to those close to him that while he would do all he could to discourage the presidential movement, he truly could not "in good conscience" refuse an unsolicited call.

Doubt has persisted that he did, in fact, discourage the efforts on his behalf; that, secretly, he encouraged them. The doubters are misled by the efforts of friends who refused to be discouraged. McGowan has stated that "the Governor had given strict injunctions to the staff against associating with these activities. Only Flanagan violated this. If the Governor had known of Flanagan's activities, he'd have kicked his ass out." Arvey, for example, knew of Adlai's injunction, and heeded it with one important, and inadvertent, exception.

The Democratic State Committee in New York had been planning a dinner in honor of Harriman to be held, as it happened, the day after Adlai issued his statement. The state chairman, Paul Fitzpatrick, had called Arvey and asked him to persuade Adlai to be one of the speakers. Arvey had called Bill Blair and the latter had accepted for Stevenson. With the issuance of his statement, Adlai told Fitzpatrick he would not appear. Arvey reports he received a "frantic" phone call from Fitzpatrick, pleading that he would be losing "my chief drawing card." Arvey told Adlai he owed it to the party to go and Adlai finally agreed on the condition that Arvey go with him and go with him to Harriman's home afterward.

At the dinner, with Kefauver as well as party leaders participating, all agreed that Adlai "stole the show" with what Arvey called a "brilliant" speech; one that contained some of the same phrases that soon would ignite the Democratic convention. As it was, the smoldering presidential fire he thought he had put out the day before was fanned into flame. On the flight home he wrote Alicia:

> It's been another awful week—agonizing last minute conferences & pressures from everywhere to "announce"; the zero hour of decision, writing the statement, opening the baseball season in Chicago, then Springfield, then Omaha, then N.Y. & now back I hope to 48 hours of peace & serious work over the weekend—then to Dallas on Monday for a full dress foreign affairs speech (not yet written); back just in time for the State Convention where they have threatened to adopt a resolution repudiating my "statement"; declaring me still the "favorite son" & starting up the whole wretched business all over again.

The Dallas speech, based on a draft sent to him by Dorothy Fosdick, was an eloquent defense of Truman's policy in Korea; it also set forth positions on civil rights and offshore oil that he knew would be unpopular in Texas. In the three months remaining before the convention he added to his busy campaign schedule in Illinois trips to Oregon, California, Washington, and Virginia, adding to the speculation that he was really running. The article on Korea that appeared in the April issue of *Foreign Affairs,* although written long before without the presidential race in mind, was cited as additional evidence. On the plane from Portland to Pasadena, he wrote Alicia in Europe: "I thought I had it [the nomination] all settled and for keeps but it seems to be hotter than ever now and I wonder if I have to issue a Gen. Sherman. It's a cocky, distasteful thing to do and I hate to earn a place in the history books by saying I *won't* do something honorable that has come to few people."

Adlai's trip to Virginia was to give the commencement address at Hampden-Sydney College and since it involved a stop in Washington, he told Flanagan to allay political speculation by issuing a press release saying it was for the purpose of discussing with the Atomic Energy Commission the possibility of constructing a billion-dollar atomic energy plant in southern Illinois. On the flight back, he again wrote Alicia, addressing her as "Birdie mine," describing his heavy schedule, the continuing pressures, and repeating, "I hate to say some further words that may look or sound as tho [sic] I deprecate the affair or the duty or whatever it is, and, you're right too, that I might well want to try it four years from now." He also lamented that his own campaign was "bogged down," and that he had not been able to make any summer plans with the boys, adding parenthetically, "Ellen on the rampage in the East I hear." This was almost an understatement.

The day after he returned, he made political speeches in Freeport and Rockford, returning to Springfield shortly before midnight and going directly to the hospital suffering severely from a kidney stone attack. The pain had mounted during the two evenings he had spent with Dorothy Fosdick in Washington and he took to the hospital with him a letter from her expressing concern for his health, urging that he consider making a speech on "freedom of the mind," and in her affectionate concern for both his physical and political troubles, quoting Matthew 26:39: "O my Father, if it be possible, let this cup pass from me: nevertheless, not as I will, but as thou wilt." It was fixed so firmly in his mind that he committed a rare gaucherie in using it in his acceptance speech a few weeks later.

Although he had spent much time at hospitals with mother, father, wife, and others, his own health was so sturdy that a boyhood broken bone had been his most serious physical problem. He was an extremely impatient patient and he remained only three days.

The kidney stone was not the only source of pain. For months, Adlai had been hearing from friends in Washington and New York that Ellen was saying outrageous things about him and their marriage. Arthur Krock had warned him of the damage she was inflicting. Then the *Time* cover story provoked furious outpourings, not only at dinner parties, but in letters to editors in various parts of the country. Some were so irrational they were ignored; but after one especially vicious comment appeared in a Chicago newspaper, her mother, Mrs. Carpenter, called Adlai in desperation asking if she should issue a statement, or if not that, what should she do?

"You must do nothing," Adlai replied, "except to love her."

Awareness that nothing could be done made the prospect of a presidential campaign even less attractive; nor was he encouraged by a letter from Bud Merwin warning him that his own newspaper, *The Pantagraph,* would not support him if he ran for President. He said it was "only fair" to tell him that while they had supported him "enthusiastically" when he ran for governor and would do so again in view of his "splendid" record, the editorial board had agreed unanimously that "there *must* be a change in our national administration," and therefore would support the Republican candidate, whether it was Taft or Eisenhower.

Friends such as Ball and Arvey saw their main task during this period as preventing Adlai from issuing a flat refusal to accept a nomination. Meanwhile, the press was reporting Truman's annoyance with Adlai and let it be known he would support Barkley. Indeed, the White House asked Arvey to persuade Adlai to nominate Barkley, but Adlai declined, saying that he had promised his support to Harriman.

The kidney stone did not relent, and after another commencement address at the John Marshall Law School on Saturday, June 21, he entered the Passavant Hospital in Chicago and the next day underwent surgery for its removal from the left ureter. As he emerged on the twenty-fifth, he diverted reporters' questions with a poem he had written:

> "What could be neater
> "Than to cheat Saint Peter
> "With a nice, clean ureter?"

On the Republican side, the increasingly bitter battle between the Taft and Eisenhower forces culminated in an uproariously contentious convention that on July 11 nominated Eisenhower. Adlai had watched the convention on the television at Bill Flanagan's home. The other, perhaps *the,* major event of the week for Adlai was the departure of Adlai III to join the Marine Corps at Quantico, Virginia.

In the intervening nine days before the opening of the Democratic convention, Adlai alternated between state business and efforts to discourage his nomination. The IVI Draft Stevenson group, down to its last one hundred dollars, had sent out a circular letter to all delegates and alternates saying, "We have no doubt Governor Stevenson, devoted as he is to public service, will respond to the call." Adlai, on July 15, sent a telegram to Walter Johnson, the cochairman and historian who would be the editor of the eight volumes of his papers: "Have just seen circular letter to delegates and am very much disturbed in view of my unwillingness to be a candidate. . . . I am grateful for your goodwill and confidence but my attitude is utterly sincere and I desperately want and intend to stay on this job, with your help I hope." Jack Arvey followed it up with a public rebuke to the committee.

Undeterred, the committee proceeded with efforts to establish a Stevenson for President office at the Conrad Hilton Hotel, the convention headquarters. It wasn't easy. Stevenson was not a candidate and they had no standing with the Democratic National Committee that controlled space allocations. Thanks to a friendly relationship with Conrad Hilton's lawyer, on Wednesday, July 16, they finally obtained a three-room suite at $150 a day and opened what was almost a parody of a campaign headquarters. The only telephone was the house phone.

Volunteers, most of them young people, crowded into the room, many of them making paper badges by hand and hand-painting signs with slogans they made up as they went along, although the favorites were GLADLY FOR ADLAI and then MADLY FOR ADLAI. Enough money was raised to order a thousand buttons saying AMERICA NEEDS STEVENSON FOR PRESIDENT. These were grabbed up instantly, and money was found to order two thousand more, and two days later another two thousand. In the midst of their congested penury, thousands of gladiolas in huge tin tubs were jammed into the rooms; a gift from wholesale gladiola growers. The gladiola-engulfed volunteers finally regained working space by dispatching the flowers to nearby hospitals.

The day the office opened, the Alsops in their nationally syndicated column announced that "the movement to draft Governor Adlai Stevenson of Illinois is now dead," and Marquis Childs in his column agreed that "Gov. Adlai Stevenson has at last succeeded in eliminating himself." As a consequence of a steady drumbeat of statements, encouragement of rumors, and a helpful roundup every day of press coverage across the country on Adlai, news-hungry reporters in increasing numbers dropped in. By the time the convention opened on Monday, not only scores of reporters but nearly three hundred delegates had come to see what was happening.

There were wholly unexpected visitors on Saturday. Sixteen-year-old John Fell, wearing one of the committee's buttons, walked in with a friend. He was quickly whisked out of sight of reporters and asked what he was doing there. He replied that he wanted to see the people who were trying to make his father do what he said he did not wish to do. He was asked several more questions, with a few interruptions from his companion extolling the virtues of Senator Taft. As soon as the hallway was clear of reporters, he was taken to the elevator. But, to Walter Johnson's consternation, John Fell was back that afternoon with his brother Borden and three of Borden's classmates from Harvard. Borden said John Fell had told him of his visit and he wanted to hear firsthand some of the things that had been explained and to ask what Johnson described as "penetrating questions, mostly about the elements that create a convention trend. . . . Then we explained that if reporters and photographers saw Stevenson's sons at our headquarters, it might give rise to charges that we were a front organization for their father. We asked them, therefore, not to come back."

"You mean never come back to the Hilton Hotel?" Borden exclaimed in disappointment. Johnson replied, "You can visit the Harriman, Kefauver, Russell and Kerr headquarters as much as you like, but never come back to the fifteenth floor." Whereupon they were taken down the back stairs to the thirteenth floor where another headquarters was located. After the nomination, when Adlai did pay the Draft Stevenson Committee a visit he had one of its buttons in his pocket. When asked how he got it, he replied: "I believe Borden and John Fell preceded me here!"

Adlai had arrived in Chicago on Friday, before the Monday, July 21, opening of the convention at which he was a delegate and, as governor, had been scheduled to give the customary welcoming address. He and members of his staff moved into the Blair family's house at 1416 Astor Street, and the quiet, sedate street soon became a shambles as television crews, reporters, and photographers moved in, trampling lawns and hedges, stringing bright lights, wires, and television cables, even parking television trucks in the narrow street and setting up temporary telephone booths.

Ellen lived nearby, and Scotty Reston and his wife, who had enjoyed her grace and skill as a hostess during the UN meetings in London, called on her. He recalls:

> She talked about Stevenson in the most outrageous way— said he was not qualified for the presidency, almost suggested he wasn't a very good husband, was bitter about what agony he had brought on her by his political career, and she was being followed everywhere. She took a pistol out of her purse and said, "I feel I have to keep this with me wherever I go." Finally I said, "It's a good thing you're talking to a guy from the New York *Times* and not the New York *News*. I'm saying this not as a reporter but as a citizen—I think it's dreadful to talk about him this way to any reporter."

For the first time in twenty years the Democrats would be nominating someone who was not an incumbent President. The rancorous disorder of the Republican convention two weeks earlier now was superseded by almost total confusion. With 1,230 votes in the convention, 615½ were needed to nominate. As the delegates began arriving, it appeared that Kefauver had 257½ pledged to him; Russell, 161½; Harriman, 112½; Kerr, 45½; and Stevenson, 41½. Other candidates and favorite sons had 231½. This count did not reflect the rising importance of the Barkley candidacy, with its White House support and its appeal to moderate southerners and big-city bosses who did not like either Kefauver or Harriman.

On Sunday the state delegations began to caucus. Adlai attended the Illinois caucus as a delegate and asked them to "abide by my wishes not to nominate me, nor to vote for me if I should be nominated." Arvey told the caucus he wanted to do whatever Adlai wanted and therefore would respect his request that Illinois not nominate him. He then added that should Adlai's name be placed in nomination, he would personally vote for him on the first ballot.

"When that happens," he said, "I consider I am relieved from any promise I made not to further his candidacy. He can not take away from me my right to cast my ballot as I wish to cast it. If I am convinced that a vote for Stevenson is a vote to unify the party and win the election in November, I will vote for him." Arvey reports that notwithstanding his declaration, Adlai came to his apartment after the caucus and said, "You got me into this, now get me out!"

At the same time, a crucial meeting of the Pennsylvania delegation was in progress. With powerful leadership in Mayor David Lawrence of Pittsburgh, James A. Finnegan, president of the Philadelphia City Council, and former Senator Francis J. Myers, the delegation was leaning strongly in Adlai's direction but they wanted to be certain he would accept. Some of them had declared for Eisenhower four years earlier and did not want, as they said, to be "left naked as a jay-bird once again."

The Draft Stevenson Committee had been trying to reassure them that it would be out of character for Adlai to refuse, and it also produced an answer to a related worry: Would anyone place him in nomination since his home state had been pledged to refrain? Archibald Alexander of New Jersey, former undersecretary of the army who had known Adlai in Washington, had come to Johnson and said if no better-known leader would place Adlai's name before the convention, he would. After Adlai heard of it and publicly asked him not to, Alexander reaffirmed his willingness to do so.

Confident of the Pennsylvania delegation, the Draft Committee leadership started trying to organize a late-Sunday meeting with delegation leaders from states where they knew the strongest support for Adlai existed—Pennsylvania, New Jersey, Indiana, and Kansas—to plan the handling of the draft movement on the convention floor. At the meeting, it was quickly agreed that Senator Myers, former majority whip of the Senate, would be the floor leader. Governor Henry Schricker of Indiana was the choice to make the nominating speech, and later, when Delaware indicated its intention to get in ahead of Indiana, an agreement was negotiated in which Governor Schricker and Governor Elbert N. Carvel of Delaware would divide the time.

When the convention met for its first session at noon on Monday, there was on the seat of every delegate a copy of *Life* magazine carrying a cover story on Adlai. For weeks, Adlai had been expressing misgivings to Flanagan about the entire project. "If this comes out before the convention it will look like I'm really a candidate." Flanagan had argued that the piece would not make much difference on the outcome of the convention, and Adlai had finally agreed to go ahead. Flanagan had taken full advantage of the opportunity. Even so, opening sessions are supposed to be routine, with the customary unwelcome welcoming speech the main item on the agenda.

But this time there was an unprecedented difference. Instead of a sparsely occupied hall, the enormous Amphitheater at the Stockyards was packed and when Chairman Frank McKinney introduced Adlai an uproar erupted. The Alsops commented: "'Spontaneous demonstrations,' with cheer leaders, organizers and demonstrators paid $5 an hour, have become a tiresome joke at our quadrennial political rallies. This demonstration for Stevenson was wholly unorganized. It made less noise than the paid-for type. But it expressed real feeling." And it went on for at least ten minutes, with delegates applauding, marching, waving state signs and a few of the volunteers hand-painted ones, and shouting, "We want Stevenson."

The speech, only fourteen minutes long, virtually decided the nomination that was to occur, after much maneuvering and a bruising battle over civil rights, on the third ballot four days later.

"I thought I came here to greet you, not you to greet me," he began in acknowledgment of the extraordinary demonstration, and then after welcoming remarks, continued:

> Here, my friends, on the prairies of Illinois and of the Middle West we can see a long way in all directions. We look to East, to West, to North and South. Our commerce, our ideas, come and go in all directions.
>
> Here there are no barriers, no defenses, to ideas and to aspirations. We want none; we want no shackles on the mind or the spirit, no rigid patterns of thought, and no iron conformity. We want only the faith and conviction that triumph in free and fair contest.
>
> As a Democrat perhaps you will permit me to remind you

that until four years ago the people of Illinois had chosen but three Democratic Governors in a hundred years. One was John Peter Altgeld, whom the great Illinois poet, Vachel Lindsay called the Eagle Forgotten. He was an immigrant. One was Edward F. Dunne, whose parents came from the old sod of Ireland, and last was Henry Horner, but one generation removed from Germany. John Peter Altgeld, my friends, was a Protestant, Governor Dunne was a Catholic, Henry Horner was a Jew.

And that, my friends, is the American story written by the Democratic party here on the prairies of Illinois.

He then recalled that Franklin D. Roosevelt had been nominated in that same hall twenty years before and had guided the country through depression, war, and toward the hope of peace in the United Nations. He jibed at Republican opposition over the years and at the battle that had taken place two weeks before.

Where we have erred, let there be no denial; and where we have wronged the public trust, let there be no excuses. Self-criticism is the secret weapon of democracy, and candor and confession are good for the political soul. But we will never appease, we will never apologize for our leadership of the great events of this critical century all the way from Woodrow Wilson to Harry Truman!

Rather will we glory in these imperishable pages of our country's chronicle. But a great record of past achievement is not enough. There can be no complacency, perhaps for years to come. We dare not just look back to great yesterdays. We must look forward to great tomorrows.

What counts now is not just what we are *against,* but when we are *for. Who* leads us is less important than *what* leads us—what convictions, what courage, what faith—win or lose. A man doesn't save a century, or a civilization, but a militant party wedded to a principle can. . . .

What America needs and the world wants is not bombast, abuse and double talk, but a somber message of firm faith and confidence. St. Francis said: "Where there is patience and humility, there is neither anger nor worry." That might well be our text.

And let us remember we are not meeting here alone. All the world is watching and listening to what we say, what we do and how we behave. So let us give them a demonstration of democracy in action at its best. . . .

Thus can the people's party reassure the people and vindicate and strengthen the forces of democracy throughout the world.

The speech had been interrupted twenty-seven times with applause and cries of "We want Stevenson." At its close, the entire hall rose in a roar. On the platform, Arvey told a neighbor, "Nobody will believe me when I tell them this is all spontaneous. He asked me not to have anything like this and I kept my word."

Outside the hall, events were adding to the move toward Stevenson. That morning Vice President Alben Barkley had ignored the advice of President Truman to meet with labor leaders one at a time and had met with sixteen of them at breakfast to enlist their support. Unanimously, they refused, and that afternoon he withdrew.

This left Truman without a candidate and Stevenson as the only middle-of-the-road possibility. A tense battle was developing between the mainly northern liberal wing of the party and the southern delegates focused on the "loyalty pledge" designed to commit the southern states to support the choice of the convention. Texas, Mississippi, South Carolina, Louisiana, and Virginia were particular objects of attack. Adlai was strongly opposed to doing anything that would drive the South out of the party, and he was increasingly concerned that Harriman, to whom he had pledged his support, had become a "disunity" candidate and thus diminished his chances to be nominated.

By Tuesday, he knew that only a flat refusal to accept could prevent his nomination. Reston wrote that he "was just a leaf on a rising stream." He remained in his State of Illinois Building office, meeting callers with the same denials, but now beginning to think about the necessity of an acceptance speech.

Tuesday also conferred miracles on the Draft Stevenson Committee headquarters. Their three rooms suddenly became fourteen. "The first thing I noticed Tuesday morning," Al Weisman remembered, "was the presence of a switchboard and everybody ordering room service. That is when I realized we'd made it. . . . Jack Kennedy and Sid Yates were in our room. So were the Shrivers. They were buttonholing delegates. We were big time."

Who picked up some of the expenses is still obscure. When the convention was over, the Draft Committee's records showed that it had raised a total of $20,300.91 and had $507.13 left to contribute to the Stevenson presidential campaign. Despite the Spartan regime that prevailed most of the time, some bills must have been sent elsewhere.

On Thursday, before the nominating process began, Adlai thought it was an essential courtesy to call President Truman, whom he knew had been supporting Barkley. But instead, the call infuriated the President and highlighted their different temperaments. Truman later wrote: "He said that he called to ask whether it would embarrass me if he allowed his name to be placed in nomination. I replied with a show of exasperation and some rather vigorous words and concluded by saying to Stevenson, 'I have been trying since January to get you to say that. Why would it embarrass me?'"

Much of Truman's annoyance sprang from awareness that even though he was President, he had lost control over the convention. His announced candidate, Barkley, had withdrawn and it was clear that Adlai was going to be nominated as his own man rather than as the President's choice. He could not help but resent the fact that Adlai, on Tuesday afternoon, had declined an invitation to dinner. Adlai explained that by dining with the President it might seem he was promoting his candidacy, in spite of all that he had been saying. To the extent that Truman's perceived influence was increased, his own would be reduced. Thereafter, despite all the surface manifestations of support, the relationship went steadily downhill.

Tuesday afternoon in *The Christian Science Monitor,* Roscoe Drummond had reported:

> This convention is jelling so speedily, the prospect is that President Truman will have no opportunity to determine the presidential nominee—even if he could. . . . They say that Mr. Truman, who can recognize a trend as well as the next politician, is ready to give his favor to Governor Stevenson. The view here is that if he does not do so shortly, he will be waving at a bandwagon that has passed by.

When Governor Schricker concluded the first half of the dual nominating speech, the convention "really went wild," according to *The New York Times,* and Governor Carvel had to deliver his half to a noisy, milling throng carrying placards around the floor. On the first ballot, the tally was Kefauver, 340; Stevenson, 273; Russell, 268; Harriman, 123½; Kerr, 65; Barkley, 48½; and others 111, with 1 not voting. As many of the pledged delegates were committed for two ballots, not much change was expected as the second ballot commenced immediately about 4:30. Kefauver and Russell gained a few, Harriman held steady, Kerr dropped out, Barkley gained 30, and Adlai 50.

During the dinner-hour adjournment, Harriman, encouraged by President Truman, decided to withdraw and throw his support to Adlai. When the third ballot began at 9:07, Governor Paul Dever of Massachusetts joined Harriman in withdrawing his own name and switching to Adlai. At that point, Senator Kefauver walked to the rostrum arm in arm with Senator Douglas, thus signaling his intention to withdraw in Adlai's favor. Despite the swelling cheers in the hall, Speaker of the House Sam Rayburn, who was presiding and was angry at Kefauver, refused to recognize him and grimly continued the roll call while Kefauver and Douglas sat helplessly on the platform. At the end of the roll call at 12:18 A.M., Adlai was 2½ votes short of a majority and only then did Rayburn recognize Kefauver. It was over. Senator Russell joined Kefauver in conceding to Adlai, and Orville Freeman of Minnesota moved the nomination be made unanimous.

A fascinating and unique chapter in American political history had reached its climax. Never had such a reluctant candidate been chosen by a convention that no one controlled. Alistair Cooke summarized its significance in these terms: "Stevenson emerged in triumph and in singularly happy independence. He owes nothing to the South, nothing to the Northern liberals. He is his own man."

Why had he been so reluctant? George Ball has provided the fullest explanation:

> Largely, I think, because he thought he could not beat Eisenhower. If it had been clear that Taft would be nominated, he would have taken a different line. He could beat Taft and would feel a duty to do so, since Taft symbolized the Middle-West isolationism against which he had long fought. But Eisenhower was an internationalist and, in Stevenson's view, a decent man who might improve the moral tone of the White House. He was affronted by the indifferent morality and untidiness of the Truman Administration and was frantic to distance himself from Truman and the messiness, which, as he repeatedly told me, proved that the Democrats had been too long in power. "Twenty years," he said, "is enough for either party." He felt deeply sentimental about Illinois, and he abhorred a partisan struggle that might set him at cross purposes with his Lake Forest friends, who had voted for him as a state governor but would vote Republican in a national election. In addition, he lived under the persistent threat of personal attack, since Ellen, now divorced, was capable of unlimited malice. Finally, he was repelled by the stultifying routine of campaigning . . . [and] he loathed the whole process of political fund raising.

Why had he nonetheless been nominated? Basically, because he was clearly the strongest candidate the Democrats could run against Eisenhower. Academics and young professionals were flocking to him in numbers that fascinated the professional politicians. Moreover, he was acceptable to moderate southerners and minimized the risk of a split in the party; he had strong support in liberal northern states, and even if Eisenhower won, his vote-getting ability would certainly help reduce losses in Congress and in statehouses. If he couldn't win, he could at least help the party cut its losses. To amateurs and pros, to northerners and southerners, to liberals and conservatives, but not to himself, he was at that moment the party's indispensable man.

CHAPTER NINE
"Let's Talk Sense"

IT WAS 1:45 A.M. when President Truman and Adlai strode across the rostrum of the convention hall, with the President, grinning, holding Adlai's hand up in a victory sign. Adlai had not left the Blairs' house far across town until the balloting had finished. Astor Street was so packed it had been difficult to move the car, and many of the streets along the way were lined with people. By the time they arrived at the Amphitheater, the exhausted delegates had become restive. They cheered the President and the nominee, then quieted down as Adlai cleared his throat nervously, fiddled with his glasses and his manuscript while trying to adjust his eyes to the blinding light. Then they rose to their feet, shouting, as his first sentence answered the question many of them had been asking all spring and most of them had been asking all week:

> I accept your nomination—and your program.
> . . . I have not sought the honor you have done me. I *could* not seek it because I aspired to another office, which was the full measure of my ambition. . . .
> I *would* not seek your nomination for the Presidency because the burdens of that office stagger the imagination. Its potential for good or evil now and in the years of our lives smothers exultation and converts vanity to prayer.

In one of his rare lapses of taste he then inserted the passage he had saved from Dorothy Fosdick's letter, not appreciating that he seemed to be comparing his situation with that of Jesus shortly before the Crucifixion:

> I have asked the Merciful Father—the Father of us all—to let this cup pass from me. But from such dread responsibility one does not shrink in fear, in self-interest, or in false humility.
> So, "If this cup may not pass from me, except I drink it, Thy will be done."

Then, after paying his respects to party stalwarts and to the delegates, he turned, in a tone of deep conviction, to what he saw as the major issues. Millions of late-night viewers and the millions more who heard broadcasts the next morning repeating the address recognized a new and stirring voice on the political scene.

> You will hear many thoughtful and sincere people express concern about the continuation of one party in power for twenty years. I don't belittle this attitude. But change for the sake of change has no absolute merit in itself. If our greatest hazard is preservation of the values of Western civilization, in our self-interest alone, if you please, is it the part of wisdom to change for the sake of change to a party with a split personality; to a leader, whom we all respect, but who has been called upon to minister to a hopeless case of political schizophrenia?
> If the fear is corruption in official position, do you believe with Charles Evans Hughes that guilt is personal and knows no party? Do you doubt the power of any political leader, if he has the will to do so, to set his own house in order without his neighbors having to burn it down?
> What does concern me, in common with thinking partisans of both parties, is not just winning the election, but how it is won, how well we can take advantage of this great quadrennial opportunity to debate issues sensibly and soberly. I hope and pray that we Democrats, win or lose, can campaign not as a crusade to exterminate the opposing party, as our opponents seem to prefer, but as a great opportunity to educate and elevate a people whose destiny is leadership, not alone of a rich and prosperous, contented country as in the past, but of a world in ferment.
> And, my friends, more important than winning the election is governing the nation. That is the test of a political party—the acid, final test. When the tumult and the shouting die, when the bands are gone and the lights are dimmed, there is the stark reality of responsibility in an hour of history haunted with those

gaunt, grim specters of strife, dissension and materialism at home, and ruthless, inscrutable and hostile power abroad.

The ordeal of the twentieth century—the bloodiest, most turbulent era of the Christian age—is far from over. Sacrifice, patience, understanding and implacable purpose may be our lot for years to come. Let's face it. Let's talk sense to the American people. Let's tell them the truth, that there are no gains without pains, that we are now on the eve of great decisions, not easy decisions, like resistance when you are attacked, but a long, patient, costly struggle which alone can assure triumph over the great enemies of man—war, poverty and tyranny—and the assaults upon human dignity which are the most grievous consequences of each.

Let's tell them that the victory to be won in the twentieth century, this portal to the Golden Age, mocks the pretensions of individual acumen and ingenuity. For it is a citadel guarded by thick walls of ignorance and of mistrust which do not fall before the trumpets' blast or the politicians' imprecations or even a general's baton. They are, my friends, walls that must be directly stormed by the hosts of courage, of morality and of vision, standing shoulder to shoulder, unafraid of ugly truth, contemptuous of lies, half truths, circuses and demagoguery. . . .

That I think, is our ancient mission. Where we have deserted it we have failed. With your help there will be no desertion now. Better we lose the election than mislead the people; and better we lose than misgovern the people. Help me to do the job in this autumn of conflict and of campaign; help me to do the job in these years of darkness, doubt and of crisis which stretch beyond the horizon of tonight's happy vision, and we will justify our glorious past with the loyalty of silent millions who look to us for compassion, for understanding and for honest purpose. Thus we will serve our great tradition greatly.

On this high note of hope, belief, and purpose Stevenson embarked on a campaign that was to become one of the most contentious, mean-spirited, and discreditable in modern American history.

Despite the hour, Adlai and President Truman moved to a small room behind the speaker's platform, where Speaker Sam Rayburn and Democratic National Committee Chairman Frank McKinney joined them to decide on a candidate for Vice President. The President suggested Senator John Sparkman of Alabama. Stevenson's liberal credentials seemed adequate to win the allegiance of the northern liberal supporters of Kefauver and Harriman, so a candidate that would attract southern support was desirable. Although Sparkman voted as a southerner on civil rights issues, his record on other issues was attractive to the liberals and he had few enemies. As soon as it was agreed that anyone who had been a presidential contender should be eliminated (which disposed of Kefauver, whom both Truman and Rayburn disliked heartily), Sparkman became the logical choice.

Presented to the convention as Adlai's choice on Saturday morning, Sparkman was nominated by acclamation; and after an appearance by the two candidates, the convention adjourned early Saturday afternoon. Earlier that morning, before going to bed, President Truman had written in longhand a note that he had delivered by messenger to Adlai saying:

> *Last night was one of the most remarkable I've spent in all my sixty eight years. . . . You have the ancestral, political and educational background to do a most wonderful job. If it is worth anything to you, you have my wholehearted support and cooperation. When the noise and the shouting are over, I hope you may be able to come to Washington for a discussion of what is before you.*

Adlai's candidacy was unprecedented not only in the way it happened but also, and perhaps more fatefully, in the total lack of preparation for it. While Eisenhower had an exceptionally talented and well-financed campaign organization working for him for months in advance of the convention, Adlai emerged from the Democratic convention not even at the goal line, but well behind it. Most of what had been put in place for the gubernatorial campaign now was needed for the candidacy of Lieutenant Governor Sherwood Dixon. What was worse, Adlai virtually banished from his presidential campaign the leaders of the Stevenson for President group. He felt that to take them in would feed the suspicion that he had conspired in their efforts to get him nominated. Some finally found low-profile functions in the Volunteers for Stevenson, but none ever became key figures. In cutting them out, he deprived himself of valuable talent and what little organization in support of his presidential candidacy existed. This self-denial was even more serious since he was determined to distance himself from the Democratic National Committee in Washington.

Thus, less than one hundred days before election, a little-known governor of Illinois, together with his personal staff and a few friends, no organization and no funds, prepared to challenge one of the best-known men in the world, a national hero to a degree rare in our history, who was backed by able people with a well-planned and generously financed campaign. Those familiar with the situation let excitement obscure their doubts as they organized an effort that, in the light of the multimillion-dollar, months and years-long campaigns of the present, seems born of the absurd.

Arriving back in Springfield on Sunday, Adlai found some twenty-five thousand people there to greet him with an ovation that brought tears to his eyes, in a rare public display of emotion, as he tried to tell them how much the years in Springfield had meant to him. "I wanted four more."

The depth of his feeling needed an outlet. On Monday, as the clock in his basement office neared midnight, Bill Blair knocked at the door.

"The caretaker has been alerted," Blair told him.

"Thanks, Bill," Adlai said quietly. "Don't let a hint of this get out, will you?"

"Not a hint," Blair replied.

Adlai then slipped out a side door of the mansion and down a dark side street to the corner of Eighth and Market where, after a brief pause to make certain he had not been followed, he hurried up the short walk to Lincoln's home. The caretaker admitted him and left. For an hour he sat alone in Lincoln's rocking chair. Beyond admitting to a few friends years later that the incident occurred, he never discussed why he did it or what he felt other than to say that on the walk back to the mansion on the dark street he felt a deep calm about the task that lay before him.

He was still governor and he had to make sure that the business of the state went forward. Since McGowan and Blair would be involved in the presidential campaign, he asked the newly arrived twenty-six-year-old Newton Minow to "stand watch" on state matters and alert him whenever there was something that required his personal attention. His confidence in the young Supreme Court law clerk was well placed; he performed admirably in the remaining months of the governor's term, including at least one serious crisis.

Meanwhile, reporters from all over the country and abroad were flocking to Springfield to learn more about this new national political figure. Consequently, a press conference was set for Wednesday. It began with jokes about the ill-fitting suit he was wearing. He explained that it had been sent to him from Spain and that the trousers were about four inches too long. One reporter said he was unaware that Sears, Roebuck had a store in Spain. Another asked who sent it. Adlai responded that it was a gift from an artist named Joseph Allsworthy. One asked if Mr. Allsworthy was a friend, another if he were an enemy. Adlai replied, "He's a friend—or was." Thus began a basically friendly, spontaneous relationship with reporters covering the campaign that survived many strains arising not only from organizational inefficiencies, but also pressures from publishers who were overwhelmingly for Eisenhower, and his own complaints later in the campaign about the "one-party press in a two-party country."

He dealt easily with questions about the governorship and his support of Lieutenant Governor Dixon as his successor. Many of the questions about campaign plans could be diverted as being premature. When asked if he were still a reluctant candidate, he replied, "No, I get more aggressive all the time." When asked if he thought his divorce would be a political liability, he replied, "I can't comment on that. I don't know. I wouldn't have thought that it would be." He was, of course, very wrong.

Surprisingly, when asked what campaign function would be filled by former Senator Francis Myers, who had been the floor manager for his nomination, he blankly asked, "Who?" He had even more difficulty when he was asked if he would retain Frank McKinney as national chairman, what President Truman's role would be, and where he would base his campaign. He was already resolved not to have McKinney, to maintain his distance from the White House and the Truman staff at the Democratic National Committee, and to make Springfield his headquarters; but the sensitivities involved required careful handling and there had not been time to think that through. The reporters sensed this and repeatedly came back to questions that might involve differences between him and the President—the Taft-Hartley Act, the administration's national health program, FEPC, and civil rights.

Adlai had settled quickly on Wilson Wyatt as his "personal campaign manager." Wyatt, who was legal counsel to Adlai's friend, Barry Bingham, and to the *Louisville Courier-Journal,* had known Carl McGowan since their service in Washington during the war. He had been elected mayor of Louisville in 1941 at the age of thirty-five and President Truman, in 1946, had appointed him the head of the National Housing Agency. A year later, he helped found and was the first chairman of Americans for Democratic Action; the following two years he was national chairman of the Democratic party's Jefferson-Jackson Day dinners. He had gone to the Chicago convention with a Kentucky delegation favoring Barkley, but had turned to Adlai when Barkley's candidacy appeared hopeless.

Soon after getting back to Springfield, Adlai called Dutch Smith, who was on vacation in Canada, to ask him if he would take the lead in setting up an organization for independent voters. Smith promptly agreed, as he did with almost anything Adlai asked of him.

The difficult problem was the chairmanship of the Democratic National Committee. President Truman was determined to have McKinney continue. Adlai was equally determined to have his own man and the decision was his to make. Ever since 1928 when the Democrats had failed to elect a Catholic as President, the party had felt obliged to have a Catholic as national chairman. Now, Catholic disapproval of Adlai's divorce made it even more necessary to have a Catholic in the post. At one point, in frustration, Adlai exclaimed, "Goddammit, can't anyone think of a Catholic?" McGowan had thought of Jim Doyle, once law clerk to James F. Byrnes on the Supreme Court and now a leading Democrat in Wisconsin (later, like Wyatt, head of the ADA), but could not reach him on the phone. In the midst of this, Adlai said, "I was lying awake last night and thought of Steve Mitchell. Mitchell is a Catholic, loyal to me, and is an alternative to McKinney."

Mitchell, of course, had been one of the original leaders of the Stevenson-for-senator/governor movement; but he had never won the support of Arvey, who was a member of the Democratic National Committee that would have to elect the chairman, and do so over the opposition of the President. Arvey was in Beverly Hills when he received a call from Adlai saying he wanted Mitchell as national chairman.

"My God, you can't do that," Arvey exclaimed. "He's had no political experience. He doesn't know one national committeeman. The chairman's job is to get the national committeemen to work for you. . . . If you get rid of McKinney, you'll displease Harry Truman and why break up a winning team?"

"I've already done it," Adlai declared.

"Then why call me?"

"Because I want you to call a meeting of the National Committee and I want you to nominate him," Adlai replied.

"You are asking me to do something that I don't agree with." But Adlai insisted, and finally, recalling all the times he had been referred to in the press as Adlai's "boss," he acceded by saying, "Okay, BOSS!"

"So I called McKinney, I had him call a meeting of the Executive Committee, and we did it," Arvey reported, adding, "I wasn't consulted: I was told."

Before the meeting took place, however, a tense internal battle had been waged. On Wednesday, August 6, during a call to President Truman accepting his invitation to lunch the following Tuesday, Adlai informed the President he had found a Catholic to replace McKinney. The President bluntly expressed what Adlai described to Mitchell as "a very definitely negative attitude." On Friday, Adlai wrote Sparkman telling him of his decision. That same day, Wyatt obtained the support of four members of the Executive Committee. Adlai talked to David Lawrence in Pittsburgh, and with these commitments, announced his choice that night. He wanted the decision to be known before McKinney's arrival in Springfield on Sunday. But the struggle did not stop there. After telling Adlai he was "very anxious" to keep the job, McKinney called the President and either he or a spokesman telephoned Adlai in an earnest but futile effort to get him to change his mind. The President apparently forgot this when he later called Adlai indecisive.

Thus was made one of the most important and controversial decisions of the campaign. The tensions that the two men had kept submerged now were in open view and would loom larger.

"Stevenson's attitude toward the President he hoped to succeed was a mystery to me," President Truman wrote in his *Memoirs*.

. . . The first mistake he made was to fire the Chairman of the Democratic National Committee and to move his campaign headquarters to Springfield, Illinois, giving the impression that he was seeking to disassociate himself from the administration in Washington, and perhaps from me. How Stevenson hoped he could persuade the American voters to maintain the Democratic party in power while seeming to disown powerful elements of it, I do not know.

Adlai's sense of the voters' concerns that prompted his decision, however, was accurate. An extensive study by the University of Michigan Survey Research Center, published later under the title, *The American Voter,* found that the public was strongly affected by the highly publicized revelations of irregularities and favoritism. The moral fiber of the Truman administration was in serious question. Indeed, Elmo Roper, in his polling activities, found that many voters feared that Stevenson, no matter how fresh or appealing he was as an individual, was a captive of party bosses they distrusted. So, the effort to give the National Committee and the campaign staff a "new look" was well conceived even though it entailed controversy and, with headquarters in both Washington and Springfield, immensely crippling administrative difficulties and confusion.

The confusion quickly produced an avoidable mistake that further exacerbated the relations with the President. The editor of the *Oregon Journal* in Portland wrote Adlai after the convention asking him if he could "really clean up the mess in Washington." Carl McGowan prepared the reply and neglected to notice that quotation marks had not been placed around the "mess in Washington" phrase to identify it as a quote from the incoming letter. Consequently, Adlai's reply read: "As to whether I can clean up the mess in Washington, I would bespeak the careful scrutiny of what I inherited in Illinois and what has been accomplished in three years." Republicans quickly seized on the letter as an admission that the Truman administration was riddled with corruption. Adlai called Truman to explain and apologize; the conversation was civil but another level of resentment was added.

Wyatt engaged in understatement when he wrote in his memoirs, *Whistle Stops:* "Almost everything had to be improvised as there had been no preparation for a candidacy that had not been sought. There was no treasury, there were no position papers, there was no staff. Unlike other presidential campaigns, it all had to be created from scratch." Given the circumstances, it is astonishing that the operation worked as well as it did; the answer, of course, is to be found in the quality of the people who rushed to give their support.

Adlai's immediate staff consisted of McGowan, Blair, Carol Evans, and Margaret Munn, joined quickly by Wyatt and shortly by George Ball. Bill Flanagan was taken off the state payroll to function as press secretary, but never was fully accepted as a part of the inner circle. From this nucleus, an organization of sorts began to take shape.

Wyatt first asked Dick Nelson, who was national president of the Young Democrats, to go off the state payroll and become an aide. He then asked Clayton Fritchey, who was on President Truman's staff, to join him in Springfield. Fritchey had been editor of the *New Orleans Item,* managing editor of the *Baltimore Post,* and had won a Pulitzer Prize while reporting for the *Cleveland Press.* He had come to Washington in 1950 as an assistant to General George C. Marshall, who was then secretary of defense. Fritchey soon recruited Phil Stern, then legislative assistant to Congressman (later Senator) Henry M. Jackson, who had also worked for Senator Paul Douglas. Victor Sholis, director of a Louisville radio and television station, former Chicago newspaperman, and assistant to Harry Hopkins; together with Louis G. Cowan, a Chicagoan who was to become president of the Columbia Broadcasting System, were the campaign specialists in their fields. For scheduling, Adlai obtained the help of Neale Roache, a thirty-nine-year-old from the Democratic National Committee who had worked with Wyatt on the Jefferson-Jackson Day dinners. For this critical function, the help of James Lanigan from Governor Harriman's staff, and Secretary of Interior Oscar Chapman also were enlisted.

As letters flooded in after the convention, Don Hyndman at the capitol tried to handle them, but was soon swamped. Wyatt brought out Charles Brewton from the staff of Senator Lister Hill. He and another man rented a room at the Leland Hotel and started rescuing letters from important figures offering help. Brewton, who had been handling political mail for years, said he had never seen letters so fervent, so sensible, or so touching.

To Carl McGowan fell the primary responsibility of recruiting those whose unenviable task was to produce speeches for a candidate determined to write his own. The result was probably the most remarkable assemblage of writing talent ever brought together for a political campaign. Incongruously housed on the third floor of the Springfield Elks Club, at least four Pulitzer Prize winners were at work virtually all the time amid the ebb and flow of ideas, rhetoric, and people. Curiously, Adlai himself recruited the man with whom he probably had the greatest disagreement.

Arthur Schlesinger, Jr., then a thirty-four-year-old Pulitzer Prize–winning historian at Harvard, and the first to arrive, thought Adlai was the most conservative Democratic candidate since John W. Davis. He believed Adlai put too much weight on wooing the independent voter, was too sympathetic to the southern viewpoint, and not sufficiently committed to civil rights, labor, or to the achievements of the Truman administration. He also thought Adlai's style was too "complex and philosophic." Nevertheless, he was probably the most effective and productive member of an extraordinary group.

David Bell, a tall, lanky thirty-three-year-old was the sole recruit from the White House staff, where he had served since 1947 after two years at the Bureau of the Budget. He was later to be an administrator of foreign aid, a vice president of the Ford Foundation and head of the Littauer School at Harvard. Dorothy Fosdick had suggested Bob Tufts, an economics professor at Oberlin who had worked with her on the Policy Planning Staff of the State Department and in the Office of Strategic Services. Willard Wirtz, at forty, was the oldest of the core group and the main link to McGowan and Adlai.

Other major "Elks Club" figures were John Kenneth Galbraith, Harvard economist and later John F. Kennedy's ambassador to India; John Fischer, editor of *Harper's* magazine; Bernard De Voto, historian and conservationist; Herbert Agar of the *Louisville Courier-Journal;* Eric Hodgins, an editor of *Fortune;* David Cohn, a well-known southern writer and associate of Senator William Fulbright; Sydney Hyman, a Washington correspondent and expert in Jewish affairs; Bill Reddig, editor of the Olathe, Kansas, newspaper and formerly literary editor of the *Kansas City Star;* and John Bartlow Martin.

Temperaments ranged as widely as the talents, but the group worked together remarkably well in spite of the lack of facilities and, even more important, lack of sleep. As many as ten people at a time occupied the big bare room with a long table down the middle for the secretaries and desks facing the wall for the writers. Four adjoining bedrooms often were occupied in shifts as work went on without regard to the clock. The first to collapse from overwork was Dave Bell. After a few days in the hospital, he returned to work, and that day Bill Reddig collapsed. Arthur Schlesinger had to be hospitalized briefly for a neglected knee infection. Later, in Philadelphia, Bob Tufts collapsed from overwork and had to be left behind.

The intensity of their dedication was even more amazing in view of their lack of direct contact with the candidate. A topic would be assigned, a draft prepared, debated, rewritten, passed on to McGowan, who would sometimes return it for revision, or do some rewriting himself, and then on to Adlai, who nearly always revised further. It was almost impossible to say who had written a speech, and often possible to say that Adlai had because his unmistakable stamp was nearly always there. Rarely, if ever, has such abundant literary talent worked so hard for so little recognition.

The sparse facilities of the Elks Club were all too typical of the physical arrangements that prevailed in Springfield. On returning from Chicago, Adlai had asked Ed Day to rent a house for campaign headquarters. "I want it small; nothing gaudy," he said. As Adlai went through the red brick house that Day had found two blocks from the mansion, he said, "These fellows we are bringing out from the East can sleep upstairs—it'll save hotel bills. They can eat here too." Then, as an afterthought, he said, "Maybe we should get an extra telephone."

Within a few weeks nearly the entire house had been taken over for Bill Flanagan's press operation alone and it was still so inadequate that a press room had to be set up in the ballroom of the Leland Hotel. In an effort to achieve some coordination, Flanagan had a switchboard installed in the kitchen of his small home, but he never did succeed in stilling the grumbling of the reporters accustomed to far better working conditions. The sign identifying this as STEVENSON CAMPAIGN HEADQUARTERS was so small—fifteen by twenty-five inches—that many missed it, but it had been made in accordance with Adlai's instructions. Wyatt still has it.

Minow slept in McGowan's house and worked in McGowan's office. Others worked on the corners of other desks in the basement of the mansion. Two floors of the Leland Hotel and additional rooms in the Abraham Lincoln and St. Nicholas hotels had to be added. With the waves of reporters, politicians, and public figures who poured in, downtown Springfield took on attributes of a refugee camp as hotel rooms were always in short supply. One day, Dick Nelson went to the airport to meet Walter Reuther of the United Auto Workers and found eight other important people arriving at the same time. Some of the more self-important were unforgiving of the lack of appropriate accommodations; others were amused and even exhilarated by what George Ball called the "ebullience" that marked the situation. Neither Adlai nor those around him had any idea of how big and complex an operation they had been plunged into.

In addition to the campaign headquarters in Springfield and the Democratic National Committee in Washington, there was the Volunteers for Stevenson, operating in virtual autonomy in Chicago. Dutch Smith and Jane Dick, the cochairs, were joined briefly by George Ball as executive director, but he quickly gravitated toward the inner circle in Springfield. He saw as his main assignment the finding of a fund raiser. He discharged this mission with brilliant success in recruiting Roger Stevens, a novice in politics who had achieved some notoriety in buying the Empire State Building and who later helped create and lead the Kennedy Center in Washington. The idea that the penniless Volunteers should pay for the bulk of the Stevenson broadcasts was such a monumental challenge that Stevens's instincts, honed in high-stake real estate, couldn't resist it. Since the networks demanded payment in advance of a broadcast, his zest for the last-minute rescue was called on so many times it must have contributed to his later success as a theatrical producer.

Between August 11 and November 6, Election Day, $749,812.32 was raised, of which $421,575.13 went for radio and television, paid for at the prevailing rate of $85,000 for a half-hour national "simulcast" on radio and television. There was a surplus of $45,625.75 to take care of late-arriving bills—ample for an organization to which few were willing to extend credit.

Volunteer groups sprang up rapidly all over the country, and all of them asking, beseeching, demanding, materials that would help them explain who this man Stevenson was, where he came from, what he stood for. After buttons and stickers were ordered, there was little money left for printing pamphlets, so a commercial publisher, Bennett Cerf of Random House, was asked to consider a paperback that would include a few of the speeches Adlai had made by then. Perhaps thinking the condition was impossible, he said he would consider it if a manuscript could be produced for him by the following Monday.

Starting Friday afternoon, Debs Myers, later managing editor of *Newsweek,* and Ralph Martin, author of a number of best-selling nonfiction books—both volunteers—persuaded John Steinbeck to write a foreword, which he did overnight; collaborated in writing a biography of Adlai; edited twenty speeches and the transcript of a press conference for publication, and hand-delivered the entire package to Cerf in New York on Monday morning. The book was on newsstands and in bookstores two weeks later. Editions sold out faster than they could be reprinted. The book was not only a valuable campaign document, it was a profitable venture for Random House and established something of a speed record for the conception-to-distribution publication of a book by a commercial publisher. It is now a collector's item.

This kind of initiative popped up all over the country, spurred by the involvement of well-known people, or bright young professionals getting their first taste of politics. John Hersey, chairman of the Connecticut Volunteers, wrote a foreword for a pictorial biography of Adlai. Archibald MacLeish was chairman of the Volunteers in Massachusetts. Robert Manning, later assistant secretary of state and editor of *The Atlantic Monthly,* was a field organizer, as was William Cary, Northwestern University law professor and later chairman of the Securities and Exchange Commission. There were, in fact, so many that the headquarters in Chicago never was able to compile even an approximate count, let alone an accurate listing. After the election, one of them wrote Jane Dick:

> *Having worked in a campaign such as ours must be something like having lived in Paris when you were twenty or discovered the "Ode to a Grecian Urn" in the midst of your first true love affair—it will always remain one of your life's peak moments, besides which there are nothing but valleys and whole eras filled with the commonplace and the lacklustre.*

Adlai's main concern and that of those close to him was not with the organization but with the substance of the campaign. Indeed, much of the disorganization inherent in having the headquarters in Springfield was a price he was willing to pay to convey the substantive message that he was not beholden to anyone for the nomination, that he was his own man, with his own agenda. His hope was to stimulate a "reasoned and precise debate" on the great issues arising from the "ordeal of the Twentieth Century." Since Eisenhower's victory over Taft represented a "victory of the constructive and progressive men in the Republican Party over its bitter and reactionary elements," the opportunity existed to conduct a high-level "national political dialogue."

Despite this hope, as early as August 4, he sent a memo to Wyatt saying he had heard that Eisenhower's general strategy was to make foreign policy, with emphasis on Korea and China, the number one issue, to have Nixon "push hard on the Hiss business," to make "every effort" to appease the conservative Taft wing of the Republican party, and to make "a big play" for the farmers. He added that "the plan is to let me develop as a shining knight until October and then hit me with horse meat, cigarette tax scandals, and whatever else they may have."

His own plan, worked out and agreed upon within the next ten days, he described later as follows:

> First, we prepared a list of some twelve or thirteen major topics or issues which I wanted to discuss, like agriculture, foreign policy, labor, national resources, inflation, corruption, etc. Feeling that the "time for a change" sentiment was the greatest hazard of all, I concluded also to devote an early speech to the vaporous anxiety of people to vote themselves out of trouble.
>
> Next, I decided that I would discuss these major questions one by one in separate speeches during September, thereby setting forth my whole program and identifying myself and my views as quickly as possible. One must bear in mind that I had not campaigned in the primaries and that my views as well as myself were little known about the country. So it seemed to me wise to take the initiative at once and set forth my position as clearly, comprehensively and unequivocally as possible, reserving October, the second half of the campaign, for the exigencies and opportunities that were bound to develop as the campaign progressed, and for amplification and rebuttal in the debate that I thought would develop.

The campaign would begin at the American Legion convention in New York in late August, and then be officially launched with a Labor Day speech in Detroit. After that would come a western trip, an eastern trip, a midwestern trip, a southern trip; West, Southwest, South, and Midwest again; then a whistle-stop trip to the East and back home again to Chicago.

The plan seemed reasonable and in large measure he held to it even though the campaign that developed bore little resemblance to what he thought it would be. The "national political dialogue" was illusory. Although it was Stevenson who was accused of "talking over the heads of people," it was Eisenhower who climbed to such a high level of generality that he seemed detached not only from issues but from the "low-road" strategy of his running mate. The detailed itineraries worked out within the overall scheduling plan were constantly subjected to last-minute changes and exhausting additions; whereas the Eisenhower campaign was so well planned it could publicize detailed itineraries two weeks in advance. Yet this chaos also produced the phenomenon of speeches that became best-selling books long after the election; speeches that remain a hallmark in American political history.

To underscore that he was still governor, he appeared at the Illinois State Fair on August 14 to introduce Vice President Alben Barkley. Then he flew to northern Wisconsin to vacation at the summer home of a Chicago friend, Dr. Clark Finnerud, followed by a corps of reporters to whose demands for a press conference he acceded. Within four days he was back in Springfield for an encounter the next day with Governor Allen Shivers of Texas that was to be one of the most revealing about his approach to politics.

It is difficult now even to imagine the intensity of the offshore-oil issue. The important states of Texas and California, along with Louisiana, were the leaders in the heated controversy over whether it was the states or the federal government that owned the oil that might lie beneath the waters off the coast. Texas claimed rights to the land extending three Spanish leagues—about ten and a half miles—into the sea, arguing that in the statute annexing Texas, the state had been permitted to keep the public lands of the Republic of Texas that had been measured in terms used by Mexico. Other states based their claims on the three-mile limit. The economic stakes were high, both for the states and for the oil industry.

President Truman, by executive order, had asserted federal jurisdiction over all submerged areas beyond low tide, and his attorney general had brought suit in 1945 in a test case to establish the validity of the order. In 1947 and twice in 1950, the Supreme Court had upheld the position that the federal government had "dominant rights." Thereupon, the power of the oil lobby asserted itself and Congress passed a resolution giving title to Texas, Louisiana, and California. Shortly before the Democratic convention, on May 29, 1952, the President had vetoed the bill, thrusting the issue into the national campaign, entangled with the question of states' rights, which also was intermingled with issues of civil rights and segregation—a thoroughly emotional brew stirred by strong economic interests.

Governor Shivers was the leader of the fight to gain control for the states. Arvey, in recognition of the critical importance of the issue to the campaign, arranged for Shivers to come to Springfield. Wilson Wyatt, who participated in the meeting, provides this report in his memoirs:

> In the presence of a small group of intimate advisors, the two met and conferred about the campaign. Governor Shivers then stated his position on the off-shore oil issue and emphasized its importance not only to Texas but to California, Louisiana, and other states bordering the oceans. Seeing that he was not preaching to the converted, he even indicated that while he would prefer an outright commitment to his states' rights view, he could go home to Texas without embarrassment if Stevenson would merely announce that he would give the matter serious study. But Stevenson told the Governor very frankly that he disagreed with him on the issue and that it was best he make a public statement of his opposition without equivocation or delay. One person gave the final and (he hoped) telling remonstrance:
>
> "But Governor Stevenson, if you insist on doing that, you can't win." Coldly and resolutely, Stevenson replied:
>
> "But I don't *have* to win."
>
> That ended the private conference and Stevenson went before the press to put the tidelands issue to rest.

But, of course, it was not put to rest. Eisenhower came out for legislation giving title of the land to the states (which didn't happen despite his election). Back in Texas, Governor Shivers said he could not vote for Stevenson because of tidelands and civil rights (which they had not discussed). Attorney General Price Daniel, a candidate for the Senate, said he could not support Stevenson, and Senator Lyndon Johnson complained that Adlai had given Shivers a weapon to beat on his (Johnson's) head. At the Elks Club that night, pride in the correctness and courage of their candidate's stand was mixed with an awareness that there was now little chance of carrying Texas.

"If we lose Texas, we lose the election," Bell said. Pointing out that Adlai could have simply stood by the Supreme Court decision without supporting Truman's veto, he wryly observed, "He sure runs a tough campaign."

Not content with meeting the issue head-on with the Texans, when he went to Louisiana later in the campaign, he opened his speech in New Orleans by repeating the position, even though he knew it was unpopular.

Wyatt, in concluding his report on the meeting with Governor Shivers, commented:

"As the campaign progressed there were many more such occasions, although few as dramatic or as costly. What earned him admiration often did not gather him support. But his candor, his honesty, and his lack of equivocation became evident to the entire country."

Four days later, Adlai flew to New York for one of the most memorable demonstrations of "his candor, his honesty, and his lack of equivocation," before the national convention of the American Legion. Seeing the police escort awaiting him as he got off the airplane, he remarked to McGowan and Schlesinger, "It's hard to tell whether I am going to be received or arrested."

Behind the lighthearted comment were weeks of thought and effort. Only a few days after the nomination, he had discussed the speech with Archibald MacLeish and they had agreed that the theme of his speech should be the patriotic ideal that held the Legion together, but that ideal also could be the screen behind which evil, such as that represented by Senators McCarthy and William E. Jenner, inflicts great damage. He had asked MacLeish to produce a draft with emphasis on "the idea of Americans first and veterans second." Then, in the note written to MacLeish on August 11, he said:

"I get so sick of the everlasting appeals to the cupidity and prejudice of every group which characterize our political campaigns. There is something finer in people; they know that they *owe* something too. I should like to try, at least, to appeal to their sense of obligation as well as their avarice."

In the letter, he enclosed some talks he had given to the American Legion in Illinois and his veto message on the Broyles bill.

From this beginning, a brief account of the evolution of the speech is indicative of the process that prevailed throughout the campaign. Arthur Schlesinger, Bob Tufts, and also Professor Walter Johnson developed drafts. They submitted their second draft to Adlai on August 18 and he returned it with suggestions. Meanwhile, MacLeish's draft had arrived, and draft 5a, which had involved most of the Elks Club residents, was submitted to Adlai on August 22. He reworked this one extensively, inserting significant additional language, and did the same with draft 6. McGowan and Schlesinger collaborated on draft 7, the speech as given, except for a few minor changes made on the plane going to New York. Many of the last revisions grew out of Adlai's concern at the belligerent tone of Eisenhower's speech to the Legion two days earlier. In it, Eisenhower had set forth what Adlai regarded as John Foster Dulles's irresponsible advocacy of "liberation" of peoples in the Eastern European satellite countries. It had evoked loud cheers from the audience.

General Eisenhower had been given a thunderous welcome by the veterans. They also had adopted resolutions that included calls for the removal of Secretary of State Dean Acheson, military victory in Korea, and better relations with Franco's Spain; in all, a general attack on Truman administration policies. The audience Adlai faced also contained many ardent supporters of Senators McCarthy and Jenner and their anti-Communist campaign.

After expressing his "warm respect" for Eisenhower's "military achievements," and describing his own war record as a "worm's eye view" as an apprentice seaman in World War I, and as a somewhat uncomfortable "top-sider" in Secretary Knox's office in World War II, he launched into his message.

> We talk a great deal about patriotism. What do we mean by patriotism in the context of our times? I venture to suggest that what we mean is a sense of national responsibility which will enable America to remain master of her power—to walk with it in serenity and wisdom, with self-respect and the respect of all mankind; a patriotism that puts country ahead of self; a patriotism that is not short, frenzied outbursts of emotion, but the tranquil and steady dedication of a lifetime. . . . This is a mighty assignment. For it is often easier to fight for principles than to live up to them. . . . Unhappily, we find some things in American life today of which we cannot be proud.

> Consider the groups who seek to identify their special interests with the general welfare. . . . I have resisted them before and I hope the Almighty will give me the strength to do so again and again. And I should tell you—my fellow Legionaires—as I would tell all other organized groups, that I intend to resist pressures from veterans, too. . . . After all, we are Americans first and veterans second, and the best maxim for any administration is still Jefferson's: "Equal rights for all, special privileges for none."

> True patriotism, it seems to me, is based on tolerance and a large measure of humility.

> There are men among us who use "patriotism" as a club for attacking other Americans. What can we say for the self-styled patriot who thinks that a Negro, a Jew, a Catholic, or a Japanese-American is less an American than he? That betrays the deepest article of our faith, the belief in individual liberty and equality which has always been the heart and soul of the American idea.

> What can we say for the man who proclaims himself a patriot—and then for political or personal reasons attacks the patriotism of faithful public servants? I give you as a shocking example, the attacks which have been made on the loyalty and the motives of our great wartime Chief of Staff, General Marshall. To me, this is the type of "patriotism" which is, in Dr. Johnson's phrase, "the last refuge of scoundrels."

The anatomy of patriotism is complex. But surely intolerance and public irresponsibility cannot be cloaked in the shining armor of rectitude and righteousness. Nor can the denial of the right to hold ideas that are different—the freedom of man to think as he pleases. To strike freedom of the mind with the fist of patriotism is an old and ugly subtlety.

And the freedom of the mind, my friends, has served America well. The vigor of our political life, our capacity for change, our cultural, scientific and industrial achievements, all derive from free inquiry, from the free mind—from the imagination, resourcefulness and daring of men who are not afraid of new ideas. Most all of us favor free enterprise for business. Let us also favor free enterprise for the mind. For, in the last analysis, we would fight to the death to protect it. Why is it, then, that we are sometimes slow to detect, or are indifferent to, the dangers that beset it?

Many of the threats to our cherished freedoms in these anxious, troubled times arise, it seems to me, from a healthy apprehension about the communist menace within our country. . . . Americans who have surrendered to this misbegotten idol have surrendered their right to our trust. And there can be no secure place for them in our public life.

Yet, as I have said before, we must take care not to burn down the barn to kill the rats. All of us, and especially patriotic organizations with enormous influence like the American Legion, must be vigilant in protecting our birthright from its too zealous friends while protecting it from its evil enemies.

The tragedy of our day is the climate of fear in which we live, and fear breeds repression. Too often sinister threats to the Bill of Rights, to freedom of the mind, are concealed under the patriotic cloak of anti-communism. . . .

There is no justification for indiscriminate attacks on our schools, and the sincere, devoted, and by no means overpaid teachers who labor in them. If there are any communist teachers, of course they should be excluded, but the task is not one for self-appointed thought police or ill-informed censors. As a practical matter, we do not stop communist activity in this way. What we do is give the communists material with which to defame us. . . .

It was always accounted a virtue in a man to love his country. . . . When an American says that he loves his country, he means not only that he loves the New England hills, the prairies glistening in the sun, the wide and rising plains, the great mountains, and the sea. He means that he loves an inner air, an inner light in which freedom lives and in which a man can draw the breath of self-respect. . . .

With this patriotism—patriotism in its large and wholesome meaning—America can master its power and turn it to the noble cause of peace. We can maintain military power without militarism; political power without oppression; and moral power without compulsion or complacency. . . .

Let us proclaim our faith in the future of man. Of good heart and good cheer, faithful to ourselves and our traditions, we can lift the cause of freedom, the cause of free men, so high no power on earth can tear it down. . . . Living, speaking, like men—like Americans—we can lead the way to our rendezvous in a happy, peaceful world.

With this speech he gave meaning to his pledge to "talk sense to the American people," and signaled what was to be perhaps the most notable personal campaign for high office in our political history. Sensing its quality, the skeptical audience responded warmly. A few days later, Nixon deplored that it "made light of the menace of communism," and "demonstrated a shocking lack of understanding" of the problem of subversion. Years later, McGowan continued to regard it as "the best day of the campaign." John Bartlow Martin wrote that the speech "stamped him as a man of courage, unafraid to tell his audiences what they did not want to hear" and that "New York's long and lasting love affair with Stevenson really began that day." It remains a landmark in American political discourse.

Adlai's genuinely "warm respect" for General Eisenhower was to be short-lived. Biographer Kenneth S. Davis, who discussed the matter with him, has written:

Stevenson in early 1952 may not have shared to the full the popular enthusiasm for the General as a potential leader, but his admiration for Eisenhower as a man and as a soldier was certainly great. . . . Stevenson believed he saw in the General a quality of moral goodness, an earnest desire to do good in the world, an innate human decency in which was rooted an apparently instinctive ability to make the proper public gesture on important occasions. The Governor in late '51 and the first months of '52 might contemplate without serious qualms the possibility of the General as President.

The first stirrings of misgivings, stimulated by the "liberation" passage in the general's American Legion speech, were pointedly expressed when Adlai went to the predominantly Eastern European population center of Hamtramck right from the official opening of the campaign on Detroit's Cadillac Square on Labor Day. Eisenhower's speech, he said, "aroused speculation here and abroad that if he were elected some reckless action might ensue in an attempt to liberate the peoples of Eastern Europe from Soviet tyranny. The anxieties of people for their relatives behind the Iron Curtain should not become a false campaign issue.

"Even if votes could be won by it, I would not say one reckless word on this matter during this campaign. Some things are more precious than votes. The cruel grip of Soviet tyranny upon your friends and relatives cannot be loosened by loose talk or idle threats. It cannot be loosened by awakening false hopes which might stimulate intemperate action. . . ."

The warning was prophetic of the helplessness with which the Eisenhower administration later watched the uprising in Hungary. It is only fair to note that Eisenhower had registered concern over the warlike implication of his earlier talk about "liberation" and had instructed his foreign policy adviser, John Foster Dulles, and others on his staff always to indicate that change in Eastern Europe should be achieved "by peaceful means." The addition of the phrase was little noted, however, as others in the campaign continued to be more bellicose in their references to the plight of the Eastern European countries, from which came many voters.

At the time, greater attention was focused on Adlai's relations with labor. Here, his profound aversion to being a partisan for any special interest clashed directly with the Democratic party's close ties to the labor movement, then engaged in a passionate campaign for repeal of the Taft-Hartley "slave labor" Act. The United Auto Workers, led by Walter Reuther, dominated the Democratic party in Michigan, and the official launching of the campaign in Detroit on Labor Day was an acknowledgment of the party's close ties to labor in general. Yet, the practices and management of some unions troubled him deeply and he could not bring himself to the all-out assault on the Taft-Hartley Act that was expected.

John Bartlow Martin has written that no speech during the entire campaign involved more work or went through more rewrites, with Willard Wirtz doing the basic drafting. The part stating he did not think Taft-Hartley was a "slave labor" act—the term that Reuther and other leaders invariably used—would be deleted by the Elks Club writers and would come back from Adlai and McGowan with the phrase again in it. Nor could he bring himself to use the buzz word "repeal."

"Stevenson could not be persuaded to call for repeal," John Kenneth Galbraith has written in *A Life in Our Times*. "He astonished and depressed us by saying that if it cost him the support of the unions, so be it."

For Adlai, more than policy was involved; a basic part of his philosophy was at the foundation of his resistance. He expressed it in a later speech at Fort Dodge, Iowa, saying: "Nobody is just a farmer, or just a farm woman, or just a businessman depending on farmers for his prosperity, or just a worker in a meat-packing plant. *The fragmentary man is a myth.*"

After identifying himself as "a fugitive from a sweat shop" in Springfield where "the speed-up is in full force," he told the throng of unionists: "I might as well make it clear right now that I intend to do exactly what I think right and best for all, for all of us—business, labor, agriculture—alike." He called Taft-Hartley "a tangled snarl of legal barbed wire, filled with ugly sneers at labor unions and built around the discredited labor injunction," and then went on to say, "I don't say everything in Taft-Hartley is wrong. It isn't. And, moreover, I'll say frankly that I don't think it is a slave labor law either. But I do say that it was biased and politically inspired and has not improved labor relations in a single plant." The next sentence was the closest he could come to using the word "repeal": "We must have a new law and my conclusion is that we can best remedy the defects in the old law by scrapping it and starting over again."

In outlining the five elements that he thought should be in a new law, he could not resist a reference to aspects that disturbed him. "The union exists for your benefit. If there is anything wrong with it, if you don't approve of the officers, if you don't like the union's policies, if there are racketeers or Communists, then it's up to you and your fellow members to do something about it. . . . But you can't do it by sitting at home and complaining."

The speech was not a success. It did not rally the unions to his side, and it did nothing to quiet the charges that he was a captive of the unions. Newt Minow, who had accompanied the governor, told a friend, "That's when, if I had any hope of winning, I knew it was lost."

The most enduring image of the day, however, was the photo taken during a stop at Pontiac, showing Adlai with a large hole in the sole of his shoe. It won a Pulitzer Prize, effectively challenged the effort to portray him as a patrician, symbolized both his parsimony and the poor prospects of his candidacy, and provided the model for a silver pin of a punctured shoe sole that remains a much-sought collector's item. When the Pulitzer award was announced, Adlai's telegram of congratulations noted it was the first time a Pulitzer had been given for "a hole in one."

Another area of difficulty was farm policy. He had a far better "feel" for the problems of the farmers than for those of workers. Soil, water, and forest conservation; rural electrification; farm-to-market roads; all were activities he could support enthusiastically; but subsidies, marketing quotas, and acreage allotments that were at the heart of the farm program bothered him deeply. What bothered him even more was that he had no better answer. In the absence of a better solution, he strongly supported the party platform calling for government support of basic agricultural commodity prices at not less than 90 percent of parity. He pointed out that the Republican platform was "aimed" at 100 percent of parity, and then asked, "How good is their aim, anyway?" in view of past Republican opposition to lower parity support.

After arriving in Kasson, Minnesota, from Denver, he delivered his "major" farm policy speech at the National Plowing Contest, following an appearance by Eisenhower, and then flew on to a rally in Cheyenne, Wyoming, and another in Billings, Montana. He awoke there the next morning to see in the *Billings Gazette* a long front-page story on Eisenhower's speech at Kasson in which it was noted that "Gov. Adlai E. Stevenson of Illinois also spoke."

His distaste for appeals to any special interest group posed continuing problems. Carl McGowan has said it was difficult to get him to speak to Jewish groups, not because he was unsympathetic to their interest in Israel but because Steve Mitchell had told him "if it was not for labor and the Jews he'd have to close headquarters in a week. Stevenson thought this was unhealthy." Jack Arvey had a somewhat different explanation: "Stevenson refused to be a demagogue. He felt he might become President and if he did he might do a great deal to ease tensions between the Arabs and the Jews but he couldn't do it if he was a partisan on one side."

The same was true with the Catholic vote, where he was in deep trouble because of his divorce and McCarthy. At one of the early press conferences, careful preparations had been made to issue a headline-grabbing statement. But the first question, after the statement had been read, was whether he would follow the example of Presidents Roosevelt and Truman and send an emissary to the Vatican. Wilson Wyatt, in *Whistle Stops,* reports:

> Adlai hesitated for a moment, and then, to the unhappiness of his supporters, stated that he thought he would not do so. This was a departure from recent precedent and clearly was disappointing to the large Catholic segment of the Democratic party. By his reply, he completely scooped his planned lead point, which was then lost in the shuffle. He told me afterward that he just thought it best to put the matter clearly on the table from the outset and not build false hopes.
>
> There was no question that his answer was politically hurtful—especially as he was a divorced man and divorce carried a political scar in those days, especially with Catholics. . . . No one would have criticized him had he held to the lead that he had planned for the conference, and stated his Vatican decision on another occasion, more conducive to his election interest. But that was not in the Stevenson character. This is but one of the many instances that were to follow in the days of the campaign.

Another followed very soon. The annual Alfred E. Smith Dinner under the sponsorship of Cardinal Spellman in New York for years had been considered a "must" occasion for political leaders. Inexplicably, when it did not fit conveniently into his campaign schedule, Steve Mitchell advised Adlai he could regret the invitation. Cardinal Spellman never forgave him.

More deeply philosophical questions inhibited his approach to the huge number of loyal Democratic votes in the black population. His stand on civil rights at the 1948 Democratic convention and his actions as governor in desegregating the Illinois National Guard, the state parks, and in handling the Cicero riot, leave little doubt about his basic position. There were some black leaders in Illinois, however, who remained disgruntled at the failure to achieve passage of Fair Employment Practices legislation, and felt that his unwillingness to "buy" the few votes needed showed lack of commitment. FEPC legislation pending in Congress and proposals to curb the filibuster in the Senate were the litmus tests with which many liberals tested commitment in the raging civil rights battle. And on both of these Adlai had mental reservations.

His failure to achieve FEPC legislation in Illinois had been a genuine disappointment (one he had hoped to erase in his second term as governor), but he was uncertain about the effectiveness of such legislation at the national level. It was partly his conviction that action on the state level would yield better results, partly doubt that discrimination was susceptible to effective legislative action, and partly concern that what he saw as a moral issue affecting the whole nation had assumed the character of a North-South political battle. It may be that his patrician background also made him insufficiently sensitive to the emotion that infused civil rights advocates. His belief that prejudice, like corruption, was individual rather than institutional in its worst manifestations clearly was out of step with the times and even with reality. Prejudice, more than corruption, had become entrenched in law and institutional conduct and seemed to call for kinds of action that instinctively he pulled back from. In ensuing years he came to recognize this state of affairs, but in 1952 he could not bring himself to make unequivocal declarations in favor of civil rights slogans any more than he could adopt organized labor's buzz words.

Early in the campaign, he went directly from the successful American Legion speech to the New York State Democratic Convention to give a speech on "equal rights" that disappointed his audience. The New York liberals had opposed the nomination of John Sparkman and Adlai began by praising him as a leader of "the new South" with a liberal record on housing and other issues. Civil rights, he said, meant equal treatment before the law, equal opportunity for education, employment, and decent living conditions. More than laws was needed.

"The fight for equal rights must go on every day in our souls and our consciences, in our schools and our churches and our homes, in our factories and our offices as well as in our city councils, our state legislatures and our national Congress. . . . And this is a job for the East, the North, the West, as well as the South." He acknowledged that the problem is "more serious" in the South but asserted that "things are taking place in the South today that would have seemed impossible only a few years ago." He said he was "very favorably impressed" with a bill in Congress that created a federal FEPC empowered to act only in states without state FEPCs and placing enforcement powers in the courts rather than administrative bodies.

This was far less than his audience wanted to hear, but he was determined not to say anything in liberal New York that he could not later say in the South.

September 20 was a curious day. The Nixon "slush fund" scandal was raging. He spoke on Korea at the graduation of Adlai III from Marine Officers Candidate School at Quantico, Virginia, and then flew to Richmond, the capital of the Confederacy. En route, he learned that a struggle was under way to desegregate the hall in which he was scheduled to speak. Virginia law required segregation in the Mosque Auditorium, but clearly he could not address a segregated audience, even if the planners had not scheduled a major speech on civil rights. Richmond authorities had assured Wilson Wyatt that they would ignore the segregation law; but there were rumors that Virginia Republicans were planning to file a formal complaint if they did. News of this debate may have explained the strange silence that enveloped the crowds lining the streets as his motorcade passed. But at the auditorium an overflow, unsegregated crowd interrupted his speech more than forty times with loud applause and friendly rebel yells.

Leaders of the powerful and segregationist Byrd machine, including Senator Harry F. Byrd, who said he was picking apples, were absent, but Governor John S. Battle gave him a warm and generous introduction. Adlai evoked loud applause as he described how the Democratic party had set "the new South" on its feet after the tragedies of the Civil War. As he set forth in terms similar to those used in New York his position on civil rights, the applause died away. Then the crowd came roaring to its feet as he declared: "I should justly earn your contempt if I talked one way in the South and another elsewhere. Certainly no intellectually dishonest Presidential candidate could, by an alchemy of election, be converted into an honest President.

"I do not attempt to justify the unjustifiable," he continued,

whether it is anti-Negroism in one place, anti-Semitism in another—or for that matter, anti-Southernism in many places. And neither can I justify self-righteousness anywhere. Let none of us be smug on this score, for nowhere in the nation have we come to that state of harmonious amity between racial and religious groups to which we aspire. The political abuse of the problem of discrimination in employment, the exploitation of racial aspirations on the one hand and racial prejudices on the other—all for votes—is both a dangerous thing and a revolting spectacle in our political life. It will always be better to reason together than to hurl recriminations at one another.

If anything, the speech to the southern audience was stronger than the one he had given in New York. If, as northern liberals charged, he was giving away too much to hold the South in the Democratic party, he failed. On Election Day he became the second Democrat since the Civil War to lose Virginia—the other was Al Smith. In addition, he lost Florida, Tennessee, and Texas, as well as most of the border states, and the Democratic majority declined in almost all the cities with large black populations. What was "too radical" in the South was "too moderate" in the North.

Assessing this aspect of the campaign, historian Stuart Gerry Brown, in *Conscience in Politics,* has written:

> Above all, he articulated a means of conciliation within the Democratic party which led directly to the enactment in 1957, by a Democratic Congress, of the first civil rights measure since the Reconstruction period, and left Stevenson himself morally and politically prepared to speak for the nation on the crisis of integration in the public schools.

CHAPTER TEN
C(2)K(1)

EXCITEMENT ENTERED THE CAMPAIGN on September 18 with the explosion of the Nixon "slush fund" story. From whatever elevation the campaign had achieved, it slid downhill from then on. The episode, even though it almost cost Nixon his place as Eisenhower's Vice President, was vastly inflated. Adlai also had a private fund, although for a somewhat different purpose. In both cases, the amounts involved were small (Adlai's exceeded Nixon's), and the purposes violated nothing more than propriety. But for days, it was a tornado tearing across the political landscape, tossing Nixon's political future on the winds, and leaving, as a lasting mark, pressure on candidates to disclose their personal finances.

The furor never would have occurred had it not been for the nature of the campaign Nixon was waging, repeatedly assuring audiences that the Eisenhower "crusade" would clean the crooks and Communists out of Washington. Stevenson, by contrast, was "a weakling, a waster, and a small-caliber Truman" who had been elected governor by a political organization with "mobsters, gangsters and the remnants of the Capone gang." Nixon persistently urged voters to "drive back to the shadowy haunts in the subcellars of American politics from which they came . . . the experts in shady and shoddy government operations." He had begun a four-day barnstorming tour in Maine on September 2 declaring he would make "Communist subversion and corruption the theme of every speech from now until election"; adding: "If the record itself smears, let it smear. If the dry rot of corruption and communism which has eaten deep into our body politic during the past seven years, can only be chopped out with a hatchet—then let's call for a hatchet."

It was in reaction to speeches of this nature, that the *New York Post,* on Thursday, September 18, produced headlines screaming: SECRET NIXON FUND—SECRET RICH MEN'S TRUST FUND KEEPS NIXON IN STYLE FAR BEYOND HIS SALARY.

The truth was much less sensational. Whatever sins Nixon may have committed, high living was not among them. Reports that a group of wealthy Californians had established a trust fund for Nixon's benefit had been circulating among newspapermen since the Republican convention. Columnist Drew Pearson, even with his penchant for scandal, had decided to ignore the story. A respected but not widely circulated Washington columnist, Peter Edson, asked Nixon about it on September 14, and the latter suggested he check with Dana Smith, a Pasadena lawyer who had been finance chairman of Nixon's race for the Senate in 1950 and was southern California chairman of Citizens for Eisenhower-Nixon. Edson was impressed with the straightforward manner in which both Nixon and Smith answered his questions.

"We realized his salary was pitifully inadequate for a salesman of free enterprise," Smith told Edson and two other reporters who also called him. When asked if Governor Earl Warren wasn't also a salesman for free enterprise, Smith had replied, "Frankly, Warren has too much of the social point of view, and he never has gone out selling the free-enterprise system. But Dick did just what we wanted him to do."

The Democrats would have fared better if they had concentrated on that last phrase rather than on the fund, but it was the fund that became the center of the storm after Edson had written a low-key, matter-of-fact story, not intending it to be a sensational exposé. It was the headline and the hot thrust of Nixon's accusations that fueled the firestorm.

Eisenhower, in his memoirs, wrote that "the storm of criticism that broke was of hurricane proportions," and that he was "bombarded" with contradictory advice concerning Nixon's continuing on the ticket. Actually, the advice was overwhelmingly in favor of demanding Nixon's resignation. The difficulty was compounded by the fact that Eisenhower's Friday-night speech in Kansas City had been advertised as an attack on corruption. Eisenhower, however, refused to be stampeded by his advisers and instead kept issuing general statements expressing confidence in Nixon's honesty. While avoiding direct contact with Nixon, his statements increasingly signaled that Nixon's counterattack on the story as a smear attempt by "Communists and left wingers" was not adequate and that a fuller explanation was necessary. "Of what avail is it for us to carry on this crusade against this business of what has been going on in Washington if we, ourselves, aren't as clean as a hound's tooth," he told reporters on his campaign train. Meanwhile, editorials across the country were two to one against Nixon. Even the staunchly Republican *New York Herald Tribune,* of which William Robinson of Eisenhower's inner circle was publisher, called for his resignation. The editorial which it was assumed Robinson wrote was a devastating blow to Nixon.

By Sunday, Nixon had decided his now famous television appeal was necessary, and although the Republican National Committee had been persuaded to pay for it, he was desperate to have some direct word from Eisenhower. When a telephone call finally was arranged Sunday night Eisenhower declined to give either advice or assurance, and Nixon, in his *Memoirs*, says he "blurted out": "There comes a time when you've either got to shit or get off the pot. The great trouble here is the indecision." Nixon concedes that Eisenhower must have been shocked by his language and that the call ended inconclusively.

Nevertheless, the Tuesday-night nationwide television speech, although derided by some as "soap opera bathos," was a great political success. The disclosure that the "slush fund" amounted to only $18,235 and had been spent largely on legitimate office expenses was lost in the response to Nixon's fervent defense of his honesty, his wife's, and his refusal to return a gift to his daughters, a black-and-white puppy named Checkers.

A landslide of approving telegrams hit the Eisenhower campaign headquarters. Sherman Adams, later the President's chief of staff, reported that Eisenhower, watching it in Cleveland, was visibly moved and when he turned from the set found his wife wiping tears from her eyes. He told her he believed Nixon was a completely honest man, but he still refrained from making a commitment to keep Nixon on the ticket. When he sent a message asking Nixon to meet him in Wheeling, West Virginia, Nixon at first refused to meet without an assurance that he would be retained. Persuaded not to hold out, he made the trip and was astonished to find Eisenhower bounding up the steps of his plane to embrace him in a big bear hug and exclaim, "You're my boy!"

Nixon was out of trouble, but Adlai was not. The day after the story broke all over the country, campaigning in Massachusetts, he responded to reporters' requests by writing out in longhand a statement saying that the important questions were: "Who gave the money, was it given to influence the Senator's position . . . and have any laws been violated? . . . I am sure the great Republican party will ascertain these facts, will make them public, and act in accordance with our best traditions. . . . Condemnation without all the evidence, a practice all too familiar with us, would be wrong." The reporters were disappointed; indeed, Steve Mitchell had issued a statement calling on Nixon to resign, and something at least as strong was expected from Adlai. Not only was the statement characteristic, undoubtedly it was also restrained by the knowledge that he, too, had a fund.

He had made no secret of the fact that a fund existed; it was mainly to augment the low salaries available for the people he wanted to bring into state government. He had talked about it openly in a speech to the Commercial Club in Chicago several years before dealing with the problems of building an effective state administration.

At the end of the 1948 campaign there had remained a net balance of $18,744.96 in the account of the Stevenson for Governor Committee. The committee thereupon wrote to him that the funds should "be subject to withdrawal for such purposes connected with the office of the Governor as Mr. Stevenson shall determine." During his first year as governor, he had used a total of $13,500 to supplement the salaries of Schaefer, Day, Flanagan, Mulroy, McGowan, Hoehler, and Mitchell. He used it also to provide Christmas gifts to office and mansion staff, to give a party for Springfield children, buy uniforms for the governor's female and male bowling teams, and for contributions to charities and flowers to sick friends.

As the fund ran out in 1950, he discussed with Dutch Smith the problem of finding ways to defray such expenses during the rest of his term. He hoped to increase supplementary payments to his staff and estimated he would need contributions of $20,000 to $25,000 per year to "enable me to do what we have talked about without robbing the children!" He entrusted the fund-raising task to Smith's discretion because he felt it important that no receiving official should know the source of the money, nor should any contributor know the identity of a recipient. Indeed, when the receipts and disbursals were made public, Ed Day wryly discovered that the $2,000 he had received coincided with a contribution of that amount from his father-in-law. Smith, as a leading insurance executive, kept meticulous records of his receipts, but after that, because the disbursals were handled on a personal basis, the bookkeeping was at best informal. None of this might have become important if it had not been for Steve Mitchell's call for Nixon's resignation.

Mitchell's statement infuriated one of Adlai's Lake Forest friends, Kent Chandler, who had been at the Commercial Club luncheon and also happened to be an executive of the family business of Jane and Edison Dick, the A. B. Dick Company. On Monday, the day before the Nixon broadcast, he released in Chicago the text of a telegram he was sending to Adlai in Springfield saying that in view of Mitchell's statement the governor had a responsibility to admit he had a similar fund, and to reveal the names of the contributors, the amounts of their contributions, and the amounts received by each state official. Adlai, in New York, issued a statement saying that it had been no secret that he had collected a fund "to reduce the financial sacrifice" of those entering public service. Naturally, reporters were not satisfied; they wanted names of contributors, recipients, and amounts.

In Springfield, a frantic effort to collect records stretched through Tuesday and Wednesday while the reporters clamored. On Thursday, a young campaign aide, Robert W. Notti, received a call from Jim Mulroy's widow, Helen, saying she had some things Jim had left that might be helpful. Notti rushed up to Chicago, and on a closet shelf they found two large suitcases filled with papers. Dumping the contents out on the living room floor, they soon found a list of contributors to Adlai's campaign containing about a thousand names. He rushed back to Springfield, and much of the campaign staff went to work calling 1948 contributors and asking them for permission to make public their names and contributions.

Realizing it would be impossible to compile a full accounting quickly enough to satisfy the reporters' demands, Wyatt, Ball, McGowan, and others recommended that he release a summary and, in addition, take the then unprecedented step of making public his income tax returns for recent years. This latter idea startled him; he treasured his own privacy and respected the privacy of others, but, reluctantly, he agreed. (When the returns were released on Sunday, he was embarrassed to discover that he had claimed a ten-dollar charitable deduction for a contribution that had been made out of the fund. In his witty speech to the Gridiron Club after the election, he said he had "won the bosom-baring and public-stripping contest.")

Although the summary statement and the exhibits represented less than full disclosure, the release of his income tax returns and those of Senator Sparkman grabbed most of the reporters' attention. With even greater reluctance, Eisenhower subsequently did declare his income (but not the substantial gifts in kind he had received). The issue then quickly died down, leaving mainly the continuing obligation pressed on many politicians to disclose their income tax returns. Adlai never ceased resenting the fact that his fund was equated with Nixon's, but both he and McGowan later commented that trying to augment salaries had been a mistake.

Adlai literally loathed Nixon. No other person aroused such disgust; not even Joseph McCarthy, whom he regarded as "a sick man" made possible by Nixon's cynical exploitation of the Communist issue. Friends who often wished he could be more of a hater were awed at the strength of his distaste for Nixon.

His contempt had begun well before 1952, during what he considered Nixon's despicable campaigns in California against Helen Gahagan Douglas and Jerry Voorhis. Nonetheless, he was surprised when Nixon launched his relentless attack on him for the Hiss deposition. He had thought John Foster Dulles's far more intimate association with Hiss and Eisenhower's presence, along with Dulles, on the board of the Carnegie Endowment for International Peace, of which Hiss had been president, would keep the issue out of the campaign. Rarely had he been so wrong.

At the National Young Republican Convention in Boston, June 28, 1951, Nixon made a speech he had been developing while making an average of three speeches a week around the country. It became his basic speech as he entered the campaign. Stephen E. Ambrose, author of definitive biographies of both Eisenhower and Nixon, has written that "for misleading allusions, half-truths, innuendos and hyperbole it was unbeatable."

Nixon asserted that "the failure of our State Department to get the wholehearted support of our allies in Korea" was one of the worst gaffes in diplomatic history, and that "Communists have infiltrated the very highest councils of this administration." He claimed that while the Hiss case was in the courts, "two judges of the Supreme Court; the Governor of Illinois, Mr. Adlai Stevenson; Philip Jessup, the architect of our Far Eastern policy; and a host of other administration officials testified as character witnesses for Alger Hiss." Only Jessup, on leave from his professorship in international law at Columbia University, was an official of the Truman administration and his role, at best, was exaggerated. "Our top administration officials," Nixon went on, "have refused time and time again to recognize the existence of the fifth column in this country and to take effective action to clean subversives out of the administrative branch of the government."

Ambrose, in his biography of Nixon, commented:

> The Administration that Nixon was accusing of being soft on Communism had, in the past five years, forced the Russians out of Iran in 1946, come to the aid of the Greek government in 1947, met the Red Army's challenge at Berlin and inaugurated the Marshall Plan in 1948, joined the North Atlantic Treaty Organization in 1949, and hurled back the Communist invaders of South Korea in 1950. . . . Nixon was talking about an Administration in which the FBI had uncovered the evidence and the Justice Department had prosecuted the case that put Alger Hiss in jail, in which the Attorney General had issued a list of Communist-front organizations and the President a sweeping executive order regarding subversives in government.

Soon after his nomination, Nixon had gone to Denver to discuss campaign strategy with Eisenhower and his staff. There is evidence that those who were then closest to Eisenhower—Paul Hoffman, Lucius Clay, and William Robinson—tried to persuade Nixon to be less strident. Hoffman followed up the meeting with a memo on his behalf and Robinson's, urging that he make "civil liberties and the rights of minorities a major theme for your addresses."

The advice was ignored. He promptly gave an interview to the *Kansas City Star* in which he described the New Deal wing of the Democratic party as "Pinks," and went on to say: "There's one difference between the Reds and the Pinks. The Pinks want to socialize America. The Reds want to socialize the world and make Moscow the world capital. Their paths are similar; they have the same bible—the teachings of Karl Marx."

Ambrose wrote: "After the Checkers speech, Nixon might have calculated that the middle of the high road was now the place for him to travel, right beside General Eisenhower. But that was neither his style nor his role. He wanted to lash out, and Eisenhower privately encouraged him to do it."

By October, his speeches were calling Stevenson, Acheson, and Truman "traitors to the high principles in which many of the nation's Democrats believe." (Following Truman's outrage that a President of the United States would be called a traitor, Nixon claimed this was a distortion of his meaning.) Another favorite line became: "Stevenson holds a Ph.D. degree from Acheson's College of Cowardly Communist Containment"; and, as a consequence, "the word of Truman and Acheson, as well as that of Acheson's former assistant, Adlai Stevenson, gives the American people no hope for safety at home from the sinister threat of Communism." In a national television speech on October 13, he said, "There is no question in my mind as to the loyalty of Mr. Stevenson," but, said Nixon, he had disqualified himself from public trust by "going down the line for the arch-traitor of our generation"—Alger Hiss. "If Stevenson were to be taken in by Stalin as he was by Hiss, the Yalta sellout would look like a great American diplomatic triumph by comparison."

Stevenson retaliated, but more often with witty jabs than direct rebuttals. Nixon, he said, was "the kind of politician who would cut down a redwood tree, and then mount the stump and make a speech for conservation."

In general, though, as George Ball as stated, "he scornfully refused to take on Nixon. He was campaigning against Eisenhower and would not demean himself by arguing with Eisenhower's hired gun." On the personal level, Adlai was frustrated by his inability to engage Eisenhower in a discussion of issues and disturbed by Eisenhower's tolerance of the kind of campaign being waged not only by Nixon but by Senator McCarthy.

Eisenhower's failure to respond to McCarthy's attacks on General George C. Marshall put the seal on his attitude. It ended whatever relaxation he felt regarding the prospect of Eisenhower in the White House. It turned a sense of duty about being a good soldier for the Democratic party into a fervent desire to win.

It is virtually impossible now to recapture the atmosphere of fear, suspicion, tension, and divisiveness that permeated the landscape; or the timidity and even paralysis that afflicted many government offices, including schools and colleges, and finally even the Army and Congress itself, as a result of the reckless charges and inquisitions launched in Wheeling, West Virginia, on February 9, 1950, by the senator from Wisconsin, Joseph R. McCarthy. Even though it is amusing now to contemplate loyalty oaths being imposed on wrestlers in Indiana or amateur fishermen in New York, calls to combat communism in Hollywood by boycotting Abbott and Costello movies, and even consideration of a name change for the Cincinnati Reds, it was a profoundly, though grotesquely, serious period in American history.

In his veto of the Broyles bill and in numerous speeches before and after that lightning-rod action, Adlai staked out very early a strong position against McCarthy and his entire campaign. For example, on June 15, 1950, in a commencement address at the University of Illinois, he had declared:

> We are behaving . . . like nutty neurotics. We . . . are nervously looking for subversive enemies under the bed and behind the curtains. We exchange frenzied, irresponsible accusations of disloyalty. "Guilt by association" has been added to our language. The slanderer is honored. The shadow of a nameless fear slopes across the land. There is talk of thought control among Jefferson's people.

Eisenhower had ample warning that a major theme of the Republican campaign against the Truman administration included personal attacks on General Marshall. Also, he had to know that most of those pushing for his nomination confidently expected he would repudiate such extremism. There had been a strong Republican reaction to President Truman's appointment of Marshall as secretary of defense, but most of them had recoiled from the fury of Senator William Jenner who took the Senate floor in April 1950 to charge that the appointment was a desperate attempt by the Truman administration to "swallow up the treachery of the past in the new treachery they are planning for the future."

"General Marshall is not only willing, he is eager to play the role of a front man for traitors," Jenner shouted. "The truth is this is no new role for him, for General George C. Marshall is a living lie. Unless he, himself, were desperate, he could not possibly agree to continue as an errand boy, a front man, a stooge, or a conspirator for this Administration's crazy assortment of collectivist cutthroat crackpots and Communist fellow-travelling appeasers." It was tragic, he concluded, that Marshall was not enough of a patriot to tell the truth "instead of joining hands once more with this criminal crowd of traitors and Communist appeasers, who, under the continuing influence and direction of Mr. Truman and Mr. Acheson, are still selling America down the river."

During this period, Senator McCarthy was merely branding Marshall as one "completely unfit" and "completely incompetent." Then, on June 14, 1951, McCarthy made a sixty-thousand-word speech on the floor of the Senate claiming that the "loss" of China and other Communist successes was the result of a conspiracy of high government officials, notably General Marshall. Marshall, he asserted, was "steeped in falsehood," and had "recourse to the lie whenever it suits his convenience." His "review" of Marshall's career as Chief of Staff in World War II, as special emissary to China, and as secretary of state implied that every success of the Soviet Union or other Communists was the product of Marshall's treachery.

"This must be the product of a great conspiracy, a conspiracy on a scale so immense as to dwarf any previous such venture in the history of man," McCarthy declared,

> a conspiracy of infamy so black that, when it is finally exposed, its principles shall be forever deserving of the maledictions of all honest men. . . . What can be made of this unbroken series of decisions and acts contributing to the strategy of defeat? They can not be attributed to incompetence. If Marshall were merely stupid, the laws of probability would dictate that part of his decisions would serve his country's interests.

(One of the decisions, of course, was to make Eisenhower the Commander in Chief of Allied forces.) Free from potential libel action because it was a reprint from the *Congressional Record,* the speech was published as a book, *America's Retreat from Victory; The Story of George Catlett Marshall.* It was in wide circulation when Eisenhower returned from Europe.

Eisenhower was indebted to Marshall as to no other man for his opportunities to achieve greatness. In 1939, Marshall told military columnist, Major George Fielding Eliot, that Eisenhower was one of about a dozen lieutenant colonels and colonels he was determined to groom for higher command. The next year, Marshall worked with Senator James F. Byrne to obtain legislation changing military promotion policy that enabled him to jump Eisenhower over the heads of more than 350 officers who were senior to him. By March of 1942, thanks to Marshall, Eisenhower in less than two years had become a major general.

Marshall pressed him on the British, who appointed him commander over all three American forces in Britain, and then, when Marshall could have had what he deeply desired, the top command for the invasion of Europe, instead, he opened the way for Eisenhower. President Roosevelt later told Eisenhower that Marshall had been entitled to the command of the invasion, but that he had been relieved when Marshall declined to put himself forward because he wanted Marshall by his side. Eisenhower's aide, Harry Butcher, in his memoirs, noted that Marshall's "whole attitude toward Ike was almost that of father to son." Eric Larabee, in his outstanding study of World War II commanders, avers that Eisenhower and Marshall "were virtually as one."

Against this background, Eisenhower's reaction to McCarthy's attacks on Marshall's loyalty as well as his competence was an intensely interesting and politically important question. For many, the question was not one of politics but of character.

Eisenhower first confronted the issue publicly when he came home to seek the nomination. On June 4, at a press conference in his hometown of Abilene, Kansas, he was asked if he would support the reelection of

Senator McCarthy. He replied he would not indulge in personalities, then added that no one was more determined than he that "any kind of Communistic, subversive or pinkish influences be uprooted from responsible places in our government." This evasive tactic was employed countless times to duck questions about McCarthy that, nonetheless, kept coming back because many were aware that Marshall had helped him to become the national hero that he was.

Marshall's biographer, Forrest C. Pogue, has noted that on November 6, 1950, some five months before McCarthy's long diatribe, Eisenhower wrote in his diary, "Marshall, the best public servant of the lot, obviously wants to quit" (as secretary of defense). The two had maintained an active correspondence that had continued after Eisenhower became president of Columbia University, but lapsed as his campaign for the nomination intensified. Promptly after the nomination he received from Marshall a handwritten letter congratulating him on his "fine victory," adding that he had "carefully refrained from any communication with you because of a continued effort to keep entirely clear of political affairs. But more than that, I felt because of the vigorous attacks on me by various Republicans any communcation with you might be picked up as the basis of some strictures detrimental to your cause."

On July 14, from Denver, Eisenhower thanked Marshall for his "fine note," and expressed astonishment at finding himself a candidate for President. "In any event, here I am," he wrote, "and I shall, of course, fight as hard as I can with the single limit on my efforts defined by honor, fairness and decency." The letter went on to say that the government "cannot stand the excesses that come about from one party domination for too long a time," and that he was "in disagreement with the present administration on many vital points of policy," and closed with "affectionate greetings" to both the general and his wife from himself and Mrs. Eisenhower. Stephen E. Ambrose, in his biography of Eisenhower, comments, "He did not thank Marshall directly for helping him by refusing to comment on the charges of treason brought against him by various Republicans, and he ignored Marshall's gentle reference to Eisenhower's new associates."

At an impromptu press conference in late August, he was pressed for a comment on McCarthy's charges against Marshall. Angrily, he arose from his chair, paced the room, and said, "There is nothing of disloyalty in General Marshall's soul," and without mentioning McCarthy, added, "I have no patience with anyone who can find in his [Marshall's] record of service for this country anything to criticize." He later said he regarded this as a definitive defense, but virtually no one else did as the vituperation against Marshall continued unabated from men he continued to endorse.

On September 9, Eisenhower's campaign train stopped in Indianapolis for a big rally at the Butler University Field House. Senator

Jenner, McCarthy's most vocal supporter in the Senate, who had characterized Marshall as a "living lie" and "front man for traitors," was on the platform with him. He did not mention Jenner by name but asked support for the entire Republican ticket "from top to bottom." Every time the huge crowd applauded, Jenner would grab Eisenhower's arm and hold it aloft in a display of joyous comradeship, and at the end jumped up and embraced Eisenhower as the flash bulbs popped. Eisenhower privately expressed his fury, but it was the implied endorsement of Jenner and the public display that got the notice. Revulsion was widespread; in New York, Stephen Young, a vice chairman of the National Young Republicans, resigned, telling reporters, "It is too much for an honest man to swallow."

Pleas to disavow both Jenner and McCarthy increased. Arthur Hays Sulzberger, publisher of *The New York Times* and one of Eisenhower's early supporters, wrote him, "If you would cut yourself loose affirmatively from McCarthy, I think the heart of the world would rise up to you." His tactic, though, was to refuse to discuss personalities, and using every device he knew to avoid the issue, he even pretended not to hear when reporters questioned him on the subject.

An early October swing through the Midwest, including stops in Wisconsin, meant the issue had to be faced. At a strategy session in New York, Eisenhower turned to Emmet John Hughes and said, "Listen, couldn't we make this an occasion for me to pay a personal tribute to Marshall—right in McCarthy's back yard?" Hughes accepted the assignment with enthusiasm. He drafted a paragraph praising Marshall as one "dedicated with singular selflessness and the profoundest patriotism to the service of America," and concluding that charges of disloyalty against Marshall presented "a sobering lesson in the way freedom must *not* defend itself."

Someone on Eisenhower's staff reported his intentions to the Wisconsin Republicans, and on October 2, when the campaign train was making an overnight stop in Peoria, Illinois, Wisconsin governor Walter Kohler, Republican national committeeman Henry Ringling, and Senator McCarthy flew to Peoria by private plane and the three of them were on the train as it moved into their state. Sherman Adams showed Governor Kohler the draft of the major speech, to be given in Milwaukee, containing the Marshall paragraph. Kohler argued that it should be removed as unnecessarily insulting to McCarthy in his home state and perhaps used somewhere else. Various members of the staff got into the argument and accounts differ on the discussion. Eisenhower's own account in his memoirs is vague, but states that at some point during the train ride he told McCarthy that at Green Bay he intended to speak out against his methods.

"If you say that, they will boo you," McCarthy told him.

With some heat, Eisenhower responded that he had been criticized before for his actions and that he would "gladly be booed for standing for my own conceptions of justice."

The event was less dramatic. Eisenhower asked the crowd "to elect the entire slate of those we have nominated on our party tickets," adding that the purpose he and McCarthy had "of ridding this government of the incompetents, the dishonest and above all the subversive and disloyal are one and the same and we differ only over methods." But, of course, it was McCarthy's methods that the national furor was all about; no one disagreed with the stated purposes.

At the stop in Appleton, McCarthy's hometown, McCarthy introduced Eisenhower and stood by him during a twelve-minute speech that made no reference either to McCarthy or his methods.

Meanwhile, while the argument over retaining or deleting the Marshall paragraph went on, key advisers such as Gabriel Hauge and Robert Cutler were telling reporters, "Just wait until we get to Milwaukee and you will find out what the General thinks of Marshall."

The event was anticlimactic. Not only was there no reference to Marshall, but the speech concentrated on Communist infiltration of government and contained the most McCarthylike statement of his campaign. The infiltration that had occurred "meant—in its most ugly triumph—treason itself." He did add that "freedom must defend itself with courage, with care, with force and with fairness."

Anticlimax or not, the speech created an uproar. Hauge considered resigning from the campaign; Senator Wayne Morse of Oregon did resign from the Republican party; Harold Stassen wrote a complaining memo, and there was a discordant chorus of editorials. Edward R. Murrow, screening the Wisconsin footage in New York, blurted out, "For Chrissake, Marshall *made* this man's career," and his *See It Now* program on Sunday was a running juxtaposition of Eisenhower and McCarthy together. About the only public figure who remained silent was Marshall.

"That he was ashamed of himself there can be little doubt," Ambrose wrote in his biography of Eisenhower.

After writing Stassen, he tried never again to refer to the Milwaukee speech. When he came to write his memoirs, ten years later, he wanted to ignore it altogether. When his aides insisted he could not simply pass it over, he wrote, discarded, wrote again, discarded again, and finally printed a version in which he said that if he had realized what the reaction to the deletion was going to be, "I would never have acceded to the staff's arguments, logical as they sounded at the time." He claimed that the reaction constituted "a distortion of the facts, a distortion that even led some to question my loyalty to General Marshall." That was as close as he ever came to making a public

apology to Marshall; whether he made a private apology or not
is unknown.

The episode finds its place in a Stevenson biography because it was
pivotal in shaping a new attitude that prevailed from then on through the
campaigns of 1952 and 1956, and, indeed, the entire Eisenhower presidency. Never again, after Eisenhower's Wisconsin trip, would Adlai refer
to "my distinguished opponent"; from then on it was usually just "the
general."

Adlai had not hesitated to seek political gain from the dilemma
posed for Eisenhower by "slanderers of his dear friend and senior officer," who were prominent in the Republican campaign. It was, he told
the Liberal party in New York on August 28, a "symbolic tragedy," because "everything that our distinguished fellow citizen has accomplished
in his great service to his country is imperilled by many men who propose
to ride to Washington on his train." But, since "you can tell the size of a
man by the size of the thing that makes him mad," he did not then believe Eisenhower would remain silent and follow what he called "the mid-
dle-of-the-gutter approach."

George Ball reports Adlai was "shocked and outraged at
Eisenhower's refusal to defend General Marshall in the presence of
Joseph R. McCarthy." Adlai had absorbed the respect for Marshall that
prevailed when he was working with Secretary of the Navy Knox;
Marshall had come to know Adlai sufficiently well at the United Nations
and through the Council on Foreign Relations to have offered him an
appointment as assistant secretary. Marshall's home in Pinehurst, North
Carolina, was near that of Ernest and Buffie Ives and occasional encounters had occurred there.

All this made it impossible for him to understand Eisenhower's
failure to respond to the McCarthy attacks. He called the Milwaukee
speech a "melancholy spectacle," adding, "My opponent has been worrying about my funnybone. I'm worrying about his backbone." James Reston observed in *The New York Times* that Adlai now was "attacking
General Eisenhower personally and trying to demonstrate that the General is not only incompetent to hold the office of the Presidency, but is
not even his own master in the campaign."

Adlai went to Wisconsin on October 8 to attack McCarthy on his
home grounds. He reminded the students at the University of Wisconsin,
"in case you have not been reading all the philosophers," that Aristotle
had said, "History shows that almost all tyrants have been demagogues
who gained favor with the people by their accusations of the nobles"; and
then exclaimed, "Way back then!" He went on to say in a pointed reference to Eisenhower as well as McCarthy: "Disturbing things have taken
place in our own land. The pillorying of the innocent has caused the wise

to stammer and the timid to retreat . . . the voice of the accuser stills every other voice in the land."

When Eisenhower's train stopped in Springfield, Adlai had state employees released from work for an hour to hear him, but it was virtually his last chivalrous gesture toward Eisenhower. Whatever respect remained was limited to "the general's" military achievements. Favorable assumptions shriveled, common ground was ignored, attacks sharpened, and hope for a reasoned discussion of issues was abandoned in favor of unilateral presentation of differing views.

Midway in his presidency, President Eisenhower happily adopted the phrase "McCarthywasm," but midway in the campaign it was still very much an "ism" expressing itself in new and nasty ways. From the outset, with Eisenhower's tacit approval, Nixon adopted as his theme for nearly every speech the "scientific" formula of Senator Karl Mundt of South Dakota—C(2)K(1)—communism, corruption, and Korea. He repeatedly rejected the idea of a "nicey-nice little powder puff duel" with someone who dismissed "the Communist menace in America as phantoms." Stevenson's election would mean "more Alger Hisses, more atomic spies, more crises." His second and final national television speech, on October 13, devoted most of the half hour to the Hiss case and Adlai's endorsement of the "arch-traitor." Meanwhile, Senator McCarthy was playing the same theme in a lower key, clumsily but deliberately confusing his reference to "Alger, I mean, Adlai Stevenson."

It had been anticipated that efforts would be made to exploit, particularly among Catholic voters, the fact of Adlai's divorce. This concern was nourished by uncertainty about Ellen's increasingly erratic behavior, not yet identified by anyone as the product of mental illness. She talked to reporters about a book she planned to write under the title of *The Egghead and I,* building on the currently popular book, *The Egg and I,* that would "expose" him and show that he was unfit to be President. Yet, when the *Chicago Daily News* ran a series of articles on their relationship, there was nothing sensational and she expressed the hope that the divorce would not influence anyone's vote. Nonetheless, rumors spread that the divorce had been caused by "other women."

The Democratic National Committee gathered information on Eisenhower's wartime relationship with Kay Summersby to hold in reserve in case it seemed useful. A leaflet began circulating saying Ellen had divorced Adlai because he was incompetent and incapable of supporting her, that he had killed a young girl "in a jealous rage" because she was interested in another boy, that his political career had been launched by Arvey, who was "Communistically saturated and a scoundrel," and by Congressman William L. Dawson, "a Negro and a Communist." Then, to rumors of rampant heterosexuality were added whispers of homosexuality.

Jane Dick recalls being summoned out of a movie to return an urgent message from a friend of hers and Adlai's, William Poole, who out of concern over a possible Taft candidacy had become chairman of the Citizens for Eisenhower in Illinois. He told her he had just learned that one of his campaign colleagues was spreading the report that Adlai was a homosexual and he was planning to issue a statement branding it as untrue. Jane advised against it, saying it would only give circulation to a rumor that would die out simply because it was so wrong.

At about the same time, a man posing as an FBI agent called on the friend of a member of the governor's staff saying he was investigating the homosexuality of Stevenson and his staff. Efforts to trace the phony agent were launched too late to succeed.

On the heels of all this, the campaign staff was told that the Republican attack was about to shift from "punks and pinks" to "punks, pinks and pansies." Indeed, the phrase did begin to pop up in McCarthy's attacks but in the general virulence of his language it escaped notice; as did the *New York Daily News* references to "Adelaide." Alarm spread, however, with word that the Republican National Committee had bought television time on Monday, October 27, eight days before the election, for a McCarthy speech to nail the "pansies" firmly onto the "punks and the pinks."

At the Elks Club it was decided that the "punks and pinks" campaign should be hit head-on in a major speech scheduled for Cleveland on October 23. As Ben Heineman and Arthur Schlesinger, Jr., went to work on a draft, debate proceeded on whether to include the "pansies" charge or to ignore it. Tension was palpable as the campaign moved into Cleveland, and alternate paragraphs dealing with the various charges were weighed.

"For three months now I have done my best to talk sensibly," Adlai told the huge audience that at first was restive and then became transfixed by what followed.

I believed with many of you that General Eisenhower's hard-won victory in the Chicago Convention was a victory of the constructive and progressive men in the Republican Party over its bitter and reactionary elements. I believed that an educational and elevating national discussion would result. But, instead, in the past two months the General has, one by one, embraced the men who were so savagely against him at Chicago. . . . It is not a campaign by debate. It has become a systematic program of innuendo and accusation aimed at sowing the seeds of doubt and mistrust.

The Republican candidate for Vice President has himself set the pace. This week and next—in these last days before the election—the Republican high command is counting heavily on this kind of campaign. Next Monday, I'm informed, the junior Senator from Wisconsin is going to make a highly advertised speech—the man who said last week that if he were put aboard my campaign train with a club, he might be able to make a good American out of me. . . . This man will appear on nationwide radio and television as the planned climax of the Republican campaign. . . . You will hear from the Senator from Wisconsin, with the permission and the approval of General Eisenhower. . . . Only last week, stung by charges that he had surrendered to the Old Guard, the General said that the decisions in this campaign "have been and will be mine alone." He added: "This crusade which I have taken to the American people represents what I, myself, believe." Crusade indeed! . . .

If the General would publicly embrace those who slandered General Marshall, there is certainly no reason to expect that he would restrain those who slander me.

He then recounted in detail his acquaintance with Hiss, the deposition he had given, and the charges being made by Nixon and other party spokesmen.

"I would suggest to the Republican 'crusaders' that if they were to apply the same methods to their own candidate, General Eisenhower, and to his foreign affairs adviser, Mr. Dulles, they would find that both men were of the same opinion about Alger Hiss, and more so," he continued. "And, more important, I would suggest that these methods are dangerous, not just to the Republican candidate, but to the processes of our democracy." He then recounted Dulles's role in the election of Hiss to the presidency of the Carnegie Endowment for International Peace, and the continuing relationship of both General Eisenhower and Dulles on its board of trustees until after Hiss's conviction; saying he did so "only to make the point that the mistrust, the innuendos, the accusations which this 'crusade' is employing threatens not merely themselves, but the integrity of our institutions and our respect for fair play."

Taking up "softness on Communism," he quoted a speech he had made in Chicago in 1946 warning that "Russia and communism are on the march. . . . We must forsake any hope that she is going to lie still and lick her awful wounds." This was made, he said, a few days after General Eisenhower had told a congressional committee, "Nothing guides Russian policy so much as a desire for friendship with the United States."

"I would never have believed that a Presidential contest with General Eisenhower would have made this speech necessary," he told the rapt audience, concluding:

I believe with all my heart that those who would beguile the voters by lies or half-truths, or corrupt them by fear and falsehood, are committing spiritual treason against our institutions. They are doing the work of our enemies. . . . Even worse, they undermine our basic spiritual values. For in the final accounting, "What shall it profit a man if he shall gain the whole world, and lose his own soul?"

The audience sat in stunned silence for a moment, and then broke into wild cheering and applause. President Truman later expressed the opinion that the speech had been a mistake. No one there that night thought so, and it may have at least partly accounted for the rambling, ineffective speech by McCarthy on Monday that did no more than rehash old material. There may also have been another reason that McCarthy's performance was blunted.

The respected columnist, Marquis Childs, has said that someone on the Democratic National Committee informed a counterpart on the Republican National Committee that they possessed a photostat of a letter General Marshall had written to General Eisenhower dealing with a report that Eisenhower and his aide, Harry Butcher, had returned to the United States briefly to tell their wives they were going to seek divorces after the war. Marshall, hearing of it, is said to have sent a note saying: "You are absent from duty without permission. If you do not return to your command immediately I shall replace you. Moreover, I know the reason for your visit here and I believe it would be very damaging to the morale of the Army and the country if this were known." The Republicans were told that if the McCarthy speech added the "pansies" charge to the "punks and pinks," the letter would be released.

Butcher did, in fact, divorce his wife after the war but the only corroboration of Childs's story is found in President Truman's conversations with Merle Miller, published in the best-selling book, *Plain Speaking.* In this version, General Eisenhower declared his intention in a letter to General Marshall and "Marshall wrote him back a letter the likes of which I never did see."

"Marshall said that if he ever again even mentioned a thing like that, he'd see to it that the rest of his life was a living hell," Miller records President Truman as saying. "General Marshall didn't very often lose his temper, but when he did, it was a corker. I don't like Eisenhower, you know that. I never have, but one of the last things I did as President, I got those letters from his file in the Pentagon, and I destroyed them."

The existence of the letter or letters or the truth of the Democrats' threat has never been established. When McCarthy made his much heralded speech, however, it had no reference to, or, as in earlier speeches, any insinuation concerning "pansies." It was clearly below his standard for vituperation, a relief to the concerned Stevensonians, and a disappointment to the Republican sponsors of his half hour on television.

It was not C(2) that dominated the final weeks of the campaign, however; it was K(1)—Korea—and it was decisive.

By 1952, the American people had become profoundly weary of the war they had supported so warmly in June 1950 when the United Nations Security Council, on the initiative of the United States, had asked member states to resist the North Korean invasion of the South. The entry of Chinese troops into the fighting, the dismissal of General MacArthur for wanting to ignore President Truman's orders and carry the war into China, stalemates on the battlefield and at the truce negotiating table, all added up to broad and deep frustration. The Taft wing of the Republican party had seized on the public restiveness to attack "Mr. Truman's war."

Eisenhower, by contrast, in Abilene, Kansas, on June 5 had said he had no plan for ending the Korean War, warned against bombing on the China side of the Yalu River as advocated by MacArthur and Taft partisans, and maintained that the United States should stand firm and try for a "decent armistice."

This moderate stand, plus the fact that Eisenhower had been Chairman of the Joint Chiefs of Staff in the Truman administration, encouraged Adlai to believe that a bipartisan approach to Korea if not to other foreign policy issues might prevail. On September 1, the official opening day of his campaign, Adlai had made a speech in Grand Rapids stating:

> I do not believe there is any fundamental issue between the Republican candidate for President and myself. As far as I know, he, like myself, approves the basic direction our foreign policy has been following. . . . He has differed sharply with members of his party who have assailed the American action to stop and turn back Communist aggression. He has gone further to set himself against the views of important members of his party who have called for enlarging the Korean war. I think he has done us all a service by saying these things.

Within a few weeks, the tone changed. In Cincinnati, on September 22, Eisenhower charged that the war in Korea resulted because the Truman administration had allowed America to become weak, had demobilized our armed forces, "abandoned" China to the Communists, and announced to the world that we had written off most of the Far East. "If there must be war," Eisenhower now said, "let it be Asians against Asians. America must avoid the kind of bungling that led us into Korea. Young farm boys must stay on their farms; the students stay in school." Then, a vague forecast of the later, decisive, thrust: "Without weakening the security of the free world, I pledge full dedication to the job of finding an intelligent and honorable way to end the tragic toll of American casualties in Korea." Later, he even contradicted his earlier stand saying,

"I have always stood behind General MacArthur in bombing those bases."

He was clearly nettled by Adlai's jibes at concessions made to Senator Taft during a meeting at his Columbia University residence on September 12. Adlai called the joint statement "the surrender on Morningside Heights," adding that "Taft lost the nomination but won the nominee." He also wondered aloud whether Taft was now a six-star general since he had obtained the surrender of a five-star officer. In Cincinnati, Eisenhower scornfully attacked Adlai's sense of humor: "Is there anything funny about the fact that they [the Democrats] have fumbled and bungled away the peace and have even gotten us into a war in Korea?"

Humor aside, for Adlai, Korea was more than a difficult political problem transferred to him by the Truman administration; it was a deeply serious issue at the heart of national interest. He saw it as the first major test of the effort to build a system of collective security through the United Nations. Moreover, Adlai III was in the Marine Corps training to go to Korea. In the midst of the Nixon "slush fund" affair, he had flown to the U.S. Marine base at Quantico, Virginia, to talk about Korea to the graduating class that included his son, making perhaps the most eloquent statement he had made since the convention:

> Why must you defend your country when your country seems to lie in peace around you? Is it because of some mistake made in the past by those older than yourselves—some failure of foresight or decision? Is it for that you must offer the sacrifice of the young years of your lives?
>
> Certainly there have been failures and mistakes. The course of human history is a record, in tragic part, of things done which should not have been done, things not done that should have been done. . . . But of one thing I, for myself, am certain and I think you also can be certain.
>
> It is not to make good the errors of the past that you are here but to make good the promise of the future. The fighting in which we are now engaged in Korea is fighting undertaken in the name of the common collective security of the great majority of the nations of the world against the brutal aggressiveness of one or more of them. . . . We and our friends found the courage to resist two years ago. It is to press that courage home, to affirm and to establish the faith that a peaceful world can in truth be built, that you and thousands upon thousands of young men like you have been asked to serve your country with the hope and promise of your lives.

This short speech solidified Adlai's desire to make a major speech on Korea; a desire shared by the Elks Club contingent who had been watching with growing irritation the attacks by Nixon and others which Eisenhower slowly was beginning to echo. Louisville was slated for a large rally on September 27, and it was decided that would be the place. Adlai discussed with Carl McGowan, George Ball, and a few others his plan to go to Korea, and then on to Japan and India after the election. However, the idea of mentioning it in a speech was discarded because it might seem like an obvious attempt to win votes. It was decided instead to make the speech a point-by-point rebuttal to Eisenhower's in Cincinnati and a broad outline of American policy in containing communism.

In response to Eisenhower's assertion that the administration had underestimated the Soviet threat, Adlai quoted Eisenhower's statement at the end of the war that he saw "no reason" why the Soviet and Western systems "could not live side by side in the world." The criticism that American forces had been demobilized too fast at the end of World War II was met with evidence that the Republicans had attacked President Truman for not moving faster, and he quoted Eisenhower himself as saying in 1946, "Frankly, I don't think demobilization was too fast." To Eisenhower's charge that the administration had withdrawn forces from Korea, he replied that the withdrawal had been recommended by the Chiefs of Staff when Eisenhower was serving as Army Chief of Staff. The charge that China had been abandoned to the Communists was met with Senator Arthur Vandenberg's testimony that defeat of the Nationalists did not result from lack of American supplies or support. The criticism of Secretary of State Acheson for excluding Korea from our defense perimeter in a speech in 1950 was unmerited since the line had been developed by the military and not by the secretary of state.

His litany of what had been achieved in Korea contained claims that history has proved wrong, such as, proving "to all the peoples of the Far East that communism is not the wave of the future, that it can be stopped," and that "we have helped to save the peoples of Indo-China from communist conquest." Other claims were more legitimate:

> We have smashed the threat to Japan through Korea and so have strengthened this friend and ally. We have discouraged the Chinese communists from striking at Formosa. We have mightily strengthened our defenses and all our defensive positions around the world. We have trained and equipped a large army of South Koreans, who can assume a growing share of the defense of their country.

The basic weakness of his position was revealed in his final words: "I promise no easy solutions, no relief from burdens and anxieties, for to do this would be not only dishonest, it would be to attack the foundations of our greatness. I can offer something infinitely better: an opportunity to work and sacrifice that freedom may flourish."

What he offered was not what the American people wanted, and on October 24, the vulnerability of his position was dramatically exposed.

Emmet John Hughes, in his book, *Ordeal of Power,* has written with justifiable pride of his role in writing the speech that sealed the outcome of the 1952 election. Handed to Eisenhower the day before its delivery, it was a thoughtful speech on the Communist challenge that ended with a pledge neither he nor the staff had ever discussed: a "simple, firm resolution," to "forgo the diversions of politics and to concentrate on the job of ending the Korean War—until that job is honorably done."

"That job," he went on, "requires a personal trip to Korea. I shall make the trip. Only in that way could I learn how best to serve the American people in the cause of peace.

"I shall go to Korea."

The politically astute Colonel Arvey, listening at home, turned to his wife and said, "That's the speech that will beat us." An Associated Press reporter on the Eisenhower train left for home saying the campaign was over.

Having planned to go to Korea himself but rejecting any public announcement as being too obvious a political ploy, Adlai immediately recognized the political impact of the Eisenhower pledge and decided to emphasize Korea in a speech scheduled for Brooklyn on October 31. In it, he dealt prophetically with a central issue in the negotiations that Eisenhower had avoided.

"The question of the forcible return of prisoners of war is an essential test," Adlai said. ". . . Fifty thousand prisoners have stated that they would rather kill themselves than return to their homeland. . . . This is the sole question remaining unresolved in the truce negotiations. Is this the question General Eisenhower intends to settle by going to Korea?" He then pointed out that various Republican leaders had counseled our negotiators to yield on the prisoner issue, and asked if Eisenhower planned to follow their advice and "give up our moral position."

He had begun the speech by dealing with those who linked "softness on Communism" at home to the impasse in Korea.

"A campaign addressed not to men's minds and to their best instincts but to their passions, emotions and prejudices is unworthy at best. Now that the fate of the nation is at stake it is unbearable."

He ended the debate on Korea with a powerful, if futile, conclusion:

> I have the profoundest sympathy for every mother and father in the United States who is affected by this tragic war. No one is more determined than I to see it is brought to a conclusion. But that conclusion must be honorable, for if we do not maintain our moral position we have lost everything—our young men will have died in vain. If we give up on this point, if we sent

these 50,000 prisoners to their death, we will no longer lead the coalition of the free world. . . .

There is no greater cruelty, in my judgment, than the raising of false hopes—no greater arrogance than playing politics with peace and war. Rather than exploit human hopes and fears, rather than provide glib solutions and false assurances, I would gladly lose this Presidential election.

Eisenhower had not thought through what he would do when he went to Korea; in fact, Hughes has said it did not enter into their conversation after the speech. But it was what people wanted to hear; and it surely lifted the spirits of the weary and frustrated troops in Korea. In the event, his trip did not end the war; it took the death of Stalin and more months of bitter negotiations by the same team of negotiators who had begun their work under President Truman before an armistice was concluded. It was, finally, the United States that made the decisive concession: The prisoners of war were not turned over to the Communists but they were allowed to "interview" them to make sure they had, in fact, defected and they were allowed to try to persuade the prisoners to return home. Some of them were so "persuaded," and thus a moral blur was spread over the armistice.

Freed from Korea, the armies of Communist China a little more than a year later moved southward toward Indochina, as Stevenson had forewarned, and the even greater tragedy of Vietnam was in the making. To this day, the armistice line remains one of the world's danger spots and American forces remain on the Korean peninsula.

Thus the major impact of the Eisenhower speech was on the election. In the early weeks of October, the Stevenson campaign had been gathering momentum; the crowds were larger, enthusiasm more manifest, and the polls were showing a shift in Adlai's direction. There was still some drama left in the final week of the campaign but it became increasingly evident that the electorate had decided that Eisenhower best met the country's needs as they saw them.

Eisenhower's Korean initiative then, and since, obscured other aspects of the campaign. Despite their eloquence, Adlai's speeches on domestic problems offered very little by way of new ideas or the "fresh look" he called for. Essentially, what he was offering was a continuation of Roosevelt's New Deal and Truman's Fair Deal. Moreover, it was a program not substantially different from the vague promises Eisenhower was making.

It was in foreign policy beyond Korea that the most notable differences arose. As stated earlier, Eisenhower, in his speech to the American Legion, had allowed Dulles to sell him on the pledge to roll back Soviet power in Europe and "liberate" the satellite countries. In the face of fearful reaction among our Western European allies and his own real-ization that the pledge on its face was a threat of war, he pulled back and did not make another speech concentrating on foreign policy until the Korean speech barely a week before the election.

In his speeches, Adlai was advocating the creation of a balance-of-power system whereby the Soviet Union and the Western powers could maintain a peaceful if competitive coexistence until such time as firmer world cooperation and stronger international institutions could be achieved through the United Nations. Moreover, the campaign revealed him as one of the first political leaders to be deeply concerned with Asia. His knowledge and understanding were limited, but he saw beyond Korea and the vindictive recriminations over the "loss" of China to the Communists. Although he saw the war in Indochina (soon to become Vietnam) as a gallant war being waged by "our French allies" against Communist guerrillas, he also warned that communism was posing as the champion of Asian peoples and attempting to identify itself with their deeply felt needs.

> When we think of Communism, we think of what we are going to lose. When many of the Asiatics think of Communism, they think of what they are going to gain—especially if they believe they have nothing to lose. . . .
>
> Across the continent of Asia more than a billion of the world's peoples are churning in one of history's greatest up-heavals. All the struggles of man over the centuries—economic, political, spiritual—have come together in Asia and now seem to be reaching a climax. The causes behind that upheaval are many and varied. But there is nothing complicated about what the people want. They want a decent living—and they want freedom.

He urged specifically that more be done for India and Pakistan, whose existence seemed lost on Republican spokesmen; that Formosa be defended; and that Asians should be assured "America will never seek to dominate their political and their economic development," but would focus on "the widening and deepening of freedom and respect for the dignity and worth of man." To the objection that such talk was visionary, he replied that "history has shown again and again that the self-styled realists are the real visionaries—for their eyes are fixed on a past that can not be recaptured."

CHAPTER ELEVEN
"Mistimed but Not Miscast"

"EGGHEADS OF THE WORLD, Unite! You have nothing to lose but your yolks!" Such was Adlai's jovial response to the charge that he was "talking over people's heads." He admitted he was doing so once when forced to speak from a railroad overpass to a throng gathered down below, but otherwise he held steadfastly to his form. None of the campaign staff ever found anyone who admitted a speech was over his or her head—it was always expressed in terms of concern about some other person.

Richard Rovere reported overhearing a bus driver tell some passengers, "I don't suppose the average fellow's going to catch on to what he's saying. But I'm telling you, this is just what *I've* been waiting for." The driver, Rovere added, was about as close to average as anyone could hope to get.

"Did I talk ever talk over people's heads?" Adlai wrote in the foreword to the book of his campaign speeches that became a best-seller.

No—and that's about the only aspect of the campaign I am sure of! . . . I think candidates for important offices . . . in this age and day should not treat us as fourteen-year-olds but as adults, challenging us, in the ancient tradition of all civilized people, with the assumption that we should and can and will respond to the appeal of reason and imagination.

Joseph and Stewart Alsop, who apparently invented the word "egghead," in their column never were very explicit as to whether it referred to Adlai and his speeches, or to Adlai and his bald head, or to intellectuals in general. Whatever its origin or intent, "egghead" entered the vocabulary, and eggs achieved an unaccustomed vogue in the campaign. When Eisenhower made an awkward and inaccurate speech about a hundred different taxes being concealed in the price of an egg, his speech promptly was dubbed "The Egg and Ike."

Other aspects of Adlai's speeches gave the staff far greater concern; the greatest being the time he spent working on them. Despite the talent and time invested by the team at the Elks Club, Adlai, usually with McGowan's help, would give each speech at least a final review and usually far more than that. His insistence on personal involvement and revisions often meant that texts would not be ready ahead of time and newspapermen missed their deadlines. Often, no time was left to determine if the text fit allotted broadcast time, with the result that concluding paragraphs were cut off the air; or, as very occasionally happened, there was leftover time for which there was no "fill."

Once, in Denver, when the camera had strained to the limit the picture possibilities of an enthusiastic audience after a speech that was shorter than the airtime, an aide standing in the wings turned to Adlai's son, John Fell, who was wildly applauding beside him, and suggested he go out and give his father a hug and tell him what a great speech it was. The ensuing scene was wonderful television. But when the camera was off, Adlai strode offstage and asked the aide if he had "put John Fell up to that." The jubilant admission was met with what the victim described as the most chilling plunge of his life into the deep freeze of Adlai's warning that if he or any other staff member "tries again to exploit my sons" it would be that person's last day on the campaign. The aide, who knew him well, knew also that it was not an idle threat.

The inability to engage the Republicans in any discussion of the issues only reinforced Adlai's determination not to let them get lost between Eisenhower's high-level generalities and the low-level personal charges of others. Thus the pleas of his advisers to spend less time on speeches and more time cultivating political leaders were not ignored but neither were they heeded.

Although it was and remains the custom of most campaigners to give a set piece in place after place with only local references changed, Adlai could never bring himself to do it. Even the newspapermen pointed out that they could not do justice to more than two speeches a day. Wilson Wyatt reports that Adlai would listen attentively in apparent agreement but soon would be back in his compartment writing something new for the next stop.

"Adlai simply could not bring himself to be repetitious, even though each audience was different," Wyatt said. "He worked on every speech as if history depended on it." George Ball, more bluntly, declared, "We used to tell him that he would rather write than be President."

Another frustration was Adlai's insistence on a carefully crafted text when those close to him knew how effective he could be without a text. The pleas for more extemporaneous short talks were unavailing.

As a consequence, the whistle-stops gyrated between jubilation and despair. When he was at ease with his text and not too exhausted from a schedule of eight to ten speeches a day, responses were warm and the mood was good. But the box score on such days was low. The rough spots were alleviated by the presence of celebrities and remarkably warm relations with the newspapermen who, almost without exception, were ardent personal partisans regardless of the stand of their papers. Early in the campaign, Lauren Bacall, Humphrey Bogart, and Mercedes Mc-Cambridge became almost constant travelers. Other actresses such as Bette Davis, Marlene Dietrich, Ava Gardner, Tallulah Bankhead, and Shelley Winters became enthusiastic supporters, but Bacall, Bogart, and McCambridge, along with Dore Schary, were the most persistently devoted to Adlai's cause.

No matter how objective their reporting, the newspapermen rarely concealed their regard for Adlai and the campaign he was waging. They would send him messages suggesting points to be made or avoided. "Say this in Erie"—followed by a draft of remarks. Or, "You really shouldn't let [so and so] ride in the car with you; he is not your kind of a guy." Midway in the campaign, Eric Sevareid of the Columbia Broadcasting System sent Carl McGowan a long analysis of the differing styles of Adlai and Eisenhower and suggesting changes. Sharply departing from a newsman's supposed aloofness, he wrote:

> In his almost painful honesty, he . . . has been analyzing, not asserting; he has been projecting, not an image of the big, competent father or brother, but of the moral and intellectual proctor, the gadfly called conscience. In so doing he has revealed an integrity rare in American politics, a luminosity of intelligence unmatched on the political scene today; he has caught the imagination of intellectuals, of all those who are really informed; he has excited the passions of the *mind;* he has not excited the emotions of the great bulk of half-informed voters, nor, among these, has he created a feeling of Trust, of Authority, of Certainty that he knows where he is going and what must be done. Eisenhower does create that feeling, or that illusion, because, God knows, he is empty of ideas or certitude himself.

Not many revealed their feelings as fully as Sevareid, but there was almost a palpable atmosphere of respect and even affection among the seemingly cynical members of the press corps, who were nonetheless uninhibited in their complaints about late-arriving texts and other inconveniences they did not have to experience on the Eisenhower train.

What was frustrating then is almost incomprehensible now as campaign managers focus on short television spots and group appearances and shun the half-hour speech that was the norm in the 1952 campaign. At the time of the Truman-Dewey race there had been only 345,000 television sets in the United States. By 1952 the number had increased almost fifty times—to 17 million—and this became the first presidential election to make substantial use of television.

Scorn and dismay swept Stevenson campaign headquarters when it was learned that the Eisenhower campaign had purchased time for television spots during the final weeks for a blitz of commercials. The general reaction was conveyed in the remark, "What do the Republicans think the White House is, a box of corn flakes?"

Some of the more sophisticated media people, like Louis G. Cowan, were keenly aware, however, that the impact would be strong, and sought to persuade Adlai to introduce some changes into the format. Most of the suggestions were rejected as unworthy efforts to manipulate the voters.

Adlai finally did agree to a "fireside chat" in place of the usual speech to a large rally. The September 29 half hour on NBC produced the largest volume of mail that had come in since the nomination. Despite that success, he refused to repeat the format until the final night of the campaign; even then, his impatience with the requirements of television resulted in his being cut off before he finished. While Eisenhower was giving his well-polished, well-timed half hour, Adlai's aides were frantically raising enough money to allow Adlai to follow him with his final five minutes over stations in New York, Boston, Chicago, and Los Angeles.

Why one so committed to the communication of ideas was so impatient with the means of communication is difficult to explain. Part of it was his background in the print media; he was more comfortable with ideas on the printed page. He had a sense of communicating with people listening to their radios, but he had watched very little television himself and was unable to sense those same people before a television set watching as well as listening. The lights, cameras, and makeup annoyed him; they smacked of show biz, artificiality, manipulation, and seemed to block him off from rather than link him to the people he was trying to reach.

One issue Adlai had not anticipated was his sense of humor. The Republicans were against it. When he was accused of making light of serious issues, he replied that "in the midst of the terrible years of the Civil War, Abraham Lincoln—and the Republican Party still claims him—at least at election time—said of humor: 'If it were not for this occasional vent, I should die.'" The *Chicago Tribune* responded by calling him "Adlai, the Side Splitter." The more his humor was deplored, the more he defied "the Republican law of gravity," and branded the GOP as Grouchy Old Pessimists. Many both laughed and winced as he jibed, "If the Republicans will stop telling lies about us, we will stop telling the truth about them," and "The Republicans have a 'me too' candidate running on a 'yes but' platform, advised by a 'has been' staff."

Although calculated at times, humor was basically an irrepressible part of his personality. At one whistle-stop where an echo kept repeating back his words, he told the crowd, "I think what I am saying is worth listening to, but it's certainly not worth listening to twice." At Notre Dame University, when a young mother, red-faced at futile efforts to quiet her crying baby, arose from one of the front rows to leave, he interrupted himself to say, "Please don't be embarrassed. I agree with you, if not with my opponent, that it *is* time for a change."

Despite the frustrations, the criticisms, and handicaps, the speeches were undeniably the most lasting and most important feature of his campaign. Writing in 1969, the historian Herbert Muller in his book, *Adlai Stevenson: A Study in Values,* observed: "Americans can still afford to read what Stevenson said at that time, for he was confronting the ultimate issues of the modern world, the fate of all mankind . . . a reader . . . will find many witty observations, much matter still well worth thinking about, and periodically memorable passages, soaring to eloquence. The speeches are still a pleasure to read and to quote."

During the campaign the speeches, clearly, were the main impetus behind the SWITCHED TO ADLAI signs that began to appear with increasing frequency. Their impact was immense, not only on radio and television, but in the press, where they won news attention, if sometimes grudgingly, from newspapers that were overwhelmingly for Eisenhower. A total of 993 daily newspapers with 40.1 million readers supported Eisenhower, whereas only 201 dailies with only one-tenth the readers— 4.4 million—supported Adlai. In at least nine states—Delaware, Maine, New Hampshire, South Dakota, North Dakota, Rhode Island, Utah, Vermont, and Kansas—not a single paper was for him. The *Milwaukee Journal* endorsed him after he had come to Wisconsin to attack McCarthy on his home ground. Other major supporters were the *St. Louis Post-Dispatch,* the *Louisville Courier-Journal,* and the *New Orleans Item.*

Many papers, *The New York Times* among them, had committed themselves to Eisenhower even before Adlai had been nominated. *The Washington Post,* for example, on March 24, declared, "It is this newspaper's hope and belief that McCarthyism would disappear overnight if Eisenhower were elected." On September 8, at a luncheon for newspaper editors in Oregon, Adlai spoke of his concern "at the extent to which we are developing a one-party press in a two-party country." Not only was an "overwhelming majority" of the press against Democrats, but against them "automatically as dogs are against cats."

Not a single mass-circulation magazine was in his corner. *Life* magazine even went so far as to say that Adlai had aligned himself with the "Acheson faction" and its "softness on Communism;" a faction that included such people as Eleanor Roosevelt, Philip Jessup, and "on the periphery . . . one finds the trail of Alger Hiss." The Acheson faction, *Life* said, had watched Communist China's victories "with feelings ranging from complacency to connivance," had "defended subversives in the U.S. Government," had been responsible for foreign policy while communism "enslaved" 600 million people. Since "treason was afoot during this calamity," *Life* concluded, McCarthyism legitimately stood on "grounds for wholesome doubt."

Many thoughtful people shared the *Washington Post*'s view that only a victorious Republican candidate could lance the boil of McCarthyism that they saw poisoning the entire body politic. A graphic but not exceptional opinion was that expressed by Joseph Alsop in a letter to Isaiah Berlin in which he said the campaign had convinced him that Adlai was "admirably qualified" to be President and that Eisenhower was not, but adding: "I find myself constantly black-mailed by the virtual certainty that we shall have a first class fascist party in the United States if the Republicans don't win. The real need for a change in this country arises, not from the decay of the Democrats, but from the need to give the Republicans the sobering experience of responsibility."

Adlai's own family newspaper, the Bloomington *Pantagraph,* had warned him as early as June that if he were nominated, the paper nonetheless would support the Republican candidate—whoever it was—because of the editors' conviction that a change in political parties was necessary. But on October 18, Bud Merwin sent him an advance copy of the editorial that would announce that the paper "for the first time in its history will not endorse either candidate." It said Adlai was qualified to be President but that it was time for a change, so the paper would "sit this one out." Adlai made no complaint. Four years later, disillusioned with Eisenhower and feeling that Adlai was free of the Truman administration, it endorsed him.

The public and the editors were not far apart. In May 1952, long before the nominating conventions, a poll by the Roper Organization commissioned by NBC showed that among those who had made up their minds 66 percent were going to vote Republican and only 34 percent were going to support the Democratic candidate. This did not include those who were undecided. When they were included, the figures were Republicans 50 percent, Democrats 25 percent, and undecided 25 percent. On September 30, a Gallup poll showed the two candidates far apart—53 to 39, with only 8 percent undecided. On October 9, Eisenhower's percentage had shrunk to 50 percent, Adlai held about even at 38, but the undecideds had risen to 12 percent. On October 25, ten days before the election, Gallup found Eisenhower slipping even further to 48 percent with Adlai gaining a point to 39 and an additional point going to the undecided, now at 13 percent. To have the undecideds increasing just ten days before the election was unusual.

It was this shift in sentiment, and the growing enthusiasm encountered on the campaign trail, that persuaded many in the Stevenson entourage that they were gaining in their uphill battle and could well win. Crowds on the final swing through California were both huge and enthusiastic. *Newsweek* reported: "Adlai Stevenson's campaign finally had caught fire. . . . He created as much enthusiasm as Dwight D. Eisenhower. . . . The Governor's advisers naturally interpreted the crowds as evidence that what they had been predicting for so long—a switch from Eisenhower to Stevenson—at last was under way."

The list of those who "switched to Stevenson" continued to grow, including such people as Henry Kissinger, who wrote Arthur Schlesinger he had been alienated by the crudity and primitivism of Eisenhower's campaign. He urged Adlai to attack more vigorously, especially on foreign policy issues, to make his points few and clear, to establish Democratic positions instead of letting the Republicans choose the battleground, and he warned that unless Adlai gained rapidly Eisenhower might win by a landslide.

Conflicting views have been expressed on Adlai's own assessment. In his preconvention appeal to Jack Arvey not to support his nomination, he had argued that Eisenhower could not be defeated. To another friend he said, "You know, you really can't beat a household commodity—the catsup bottle on the kitchen table." But, once nominated, he never let this thought surface again until years later when he told Lillian Ross, "To run as a Democrat in 1952 was hopeless, let alone against the Number One war hero." Yet, "could anyone in good health and already in public life refuse the greatest honor and greatest opportunity in our political system?"

In any event, once nominated he campaigned with both vigor and conviction. George Ball is among those who believe he thought he was going to win. Carl McGowan is less certain, believing his expressions of confidence were addressed to maintaining the morale of the campaign workers. His own morale was remarkable. He would grouse about details of arrangements or the need for improving the content of his talks, but even in moments of extreme fatigue he was the most buoyantly confident member of the entourage.

One of the great anomalies is the image of Stevenson as an indecisive man that emerged from the campaign and has persisted in the public mind as one of his distinguishing characteristics. In the absence of what George Ball called "the institutionalized candid friend," a wife, he was almost indiscriminate in giving vent to what was on his mind. But it was more complicated than that. As a lawyer, he liked to examine many aspects of a matter before reaching a conclusion. Adlai's difficulty was that he did this aloud almost without regard to who was listening; indeed, he often would state positions simply to elicit a reaction. But there is not a single person who worked with him closely as governor or as candidate in 1952 who will tolerate the suggestion that he was indecisive.

It was President Truman who pinned the label to him most firmly. Adlai's efforts to be polite in rejecting the President's proffer of the nomination served mainly to persuade the latter that Adlai could not make up his mind. The trouble was he had not made up his mind the way the President desired.

Truman's strong convictions and Adlai's intellectual style made almost inevitable this gap in understanding, even though the basic impetus was decisive action—such as the determination to replace Frank McKinney as national chairman, to have the headquarters in Springfield rather than Washington or New York, to conduct the campaign as one who was not the "captive" of the President, of organized labor, or anyone else. The courage of these actions, and of stating his positions bluntly to those most unfriendly—anti-McCarthyism to the American Legion, tidelands in Texas and Louisiana, civil rights in Virginia—was not lost on those close to his campaign who frequently wished he would be less decisive.

His secretary, Carol Evans, has said: "I never once knew him to be indecisive in matters having to do with public affairs or with the public interest. He was decisive and he was honest. The very few times I knew him to be indecisive were when he was required to make decisions about himself."

Carl McGowan, who faced more tough problems with him than anyone else, has said: "He was quick and decisive on the issues that came before him. Occasionally, he would drive us up the wall on such questions as to whether he would spend the weekend in Chicago, but if a public matter arose, it was handled with despatch. We never had any trouble getting him to face hard choices or make hard decisions."

Responsibilities of the governorship did not go away during the campaign. During the weekend of October 26, a prison riot had begun at Menard Prison, in southern Illinois. The rebelling inmates held seven guards as hostages. Minow had sent Michael Seyfrit, the director of public safety, and Adlai's investigator, Michael Farrin, there, and was keeping McGowan informed at each stop of the whistle-stopping campaign train. By Thursday, October 30, as they moved through Pennsylvania toward a major speech in Pittsburgh, with introductions to be given by CIO president Philip Murray and Mayor David Lawrence, the situation at the prison was becoming more serious. Lieutenant Governor Sherwood Dixon and parole board chairman Joseph Lohman now were there.

Minow told McGowan that the inmates were going to be given one more chance to release the hostages unharmed, but if they refused, state police were going in for them the next morning with guns. Dixon felt obliged to call McGowan and inform him of the plan.

"I immediately made the arrangements for the trip back," McGowan recounted later.

> I knew that Stevenson had the same close feeling for the state police I did—a force he had taken out of politics and built up— and I knew he would want to be with them. When I told him of the plans he approved without a flicker of hesitation. We also thought that, when the rioters knew the final authority was there on the spot, they would feel there was no more room for delay and bargaining, and that it might help to prevent bloodshed.

After the speech, with McGowan, Blair, Flanagan, Ball, Schlesinger, and a few newspapermen who insisted on coming, Adlai slipped away from the cheering crowd for the flight to Menard. John Bartlow Martin has described the situation as follows:

> The decision to go to Menard, taken so automatically, looked to outsiders extremely difficult. Some Stevenson aides felt he had little to gain and everything to lose. If he compromised with the inmates, he would be criticized for "coddling convicts." If he ordered the state police to storm the cell blocks, hostages or state policemen might be killed, and Stevenson might be accused of playing politics with people's lives. The most he could accomplish would be to quell the riot. He would get little credit for that. And furthermore, Lieutenant Governor Dixon did not want Stevenson to go, for Dixon, running for Governor, had tried to quell the riot and failed; if Stevenson now succeeded, Dixon would be hurt politically. But Stevenson was still Governor, campaign or no campaign, and the responsibility was inescapably his.

Martin described Menard Prison as "probably the worst penitentiary" in Illinois.

> Guards were hired on a spoils politics basis. Some sold contraband to the inmates and stole from the state. . . . The psychiatric section caused unrest in the prison at large. Homosexuality was widespread. Stevenson had tried to tighten up Menard. There were reports that old-time guards who resisted change told inmates, "This is your chance." That is their chance to make trouble while Stevenson was campaigning for President.

Inmates had created a disturbance in the dining halls, seized seven hostages and locked them in with 350 convicts on the high seventh tier. Inmates in the psychiatric division seized other guards, and, flashing knives, threatened to kill them. Tension was rising as Adlai arrived at 4:00 A.M. and went over the plans. At 6:00 A.M., state police carrying submachine guns, shotguns, and revolvers moved into the prison chapel facing the cell house where the hostages were being held and about 100 guards, some armed and some with clubs, went into the prison yard. At 10:05, Adlai, Public Safety Director Michael Seyfrit, and the guards moved into the yard, and Adlai stood in full view beside Seyfrit who read over the loudspeaker an ultimatum he and McGowan had helped draft.

"We are going into the cell house with state police armed with guns, we will use whatever force is necessary to restore order. Bring those guards out and bring them out unharmed."

Then he and Adlai moved toward the north door of the cellblock as troopers were told to use acetylene torches on the north and south doors that had been barricaded with chains. Seyfrit kept yelling through the loudspeaker, "Get back to your cells" as the state police rushed into the cell house. At 10:25 the first two hostage guards came out the north door. Five minutes later, the third appeared. A prisoner struggling with a guard was shot and later died. A few minutes later as random shots were heard, the remaining hostages emerged. By 10:42, the troopers and guards reported "all secure" with prisoners back in their cells. Adlai walked the tiers of the cells, saying not a word to the prisoners, then went to the prison hospital to talk to the guards. Then he left to rejoin the campaign in New York. The election was only five days away.

On Saturday, November 1, the campaign train rolled through Ohio and Indiana toward Chicago, stopping for eight rear-platform speeches, the last one at Gary, Indiana, shortly after five in the afternoon. Still to come was the climactic rally at Chicago Stadium at eight. The crowd, recruited by the powerful Cook County machine, rose out of sight among the beams and rafters of the huge stadium to cheer the candidates for state office before Adlai's speech scheduled for nine-thirty on national radio and television. Lieutenant Governor Dixon was introduced as the hero of the Menard riot. He introduced Adlai.

"Tonight we have come to the end of the campaign, and a long, long journey—and I have come home to old friends and to familiar surroundings. . . . There have been times when I have wondered whether you, my friends here in Illinois, couldn't have found some easier way of getting rid of me," Adlai began. Responding to the enthusiasm of the crowd, he poked fun at the Republicans and exuded confidence in victory. Then he closed with a passage that brought even the newspaper reporters to their feet to join the rousing ovation; some of them, like many others in the throng, with tears in their eyes.

I wish you could all have made this two-month journey with me. No American could travel the long road I have traveled and not find his faith renewed, his faith in his country and its future.

I have traversed the New England hills, ablaze with autumn color, and felt the touch of the soft air of the Southland.

I have flown over the mighty mountains to the Golden Gate and the blue Pacific.

I have flown over the fir-clad slopes and the rolling wheat-lands of the great Northwest, and over the lonely cattle lands of the old Southwest.

I have traveled the route my forebears followed westward to Illinois. I have seen the old stone houses in the Pennsylvania hills, and I have come home to the sweep and the swell of the free soil of our beloved Illinois.

I have seen an America where all of the signs read "Men at Work."

But we have much to do in this century in this country of ours before its greatness may be fully realized and shared by all Americans.

As we plan for change let us be sure that our vision is high enough and broad enough so that it encompasses every single hope and dream of both the greatest and humblest among us.

I see an America where slums and tenements have vanished and children are raised in decency and self-respect.

I see an America where men and women have leisure from toil—leisure to cultivate the resources of the spirit.

I see an America where no man is another's master—where no man's mind is dark with fear.

I see an America at peace with the world.

I see an America as the horizon of human hopes.

This is our design for the American cathedral, and we shall build it brick by brick and stone by stone, patiently, bravely and prayerfully. And, to those who say that the design defies our abilities to complete it, I answer: To act with enthusiasm and faith is the condition of acting greatly.

The next morning, *The New York Times* carried the text of "I See America" on its front page.

Also reported was the detonation on Eniwetok of the first hydrogen bomb—a new dimension in destruction had been added to mankind's capacities.

The final weekend Adlai spent working in Springfield, except for church and a reception in Bloomington on Sunday. On Monday he flew back to Chicago for the closing fireside chat that he kept reworking until it was so long that he was cut off the air before he had finished.

"Looking back, I am content," he said. "I have told you the truth as I see it. I have said what I meant and meant what I said. I have not done as well as I should like to have done, but I have done my best, frankly and forthrightly; no man can do more and you are entitled to no less."

Exhausted, he went home with Dutch and Ellen Smith. In August, Ellen had written him an affectionate letter thanking him for asking her husband to be cochairman of the Volunteers and adding, "I want you always to bear in mind that we will love you in the rains and blizzards of failure and adverse criticism as well as in the fair weather of success." Dutch never believed for a moment that Adlai could win, but it did not curtail either the tenacity or the generosity of his support. Retiring to the home of such devoted friends at this crucial point in his life was appropriate for a man who had no true home of his own.

Tuesday morning he went to Libertyville to vote. A country schoolhouse at Half Day housed the polling place, and outside the PTA had set up a tent to serve coffee and doughnuts to the Stevenson staff and press. After voting, he chatted with neighbors and friends, many of them wearing I LIKE IKE buttons, and then gathered the schoolchildren around him.

"I would like to ask all of you children to show, by holding up your hands, how many of you would like to be Governor of Illinois, the way I am." He counted the hands, and said, "Well, that's almost unanimous. Now, I would ask the Governors here if they would like to be one of you kids." With a whoop his hand shot up. Then, in a more serious tone, he went on:

> I don't know whether you understand what is going on here this morning very well. I am not sure I do myself. But what you see here is something that does not happen everywhere in the world. Here are a lot of your parents and your neighbors going over to the schoolhouse to cast their vote. That means they are deciding for themselves who is going to lead them. . . . What that means is, we decide who governs us. It is not everybody in the world who can do that. These are the things you read about in the history books, that your ancestors have been struggling for for generations—not only to get the right to govern themselves but to keep it. Perhaps the main thing you will remember about this day is that you got half a day off from school. I am sure I have enjoyed this as much as you have and what I would like to do is to spend the recess playing in the yard.

He asked what they would play and when shouts of baseball, football, and other sports went up, he asked, "Wouldn't anybody like to play a game of mock politics?" One boy replied, "We don't like mud fights."

He laughed and then after a few more minutes, almost sadly, said, "Goodby kids. I hope you will all come over and see me on St. Mary's Road, but I am not over there very often any more." With that, the motorcade took off for the airport and Springfield. The mood on the plane was subdued; nevertheless, all those on board professed belief in victory in the five-dollar pool on electoral votes. Two, including Bill Blair's, were just above the margin needed. Adlai's slip, that Bill Blair kept, predicted 381 electoral votes—a landslide!

The day before, Carl McGowan had handed Adlai a note:

"I don't know who is going to win *tomorrow,* but it is clear to me that *today* all of the honest and sensitive and intelligent people in this country know who should. Who can say, then, that victory has not already come."

The Leland Hotel ballroom was filled with campaign workers and celebrities to watch the returns on the huge scoreboard at one end of the room and, hopefully, to celebrate what they saw there. Jubilation died early. Family and close friends gathered around portable radios in the mansion while Adlai worked on state business in his downstairs office, listening to a tiny radio on the corner of his desk.

About nine o'clock Bill Blair came into the office. Adlai, who knew perfectly well what the trend portended, said cheerfully, "Well, Bill, which is it to be—A or B?" referring to two statements he had written out, one acknowledging victory, the other conceding defeat.

"I'm afraid it's B, Governor," Blair replied.

"Okay," Adlai said. His tone was casual. His face was calm.

A short while later, his friend from Princeton days, Jim Oates, went into the office.

"I was pretty sunk," Oates recalled. "But he said, 'What the hell's the matter with you—don't you realize this is going to save me a hell of a lot of work?'"

By ten-thirty he wanted to send the telegram of congratulations he had written to Eisenhower, but Steve Mitchell dissuaded him on the ground that conceding early might damage the prospects of congressional candidates. Meanwhile, in his suite at the Commodore Hotel in New York, Eisenhower was repeatedly asking, "What in God's name is the matter with that monkey?" His choice of words was not accidental. His dislike of Adlai began early and grew. When he had heard Adlai's acceptance speech and the reference to the Garden of Gethsemane, he had snapped off the television set exclaiming, "I think he's a *bigger* faker than all the rest of them."

At 12:40 A.M., Adlai refused to wait longer and went over to the Leland to read before the television cameras the telegram to Eisenhower he had written in longhand.

"The people have made their choice and I congratulate you. That you may be the servant and guardian of peace and make the vale of trouble a door of hope is my earnest prayer. Best wishes. Adlai E. Stevenson."

Then to the crowd, most of whom wept as they also cheered, he said:

The people have rendered their verdict and I gladly accept it. General Eisenhower has been a great leader in war. He has been a vigorous and valiant opponent in the campaign. These qualities will now be dedicated to leading us all through the next four years. . . .

That which unites us as American citizens is far greater than that which divides us as political parties. I urge you all to give to General Eisenhower the support he will need to carry out the great tasks that lie before him. I pledge him mine.

We vote as many, but we pray as one. With a united people, with faith in democracy, with common concern for others less fortunate around the globe, we shall move forward with God's guidance toward the time when His children shall grow in freedom and dignity in a world at peace.

That was the end of his prepared text. Then he added:

Someone asked me, as I came in, down on the street, how I felt and I was reminded of a story that a fellow townsman of ours used to tell—Abraham Lincoln. They asked him how he felt once after an unsuccessful election. He said he felt like a little boy who had stubbed his toe in the dark. He said that he was too old to cry but it hurt too much to laugh.

Borden and John Fell, who were present, reacted in stiff-upper-lip style. Borden commented it would take him at least a year to pay off his election bets. John Fell said wistfully to a friend, "It would have been nice to be a son of the President for a little while."

As Adlai left the ballroom, his secretary, Carol Evans, said he seemed startled to find her crying. Actually, many in the ballroom were sobbing aloud and millions of others sitting before their television sets that night also responded to the Lincoln story with tears in their eyes.

At the Commodore, Eisenhower did not wait to hear it. As soon as he was told that Adlai was about to make a concession statement, he snapped off the set and went down to the ballroom. After a short speech to his supporters, he and his wife drove up to the President's House at Columbia University. A polite but formal telegram was sent to Adlai saying: "I thank you for your courteous and generous message recognizing the intensity of the difficulties that lie ahead. It is clearly necessary that men and women of good will of both parties forget the political strife through which we have passed and devote themselves to the single purpose of a better future. This I believe they will do. Dwight D. Eisenhower."

As Adlai returned to the mansion, he found some people leaving, thinking he would want to be alone with family and close friends.

"Where's everybody going?" he challenged them. "Let's go upstairs and celebrate my defeat."

George Ball has written in his memoirs that the "mixed group" included

> a number of Adlai's Lake Forest friends, most of whom had, as they smugly announced, voted for Eisenhower, including one gloating female whose pneumatic bosom was asserted by a diamond Eisenhower pin. When another guest said, "Governor, you didn't win, but you educated the country with your great campaign," Stevenson replied pointedly, "But a lot of people flunked the course."

Ball added that

> ten years later listening to another candidate who had just lost an election for Governor of California, I thought of the stark difference in style and quality of the two men. Stevenson told an Abraham Lincoln anecdote. . . . The other candidate's comment—so different in spirit—was quite as much in character: "Now you won't have Dick Nixon to kick around any more."

In an earlier book, Ball described the balance of election night in these words:

> Adlai was remarkably composed and serene, the only blithe member of a doleful group. He had no taste, he said, for political wakes—"especially when I'm the corpse." He consoled us as though we, not he, were the losers; at one point disappearing into the kitchen for a jeroboam of victory champagne someone had sent him. Always the Scotsman, he insisted on not wasting it. Always the considerate host, he insisted on pouring it himself.
>
> Finally, he announced that since he had lost the election the least he could do was to make a toast. And so, with Adlai, we all raised our glasses while he offered a tribute to "Wilson Wyatt, the best campaign manager any unsuccessful politician ever had."
>
> He described himself wrongly, of course, as we all knew. He was no "unsuccessful politician," but a brave leader who had given a whole generation of Americans a cause for which many could, for the first time, feel deeply proud—a man of prophetic quality who, in Arthur Schlesinger's phrase, "set the tone for a new era in Democratic politics."
>
> Only one person present that evening would have dared to call Adlai Stevenson "unsuccessful"—and we loved him for it. For we had each of us, at different times and in different ways,

discovered that sense of decency and proportion, humility and infallible good manners which led him so often to understatement—particularly when he spoke of himself. And we would not have had him otherwise.

An unprecedented number of Americans had voted—61,637,951. Eisenhower received the votes of 55.1 percent of these—33,936,234. Adlai's total of 27,314,992 was the largest vote of any defeated presidential candidate. Aside from Eisenhower, only Franklin D. Roosevelt in 1936 had surpassed, and by less than 165,000, Adlai's total. Eisenhower's proportionate vote was less than those received by Roosevelt in 1932 and 1936, Hoover in 1928, and Harding in 1920. So there was some comfort for him in the numbers.

The defeat in the Electoral College, however, was massive, 89 votes to Eisenhower's 442. Adlai carried only nine states—all of them southern or border states. The extent to which it was a victory for Eisenhower rather than the Republican party was indicated by the fact that Republican gains from the landslide totaled only 22 seats in the House—just 3 more than needed for control—and only 1 seat in the Senate—just enough to make Nixon's vote the one to break the 48-to-48 tie. Eisenhower ran almost 6 million votes, or 10 percent, ahead of his party.

Official party reports listed Republican expenditures at $12.2 million on the national level for Eisenhower and less than half that for Stevenson, $5.1 million. The Volunteers reported expenditures of just over $750,000.

Looking back on the campaign, it now seems curious that everyone felt he should fight the battle on issues defined by the Republicans—corruption, communism, and Korea. He could have concentrated more on Eisenhower's lack of experience with civilian problems and Republican obstructionism on domestic programs such as social security. But he and his staff remained preoccupied with Republican issues. On balance, however, it is doubtful if any different tactics would have changed the result.

Adlai himself rather accurately assessed the situation in writing later, "As the battle of words progressed, I felt more and more that people cared little about the issues and party records, or about precise definitions of positions. They were weary of conflict, impatient and eager for repose." The deep feeling among the electorate that it was, indeed, time for a change, and frustration over the war in Korea, plus Eisenhower's status as a national hero and his appealing personality, made his victory a virtual certainty.

Why, then, does the 1952 campaign stand out so prominently on our political landscape?

Stephen E. Ambrose has written:

Few of the participants could look back on it with pride. . . . There was Eisenhower himself, usually so careful to hold to the high ground, being dragged in the mud, forced to stand next to Senator Jenner of Indiana, who had called George Marshall a traitor. Eisenhower's closest friends hung their heads in shame when he failed to defend General Marshall. . . . One participant who could take some pride in his performance was Adlai Stevenson. He was not only witty, but thoughtful, intelligent, concerned and committed. He envisioned an America that would be caring and sharing. He offered a domestic program that would build on and extend the social gains of the New Deal. His speeches, his vision, his personality won him millions of loyal and enthusiastic followers. Many of them loved him not least because he was the most successful Democrat in getting under Nixon's skin. What Stevenson could not do was cut into General Ike's tremendous popularity.

The last sentence may be a slight overstatement. Elmo Roper, comparing the actual votes with his earlier polls of voter preference at the beginning of the campaign, concluded that between 6.5 and 11.5 million voters either had moved from being undecided or had actually switched to Adlai. Although the early undecideds created some uncertainty, he thought it reasonable to assume that Adlai had changed more votes than ever before in a presidential election and had narrowed the gap between himself and Eisenhower by some 10 million votes.

The figures carry another message. More voters than ever participated in the political process, stimulated by a national hero on one hand and a new voice on the other; and both were men of outstanding qualities. They made people feel it was important to cast their votes.

Despite vicious utterances by lesser figures, Eisenhower managed to remain aloof from the shocking excesses and stand out as an encouraging and even inspiring figure. Adlai, as a political unknown, had a far more difficult task to perform in less than four months. In the end, it was not the number of votes he received but the voters he aroused that was significant. They were the young, the idealistic, the emerging postwar generation groping for a just and better America. He was a promise of what politics might be, and a call to enter political life. He sounded themes they wanted to hear: the responsibilities of freedom, the discipline of democracy, and the necessity of recognizing that the first and last issues of democracy are moral issues.

"My tiny world seemed suddenly to widen," Richard N. Goodwin, then a college senior who was to become an assistant to both Presidents Kennedy and Johnson, has written about the impact on him as "the ringing phrases tumbled like sower's seeds on unplowed ground."

Summarizing the reaction of many in his generation, Goodwin wrote:

The pursuit of power, and its use, were not solely the object of greed and "vaulting ambition" but infused with service and nobility and the love of others. . . . He revealed a world we already sensed was there, bared challenges we were aching to undertake. The words were the words of sacrifice, but the music sang of meaning and purpose to a young man. . . . And all these principles, and many more, he suffused with another welcome and shining truth: the pursuit of national interest was not inconsistent with the desire for justice and dignity and well-being for all the people of the world—that there was no basic unresolvable contradiction between realistic policies and high ideals. He told us our sights were too low, the course we had charted too narrow. . . . He told an entire generation there was room for intelligence and idealism in public life, that politics was not just a way to live but a way to live greatly, that each of us might share in the passions of the age.

This eloquence seems far removed from the energetic disorder of the uncounted Volunteers for Stevenson offices across the country where young people were the conspicuous center of the turmoil. Their spontaneity, enthusiasm, and buoyancy were a new phenomenon and were destined to affect profoundly the future of American politics, not the least of which was the election of John F. Kennedy.

Washington Star columnist, Mary McGrory, remembers listening with her brother in New Hampshire as Adlai's acceptance speech on the radio "fell in our unbelieving ears. Politically speaking, it was the Christmas morning of our lives."

After the election, Adlai received an unprecedented avalanche of letters and telegrams from people who had voted for Eisenhower but felt compelled to tell him how much they admired him. Typical was one from Walter Lippmann saying, "You have won everything that a good man could want except only the election. That was impossible for a Democrat to do this year. You should think of your campaign as the beginning. Affectionate regards."

Even as staunch a Democrat as Hubert H. Humphrey wrote in his memoirs, *The Education of a Public Man,* that although "Adlai Stevenson was a brilliant man and thoroughly qualified to be President of the United States, a man who would have brought great honor and distinction to the office, it is a simple fact that the election of Dwight Eisenhower permitted substantial defusing of the explosive nature of American politics."

George Ball regarded the 1952 campaign as the "highest achievement" in Adlai's career, "lifting political discussion to a level of literacy and eloquence, candor and humor that tapped unsuspected responses in the American electorate." Carl McGowan, as he did so often, best assessed the situation by saying, "He was mistimed, but not miscast."

CHAPTER TWELVE

"A Funny Thing Happened . . ."

"COME IN, GENTLEMEN, WE'RE serving fried post-mortem on toast."

This was the cheery greeting extended to newsmen as they arrived at the mansion the morning after the election. There was no trace of bitterness, of regret, and little even of fatigue, as Adlai turned that very day to two tasks immediately at hand: a workmanlike conclusion of the governorship that would end on January 12, and dealing with the extraordinary outpouring of telegrams and letters that began the day after the election—many of them explaining apologetically why they had not voted for him.

His approach to the final days of the governorship was laid out in a memorandum to the president of the Illinois Civil Service Commission, Maude Myers, on November 7. After stating his concern that the pending turnover of the state government and disappointment in the election might result in "a letdown on the part of key officials and State employees generally," he expressed appreciation that some of the reaction might stem from personal loyalty to him, and then added:

> An even more basic loyalty is that which we owe to the people of Illinois; and it can be discharged only by rigorous adherence to the highest standards of public service during the remainder of our terms. It is my earnest desire that we turn the State government over to the new administration in first-rate condition. . . . We started this administration with a new concept of public responsibility; and we must end it that way.

His concern extended also to the Illinois Democratic political organization, especially in the downstate areas where the party suffered from chronic weakness. His effort to establish a program of party development failed mainly because of opposition from leaders in the legislature who preferred control over the existing mechanism, however weak, to possible inroads from people he attracted to the party—especially since they showed an unfortunate tendency toward honesty.

The last weeks were filled also with efforts to help people he had recruited find new jobs outside of government. Fortunately, the reputation for high quality that had resulted from the attention to bringing in capable people produced far more success than the attempt to strengthen downstate political organization.

In his final report to the people of Illinois on January 7, 1953, he listed four areas in which "I would wish history to judge the total worth of my administration." The first was the highway program. Work in progress in 1952 was more than twice that of any previous year. Next was education. State aid to public schools had been almost doubled during the four years. Elementary schools rated "inferior" had been reduced from one half to one fourth of the total since 1949, and the "inferior" rating for secondary schools had been cut from one half to one fifth. The third area of improvement was in welfare services and administration, most notably improved care and treatment for the mentally ill. Finally, he noted improved personnel policies and recruitment. Here he pointed to the removal of the state police from politics; the extension of the civil service system to 70.3 percent of total personnel as contrasted with 53 percent at the beginning of his term; training programs in welfare, revenue, public safety, and other departments needing trained career personnel.

"To the people of Illinois who have honored me so generously, and to the associates in this great undertaking, whose friendship and loyalty have meant so much to me, I shall be eternally grateful. And now, with a full heart, I bid you goodbye."

He was out of a job. November and December had produced a number of suggestions and offers, but there had been very little time to give thought to what he would do next.

First, there were the letters and telegrams. They were awesome—in quantity, quality, and diversity, in terms of geography as well as people. He was astonished at the extent to which his speeches had been heard and read in Europe, Africa, and Asia as well as at home. He asked Newton Minow to see to it that all of them received replies, giving to him only the few that clearly called for personal attention. Before the end of the first day, Blair and McGowan were drafted to help sift through the paper landslide. Soon it was obvious that a corps of volunteers, and, for most of the letters, a form reply, were going to be required. When a letter was dropped on his desk addressed simply "To the Man who said what he ment [sic]and—ment [sic] what he said, Springfield, Illinois," he could no longer resist plunging into the growing pile himself. By November 14, there were more than fifty thousand; by January the estimate reached a hundred thousand including more than three hundred invitations to speak.

Letters from young people, like the one who could not spell "meant," enchanted and often moved him. Seventeen members of the Air Force, an enlisted man in Korea, a nineteen-year-old Japanese, a thirteen-year-old schoolboy in New Rochelle, New York, students at Columbia University who reported the flag there was flying at half-mast, and others had their messages rescued from the form letter pile so that Adlai could respond personally to the enthusiasm and fresh involvement of young people in politics.

General Marshall sent a longhand note saying: "I send you my sympathy over the results of the campaign. You fought a great fight. Your political speeches reach a new high in statesmanship. You deserved far better of the electorate, but you will be recognized increasingly as a truly great American."

Albert Einstein, UN Secretary General Trygve Lie, Winston Churchill, Eve Curie, Reinhold Niebuhr, Carl Sandburg, John Steinbeck, Henry Steele Commager, Norman Cousins, Brooks Atkinson, and Helen Keller are a sample of the people who wrote thoughtful letters about the meaning of the campaign to them and who elicited thoughtful replies.

An early telegram from Hubert Humphrey, saying that Adlai's campaign and candidacy were "two of the finest things that have ever happened to American politics," urged him to continue to be the leader of the Democratic party. This theme became increasingly prevalent and was led by President Truman.

Leadership of the party at the outset meant little more to Adlai than paying off the campaign deficit for which he felt a personal responsibility. It amounted to what was, in his fiscally conservative mind, a staggering total of $800,000, but only a jiggle on the rising chart of today's campaign costs.

As he prepared to leave Springfield, he had nothing definite to return to—no wife, a house he loved but no one there; a profession, but no base; and hundreds of people with proposals, many of them self-aggrandizing efforts to exploit his celebrity. His old firm would have him back but under circumstances that might restrict his political freedom; other law firms beckoned, Ball's and Heineman's among them; there was the possibility of establishing his own firm with McGowan, Blair, Minow, and others. Offers of editorships, lectureships, columns, television commentaries, and academic positions piled up along with proposals for books, including urgent proposals from Harper and Brothers, Doubleday, and Random House to publish his campaign speeches. On December 9, he turned the problem over to his old friend in New York, Lloyd Garrison, as his short-term plans fell into place.

He would accept the offer of the Sidley firm to give him office space for himself, Bill Blair, Carol Evans, and Phyllis Gustafson. He wanted to keep Carl McGowan and Bill Flanagan, but since there was no arrangement that seemed right for them, McGowan joined a law firm and Flanagan joined a Chicago public relations firm. Adlai would edit a book of his campaign speeches and do most of it during a vacation in Barbados. He would make speeches at party fund-raising functions to reduce the deficit, and then about March 1, take off on an extended trip around the world during which he would not only educate himself but think through his longer-range plans.

Events, as usual, did not permit such an orderly progression; the chief problem arising from struggles to gain control of the Democratic party. Unlike most defeated candidates, he was not subjected to strong personal criticism for his conduct of the campaign. The recognition that Eisenhower was unbeatable was too widespread to permit that, but this did not mean he was without enemies in the party, most of them entrenched in the conservative southern wing.

After the election, the party found itself split into three main segments. President Truman remained the accepted leader of the segment composed of the big-city machines and the conservative labor unions. Steve Mitchell, as Adlai's man, was national chairman; but traditionally the National Committee's power stemmed mainly from the White House, and Mitchell not only lacked that backing but he had not developed strong relationships with national committeemen or state organizations, many of which were locked in their own struggles for power. Adlai's power base, such as it was, consisted of the liberal-academic-intellectual community, the Americans for Democratic Action, and liberal unions such as Walter Reuther's. The real power was in the hands of the Democrats in Congress and there the conservative southerners were in control.

When the parties caucused on January 2, control of the majority Republican party was won by the Taft wing in both the House and the Senate. For the minority Democrats, Sam Rayburn became floor leader in the House and his fellow Texan and protégé, Lyndon B. Johnson, was elected leader of the Senate. Veteran Washington political observer, Thomas L. Stokes, wrote in his syndicated column: "The people, including many Democrats, voted for Gen. Eisenhower. What they get in Congress is Senator Taft. Likewise, what might be called the 'Stevenson element' in the Democratic party . . . is much in the minority in Congress so far as power and voice are concerned." Rayburn had actively supported the Democratic ticket in the election. Johnson's support, with an eye on the Shivers/Daniel bloc, was more ambiguous. When an effort to stop Johnson's bid for leadership was initiated by two friends of Adlai's, Senators Paul Douglas and J. William Fulbright, Johnson immediately assumed that Adlai was part of, if not behind, their campaign. Adlai thereupon became a target of the love-hate courting and undercutting that was such a remarkable aspect of the Johnson persona and which lasted until Adlai was in his grave.

Given this situation, Adlai wisely avoided either an overt bid for leadership or an expression of ambitions for 1956 that would have invited confrontation. Instead, he opted for emphasis on fund raising; the avoidance of any challenge to the southern wing, which he felt was central to the future of the Democratic party; and a long absence from the country that would last from March into August. This is the background that must be kept in mind in looking at the exceptionally active five months that intervened between the election and the departure on the round-the-world trip.

As early as November 7, President Truman had wired his hope that Adlai would, as head of the Democratic party, revitalize the Democratic National Committee to work for the recapture of the Congress in the 1954 elections. Adlai had responded promptly and favorably to the suggestion that they "discuss political matters to our hearts content without fear of interruption or of being overheard."

On December 3, he flew to Washington where he was almost mobbed by a huge airport crowd shouting, "We want Adlai." When he arrived at the White House an hour late, President Truman was, even so, waiting for him under the north portico entrance and arm-in-arm took him into the White House. They talked until almost 11:00 P.M., and then Adlai was shown upstairs to the Lincoln Room. The next night, from the Lincoln Room, he wrote Jane Dick describing how the weight of history kept him from sleeping. He was nevertheless buoyed, he said, by the message he was tempted to send the President-elect: "Dear General—I got here first, pal! Yours, AES."

The second morning of his stay, Press Secretary Roger Tubby took him to the White House press room to meet a large gathering of newspaper and broadcast reporters. The questions elicited a definition of the party's role in opposition—a role it had not played since the days of Herbert Hoover—one that with little elaboration he held to in the months ahead. There would be no opposition for opposition's sake; the interests of the party "must be subordinated to the interests of the nation and the dispatch of the public business." The instrument "of being a constructive and wholesome influence in our public life will, of course, be the Democratic leadership in Congress." He repeated that "good government is good politics." His plans for public speaking were not aimed at criticizing the new administration but at reducing the party deficit. He added that he and the President had agreed that Steve Mitchell would stay on as National Committee chairman.

That night, the President and Mrs. Truman hosted a dinner that included nearly all the members of the President's Cabinet, Chief Justice and Mrs. Vinson, Associate Justice and Mrs. Clark, General and Mrs. Marshall, and former Vice President and Mrs. Wallace. The President clearly was extending himself to be cordial to Adlai and to signal his support for Adlai as the leader of the party.

On December 12, Adlai was back in Washington, this time with Adlai III. Adlai and Vice President-elect Nixon had been invited to speak at the annual dinner of the famed Gridiron Club composed of the elite of the Washington press corps and more than five hundred leaders in government and business from all over the country. Truman deliberately stayed away from the dinner to leave the spotlight to Adlai, whose speech was a triumph. For the first time, the club's off-the-record rule was breached and a printed copy of his speech was privately distributed. It began with a line that brought down the house, but strangely forecast political developments of the months ahead.

A funny thing happened to me on the way to the White House!—Let me tell you about it.

While I did not carry many states, I seem to have run way ahead in the Fourth Estate, excluding, of course, you publishers. I can think of no state I would rather have carried, and perhaps I should begin by apologizing to those of you who work for a living and who thought I was out in front somewhere beside Mississippi, Britain and France. The fact was, of course, the General was so far ahead we never saw him. I was happy to hear I had even placed second. . . .

At that Gridiron dinner just four years ago the newly elected Governor of Illinois sat down there with you common people—which reminds me that I rather enjoy talking over your heads—at last! . . . I, a Democrat, had just been elected Governor by the largest majority ever received in Republican Illinois. And here I am, four years later, and just defeated by the largest majority ever received in Democratic America. . . .

I wonder if I'm not entitled to some kind of a record. Did anyone starting from scratch ever *enter* our public life with such widespread approval, and then *leave,* with such widespread approval—all in the space of four years? Frankly, I think the chroniclers of our time have overlooked the meteoric beauty and brevity of my political career.

I am happy that almost 27 million voted for me. I was a little baffled by the emergence of that word "egghead" to describe some of my supporters—a word which I am glad to bequeath to the nation's vocabulary. It seems to have been first used to describe the more intelligensiac members of that lunatic fringe who thought I was going to win. I am happy to note that you have refrained from saying of the eggheads that the yolk was on them! . . .

I have not compared notes with the President-elect on how he enjoyed the campaign. Indeed, now that the affair is over, I hope some time to know him, which recalls many editorials and articles you gentlemen wrote last spring about how I wanted to run against Senator Taft but not the General who was my old friend. It has seemed to me odd that the simple truth that I did not want to run against anyone had so little news value.

I would tell him that for my part I enjoyed the campaign—in spots. There were times, I confess, when I . . . felt like I wouldn't do it to a dog. Let me add, by the way, that, like every red-blooded American, I too own a dog. It was not a campaign contribution. And I think the General would say to me there are times when he wishes he were in my shoes—you see I had them fixed.

And now that the tumult and shouting have died and Walter Lippman[n] and Joe Alsop have gone back to writing the next chapter of the Doomsday Book, how does the vanquished hero feel, and what of the future?

Well, gentlemen, there are certain pleasurable aspects of defeat. Although there seemed little perceptible editorial enthusiasm for me during the campaign, except in some of the better papers, I have been stirred by the virtues which so many assayists (essayists) discovered in me the moment it was discovered that the outs were in. Much of this comment seemed to suggest that it couldn't have happened to a nicer guy. And, lest you get ahead of me, I say I couldn't have lost to a nicer guy. And I'll still think so, even if the boys are not out of the trenches by Christmas!

Then there were the letters. We gave up counting before long and began to weigh them. So many of them were from people who voted for the General, and evidently felt they owed me an explanation; curious why people will go to all that trouble to write a long letter when a little X in the right place would have been so much easier. . . .

As to my future: Well, there are those like the man who changed the sign on his car after the election from "Switched to Stevenson" to "Switched, Bothered and Bewildered," who feel I should devote my classic talents to the welfare of mankind by frequent talking; then there is a smaller group who insist that God, and/or the election, has appointed me the scourge of the Republican party; and finally there is the much smaller group that feel that it is not wholly unworthy or improper to earn a living. My sons are numbered in the latter group. . . .

To those of us who constitute what I trust will be known as the responsible opposition, these are times of unusual complexity. Mention of Mr. Taft suggests, for example, that for the moment, at least, we Democrats are intruders in a family quarrel. Indeed it is difficult, for the present, to be certain whether we Democrats will be disagreeing with the new President, or acting as his bodyguard.

But whatever happens to the Republicans, the Republic will survive. I have great faith in the people. As to their wisdom, well, Coca Cola still outsells champagne. They may make mistakes. They do sometimes. But given time they correct their mistakes—at two or four year intervals. . . .

Every lesson of history is that democracy flourishes best when speech is freest. No issue is more important—and more troublesome—in this time of conflict with massive repression than the preservation of our right to bore each other. . . . Never was the responsibility of the majority press greater to make clear that it is concerned about the freedom of all Americans, and not merely about its own liberty to agree with itself. Your typewriter is a public trust. Its sound may be the most beautiful sound you know, but it has meaning and justification only if it is part of the glorious discordant symphony of a free society.

Vice President-elect Nixon also spoke. No exception was made for his remarks and they went unreported.

At almost the very hour General Eisenhower was being inaugurated President of the United States, Adlai left New York for Barbados. His note that day to Alicia Patterson, to whom more than anyone else he communicated his innermost thoughts, said, "I've no regrets; did the best I could, didn't trim, equivocate or clasp dirty hands."

This vacation, though, did not involve Alicia. He had accepted an invitation from Ronald and Marietta Tree to come to their estate in Barbados. With him on the airplane were Jane Dick, who would continue to be a close friend all of his life, and Marietta, whose close relationship was now beginning. Letters from Dorothy Fosdick had tapered off during the campaign; those with Alicia had lost some of the usual warmth, due probably to the pressures of the campaign and illness that she suffered in its final months. Alicia would remain close, however, even as the friendship with Marietta flourished.

Elegantly beautiful, well-informed and intelligent, she exuded the sophistication of a distinguished family that included a grandfather who was the founder and longtime headmaster of the famous Groton School, and a brother, Endicott Peabody, who had been governor of Massachusetts. During her junior year in college, in 1939, she had married a young lawyer in New York and had gone to work at *Life* as a researcher to support their daughter when he went into the Army as a private. At *Life,* she also became a shop steward in the Newspaper Guild and by the 1944 presidential election she was a vice chairman of the New York CIO Political Action Committee. She and her husband were divorced after the war and in 1947 she married Ronald Tree, who was some years older than she, and they went to live in England.

Tree was the son of Ellen Field, daughter of the first Marshall Field. He had been born in England and his first wife was a niece of Lady Astor. He had been elected to Parliament and served in Churchill's junior cabinet during the war. He and Marietta had entertained Adlai and Ellen at the family's great estate, Dytchley (now an important conference center), when Adlai was in London for the preparatory session of the United Nations. By the 1952 campaign, the Trees had moved back to the United States, and the friendship took on a new dimension when, after one of Adlai's early campaign speeches, Marietta encountered Bill Blair, a friend from their teenage years, when their families vacationed near each other in Maine. The invitation to recover from the campaign in Barbados had been repeated several times and was accepted within a few weeks of the election.

By the time Adlai left, Garrison had concluded negotiations on writing commitments that made certain the three weeks would not be without work. It was agreed he would make a selection of campaign speeches and write an introduction that would be published by Random House.

In addition, Garrison had concluded negotiations with Gardner Cowles at *Look* magazine that called for Adlai to travel around the world, at *Look*'s expense, with a party that would include in addition to himself, Bill Blair; *Look*'s European editor, William Attwood; and a photographer. He agreed to write ten articles of about thirty-five-hundred words each on England, Germany, Italy and the Vatican, Israel, the Arab world, India and Nehru, Indochina, Formosa and Chiang Kai-shek, Korea and Japan, and a summary article. They were to be cabled back for publication while he was still abroad, but *Look* would not alter or censor them; Garrison would approve all final proofs and layouts. *Look* agreed to pay $50,000 for the first world publication rights, with Adlai retaining all reprint or book rights. Moreover, to reduce the tax burden, it was agreed that Adlai would write two more pieces in early 1954 and 1955 on subjects to be agreed upon later at $5,000 each. Thus, the income could be spread as $20,000 per year for each of the three years.

For three weeks he combined writing with occasional tennis and swimming, and frequent evening partygoing. Adlai had a cottage to himself where he worked every morning and nearly every afternoon. One afternoon, Marietta unexpectedly encountered his lifelong love of the sun and disdain for clothing. She, Jane Dick, and Adlai were walking along a public beach in their swimming clothes when suddenly Adlai took off his trunks and ran naked into the surf. Shocked, Marietta ran up to the house for a big beach towel to give him as he came out of the water. "He had absolutely no modesty," she later commented. Visitors to the Libertyville farm, when their arrival was not anticipated and they encountered him out in the sun with few if any clothes on, had discovered that long ago.

He arrived back in New York on February 11 with the introduction and selections for *Major Campaign Speeches of Adlai E. Stevenson, 1952,* virtually completed, and work well advanced on his first postelection political speech three nights later at the Waldorf-Astoria in New York. Seventeen hundred party politicians and Volunteers crowded the huge ballroom for brief speeches by Margaret Truman, Averell Harriman, Sam Rayburn, Lyndon Johnson, Herbert Lehman, and a "major" speech by Adlai. In it he laid down a political strategy that would not win for him in 1956 but would be central to the election of John F. Kennedy in 1960.

With a bow toward the congressional leadership, he outlined the role of the opposition.

> We shall fight them to the end when we think they are wrong. But our central purpose, our guiding light, must be something different: It must be to keep on working positively and constructively for the good of the country. Of course, it is easier to express these lofty sentiments than to practice them. Undoubtedly we will have our partisan moments. But let us never be content merely to oppose: let us always propose something better. . . . Our job is to make the Democratic party stand for sound and progressive policies, so that it will attract honest, forward-looking and independent-thinking citizens.
>
> Last fall there was a formidable upsurge of interest by the people of our country in politics. Men and women took part in the campaign who had never before participated in political activities. . . . These people are the new blood of our political life. We need them, and to keep them we must have programs and candidates which will command their active allegiance.

He then proceeded to have a partisan moment of his own as he described the Republican party attempt at "government by business men." The experiment, he said, deserved a fair test, but warned of the "tendency to mistake the particular interest for the general interest," and he quoted the "immortal thought" of Secretary of Defense-designate Charles E. Wilson, president of General Motors, that "what is good for General Motors is good for the country."

Thus he defined what would become a major issue in the 1954 midterm elections, and the 1956 and 1960 presidential campaigns. Then he took up what would be a second major theme: foreign policy. Responding to a speech in which Secretary of State Dulles had warned that it might be necessary "to give a little rethinking to America's own foreign policy in relation to Europe," Adlai said:

> The last thing we want, I would suppose, is to stand alone against this threat [from Soviet ambitions]. . . . Our allies share with us not only bases and raw materials and manpower but— more important—the common faith in the worth of free men which is our most potent weapon. We need them as they need us. . . . We want understanding from them of our problems and heavy tax burdens, even as we patiently try to understand their difficulties. . . . We have heard much about the new "psychological" offensive; but we will frighten no Russians by threatening financial sanctions against our allies. . . . A genuine partnership operates through consultation and persuasion. . . . Ours must be the role of the good neighbor, the good partner, the good friend—never the big bully.

McCarthyism and race relations were saved for the end.

> Our farms and factories may give us our living. But the Bill of Rights gives us our life. Whoever lays rough hands upon it lays rough hands on you and me. Whoever profanes its spirit diminishes our inheritance and beclouds our title to greatness as a people. If we win men's hearts throughout the world, it will not be because we are a big country but because we are a great country.
> Only a government which fights for civil liberties and equal rights for its own people can stand for freedom in the rest of the world. Only a people who can achieve the moral mastery of themselves can hope to win the moral leadership of others. . . . The Democratic party understands the nature of the contemporary challenge. . . . And because the Democratic party understands the challenge of history, history will reward it once again with responsibility.

The speech was a success. President Truman, listening to it on the radio at his home in Independence, Missouri, immediately sent a telegram pledging support. He asked for an autographed copy and reported that his daughter told him the speech "was about the best she had ever heard and she was talking to her Dad when she said that."

Adlai returned to Washington in a private railroad car on Sunday with Sam Rayburn, Senators Johnson and Robert S. Kerr, Averell Harriman, and others, then to lunch at Rayburn's with the House Democratic leadership, on to a reception at the Women's National Democratic Club for Democratic members of the House and Senate. Monday morning he had breakfast with the liberal House Democrats, visited National Committee headquarters, met with Senate Democrats, and went to a reception for campaign contributors and a political dinner.

The turnouts at the Capitol were startling. Hundreds of legislators and staff aides lined up to shake his hand. In the caucus room of the old House Office Building, about four hundred, including the Republican speaker, Joseph Martin, greeted him as Sam Rayburn stood beside him in the receiving line. On the Senate side, Lyndon Johnson, who had earlier declined an invitation to come to Springfield, presented him to the hundreds who had waited outside the Senate Democratic conference room. Of the forty-seven Democratic senators, thirty-four were there, among them Senator Richard Russell, a key leader of the southern bloc whom Adlai had been courting quietly in his determined effort to build bridges between the liberal northern wing and conservative southern wing of the party. The only significant absentees were Senators Price Daniel from Texas, Harry Byrd from Virginia, and Pat McCarran from Nevada, whose committee's civil rights record Adlai had attacked.

At intervals he had also been calling on the ambassadors of countries he was planning to visit, and on Tuesday, Secretary Dulles, with four high State Department officials, gave him a briefing on those parts of Asia and Africa that were on his itinerary. President Eisenhower gave him a lunch, including some twenty congressional leaders from both parties, which was preceded by a half-hour private visit that he wrote the Trees was "uninformative."

As he returned to Chicago on Wednesday, he could look back on a week that may not have added up to the "triumphal" description of many writers, but had certainly helped him gain ground in the quiet struggle with the southern conservatives for control of the party.

After a few days of putting his personal affairs in order, Adlai proceeded to San Francisco for another Jefferson-Jackson Day gathering with Democrats from western states on February 26 that would raise another $50,000 to retire the election debt. In his speech, he repeated the themes of the New York talk, but added a sharp reply to the comment in President Eisenhower's State of the Union message that the Seventh Fleet would "no longer be employed to shield Communist China" from Taiwan. It was "unworthy and misleading," he said, to imply that "President Truman's purpose had been to protect Red China rather than Formosa." He also referred to the controversial offshore-oil issue, warning that it could "set in motion the piecemeal dismemberment of our great public domain which is held for the benefit of all the people of the United States." California oil interests were not pleased, but the public reception again was enthusiastic.

Carol Evans and Bill Blair were waiting for him at Palm Springs with piles of correspondence that needed handling before his departure. By now, Carol Evans had become so familiar with his style that she could produce the artful and often humorous short note so skillfully that only a few of the knowledgeable could detect her hand, even in the signed initials. Even so, there were still hundreds that had been winnowed from the thousands for him to go over personally.

As in Barbados, the work-filled days were leavened by occasional tennis and fun-filled dinner parties. This time it was Lauren Bacall who was the center of attraction. She and Humphrey Bogart had been ardent campaigners and had been with him in Springfield the night of the election. Bogart was working on a film but Bacall eagerly accepted an invitation from friends in Palm Springs to be with them during Adlai's stay there.

The first night she was there, at a small dinner party, she asked him what his favorite song was. "After what I've been through," he replied, "it has to be 'The Battle Hymn of the Republic.'" Writing of these few days in her autobiography, *By Myself,* she said:

> I savored every second. The truth is I had fun with him—and it was a new kind of fun. . . . He was someone I could look up to—his mind excited me—and his flirtatiousness encouraged me. And some of his friends and the people around him also encouraged me—they said it was good for him to have me around, he enjoyed my company, felt easy and relaxed with me, I took his mind off his heavy responsibilities. . . . So, short of leaving husband and home—which I had no desire or intention of doing—I would see him when I could. . . . Adlai Stevenson was someone worth putting myself on the line for, worth fighting for.

A huge bundle of letters still to be answered went into his bags as he prepared to sail on March 2. While he fretted over them, he left full of enthusiasm for this new adventure and confident that leadership of the party would not be wrested from him during the absence that would last until August 20. During that period, in which the loser in the election steadily would be strengthening his hold on his party; the winner, President Eisenhower, would be losing control of his. A funny thing, indeed, was happening.

CHAPTER THIRTEEN

"Chronic Stamina" Encounters McCarthy

TRIUMPHAL RECEPTIONS IN TWENTY-NINE countries lay ahead of the Stevenson party that boarded the S.S. *President Wilson* on March 2. In country after country, an astonished Adlai would exclaim, "Haven't they heard who won the election?" His thought that he could travel as a private citizen on a quiet trip of "self-education" proved to be wildly unrealistic. In dealing with the thousands of letters and telegrams after the election, he had not focused on the multitude from abroad and had little awareness of how widespread was his reputation as an articulate spokesman sensitive to the problems of people everywhere.

In addition to Bill Blair and Bill Attwood from *Look,* he was joined by his old friend and publisher of the *Louisville Courier-Journal,* Barry Bingham, and Dr. Walter Johnson, University of Chicago historian. Adlai had persuaded *Look* to forgo the photographer who had been in the original plan in favor of Johnson, who had been a leader of the Draft Stevenson movement but whose presence was due to the fact that, as chairman of the Fulbright Educational Exchange Program, he had visited many of the countries on their itinerary. Adlai had persuaded *Look* that it would be useful to have someone with him who could gather information from intellectuals and people in opposition movements. With Bill Blair's remarkable skill and tact in handling logistics and appointments, the group was well-balanced except for what Attwood described as one "incurable defect"—Adlai "suffers from chronic stamina."

Adlai was determined to talk to all sorts of unofficial people: journalists, educators, students, trade union leaders, writers, businessmen, and did not want to be drawn into rounds of official receptions and dinners. He wanted to gain as perceptive a view of each country as such brief visits would allow. The object, he repeated again and again, was to listen and to learn. He had brought a number of books about the areas to be visited, but, as usual, did very little reading. Much of the time on the five-day voyage to Hawaii was spent working on correspondence, which had been vastly augmented in San Francisco. He especially delighted in a telegram saying, "You are better in defeat than Eisenhower is in de head."

Warnings that the "listen and learn" objective would be under constant attack also began coming in. In response to the numerous radiograms asking him to speak during the two days they would be in Honolulu, he grudgingly accepted invitations from Frank Fasi, Democratic national committeeman of Hawaii, to appear on television; the Territorial Legislature; and, naturally, the Princeton Club. Its overwhelmingly Republican membership presented him with a scroll summarizing his virtues "now that your political career is over." But before the two days were finished, he had also met with the Hawaii Statehood Commission, Admiral Arthur W. Radford and the naval staff at Pearl Harbor, a Democratic fund-raising luau at the Chinese-American Club, and a number of small private groups during a whirlwind tour of the island. His reaction, as they boarded the Pan American Clipper for Wake Island and Japan was, "No more receptions, no more flashbulbs, no more speeches, no more handshaking, and no more politics." He was ludicrously mistaken.

At his late afternoon arrival in Tokyo, the throng that met him was described by the Tokyo *Evening News* as "the vortex of a shoving, jabbing, prodding maelstrom of animate flesh." The paper, for its part, greeted him by printing the text of his welcoming speech at the Democratic convention.

It is difficult now to recapture the precarious state of the political, economic, and social structures of Japan in early 1953. Prime Minister Shigeru Yoshida had not yet consolidated his political leadership and was under siege from the right and, most vigorously, the left. The economy seemed in danger of being overwhelmed by too many people, too little land, too few resources, and too few opportunities for finding markets abroad. Japanese intellectuals, as was pointed out in the excellent briefing arranged by Ambassador Robert Murphy, were mainly Marxist-oriented and so isolated from outside contacts since the early 1930s that they had little knowledge of current world realities and were a generation behind thinkers in Europe and the United States.

The plans for fanning out were quickly put into action as Adlai discovered with dismay the difficulties of avoiding formalities in Japan. While Adlai, usually with Blair, was making required calls on the prime minister, the leader of the opposition Progressive party, and the head of the U.S. Far Eastern Command, General Mark Clark; Attwood and Bingham were meeting with foreign correspondents, and Johnson was at Tokyo University, or interviewing such people as Wolf Ladejinsky, the land reform expert. Attwood also interviewed Professor Lawrence Battistini, who had been in Japan for seven years and had prepared for Adlai a long memorandum warning that the United States was losing out in Asia because of identification with militarism and colonialism. When Attwood gave the memo to Adlai with the remark that some of the comments sounded heretical, Adlai replied, "What's wrong with heresy? We need it."

The unavoidable speech to the America-Japan Society produced the largest turnout in its history. Adlai told the throng that the purpose of his trip was "to find out something about Asians to tell Americans when I get back." He then expressed a vision unspoken by an American political leader up to that time:

> Across the continent of Asia more than a billion of the world's peoples are churning in one of history's great upheavals and convulsions. All the struggles of man over the centuries— economic, political and spiritual—have come together in Asia and now seem to be reaching a climax. The causes behind that upheaval are many and varied. But there is nothing complicated about what the people want, at least that's what we think. What they want is simply a decent living—and they want some measure of freedom for themselves and their countries. . . . I believe we may in time look back at Korea and the events of this post-war period here in Japan, our reconciliation and community of friendship and common peaceful purposes, as a major turning point in history—and a turning point which led not to another terrible war, but to the first historic demonstration that an effective system of collective security is possible.

The party was scheduled to fly to Ōsaka at nine the next morning, but before sunup Adlai roused Blair and Johnson saying he had arranged to visit a fish market and vegetable market. Thus they learned early of his insatiable interest in markets and bazaars wherever they were. The trip to Ōsaka was planned primarily to see the shrines and temples there and in the ancient capital city of Kyōto, but after landing, Adlai insisted on stopping unannounced at an industrial plant along the way where he plied the stunned assistant manager with questions about wages, working conditions, and pricing.

At eight the next morning he was at Doshisha University for a meeting with students and faculty who told him that 80 percent of the students were Marxist-inclined and were watching with interest the "progressive reforms" being carried out in China. Their questions were full of Marxist clichés and complaints about the disorder caused by the democratic system the United States had "imposed" on Japan; then one demanded to know, "Just what is democracy, anyway?"

"Democracy," he told them, "is honest disagreement. It is the right to hold the opinion you believe in, and to fight for it with self-respect and determination. The virtue of democracy is not cold order. It is the heat of men's minds rubbing against each other, sending out sparks. It is liberty with responsibility. It is a struggle that never ends and is always worth the fight." For Japanese students to have freedom, he told them, they would have to learn not to go to either the extreme right or the extreme left whenever a problem occurred. He was greatly disturbed, he said, that so many Japanese intellectuals were not offering leadership. "The trouble with intellectuals is that they see so much they do not always see things very clearly and, as a result, the intellectual is apt to be wobbly." Thus spake Mr. Egghead.

En route to Korea, he studied carefully a memorandum prepared for him by Donald Kingsley of the United Nations Korean Reconstruction Agency that was to be reflected in his thinking for years to come. Necessary military pressure in Korea and elsewhere on the periphery of Soviet expansion could never be more than a primary step, Kingsley wrote. "Ideas, when related to the legitimate aspirations of men, have never been defeated militarily." The Communists in Asia were promising people three basic things: (1) land reform—an end to landlordism and the right of the peasant to the products of the land he worked; (2) national and cultural independence from Western colonialism; and (3) peace. The United States could not meet these challenges "by lectures on freedom of speech, constitutional rights, the American standard of living, television or free elections." To defeat the Communists the United States should "focus on where they are the weakest—namely, in that of performance." Throughout Asia and the Middle East, the main problem was to assist people "to improve their own living standards, while assuring them of their independence. In simplest terms, what they want is respect and rice. If we can solve this problem we can stop Communism."

"Respect and rice," in that order, became the theme, along with that of "the revolution of rising expectations," in countless speeches Adlai made during the rest of his life.

As the plane came down at Pusan, where the Korean government had fled from the Communist attack, he was amazed at the hundreds of Korean dignitaries and American GIs gathered to greet him. "Oh God, don't they know I lost the election?" he said. They knew, but they also were resentful that President-elect Eisenhower had not stopped in Pusan during his trip to Korea. Thousands upon thousands of schoolchildren lined the dusty road into Pusan and there were WELCOME STEVENSON banners sprinkled through the crowd.

Adlai was again impressed by the high quality of the briefing offered by the ambassador and his staff, after which the formula employed in Japan went to work: Adlai, Bingham, and Blair meeting with the acting prime minister, the foreign minister, members of the National Assembly, United Nations officials, and making a quick flight to Cheju Island to see the training program of the Republican Korean Army; Attwood meeting with faculty and students at Ewha University in the cluster of wooden shacks in which they were carrying on until they could return to Seoul, and with experts on the embassy staff; and Johnson, with United Nations relief-and-reconstruction officials and the leadership of Chosŏn Christian College.

Early the next morning, Monday, March 16, after a stop at the Korean Army's officer training camp, they arrived in Seoul and were driven directly to tea with President Syngman Rhee. One of his first comments was, "The Democrats saved Korea. I hope now the Republicans will finish the task." Adlai smiled and replied, "I hope so, too." Meetings with Korean officials and American Army and Air Force officers filled the afternoon, before dinner as the guest of the president, followed by a late-night meeting with newspaper reporters at the local press club. Adlai never stopped asking questions.

Early the next morning, accompanied by General Maxwell Taylor, they flew to the forward lines. They trudged up a ridge to look at the Chinese lines about a thousand yards away and chat with soldiers while occasional artillery shells rustled overhead and air strikes thudded on neighboring ridges. When a mortar exploded a few hundred yards away, General Taylor hustled the group down the ridge to a safer spot. Back in Seoul, the dust-caked, bone-tired group showered and were off to a reception given by the mayor of Seoul, followed by dinner with General Taylor and his staff at which a remarkably frank and revealing discussion ensued.

Adlai said he was concerned that Eisenhower had placed himself "over a barrel" by promising a quick solution in Korea. Many at home thought that increasing the Republic of Korea Army was a way out. Others wanted to wage full-scale war even if it meant war with China. He asked, "What will be the cost of an all-out attack? What will be the cost of a stalemate?" Cautioning that his opinions were personal and not for publication, Taylor warned that the ROK forces were overestimated; they were excellent as a defensive force and increasingly could assume more front-line duty but only if the current stalemate continued. The forces under his command, Taylor stressed, could not launch a crippling attack and such an effort would require stripping other vital areas of troops or an all-out mobilization at home. The idea of "unleashing" Chiang Kai-shek and invading the mainland was mostly talk and impractical.

If it all added up to a bleak picture, he wanted to leave Stevenson with one optimistic note. He recalled that in Berlin when the Russians realized the United States could not be dislodged and would persist with the airlift, they ended the blockade. The Chinese were hurting more than we were. No one could be sure how long they would keep it up, but a little more patience on our side would most likely produce results.

Patience did have its reward. Five weeks later, armistice talks began, and four months later they were concluded. But American troops remain in Korea to this day.

A visit to a Korean orphanage, an aircraft carrier at sea, and a farewell session with President Rhee concluded the Korean experience. As they were leaving, General C. J. Ryan admiringly commented to Attwood, "Do you realize he has spent more time looking at the ROK Army than any other visitor to Korea?"

Back in Japan, after a late-night arrival, he was up early to go looking for a cutaway for the protocol visit to the emperor, and then into the countryside with Wolf Ladejinsky to inspect Japanese farming at first hand. When it was jokingly suggested that if he really wanted to get a feel of it, he should take off his shoes and wade through the rice paddies. "Oh, if I did that," he replied, "I would probably encounter Mrs. Roosevelt coming from the opposite direction."

In Taiwan, where they arrived in the early dawn, the pace was much the same except that Generalissimo Chiang Kai-shek made a determined effort at persuasion. Attwood, in his memoirs, *The Twilight Struggle,* observed:

> While Chiang Kai-shek figured he had the Republicans in his pocket, he wasn't so sure about the Democrats. So he saw Stevenson three times—twice privately and once at a stag banquet for our party. . . . Everything he said during these meetings was a repetition or variation of one of his answers in the transcript of his first talk with Stevenson: "Elimination of the Chinese Communists on the mainland is a prerequisite to a final solution of the Korean war. Minus this, Russia will become a strong power and the war will go on. So the recovery of the Chinese mainland is an imperative necessity."

At the stag dinner, the generalissimo maintained that his forces could retake the mainland if the United States would merely divert to him 20 percent of the military support then going to the American and UN forces in Korea.

Shortly after they had returned to the guesthouse from the dinner, General Sun Li-jen, commander of the Nationalist Army who also had been one of the guests, arrived unannounced and asked to speak to Adlai alone. He was ill at ease and spoke in a low voice, clearly fearing the presence of hidden microphones. He praised the work in China of General Joseph Stilwell whose dismissal Chiang Kai-shek had demanded, and said that General Marshall had been absolutely right when, during his mission to China in 1946, he had criticized the Nationalist government as corrupt, inefficient, and without popular support. Now that 2 million people from the mainland had taken over power from the 6 million Taiwanese, the secret police were maintaining rigid thought control and Chiang and his son were ruthless and relentless in suppressing any opposition to themselves.

He agreed that the figure of 400,000 to 600,000 Nationalist troops that had been touted in the United States was greatly exaggerated; the number was closer to 150,000. Although the average age was twenty-nine, they were a good army. But if they were going to invade the mainland, the United States would have to mobilize if it was really going to help. He thought they could get somewhere on the mainland, but that their present leadership was concerned with personalities and personal power rather than with the nationalism and democracy of Sun Yat-sen's revolution. It was a sobering encounter, particularly in view of the high personal risk the general had been willing to take to have it.

In his report for *Look,* Adlai made three main points: (1) The Chinese were creating an impressive demonstration of good administration in Taiwan. He had been especially impressed by the work of the Joint Commission for Rural Reconstruction. (2) There was dissatisfaction at many levels with police-state methods. (3) The Nationalist Army was not as strong as many people thought. His earlier defense of heresy now came into focus, because these last two points at least bordered on heresy so far as the conventional wisdom in the United States in 1953 was concerned.

In Hong Kong, the presence of former *Chicago Daily News* correspondent Albert Ravenholt, now working with the American Universities Field Staff, greatly assisted his fact gathering. Ravenholt soon had them at the fishing village of Aberdeen, walking on sampans and junks, going through a fish market, then into the back alleys of Victoria chatting with shopkeepers. At one point, Adlai exclaimed, "I'm getting more out of this than interviewing Chiang!"

Ravenholt arranged a series of meetings with "old China hands" from a variety of countries and backgrounds, and Adlai combined with his own cross-examination of them a testing of what he had been told in Taiwan. There was then concern that Mao Tse-tung might seek to extend his victories into Hong Kong itself, but he was assured that the Communists needed it as a listening post and as a source of foreign exchange. The extent to which this economic support was coming from our allies angered him. On the central question of whether an invasion from Taiwan by Nationalist forces was feasible, the answer from all was the same: It was not.

In a dispatch to the *Daily News* after his departure, Ravenholt wrote that "Stevenson's fact-finding trip through Asia is emphasizing one of America's major national handicaps. This is the failure of its political parties to develop the staff of trained specialists needed to evolve policies that take account of America's world-wide involvement."

Arriving in the Philippines in the midst of a presidential election, Adlai said he felt very much at home, and enjoyed especially the ability to look at the campaign more objectively. Awaiting him was the ambassador, Admiral Raymond Spruance, who had known him when he was assistant to Secretary of the Navy Frank Knox, and also a boisterous crowd of reporters, officials, diplomats, and private citizens.

Admiral Spruance, knowing that President Elpidio Quirino was arranging at least two meetings with Adlai, invited a variety of guests to dinner, including, in addition to the foreign minister, two opposition leaders, and the Nacionalista presidential candidate, Ramon Magsaysay. General Magsaysay, along with two armed bodyguards, came early for a lengthy private meeting during which he emphatically warned of the corruption that might end in stealing the election. Magsaysay had achieved fame as a guerrilla leader during the Japanese occupation; and when, in 1950, General Marshall, as secretary of defense, had warned President Quirino there would be no more United States aid unless steps were taken to stop the corruption of the Philippine Army, Magsaysay had been appointed minister of defense. He had reorganized the army and had launched an effective campaign against the Communist-led Hukbalahaps. But just a month before Adlai arrived, he had resigned in protest over the continuing widespread corruption in the Quirino government and failure to initiate social and economic reforms needed to weaken the base of the guerrilla movement. Adlai found him so impressive, he asked him to remain behind after dinner for further conversation and stopped by his house during a tour of the city the next day for two more hours of conversation.

The embassy briefing the next morning focused on the report of a mission President Truman had sent to the Philippines in 1950, headed by Undersecretary of the Treasury Daniel W. Bell. It remains such a largely unfinished agenda, it merits summarizing still: (1) Revise the tax structure to increase the proportion of taxes collected from high incomes and large estates and curb the tax evasions of the rich: (2) Increase agricultural production by breaking up large estates and selling the land to the tenants, establishing rural credit facilities, opening new land for homesteading, and improving research and extension services: (3) Expand power and transportation facilities and encourage industrial development: (4) Implement social reforms, including a minimum wage, labor unions, improved health, education, and housing: (5) Reform public administration to ensure honesty and efficiency in government.

At the summer capital city of Baguio, President Quirino staged a huge luncheon with members of his own Liberal party in attendance, at which he lavishly praised Adlai, who deftly ignored the president's campaign remarks and with equal deftness concentrated on another sensitive topic—the need for mutually beneficial economic relations between the agricultural Philippines and industrial Japan. The president had lost his wife and two children in the war, Foreign Minister Elizalde's brother had been beheaded by the Japanese, and anti-Japanese feeling was intense and widespread. At a press conference immediately after Adlai and Admiral Spruance had left, President Quirino endorsed Adlai's comments on Japan, but vigorously attacked the United States embassy for "meddling in local politics."

Amid meetings, he finished the *Look* article and visited the Los Banos Agricultural College, where some of the most lasting economic benefits to the Philippines were just beginning to take shape, including the development of "miracle" rice that has profoundly altered the life of farmers throughout Asia. At his final press conference, as at nearly all the others since his arrival in Tokyo, he was asked to comment on President Eisenhower's campaign speech in October in which he said "Asians should fight Asians." He replied simply that the Korean War "is not a matter of race—it has to do with principles."

In his *Look* article, he stated firmly that Magsaysay "could write a bright new chapter in the chronicles of Philippine politics"—which he did until his career was cut short in an air crash. His conclusions foretold what some of the best-informed observers of the Philippines are writing as the Aquino government approaches the end of the 1980s: "I feel a cautious optimism that this ambitious, self-respecting people can set their political house to rights, tighten their belts and settle down to the long, hard business of developing their great human and natural resources, raising their standard of living and building a stable society."

As he approached Vietnam and Cambodia, he could not know that the issues awaiting him there would shadow, and probably shorten, the final years of his life. It had been only twenty-three days since he had first landed in Japan. Now, five countries and an overnight stop in Singapore later, a letter written on the airplane to Jane Dick was a capsule of his state of mind:

It's just one war after another here! The pace has been too fast and I haven't slept well—to bed last night at 12 (after writing 23 letters of thanks to people along our route) and up this morning at 5—officials, functions, heat, interviewing, writing, packing, unpacking and the ubiquitous photographers and newsmen day

*after day. Besides, I'm afflicted with a misfortune too embarrass-
ing to mention!*

Saigon was a continuing and only sporadically successful struggle to
avoid being hemmed in by officialdom—American, French, and Vietnamese. Adlai would be hearing the official line while his companions
would be hearing from newspaper correspondents that Ambassador
Heath was so committed to the necessity of the French presence that he
would allow no reports critical of the French to be transmitted back to
Washington. The United States was already spending almost a million
dollars a day to supply the French effort to sustain their colonial empire,
which nearly everyone outside officialdom told them was slipping away
and would end in the hands of Vietnamese nationalists, but whether
Communist or non-Communist was not yet clear. Few thought the remote, French-installed emperor Bao Dai was a match for the Communists' Ho Chi Minh. Even officialdom almost unanimously proclaimed the
war was at least as much political as military, but few would make critical
assessments either of French policy or of the inefficiency or corruption of
Vietnamese officials.

Supreme Court Justice William O. Douglas had recommended to
Adlai that he see Captain Edward Korn at the embassy. Johnson showed
Korn a list of Vietnamese names that Adlai had brought with him. With
surprise mixed with admiration, Korn exclaimed, "This is the best list of
nationalists-neutralists conceivable. Where did you get it?" Johnson explained that a Catholic priest who was Asian had come to Adlai's office
before they had left Chicago, and although he refused to give his name,
he urged Adlai to see the people on the list. By the end of the visit,
almost half of them had been seen and provided much of the best information they obtained.

At Hanoi, much of Adlai's time was taken up with briefings by
French military commanders who, in the 1950s, spoke in almost the same
terms our own generals and statesmen did in the 1960s. Thirteen months
after Adlai received optimistic estimates, the French were overwhelmed
at Dien Bien Phu and swiftly withdrew from the war.

From Hanoi, they flew across Laos to Siem Reap, Cambodia, to see
the awesome ruins of Angkor Wat. For two hours, Adlai wandered
through the temples, inspecting the intricate carvings and the golden
Buddhas still resisting capture by the jungle. When he found several of
his aides lagging behind on the hot climb to the top of one of the temples,
he shouted back, "What's the trouble with you fellows? Mrs. Roosevelt
climbed this pyramid." But his favorite encounter was reported by Barry
Bingham in these words:

Suddenly the air was rent by a voice raised in purest Amer-
icanese. "Ad-lie, Ad-lie!" it called, following the common mis-

pronunciation of his name. A large, amiable, overheated American lady came steaming up, her camera bumping at her ample bosom. "Ad-lie," she cried, "I've been saving my last film for a picture of a water buffalo, but I think I will take you instead!"

Bingham said Adlai was still laughing days later.

He was photographed as well with a pair of sacred white elephants, which, he noted in a letter to Marietta and Ronald Tree, really were pink and ought to be investigated promptly by Senator McCarthy.

Along the way, Adlai visited, as always, the markets, but also, refugee camps, a school for illiterates, an orphanage. One night in Saigon, after a bountiful French meal at the Majestic, he and Attwood slipped off for a walk along the riverbank a few blocks away. Everywhere there were people lying on the ground in rags, whole families huddled under cardboard shelters on the muddy bank, naked children and emaciated mothers begging for food. "How can we even talk about these people fighting to defend freedom and democracy?" Adlai asked Attwood. "What do words like that mean to them?"

In his article for *Look,* he urged unequivocal independence, a buildup of Vietnamese forces, free elections, land reform, and United States participation in policy-making if we were to bear so much of the economic burden. They were recommendations that might have worked in 1945, but by 1953 they were too late. The "domino" theory that was so fatefully to influence American policy was also set forth in these words:

From a look at the map, we can readily see why Indochina must be held. The rice-rich associated states are the strategic gateway to all of Southeast Asia. If Viet-Nam falls, all of Indochina is doomed; Thailand and Burma would be in mortal danger; Malaya and Indonesia would be exposed and vulnerable. If this vast area of the world, with its 175,000,000 people, its tin, rubber, minerals and oil, is absorbed into the Moscow-Peking empire, the still vaster nations of India and Pakistan would quickly lose any freedom of action. All Asia would slide behind the Iron Curtain.

There is some question whether Eisenhower or Adlai first enunciated this domino theory, which also motivated Presidents Kennedy and Johnson. In any event, all of them were wrong. Nations and peoples do not respond like unthinking dominoes. But it took a terrible toll of lives and treasure to find that out, and there is great uncertainty that the lesson has yet been really learned.

Tribesmen aiding British forces in the Malaysian jungle present one of their blowpipes to Adlai, but he declined their offer of poison-tipped arrows, saying he had seen enough of those in the 1952 campaign. *(Photograph by William Attwood. Used with his permission.)*

Queen Elizabeth II and Adlai discuss their choices at the races at Goodwood in 1953. *(Photograph by William Attwood. Used with his permission.)*

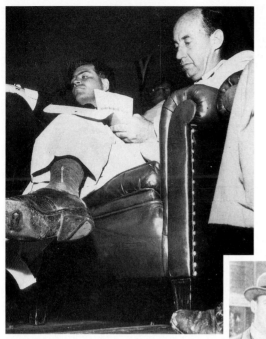

Left: This Pulitzer Prize photo with its worn-through shoe became a Stevenson symbol and accurately reflected his thrifty nature. Taken with Michigan Governor G. Mennen Williams during the 1952 campaign, it prompted hundreds of people to send him shoes. Climbing a mountain in Switzerland in 1965, he confided to Mr. and Mrs. Philip Klutznick that the battered shoes he was wearing were among the many he was still trying to wear out. *(AP/Wide World Photos)*

Right: Six days before the 1952 election, Adlai made a middle-of-the-night flight to try to avert violence in the riot that had broken out at Menard prison. The riot was ended with but one prisoner wounded (who later died). With machine-gun–carrying guards still on alert, Adlai confers in the prison yard with Lieutenant Governor Sherwood Dixon before flying to rejoin the campaign in New York that afternoon. *(Chicago Sun-Times Photo)*

Left: Mrs. Ronald (Marietta) Tree and Mrs. Edison (Jane) Dick, close and long-term friends, join Adlai on January 20, 1953, for a vacation at Barbados, British West Indies, where Adlai edited what became a best-selling book of his 1952 campaign speeches. *(AP/Wide World Photos)*

In the early morning hours of July 26, President Harry Truman, with a "Here's your man!" wag of the thumb, presents Adlai Stevenson to the Democratic National Convention as its 1952 candidate for President. *(Chicago Sun-Times Photo)*

Alicia Patterson, publisher of *Newsday,* was the one whom many felt Adlai should have married. Their intimate though sometimes stormy relationship lasted until her death two years before his. This picture, with William McCormick Blair, was taken during the 1952 campaign. *(AP/Wide World Photos)*

Adlai, working late as he often did, in his ground-floor office in the Executive Mansion at Springfield. *(Copyright by Cornell Capa/Magnum)*

Laughter over the governor's efforts to say repeatedly, "Dairy Cream Dream Queen" (whom he was about to crown at the Illinois State Fair), almost broke up this group picture in the Executive Mansion. Shown are William McCormick Blair, Eunice Kennedy (soon to become Mrs. Sargent Shriver), Adlai, Susan and Porter McKeever, Dorothy Fosdick, and Ernest Ives.

Adlai seized every opportunity to engage in a wide variety of outdoor sports with his sons. This picture, taken during his term as governor, shows all but Adlai III returning with a pheasant. *(Courtesy of Mrs. Nancy Stevenson)*

Carol Evans, Adlai's secretary for many years, became adept at the witty, brief personal notes that streamed from his office to friends and admirers all over the world. This photograph was taken early in his term as governor. *(Courtesy of Carol Evans)*

This 1948 picture with John Fell on the farm at Libertyville remained one of Adlai's favorites. *(Chicago Photographers, courtesy of Mrs. Nancy Stevenson)*

At the San Francisco Conference that established the United Nations, Adlai was designated as the "official leak" of the United States delegation. Members of the delegation seated around the table are State Foreign Relations Committee Chairman Senator Tom Connally, Secretary of State Edward R. Stettinius, Jr., Senator Arthur H. Vandenburg, Representative Charles A. Eaton, former Governor of Minnesota Harold E. Stassen, Assistant Secretary of State Nelson Rockefeller, Adlai, and John Foster Dulles. Missing from the photograph are Barnard College Dean Virginia Gildersleeve, House Foreign Affairs Committee Chairman Sol Bloom, and former Secretary of State Cordell Hull. Others shown are delegation advisers. *(Courtesy of Papers of Adlai E. Stevenson, Princeton University Library)*

Summers at Charlevoix were among the happiest in Adlai's life. Here he is in 1904, flying a kite, with Buffie on his right. *(Courtesy of Mrs. Ernest L. Ives and Papers of Adlai E. Stevenson, Princeton University Library)*

Adlai at Montreaux, Switzerland, September 1920 *(Courtesy of Mrs. Ernest L. Ives and Papers of Adlai E. Stevenson, Princeton University Library)*

Ellen Borden Stevenson's delight in costume parties, as well as her beauty, are caught in this *Chicago Tribune* society-page photograph in the early years of their marriage. *(Copyright © by Chicago Tribune Company, all rights reserved, used with permission)*

The aristocratic bearing of Adlai's mother, Mrs. Lewis Stevenson, is evident in this prized family portrait. *(AP/Wide World Photos)*

Adlai's father, Lewis G. Stevenson, with Adlai and Buffie on the steps of their summer vacation home at Charlevoix, Michigan *(Courtesy of Mrs. Ernest L. Ives and Papers of Adlai E. Stevenson, Princeton University Library)*

At the 1956 Democratic National Convention, Mrs. Eleanor Roosevelt was Adlai's most tireless and eloquent supporter. Here she appears before a delegation to counter the opposition of former President Truman. *(Copyright by Cornell Capa/Magnum)*

Overcoming opposition led by former President Truman, Adlai accepts the nomination of the Democratic National Convention as its 1956 candidate for President. *(Copyright by Cornell Capa/Magnum)*

The bizarre behavior of Adlai's divorced wife, Ellen, at the wedding of Adlai III and Nancy Anderson reduced the bride to tears. But Adlai's happiness in his son's marriage, so evident at the June 1955 wedding in Louisville, Kentucky, continued throughout his life. *(INP Photo)*

Willard Wirtz and Arthur Schlesinger, Jr., helping Adlai draft his telegram to President Eisenhower conceding defeat in the 1956 election. Adlai's son, John Fell, is visible in the mirror taking the picture. *(Copyright by John Fell Stevenson/Magnum)*

Wilson Wyatt called this picture, taken following the 1956 defeat, "The Morning After." A quip of Adlai's must account for all the smiles of these close campaign associates—it could not have been the results. Newton Minow, Clayton Fritchey, Thomas K. Finletter, Willard Wirtz, Matthew McCloskey, Adlai, Wilson W. Wyatt, James A. Finnegan, William McCormick Blair, Arthur E. Schlesinger, George W. Ball. *(Courtesy of Wilson W. Wyatt)*

The Honorary Degree from England's Oxford University in 1957 was probably the most cherished among the many Adlai received, and he wore the academic robe whenever it was appropriate. His pleasure is clearly evident as the Public Orator, T. J. Christie, accompanies him in the academic procession to the Sheldonian Theatre for the ceremony. *(AP/Wide World Photos)*

With the Soviet Union's Nikita
Khrushchev on the Iowa farm of
Roswell Garst, who stands behind
them. This photograph was taken by
Adlai's youngest son, John Fell.
*(Copyright by John Fell
Stevenson/Magnum)*

Adlai's appearance on the floor of the 1960 Democratic Convention in Los
Angeles sparked a wild, spontaneous demonstration and kindled hopes that he
would be chosen over Kennedy and Johnson. *(Courtesy of Adlai Stevenson III
and Papers of Adlai E. Stevenson, Princeton University Library)*

Adlai with his partners on the last day of their law firm. As he left to assume his post as U.S. Ambassador to the United Nations, and Blair, Minow, and Wirtz also prepared to join the Kennedy administration, he commented, "I regret I have but one law firm to give to my country." William D. McDougal, Jr., William McCormick Blair, William Wirtz, Adlai, Newton Minow, and John Hunt. *(Courtesy of William McCormick Blair)*

With President Kennedy in the Oval Office of the White House, February 1961. *(Copyright by Inge Morath/Magnum)*

Caught in earnest consultation during the Security Council recess, UN Secretary General Dag Hammarskjöld and Adlai demonstrate the lively and trusting relationship that had such constructive consequences. *(Copyright by Inge Morath/Magnum)*

The almost spiritual quality of the relationship of Adlai and Mrs. Roosevelt is captured in this photograph taken during a meeting at the United Nations. *(Copyright by Inge Morath/Magnum)*

Smiling bystanders are too stunned to realize Adlai has been hit on the head with the sign of the woman picket with tongue stuck out. Asked by Dallas police if he wanted her arrested, he replied, "I don't want to send her to jail. I want to send her to school." Also spat upon and jeered, he considered warning President Kennedy against going to Dallas the following month. *(Courtesy of Papers of Adlai E. Stevenson, Princeton University Library)*

On August 6, 1964, two days after the Tonkin Gulf incident, President Johnson gave UN Secretary General U Thant the "full treatment" of a helicopter flight to the White House lawn, a working lunch with Secretary of State Rusk and a formal White House dinner in a futile effort to win support for his Vietnam policy. Ranged beside the helicopter on arrival are Adlai's deputy, Ambassador Charles Yost, Mrs. Johnson, U Thant, the President, Adlai, and UN Under Secretary-General Ralph Bunche. *(USIA/United Nations photograph courtesy of Papers of Adlai E. Stevenson, Princeton University Library)*

Taken on the Libertyville farm a few weeks before the 1952 Democratic National Convention, this photograph forecasts the wish expressed to Eric Sevareid just before Stevenson's death in London in 1965: "For a while, I'd really just like to sit in the shade with a glass of wine in my hand and watch the dancers." *(Copyright by Cornell Capa/Magnum)*

Doonesbury

BY GARRY TRUDEAU

Adlai's ability to inspire young people is dramatized in this *Doonesbury* cartoon by Garry Trudeau in 1984, nineteen years after Adlai's death.
(DOONESBURY/copyright © 1984 by G. B. Trudeau. Reprinted with permission of Universal Press Syndicate. All rights reserved.)

In Indonesia, he found Chester Bowles, together with his family, en route home from his successful ambassadorship in India. Bowles reported that, as in the countries Adlai had visited, Eisenhower's remark that "Asians should fight Asians" had had a "devastating impact" on India. It was essential to have an economic policy for South and Southeast Asia that would not be dominated by military considerations. We should extend aid, however, only if governments agreed to implementing tax systems that included taxing the big landlords, and land reform.

Adlai was eager to learn about the new young republic. Its magnitude and potential were known to only a few Americans. The island of Java, slightly smaller than Illinois, had a population of more than fifty million and was one of the most densely populated areas in the world. And it was but one of more than thirteen thousand islands, nearly one thousand of them with permanent settlements, in the huge archipelago that stretched over areas longer than the width of the United States to make it the sixth largest country in the world.

Since the recently won war for independence from the Dutch, a provisional constitution had been drafted, but there had not yet been elections. Members of the parliament were in effect appointed by President Sukarno to represent various groups and regions, and nine different political parties were represented in the seventeen-member cabinet. Unlike the British in India or the United States in the Philippines, the Dutch had not educated or trained the Indonesians, so that, all things considered, it was almost a miracle that there was as much stability as Adlai discovered. President Sukarno surprised Adlai with his detailed knowledge of American history as he argued that of all the people on earth, Americans should understand from their own revolution Indonesia's desire to avoid involvement in the rivalries between the United States and the Soviet Union.

Interviews with leaders in the variety of political parties provided some understanding of the suspicion of outsiders that he encountered in nearly every conversation. On at least one occasion, he could not resist saying that "ignorance about the United States is one of the most disturbing things I have noticed on this trip . . . ignorance of how we live, of the amount of taxes we pay, of our motives in helping to strengthen the free world." He chided one group for acting as though receiving American aid was almost a right. Though blunt, it was said in a tone that left his listeners impressed and eager to continue the conversation.

His crystal ball was clear as he wrote for *Look:*

> Indonesia's basic problems are economic rather than political. They stem from a badly distributed population and low productivity. . . . Life expectancy here is about 32 years. . . . What's ahead for Indonesia politically is hard to predict. . . .

Nevertheless, I'm optimistic about the future of these friendly, cheerful people who have achieved nationhood unprepared and in violence, and in a trying and perilous time. . . . The hunger for knowledge and education is heartening, and their independent-mindedness is itself a safeguard against dictatorship.

History has proved him largely right.

Lessons in terrorism, blunt encounters with ethnic rivalry, and a narrow escape from death highlighted the visit to Singapore and Malaya.

In the British high commissioner for Southeast Asia, Malcolm MacDonald, and the high commissioner for Malaysia, General Sir Gerald Templar, Adlai met two of the best-informed, most vigorous and colorful figures in the entire region. Confronted by well-armed and well-trained guerrillas in a vast jungle, they nevertheless exuded well-justified confidence in their ability to reduce the terrorist threat and move toward independence.

Adlai was told that four fifths of Malaya was jungle with trees two hundred feet tall. The thick top foliage meant that even on the brightest days it was like a cathedral at night and the undergrowth was "awful and horrible." Food could not grow under such trees so the terrorists were forced to make clearings to grow tapioca. This enabled the British to spot the clearings from the air and bomb them. This drove the terrorists to raid plantations on the edges of the jungle with such violent methods and indiscriminate killing that they lost the support of the ordinary people. By 1953, the effort to cut off food supplies was having notable success; captured guerrillas were in "terrible" physical condition and the attacks, while fewer, were more desperate and bloody.

The British recognized that colonial rule was at an end and were determined to leave behind an independent Malaya, but they were in the odd position of having to deal with pleas from Malayan nationalists not to leave too hastily. Ethnic tensions among the majority Malays, economically powerful Chinese, Indians, and Pakistanis were high and political rivalry was divided into a multitude of factions. On a tight schedule, efficiently managed by his British hosts, Adlai managed to have individual discussions with leaders of the major factions and of the trade unions, and to visit various towns and estates, schools and hospitals. At one native kampong, he was presented with a blowgun and poisoned arrows. When he was invited to try it, he laughingly declined, "until I have a Republican in the sights." At another, where he was introduced to the half-naked headman, he said, "Hello, boss. How's the precinct?" His companions said that by the time he left, the kampong seemed to be safely Democratic.

Most of this travel was made in General Templar's bulletproof car, escorted by two armored cars bristling with twin Bren guns. But to get to the kampongs in the jungle, the car and escorts had to be left behind, and they bounced and slid over the jungle trails through drenching monsoon rain, in a British Land Rover.

Early the next morning, the party was flown in two helicopters to a kampong deep in the jungle and they then hiked a jungle trail to a river where a patrol was returning from an all-night search for terrorists. From there, he was flown to a jungle clearing so small that only one helicopter at a time could go in. After talking to the patrol resting there following their jungle probes, the first helicopter, with Attwood, Blair, and Robert Hewitt of the Associated Press, took off. Adlai, Bingham, Johnson, and Major-General W. H. Lambert climbed into the second. They were aloft barely two minutes when the motor began clanging and smoke poured into the cabin. The big propeller slowed and the helicopter began dropping toward the jungle. The pilot spotted an abandoned clearing and skillfully maneuvered the disabled copter toward it. It made a sickening thud into the trees and then, miraculously, slid off and the pilot landed it upright in a rice paddy. The British general jumped out with revolver in hand—the only weapon available. Adlai climbed out behind him, sinking into the mud up to his knees, and imperturbably expressing his admiration for the pilot.

While General Lambert anxiously scanned the edge of the clearing for guerrillas, the other helicopter flew to a clearing where there were British soldiers, left the rest of the party, and flew to rescue Adlai. Within fifteen minutes of the crash landing, he was in the second helicopter on the way back to Kuala Lumpur where an alarmed General Templar was waiting. His comment to Adlai, however, was, "Well, Governor, I hope you don't think I laid that one on."

Reporters also had gathered at the airport, and when they questioned him about the crash, he made light of it saying, "I'm glad nobody reminded me that it was an American helicopter with an American engine." One reporter observed to a colleague that almost any other political figure, even if admitting the helicopter was American, would have blamed the accident on poor British maintenance. The comment indicated the solid impression he had made; one that was reinforced by a blunt encounter with a delegation of pro-Kuomintang leaders.

Adlai was handed a statement asserting that the United States must help Chiang Kai-shek free China of communism and the United Nations forces must continue to fight in Korea rather than to seek a truce. After reading it, Adlai said to them:

"You want America to shed its life in Korea, the French to do the same in Indochina, and the British to do it here. Now tell me, how many Chinese have volunteered to fight in the security forces here or in the police to go after the Chinese Communists in the jungle?"

There was a long discussion in Chinese, and finally he was told:

"You have to be a British subject before you can join the army and you have to speak English. This prevents us from joining."

"There are lots of young Chinese who can speak English and are British subjects. Yet only a few of them are fighting. It would be better grace when you ask the United States to fight in Korea, if you people would fight and put up money for the struggle here in Malaya."

After another lengthy conversation in Chinese, they decided to end the interview, saying, "If we can organize our own army, we will fight." But Adlai did not let it end there. "If you really want to organize an army, why don't you go to General Templar and say that you will fight, so the British can get out of here, which they want to do." As they hastily left, the American consul general, Charles F. Baldwin, told Adlai the statement about British restrictions on enlistments was "a lot of nonsense."

Adlai's article dealt at length with the rivalry of the ethnic groups and the grim nature of the jungle warfare, but was positive in his assessment of Malaysia's future. Once again, he was right.

Despite the presence of an exceptionally knowledgeable ambassador, Edwin F. Stanton, the visit to Thailand was one of the least illuminating and most frustrating; owing largely to the charming evasiveness of the Thais. Their charm was matched only by the corruption that was the accepted norm among the ruling elite, just as bloodless coups among competing military cliques were the accepted way of changing governments. Outbreaks of violence and instability on the northeast frontier with Indochina seemed to be of less interest than the "ice-cold war" in Bangkok between rival politicians who controlled the Coca-Cola and Pepsi-Cola concessions. Rounds of interviews and visits to remarkable temples did not interfere with Adlai's persistent interest in markets, which he insisted in sharing with the others, sometimes at 5:00 A.M.

Burma was a surprising contrast, beginning with the large number of Burmese at the airport wearing Stevenson campaign buttons. The Burmese passion for gambling had led to four-to-one bets on a Stevenson victory, but their losses only seemed to enhance his popularity. The greeting also ran counter to a strong current of anti-Americanism flowing from the presence in northeast Burma of Chinese Nationalist troops who had fled before the Communist forces and were being supplied from Taiwan via Thailand, presumably with American support. Among those who insisted on entertaining him was the Trade Union Congress of Burma, who for the first time for any American, honored him at a luncheon. At a dinner given by President Baw U, he met the secretary of the ministry of information, U Thant, who was later to be a respected colleague at the United Nations.

Adlai did not escape anti-Americanism entirely, but most of it was focused on Eisenhower's "Asians should fight Asians" statement, and for the first time, it was also directed at Senator McCarthy. Officials, journalists, students, all pressed him about the report that McCarthy had just "forced" the U.S. Information Agency to investigate his writings and those of Mrs. Roosevelt "for any Communist leanings." "How do you Americans think you can ever be a world leader if you act this way?" one asked. Adlai expressed his contempt for McCarthy but emphasized that the senator should not be confused with the whole country.

The vigor of the hospitality was not reflected in the country itself. Burma, sadly, was in shambles, and, more sadly, remains so.

The India at which Adlai arrived on April 28 was only six years away from the bloody partition of the subcontinent into two nations that precipitated a horrible communal conflict in which uncounted millions had died. It was entering only the second year of its first five-year plan to begin developing this huge, divided, multilingual, largely illiterate, poverty-plagued land. Again, an extraordinary number of reporters were awaiting him at the steamy Calcutta airport, only to be disappointed by his insistence on withholding comments until the end of the trip and his resolve not to make a speech while there. Later, it was charged that he had been "gagged" by John Foster Dulles and the CIA.

Adlai plunged immediately into long conversations with West Bengal leaders, including the directors of the vast Damodar Valley project modeled after the Tennessee Valley Authority, under way northeast of Calcutta and embracing a system of dams to prevent floods, irrigate a million acres of land, produce 400,000 kilowatts of power, and encourage a complex of steel mills and related factories. He visited it the next day in 110-degree heat, climbing up and down the earthen embankments and commenting on the "gallantry" of the men lifting huge rocks up to the heads of women by whom they were carried off to trucks.

From the Damodar Valley project, the party flew directly to the holy city of Benares. His companions sighed in resignation as he rejected the tea the hotel manager had waiting for them, saying, "I'm an impetuous tourist. I don't want tea. I want to see the people and the temples." After a full day, Bingham described the night in Benares:

> We were sharing a room in a small hotel. When we went to bed we found ourselves almost smothered under mosquito netting, with no breath of air coming through the staring windows. Each of us tossed and turned in his bed for a while, remembering the burning ghats we had seen that day loaded with corpses, remembering, too, the wrecks of humanity we had seen creeping through the streets, people who had come to die in the holy city by the Ganges. After a while we gave up and began to talk. We talked all night, until a pale light came to herald another burn-

ing day. An hour later Adlai was up, apparently rested and ready to continue the inexorable schedule.

Adlai was out of the hotel by 6:00 A.M. for a Ganges boat ride postponed from the night before, and by noon was on the plane to visit the Taj Mahal at Agra, before proceeding on to New Delhi where Ambassador George Allen, a host of Indian officials, and an even larger number of reporters were waiting to greet him. The evening was spent obtaining from *New York Times* correspondent Robert Trumbull and his wife a briefing on Jammu and Kashmir to which he flew the next morning at 6:30.

The Indian Army's occupation of much of Kashmir and the danger of conflict with Pakistani troops in the remaining portion of the area was a passionate issue that confronted him at every stage of his sixteen days in India—the longest in any country on the trip—and ten days in Pakistan. A precarious ceasefire had held since 1949, but questions of a plebiscite and the future hung heavily over both countries. Not conflict, but escape from the shriveling heat and three days to write and rest on a Kashmiri houseboat were the main preoccupations of the party. Both Attwood and Johnson were ailing; only Blair was managing to keep up with Adlai.

Sheikh Mohammed Abdullah, the chief minister of Jammu and Kashmir, saw to it in two long meetings and a dinner with his cabinet that Adlai was fully briefed on their position in the conflict. (Not long after Adlai returned home, Prime Minister Nehru arrested Abdullah and parts of the Indian press accused Adlai of conspiring with Abdullah to declare the state independent of both India and Pakistan.) He also told Adlai that Asians distrusted America because of its support of colonial Britain and France. "Americans must understand the aspirations of Asia," he continued. "You must not be so strongly anti-Communist that certain people can blackmail you. . . . Chiang Kai-shek in China did this to you." A member of his cabinet added that Americans cannot fight Communists just with guns, but must also win the hearts and minds of people. Adlai interjected that that sounded like one of his campaign speeches. The minister startled him by saying it was, and that they had read his speeches in *The New York Times* every day during the campaign.

Back in Delhi for the beginning of his "unofficial official" visit, Adlai was housed in the presidential palace. On his arrival, he was ushered in to an immediate meeting with Prime Minister Nehru for an especially warm opening conversation. "I have looked forward to meeting you for a long time," Nehru said, forgetting that a few years earlier, while presiding at a Council on Foreign Relations luncheon, Adlai had reduced Nehru, himself, and the audience to helpless laughter when he asked everyone to remain seated "until the Prime Minister passes out."

After lunching with Ambassador Allen and members of his staff, and meeting with the president, vice president, and members of India's Planning Commission, Adlai and Bingham dined alone with Nehru. Bingham wrote of the dinner:

> The play of intellect between Stevenson and Nehru was fascinating to observe. Adlai was of course noted for his command of English. Nehru, who was said by Gandhi to have dreamed in English, showed the same delicate grasp of the nuances of the language. These two men, from opposite ends of the world, talked as though they had enjoyed an intellectual friendship for decades. Each spoke lucidly and with candor.

During the dinner Nehru predicted the eventual break between Russia and China. "It is inconceivable to me," he told Adlai, "that Mao will accept the position of being a satellite."

Early the next morning, Adlai was en route to see a community village project being helped by the Point Four program some eighty-five miles from Delhi. There, new plows were breaking up the sun-baked earth, wells were being dug, and small industries were being developed. Blair's insistence back in Delhi that the evening be devoted to writing some three hundred "political" letters and postcards was met with grumbling that was only stilled when he was shown a review of the book of campaign speeches that had been published in their absence. Written by James Reston of *The New York Times,* it described them as "something extraordinary in the political life of the Republic . . . undoubtedly the finest collection of speeches made by any Presidential candidate since Wilson and maybe in this century . . . surely among the finest ever crowded into a single Presidential campaign by a single individual."

On May 7, Blair and Bingham, under protest, left with him for Madras, Trivandrum, and Bombay. Adlai explained in a letter to Jane Dick that Attwood and Johnson were ailing "but the old man came to see and by God he's going to see!!" Communist influence was strong in southern India, especially in Travancore and Cochin, but the welcome given him in Trivandrum was so rousing that the local Communist party leader was overheard saying: "Dash it all! First we have [Ambassador] Bowles to contend with; then Mrs. Roosevelt had to come here—now we have Stevenson. And they're all so dashed human and attractive that it undoes months of propaganda on our part."

The rounds of interviews and sightseeing were as relentless as the letter to Jane Dick suggested, and they continued through the final days in Delhi that included a meeting with some hundred members of parliament and a packed press conference. Questions about Senator McCarthy were interlarded with inquiries about his reactions to India.

In the conference, as in the *Look* article that followed, Adlai chose to describe India's position as one of "noninvolvement" rather than neutrality. He wrote:

The great contest in Asia is between the totalitarian and the democratic approach to the development of backward areas. Thus it seems far more important for India to strengthen her fledgling democracy than to proclaim her allegiance to "our side" in foreign affairs. For a healthy democracy, even in a "neutralist" India, will be a stronger bulwark against communism in Asia than a shaky, uncertain state—no matter how loudly pro-American or anti-Communist its leaders speak. . . . On balance, I think the prospects for a free India are good.

Many of the same issues dominated his ten days in Pakistan, although they were usually cast in a religious perspective and required an intense effort on Adlai's part to understand the functioning of a theocratic state. He immediately established a warm rapport with Foreign Minister Sir Zafrullah Khan, a target of the conservative mullahs, who would later be a colleague at the United Nations and end his career on the World Court. In Karachi, as in Delhi, he was impressed with the quality of Chargé d'Affaires John Emmerson and his staff at the United States embassy.

At Lahore, as he walked happily through the narrow, teeming streets of the old walled city, one of the Pakistani officials was heard to comment that Adlai was "insane to want to rub shoulders with the masses." From there, he flew to Peshawar in the North-West Frontier Province, where cars were waiting to drive through the Khyber Pass to the Afghan border. At the entrance to the pass, there was not only an honor guard of frontier scouts, but tribal chiefs had come in from the surrounding mountains to greet him. They covered him with garlands of flowers and presented a pair of highly decorated sandals, explaining they were worn by bridegrooms, and as he tried to put them on he assured the chiefs that he was available. The next stop was Rawalpindi, where the headquarters of the Pakistani Army was located. The full schedule included a flight over Gilgit Province, Swat, and other mountainous regions, but heavy clouds blocked the passes.

Told that the flight would be delayed two hours, Adlai turned to Johnson and said, "Walter, let's go and see Alexander the Great's village."

Johnson's curiosity was aroused. "As an historian, I knew Alexander had gotten into India but I did not know he had founded a village. As we approached it, Adlai said, 'When do you think he founded it?' I did some arithmetic and said, 'About 326, Governor.'"

"No, Walter, no," Adlai replied. "I think it was 322."

"Sure enough," Johnson said later, "when we got there we found a plaque in the village saying 322 B.C." Johnson kept brooding over how Adlai could have known about that village. He would get his answer four countries later in Lebanon.

Adlai summarized the impact of Asia for *Look*'s readers in this passage:

For a long time, the peace and destiny of the world were decided by the balance of power in Europe. Now a new factor has emerged. What happens in free Asia can upset the balance of power and of principle in the world.

Fortunately, its present leaders hate tyranny and dictation. They fought and suffered for freedom and independence. They believe, passionately, for the most part, in representative institutions; and many still look to revolutionary, democratic America for inspiration and encouragement.

But their countries are poor and backward. Their peoples know little of democracy and the blessings of human freedom, but they want to eat every day—and they mean to do it.

The next few years will tell whether these leaders can make democracy work in this great new area of decision—Asia."

At the airport in Dhahran, Saudi Arabia, another colleague from his UN days, Ambassador Raymond Hare, was awaiting him with the happy news that he, Blair, and Johnson would be staying in air-conditioned comfort at a guesthouse provided by Aramco, the Arabian American Oil Company. (Bingham had left for home and Attwood had gone ahead to Cairo.)

Although oil had been discovered in the 1930s, it was only in 1948, five years earlier, that oil had begun to produce large revenues for both Aramco and Saudi Arabia. There was little in the form of government; King Ibn Saud was the absolute monarch who ruled by decree. There was slavery; even a slave market. However, the technical training programs initiated by Aramco for its twenty-five thousand Arab employees were beginning to create a middle class and change was in the air.

Adlai was warned that although Israel might not enter the conversation very often, emotions on the subject were intense. More likely, the conversations would be directed toward Saudi claims to the oasis of Buraimi, unimportant until the discovery of oil, located on the kingdom's undefined southeastern border. Hare also stressed the king's determination to prevent Iraq, Jordan, and Syria from forming "a greater Syria," and his unhappiness at the replacement of the monarchy in Egypt with a republic just the year before.

Flown to Riyadh for an audience with the aging king, Adlai was then treated to an awesomely sumptuous dinner with the king, Crown Prince Saud, Prince and Foreign Minister Faisal, and a number of other sons. This was followed by a midnight supper at Prince Saud's palace. Conversation throughout followed Hare's predictions, with Israel being referred to, but not mentioned by name and being alluded to, as the "cancer placed in our hearts." Prince Saud during a stroll through a beautiful garden added that because Israel was an aggressor nation, "anyone who supports our enemy, Israel, is our enemy as well."

When Adlai returned to the mud-brick palace that had been assigned to him, he found a representative of the king waiting to present him with a curved Arabian sword and a gold case made from hammered British sovereigns. His somewhat equivocal expression of appreciation was interrupted by the entry of two servants staggering under the weight of a huge oriental rug, which they rolled out before him. He turned to Hare pleadingly and asked, "Can't I thank them very much and refuse it?" The ambassador shook his head and said, "You'll have to take it and get it out of the country, because the king will know if you don't." (The rug was shipped from Dhahran to Libertyville.)

Even though it was 1:00 A.M. when they landed in Cairo, Foreign Minister Mahmoud Fawzi as well as the deputy chief of the United States embassy, G. Lewis Jones, were waiting, along with a sizable crowd, to meet him. From both Lewis and Fawzi he quickly received lessons in the intensity of Egyptian nationalism and her hatred of England even more than of Israel.

From the Egyptian point of view, Britain was the enemy. Since it had invaded Egypt in 1882, it had promised sixty-six times to evacuate the country. Now, in 1953, it had eighty thousand troops, almost twice the number of the Egyptian Army, stationed in the' Suez base that stretched nearly a hundred miles along the canal. The Egyptian military leaders who had taken control of the government the year before were intent, above anything else, on ousting the British, which, in 1954, they did. At the time of Adlai's visit, however, the British were as convinced that the Egyptians were not capable of operating the Suez Canal, especially in time of war, as the Egyptians were determined to gain sovereignty over it. The Egyptians were willing to retain British technicians, provided that all instructions to them were transmitted through Egyptian authorities. The British did not trust the Egyptians to do this faithfully.

Adlai pursued the issue in talks with all the Egyptian leaders and Britain's top diplomatic and military officials. The latter arranged for him to fly up and down the base, telling him he was the first American, civilian or military, to see how extensive the base was. Adlai came to the conclusion that the positions of the two sides could be reconciled, and told them so. Both were polite, but unconvinced, and British stubbornness finally lost out to Egyptian determination. Egyptian nationalization of the canal in 1956 was to have a dramatic impact on Adlai's second bid for the presidency.

Borden's arrival prompted a day off to fly to Luxor to see the ancient monuments. Adlai described the Temple of Karnak as "the biggest thing

in ruins," to be recommended "to anyone suffering from self-impor-
tance." As usual, during such an excursion, Attwood and Johnson remained in Cairo to interview a number of people, mainly Egyptian
educators and foreign correspondents.

Adlai's tour of farm villages left him depressed, as he learned that
half of Egypt's children died before reaching the age of five. Some land
reform had begun and the Aswān High Dam that would increase the
country's irrigated land by one third was being discussed, but economic
development was deep in the shadow of the Suez issue, which was almost
the sole subject pursued at his final press conference on June 2.

"Two burning issues kindle the passions of the Middle East," Adlai
told the readers of *Look.*

> —the great British base along the Suez canal and Israel's lusty
> little beachhead in a hostile Moslem world. Both are over-
> charged with emotion and both threaten stability and progress in
> the Middle East. . . . The Arab nations face the same staggering
> social, economic and political problems as the new Asia: igno-
> rance, poverty, disease, feudalism, instability. These are the *real*
> problems, but "imperialism" and "injustice" are the universal
> preoccupations. Over here, communism is remote and for to-
> morrow; Suez and Israel are next door and for today.

Five days were allotted to Lebanon, Syria, and Jordan. The United
States ambassador in Beirut, Harold B. Minor, gave the party a blunt
briefing, more sobering in retrospect by its familiarity some thirty-five
years later. Institutions such as the American University of Beirut, which
had been established in 1866, and the fifty-fifty profit sharing of American
oil companies, had won goodwill for the United States. It had been dissi-
pated, however, by support of Israel. Arabs viewed Israel as an "American creation." The entire area, Minor warned, was on the point of
turning against the United States unless it gave evidence that it stood for
equal treatment for all countries and preference for none. Otherwise,
there would be increasing Soviet intrusion, and increasing violence, especially if there was not a settlement of the Palestine refugee problem.

He conceded that lack of unity among Arab states complicated the
problems. Terrorists and fanatics made it difficult for Arab leaders to be
conciliatory toward Israel, as was demonstrated by the assassination two
years earlier of King Abdullah of Jordan while working on an agreement
with Israel.

Similar views were expressed at a meeting with some twenty faculty
members, American and Arab, at the University of Beirut. Reasonable
Arabs, they told him, knew Israel should not be driven into the sea, but it
was essential that the three resolutions adopted by the UN should be

implemented—internationalization of Jerusalem, rectification of boundaries, and repatriation and/or compensation to the refugees. Again and again, in Jordan and Syria as well as Lebanon, the importance of acting on these three resolutions would be stressed. And, each time, Adlai would express doubt that all three could be achieved.

Only once, in a meeting with three Socialist leaders, did an issue other than Israel figure prominently in the conversation.

"Because of your fear of Communism you back whatever government you find in power, like Franco in Spain, regardless of whether it is reactionary, fascist, or progressive," they told him. "Americans should not talk so much anti-Communism and instead talk in terms of positive social reform. If you did that, the Communists would crumble all over the Arab world."

The final night in Lebanon, President Camille Chamoun gave a large dinner party, and the next morning drove with Adlai over the mountains and into the green Bekáa Valley to lay the cornerstone of a barn that was to be part of a large Point Four–Lebanese modern livestock and experimental demonstration farm. There they parted, with the Stevenson party driving to the Greco-Roman temple site at Baalbek. Adlai took Johnson aside and said, "Let the guide take care of the others and you and I go off by ourselves." He wanted to take advantage of Johnson's scholarship as an historian, but he was the one who was soon explaining the meaning and history of the great columns standing amid the ruins.

Finally, Johnson turned to him and said, "Look, Adlai, ever since you told me the date of that village Alexander the Great founded in Pakistan, I've been wanting to ask you, where did you learn all this?"

Johnson reports that, with a twinkle in his eye, Adlai said, "I'm sure it comes as no surprise to you, Walter, that I was sort of bored by the law. "So I used to sneak out of my office downtown and come out to the university [of Chicago] and listen to [James] Breasted's lectures on the Middle East and Asia."

"And you never forgot a damn thing he ever said to you, either, did you?" Johnson asserted.

Adlai paused for a moment and then said, "I guess I didn't."

It was a dramatic example of how he had acquired so much of his learning. The extent of his reading certainly did not merit the reputation he had gained as an intellectual, but his capacity to learn and remember through listening was phenomenal.

After a picnic lunch amid the ruins, they drove to the Syrian border where Syrian officials and United States embassy representatives were waiting to take them directly to the president, former army chief of staff General Adib Shishikli, who had seized control of the government in 1951. Shishikli tempered his criticism of United States policy by saying, "Israel is here to stay"; then repeated the three requirements for peace Adlai had heard elsewhere. He also talked about his plans for economic development: Work to develop Syria's only important harbor at Latakia was already under way, and there were plans for roads, and dams for irrigation and hydroelectric power. "The United States should see that its aid to Israel and to the Arabs was not used by them to fight each other," he declared.

The next afternoon, the party flew to Amman, Jordan's capital, in an old seven-seat biplane Attwood had chartered. They were not reassured when the pilot claimed they were flying low so they could see the parched desert that needed irrigation. The real reason, they believed, was to be ready for a quick landing should the engine die.

Eighteen-year-old King Hussein was not in the country, and Adlai spent much of the time with the famous and colorful commander of the Arab Legion, Lieutenant-General John Bagot Glubb. Then the party left for Jerusalem with an armed escort of Arab Legionnaires, stopping en route at a refugee camp at Jericho, which Attwood described in his diary as "a vast conglomeration of mud huts where 90,000 people are existing and rotting of idleness." All told, the refugee population of 460,000 accounted for nearly half of Jordan's total population.

"My last day in the Arab world," he wrote in his *Look* article,

> a Sunday, I wandered about Bethlehem and Old Jerusalem through the imperishable scenes enlivened by names that never die. . . . I thought, too, about how much in common have the Arabs, Jews and Christians who have shared the Sacred City for so long; how their common inspiration—faith in one God— sprang from these same rocky hills and deserts; how Jews and Arabs lived together here in harmony for 1,300 years; and how the great concepts that unite us converge within the walls of old Jerusalem. Surely here, one would think, we could settle our differences in the face of peril to our common faith in God. Instead, ill will is growing like the weeds that sprout amongst the rubble of Jerusalem's no man's land.

With United Nations soldiers as escorts, the party was driven through the Mandelbaum Gate and across the no-man's-land that separated Israeli Jerusalem and Jordanian Jerusalem. Suddenly, as Adlai wrote later, they were struck by

> the abrupt change in living standards—no one is barefoot, no one is dressed in rags. Then you notice the modern European aspect of the New Jerusalem, the bustling crowds, the new construction. For the Jews are moving their capital to Jerusalem in spite of the talk of internationalization and in spite of the city's division and location, because, as one said to me, "Jerusalem has a meaning for Jews which no Gentile can understand."

The Israelis had kept themselves well-informed on Adlai's travels and were concerned that he may have been overly persuaded by the Arabs, so they spared no effort to give him their side of the issues. Prime Minister David Ben-Gurion saw him promptly and stressed his determination to "rebuild the desert. . . . We must build a civilization based on our Bible but in the context of modern civilization. It has to be done and therefore we believe it can be done."

Probing for some area of possible conciliation with the Arab states on the refugee problem, Adlai drew from the prime minister a blunt declaration that bringing the refugees back would mean the destruction of Israel, but that Israel was willing to compensate those who had left property behind. He confessed, however, that he did not know where the money would come from.

At a later, even longer meeting, the foreign minister, Moshe Sharett opened the discussion by saying, "I know the refugees prey on your mind—it does on ours. It is the main stumbling block to peace." His remarks, however, were only a slightly milder restatement of the prime minister's views. This conversation also produced the only reference to the Soviet Union that was made during the five-day stay. Sharett felt that since the death of Stalin, "blustering and intimidating" had moderated but that restoration of diplomatic relations was not likely in the near future.

As he traveled around the country, Adlai became increasingly concerned about the Israeli economy. Although Israel had a highly trained and able population in which nearly a third were professionals or experienced managers, their contributions were diluted by powerful inflationary forces. Defense expenditures, for example, consumed nearly a third of the national budget; nearly 70 percent of its food was imported; shortages of foreign exchange to buy raw materials kept industry from operating at full capacity; only about a fifth of the foreign currency spent was earned in Israel, the balance came from investments, loans, and gifts from abroad, mostly from American Jews and the United States government. Of the previous year's budget, almost three fourths came from abroad.

Adlai's *Look* article reads as if it had been written today:

> I was both exhilarated and depressed by what I found in Israel—exhilarated by what had been accomplished by the pride of the ordinary people (like the taxi driver who boasted of what "we Jews" are doing to irrigate the Negev desert) and by the vision in Israel of a better future for all of the Middle East.
>
> And I was depressed by the gulf that separates Israel from the Arab world and by the bleak facts of her economic life. . . . The good will of her neighbors is as vital to Israel's survival in the long run as aid from abroad is today. Israel's many friends in America should remember that good relations between Jews

and Arabs are the only alternative to endless contributions of money to a permanently beleagured fortress surrounded by embittered neighbors.

And "peace" is not just a word in a treaty which, signed today, means friendly relations tomorrow. Real, enduring peace is a state of mind which will only stem from mutual confidence and a community of interests between Jews and Arabs. . . . The Middle East is smoldering with anger. Yes, and with nationalism, pride, mistrust and temperance too. Demagoguery and inflamed public passions make reasonable, effective leadership difficult on both sides.

The article's objectivity explains the remark of an Israeli official after his departure: "He's too bi-partisan for us."

A rest stop in Cyprus was scheduled just in time. In fact, Adlai was so groggy he automatically began asking the United States consul general who was there to meet him questions about the island's population, economics, and politics. Attwood had to remind him that this was one place "where he didn't have to know a damn thing or write a damn line about it." Attwood later observed that when Adlai was extremely fatigued he would mix "bewildered enthusiasm with engaging spontaneity." He recalled that when Adlai first met Mrs. Attwood, who joined them in Cairo, "for the first half minute he had no idea who I was introducing him to and he gave her the quick smile and hearty handshake; then when he realized who she was he suddenly patted her cheek and explained, 'Why bless you my dear—we've been chasing you for 15,000 miles.'"

Thanks to Bill Blair's alert guardianship, they managed to elude persistent efforts by Archbishop Markarios to enlist them in the islanders' disputes with the British. Despite attempts to entrap him during his sightseeing, on the beach, and at the airport, he escaped to Turkey uncommitted.

Now, for the first time since leaving San Francisco more than three months ago, he entered a country he had visited before. The unpleasant memories of his 1926 struggle to get a visa for his trip to the Soviet Union were eclipsed by his enthusiasm for the bazaars. Also, the almost brutally blunt talk of the Turks, the strength of their opposition to the Soviet Union, and the vigor and vitality of their economy and young political institutions fascinated Adlai. Turkey's commitment to the war in Korea was so strong, Adlai discovered, that the barbed-wire entanglements around the port of debarkation were not to keep soldiers from going AWOL but to prevent others from sneaking in and *going to* Korea.

Most exciting to him was the economic progress of the fledgling democracy. "Since the Truman Doctrine brought American aid and advice to threatened Turkey in 1947," he wrote, "wheat production has doubled

. . . cotton production has trebled; highway mileage has risen from 6,000 (mostly mule tracks) to 16,000 miles of all-weather roads; port facilities have increased ten-fold . . . average per capita income is up from $150 to $175 per year, and the gross national product has risen 30 per cent." In concluding that Turkey was "one of the wonders of modern history," he conceded that his enthusiasm might be enhanced by the fact that the party in power was the Democratic party.

Events at home now began to intrude on the months-long preoccupation with new experiences. Bill Blair had been routinely refusing the invitations to speak that began to come in mounting volume, but an urgent recommendation from Steve Mitchell for a big homecoming rally in Chicago that would also raise funds for the party was promptly accepted.

Adlai was very disturbed by the increasing impact of McCarthyism on the American position overseas. From occasional questions at press conferences at the outset of the journey, the issue had grown into obvious morale problems at the embassies he visited. Now, in anti-Communist Turkey the counterproductive reaction to McCarthyism was thrust at him. In February, Secretary of State Dulles had issued a directive to the United States Information Agency that "no material by Communists, fellow-travellers, et cetera, will be used under any circumstances." Sometimes derisively and sometimes seriously, Adlai was asked to define "et cetera." In Turkey he was confronted with the fact that "et cetera" had been defined to embrace the removal from the Ankara USIS Library of Dashiell Hammett's mystery stories, *The Thin Man* and *The Maltese Falcon,* and Chaucer's *Canterbury Tales* with illustrations by Rockwell Kent.

One of the first questions he was asked as he arrived in Yugoslavia sprang from the recent tour of Europe by McCarthy's staff associates, Roy M. Cohn and G. David Schine. They had been asked how aid to Communist Yugoslavia could be justified even though it had broken with the Soviet Union, and they had replied they wanted to think about it. The same question was asked Adlai as he stepped off the plane in Belgrade. "The need to resist Soviet aggression is sufficient justification for American aid to Yugoslavia," he replied. The United States chargé d'affaires, Woodruff Wallner, had diverted Cohn and Schine by telling them on their arrival, "Boys, you are now in the fightingest anti-Soviet country in Europe." That seemed to divert them, he told Adlai, and they did not cause much trouble during their visit. Nonetheless, when Adlai asked President Tito if there was a likelihood of his visiting the United States, the reply was, "I would like to very much, but I don't suppose McCarthy would let me in!"

Yugoslav officialdom was eager to lay before Adlai their thinking about the Soviet Union, the reasons behind the break between the two Communist countries, the changes being made in their economic system as they moved away from the Soviet model, and the progress made in rebuilding their war-ruined economy. In a Yugoslav Air Force plane provided by President Tito, the group toured the country—Zagreb, Dubrovnik, Skopje, and Tito's island retreat at Brijuni.

There, in long discussions alone with Adlai, Tito spoke frankly about the post-Stalin leaders of the Soviet Union, all of whom he had known, and warned that a change in tactics by the new regime must not be mistaken for a change in expansionist objectives. The signal for real change will come, he said, "when force and violence are replaced by consent and cooperation, when the brutal autocracy of the police state is replaced by democratic socialism." When Adlai remarked that Stalin might be compared with Peter the Great, Tito cried, "No! No! Not Peter the Great—Ivan the Terrible!" At one point, Tito proposed a toast to 1948—the year Yugoslavia broke with the Soviet Union and Adlai was elected governor of Illinois. In his notes on the day on Brijuni he wrote, "A place to revisit." It was the first time that comment had been made during the entire trip, and Yugoslavia retained a place in his affections for the rest of his life.

In Greece, Adlai began to condense his travel schedule as he felt more familiar with Europe and the conditions prevailing there. Also, he wanted to spend more time with Borden and with John Fell, who would be joining them in Italy. Borden was with him as he visited a parade of Greek officials and leaders of opposition parties, as well as lunched with the king and queen, who talked about their plans to visit the United States. Queen Frederika made a date with them for a chocolate soda at an American drugstore.

Mrs. Roosevelt arrived, en route to Yugoslavia to interview President Tito. She and Adlai spent an afternoon together, talking mainly about the political situation at home. To her, and to the readers of *Look,* he expressed admiration for the achievements of the Truman Doctrine and the Greek-Turkish aid program. "With that bold and historic decision, the Eastern Mediterranean was secured and the tide began at last to turn against Moscow," he wrote. Three prime ministers, past and present, had told him, "We owe our freedom and rehabilitation to the United States; because our danger was greatest, our gratitude is greatest."

Attwood's diary reports that on the plane to Rome the British ambassador to Greece sat down beside Adlai and told him that "on instructions from my government," he had just read *Major Campaign Speeches, 1952.* Adlai laughed and remarked that if the ambassador had been working for the United States government in these McCarthyite days he might have been instructed not to read it.

Italy was in the midst of one of its recurring political crises, with the Communists threatening to gain power, and Adlai quickly found himself in a round of meetings with a variety of political leaders, beginning with

Prime Minister Alcide de Gasperi. His experience just ten years earlier in heading the mission to study the reconstruction of Italy's economy now proved to be helpful in assessing the personalities and political forces in fierce contention.

On his last day, July 6, Adlai described to a large press conference the physical reconstruction that had occurred since he had been there and praised "the spectacular recovery of an indomitable people." Italians at the moment were not hearing much favorable comment from Americans and the remark won him many friends.

He could not escape McCarthyism, however. He was asked if he agreed with Mrs. Roosevelt's comment in Athens that Senator McCarthy was doing the United States "a great deal of harm abroad." He responded: "Mrs. Roosevelt must have traveled in some of the same places to which I have been. I have expressed myself before on this subject, and I may say more after I return to the United States." With only a few lapses, this was the answer he held to as the question constantly recurred at every press conference for the remainder of his stay in Europe. Although he tried to maintain restraint on the subject in press encounters, it figured in most of the private conversations from then on.

In Vienna, the press officer at the embassy, Bernard McGuigan, confided that he was resigning because the McCarthy issue had robbed his work of its satisfaction and that the April visit of Cohn and Schine had a "disastrous" impact on American prestige. The wife of his longtime friend, Ambassador Llewellyn Thompson, confirmed that morale of the embassy staff had been seriously affected.

Before leaving Vienna for Berlin, Adlai made a broadcast for Radio Free Europe expressing American solidarity with the peoples of Eastern Europe and praising the courage of the workers in East Berlin, who, on June 17, had launched riots in protest against policies in the Soviet zone of occupation. For several hours the workers actually had control of East Germany's major cities until overcome by Russian tanks and troops that came to the assistance of East German soldiers.

By the time the group reached West Berlin, where Ernest L. Ives, Adlai's brother-in-law, joined them for the remainder of the trip, reports were circulating of the arrest and execution of Lavrenti Beria, one of the trio who had taken over leadership after Stalin.

Mayor Ernst Reuter and a large group of officials, along with more cameramen than he had seen since Tokyo, greeted him at the airport. The next day, after a luncheon given by the city council in his honor, Adlai was asked by Mayor Reuter to deliver a personal message to President Eisenhower. He explained that he knew Eisenhower well and respected him but could not understand what was happening. Please tell him, Reuter said, that "American prestige has been injured almost beyond repair in Europe during the past few months." He hoped the President would do something about it—and McCarthy—while there was still time. "McCarthy," he said, "has done more to hurt America abroad in eight months than Soviet propaganda did in eight years."

Not long after the lunch, Adlai and his companions were staring into the muzzles of Soviet submachine guns. Accompanied by Cecil B. Lyon, the Berlin representative of the U.S. High Commission, they had driven into the Soviet sector to the bunker where Hitler had died. As Adlai clambered over the broken concrete, Attwood and Blair took pictures. Suddenly, they were surrounded by East German soldiers, and cars were parked in front and behind to prevent escape. One of the soldiers, repeating what had been said in German by an officer, loaded his submachine gun, poked it through the window, and said, "You move and we shoot."

Lyon pointed to the flag and official identification on the car and demanded that the soldiers contact the Soviet ambassador and return with Russian officials who were responsible for the area. Instead, the Germans insisted that the Americans go with them to headquarters. Lyon refused, and finally, the Germans agreed to send a messenger to the Soviet embassy. For about twenty minutes, Adlai paced up and down asking questions about slogans on banners hanging from nearby government buildings and being followed by two policemen with Soviet machine pistols slung in front of them. Then, a motorcyclist arrived with a message that they were to be released on condition that all film was to be surrendered. They should have known better, they were told, since "it was well known" that foreigners were forbidden to take pictures in America.

The rest of the visit, which included the West German capital of Bonn, was almost a triumphal progression. Adlai was feted at a dinner given by the British, French, and American commanders of the Allied forces in Berlin, at a lunch given by Dr. James Bryant Conant, the United States high commissioner, and a reception by the German government.

The effort to postpone comment on Senator McCarthy became particularly difficult with the dismissal of Theodore Kaghan, public affairs officer in Berlin, by the U.S. Information Agency after the senator had attacked him. This had been done despite supporting letters from Mayor Reuter and ex-Chancellor Figl of Austria testifying that he was an ardent anti-Communist.

The reception in Germany, however, was only a foretaste of what was awaiting Adlai in Paris, starting with photographers' insistence that his picture be taken with the engineer of their overnight train from Berlin and the four telephones that were ringing simultaneously and constantly as they checked into their suite at the Hôtel Georges V^e. The first day was occupied by an embassy briefing, a meeting with President Vincent Auriol, a reception in his honor given by the Committee on Cultural

Freedom, and finally a quiet family dinner at the restaurant on the Eiffel Tower with John Fell, Mr. and Mrs. Ives, and a cousin, Lady Mary Bailey. It was merely a warm-up for the second day.

It began at breakfast with René Mayer, chairman of the High Authority of the European Coal and Steel Community, followed by a meeting with Premier Joseph Laniel, and a long luncheon that included Pierre Mendès-France, a future prime minister; Pierre Lazareff and Hervé Miller, publisher and director of *France-Soir;* J.-C. Servan-Schreiber, editor of *L'Express;* Maurice Schuman, then undersecretary of foreign affairs, and General Corniglion-Molinier, minister of state. Indochina, and, once again, McCarthyism, dominated the conversation.

"We Americans seem to be losing confidence in ourselves at the very moment when the Soviet Empire is showing signs of internal weakness and when Europe seems to be trying to go its own way independent of American leadership," Adlai observed toward the end of the discussion. "This is the moment when a united free world should be ready with a dynamic policy to exploit the possibilities inherent in the fluid situation behind the Iron Curtain."

Following lunch he went to a briefing at the offices of the U.S. Mutual Security Agency. As he approached, employees leaned out the windows applauding and showering him with confetti. Then back to the hotel to meet with former Premier Antoine Pinay, and on to a dinner with American and French newspapermen at the home of the Attwoods. Germany, the European Defense Community, the Soviet Union, were lively topics of discussion, with Adlai acting "like a moderator trying to extract the hard facts from the general free for all," as Attwood wrote in his diary, until the subject arrived, inevitably, at McCarthy.

Attwood's diary entry continues:

> [Adlai] said his hope was that sooner or later the conservative Republicans would declare war on the guy. For he feels that McCarthyism is bigger than the partisan issue and realizes that if liberal democrats like himself launch the attack . . . it may only help solidify the Republicans. . . . Stevenson confessed that he wished he were somebody like Jim Duff, a tough hard-bitten Republican [senator from Pennsylvania]; if he were he would go out around the country and call McCarthy "a lying son of a bitch" who is the Kremlin's best friend in America. . . . In other words, defeat McCarthy with his own weapons. It has been obvious on this trip through Europe that Europeans tend to equate McCarthy with Fascism—and Stevenson, I think, is not sure that they may not be right. . . . He admitted that he can't explain the President's inaction on the matter but said that if he is doing it for political reasons then the menace of McCarthy is very great indeed.

Adlai began the next day with a lengthy talk with Jean Monnet, chairman of the European Coal and Steel Community, and then, to escape the incessant calls at the Georges V^e and to find time to work on his *Look* article, he and the Attwoods drove to the home in Versailles offered to him by Mr. and Mrs. David K. E. Bruce. Even there, there were interruptions for a meeting with Senator William Fulbright who had arrived from Washington, a call on General Alfred Gruenther, Supreme Commander of NATO forces, and three young Frenchmen representing left-of-center youth groups. Adlai stayed up until 3:00 A.M. working on the article.

On the last day of his tour for *Look,* he told a large press conference, the experience had been "fascinating, fatiguing and fattening."

Adlai loved England; some of his happiest and most satisfying times had been there, where warm, personal hospitality was everywhere. His first act was to go out and rent a pair of striped pants, a cutaway coat, and a gray topper to attend Queen Elizabeth's final Buckingham Palace garden party of the year. He spent the weekend as the guest of Lord Salisbury, the acting foreign secretary; a weekend enlivened by reviews in the Sunday papers of the British edition of *Major Campaign Speeches, 1952.* Sir Harold Nicolson wrote in the *Observer:* "Much as I like Ike, I should assuredly have voted for Stevenson, together with 27 million of the very best Americans." The BBC produced a special program of the "Speeches of Adlai Stevenson," in which the commentator described them as the "only really interesting and responsible political speeches the world has heard since the end of the war." By November, the British edition had sold what was considered to be a phenomenal fifty thousand copies.

However, a press conference, "probably the biggest" in London since the end of the war, on July 28, and a BBC panel discussion with a group of British editors the next night, disappointed many of his British admirers. His positions on the Soviet Union and the French in Indochina and his opposition to Communist China's admission to the United Nations were part of what was looked upon as general American inflexibility. *The New Statesman and Nation* commented that "he should never have become the darling of American progressives," adding that "the trouble about Mr. Stevenson is that although he would have made a better Republican President than General Eisenhower, he was selected as a Democrat."

With Attwood, Adlai retreated to Herbert Agar's estate in Sussex to complete work on his final article for *Look.* The Agars took Adlai with them to the races at nearby Goodwood, where he was summoned to join Queen Elizabeth in the royal box for tea. Also, while he was with the Agars, reporters called to inform him of the death of Senator Robert A. Taft, to which he responded: "Senator Taft enjoyed all the inducements to a safe and tranquil life. Instead, he followed in his father's footsteps and chose the toil and peril of public life to serve his country as he saw fit. I hope his example will be followed by many Americans." The other item of news he received there was that Adlai III, an officer in the Marine Corps, was about to be sent to Korea. He promptly telephoned his son in California and proposed flying there to say good-bye but was dissuaded from doing so.

During the two weeks in England, Adlai also saw friends such as T. S. Matthews, Robert Sherwood, Arnold Toynbee, Douglas Fairbanks, Jr., and Lady Astor, dined with leading British intellectuals assembled by Geoffrey Crowther of *The Economist,* had an off-the-record session with American correspondents in London, lunched with leaders of the British Labour party, sat in the House of Commons and then met with the British-American Parliamentary Group in the Members Dining Room, made a brief speech to the English Speaking Union, dined with Ambassador and Mrs. Winthrop Aldrich, and, most memorably, drove to Chequers for a lengthy lunch with the aging and ailing Sir Winston and Lady Churchill.

Years later, Attwood summarized his round-the-world experience with Adlai in these terms: "When we first met . . . I was a contented apolitical magazine writer. Because of him, I became, among other things, a Democrat, a U.S. Ambassador, and, I hope, a better American. I may even have become a better writer."

CHAPTER FOURTEEN
Titular Leader

ANY DOUBT THAT POLITICS was awaiting Adlai was dispelled by the presence at the airport of leading New York Democrats, including State Chairman Richard H. Balch and Averell Harriman, who took him off to the Biltmore Hotel for a press conference with some 250 reporters and photographers. He told them he would hold off making a report "on my long journey" until a speech in Chicago on September 15. Nevertheless, he went out of his way, without referring to McCarthy, Cohn, or Schine, to state that he was "proud of the Americans representing us abroad and of the goodwill and respect they enjoy in their stations . . . which have been sadly undermined of late from home." He ended the statement with praise for the Democratic minority in Congress, which had "made a record of which I for one am proud and thankful, and for which the President should be even more thankful. This has been opposition at the best."

Adlai avoided direct answers to questions of whether he regarded himself as the Democratic party's leader, and after a luncheon given by the Democratic State Committee, calls to ex-President Truman, Senator Lyndon Johnson, and Speaker Sam Rayburn, he was off to Chicago and Libertyville.

Jack Arvey, Steve Mitchell, State Chairman Jim Ronan, Mayor Martin Kennelly, and reporters were at the airport. Before escaping to Libertyville he told them he thought the Democrats had an "excellent" chance of winning the off-year 1954 elections, that under no circumstances would he run against Paul Douglas for the Senate, that Eisenhower had invited him to visit and report on his trip, and that he would support Mitchell against any effort to replace him as national chairman.

On Monday, when he arrived at the office, he found 450 invitations to speak. (Bill Blair and Carol Evans had already weeded out the less important ones.) Unless the invitations had potential for a major fund-raising event or had some other special attribute, they were routinely declined. The staff shielded him as he sought to catch up on correspondence, spend time with John Fell, and rest. The latter was interrupted repeatedly by such incidents as the group of Yale students en route to New Haven from the West Coast who found their way to Libertyville and asked to spend the evening with him. Adlai also worked on a speech to be given at a big Democratic dinner in Chicago on September 14, and another to be nationally televised from the Chicago Civic Opera House the following evening.

What had begun as a Stevenson homecoming was turning into a major between-elections Democratic conclave. At the Democratic dinner, Arthur Schlesinger, Jr., thought that Sam Rayburn's speech was "dull," Truman's "routine," others "tedious," and by the time Adlai's turn came "the room was filled with sodden and restless Democrats." But when Adlai began, "they all sat up as if an electric current had been shot through them. His speech was a triumph."

A packed Civic Opera House, with Democratic leaders from all over the country, and a national television audience heard his report, which described the trip graphically, country by country, and set forth observations that were harbingers of issues that were to mark the 1956 campaign.

> We must think afresh; and, I believe, in terms of a European system of durable assurances of non-aggression—for Russia, as well as for France, Germany, and the rest of us. . . .
> There is anxiety lest the shaping of our policy may be slipping from the respected hands of President Eisenhower into the hands of men less concerned with strengthening our alliances abroad than with appeasing our isolationists at home.

Then, foreshadowing his advocacy of a nuclear test ban treaty, he stressed that "a new fact confers a grim and pressing urgency on the international situation—the hydrogen bomb. For some years efforts toward the limitation and control of armaments have been stalemated"; and he called for "initiative in re-exploring the possibility of disarmament."

When the cameras were turned off, he spoke extemporaneously to the Opera House audience in terms many thought were more effective than the televised speech. The report indicated, he said, that "my cup of defeat has been sweet, indeed. After all, General Eisenhower has been to Colorado and look where I've been." Then, more seriously, he said he had made the trip because he feared that most Americans really preferred to avoid foreign involvements—that the ideal was isolation but the reality was involvement. Foreign affairs, however, "will be the most important and the most difficult, the most intricate problem for the Administration in Washington and for us as citizens for years to come."

The speeches and the Democratic conclave had succeeded in many ways. The Democrats had raised nearly $150,000 of the remaining campaign debt of $275,000. Disputes over civil rights, leadership of the Democratic National Committee, and other issues had been avoided; an image of a strong and united party had been projected. Hope that the 1954 elections might bring control of both House and Senate began to take solid hold. Adlai had seized and would continue to hold the spotlight. The world tour had been a vital part of his surge from overwhelming defeat back into leadership. Moreover, it was a major element in the shaping of what he was to be in the remaining years of his life.

In the fall of 1953, President Eisenhower maintained his stature as a commanding leader despite apparent inaction amid the mounting turmoil over Senator McCarthy and division within his own party. Paradoxically, Adlai appeared to be uncertain, vacillating—indecisive—as he actually moved purposefully into genuine leadership, even though the tools of power were in the hands of others, most notably Speaker Sam Rayburn and Senator Lyndon Johnson.

Adlai's role was obscured by what would become the too familiar process of self-denigration and denial of ambition while he was, in fact, working quietly to solidify his position. He knew, as he wrote later in the introduction to *What I Think,* that the role of titular leader of a party out of power "is a very ambiguous one." Indeed, he often referred to himself as the hind-tit-ular leader.

> The titular head has no clear and defined authority within his own party. He has no party office, no staff, no funds, nor is there any system of consultation whereby he may be advised of party policy and through which he may help to shape that policy. There are no devices such as the British have developed through which he can communicate directly and responsibly with the leaders of the party in power. . . . He has—or so it seemed to me—an obligation to wipe out the inevitable debt accumulated by his party during a losing campaign, and also to do what he can to revive, reorganize and rebuild the party.

From Independence, Missouri, Mr. Truman was urging him to assume leadership, but Adlai knew that the center of action that was defining party policy was in Congress and that to move out in front too fast would invite opposition from the Democratic leaders there. Speaker

Rayburn had been a consistent friend, but he was deferring increasingly to his protégé, Lyndon Johnson, who was capable of mobilizing a formidable bloc of southern and other senators if his jealous nature sensed a challenge. Accordingly, Adlai set out to strengthen his own relationships with the Democrats in Congress, while setting up an informal and unobtrusive brain trust, to study issues and feed him ideas and speech drafts, that he would use in an increasingly intensive effort to elect Democrats to Congress and, by so doing, build his own network of support. It is difficult now to establish how consciously this two-front campaign was conceived; but it was done so adeptly and effectively in the short span of fourteen months that it is equally difficult to believe it was inadvertent.

The work that began with the so-called Finletter Group had an impact—largely unrecognized—that lasted through the 1956 campaign and significantly shaped the programs of the Kennedy and Johnson administrations. To some, this was Adlai's most valuable contribution to American history.

It is not unusual for supporters of a losing candidate to want to continue the fight, but the enthusiasm usually fades quickly. This was not the case with a hard core of Stevenson supporters. Within two days of his return from his service as ambassador to India, Chester Bowles wrote urging Adlai to speak out on what he regarded as the administration's mistakes. Adlai replied on August 31 that he would be going east in late September and hoped "we could foregather at your place and with George Kennan for some deliberate talks." The same day, he wrote Kennan, former ambassador to the Soviet Union and head of the State Department Policy Planning staff, asking for a copy of a speech and adding, "I hope very much we have an opportunity to talk sometime this autumn." That day, too, he talked with Tom Finletter about the impact of budget cuts on foreign and military aid and suggested for his September trip east "an evening, perhaps with some others, for some skull practice." Also that day, and probably not coincidentally, Arthur Schlesinger sent him a bulging envelope that included material from Dave Bell and Bob Tufts from the Elks Club group, and a memorandum on social security by Elizabeth Wickenden.

Schlesinger has reported that he and Finletter and John Kenneth Galbraith had been discussing the need to expose Adlai to ideas on the developing issues that would "help him overcome his upbringing," which Schlesinger and Galbraith felt was too patrician. (It has been customary to underestimate his sentimental attachment to his Lake Forest friends and overestimate their impact on his thinking.) Of Finletter, Schlesinger has said, "He was older than all of us. He was identified with airpower and hard-nosed things like that. This gave weight to his views that Ken Galbraith and I did not have with Stevenson." Actually, Adlai had known Finletter in Washington during the war when he was a special assistant to the secretary of state and at the UN conference in San Francisco where he was a consultant to the United States delegation. He had been Truman's secretary of the air force and was later to be ambassador to NATO in both the Kennedy and Johnson administrations. He was, in addition, a successful lawyer in the prestigious firm of Coudert Brothers and a respected member of the New York establishment.

During the mid-September Democratic conclave in Chicago, Adlai talked to a number of people about finding ways to work out policies for the future, which prompted a letter from Charles S. Murphy, who had been on the Truman White House staff, suggesting that a policy planning program should be set up in the research division of the Democratic National Committee. He had a source from which he could get funds for such an undertaking but it might involve his participation in a paid position. Adlai suspected that the source of the funding was the CIO and there is some belief that this caused him to drop the idea of establishing the project in the National Committee with Murphy's participation.

On September 23, a somewhat similar suggestion came from Galbraith. He told Adlai he had been discussing with Harriman and Schlesinger the question of "how can we do the most to keep the Democratic party intellectually alert and positive during these years in the wilderness? We have all told ourselves mere opposition is not enough. Yet it would be hard at the moment to say what the Democratic Party is for." The party should present a program to the people if it was to attract and hold young voters and offer an alternative to Republicanism. This called for, Galbraith thought, "some organization in or adjacent to the Democratic party" that could reach out to specialists for position papers. "As the party of the well-to-do, the Republicans do not hesitate to use their dough," he wrote. "As the party of the egg-heads, we should similarly and proudly make use of our brains and experience." The papers would be "sifted, discussed and worked over"; what would then be done with them was less important than the discussion itself, although clearly they could be a reservoir of ideas and speech material for members of Congress and candidates. Adlai's response was that it was "a perfect statement of our problem, which I have thought about for a long time."

The weekend of October 3 and 4, Adlai, Finletter, and Kennan met at Bowles's house in Connecticut, and the Finletter Group was born.

"The idea of a 'cabinet,' an organization in opposition, a shadow organization, was in my mind for a long time," Finletter recalled years later.

> I was always horrified by a party in opposition being unable to find out what the policies were and so on. That weekend we went up on the train and spent the night and talked about the idea. From then on it was a fact. I was the one that called the meetings and saw to it that the papers got written and so on. . . . I remember Kennan's including himself out, he felt he

had to stick to his knitting in Princeton. . . . They were ad hoc meetings. . . . I never worked with more intelligent and devoted people in all my born days. Not everybody wrote papers. . . . The papers were written and discussed and sent back again and again for revision. . . . The quality of the discussion was the important thing. We spent *hours* together. These were men with first-class brains.

At the same time, John Sharon in George Ball's Washington law firm proposed the formation of a group of young lawyers in Washington to prepare papers on various issues for Adlai's use. Because of the initiative under way in New York, Adlai hesitated, but then encouraged Sharon to go ahead. He decided that having more than one center of activity might reduce the appearance of an organized campaign on his part. This was an important reason why he also attended few meetings of the Finletter Group, although he maintained close touch, suggesting people and subjects and giving encouragement through individual contact and the use of material in his own speech writing. On October 16 he had written Galbraith, "I am eager to avoid any impression that this is a Stevenson brain trust operation."

By the end of October, Finletter had assembled the first meeting; he reported to Adlai on November 2 that a paper by Galbraith on agriculture and another on budget and fiscal issues by Richard Musgrave of the University of Michigan had been approved by a group that also included Roy Blough, University of Chicago economist who had been on Truman's Council of Economic Advisers; Richard Bissell, MIT economist; Paul Appleby, Syracuse University economist who had been in Roosevelt's Department of Agriculture; as well as Harriman, Galbraith, Schlesinger, and Clayton Fritchey, now editor along with Phil Stern of the *Democratic Digest*. Moreover, assignments had been made for additional papers: Bissell on foreign trade; Bernard De Voto on natural resources; Alvin Hansen on monetary policy; Arthur Maass on public power; Chester Bowles on economic development; and Roswell Gilpatric, New York attorney and Finletter's undersecretary of the air force, on defense. These, and others, wrote position papers throughout 1954.

John Bartlow Martin assessed the effort in these terms:

The Finletter Group laid the groundwork for the 1956 campaign. . . . After 1956 the Finletter Group as such was dissolved—but a Democratic Advisory Council . . . continued to hammer out papers on issues. And then . . . in 1960, these position papers became the basis of the New Frontier and the Great Society. Indeed, much of the legislation that became the law of the land under Presidents Kennedy and Johnson, particularly social legislation, can be traced back to those discussions in Tom Finletter's apartment.

The intellectual probing of the Finletter Group was in sharp contrast to the emotional political turmoil gripping the country on Adlai's return as a consequence of the activities of the senator from Wisconsin. On his second day in office, Eisenhower learned that McCarthy was holding up the nomination of his friend and former Chief of Staff, General Walter Bedell Smith, as undersecretary of state. Since the war, Smith had served as head of the Central Intelligence Agency and as ambassador to the Soviet Union, where a McCarthy target, John Paton Davies, had been on his staff. Smith had defended Davies as "a very loyal and capable officer." In McCarthy's eyes, such an endorsement made Smith a possible "fellow traveler." The President called Senator Taft and told him to put an immediate stop to this nonsense about his friend "Beetle." It worked.

Then came the nomination of Dr. James B. Conant, president of Harvard University, to be United States high commissioner in Germany. McCarthy informed the President he would oppose the nomination because Conant had once said there were no Communists on the Harvard faculty—a statement so outrageous in McCarthy's eyes that it could only be made by someone who was at least pink. This time the President had Vice President Nixon talk to McCarthy but had to follow that up with a personal call as well before McCarthy said that even though he was opposed to the appointment he would not "make a row."

Two days later, on February 5, the President sent to the Senate the name of Charles E. "Chip" Bohlen as ambassador to the Soviet Union. For McCarthy, that did it. Bohlen was a career foreign service officer, which by itself made him suspect; but worse, he had been at Yalta and at his confirmation hearing he had defended the agreements reached there as the best that could have been obtained at that time. McCarthy then obtained FBI reports that contained vague suggestions about possible homosexuality and he demanded that they be made available to the Senate before the Senate voted on the confirmation. The President refused and sent Nixon to talk to McCarthy, with less success. Emmet John Hughes reports in *The Ordeal of Power* that Major General Wilton B. Persons, also of the White House staff, told him: "McCarthy had two speeches ready to use in fighting us. Both were pretty rough, but one was *real* dirty. So he [asked Nixon] which he ought to give. So Dick told him— and he didn't use the real *dirty* one."

This was then considered a victory, even though the bitter and heated Senate debate over Bohlen lasted from March 23 to 27. The President's refusal to make raw FBI files available had been defused by a compromise that allowed Senator Taft and Senator Sparkman to examine the files. After they reported to the Senate that there was nothing in them, Bohlen was confirmed by a vote of 74 to 13, with 11 of the 13 votes in opposition coming from Republicans.

The confirmation battles, however, were merely smoke signals warning of what was still to come. With Republican control of the Senate, McCarthy became chairman of the Senate Committee on Government Operations, where, Senator Taft said, "he can't do any harm." But the Wisconsin senator knew he had a hunting license in the authorization of the Permanent Subcommittee on Investigations, of which he made himself the head, to conduct "the investigation of the operation of all government departments at all levels, with a view to determining their economy and efficiency."

In mid-February, McCarthy launched an investigation of the Voice of America, which had ten thousand employees, nearly 40 percent of the total personnel of the State Department, and each day transmitted on various frequencies fifty hours of programs in as many languages, and had a budget of $100 million. Within months, three successive heads and some eight hundred employees of the Voice resigned. From the Voice, McCarthy had moved into the operations of the associated U.S. Information Service and its libraries in sixty-three countries. His charge that thirty thousand books in the libraries were written by Communists had resulted in a frantic removal of books from shelves and even actual book burnings. These were the actions behind many of the expressions of dismay and disbelief from people high and low that Adlai had heard during the latter phase of his trip.

Meanwhile, McCarthy had added to his staff as assistant counsel, at the urging of Joseph Kennedy, his son, young Robert F. Kennedy. He and LaVern Duffy, produced the most solid piece of staff work in the committee's record, and, in so doing, produced a different kind of crisis. They looked into trade being carried on with Communist China by the allies of the United States, and their hard, detailed work revealed that since the outbreak of the Korean War, 75 percent of all ships carrying goods to mainland China had sailed under Western flags, most of them while the Chinese were fighting against UN troops in Korea, including troops from the very countries engaging in the trade. On the basis of this information, McCarthy secretly opened negotiations with Greek owners of 242 ships and announced on March 28 an "agreement" with the owners to break off all trade with Communist China.

Actually, the American and Greek governments had just finished an eighteen-month negotiation ending in agreement "to prohibit the shipment of strategic materials by Greek ships to the Peiping regime." More basic was the question of a senator engaging in foreign policy negotiations. Harold Stassen, the head of the Mutual Security Agency, told McCarthy that such agreements could only be made between governments and that he was "undermining" objectives of the government. The next day, when asked at his press conference, the President agreed that congressional investigators had no power to negotiate but that Stassen must have meant "infringement" rather than "undermining." Stassen took the slap on the wrist; Nixon and Dulles got together with McCarthy, and the issue gradually died away. But others were soon to arise.

McCarthy chose Dr. Ralph Bunche, the 1950 Nobel Prize winner and the top American in the United Nations Secretariat, as a major target. The President learned that McCarthyites in the FBI were passing to McCarthy charges that Dr. Bunche, a black, was a Communist. According to Eisenhower biographer, Stephen E. Ambrose, the President told his aide in charge of relations with minority groups, Maxwell Rabb, that "Bunche is a superior man, a credit to our country. I just can't stand by and permit a man like that to be chopped to pieces because of McCarthy. This report will kill his public career and I am not going to be a party to this." He had Rabb go to New York and tell Bunche that the President was ready to support him in public. Bunche told him that he would face the charges directly before the House Committee on Un-American Activities, which he did successfully the following month. While the hearings were in progress, the President invited Bunche to dinner at the White House—secretly.

The President, though furious, steadfastly avoided public confrontation with McCarthy. He was convinced that, sooner or later, McCarthy would destroy himself and Eisenhower was willing to pay the price of sacrificed careers and political turmoil for the votes of pro-McCarthy senators. Although Adlai had promised in Europe to speak out on McCarthy when he returned home, he, too, held back in the belief that it would be more effective if "the conservative Republicans would declare war on the guy."

President Eisenhower opposed McCarthy's methods but shared his objective of ridding the government of Communists. Consequently, early in his administration, he had issued Executive Order 1040, which combined the separate loyalty and security programs that existed under Truman. One covered all employees and enabled the government to fire anyone when there was a reasonable doubt of loyalty. The other applied to eleven "sensitive" agencies, including the Departments of State and Defense, and provided for dismissal of employees if their bad habits, which included such things as drinking, loose talk, and homosexuality, or subversive activities, made them risks to the national security. This combined order was the administration's "new broom" for sweeping subversives out of government. Hoping to take media attention away from McCarthy, the President led discussions at Cabinet meetings in late September and early October on how to get favorable attention for the results of the new executive order. He wanted to know how many Communists had been found, how many had been dismissed.

A somewhat chaotic discussion ensued, as there had been a wholesale dismissal of federal personnel by the new administration for many reasons, including budgetary and patronage ones. Finally, Attorney General Herbert Brownell came up with a figure on the number of security risks fired by the administration, and, at a press conference on October 23, James Hagerty announced on behalf of the President that 1,456 persons had been driven from the federal payroll. Were they all spies? the reporters asked. No, that had not been said. Were they all Communists? No, not exactly, but they were all security risks. From then on, for weeks, a numbers game ensued, with the President announcing at one point the removal of 2,427 security risks, until it was finally admitted by an administration spokesman that only one alleged active Communist had been found.

It was in this atmosphere that Attorney General Brownell got the President's approval to revive the Harry Dexter White case in the belief that it would show McCarthy and his supporters that Eisenhower could be trusted to carry on the hunt against Communists in government. (McCarthy, in private, was calling the President "Stupe.") On November 6, in a speech before the Executives Club in Chicago, Brownell charged that President Truman himself had promoted the now deceased White, a Treasury Department official, in spite of evidence the FBI had given him that White was a Soviet spy. The charges had been made by ex-Communists Whittaker Chambers and Elizabeth Bentley in 1946; White had denied it, and a federal grand jury had refused to indict. Truman had read the report, had decided the charges came from "a crook and a louse," and that the only new information was that White had shown "friendliness toward Russia" during the war, as, indeed, many Americans had, including President Eisenhower himself in testimony before Congress.

The implied accusation that a President of the United States had not only harbored but actually promoted a known Communist spy, made by the attorney general with the approval of the President, sparked a firestorm. Chairman Harold Velde of the House Committee on Un-American Activities issued subpoenas to appear before his committee, not only to Mr. Truman but to former Secretary of State James F. Byrnes and Attorney General Tom Clark. All were refused. Truman went on national radio and television to say that Brownell had lied. Eisenhower was subjected to one of the most difficult and hostile press conferences of his eight years in office. Because Truman had mentioned McCarthy, the latter demanded and got equal time, in which he declared that Communists in government would be a major issue in the 1954 elections.

On November 11, Adlai issued a statement calling the subpoenas "reckless," disrespectful "partisan showmanship," and adding, "It is infamous that the man who has done more than anyone else to organize and fortify the free world against Communism should be subjected to such malicious political attack." More important, whatever hope Adlai retained that the President would restrain McCarthy now was gone and he began listening to those counseling him to speak out. From this point on, it was no longer a question of whether, but when, and in what circumstances.

The first opportunity was a speech before the Georgia legislature on November 24 when he reminded the southerners that "by this identical tactic of smearing the Democratic party as the party of disloyalty the Republican party kept itself in power for a generation after the Civil War." Now, he continued, "they are waving not the Bloody Shirt, but the Red Shirt—at a former President of the United States."

He happily interrupted his work on this speech to send a note of congratulation to General Marshall on winning the Nobel Peace Prize. (Marshall had attended President Eisenhower's Inauguration, but Mrs. Marshall had refused to go despite her husband's urging.)

Adlai next chose a less political setting to speak indirectly to President Eisenhower in an address to the Association of American Law Schools in Chicago on December 28 that he titled "The Reputation of the Government."

"There is too little appreciation of the wounds which government itself receives when private reputations of its citizens are insecure against official attack," he declared. There was no doubt in anyone's mind at whom the next passages were directed:

> Leadership to be greatly served must be cloaked in greatness. Idealism at the center must not be frayed around the edges. . . . The tyrants, *and the political opportunists who use them,* do the same kind of damage as the dishonest and the disloyal. They chip away at the pride which American citizens have in their government—a pride which is a corollary to the principles of decent, effective, fair government.

It was not until March 7, however, at a Democratic National Committee fund-raising dinner in Miami, that Adlai delivered the sledgehammer blow that would significantly affect the course of events leading to McCarthy's downfall.

So commanding was the McCarthy presence that when the appropriation for his permanent subcommittee came before the Senate in February, there was exactly one senator, William Fulbright of Arkansas, who dared to vote against the $214,000 that was proposed. Yet, beginning in mid-month, a new uproar began over the case of Major Irving Peress, a dentist at Camp Kilmer, New Jersey, who had refused to answer McCarthy's questions about alleged Communist activities. Peress's discharge had led to demands for Army records, which Peress's superior, Brigadier General Ralph W. Zwicker, with War Department approval, declined to provide. This prompted McCarthy to shout at Zwicker that he was "a disgrace to the uniform. . . . You are not fit to be an officer. . . . You're ignorant." Secretary of the Army Robert Stevens then directed General

Zwicker not to appear again before the McCarthy committee and announced he would appear in Zwicker's place. Frenzied meetings among Republican leaders in both the executive and legislative branches, and a flurry of statements, including a long one by the President at his March 3 press conference, left the situation in heated confusion.

Adding to Adlai's anger and disgust were activities being conducted under the auspices of the Republican National Committee. During the traditional Lincoln Day celebrations in January and February, the committee had arranged for McCarthy to give a series of speeches in various parts of the country on the theme, "Twenty Years of Treason," and other Republican speakers took up his charge that the Democratic party was a party of war, crisis, subversion, and treason.

Among those who joined in the chorus was a major leader of the liberal wing of the Republican party that had sponsored President Eisenhower's candidacy, former Governor Thomas E. Dewey of New York. On December 16, in Hartford, Connecticut, he had said: "Remember that the words, Truman and Democrat, mean the loss of 450 million Chinese to the free world. Remember the words, Truman and Democrat, mean diplomatic failure, military failure, death and tragedy." He added that the Democrats feared "the American people will discover what a nice feeling it is to have a government that is not infested with spies and traitors."

Adlai had first planned to speak on economic issues in Miami. Then a January speech by Secretary of State Dulles had turned his attention to foreign policy. But the Lincoln Day speeches and developments at the McCarthy hearings brought out the long yellow pad on which, on February 24, he began to draft his thoughts on "Crusades, Communism, and Corruption." The speech went through at least eight drafts, with others making suggestions. The speech as delivered, however, was basically the one written in longhand on February 24. It was a slashing attack.

> This has been a fateful week in the history of American government. We are witnessing the bitter harvest from the seeds of slander, defamation and disunion planted in the soil of our democracy. . . . Those of us—and they are most of us—who are more American than Democrats or Republicans count some things more important than winning or losing elections. There is a peace still to be won, an economy which needs some attention, some freedoms to be secured, an atom to be controlled—all through the delicate, sensitive and indispensable processes of democracy—processes which demand, at the least, that people's vision be clear, that they be told the truth, and that they respect one another.

Having set this perspective, he went on:

> It is wicked and it is subversive for public officials to try deliberately to replace reason with passion; to substitute hatred

for honest difference. . . . When one party says that the other is the party of traitors who have deliberately conspired to betray America, to fill our government services with Communists and spies, to send our young men to unnecessary death in Korea, they violate not only the limits of partisanship, they offend not only the credulity of the people, but they stain the vision of America and of democracy for us and for the world we seek to lead. That such things are said under the official sponsorship of the Republican party in celebration of the birthday of Abraham Lincoln adds desecration to defamation. This is the first time that politicians, Republicans at that, have sought to split the Union—in Lincoln's honor.

This system of ours is wholly dependent upon a mutual confidence in the loyalty, the patriotism, the integrity of purpose of both parties. Extremism produces extremism, lies beget lies. The infection of bitterness and hatred spreads all too quickly in these anxious days from one area of our life to another. And those who live by the sword of slander also may perish by it, for now it is being used against distinguished Republicans. We have just seen a sorry example of this in the baseless charges hurled against our honored Chief Justice [Earl Warren]. And the highest officials of the Pentagon have been charged with "coddling Communists" and "shielding treason." General Zwicker, one of our great Army's finest officers, is denounced by Senator McCarthy as "stupid, arrogant, witless," and "unfit to be an officer," and a "disgrace to the uniform." For what? For obeying orders. This to a man who has been decorated thirteen times for gallantry and brilliance; a hero of the Battle of the Bulge. When demagoguery and deceit become a national political movement, we Americans are in trouble; not just Democrats, but all of us.

Before moving to fix responsibility, he briefly catalogued the impact of McCarthyism:

Our State Department has been abused and demoralized. The American voice abroad has been enfeebled. Our educational system has been attacked; our press threatened; our servants of God impugned; a former President maligned; the executive departments invaded; our foreign policy confused; the President himself patronized; and the integrity, loyalty and morale of the United States Army assailed.

The object of all of this is—not only the intimidation and silencing of all independent institutions and opinion in our society, but the capture of one of our great instruments of political action—the Republican party. The end result, in short, is a malign and fatal totalitarianism.

And why, you ask, do demagogues triumph so often? The answer is inescapable: because a group of political plungers has persuaded the President that McCarthyism is the best Republican formula for political success. Had the Eisenhower administration chosen to act in defense of itself and of the nation which it must govern, it would have had the grateful and dedicated support of all but a tiny and deluded minority of our people.

Yet, clear as the issue is, and unmistakable as the support, the administration appears to be helpless. Why? . . . A political party divided against itself, half McCarthy and half Eisenhower, cannot produce national unity—cannot govern with confidence and purpose. And it demonstrates that, so long as it attempts to share power with its enemies, it will inexorably lose power to its enemies.

Perhaps you will say that I am making not a Democratic but a Republican speech; that I am counseling unity and courage in the Republican party and administration. You bet I am!—for as Democrats we don't believe in political extermination of Republicans, nor do we believe in political fratricide; in the extermination of one another. We believe in the republic we exist to serve, and we believe in the two-party system that serves it—that can only serve it, at home and abroad, by the best and the noblest of democracy's processes.

He then recounted the changing "numbers game," in regard to security risks, concluding that after all the claims

the only thing we know for sure is the government's reluctant admission that out of more than two million federal employees only one alleged active Communist has been found.

The President has said he disapproves of all these goings on—this slander and deceit, this bitterness and ugliness, these attempts to subordinate a nation's common purposes to a divided party's political ambitions. He has said so repeatedly in statements to the press—but the nation's ideals continue to be soiled by the mud of political expediency. . . .

Now, more than ever, America must be a citadel of sanity and reason. We live in a troubled, dangerous world where the great issues are peace or war and the stakes are life and death.

He then turned to a discussion of foreign and defense policy, but returned at the end to another appeal for reason and unity.

I hope we can begin to talk with one another about our affairs more seriously, moderately, and honestly, whether it be our foreign policies or the patriotism of our people and public servants. There has been enough—too much—of slander, dissension, and deception. We can not afford such wastage of our resources of mind and spirit which still surges so strongly through the hearts and minds of America.

He had made the speech in spite of the misgivings of leading Democrats, including not only Senators Lyndon Johnson and Richard B. Russell, but even Senator Hubert Humphrey and other liberal senators, who feared it would backfire on Democratic candidates in the coming congressional election. The reality was quite different and Senator Humphrey was among the first to write Adlai to say he had been wrong. Such members of the Republican establishment as John J. McCloy wrote him notes of approval and commendation.

The next day, the Republican National Committee, after consultation with the President, announced that Vice President Nixon and not Senator McCarthy would reply to Stevenson. The following day, March 10, President Eisenhower, at his press conference, denied that the Republican party was half Eisenhower and half McCarthy, and then commended Vermont Republican senator Ralph Flanders for accusing McCarthy of "doing his best to shatter" the Republican party. On March 13, Vice President Nixon, speaking for the Republican party and the administration, officially repudiated his personal and political friend, McCarthy, saying on national radio and television, "Men who in the past have done effective work exposing Communists in this country have, by reckless talk and questionable method, made themselves the issue rather than the cause they believe in so deeply."

McCarthy's downfall set in swiftly. He held the spotlight from April 22 to June 18, during the balance of the so-called Army-McCarthy hearings. On June 12, Senator Flanders moved in the Senate to strip McCarthy of his powers, and on July 20 he followed it up by calling on his Republican colleagues to join him in a formal resolution of censure. A six-man panel to report on the question of censure was set up on August 3, and on September 28 it unanimously recommended censure to the full Senate. Discussion was postponed until after the election. On December 3, the Senate voted 67 to 22 to condemn the conduct of Senator McCarthy. The reign of fear, if not of terror, was at an end. To the extent that there was an authentic spokesman for the movement that ended the McCarthy era, it was not the victorious President but the defeated candidate.

Democratic leaders in the Congress had watched the fight against McCarthy from the sidelines. A few had cheered, but often after asking reporters not to use their names. More thought Adlai was foolhardy and would wind up hurting the party and, without regret from some of them, destroying himself. As McCarthy's fortunes had dimmed, for Adlai, so did the word "titular" preceding that of "leader." The struggle to eradicate that designation was more subtle and prolonged, but it, too, moved forward persistently through the fall of 1953 and the elections of 1954.

In addition to the activity surrounding the Finletter Group, Adlai began by letter and telephone to establish contacts that had lapsed despite the awesome volume of correspondence he had maintained during his travel abroad.

The next overt foray after the September party conclave was the trip to Atlanta on November 23 and 24, at which he spoke to the joint session of the Georgia General Assembly. The ground had been well prepared. He was met at the airport by Governor Herman Talmadge, and ushered to a press conference. Since Georgia was one of Eisenhower's favorite golfing haunts, Adlai used golfer's language and told the reporters that the Democrats intended to shoot 108—"Out in 52 and back in 56." He called on Senator Russell, former Governor Ellis Arnall, leaders of the AFL and CIO, and attended receptions given by a Negro group and by a Princeton group, before spending the night as the guest of Governor and Mrs. Talmadge. The speech the next day, on which he had received valuable help from Ralph McGill, the editor of the *Atlanta Constitution,* and in which he gracefully acknowledged that the state had given him his biggest majority in 1952, was a success.

From Atlanta, Adlai went on to Montgomery, Alabama, where he was met at the airport by Senator John Sparkman and Governor S. Gordon Persons. It was Thanksgiving weekend and former Senator Millard Tydings of Maryland took him, Borden, and John Fell duck hunting.

Next, on Friday, December 11, he went to Philadelphia, where the Democratic party was holding a weekend of workshops, speeches, and receptions. On Sunday he went on to New York, where he received an honorary Doctor of Laws degree at a Yeshiva University banquet and spoke about "the great split in the soul of twentieth century man—intellectual expansion and moral contraction." On Monday, UN Secretary General Dag Hammarskjöld gave him a lunch, after which he had a meeting with the United States district attorney in New York to discuss the question of Communists in government, and then returned to Chicago.

After the Christmas lull he began the year that was to test his political leadership with a New Year's Day statement on the preservation of human freedom followed by a broadcast calling on the Democratic party to "distinguish between the occasion for partisanship and the time when peril demands unity, to offer constructive alternatives and "the best candidates," to appeal in the forthcoming campaign "not to emotion but to reason," and to "hold fast to our liberal humane traditions."

Politics was occupying him in other ways as he involved himself in the reelection of Senator Paul Douglas; the impending candidacy of his friend Richard L. Neuberger in Oregon; meetings with loyal supporters such as Senator Mike Monroney who had run, almost single-handedly, the Speaker's Bureau in the 1952 campaign; and a lively correspondence with people all over the country.

The correspondence and telephone calls took on new urgency after the January 12 speech of Secretary Dulles replacing the Truman policy of "containment" of Communist expansion with that of "massive retaliation," suggesting that if the Soviet Union or China started local wars they could expect a nuclear attack on them directly. Adlai asked George Kennan at Princeton for his views, got memos on the inability of the Air Force budget to back up the Dulles policy and on its impact on NATO. He began a correspondence on the subject with Paul Nitze at the Johns Hopkins School of Advanced International Studies, who, despite his Republican credentials, had been dropped by Dulles as Kennan's successor as the head of the State Department Policy Planning staff because of his service in a Democratic administration.

Directly and through intermediaries he was also developing, with some difficulty, his relations on Capitol Hill. Those with Speaker Rayburn were comfortable, but with Senate Majority Leader Johnson there was tension on both sides. Adlai was scornful of Johnson; the latter's attitude was summarized in such colorful phrases as: "That fat ass, Stevenson—he's the kind of man who squats when he pees."

Illness and surgery for kidney stones in April and a long recuperation slowed but did not stop the political activity. The Gallup poll showed he was the choice of 67 percent of the Democrats for their candidate in 1956, but he was concentrating on congressional candidates and issues such as McCarthy, "massive retaliation," the Bricker amendment proposing severe restrictions on the foreign policy powers of the executive branch, and racial issues that came to the forefront after the May 17 Supreme Court ruling that declared racial segregation in public schools unconstitutional.

His first speech on this latter issue was somewhat less than forthright. It was made on May 27 in Meridian, Mississippi, and only by implication gave support to the Court's decision. His emphasis on equal opportunity, better education, better job training, and voting rights rather than the enforced integration demanded by many seems more prophetic now than it did then, particularly to his liberal supporters. The fact that the speech was given in Mississippi only ten days after the Court decision may be a partial explanation of his caution, but in the weeks that followed his ambiguity gained clarity only in contrast to the even foggier vagueness of President Eisenhower.

Sustained and hectic political activity filled the summer and fall. In June, he campaigned in Michigan and Indiana for local candidates, most earnestly for John Brademas, one of the many bright young men he had helped to bring into political life who was later to be Democratic whip of the House and president of New York University. A "vacation" in the Northwest and Alaska was planned for maximum political effect. That fall, Alaska went Democratic. The territorial treasurer wrote Adlai that he was "convinced that your visit gave the people the big push that culminated in the landslide."

Montana, Kansas, Nebraska, Illinois, Iowa, South Dakota, and Ohio were covered before the campaign began formally in Indianapolis on September 18. By Election Day, he made eighty speeches in thirty-three states.

Toward its end, the campaign turned nasty. With McCarthy in decline, Vice President Nixon once again took command of the low road. In Wyoming, Senator Joseph O'Mahoney was being called a foreign agent; Senator James Murray in Montana was confronted with pamphlets calling him a red spider; the loyalty of Senator Douglas was under attack in Illinois; and in New York, Harriman's integrity was called into question. Nixon's own speeches did not stray far from the innuendos and charges he made during the 1952 campaign. Adlai characterized Nixon's campaign speeches as "McCarthyism in a white shirt." The President wrote Nixon congratulating him on his "effective work" in the campaign.

At the outset of the campaign, the President had remained aloof, but on October 7, during a six-week vacation in Denver, Governor Tom Dewey warned him that "the Republican Party is going down the drain." This was followed by a message from Gabriel Hauge, then on the White House staff, that the polls showed a sizable shift toward the Democrats that could well give them control of the Congress. If that happened, Hauge stressed, "the extreme right wing will try to recapture the leadership of the party." The President heeded this warning and in the second half of October he traveled more than ten thousand miles and made nearly forty speeches, mainly in states where moderate Republicans needed help.

On Election Day, the Democrats won 53 percent of the popular vote. The Republicans lost seventeen seats in the House and two in the Senate. The Democrats not only won control of the Congress, but added nine governors to their total. Without Eisenhower's last-minute campaigning, most observers believed, the losses would have been much greater.

For Adlai, the next few days were filled with sending and receiving congratulatory messages. He could do for others what he could not do for himself in a head-on contest with the popular President. He had put his prestige on the line in the campaign and had forced the President to do the same. He might remain the public's second choice, but he had placed many Democrats around the country in his debt, strengthened his position in the party, and left few observers in doubt that if he wanted it, the nomination in 1956 would be his.

*   *   *

If there was purposeful direction, and even some order, in his public life, that definitely was not the case in his personal life. It was marked by uncertainty, confusion, and physical as well as psychological pain. Even the joy of Adlai III's engagement and wedding were scarred by Ellen's increasingly bizarre behavior. The indecisiveness that could not be found in his relation to public issues was evident in his handling of the personal matters that confronted him on the return from the round-the-world trip.

Ellen's divorce had come early in the governorship. The demands of that period and of the presidential campaign, followed promptly by five months of travel abroad, had enabled him to sublimate the profound impact of losing a home life of his own. Now, as he watched the flowering of his son's romance amid thorns from Ellen's erratic opposition, yearnings for an idealized home base grew more intense, even as he permitted the campaign to scatter the focus.

While in training as a tank officer at Fort Knox, Kentucky, Adlai III had met Nancy Anderson, daughter of an advertising executive well known to his father's friends, the Barry Binghams. They saw each other frequently, and, after he was transferred to Japan in July 1953, then to Korea six months later, he had written her almost daily. Both Ellen and Adlai were aware of the developing romance. Adlai, in his trips to Louisville, had met the Andersons and liked them immensely, but Ellen had not.

Adlai III returned from Korea in July 1954 and, getting off the plane, realized for the first time that something more profound than the changeability of an artistic temperament impelled his mother. As he walked down the steps from the airplane in his captain's uniform, a news photographer's bulb flashed. Instead of greeting her son, Ellen whirled on the photographer and told him he should be taking her picture, not Ad's, as he was known to all but his father, who generally called him Bear. When she turned back to her son, she still did not greet him but berated him for being a publicity seeker.

In the car on the way home, she continued the criticism, telling him he should stand on his own two feet and not try to "cash in" on his father's name, adding also that she was the prominent member of the family and the one who should have been photographed. Under questioning at the 1966 legal proceedings, in which all three sons and Ellen's mother, Mrs. John Carpenter, joined to have her declared incompetent and a conservator appointed to manage her financial affairs, Ad testified that at no point did his mother say hello to him, kiss him, or congratulate him on his service as a Marine officer. Instead, after they arrived home, she asked him about his service ribbons only to tell him they amounted to nothing.

Ad's announcement that he was going to see Nancy in Louisville was met with fierce opposition. He had been gone a long time and should see other American girls, he was "an easy prey for a predatory woman." Ad went, and a couple of weeks later brought Nancy back to meet Ellen at her house in Half Day, and Adlai at nearby Libertyville. Nancy recalled that at the beginning she was greeted with warm, even affectionate, cordiality, marred only by an occasional reference to "nicer girls that Ad knew." But on the second night when they returned late, Ellen was waiting to berate them both for their behavior and to accuse Nancy of being a "bad influence" in terms Nancy has chosen not to remember.

A second visit followed a similar pattern. After a happy visit, Ellen suggested they pick some sweet corn to take back to the Andersons in Louisville since Ad was driving Nancy back. Ellen made a joyful game out of the corn picking, but as they neared the end she suddenly turned on Nancy shouting, "What are you trying to do? Why are you in such a hurry to take all of the corn out of my garden? What makes you so nervous and greedy?" The corn picking was ended quickly and the couple left for Louisville.

Adlai and his prospective daughter-in-law had liked each other from their first meeting. She responded to his keen interest in her and he was enchanted by her. He took both of them with him when he went to Springfield to speak at the state fair, and to the family home in Bloomington, and he regaled them with stories of his travels in the state during his governorship and of Illinois's history. To this day, Nancy recalls these early times together with sparkling eyes and affectionate laughter.

Ad enrolled in Harvard Law School in the fall, and the engagement was announced in Louisville on September 12. Two nights before in Chicago Ellen had given a preengagement dinner party at which most of the guests were her son's friends. At one point, when she was out of the room, Ad's roommate at Harvard, Bass Robinson, mentioned he had a stiff neck and Nancy had gotten up to massage it. Returning, Ellen immediately charged Nancy with "soliciting" another man, and shouted, "You get away from him, you nasty girl." On this note, the party ended. Consequently, Ellen's presence at the Louisville engagement party, which her ex-husband also attended, was not a relaxed occasion. Adlai stayed on for a few days, however, having a good time with the Barry Binghams, the Wilson Wyatts, and the Andersons, with whom he found it easy to become good friends.

More serious were the telephone calls that Ad at Harvard and the Andersons in Springfield began receiving at all hours of the day and night. The general substance was that the Andersons were social climbers who were trying to take advantage of the Stevenson name; marriage to the daughter of such a family was not to be allowed. Nancy recalls her mother hanging up the telephone on several occasions with tears staining her face. Actually, the Andersons seriously discussed the possibility of canceling the engagement and were concerned that a person so mentally unstable should be their daughter's mother-in-law and a grandmother of her children. They finally agreed that marriage plans could go forward on the condition that the young couple seek professional counseling.

Adlai, in the midst of the congressional campaign, was writing Mr. Anderson, Nancy, and his son, showing his understanding of the stresses that were being imposed on them and assuring them all would be well.

Inwardly, however, he was in turmoil. The evidence appeared only occasionally in the presence of those closest to him. There were unusual flashes of anger at Bill Blair; moody, distracted periods during visits of good friends at Libertyville; and unaccustomed expressions of concern about the impact Ellen's behavior was having not only on Adlai but also Borden and John Fell. Difficulties arose, for example, from an invitation to John Fell to join the William Benton family on their yacht in the Mediterranean that required Ellen's permission, which was not forthcoming, and Adlai felt powerless to intervene. Most of the time he submerged his emotions in sheer activity, not all of which was political campaigning.

He had agreed to give lectures at Harvard, Princeton, Columbia, and Vassar. In addition, he was making notes for a never-to-be-written book that he had discussed with Walter Johnson during the trip, weighing business offers, considering what he should do to earn a living, and perhaps more seriously than at any later time thinking about getting married— although utterly vague as to whom.

His letters to Alicia Patterson took on renewed warmth. He met Barbara Ward—Lady Jackson—and began one of the most important relationships of his later years. Marietta Tree had come to the Democratic rally in Philadelphia, returned to New York with him, and from then on his communications were more often addressed to her than to "the Trees." His friendship with Lauren Bacall received publicity in an article she wrote in *Look* in late 1953, entitled "I Hate Young Men," and putting Adlai at the top of the list of six she found attractive. Marlene Dietrich, not to be outdone, asked for an autographed photograph, and asked him to find a way to come to her since any initiative on her part would be publicized. With Agnes Meyer, whose husband published *The Washington Post,* he began what she described as "a very personal friendship . . . a beautiful and incredible friendship . . . harder than a love affair."

In the midst of all this, Adlai had two brushes with death—one fleeting and the other painfully prolonged.

On August 5, flying from Great Falls, Montana, to Denver, the commercial plane in which he was traveling was struck by lightning. An emergency landing was made at Billings. After two hours of inspection and radio repair, the flight proceeded. Adlai's calm through it all was characteristic, but it was perhaps reinforced by the far more serious threat from which he was still recovering.

The kidney stone problem that had hospitalized him in 1952 struck again on March 28, while he was horseback riding with Jonathan Daniels during a visit to the Ives home at Southern Pines, North Carolina. After three days at the Duke University Hospital he was released to return to Chicago. There, a stone below the kidney "bit me savagely," and on

April 12, he underwent major surgery at Passavant Hospital for removal of the stone. When he was released on April 20, he expected his convalescence to take six weeks, but despite his rugged constitution, recovery was slow and painful, with discomfort, nausea, and dizziness continuing as he embarked on the speaking schedule that began May 26.

Although Adlai fussed and fretted at the enforced idleness, the illness gave him time to decide that the projected book on the world tour was an impractical idea and to concentrate on the university lectures. As it happened, the Godkin Lectures at Harvard became the substitute, and the best-selling of all his books.

The academic lectures strengthened his image as a world statesman; the November elections strengthened his position as a political leader.

Adlai's interest in young people, which had prompted his acceptance of the university invitations, was reciprocated. At Harvard, in a mid-March Massachusetts chill, one young lady arrived outside Sanders Theater with a sleeping bag twenty-four hours before the first lecture was to begin. She was wise, because a line began to form before noon on the day of the talk, with many bringing box lunches and camp stools. By lecture time, loudspeakers had been installed in two other halls; some fourteen hundred people jammed themselves into Sanders, and untold numbers gave up and went home.

The first of the three lectures he entitled "The Ordeal of the Mid-Century." As he had worked on it, he told the audience, he was reminded of the classic phrase "that never occurred to Horace: 'Via oviciptum dura est,' or, for the benefit of the engineers among you, 'The way of the egghead is hard.'" At mid-century, he said, "great movements and forces" were converging "in a world revolution of which communism is more the scavenger than the inspiration." He traced the shift in world power from the Tigris and Euphrates valleys to successive centers of civilization that now focused on "two new colossi, the United States and the Soviet Union."

Asserting that "there is more real security in Americans in understanding than in H-bombs," he described what he saw as basic differences between the two superstates. "Our political institutions have matured around the idea of popular consent as the only valid basis of government and political power." By contrast, he quoted Alexis de Tocqueville's 1835 observation that in Russia the principal instruments of government had been despotism and slavery. Russia had lived in insecurity for centuries, suffering five invasions from the West since 1610, whereas the United States "only now, with the development of the long-range bomber and the guided missile is experiencing for the first time the sensation of vulnerability." Except for its treatment of the Indians, the United States had "disclosed little expansionist tendency," whereas Russia "has been consolidating her vast land mass, one sixth of the earth's surface, and, in the process gobbling up all manner of peoples linguistically and ethnically unrelated." Nonetheless, the non-Western majority of the world associates the United States with the expansionism of European colonialism "and finds the West guilty of aggression as charged in the Communist indictment."

Now, however, the "technological revolution . . . has made our geographies obsolete and also many of our concepts of power and warfare. With that, he described his world tour, which was really, he said, a tour of three worlds: Communist, Allied, and uncommitted. He gave the United States high marks for its "decision to shoulder the burdens of great power in the world," referring specifically to the Marshall Plan, NATO, Korea, and a general desire to "build the free world's moral, economic and military viability to the end that the weak and strong can be independent; can live in peace and each work out its own way of life."

He then expressed deep concerns about the misunderstandings and misconceptions he had found—our militarism, materialism, wealth, impulsiveness, unreliability, and disunity.

> Ignorance, propaganda, and our own behavior discolor and distort the vision of America.
> It has fallen to America's lot to organize and lead that portion of the world which adheres to the principle of consent in the ordering of human affairs against its first attack in several hundred years. . . . The quest for peace and security is not a day's or a decade's work. For us it may be everlasting.

"Perpetual Peril" was the title of the second lecture. Two "immense facts" dominated the scene at mid-century. The first was "the revolution of rising expectations and the new political independence of masses of awakening peoples." The second was the "constant overhanging threat of aggressive communism to national independence and to our concepts of political freedom and individualism." We tended to focus on the second of these while much of the rest of the world was engaged primarily by the first.

"They have not yet solved the tremendous problems of poverty, illiteracy, administrative inexperience, economic underdevelopment, political instability and decaying feudalism." In that world, he stressed, "slogans like 'massive retaliation' are no answer and nuclear intimidation no solution."

Western technology, however, "has shattered time and distance and released sources of energy beyond our comprehension" and "poverty, hunger, disease and servitude are not the immutable destiny of the long-suffering two-thirds of the human race who are largely colored. This revolution of rising expectations, this awareness that there can be relief and improvement . . . is a product not of communism but of our own industrial revolution and material progress."

The most important issue of our time is whether "Operation Bootstrap" could be won by "democratic, voluntary methods." After surveying efforts to help, he asked, "Where are we?"

An "unsteady equilibrium" had been achieved, he answered, and "we are now settling down for a long endurance contest." The world had moved toward a balance of power that must be maintained "until we can move on to a satisfactory international system for the limitation and control of military power, and ultimately . . . to the realization of our dream of peace by the concerting of all interests among all nations, great and small."

Beyond the "cold confines of the cold war," he foresaw the development of European unity. But in Asia, the situation was more uncertain.

> Civilizations are very old, but political independence is very young. In the new states the economies are shaky, public administration is weak; they are hungry and poor, sensitive and proud. Nationalism is rampant. And the West, identified with the hated colonialism, is suspect. . . . But in spite of all their doubts and difficulties the devotion of the leaders of Asia to the democratic idea of government by consent rather than force is impressive, as is the decisive manner in which so many of the new countries of Asia have dealt with violent Communist insurrections and conspiracies. . . .
>
> The tempered use of our power, the sympathetic understanding of people's "yearning to breathe free," the modest proffer of our ideas and faith—these constitute the true resources of America and the treasured hope of our civilization. Until the long labor is achieved, perpetual peril will be our lot and our condition.

The final lecture dealt mainly with what he regarded as the intangible aspects of "America's Burden." He began by again drawing on observations made during his trip to Asia and his conclusions as to Asia's new importance.

> Stability and indigenous strength in what remains of free Asia can only be established in the long run by the will and work of the people themselves. . . .
>
> In Asia, now, India and Japan are the anchors of the free world. With them rests the balance of power; as they are strong and free their non-Communist neighbors will draw increased strength in the alternative to China and communism. . . . China may in time become an even greater influence for good or evil in

the world than its partner in the vast Chinese-Russian heartland stretching from the Danube to the Pacific. . . . The Chinese may prove much wiser and cleverer than the Russians under Stalin. . . . The United States will soon have to formulate a reasoned policy with respect to China. We will shortly have to evolve the minimum conditions on which we are willing to live with the Chinese Communists, with the probability that, as in Europe, the ideological contest will go on for a long time.

He then turned to what he believed the conditions he had been describing in all three lectures required of Americans.

The challenge to us is to identify ourselves with this social and humanitarian revolution, to encourage, aid and inspire the aspirations of half of mankind for a better life, to guide these aspirations into paths that lead to freedom. . . . One of our hardest tasks—if we hope to conduct a successful foreign policy—is to learn a new habit of thought, a new attitude toward the problems of life itself. . . . Americans have always assumed, subconsciously, that all problems can be solved; that every story has a happy ending; that the application of enough energy and good will can make everything come out right. . . . If one diplomat can't come up with the answer, fire him and hire another—or better yet, hire ten. And if that doesn't solve it, some Americans conclude that there can be only one explanation: treason.

Our first job, it seems to me, is to school ourselves in cold-eyed humility; to recognize that our wisdom is imperfect and that our capabilities are limited. . . . So the first step in learning our new role in world affairs . . . has to be taken by individual Americans, in the privacy of their own homes, hearts and souls. It involves a . . . recognition that we are never going to solve many of the hard problems of the world, but will simply have to learn to live with them, for years and maybe for centuries. . . .

Another lesson that we shall have to learn is that we cannot deal with questions of foreign policy in terms of moral absolutes. Compromise is not immoral or treasonable. It is the object of negotiation and negotiation is the means of resolving conflict peacefully. . . . Experience suggests that it has not been easy for men to learn the wisdom and virtue of tolerance for ideas and ways of life which deeply offend the cherished tenets of their own faith. In times past men of fervent faith regarded religious tolerance as a sign of moral weakness rather than moral strength. It seems that only when warring faiths have become convinced that they must choose between common survival and mutual extinction do they agree to live and let live. . . . We shall have to listen as well as talk; learn as well as teach. And I sometimes think that what America needs more than anything else is a hearing aid.

America's greatest contribution to human society has come not from her wealth or weapons or ambitions, but from her ideas; from the moral sentiments of human liberty and human welfare embodied in the Declaration of Independence and the Bill of Rights. . . . The reservoir of good will and respect for America was not built up by American arms or intrigue; it was built upon our deep dedication to the cause of human liberty and human welfare. . . . Now at maturity we shoulder the heaviest burdens of greatness, for in the last analysis the epic struggle of our civilization, for government by consent of the governed, will be determined by what Americans are capable of. In bearing burdens, in ennobling new duties of citizenship, is the greatness of men and nations measured, not in pomp and circumstance.

A remarkable aspect of the lectures was their emphasis on Asia. Few, if any, American leaders had even begun to put Asia in such a prominent position in assessing the nation's interests. The phrases, "revolution of rising expectations," may have originated elsewhere; but it was these lectures that moved the idea to the center of awareness and of policy. Although he stopped short of advocating recognition of Communist China, he placed both China and the Soviet Union in the context of history and of policy, which was rare to the point of daring in the emotional aftermath of Korea and in the depth of the cold war. They solidified his position in the liberal and academic communities and provided an amazingly prophetic framework for much of what he would later say and do.

Only three days later, Adlai was at Princeton for the senior class banquet. His speech there dealt with one of his deepest convictions: the educated citizen's responsibility for public service. He began by pointing out that political organization in the United States consisted of some 155,000 governing units, including school boards, conservation districts, municipalities, states, nation, and so on, and was operated by some one million elected officials and six million full-time employees.

Our government is so large and so complicated that few understand it well and others barely understand it at all. Yet we must try to understand it and make it work better.

For the power, for good or evil, of this American political organization is virtually beyond measurement. The decisions

which it makes, the uses to which it devotes its immense resources, the leadership which it provides on moral as well as
material questions, all appear likely to determine the fate of the
modern world. All this is to say that your power is virtually
beyond measurement. . . . You dare not . . . withhold your attention. . . . If those young Americans who have the advantage
of education, perspective, and self-discipline do not participate
to the fullest extent of their ability, America will stumble, and if
America stumbles the world falls. . . .

Participating in government in a democracy does not mean
merely casting a ballot on election day. It means an attitude, a
moral view, and a willingness to assume a day-to-day responsibility. How many good citizens do you know who constantly
deplore waste, inefficiency, and corruption in government, and
who also go out and ring doorbells for candidates they believe
in? Not very many. Far more say, "Politics is dirty" . . . and far
more use the word "politician" as a term of opprobium, disrespect, and dishonor—and this in the land of Washington, Jefferson and Lincoln. . . .

People get the kind of government they deserve. . . . It is
the duty of an educated man in America today to work actively
to put good men into public office—and to defend them there
against abuse and the ugly inclination we as human beings have
to believe the worst. We . . . have placed all our faith . . . all of
our hopes, upon the education, the intelligence, and the understanding of our people. We have said ours is a government conducted by its citizens, and from this it follows that the
government will be better conducted if its citizens are educated.
It's as simple as that.

But there remained the question of "whether we have reached the
awful pinnacle of world power too soon, before we have sufficiently ele-
vated our national mind to lead the world wisely." He said that "nothing
had been more disheartening" in recent years "than the growth of the
popularity of unreason—of anti-intellectualism," and he urged the se-
niors

not to be afraid of unpopular positions, of change. . . . If we
can't look to people like you . . . then where can we look? . . .

Your days are short here; this is the last of your springs.
And now in the serenity and quiet of this lovely place, touch the
depths of truth, feel the hem of Heaven. You will go away with
old, good friends. And don't forget when you leave why you
came.

At the Columbia University Bicentennial Conference on June 5, he spoke after President Eisenhower. He began by expressing his concern over the "malice, distemper, and the new fashion of being cynical, sarcastic, skeptical, deprecating about America or fellow Americans"; and then declared: "If we doubt ourselves we will persuade no one. If we doubt our mission in the world, we will do nothing to advance it. And if we are craven before the slanders that fill our ears we will secede from each other. . . . The plain truth is that we here in America have written the greatest success story in human history."

He then reviewed material progress and stressed that productivity had been increased, and distribution improved

by putting government to the service of the people. . . . The child labor laws, wage and hours laws, the anti-trust acts, banking legislation, rural electrification, soil conservation, social security, unemployment compensation, the graduated income tax, inheritance taxes—it may be too much to say that all this and more amounts to a bloodless revolution, but it certainly amounts to a transformation of our economic and social life. . . .

Too many of our people still dwell in wretched slums or on worn-out land. Once again our top-soil, our national skin, is blowing away out on the plains. Our schools and our hospitals are over-crowded; so are our mental institutions and our prisons. Too many of our cities are wasting away from neglect. And how can we boast of our high estate when more than one of every ten citizens still do not enjoy fully equal opportunities?

Turning to foreign policy, he pointed out that "we have successively and emphatically renounced first imperialism, then isolation, and finally our historical neutrality. . . . Twice America has tipped the scales for freedom in a mighty global exertion."

America now faced the "danger of falling into a spirit of materialism . . . a moral and spiritual vacuum"; but there was greater evidence of "a deep, intense longing for a vision of a better life not in a material, but in a spritual sense; for love for human solidarity. There is hunger to hear a word of truth, a longing for an ideal, a readiness for sacrifice."

Amid doubts and difficulties there is reason to be "proud of what freedom has wrought—the freedom to experiment, to inquire, to change, to invent." To solve our problems now, he concluded, we can continue to look to "individual Americans, to their institutions, to their churches, to their governments, to their multifarious associations—and to all the free participants in the free life of a free people," and, "finally, to the free university whose function is to search for truth and its communication to succeeding generations. Men may be born free; they cannot be born wise; and it is the duty of the university to make the free wise."

Taken together, these three engagements and their five lectures made in less than three months, provide the clearest and deepest view that we have into the mind and the heart of Adlai Stevenson.

CHAPTER FIFTEEN
Eager Candidate

THE 1956 CAMPAIGN WAS viewed by some as a disaster, by others as a triumph, by still others as both. Beyond argument, it was an overwhelming and even humiliating defeat. The disaster was rooted in the public's impenetrable faith in Ike. The triumph came later as the quality of the ideas floated found harbor in the Kennedy and Johnson years. Yet the defeat, however inevitable, was significantly augmented by Adlai's failure of leadership.

Not long after the 1956 election, when a friend expressed concern about the way the campaign had gone, his reply was: "In 1952 I did it my way and got licked. This time I thought I owed it to the pros to do it their way. I deserved what I got, but the country doesn't deserve what it got." That comment summarized much of what was wrong in the campaign and also the depth of his feelings about the issues that were involved.

The first major difference from the 1952 campaign was his lack of reluctance. He was running at home even while traveling around the world. His campaign, though not explicit, began as soon as he got off the airplane on his return. To be sure, through the 1954 congressional elections, his activity was cast in terms of paying off the campaign debt and electing a Democratic Congress, but it was aimed as well at the 1956 presidential election. As usual, he would express doubts, ask people if they thought he should run, and otherwise seek reactions in ways that fed the idea that he was indecisive; but those close to him knew that he was planning to run again.

A similarity with 1952 was doubt from the outset that he could overcome Eisenhower's popularity. Wilson Wyatt, in his memoirs, tells about returning with Adlai from a vacation in Jamaica in early 1955:

> He turned to me, as the plane was coming down in Miami, and said: "Do you think I should run in 1956?" I answered with an emphatic "Yes." He then asked a question I would have given my eye teeth not to have heard, "Do you think I will win?" And, hesitantly but clearly I said, "No, I don't think so." He then asked, "Then why do you think I should run?"

Wyatt cited the influence Wendell Willkie's campaign had on the Roosevelt administration as illustrating the impact of even an unsuccessful effort and insisted "that the leadership he would give, even though defeated, would be invaluable to his party and to the nation." Adlai did not demur.

The question of electability nevertheless gave rise to frequent suggestions that a second candidacy should be postponed until 1960. Adlai discarded that notion very early. Nineteen fifty-two had taught him that it was difficult, if not impossible, to determine the time of opportunity. To try to evade the nomination in 1956 almost certainly would raise formidable obstacles to a bid in 1960. Overriding all other considerations, though, was the conviction that discussion of important public issues could not be postponed. Conscience, far more than political analysis, determined the decision to run. This same conscience, when it conflicted with political advice, sowed much of the disorder that would later arise. In addition, an almost incredible sequence of events would crowd more confusion on to the playing field.

"In 1956 Stevenson had to run," J. Edward Day has written,

> . . . because he had to be true to his devotion to forthrightness and to "talking sense." To him the Eisenhower performance was an infuriating exercise in Madison Avenue gimmickry. Stevenson had to speak up against what to him were drift and blandness. In 1956 he was not a reluctant candidate. To suggest that he should have sat back, refusing to run, hoping to get the nod in 1960, is to ask that Stevenson should have been something he wasn't: cunning, contriving, and highly adjustable in his convictions.

The second major difference was the preparation, nonexistent in 1952, but now signified by the work of the Finletter Group and solidified by a close relationship with the Democratic National Committee. Sadly, the ultimate result was a surplus and a confusion of counsel that eluded the firm direction of the candidate.

A seeming contradiction of much of the foregoing was the conclusion of the speech he made to the Democratic National Committee meeting in New Orleans on December 4, 1954. After his prepared address, he read a handwritten statement which concluded:

> But now I must devote more time to my own concerns. So if henceforth I cannot participate in public and party affairs as vigorously as in the past, I hope you will understand and forgive me, and I assure you that it reflects no lesser interest in our party's welfare and no ingratitude for the inspiration and encouragement you have given me in such abundance.

Within two days of the New Orleans statement, however, Lloyd Garrison in New York sent Bill Blair a long letter about the fund-raising efforts under way to finance Adlai's political activities aimed at the 1956 nomination, and making clear that the matter had been discussed with Adlai in considerable detail.

Some thought his objective was to encourage his supporters to express their wishes. Others thought he sought a brief breathing space to attend to personal affairs—mainly, establishing a law office and the wedding of Adlai III.

Newt Minow found space for the law firm at 231 LaSalle Street, a building housing the Continental National Bank and a number of other law offices. Opened for business at the beginning of 1955, the firm consisted of Adlai and Willard Wirtz as the senior partners, plus Minow and Bill Blair. Each of them had comfortable, well-appointed offices. There were two more offices for the four secretaries, Carol Evans, Phyllis Gustafson, Florence Meadow, and Juanda Higgins, and two walnut-paneled reception rooms.

The firm was successful from the outset; in fact more clients were refused than accepted. Wirtz was a recognized expert in labor arbitration cases. Out of seventeen additional clients that paid fees of $112,258 in the first year, Adlai was actively engaged in handling five. The largest was the Radio Corporation of America, which had retained him as counsel in an antitrust suit brought against it by Zenith Radio Corporation. His other clients included Reynolds Metals Company; the Lindsay Chemical Company; Leon Tempelsman and Son, diamond importers and toolmakers; and a French company, Lambert and Company.

Francis Plimpton has reported that colleagues in the New York legal establishment familiar with the RCA litigation greatly admired the work that Adlai did on the case. Minow has said that "the grubby details bored him, but he was a good negotiator." This attribute was especially useful to Reynolds Metals, which was interested in making aluminum in Ghana and Jamaica, and to Tempelsman in negotiations with the De Beers diamond syndicate in South Africa. Not all the clients were corporations. Work was done for the Air Line Pilots Association, the Field family, for

Marietta Tree, for Mary Lasker, and others. Minow recalls a friend sending him the case of a young man denied an honorable discharge from the Army on grounds of being a security risk. Minow believed the man had been accused unjustly, but because of Adlai's political position he hesitated and then sought Adlai's advice.

"Are you sure he is telling the truth?" Adlai asked. When Minow said he was, Adlai asked what the problem was in that case. Minow replied that he was concerned that taking on a loyalty case could end up embarrassing Adlai. Minow reports Adlai looked astonished and then said, "If I ever succumb to that, I might as well quit practicing law." Minow won the case.

It was soon clear that the firm could quickly develop into one of Chicago's most successful, but the case load was held down deliberately. Part of it was due to the planning for 1956, but also requests flowing from the campaigns of 1952 and 1954 did not subside and consumed much staff time. Adlai received about 150 letters a day. Carol Evans handled many of the personal letters. Although she could respond to most in Adlai's style, she also had an instinctive sense for the ones he would want to see. An example was a letter from a mother he did not know asking him to write a letter to her ill son to speed his recovery. He wrote the letter himself. Blair handled the speaking invitations, which averaged about ten a day, plus other political correspondence and requests for appointments. By now, the office had names and addresses of some sixty thousand political supporters arranged on three- by five-inch cards and filed by state and city. Literally thousands of messages were sent to local Democratic organizations, labor unions, Jewish, veterans', and farmers' groups, testimonial and fund-raising dinners, dedications, anniversaries, cornerstone layings, and so on.

So many people arrived unannounced to see Adlai that he tried to get work done by spending much of the week in Libertyville and crowding appointments into one or two days in town. Then he would usually lunch at his desk from a brown paper bag, and if he had a luncheon appointment he would simply order an extra sandwich. During this period, his new partners were astonished at the diversity of his friendships. He moved easily between the Morrison Hotel's Democratic precinct captains and the Republicans of Lake Forest. "Many who progress kiss their old friends good-by," Minow observed. "He never did that. He never closed a door." And it was not simply the politician's ploy; he maintained friendships with people he knew would never vote for him. His colleagues marveled also at the extent to which the children of his friends became his friends. They were legion, and their letters were among those Carol Evans would not intercept.

The RCA case and negotiations in Jamaica for Reynolds Metals took up much of his time in the first few months of 1955; but on April 18 he and Bill Blair left for Africa, partly for business but even more because it was a part of the world he had not seen and felt he should know about. He visited Kenya, Rhodesia, the Belgian Congo, the Union of South Africa, the Gold Coast, and Swaziland and along the way wrote another article for *Look*. For much of the trip, he and Blair were joined by the Lloyd Garrisons and by Mr. and Mrs. Cass Canfield of Harper and Brothers.

Garrison's long involvement with the Urban League and the National Association for the Advancement of Colored People made him sensitive to the fact that Adlai's schedule had him meeting important whites, but no blacks. In each country he would look for black lawyers. In Kenya, he discovered there was only one, who took them to visit a prison camp where members of the terrorist Mau Mau tribe were being held; some of them his clients. In South Africa, the law forbade gatherings of more than three or four blacks, so Garrison arranged for a dozen to meet at night in a basement with lights off in a private home on the outskirts of Johannesburg.

At the airport, as he was leaving Johannesburg, Adlai held a press conference at which he said:

> I would express the hope that the people of this lovely land take care lest fear lead them along the wrong path. . . . Responding to questions that have been sent me from all sides, and speaking with utmost diffidence, I cannot foresee the success of Apartheid as applied to industry and economic development with any confidence. And let me add I have grave misgivings about efforts to arrest the progress of a whole race when the rest of the world is moving rapidly in the other direction. It is seldom wise to close safety valves.

This, in 1955.

On the way home the plane was delayed for repairs in Dakar and he took advantage of the time to write a twenty-three-page "Memo to the Boys" on the month in Africa. It was filled with descriptive and factual reporting, political analysis that does him credit after all the intervening years, and humor. He told the boys he had heard the price of wives "is rising alarmingly," and assured them "I won't be stampeded into making a purchase!" Later he expressed disappointment at not seeing Dr. Albert Schweitzer, "whom many call 'the greatest living man'. . . . I wanted also to confirm the epitaph he has written in case he is eaten by cannibals: 'He was good to the last.'" (Schweitzer, for his part, wrote Adlai expressing regret they had missed each other, adding that he liked Adlai's Unitarian mentality since "religious thought free of dogmatism" was important to the "creation of a spiritual civilization.")

"I often asked Africans in what order progress should come—economic opportunity, political participation, education or respect," he concluded. "Almost always the educated ones said recognition and respect. . . . But everywhere, with the exception of South Africa, it is the same—the African is advancing. Indeed, the question is not *if* he is advancing, but *how* and *how fast*."

The boys were never far from Adlai's mind, but in these months he was most deeply concerned about Ad's wedding plans and the problems arising from Ellen's conduct. He hoped to dispel some of the tension that lingered from Ellen's attack on Nancy with a reception at the Onwentsia Country Club the day after Christmas. He and John Fell spent Christmas with Ad, Nancy, and her parents in Louisville, after which it was planned that all would return together to Lake Forest for the reception. As Nancy and her mother were packing, Mrs. Anderson answered a telephone call from Ellen. In her later testimony, Nancy said, "She said to Mother, 'I forbid you to come up here, and I forbid you to . . . capitalize on the Stevenson name. You are just social climbers.' And I could hear because her voice was very loud and it carried through the telephone into the room and—well, my mother was understandably very upset." Mr. and Mrs. Anderson canceled their plans to attend the party at which all were to meet Adlai's law partners and friends.

Afterward, Nancy wrote a warm, understanding, appreciative, and reassuring letter that ended: "I understand many things about Mrs. Stevenson—I hope you won't worry about my feelings—mine are more easily protected than Ad's. We will try to keep from being disturbed. . . . Oh—enough of all this—they are stumbling sentences which are, in a sense, just a round about way of saying that I love Ad very much, you've given us a great deal and we love you." Adlai's reply to this "charming" letter ended: "A new daughter is the best thing that has happened to me or any of us for a long while, especially one who is so understanding and patient with all the difficulties she has encountered. Ad is not the only one who loves you—we all do." In a postscript he reported that her parents were having dinner with him on Saturday night.

The storm passed briefly but blew up even more alarmingly when the Andersons, thinking it would ease matters if Ellen and Adlai were not at the same social event, suggested two prewedding parties in June. The consequence of that effort is indicated by an April 6 letter Adlai wrote to "Dear Bear":

I can imagine the trouble you had with Mother. I had it too and the Andersons had it worse than ever before. I talked with Warwick yesterday and found him really shattered this time. I think they are worried about Nancy having to be exposed to this sort of thing but I did my best to try to reassure them. . . . I just hope that with your help we can all come to understand this situation a little better and handle it a little better. Warwick and I decided not

to decide what to do yet and think things over a while until per-
haps Mother's passion had cooled.

Ad told his father he was flying out to Louisville for the weekend
"because Mr. Anderson really is beside himself and because I think
Nancy may break down if she has to go through much more. . . . I'm
getting some professional advice about mother—I refuse to live a married
life exposed 24 hours a day to her vindictiveness and she's getting worse."

Anderson's emotional turmoil was revealed in two letters he wrote
Adlai in quick succession. In one, he said Ad was appeasing his mother,
temporizing, refusing to face the truth, and suggested that Adlai was
doing the same. He urged that Ad be told the truth and made to face it,
that professional advice should be sought and that all should join in resisting Ellen's demands because the situation was becoming "intolerable." He also said he cared nothing about the details of the wedding—if,
indeed, there was to be a wedding—but he cared deeply about his daughter's happiness and they had to face the fact that Ellen was threatening
the success of the marriage. He also reported that Ellen had telephoned
one of their Louisville friends late at night to warn them she was going to
expose the family row in the press.

Adlai's reply was strong and direct.

> *In the first place, Adlai knows and has known for a long*
> *time literally everything that I know about her case professionally.*
> *No one has been able to induce her to see a psychiatrist since I got*
> *her to see one in Boston in 1942. As to "appeasing" her, I think a*
> *semantic debate would serve no purpose. I have not thought of it*
> *as appeasement nor have I ever seen any indication on Adlai's*
> *part of giving in, although he has frequently cut off or just with-*
> *drawn from the arena, if I make myself clear.*
>
> *I am afraid I cannot foresee the same disaster to their mar-*
> *riage that you do, although I have little doubt that she is and will*
> *continue to be a source of infinite difficulty and that that must be*
> *a hazard Adlai and Nancy will have to face. . . .*
>
> *Perhaps he has not "faced the facts" in their full import, and*
> *I have been loathe to do anything to set son against mother. I*
> *thought it better to let it take its own course than that she or any-*
> *one could find confirmation for her suspicions and justifications*
> *for her injury in that direction.*

He then counseled them to do whatever they wished about the parties, including having none, and ended:

"I am sorry to hear that there have been visible damages to the
children. I had not detected it in Adlai and I wish I could somehow make
amends to Nancy for the unhappy situation which she has become in-

volved in. . . . I can only say I am sorry and disappointed, and you are doubtless right that I have not done a very good job of it all." He then added a postscript: "I wonder sometimes if you and Mary San would have more respect for Adlai if he had behaved with less compassion and consideration for his mother. . . . After all, she is his *mother.*"

He sent a copy of his letter to Ad with a note saying, "Now pay attention to your work and forget all this business. It will work out as it always has, and a son who behaved with less compassion and consideration for his mother than you have I would not have much use for."

In addition, he called Ellen's mother, Mrs. Carpenter, who happened to be in Chicago and requested her to talk to Ellen and to Mrs. Anderson. In spite of his counsel to Ad to "forget about this whole business," he tried to arrange a family meeting in Washington, where he would be the night of April 16 for a dinner in honor of Speaker Rayburn, "to discuss all our family plans and problem." Borden managed to get leave from his Army camp in North Carolina and Ad arrived from Louisville "feeling better about the latest crisis with his mother."

The next day in New York, Adlai arranged through William Benton to have Borden transferred from psychological warfare to the Army Signal Corps's motion picture division, and set up an appointment for Ad to talk with Dr. Carl Binger, a psychiatrist he had previously consulted about Ellen. Consequently, when he returned from Africa in mid-May, there was a letter from Ad reporting:

> There's no question in his mind but that mother is a paranoid. . . . There's very little hope of the condition ever improving. There's good chance of the condition deteriorating. . . . He says the only thing to do is to remove yourself as far as you can in good conscience. . . . He says I should never expose Nancy to her. He says there's fortunately time to consider whether she should even be permitted to come to the wedding—lest she make some cynical remark at the "forever hold your peace" moment in the ceremony. Mother called the other night and I had to hang up again.

Ellen's aunt, Lady Mary Spears, had written to ask if there was anything she could do to be helpful. Adlai thanked her and explained that Ellen suffered "an illness well-known as persecutory paranoia and it is not very likely that much can be done or that it will improve.

When he flew to Louisville with the Edison Dicks on June 24 for the wedding, he learned from the Andersons that the "extreme difficulties" had continued and the barrage of phone calls from Ellen had not ceased. Although sometimes they had to hang up on her, they now felt better able to deal with the calls. Borden drove Ellen to Louisville and on the way she showed him a pistol she was carrying in her purse as protection against "Chicago politicians." Borden checked it and it was not loaded. She wore black to the outdoor wedding ceremony at the bride's home. The orchids Ad gave her she threw to the ground. During the ceremony, when the minister referred to Ad as "Adlai Stevenson, Junior," she interrupted saying, "That is not his name." When the couple went to greet her after the ceremony, followed by a photographer, she snapped, "Why is this photographer here at the wedding?" Nancy wept and Ad drew her away.

To most observers, though, it was a happy and beautiful wedding. As Nancy and Ad left on their honeymoon, Adlai's only expressed misgiving was that their Canadian camping trip scheduled too many nights in sleeping bags.

In the midst of these family concerns, a development of profound concern to Adlai—and to the country—was occurring on the foreign front. We now know that the Joint Chiefs of Staff five times recommended the use of atomic weapons in defense of islands now almost forgotten—Quemoy and Matsu. President Eisenhower fortunately vetoed the recommendations each time and the country did not learn how close it had come to a nuclear war.

When the Democrat-controlled Congress convened in January 1955, it had before it for approval a treaty of mutual defense between the United States and the Republic of China, which then included Taiwan (Formosa), the Pescadores Islands, and a number of small islands between Taiwan and the mainland, notably Quemoy, Matsu, and the Tachens. These latter islands, the President asserted to General Alfred Gruenther, "have always been a part of the Chinese mainland both politically, and, in effect, geographically"; some of them being within "wading distance" of the mainland.

The importance of the islands arose from the possibility that they could be the stepping stones for the often proclaimed return of Nationalist forces to the mainland, or, in reverse, a Communist invasion of Taiwan. For months both the Nationalists and the Communists had been engaged in provocative actions centered on Quemoy and Matsu. Communist shelling from the mainland had begun the previous September. There is now evidence that there was CIA involvement in the small Nationalist raids on the mainland. In any event, the treaty proposal was spurred on by almost daily clashes and a broad consensus that a threat of war existed.

While the Senate was deliberating, the President sent a special message to Congress requesting authority to defend Taiwan and the Pescadores, and stating that this might include "closely related localities." There was no doubt that this phrase referred to Quemoy and Matsu. Within days, the Democratic Congress, with only three dissenting votes in each house, approved the President's request. Fears of war mounted in the early spring. At one point, the President commented that the basic foreign policy idea of his leader in the Senate, Senator William Knowland, was to develop high blood pressure at the mention of China. Amid the noisy sword-rattling of Senator Knowland and his colleagues, Admiral Arthur W. Radford's open advocacy of a nuclear assault on mainland China, and Secretary of State Dulles's more ambiguous threats, congressional Democrats remained quiescently uncritical.

In early January, Adlai had begun corresponding with a variety of people about his concern over the mounting crisis. In the ensuing weeks, this involved exchanges with Benjamin V. Cohen, with whom he had served on UN delegations; Dean Acheson; Chester Bowles; Everett Case, president of Colgate and Princeton classmate; James P. Warburg, Paul Nitze; Bob Tufts; Arthur Schlesinger, Jr.; and others. He moved carefully because of the support the Democrats in Congress, and especially those in the Senate, were giving to administration policy.

With the help of Senator William Fulbright he arranged dinner meetings in Washington in early February that included Senators Lyndon Johnson, Russell, Jackson, Smathers, and Stennis the first evening and then, with Senator Lister Hill acting as host, a second dinner with Senators Holland, McClellan, Scott, Hennings, Mansfield, O'Mahoney, and Ervin. He also called on Speaker Rayburn, Senator Sparkman, and Senator Douglas. On his return to Chicago, he wrote Ben Cohen on February 15 that he "found them almost uniformly skeptical of the treaty but loathe to vote against it for fear of misunderstanding."

The unease on Capitol Hill and in the country grew sharply in March, however, when Secretary Dulles explicitly stated that American support for the offshore islands would "require the use of atomic missles." This was enhanced on March 16 when the President followed up this statement with the comment that tactical nuclear weapons could be used "on strictly military targets," and adding, "I see no reason why they shouldn't be used just exactly as you would use a bullet or anything else."

By this time there was no longer any question in Adlai's mind about speaking out against administration policy. The only questions were when, and how best to avoid resentment among congressional Democrats. He spent the first weekend in April in Libertyville writing answers to Mr. Anderson's two anguished letters and drafting a speech on Quemoy and Matsu. Both crises occupied him throughout the next week. He gave advance notice of his intent to Rayburn, Johnson, and Senate Foreign Relations Committee chairman Walter George, and elicited comments on his first draft from Acheson, Ball, Cohen, Fritchey, Nitze, Stern, and Tufts. As so often happened, after having been worked and reworked right up to the last minute, the speech was essentially the same as his original draft. Adlai looked upon it as his most important speech since the all-out attack on McCarthy, and the press was giving a strong advance buildup for the radio broadcast on Monday, April 11.

He began by recalling that it was just ten years since the founding of the United Nations with its "charter of liberation for the peoples of the earth from the scourge of war and want," but now, "despite uneasy truces in Korea and Indo-China, our country once again confronts the iron face of war—war that may be unlike anything man has seen since the creation of the world, for the weapons man has created can destroy not only his present but his future as well."

He moved quickly onto the offensive by saying the "hazard of war" hinged on "small islands that lie almost as close to the coast of China as Staten Island does to New York," adding that "I have the greatest misgivings about risking a third World War in defense of these little islands in which we would have neither the same legal justification nor the same support as in the defense of Formosa." Are we, he asked, "prepared to face the prospect of war in the morass of China, possibly global war, standing almost alone in a sullen world?"

He expressed special concern at the pursuit of a policy opposed by our allies. They were needed, he said, "because we have only six percent of the world's population . . . because the overseas air bases essential to our national security are on their territory . . . because they are the source of indispensable strategic materials," and because of "the moral strength that the solidarity of the world community alone can bring to our cause." He warned that the division from our allies over the islands "is, in my judgement, a greater peril to enduring peace than the islands themselves."

From this base, he put forward his own suggestions: Consultation with other states to "ask them all to join with us in an open declaration condemning the use of force in the Formosa Strait, and agreeing to stand with us in the defense of Formosa against any aggression, pending some final settlement of its status—by independence, neutralization, trusteeship, plebiscite, or whatever is wisest." He maintained that such a declaration would place the responsibility for war, should it come, on the Communists and would reunify the free world.

He then made a detailed and stinging criticism of administration policy and "the yawning gap between what we say and do"; starting with Vice President Nixon's talk a year earlier about sending troops to Indochina, the "brave talk about liberation that raised such vain hopes among people behind the Iron Curtain," the "dire threats of instantaneous and massive atomic retaliation," the President's announcement "that he was unleashing Chiang Kai-shek . . . presumably for an attack on the mainland," when "it was apparent to everyone else, if not to us, that such an invasion across a hundred miles of water by a small, overage, underequipped army against perhaps the largest army and the largest nation on earth could not possibly succeed without all-out support from the United States."

Declaring that "we must renounce go-it-aloneism," he stressed:

If the best hope for today's world is a kind of atomic balance, the decisive battle in the struggle against aggression may
be fought not on battlefields but in the minds of men, and the
area of decision may well be out there among the uncommitted
peoples of Asia and Africa who look and listen and who must,
in the main, judge us by what we say and do. . . . We will win
no hearts and minds in the new Asia by uttering louder threats
and brandishing bigger swords.

He then closed with this plea:

Let us stop slandering ourselves and appear before the
world once again—as we really are—as friends, not as masters;
as apostles of principle, not of power; in humility, not arrogance; as champions of peace, not as harbingers of war. For
our strength lies, not alone in our proving grounds and our
stockpiles, but in our ideals, our goals, and their universal appeal to all men who are struggling to breathe free.

Historian Stuart Gerry Brown in his book, *Conscience in Politics,*
assessed the impact of the speech in these words:

There is no doubt that, partisan though he was, he spoke for
the great majority of Americans. The next day, April 12, as
though he had never suggested military intervention in the islands, Secretary Dulles said that Stevenson's proposals "copied"
those of the administration. "Mr. Stevenson," he said, "has in
fact endorsed the administration's program in relation to Formosa." Whether the Secretary's words meant what they seemed
to say or were merely politic, there is no doubt that national unity
on the Formosa question followed Stevenson's speech. . . .
There is no reason to suppose that President Eisenhower
ever personally wished to go to war over Quemoy and
Matsu. . . . But Eisenhower was under severe pressure from
leaders of his own party and from Nationalist China. Stevenson's intervention on behalf of a peaceful solution provided
Eisenhower with the unity of American opinion he required to
resist these pressures.

The issue would arise again in the fall of 1958 and much the same
pattern would be repeated: threats of war, invocation of the Formosa
Resolution, a Stevenson speech this time backed up by Senate Foreign
Relations Committee chairman Green as well as public opinion, reduction of the Nationalist garrisons on the islands, and the end of the shell-

ing. By late October, Quemoy and Matsu retreated from the brink of war to near oblivion in the mists of history.

With the late June wedding over and Nancy and Ad off on their honeymoon, Adlai's main focus was the domestic political scene that soon would be thrown into disarray by President Eisenhower's heart attack.

At midyear in 1955, the Gallup poll found only 16 percent of the people expressing dissatisfaction of any sort with President Eisenhower. Richard Rovere, one of the keenest Washington observers of the time, wrote in *The New Yorker,* "It is a decade at least since there has been anything approaching the present degree of national unity." Some Democrats took comfort from the 1954 congressional elections plus the continuing feuds within the Republican party and voiced optimism about the 1956 presidential election, but there were few signs of major difficulties facing Adlai in moving toward nomination, and probable defeat.

This was the general atmosphere in mid-June when Steve Mitchell and a few others, after talking with Adlai, established a Steering Committee to Secure AES Nomination in 1956. During the summer, this small group began actively rounding up delegates and discussing what primaries, if any, Adlai should enter. This was to be the first election in which primaries were to have any significant role, and even then, they were to be held in only nineteen states.

Adlai tried to warm up his relations with Truman by arranging a meeting during the latter's forthcoming visit to Chicago for a Shriner's parade, but notes Adlai sent hardly advanced his objective. He used phrases such as "communion with you," and "motor you out to Libertyville," which could not have hit a responsive chord in Mr. Truman's more rugged phraseology. He said his aim was to restore public interest in government and have the Democrats nominate the strongest candidate, whoever that might be. It was a clear reflection of their differing wavelengths: What was high-minded to Adlai was softheaded to Mr. Truman.

The weekend of August 5, Adlai convened the steering committee at Libertyville. The first item on the agenda was, "Should AES be a candidate?" Adlai began the meeting by saying it was an open question although he had to know the question already was answered by the invitation and their response to it. The meeting quickly moved to a vigorous discussion of what all knew they were there for: the timing of an announcement, fund raising, staffing, the role of a revived Volunteers group, primaries, issues, overall strategy—the nuts and bolts of a campaign machine.

The Truman meeting and the Libertyville conference—both intended to advance an already decided upon candidacy—are good examples of the behavior pattern that made it so easy to label him a Hamlet and needlessly sow doubts in the minds of those who did not know him well. He always seemed to want to give people an opportunity to escape from any obligation they might feel they had to him. It was behavior that still stimulates searches for understanding in such elements of his past as the shooting tragedy of his childhood, the unhappy marriage of his parents, or the failure of his own marriage that he persisted in attributing to some shortcoming of his rather than to the destructive nature of his wife's illness. This questioning of himself was in stark contrast to the utterly objective, sometimes almost ruthless, qualities of mind and action that were evident when impersonal matters were involved. It is around this contrast that questions revolve about the kind of President he would have made. The 1956 presidential campaign confuses the picture because the personal and impersonal became so intertwined.

The day after the Libertyville meeting, Adlai began a series of lunches, dinners, and meetings with governors arriving for a governors' conference in Chicago. He also gave a big dinner at the downtown Tavern Club for both governors and the press at which he said he would announce his 1956 intentions in November (as had been agreed upon in Libertyville). That same day, Ellen gave a press interview claiming she had planned to give a reception that week for Ad and Nancy but the Democrats had forced her to cancel it. "They didn't want the publicity of our divorce ruining the [Governors'] Conference," she was reported saying. She also went on to call Adlai a "Hamlet" who "can't make up his mind" about running for President, adding, "That's why I don't think he'd make a good President." She asserted that Adlai did not want to run against Eisenhower "because he knows he can't beat him. He wants to wait, but he knows if he does he's politically dead." Understandably, the interview was very upsetting to Adlai but he said nothing.

A more sensitive insight was contained in a remarkably affectionate letter he received at the same time from Agnes Meyer, in which she began by chiding him for his "self-distrust" and for saying, "I wish I had a stronger heart for the work ahead."

> *Don't for a moment think that my recognition of who you really are and of the great human being God meant you to be, is feminine sentimentality. . . . Whether you are elected to the Presidency or not, you are bound to become the nation's outstanding leader if only you can overcome a deep psychopathic fear of your own greatness and destiny. What the origins of this emotional block may be I do not know since I have never had a chance to talk it over with you, but ever since we had our only meeting, I have allowed the passionate and disinterested sympathy I feel for you to stream out towards you. For I realize that whatever my reason, my political training and my wide connections can do for*

you—all this is secondary to your own need for love and for a faith in you that is far stronger than your own.

No letter or interview comes closer to the heart of the Stevenson enigma, and, characteristically, his reply evaded the personal issue:

No, you are wrong, I insist. It isn't just self distrust; it is prior experience and a genuine anxiety to be sure the Democratic party is doing the best thing for it and its cause, which is the restoration of public interest in government. However, let us not argue about my frailties, of which I have a great many; nor will I argue about my virtues of which I am afraid you see more than there are. I am, in fact, quite ready for the task, if equally ready to see someone else, and I would hope a better man, to undertake it.

With the governors gone, Adlai looked forward to a relatively quiet summer. He took with him on vacation at the Smiths' Desbarats, Ontario, summer place memos from the Libertyville meeting and the Finletter Group. One of them set forth what was to be the theme of the campaign: "We have a new age, a new prosperity, increasing leisure. Before us there is a vision of a New America." The campaign should focus "on the substance of this vision, and what we are doing, which we can do on a large scale, and practically, to realize it."

Another paper, calculating Democratic chances, said "nothing will have happened to shatter Eisenhower's popularity and the national mood of complacency and apathy on which his popularity rests." Therefore, Adlai should begin early to identify himself with "a wide variety of local issues," public power in the Northwest, unemployment in New England, farm problems in the Midwest, and so on. He should start early in the spring of 1956 to make informal, hand-shaking trips around the country, making short speeches, attending conferences and conventions, especially union conventions, and concentrating on small places that would be bypassed in the fall. September and October would be devoted to getting out the vote in the big cities and major speeches on national telecasts. Foreign policy did not present effective campaign issues so domestic issues should be central. Since the election was almost certain to be close, the selection of a running mate was especially important, and Estes Kefauver seemed the best possibility.

With plans in place, life proceeded with unaccustomed calm. Ad and Nancy were at Libertyville, and Adlai was indulging his unfailingly hearty appetite in the glories of Nancy's cooking. The resulting threat to his waistline he sought to divert in vigorous tennis matches that were marked by mean splices, cuts, placement shots, and good net work. John Fell joined them after a tour of Europe. Harry Ashmore agreed to resign as editor of the *Arkansas Gazette* to join the staff to write and handle press relations. John Brademas, who had lost his first race for Congress in Indiana by a narrow margin, agreed to take charge of research on issues and coordinate the work of the Finletter Group with the research capabilities of the Democratic National Committee. In early September, Ad and Nancy joined him on a business trip to Haiti and Jamaica for the Reynolds Metals Company. En route, he met with the Finletter Group in New York to discuss the content of his announcement and the assignment of topics to various task forces.

Work was completed on an article that would appear in the October *Fortune* expressing "My Faith in Democratic Capitalism." His strong attacks on the domination of the Eisenhower administration by "big business" made a broader statement of his views desirable. Eric Hodgins, an editor of *Fortune,* was eager to collaborate.

The relationship between business and government was "essentially one of cooperation between two institutional forces wholly dependent upon each other," he wrote, adding that postwar prosperity "has been due in large measure to processes in which government and business have in effect played complementary and co-operative roles." He cited examples such as taxpayer paid roads opening the West, power and irrigation projects, protection of infant industries, and second-class postal rates that subsidized newspapers and magazines.

In the technological age there must be an ever closer "interdependence." However, this required care to avoid confusing the respective functions of government and business. "Although commercial interests and national interests can and usually do walk a certain distance hand in hand, no full identity between them can ever be forced, and any attempt to force it would be apt to end in misery, or disaster, or both—and for both."

He continued the theme in a late September speech at the University of Texas, expanding on the "unique partnership between government and private enterprise, a mixed economy that is the despair of doctrinaire reactionaries as it is of doctrinaire radicals."

Everything was proceeding in an orderly manner. Then, during the night of Friday, September 23, in Denver, after playing twenty-seven holes of golf, President Eisenhower had a heart attack. The immediate conclusion was that if he lived to complete his term, he certainly would not seek reelection.

Until then, the Democratic nomination held few attractions; Governor Averell Harriman and Senator Kefauver had little difficulty in restraining their ambitions and had been in cordial communication with Adlai. Now, all calculations began to change.

Newt Minow recalls he was playing golf that afternoon when his wife transmitted an urgent call from Adlai to join him in Libertyville. There were about thirty reporters there, who believed that Eisenhower was dying and wanted a statement. Moreover, Adlai was scheduled to go to Texas on Wednesday to speak at the University of Texas and see Rayburn and Johnson; Blair was ill, he needed help. Minow quickly joined him.

Adlai spoke to the press briefly and then prepared a more formal statement to be read the next day to press and television. It said: "President Eisenhower's health is a matter of concern to the whole world. The news of his heart attack is very distressing, and—as I said yesterday—I am sure *all* Americans, regardless of political or other differences, share my anxiety and on this Sabbath day earnestly pray for his speedy and total recovery."

Before he left for Dallas, a close associate of Governor Harriman's, George Backer, arrived in Chicago to tell him that Harriman had decided to seek the nomination. In Texas, where Johnson was recovering from his own heart attack, both he and Rayburn told Adlai it would now be necessary for him to run in the primaries. There, and back in Chicago where Blair, Wirtz, Arvey, Finnegan, and Senator Hubert Humphrey all told him the same thing, he was resistant.

Primaries, inevitably, focused on local issues that were difficult, if not impossible, to relate to broader national and international issues. Adlai felt, therefore, that the kind of campaigning that was required was demeaning of the candidates and unworthy of the office. "I'm not running for sheriff," he would complain to his staff. However much the prospect of the primaries repelled him, he was no longer a free agent. Too many people had invested in his cause, too many staff commitments had been made. Also, allegations that he wanted the nomination handed to him on a platter aroused resentment in a man who had never shrunk in fear from a fight. Moreover, he was convinced that of all the likely candidates, he had the best chance of winning and was the best man to use the office of the presidency to advance the general welfare.

He acceded to the unanimous judgment of his colleagues, and it may have been one of the biggest mistakes of his career. It could be argued that he was so clearly the dominant candidate, he could have ignored the primaries in the nineteen states that held them and still have been the choice of the convention. Certainly, he would not have entered the election campaign exhausted in mind, energy, spirit, and willingness to exert firm guidance over a committed and creative staff. As a result, the "New America" theme lost whatever coherence it might have had.

The inner conflict between primary political necessity and statesmanship was illustrated by a statement issued in mid-October on farm policy—an issue on which he always had difficulty because none of the prevailing views seemed to him to be sound, though he had no proposals of his own to offer. He was under intense pressure to endorse a return to rigid high-price supports for basic crops in place of the flexible supports adopted by the administration. In a speech prepared for the state Democratic convention in Wisconsin on October 7, he had resisted those pressures, but resorted to vague calls to "explore new techniques," for "such devices as production payments," and for other measures to reduce over-production and conserve soil. His advisers fumed that he was throwing away the one clear vote-getting issue the Democrats had in the Midwest. So, to counter a speech Governor Harriman was to make in Des Moines, he issued a statement favoring price supports at 90 percent of parity. He didn't like the statement as it was being prepared, and when it was publicly described as a cheap political expedient, he engaged in an uncharacteristic display of resentment toward the staff that was a harbinger of the tensions, with them and within himself, that were still to come.

The incident demonstrated also that now it was the nomination and not the election that was important. Space and staff grew swiftly. Down the hall from Adlai's office was an office for Finnegan and Henry Raskin. Down another hall was a large room where volunteers and two paid workers did mimeographing, mailing, file keeping, and other details of campaigning. Nearby were offices for Ashmore and Brademas, who soon acquired a young assistant, Ken Hechler, who also would go on to Congress later. Roger Tubby, who had been President Truman's press secretary, arrived with an assistant, C. K. McClatchy, whose family owned a chain of newspapers in California. A few blocks away, Jane Dick and Barry Bingham, as cochairs, and Archibald Alexander as executive director, set up offices for the Volunteers that this time would be called the National Stevenson for President Committee. It was all still unofficial and unannounced, but it all suggested an eagerness to run.

The political climate heated up in October's cool as doubt that President Eisenhower would recover gradually was replaced by doubt that he would seek reelection; with both doubts increasing the number and intensity of the meetings and maneuverings. President Truman, in New York, said that if he were a citizen of that state he would support Harriman, and pointedly did not say what he would do if he were a citizen of Illinois. Kefauver was in Europe and there was much speculation on his plans, particularly after people all over the country began receiving postcards from Moscow. The question was raised whether he could be persuaded to accept the vice presidential nomination. Adlai resisted this idea on the ground that Kefauver, according to Johnson and Rayburn, was "the most-hated man to serve in Congress for many years."

Amid it all, Adlai received expressions of support from Senators Monroney of Oklahoma, Anderson of New Mexico, Muskie of Maine, Neuberger of Oregon, Kennedy of Massachusetts, and, most important, Senator Lehman, the respected leader of New York Democrats whose public endorsement was a major blow to Governor Harriman. Congressman Hale Boggs of Louisiana reported the support of several southern governors. From Governor Edmund Brown in California came an assurance that would evoke rueful recollections: Adlai "need have no fears whatsoever" about being able to defeat Kefauver in California with only a "minimum" amount of campaigning.

With such broad expressions of support, confident plans were made on October 20 to announce Adlai's candidacy on November 15, two days before a meeting of the Democratic National Committee in Chicago; and entry into the Minnesota primary on November 16; the California, Florida, and Pennsylvania primaries on December 14; and Oregon at a later date.

He also found time before the National Committee meeting to speak at Queens College in Toronto on United States-Canadian cooperation and receive an honorary degree; he received another from the University of Virginia, where he spoke at the opening of the Woodrow Wilson Centennial celebration. This November 11 speech exemplified what he wanted to establish as the character of his campaign. Woodrow Wilson gave him the opportunity to promote the Democratic party; the occasion gave him an opportunity to attack Eisenhower policy in the Middle East, and advance ideas of his own. Later events confer historical interest on what he said.

Citing the mounting violence between Israel and its Arab neighbors, he warned that "unless these clashes cease there is danger of all-out war developing while we debate which side is the aggressor." He said that "a major effort of statesmanship is required if we are to avert . . . disaster in this troubled area." The immediate requirement was to "make it emphatically clear that the status quo shall not be changed by force." He deplored that "we have shown little initiative within or outside the United Nations to prevent these clashes," and then suggested: "After years of experience it would seem the only way to avoid bloodshed and violence along the border is to keep the troops of these antagonists apart. And I wonder if United Nations guards could not undertake patrol duties in the areas of tension and collision. Certainly both sides would respect United Nations patrols where they do not trust each other." These thoughts would receive serious attention a year later—at the outbreak of the war that would seal the election.

The announcement of his candidacy on November 15, in spite of all the advance discussion, was a bland statement and left many questions unanswered until a press conference the following day. It was then that Adlai said he would enter the Minnesota primary and probably other primaries, that there would be no deals on the vice presidency and that the convention should make the choice with great care, that Jim Finnegan would be his campaign manager, and that if Eisenhower decided to run his health would be a "consideration" but not an issue. Likewise, his speech to the National Committee meeting was moderate, as Johnson and Rayburn had advised, avoiding attack on the President, though not the administration, and rejoicing in his progress toward recovery.

There were cordial meetings with a wide range of party leaders, although some of Chicago's ward heelers snubbed him. The most ominous development was a complaint from Senator Kefauver that the National Committee was giving Adlai all the radio and television time and favoring him in other ways. But, generally, the way ahead looked clear in spite of uncertainty over the President's condition and plans. Little did he realize that he was about to be challenged in one of the most vigorous and exhausting primary campaigns the country had yet known.

At the close of the National Committee meeting, the campaign plan agreed upon earlier was put into action. He campaigned in Florida for four days and then went on to Oklahoma City to speak at the national convention of the Young Democrats, and back to Chicago where, the next morning, he had breakfast with Senator John Kennedy. On December 6, he flew to New York to speak at the unity convention of the AFL-CIO, attend fund-raising functions and see Jewish and Negro leaders. From there he flew to Arkansas for a few days of hunting with Senator Fulbright and other leading politicians of that state.

Back in Chicago, on December 14, he issued a statement saying he would enter primaries in California, Florida, Pennsylvania, and Illinois in addition to Minnesota. These would "provide for expressions of preference on a regional basis in the East, Midwest, South and West." The next day, he received a telegram from Senator Kefauver informing him:

"I shall announce my candidacy for the Democratic nomination tomorrow. I want you to know that my effort will be devoted to pointing out weaknesses in the Republican administration and I shall endeavor to keep and improve the unity which our own Democratic Party has today."

Adlai promptly issued a statement saying: "Senator Kefauver is an esteemed friend and I say, come on in; the water's fine. I am glad to hear that he wants to increase the unity and strength of our party. Certainly we shall need unity and strength next November for the important contest."

Adlai had looked forward to a quiet family Christmas, but on Wednesday, December 21, when he arrived at the office, he learned that John Fell had been seriously injured on his way home from Harvard. He had been driving his father's Chevrolet with three passengers, classmates whom he counted among his closest friends. On U.S. 20 near Goshen, Indiana, coming over a hill, his car had been hit head-on by a truck that had been trying to pass another. The two boys sitting beside John Fell in the front seat were killed instantly. The one boy riding in the backseat was seriously injured. All three boys, and their parents, were friends of Adlai's as well. John Fell sustained a broken jaw, a lacerated mouth, the loss of upper teeth, and more seriously, a shattered kneecap. No blame attached to John Fell; indeed, the driver of the truck was indicted for reckless driving and involuntary homicide.

Adlai immediately arranged to charter a plane to fly to Goshen and called the parents of the dead boys, offering to take them with him. They declined, and accompanied by Mrs. Carpenter, John Fell's grandmother; Bill Wirtz; Roger Tubby; and a doctor, he flew to Goshen. The next day they brought John Fell to the Passavant Hospital in Chicago in an ambulance. Ellen was waiting for them at the hospital.

"I am the most fortunate parent in the world that he is still alive," Adlai told a friend. But his own childhood accident must have been on his mind as he wrote Agnes Meyer, "He will be alright in time—or almost alright—but who knows what the death of two of his dearest friends beside him in the front seat will do and mean inwardly."

Calls, cables, telegrams, letters, poured in, including messages from President Eisenhower, Mr. Truman, the president of Uruguay, and Senator Kefauver. There were so many that, reluctantly, he agreed that a printed reply had to be sent, but he rejected a routine acknowledgment and drafted a personal response:

> While his body is recovering rapidly, the spirit will be slower to mend. But faith and love are healing powers, and there is a great reservoir of both in the world. They are lifting John Fell on a warm sustaining flood and will restore him in time, I know. Our greater anxiety is that the families of all his beloved friends will be given the strength to live through and beyond this tragedy.

Later, reporting John Fell's progress to a friend, he said, "He won't be crippled at all. It looked at first as though he would be, but the doctors say he will make a complete recovery." Then, after a pause, and in a different tone of voice, he added, "That is, a complete physical recovery. Of course, a thing like this, it leaves scars on the spirit. They'll always be there."

Religion, which might have given him some solace at this time, became instead the cause of bitter attack and misunderstanding. Quietly, and seeking to avoid publicity for what he regarded as a very personal matter, he became a member of the First Presbyterian Church in Lake Forest on October 2. A few weeks later his action found its way into the news when a member of the church's session inadvertently mentioned it to a reporter. Adlai was utterly astonished by the furor that followed. Many of the hundreds of irate letters were from Unitarians who charged that he had deserted religious liberalism, and from others who asserted that it was an insincere, cynical, politically motivated act. One of the first and calmer letters was from the Reverend Kenneth Walker of the Unitarian Church in Bloomington; and to him Adlai replied:

> The story about the church business is not complicated. While in Springfield there was no Unitarian Church and I at-

tended the Presbyterian Church, and became a devoted admirer of Dick Graebel, the minister whom I believe you know [and who would preside at Adlai's funeral]. Somewhat at his instigation, when I returned to Lake Forest, there again being no Unitarian Church, I attended the Presbyterian Church from time to time where my old friend Bob Andrus is the pastor. Feeling the want of some church identification thereabouts, I concluded to formalize my membership. Meanwhile, I shall continue to go, when circumstances permit, to the Unitarian Church . . . and I consider myself no less a Unitarian than before. I hope there is nothing wrong with this. My understanding was that Unitarians have no objection to membership or association with other churches. . . . Moreover, as you also know, my father's family have been Presbyterians for generations. I had not thought this would cause any anxiety.

But it did cause considerable anxiety, and finally, Andrus and Graebel, joined by Walker and another Unitarian minister, the Reverend Jack Mendelssohn, jointly drafted a letter to Adlai saying he could belong to both churches without "inconsistency." They added: "While we understand you respect theologians, we know that doctrinal rigidity has never limited the comfort you find in Christian faith, fellowship and worship." They understood he would

maintain your lifelong affiliation with the Unitarian Church of Bloomington, your home town. Descended from active Unitarians on your mother's side, and equally active Presbyterians, including many ministers, on your father's side, we understand perfectly that you have found a local church home without forsaking a lifelong commitment and that you have also united your parental religious endowments.

The critical comment that continued to arrive required two different form letters and in many the letter signed by the two Presbyterians and two Unitarians was included. The "Merry Christmas" that ended most of the letters seemed to be an anachronism; a turning of the cheek rather than a joyous Christian wish. Even his devoted admirer Agnes Meyer wrote deploring his political use of religion. In a long reply, he said he was "disturbed" because such a reaction on her part "must reflect a broader cynicism." After recounting the circumstances, he said, "I will try to tell you all about religion in my life which came late and emphatically and has been a solace and strength I had not known."

In these sad and anxious circumstances he entered 1956; the most hectic, chaotic, frustrating, exhausting, and, in many respects, humiliating year of his life.

CHAPTER SIXTEEN
"This Will Lose You Votes"

THE FATEFUL YEAR BEGAN in tension. Watching John Fell's convalescence required care to avoid crossing paths with Ellen; he wanted to spare John Fell any consequence of her unpredictable but often vindictive behavior. To most friends he sent optimistic reports of his son's recovery, but he revealed his deeper feelings in a comment to Arthur Schlesinger: "He will always bear the scars of this. It will be an eternal nightmare for him." The controversy over religion was unsettling; particularly since it was so unexpected. The issues and activities that would plague him throughout the year surfaced very early: Israel and the Middle East, civil rights, defense, staff and fund-raising, the vagaries and vicissitudes of primary politics especially, and an election that could not be won.

An uncharacteristic clash with newsmen, with whom he was generally at ease, on the CBS-TV network program, *Face the Nation,* on January 8, signaled his state of mind. The questioners' confrontational tactics that normally would have been handled with wit and good humor led to open quarreling. Although public comment was favorable, Adlai was furious. He told Schlesinger the whole program had been cheap, undignified, and useless and went on to irritated complaints about the mechanics of filing for primaries and such irrelevancies as serving as a disc jockey for the March of Dimes campaign, the inadequacies of staff, lack of adequate speech preparation, the pressures of special interest groups in general and Zionists in particular. It was a revealing and ominous episode.

That same day, January 8, President Eisenhower, in Key West, Florida, held his first press conference since summer, announced he was returning to Washington to assume "the full duties of the presidency," and deftly handled questions about his health, and whether or not he would seek reelection, while leaving a strong impression that he would.

Much of Adlai's annoyance was arising from Jewish and black leaders who had been supporters in 1952, but now felt he was too lukewarm in his support for issues close to their hearts. His 1953 article in *Look*, titled "No Peace for Israel," had led to continuing criticism from Israel's supporters that he was "too objective." His basic difficulty was that he persisted in thinking in terms of how a Middle-East settlement might be achieved if he were President rather than, as a candidate, winning the votes of Israel's partisans.

At about this same time, Finnegan received from Jack Arvey a report on mail he was receiving from Jewish friends whose criticisms aroused "nervousness, apprehension and fear." Finnegan collected an exchange of correspondence between a California rabbi, Alvin I. Fine, and Chicago Rabbi Jacob Weinstein in which the latter defended Adlai's position and included quotations from recent statements by Adlai and personal testimonials from others that could be sent out to critical correspondents.

To this was added a carefully drafted statement sent to a meeting of the American Jewish Committee on January 23, which stressed that the United States should "arrest the frightening tensions in the Middle East, not only for the sake of Israel but its Arab neighbors as well." It recommended

> the restraining effect of an equitable balance of armed strength between Israel and her neighbors. And I think the security of all these states should be guaranteed by the United States, and also by France and Britain who joined with us in the tripartite declaration against change by force. I have suggested, too, that one way to make such a guarantee effective would be to keep Israeli and Arab forces apart by substituting United Nations patrols in the areas of tension and collision on the borders. . . . I think this country should reassert its fundamental friendship for both Israel and the Arab states. . . . Once the Arab states recognize and accept the permanency of Israel, then the real community of self-interest in the Middle East would become apparent and we can help solve the border adjustments, refugee resettlement and other obstacles . . . to peace and economic progress.

These and similar efforts were only partially successful. The dissatisfaction continued. Years later, Rabbi Weinstein said:

> The newly established state of Israel was still on shaky legs and ardent Zionists were eager to get the firmest commitments

from candidate Stevenson. They were so absorbed in the right-
ness of their cause and so completely persuaded that any right-
thinking man would see eye to eye with them that they were
often impatient with the Governor's insistence on objectivity
and his image of himself as one who might be in the mediator's
position as President and therefore not free to show too partisan
a hand.

Arvey later told an interviewer:

He had a big hope, by reason of his many contacts with the
Arabs and with the Jewish communities throughout the world
that he would be able to act as a mediator and get them together
at the conference table. . . . One of his great regrets, great disappointments, and a matter of great distress to him was that he
was not understood by many of his Jewish-American friends,
that they doubted his belief in the State of Israel.

Adlai's instinctive resistance to pressure groups, even when he
agreed with their basic objectives; his abiding desire to bring parties to a
dispute together; his tendency to look at a set of issues in terms of what a
President should *do* rather than what a candidate should *say,* also created
similar problems in relation to the most emotional of domestic issues—
civil rights.

Accused by northern liberals of pandering to southern white voters,
and by southerners as being a captive of liberals and blacks, he left both
unhappy by refusing to take positions that would satisfy either. In the
midst of demands for the use of force, if necessary, to enforce the Supreme Court's ruling, and the emotions aroused by the murder of four-
teen-year-old Emmett Till, a black Chicagoan killed while visiting
relatives in Mississippi, he persisted on a course of moderation that was
distinctly more restrained than Harriman's, and was perceived as more
moderate than Kefauver's equivocal statements. Many found it difficult
to distinguish his position from Eisenhower's even though Adlai was
more forthright in declaring that the law must be enforced.

His major concern was to find ways to push the South toward com-
pliance without promoting confrontation. This fit the concept of "gradualism" that was anethema to civil rights advocates. His mail on this
subject grew in volume and insistence, and again resistance set in along
with some resentment at being misunderstood. The fact was, however,
that his lack of emotional commitment obscured his convictions, and his
legal training dominated both.

Adlai flew to Minneapolis on January 17 to file as a presidential candidate and spent a day almost typical of the Minnesota primary campaign

that was to follow. He met with Governor Orville Freeman and other state leaders in the governor's office, went to a luncheon meeting in St. Paul, held a press conference at the state capitol building, went to the Ford plant to shake hands during the change in shifts, met Volunteer groups, attended a reception, and returned to Chicago.

A few days earlier, he had entertained at Libertyville Roger Stevens and others who would be his major fund raisers. Raising money for Adlai would have been difficult under any circumstances, but he made it even more so. Roger Stevens said that his one instruction from Adlai in 1952 was "No commitments." An offer of a large contribution was refused, for example, because it stipulated that the donor was to have ten minutes entirely alone with the candidate for an unspecified purpose. "Later, in 1956, when he asked me to do it again," Stevens recalled, "he said, 'I want you to do it because I don't think you'll make any commitments on behalf of me, not even for embassies—which is a habit of most fund-raisers.'"

Israel and civil rights gave special concern to the fund raisers because New York and California were the major sources of support, with Washington not far behind. Chicago, and especially Lake Forest, were disappointing. Texas was almost a blank. A member of the Reynolds Metals family gave $50,000 in the primary and another $50,000 in the fall campaign. In all, about $1 million was raised for the primary, and about $4 million for the fall campaign, not counting local or labor union spending. These figures seem ridiculously low now when the ceiling for primaries alone is $27.6 million, and the federal government grants each candidate $46.1 million for the fall campaign with another $8.3 authorized for each from their respective national committees, plus a battlefield littered with loopholes.

All these strains were coming together on January 23 as Adlai left for California on his first campaign trip of 1956. It would have been better if he had stayed at home. He was tired and he spent a week at Bill Benton's home in Phoenix, with Carol Evans and Bill Blair, working on correspondence and speeches for a busy California schedule. He began in Sacramento with a press conference, a farm meeting and reception, and a speech at the state fair grounds. On February 1, he campaigned in the San Francisco area, ending the day with a light, humorous speech at the Oakland Municipal Auditorium that evoked frequent laughter and applause. The next two days were filled with campaign stops in the Bay area.

It was felt that by overcrowding his schedule he could demonstrate his own vigor in contrast to Eisenhower's illness. It was a mistake. He arrived in Fresno for the most important speech of the trip before the California Democratic Council without having been briefed on the occasion or the audience because all assumed the predominantly young, intellectual, and suburban audience was for him enthusiastically.

John Bartlow Martin has reported that the speech was "a political disaster," and it was referred to thereafter as "the Fresno fiasco."

It was lofty, thoughtful, and almost nobody in California liked it. . . . Kefauver spoke the same day Stevenson did, delivered an all-out attack on the Republicans, and took the CDC by storm. From that day on, all through the long spring primary, Stevenson was fighting to regain the ground he held before Fresno. On few occasions has a single speech made more difference . . . the volatile California electorate, regarding Stevenson as a has-been because of the Fresno speech, turned wholeheartedly to Kefauver.

The atmosphere did not improve when Adlai went on to Hillcrest Country Club in Los Angeles for a fund-raising breakfast with its wealthy Jewish membership. Their commitment to Israel was such that some of the questions verged on the hostile. "We raised $55,000 or $60,000, but it was very unpleasant," Roger Stevens reported.

The ill wind continued at a press conference the next day when Adlai's commitment to enforcing the Supreme Court decision on desegregation was lost in his opposition to a proposal by Representative Adam Clayton Powell of New York that would deny federal aid to schools that practiced segregation. A few days earlier, President Eisenhower's similar stand had made him the focus of charges of "gradualism," and Adlai had moved into that line of fire. The worst suspicions of his worried liberal supporters were confirmed the next day at a meeting with Mexican-Americans and blacks in the heart of Los Angeles's black district when the word "gradually" crept into an answer to a question.

From San Diego, where he had gone to work and to recover from his battering, a letter to Agnes Meyer portrayed a situation over which he rarely gained control.

> I am more tired than I should be, but find a peculiar resilience that I hope endures a few more months of this ordeal. But I do not enjoy it, and what makes me uncomfortable and depressed is the rapid sequence of total surprises with no preparation or previous indoctrination. I have never enjoyed slapstick politics or extemporaneous speaking, and that seems to be all that is contemplated. The result, of course, is that the image comes out confused and the misquotations are at least as numerous as the accuracies. It is an awkward position for me to be in when I am trying to be the "responsible" candidate and most of the pressures are either for irresponsibility or banality.

Despite the bruises, he persisted in a similar vein at a press conference in Portland, Oregon. The negative reaction prompted the issuance of a "clarifying" statement that was of little help. George Meany, president of the AFL-CIO, attacked his views, and even his major supporter in New York, Senator Herbert Lehman, wrote him a long letter "expressing my sense of disquietude" and warning him that the words "gradualism" and "education" had been "used by apologists for discrimination and injustice for many years." Some editorials were praising him for his "courage, character and integrity," but, as Eric Sevareid acknowledged in his CBS commentary, Adlai's "calmness and common sense" had "cost him dear, politically, among some Negro and some labor groups." His most outspoken defender was Eleanor Roosevelt, whose friendship and loyalty had long been evident and would grow in strength and importance.

To these unsettling experiences, as he went on from California and Oregon to Washington and Utah, were added ominous reports from Minnesota, where the March 20 primary was rapidly approaching with unexpected signs of widespread support for Kefauver. Both Senator Hubert Humphrey and Governor Orville Freeman, who had encouraged Adlai to take the outcome for granted, were beginning to sense that Kefauver was gaining ground. Nonetheless, overconfidence continued to reign as Adlai spent the latter part of February in the East, where he was when President Eisenhower announced on February 29 that he would run again.

The next day, Adlai flew to Minneapolis to begin a campaign that was perceived to be against Eisenhower rather than Kefauver. A grueling week-long schedule took him to all parts of the state for scores of appearances in which Kefauver's name fails to appear in any transcript. One of the most positive results was a speech on civil liberties and civil rights at the University of Minnesota that appealed so much to Senator Lehman that he inserted it in the *Congressional Record* and reaffirmed his support. But the best news was a letter from Ad saying that he and Nancy were going to have a baby.

So confident was everyone that for the next week Adlai chose to work at home, speak in Detroit, and not return to Minnesota until March 14, just six days before the primary. By then, Kefauver's effective campaigning was joined to accumulating evidence that the Republicans were encouraging their faithful to vote in the Democratic primary for Kefauver as part of a "stop-Stevenson" effort. Adlai's Minnesota sponsors, concerned but still confident, set up what was, almost accurately, called a "murderous" schedule, involving meetings at half-hour intervals at towns twenty to thirty miles apart, which had to be reached by "wild rides on icy roads" or by small planes in hazardous weather. It was, literally, exhausting. Worse, the hectic effort enhanced the impact of the disaster that followed. Kefauver won 56 percent of the votes and twenty-six of Minnesota's thirty delegates to the national convention. Out of a total of over 300,000 votes, Kefauver had led by some 60,000.

As before, Adlai functioned best in the face of adversity. As the early returns spelled defeat, Finnegan and his staff met to consider withdrawing from the California and Florida primaries. The gloom was so pervasive that at one point Roger Tubby left the room and returned with a copy of James Joyce's *Finnegan's Wake* and presented it to Finnegan. After contemplating it a few moments, Finnegan looked up and told the group, "Well, I guess we've had our wake. Now let's get back to work." The pessimism remained so strong, however, that Finnegan advised Adlai, who was in Libertyville, not to issue any statement that night but to wait to comment at a press conference that had been scheduled for the next morning in anticipation of a victory. Instead, Adlai insisted on declaring immediately that he was in the primaries to stay, and at the press conference the next morning he was cheerful and positive.

"Senator Kefauver has won the first round and I congratulate him," he told the press conference.

> As for myself, I will now work harder than ever, and I ask
> my kind friends everywhere to redouble their efforts, too. As I
> said last night, my plans are not changed, and neither are my
> ideas. I have tried to tell the people the truth. I always will. I
> have not promised them the moon. And I never will. This may
> not be the way to win elections but it is, in my opinion, the way
> to conduct a political campaign in a democracy.

Asked by a reporter if in the future he would spend more time shaking hands, he grinned and said it was apparent that "a certain identity is established between the shaker and the shakee."

The response to defeat revealed Adlai's inner strength, but it also revealed a lack of rapport with his staff and an ineffective working relationship that he permitted to go unresolved through the entire campaign. George Ball wanted to bring Wyatt back; Schlesinger suggested that Finletter be made executive director of the campaign; Finnegan recognized disorganization and asked Minow to help coordinate the campaign. There was much milling about, but little change.

It was Adlai who decided to go to California promptly and deliver "fighting" speeches in Los Angeles and San Francisco to "put out the Kefauver fire." Wirtz, Ashmore, and Martin each worked on drafts of the Los Angeles speech, and at the airport he was presented with three that differed in both tone and substance. A delayed departure gave him time to complete a speech that was telephoned to Minow, who telephoned it to Los Angeles to be put on a TelePrompTer for the telecast that night. Their arrival was so late, he had to be flown to the studio by helicopter.

In spite of conflicting drafts, the Los Angeles speech was effective, probably because Adlai had written nearly all of the final version himself.

He no longer held back from attacking Kefauver. Kefauver's charge that Adlai's support came from "bosses" and "a machine," the senator knew, "is not so. These tactics can only weaken and divide the party and thereby help the Republicans. And when I read in the papers . . . that I'm more concerned about issues than about people—well, frankly, it makes me disgusted, and then it makes me just plain mad." His 1952 pledge to state the same position in all parts of the country "will not be changed to meet the opposition of a candidate who makes it sound in Illinois as though he opposed Federal aid to segregated schools, in Florida as though he favors it, and in Minnesota as though he had not made up his mind."

He restated his own position on desegregation in terms that conveyed deeper conviction about enforcing the Supreme Court decision than had been perceived up to then. He answered the attacks of Israel's advocates by calling on the administration to "make it unmistakably clear that Israel was here to stay" and that it "would not tolerate any alteration in the status quo in the Middle East by force."

The response was so favorable that he dropped his insistence on a different speech for San Francisco and instead did some rewriting that took into account the importance of union support in the Bay area. Even so, he finished the San Francisco speech in his hotel room just in time to get to the studio. As a consequence, he disappointed two leaders of the black community who had been waiting to see him by giving them only a quick handshake on his way out.

Confusion marked the arrangements all along the way and illustrated general disorganization among California Democrats on whom the Chicago staff had relied. Adlai's supporters were alarmed by ominous reports of the enthusiasm aroused by Kefauver's energetically informal and personalized campaigning.

After Minnesota, a California victory was absolutely essential, and it was in doubt. Indeed, the staff was awash in gloomy reports. Finnegan thought it was too risky to run in Oregon. Polls showed Adlai in trouble in Illinois and Montana. Kefauver was making great progress in Florida. Adlai should "come down off Cloud Nine." He should issue a statement on Israel; he should pay less attention to foreign policy; he should pay more attention to foreign policy. He should make a stronger appeal for the farm vote; for the votes of the elderly; and on and on. In the absence of the calm, firm hand of Carl McGowan, from the 1952 campaign, a veritable cacophony of advice from uncertain "pros" and more certain nonpros engulfed him.

The impact on him personally was a shock to the members of the National Stevenson for President Committee that gathered in Chicago in early April. "He looked exceptionally tired; sad, gentle and charming in manner; and the total impression was rather heartbreaking," according to Schlesinger. Marietta Tree said, "He was so exhausted he was making no sense . . . I was horrified at his condition, so horrified that I almost lost faith in him."

This was the setting from which he embarked in mid-April on an unrelenting campaign that would persist, with few breaks, through the convention in early August and on to the election in November. The uncoordinated, often conflicting even if excellent counsel, and the profligate expenditure of his physical and emotional energy, may not have changed the outcome but they exacted a very costly toll. The wonder is that he managed somehow in the midst of it all to develop ideas that would have historic impact. The earliest and one of the most significant originated with him rather than the Finletter Group. It was a political mistake, and perhaps one of his most important contributions. That was his proposal to stop the testing of nuclear weapons.

Adlai's service at the United Nations had made him thoroughly familiar with the "Baruch" proposals that would have placed the ownership of atomic materials in the hands of an international agency. Moreover, during his service in the Navy, Carl McGowan had worked on the Acheson-Lilienthal report, on which the proposals were based. The proposals had foundered on Russian opposition, but the subjects of atomic energy and arms control remained a lively topic that Adlai had continued to follow. His world tour, and the growing concern over the effects of fallout of strontium 90 from nuclear explosions, prompted him to ask questions on the issue in numerous letters and conversations. With the advent of the hydrogen bomb, his concern intensified.

In late February, Adlai had met in New York with Atomic Energy Commissioner Thomas E. Murray, who was known to favor suspension of testing, and had continued the discussion with financier Frank Altschul, a leading figure of the New York Council on Foreign Relations. Altschul strongly warned him that the idea was politically dangerous. The record suggests that this was his first serious discussion of the testing issue; thereafter the subject appeared in exchanges with George Kennan, Benjamin V. Cohen, Jerome Wiesner, Finletter, Schlesinger, Tufts, and others. He became convinced that the risks in unilateral suspension had been greatly reduced by advances in the ability to detect explosions. In fact, President Eisenhower had said that "tests of large explosions, by any nation, can be detected when they occur." He was convinced, too, that some initiative on our part would restore our moral leadership, especially in Asia where the first bomb had been dropped and where, in a recent test, Japanese fishermen had been severely burned.

When he first accepted the invitation to speak to the American Society of Newspaper Editors on April 21, his intention was to speak on foreign policy and defense. The first draft, prepared for him by Schlesinger, contained no reference to the suspension of tests.

The actual speech was written by Adlai in a Philadelphia hotel room a day or two before it was to be given in Washington and he kept working on it right up to the moment of delivery. He consulted widely, but the final product was his own.

The largest portion of the speech was, indeed, a vigorous attack on administration foreign policy. He spoke of the "great, creative years" under the Democrats that resulted in the UN, the Truman Doctrine, the Berlin airlift, the Marshall Plan, Point Four, NATO, and the Korean War, and called on the editors to "compare that extraordinary outburst of creativity with the sterility of the past three years." He charged that "the United States has come dangerously close to losing, if indeed it has not lost, its leadership in the world—economically, militarily, and worst of all, morally." He cited a poll taken a year earlier in Calcutta in which the respondents, nineteen to one, thought the United States was more likely than Russia to start a war.

In making these charges, he was on solid ground. A poll of the editors found them agreeing, by a margin of two to one, that the United States was losing the cold war.

Adlai went on to assert that the administration was failing to respond to "an extraordinary age which has witnessed the coincidence of technological, political and ideological revolutions." He then recognized "the obligation to measure criticism by affirmative suggestion." His first point called for altering style to manifest "a decent respect for the opinions of others," arguing that "foreign policy is not only *what* we do, it is *how* we do it." His third point contained specific suggestions for a "basic revision of our method of giving aid." It was his second point that broke new ground and was the heart of the speech.

> I believe we should give prompt and earnest consideration to stopping further tests of the hydrogen bomb, as Commissioner Murray of the Atomic Energy Commission proposed [in hearings nine days earlier before a Senate Foreign Relations subcommittee]. As a layman I hope I can question the sense in multiplying and enlarging weapons of a destructive power already almost incomprehensible. I would call on other nations, the Soviet Union, to follow our lead, and if they don't and persist in further tests we will know about it and can reconsider our policy.
>
> I deeply believe that if we are to make progress toward the effective reduction and control of armaments, it will probably come a step at a time. And this is a step which, it seems to me, we might now take, a step which would reflect our determination never to plunge the world into nuclear holocaust, a step which would reaffirm our purpose to act with humility and a decent concern for world opinion.

Four days later at a press conference, the President dismissed the suggestion. "It is a little of a paradox to urge that we work just as hard as we know how on the guided missile and that we stop all research on the hydrogen bomb, because one without the other is useless." Adlai had not proposed stopping "all research" on the bomb, only testing; but that was just the beginning of the misrepresentation and distortion that were to follow. Other administration spokesmen treated the proposal with ridicule and contempt, suggesting it was foolhardy and presumptuous of Adlai to make such a proposal to such a great military leader. They would continue to do so—until after the election.

This was not the only speech that would have a future. A few days earlier in Miami, he had made a speech on health issues that he would continue to develop throughout the campaign until it described a program close to what we now call Medicare. But at the time it was lost in the scurrying that surrounded Adlai's determination to "run like a singed cat."

The lack of direction suggested by that figure of speech was evident as he traveled to Florida, Pennsylvania, Washington for a United Auto Workers' conference, New York, back to Florida, Chicago for eleven hours, Oregon where he made as many as sixteen different whistle-stop speeches a day, California for more extended and even more hectic barnstorming, making more than fifty speeches in a single week, back to Oregon, then on to Florida, and back to California, all in less than six weeks before the California June 4 primary.

Such a schedule would have been backbreaking under the best of circumstances but Adlai's determination not to repeat himself made it mindbreaking as well. He was constantly talking about the need for an all-purpose speech, but when one was composed that he liked, he would use it two or three times, get bored with it, and insist a new speech was needed.

Sanity was preserved by the heroic efforts of Brademas and Hechler, who had compiled a veritable encyclopedia of the views he had expressed over the years, issue by issue, which they kept updating in a set of thick books they called the "Adlaipedia." It served two purposes: to provide a reservoir of ideas from which short speech segments could be drawn on a wide range of subjects—aging, health, depressed areas, conservation, small business, foreign policy, and so on; and to provide a ready reference to meet his lawyer-based respect for precedent and his conscience-based desire to be consistent. By convention time they had compiled background notes and position papers on 180 different issues.

Most aggravating of all was the unceasing demand to pay homage to local issues. Later, Adlai mocked himself by describing how he "bitterly denounced the Japanese beetle and fearlessly attacked the Mediterranean fruit fly." More seriously, to his associates, he would ask if such matters really deserved "so much attention from candidates for the highest temporal office on earth. Isn't it time we grew up?" At other times, more impatiently, he would exclaim, "Campaigning like this makes a whore out of you!" In a more considered comment, he said that "the hardest thing about any political campaign is how to win without proving you are unworthy of winning."

"In Florida," Maury Maverick, Jr., recalls,

> everybody thought he should talk about catwalks on bridges where old people could go and fish. People would keep pushing him, and he would say, "The world is in too much trouble to talk about catwalks. I'm going to talk about international affairs." And we would say, "But people down here don't want to hear about international affairs." His answer would be, "Then I have an obligation to tell them." And he did. Then Estes Kefauver came on, and what did he talk about? Catwalks."

Kissing babies, putting on cowboy hats, Indian headdresses, or otherwise cultivating an image, made him feel uncomfortable, and he would show it. Harry Ashmore tells of an incident representative of his aversion to being someone he wasn't. As they were leaving a small town in Florida, Ashmore told him it had been a successful stop, except for one thing:

"When you are shaking hands in a supermarket and a little girl in a starched dress steps out of the crowd and hands you a stuffed alligator, what you say is, 'Thanks very much, I've always wanted one of these for the mantelpiece at Libertyville.' What you *don't* say is what you *did* say: 'For Christ's sake, what's this?'"

According to Ashmore, Adlai was so delighted at this advice that he told it on himself at the next stop, "thereby losing another hundred votes to Kefauver, who was born knowing what to do with stuffed alligators."

Yet, paradoxically, there were many occasions on which he would break off a morose or irritable session with staff people in the bus or on the train and walk out into a crowd exuding charm and good humor. John Bartlow Martin recounts an incident in Long Beach, California, when he got off the bus and, instead of going to the speaker's stand, walked over to a park and started playing croquet with several old men there.

> He seemed to enjoy every minute of it, one would have thought he had come all the way to California for the sole purpose of playing croquet with these people. Yet a few minutes before on the bus he had been complaining to his staff about the next day's schedule. . . . He turned outward, to the crowd; and when he left the bus he seemed . . . a close friend of the people waiting outside.

There were still other contradictions. After complaining that he didn't have time to finish a speech he was working on, he stopped to write a warm, affectionate note to Marietta Tree's daughter, Penelope, on her sixth birthday. At one of the most intense periods of the California campaign, he rejected the advice of his California managers and boarded a midnight plane to get to the funeral of his friend and distant relative, Senator Alben Barkley, in Paducah, Kentucky.

Victories that boosted morale more than they increased the delegate count began to occur. Alaska, the District of Columbia, New Jersey, Illinois, and a write-in vote in Oregon led up to Florida where Kefauver was thought to be ahead. There the campaign became more bitter. Kefauver augmented charges of alliances with "bossism" with suggestions of Mafia ties, indifference to the elderly, and racism. In their worry, Adlai's advisers arranged for the first election-year debate in history between two presidential candidates on nationwide television and radio. However, the result, in the words of George Ball, "proved not so much a disaster as a bore." Adlai won Florida by just 12,000 votes.

On Election Day in California, Martin was asked to prepare two statements—one for victory and one for defeat. It was soon apparent, however, that the latter would not be needed. Adlai won California with 1,139,964 votes to Kefauver's 680,722—almost double the most optimistic estimates of his staff. The result was so cheering that no one stopped to ask why the staff had been so far off the mark.

After California, attention turned to seeking support of delegates from the more numerous nonprimary states. But the impact of the primaries lingered. They had cost about $50,000 more than the $1 million that Stevens had raised, "with no commitments," he assured Adlai. As appalled as Adlai was by the expenditures, there was an even higher cost.

"The primaries destroyed his élan and his resilience," George Ball has written. "No longer was he a confident, ebullient candidate; the querulous note was heard far too often as he looked toward the impending campaign as an ordeal rather than an opportunity." Also, Jane Dick had written him prophetically, "I don't think you have any idea how tired you are. I do know. I have been deeply concerned. . . . In my considered judgement, this *one factor* of wearing you out, until you are just an animated shell of the *real* Adlai—has been *the major mistake* of the [primary] campaign."

The most positive aspect of the entire experience was the unstinting support of Mrs. Eleanor Roosevelt. Behind her frequent encouraging notes to him were countless efforts in his behalf, especially in meeting Governor Harriman's challenge in New York, statements in support of his civil rights stand, and a day of campaigning in California that undoubtedly was a major factor in his overwhelming endorsement from black voters despite the expressed opposition of the NAACP. In one of his notes to her after the California primary he told her that that day "was more valuable than anything that had happened."

In late June, Kefauver began making conciliatory gestures and on July 26 announced his withdrawal from the contest. Governor Harriman, however, encouraged by President Truman, continued to seek delegates in the nonprimary states; so the contest continued as Adlai traveled on his own delegate search from New England to Washington, Colorado, Wyoming, and Nevada. He also quickly decided that a proposed trip to the Soviet Union being urged by Barry Bingham and other advisers was no longer practical.

Another overshadowing question mark was President Eisenhower's health. On June 7 he had been stricken with an attack of ileitis that required an immediate and serious operation that same night, between 3:00 and 5:00 A.M. The consequences of such a long operation on a heart attack victim aroused great concern, and questions about his remaining a candidate and who the vice presidential nominee might be. On the Democratic side, Governor Harriman promptly made a formal announcement of his candidacy.

Adlai seemed to have no doubt that the President would stay in the race. Four days after the operation he wrote his friend, Gerald W. Johnson at the *Baltimore Sun,* "I have no doubt the attitude will be: if he can walk he can run." Gone was the respectful attitude of 1952, as he added: "Instead of giving the people a better understanding of the world and its grim realities he accentuates all the national feelings of complacency and moralizing. The 'father figure' has given his family such a diet of sugar that it is suffering from fatty degeneration and a flabby America means a flabby free world."

None of this suggested he had become optimistic about defeating Eisenhower. On the eve of the Democratic convention, a Gallup poll showed 61 percent for Eisenhower and 37 percent for Stevenson.

On Saturday, August 11, the weekend before the convention opened, President Truman, after several days of building up expectations about his intentions, announced he favored Governor Harriman. In a hard-hitting press conference he declared that Adlai did not have the experience to be President while Harriman had "the ability to act as President immediately upon assuming that office, without risking a period of costly trial and error." He asserted he would fight with every ounce of his strength to stop Adlai.

Mrs. Roosevelt promptly admonished Mr. Truman, declaring that Adlai had more experience than Governor Harriman to equip him to be President, and adding that older people like herself and Mr. Truman should leave the political situation to people younger than themselves. She then joined Adlai, young Ad, Nancy, and John Fell, for a weekend-long round of visiting caucus after caucus to gain pledges of support and reaffirmation of old ones. (Borden was in the Army in Hawaii.) Mrs. Roosevelt continued her vigorous and effective campaigning right up to the balloting on Wednesday. Mr. Truman had retaliated on Tuesday by calling a second press conference to attack Adlai as a "conservative" who follows the "counsel of hesitation" and "lacks the kind of fighting spirit we need to win."

For a brief period, it seemed that Adlai's nomination might be blocked by Truman's activities, plus furious southern reaction to Adlai's support of "unequivocal approval" of the Supreme Court's decision on school desegregation in the party platform, and the activities of a few favorite sons, most notably Lyndon Johnson. But by the time the youthful senator from Massachusetts, John F. Kennedy, placed Adlai's name in nomination on Wednesday evening, the outcome was no longer in doubt. Pennsylvania's vote gave Adlai the 686½ needed for nomination, and by the end of the first roll call, the tally stood at 905½ for Stevenson, 210 for Harriman, and 80 for Johnson. With a roar, the convention then voted to make the result unanimous.

During the balloting, Adlai had left his office at 231 South LaSalle and rushed, with police escort, to the Amphitheater, where backstage he quickly became engaged in a heated argument. For weeks he had been thinking about the vice presidential spot, which had assumed additional symbolic importance in light of Eisenhower's illness. His personal preference was either Humphrey or Kennedy. The latter's religion created problems and, in addition, Speaker Sam Rayburn bitterly opposed "that little pissant." Kefauver had strong supporters, but Adlai was not one of them.

His decision to dramatize the importance of the choice of a possible successor to a President by making it a convention decision rather than a personal decision ran into strong opposition from convention chairman Rayburn, supported by Johnson and national chairman Paul Butler. Adlai's decision was a surprise also to Jack Arvey, Mayor Richard Daley, Mayor David Lawrence of Pittsburgh, and Governor Abraham Ribicoff of Connecticut, who were present, but they endorsed the idea. For fifteen minutes the argument raged, as tempers flared and harsh words were exchanged.

"Are you absolutely sure this is what you want to do?" Rayburn finally asked.

His face flushed, but his voice calm, Adlai replied, "It's what I want to do, Sam."

Rayburn marched out onto the podium and told the cheering delegates: "I have the unusual privilege of recognizing a gentleman whom, I think, you will recognize when he comes on this platform. He is here, not to make his acceptance speech, but to greet you and make an announcement."

The unprecedented action he then proposed, he was convinced, served not only the political interests of 1956 but the national interests of the future.

"The American people have the solemn obligation to consider with utmost care who will be their President if the elected President is pre-vented by a Higher Will from serving his full term," he told the dele-gates.

> It is a sober reminder that seven out of 34 Presidents have served as the result of such indirect selection. . . . The choice for that office has become almost as important as the choice for the Presidency. . . . I have decided that the selection of the Vice Presidential nominee should be made through the free processes of this Convention so that the Democratic Party's candidate may join me before the Nation not as one man's selection but as one chosen by our Party as I have been chosen.

The stunned surprise of the convention was followed by wild ap-plause and then by a scurrying for delegates by supporters of Humphrey, Kennedy, and Kefauver. Humphrey's candidacy was fatally wounded by the results of the Minnesota primary, and the contest quickly centered on Kennedy and Kefauver to provide, the next day, the most exciting after-noon of the convention. Widespread dislike of Kefauver was balanced by concern over Kennedy's religion and a vote he had cast against a Demo-cratic bill calling for high rigid farm price supports a few months earlier that would cost votes in rural areas where Kefauver was strong.

Adlai later admitted that when he threw the convention open, he fully expected Kennedy to win—that was why he had asked Kennedy to nominate him. But having taken the step, he was determined to hold to his promise not to influence the result and he instructed his staff to take no part in the contest. Kefauver, on the second ballot, received 755½ votes to Kennedy's 589 and became the nominee. Some of the Kennedy people, but not the senator, never forgave Adlai. Senator Kennedy later acknowledged that had he, as a Catholic on the national ticket, gone down to defeat with Adlai, he very likely would not have become Presi-dent.

Although interrupted by fifty-three bursts of applause, Adlai's accep-tance speech was an anticlimax. He launched the "New America" theme while at the same time decrying the Republican attempt to "merchandise candidates like breakfast cereal," to "cynically covet" Eisenhower as a candidate but "ignore" him as leader. We were, he said, "losing the cold war. We chat complacently of this and that while, in Carlyle's phrase, 'Death and eternity sit glaring.' . . . It is time to get up and get moving again." The rhetoric was lofty but the content was diffuse, unfocused, and disappointing.

Flying the banner of "Peace, Progress, Prosperity," the Republicans in San Francisco the next week quickly affirmed the Eisenhower/Nixon ticket. Ironically, while Adlai's decisive and unprecedented stand on the vice presidency had the appearance of indecision, Eisenhower's stand in regard to his running mate had been marked by indecision. His authoritative biographer, Stephen E. Ambrose, reports that after his ileitis attack his private conversations frequently expressed concern over the possibility that Nixon would reduce his margin of victory and jeopardize regaining Republican control of the Congress. His diary, his conversation, and his correspondence reveal that his personal choice was Robert B. Anderson, who declined. "Having failed to persuade Anderson, Eisenhower returned to his passive role in the selection of his running mate," Ambrose has written. "He was detached and seemingly uninterested" and "almost seemed to enjoy keeping Nixon in a state of high tension."

"Given Eisenhower's health and age, the chances of the VP nominee of 1956 becoming President sometime before 1960 were high," Ambrose continued. "Potentially, Eisenhower's choice of a running mate in 1956 was among the most important decisions of his life. While it is true that he did not choose Nixon, it was also true that he did not reject Nixon." This does seem, as Ambrose says, strangely "detached."

Eisenhower's campaign began in calm; Adlai's began in conflict. His closest advisers wanted Finnegan to be elected National Committee chairman in place of Butler. As Adlai hesitated because of an earlier commitment he had made to Butler, intense, emotion-wracked maneuvering set in. Finally, a grudgingly accepted compromise continued Butler in his job with curtailed powers and designated Finnegan as campaign manager. It was an ominous beginning. The arrangement actually worked better than anyone anticipated, but the incident symbolized the divided nature of the campaign, with Adlai himself the core of the problem. The campaign strategy agreed upon not only ignored his state of exhaustion but was based on assumptions contrary to his character and temperament.

Most of the brainwork, the actual writing of speeches and policy statements, was to be done by trusted staff and volunteers, leaving him free to concentrate on public appearances and personal contacts. In retrospect, it is difficult to understand how such a miscalculation of the candidate could have governed the campaign.

In an interview with his first biographer, Kenneth S. Davis, in the midst of it, Adlai implicitly recognized the contradiction in the agreed-upon plan by saying:

> What I ought to do is what everybody tells me to do—delegate the "creative" thing (which is what I *like* to do, it's the fun of my life) and concentrate on the "executive," because so much of the latter is stuff that just can't be delegated. There are so many people who have to be dealt with on the top level, you know. They have to see *me,* or talk to *me,* and nobody else.

And there are decisions to make, operating decisions, which nobody else can make.

The contrast with Eisenhower's approach to the campaign could
hardly have been portrayed more sharply.

Another irony was embedded in the decision that Adlai should engage in a public display of energy and stamina that Eisenhower could not
match and thus indicate the contrast between a relatively young man in
vigorous health and an aging man with heart and digestive problems. It
seemed like a good idea, but the implementation was devastating. The
travel and speaking schedule that was worked out entailed almost unceasing, round-the-clock activity from mid-August right through November's
Election Day. In addition to incessant travel, there were as many as five
speeches in a single day, constant meetings with local Democratic groups
and candidates, and dozens of full-length speeches. In all, he traveled
about fifty-five thousand miles and made more than three hundred
speeches. It would have been a man-killing schedule for one starting out
completely rested, which, of course, he was not.

Moreover, Adlai was inherently incapable of delegating "the 'creative' thing." He initiated and was deeply involved in the nuclear test ban
and draft suspension issues. Nor could he remain aloof from the policy
statements, averaging ten thousand words each, in which were spelled out
the "New America" program for education, health, older citizens, resources and power, agriculture, depressed areas, civil liberties, and civil
rights.

The consequence was just the opposite of the plan. On TV screens
and in personal appearances he often appeared tired, driven, harassed,
and lacking in control. Without time to absorb the content of his
speeches, their delivery was often stumbling, uncertain, unconvincing. By
contrast, with careful scheduling and the skillful production assistance of
actor Robert Montgomery, Eisenhower would appear in parades, on platforms, and home screens looking more relaxed, vigorous and often even
younger than Adlai, his junior by ten years.

The decision to keep foreign policy in the background and concentrate on domestic issues was another basic misjudgment. It ignored the
candidate's profound interests in the area that, if allowed full expression,
would have provided a better base for meeting the foreign policy crises
that dominated events in the crucial days before the election.

Emmet John Hughes recalls encountering Jim Finnegan about two
weeks after the election and asking questions about some of the mishaps
of the campaign.

"Very simple," Finnegan replied. "We had two groups of people
supposedly joined in running this campaign. There were the politicians—
and the intellectuals. And for some reason, the politicians were determined to try to make decisions as if they were intellectuals. And all the

intellectuals insisted on trying to think and act like politicians. What the hell could you expect?"

He was describing the division not only within the staff, but within Adlai himself. He knew that to defeat an immensely appealing personality he had to win back the active support of normally Democratic voters who had deserted the ticket in 1952. That called for attacking a record he felt fully deserved attack, but it also meant engaging in the "Give 'em hell, Harry" tactics that Truman had used so effectively in 1948 but were alien to Adlai. The intellectuals he had won on the high road in 1952 would remain faithful; to win, he was told, he had to woo the "regulars" who preferred the low road. He accepted the advice, believing the combination of the eggheads and the regulars might just be enough to win. The trouble was that he never felt comfortable on the low road and kept hopping up to the high road, so that the campaign assumed an ambivalence that disappointed everyone.

History gives Adlai high marks on the major issues of the campaign, but that is because the judgment is based on material that was more effective in influencing later policy than in winning votes. It is now clear that some of the positions he insisted on taking simply because he thought the issues were important cost him dearly in votes.

"One of my keenest disappointments in the 1956 campaign was its failure to evoke any real debate of the issues," he wrote later. "In the climate of opinion which then prevailed, it was easy—and politically astute—for my opponents to brush them aside. Yet the illumination of problems, needs and dangers, and alternatives for dealing with them are the very purpose of a campaign, especially for the Presidency."

It is highly doubtful that a partisan campaign is the best place to achieve a considered examination of issues and alternatives, and Adlai seemed almost destructively committed to the foregoing statement of a campaign's purpose. He wanted desperately to win, but his idealism erected barriers.

John Brademas recalls that in the midst of the campaign, however hectic the pace, the surest way of getting Adlai's undivided attention would be to say to him, "Now, Governor, probably this is going to lose you votes, but you ought to say it anyway," whereupon he would "push aside whatever else was demanding his attention and say, 'Tell me more.'"

The proposals to ban nuclear testing and to terminate the military draft are outstanding examples. Some of the political professionals estimated that his stand on these issues cost him three million votes. Willard Wirtz, who with Ben Cohen played the major role in preparing his statements on the test ban, has said:

> He knew it would not be a political plus. He just thought it
> was a critical issue. It was because he was so determined that the

issue be considered on its merits rather than in a political context that he chose to make it early to the Newspaper Publishers Association. Many of us felt it was almost incredible that he would choose to make the speech. But there was no hesitation in his mind about giving it. He felt that what he believed had to be said. Moreover, he felt that anyone who was entitled to be President had to speak out on this issue.

The distortion of his April statement by President Eisenhower and other administration spokesmen had rankled Adlai and he chose, against advice, to return to the subject promptly after the convention before the most difficult of audiences; again, the American Legion, in convention in Los Angeles on September 5. He also chose to double the danger by proposing an end to the military draft.

Emmet John Hughes, Eisenhower's most effective speech-writer, recalls in *The Ordeal of Power,* "my own incredulity" when Press Secretary James Hagerty joined him at lunch in the White House "mess" to report Adlai's speech. "From the standpoint of the White House, it would have been impossible to have wished for a greater political gift." Hughes and others in the White House were concerned about many aspects of the administration's defense and foreign policies but they now immediately perceived the opportunity to divert attention from their vulnerabilities.

Actually, the President himself had been moving toward favoring a test ban even while dismissing Adlai's proposal as a "theatrical gesture." Ambrose, in his biography of Eisenhower, records an August 30 letter to Admiral Lewis Strauss, chairman of the Atomic Energy Commission, in which the President wrote, "I have spoken to you several times about my hope that the need for atomic tests would gradually lift and possibly soon disappear." He added that Columbia University physics professor Isidor Rabi had just told him it was now possible to stop testing, and concluded, "I should like to talk to you about this when you have an opportunity."

This record makes it difficult to understand Eisenhower's strong and uncharacteristically emotional reaction to Adlai's initiative. Ambrose reports his reaction as "scathing," and that "insofar as there was a reason for his increasing contempt for Stevenson, it was the inept and confused way in which Stevenson raised and used the issue."

To be sure, Adlai's position lacked technical precision and was calculated to open discussion on an issue the President, according to Ambrose, felt "was far too complex and dangerous to be discussed in a political campaign." However, increasingly and in public, it was a subject on which thoughtful, well-informed people, understandably, could and did disagree. Also, the President had not hesitated, for political reasons, to brandish the atomic weapon during the Quemoy-Matsu debates. But if it seemed ill-advised for a civilian political candidate to challenge a revered military leader and President on such a matter, raising the draft issue seemed even more foolhardy.

"Until there is world-wide agreement on a safe, effective system of disarmament we can not abandon armed deterrents to war," Adlai told the American Legion.

> . . . It seems clear that we must rethink the problems of military strategy and military requirements in this atomic age. Many military thinkers believe that the armies of the future, a future now upon us, will employ mobile, technically trained and highly professional units, equipped with tactical atomic weapons. Already it has become apparent that our most urgent need is to encourage trained men to re-enlist rather than to multiply the number of partly trained men as we are currently doing. We can now anticipate the possibility—hopefully but responsibly—that within the forseeable future we can maintain the military forces we need without the draft.

Adlai made a serious mistake in not spelling out in greater detail the reasoning behind the draft proposal. Indeed, he had done that in an earlier version but, in cutting, he made successful attack much easier. The President responded at a press conference a few days later: "I see no chance of ending the draft and carrying out the responsibilities for the security of this country that must be carried out." Then, in a September 17 speech, he declared that draft suspension, "I state categorically—cannot be done under the world conditions of today," and branded the test ban proposal as "a theatrical national gesture."

Others joined in the attack. Former Governor Thomas Dewey called the test ban proposal "an invitation to national suicide," from a man who was engaging in the "most dangerously irresponsible scaremongering by any political candidate." Later, after Soviet Premier Nikolay A. Bulganin proposed a U.S.-U.S.S.R. agreement to ban tests, he called Adlai "a spokesman for the proposals of Moscow." Vice President Nixon's contributions included calling the test ban "catastrophic nonsense," and the draft proposal "irresponsible."

The administration was intent on pursuing what it saw as its advantage. When a reporter, at the President's October 11 press conference, said he had learned from "reliable sources" that both of Adlai's proposals were under consideration within his administration, the annoyed President declared, "I have said my last word on these subjects."

But after speeches by Adlai on October 15 and 18, the President on October 19, in a speech at the Hollywood Bowl, stated that "the man who today dismisses our military draft as an 'incredible waste' is a man who, while I do not question his sincerity, is speaking from incredible folly, or incredible ignorance of war or the causes of war." Five days later he returned to both issues in a Republican television program, followed by a lengthy formal statement on the bomb issue. Adlai then, on October 29, issued a "program paper" that was the fullest exposition of his position; but by then, a week before the election, it was too late. By then, too, partisans on both sides of the question were issuing statements that contributed as much confusion as enlightenment.

The ultimate confusion, though, was provided by Premier Bulganin's letter to Eisenhower suggesting a test ban as "the first step toward the solution of the problem of atomic weapons" and noting with approval that "certain prominent public figures in the United States" were advocating such action. Prevailing public opinion regarded anything endorsed by the Russians as inherently dangerous to the United States.

Eisenhower, Adlai, and the press rejected what all regarded as a blatant interference in the election. Nixon rose to the opportunity by calling Adlai a "clay pigeon" for Soviet sharpshooters, and his proposal "the height of irresponsibility and absurdity." Eisenhower, however, according to Ambrose, "wanted to de-emphasize the issue, not highlight it as Nixon was doing." Ambrose adds: "Eisenhower knew he had Stevenson beat anyway. When his son, John, told him, about this time, that 'You've got to get moving. You're going to fall behind,' Eisenhower, laughing, said, 'This fellow's licked and what's more he knows it! Let's go to the ball game.' With that, they were off to see the opening game of the World Series."

He knew he had won the argument, although Adlai finally won the verdict. On October 31, 1958, a test ban suspension was put into effect by President Eisenhower's decree, and formal negotiations for a test ban treaty began. Acceptance of Adlai's arguments on the draft would come even more swiftly—after the election.

So many of the proposals advocated in the "New America" program have become such an accepted part of American life that the speeches and papers advancing them now make rather dull reading; of interest mainly because of their historical significance. Undeniably, they are more thoughtful and more informed than the speeches of 1952; but the rhetoric, though often lofty, does not ignite the excitement of those speeches made four years earlier.

By 1956, it was recognized that the public's attention span for serious material on radio or television was sharply limited. A few major events were allotted a half hour on television, but five-minute and one-minute "commercials" increasingly became the favored method of communication—much to Adlai's disgust and even anger. Louis Cowan, a successful television producer who would become president of CBS, and who had labored in 1952 to make Adlai more amenable to television, now enlisted the help of Edward R. Murrow. Despite the high regard Adlai and Murrow had for each other, the attempt was a failure. Never at ease before a television camera, Adlai was repelled by the requirements of short, staged appearances and resisted them stubbornly. As a consequence, some of his best and most eloquent statements in 1956 were delivered to audiences of only a few hundred people.

Given this situation, a new way had to be found for the extended analysis and exposition of major issues that he thought were the most important aspects of a presidential campaign. The innovation hit upon was a series of program papers on a wide variety of issues. After the election, combined with major speeches, and edited by Seymour Harris, John Bartlow Martin, and Arthur Schlesinger, Jr., they were published in a book called *The New America*.

Strangely enough, school desegregation, which had aroused so much emotion during the primaries, did not figure prominently in the fall campaign. Eisenhower virtually ignored the question, and Adlai had been bruised by it. Nonetheless, before a prosegregationist crowd in Little Rock, Arkansas, he went beyond saying that the law had to be enforced to add that he regarded the Supreme Court decision to be morally right. Some of his staff had almost desperately urged him to avoid the statement, but to their surprise, the audience applauded loudly. The approval, they agreed later, was more for his courage and honesty than for his position. Eisenhower, on his brief swing through the South, failed even to mention desegregation.

The farm issue was another on which the administration was vulnerable, and though Adlai engaged in rhetorical attacks he did not push it as much as his staff urged because he disliked being negative, was uncomfortable with the prevailing wisdom in the party, and was uncomfortable with himself for not having any better ideas to offer.

Proposals to meet the "crisis in education" built on his experience as governor, with the addition of strong endorsement of the then controversial idea of financial support from the federal government. He proposed federal assistance for school construction and teacher training, federal college scholarships, fellowships and loans, the expansion of foreign exchange programs, and the expansion of vocational and adult education. Two years later, the Eisenhower administration responded to the challenge of the Soviet launching of Sputnik with the National Defense Education Act of 1958, with special emphasis on assistance to science education. Kennedy picked up the broader approach Adlai advocated, and in 1965, President Johnson broke the traditional resistance of Congress and large-scale federal aid was adopted.

To help economically depressed areas, Adlai called for the enactment of the Douglas-Flood bill then pending in Congress, and which later was twice vetoed by President Eisenhower. In President Kennedy's first year in office it was signed into law as the Area Redevelopment Act.

The program on health was based on shocking statistics. The Department of Agriculture was spending more money for research on plant and animal diseases than the Public Health Service was spending on cancer, heart disease, arthritis, and mental illness altogether. "Last year," he said, "the government spent more money for eradication of hoof and mouth disease in cattle than on mental illness—which afflicts nine million people." Another grim contrast showed Americans spending less for medical research than for tombstones.

Adlai recommended programs to encourage young people to enter medical research as a career; to provide improved laboratory facilities, additional research funds, federal loans and scholarships for medical education; to expand the Hill-Burton program to build more hospitals, and he urged consideration of various proposals to make comprehensive health insurance available to all on a voluntary basis. All of this was done over the next nine years, except for providing health insurance, which was restricted to the elderly.

The most novel proposals related to older people and marked a signal advance over positions taken by major national figures up to that time. Adlai recommended lowering the retirement age for women from sixty-five to sixty-two years, and permitting retired persons to earn more than $1,200 without losing their social security benefits. Congress later adopted these recommendations. He proposed federal financing for housing for the elderly, and in 1962 Congress passed the Senior Citizens Housing Act. He urged Congress to consider "adding a program of hospital insurance for the old to the present Old Age and Survivors Insurance system." Finally, in 1965, what we now call Medicare was enacted.

Given Adlai's fiscal conservatism, he insisted on giving attention to how the various programs were to be financed. The paper, issued in the final days of the campaign, was not one of the best. Essentially, it maintained that the money would come "from the great and constantly increasing productive capacity of the United States." Uninterrupted economic growth meant a gain in productive capacity of $15 to $20 billion a year, and the prospective programs could be paid for out of these gains. The power to tax, he said, should be used "as a balance wheel to help keep a stable economy," with a balanced budget when economic activity was high and deficit financing in the face of recession. Its weakness, though, went entirely unnoticed in the ominous developments that dominated the days before the election.

The outbreaks of conflict in both Eastern Europe and the Middle East on the eve of the election were, at least in part, tragic failures of the Eisenhower/Dulles foreign policy that, paradoxically, ensured Eisenhower's reelection. It is almost certain he would have been elected anyway, but it is justifiable to question whether he would have won such a crushing victory had it not been for these almost simultaneous upheavals.

From the beginning, Adlai had been scornful of the "liberation" policy toward Eastern Europe as one that was trouble-making bluster in the absence of ability to give effective help to those seeking liberation. The publication of Khrushchev's secret speech to the Twentieth Party Congress condemning Stalin had sparked disturbances and riots in Poland that swept away the Soviet-dominated government and brought in Wladslaw Gomulka, whom the Soviets had dismissed earlier as a Titoist. On October 22 this successful defiance set off demonstrations throughout Hungary with demands that Imre Nagy, whom the Soviets had deposed in 1955, be returned to power.

The uprisings were spontaneous, but there is no doubt that Voice of America and Radio Free Europe broadcasts and CIA-assisted resistance cells had encouraged them. Yet, as Ambrose observes, "liberation was a sham. Eisenhower had always known it. The Hungarians had yet to learn it." So had many of the Republican orators who greeted the uprisings with claims that they proved the success of the administration's "liberation" policies. They quickly lapsed into silence, however, when, on October 26, Soviet troops and tanks entered Hungary in force, brutally and bloodily crushing the resistance. Whatever the administration's role had been, it was a disaster. But the President's calming assurance that we would not become involved strengthened the public's image of their leader as a man of peace.

Even more threatening were the developments in the Middle East. Adlai had returned from his 1953 trip deeply concerned at the British stance toward Egypt and the Suez Canal. His writings and warnings were sadly prescient. Much of the opposition he encountered from Jewish voters arose from their sense that he was too evenhanded in appraising Israeli-Arab issues, and their emotions intensified as they watched the administration's courtship of Premier Naguib that began in 1953.

With the accession of Gamal Abdel Nasser in 1954, the courting continued even after he obtained heavy arms from the Soviet Union in a secret deal that ushered in a growing volume of anti-Western propaganda. Israel's request for arms, supported by the British and French, had been refused. The British were persuaded to join in offering a massive economic-aid program including help in building the Aswān High Dam. The offer dangled while Nasser energetically sought to consolidate opposition to Britain, France, and Israel throughout the area. Israel's repeated pleas for arms to restrain Nasser continued to be rebuffed. Then, in an abrupt reversal in July 1956, the offer of help on the Aswān dam was withdrawn in terms calculated to humiliate Nasser and damage his prestige in the Arab world. Nasser's response was prompt seizure of the Suez Canal. Britain and France demanded that the canal be internationalized—by force if necessary—but were restrained by Dulles who engaged in almost frantic efforts to find an acceptable compromise in the situation he had done so much to create.

By October, Britain and France were convinced that their vital access to the canal was going to be cut off by Nasser and that he was planning to take over their Middle Eastern bases and cut off their oil supplies. Israel also believed Nasser was about to attack her. And all three had given up hope that the United States would help them resolve a crisis that seemed to them to involve their survival. On Monday, October 29, Israeli troops and tanks thrust deep into the Sinai Peninsula. By Tuesday, October 31, the British were bombing Egyptian airfields, Israeli troops had sealed off the Gaza Strip, and Anglo-French landing forces were moving toward Suez.

The Russian alliance with Egypt and the mobilization of Soviet forces for the Hungarian uprising made World War III seem very close. However, Ambassador Henry Cabot Lodge, at the UN, soon found himself strangely allied with the Soviet Union in opposition to our longtime allies and friends. He sought support for a ceasefire order, but when the vote came on October 30 the British and French vetoed it as well as another by the Russians calling on Israel to pull back to the starting line. Thereupon, Lodge went to the General Assembly with a proposal uniting the American ceasefire proposal with the Russian injunction on Israel to withdraw, and adding a call to all UN members to refrain from the use of force and to participate in an embargo against Israel unless it withdrew.

By the time the Lodge proposal was adopted on Friday, November 2, by a vote of 64 to 5, Israeli forces had taken the Sinai and the Gaza Strip, five thousand Egyptian prisoners, and large quantities of Soviet-made arms. British and French planes continued to bomb even after the Egyptian Air Force had been destroyed. Their troops had not yet landed, but due more to ineptitude than resistance.

Then, on Sunday morning, tension was heightened as 200,000 Soviet troops and some 4,000 tanks moved into Budapest. Nagy fled to the Yugoslav embassy, later to be seized and executed. The Russians installed János Kádár, and ruthless suppression of the freedom fighters began as they pled for the help they thought Radio Free Europe and Dulles's speeches had promised them. The next day, the day before the election, British and French troops landed in Egypt; Bulganin sent word to Britain, France, and Israel that the Soviet Union was ready to use force to crush the aggression. His message contained a thinly veiled threat of the use of nuclear missiles against London and Paris unless the forces withdrew; moreover he proposed to President Eisenhower that the United States and the Soviet Union join forces, march into Egypt, and put an end to the fighting.

This was the situation as the American people headed toward their polling places. Their votes were cast amid the threat of war. Yet, within days, the fighting stopped, Anthony Eden resigned as prime minister, UN forces were on their way to serve as a buffer between Egypt and Israel as Adlai had advocated more than a year before, and President Eisenhower announced willingness to accept 21,000 of the 150,000 Hungarian refugees, the only Hungarians our policy had "liberated."

In his assessment of the election-eve scene, Adlai said:

Here we stand today. We have alienated our chief European allies. We have alienated Israel. We have alienated Egypt and the Arab countries. And in the UN our main associate in Middle Eastern matters now appears to be Communist Russia— in the very week when the Red Army has been shooting down the brave people of Hungary and Poland. We have lost every point in the game. I doubt if ever before in our diplomatic history has any policy been such an abysmal, such a complete and catastrophic failure.

Earlier in the previous week, he had thought that these events would start a surge in his direction. He soon realized that, on the contrary, the impulse of the American people in a crisis is to rally behind the President, whoever he may be, and especially when he is a military hero who has brought peace. Given a week or more, the voters might have realized much of the truth in what Adlai had said, but they were not prepared to think about it in the midst of crisis.

The frustration of this realization, caused him to make his most serious lapse in taste if not in political judgment. Toward the end of the final speech in Boston, he said:

Distasteful as this matter is, I must say bluntly that every piece of scientific evidence we have, every lesson of history and experience, indicates that a Republican victory tomorrow would mean Richard M. Nixon would probably be President within the next four years. I say frankly, as a citizen more than a candidate, that I recoil at the prospect of Mr. Nixon as custodian of this nation's future, as guardian of the hydrogen bomb, as representative of America in the world, as Commander-in-Chief of the United States armed forces. Distasteful as it is, this is the truth, the central truth, about the most fateful decision the American people have to make tomorrow. I have full confidence in the decision.

It was an uncharacteristic and unworthy note on which to end the campaign. It can only be explained by his acceptance of advice that concern over Eisenhower's health was his last best chance for winning. The outlook had never been good; an encouraging upswing had been noted in the late weeks, then Suez had plunged everything into uncertainty, and he succumbed to an act of desperation. He was an idealist, but he also wanted to win. The price he paid in stepping out of character appalled some of his closest friends and haunted him.

Adlai had intended to make this election-eve speech in Chicago, but on Sunday afternoon he had received a jubilant message from Ad, who had returned to the Harvard Law School, announcing that Nancy had given birth in Boston's Lying-in Hospital to a boy, who had been named Adlai Ewing Stevenson. Adlai immediately revised his schedule and the next day, with John Fell and Borden, he flew from Minneapolis to Boston. Photographers surrounded them as the whole family, so rarely together, surveyed the plump, brown-haired, one-day-old grandson who slept on as flash bulbs popped. "He must be a born pol," Adlai laughed, and threatened to "punch in the nose" anyone who said the baby looked like him.

Visit over, final speech given, numb with fatigue, he flew back that same night to Chicago, and the next day voted at Half Day. He did not have to wait long for the results. With family and a few friends, some twenty in all, he shared a buffet dinner in the President's Suite of the Sheraton-Blackstone. The atmosphere has been described as reflecting the candidate's mood: tired but smiling, a bit rueful yet gay, expecting the worst but not conceding it. By nine o'clock he left his party to confer with Jim Finnegan and Bill Wirtz on arrangements for his concession statement and then went into his bedroom to write it.

In Washington, at the Sheraton Park, Eisenhower, with his close associates, waited impatiently for Adlai's concession, but when informed it was coming, he declared, "I went through this whole campaign without listening to him, and I'm not going to start now. . . . Listen, I never personally received anybody's sword in the war. I had the Germans surrender to someone else, and that's the way it's going to be now. *You* fellows watch. I appoint you to receive the surrender." And with that he strode from the room.

The defeat was overwhelming. Eisenhower's 35,590,472 votes exceeded Adlai's 26,029,752 by nearly 10 million, a margin almost 50 percent larger than in 1952; his electoral votes were only 73 compared to Eisenhower's 457. He had carried only Missouri and six southern states.

Shortly after midnight, Adlai walked across the street to the Conrad Hilton where some twenty-five hundred supporters were waiting, many of them tearfully, in the Grand Ballroom. He smiled, waved, joked, and exuded such cheer that smiles quickly replaced the tears. He read the telegram he had sent President Eisenhower, then paused, looked at the crowd, and said, "Now, let me say a word to you, my supporters and friends, all over the country."

After paying tribute to Kefauver and the campaign workers, he went on:

> The people have made their choice in a vigorous partisan contest that has affirmed the vitality of the democratic process. . . . There are things more precious than political victory; there is the right to political contest. . . . I have tried to chart

the road to a new and better America. I want to say to all of you who have followed me that I am supremely confident that our cause will ultimately prevail, for America can only go forward. It cannot go backward or stand still.

As he came to the end of his prepared statement, his smile broadened and he concluded: "Let there be no tears for me. If I have lost an election, I have won a grandchild."

Borden grasped his father's right hand and lifted it high in the traditional gesture of victory.

CHAPTER SEVENTEEN
Fulfilled Prophecies

"AFTER ALL THOSE ISRAELI bond rallies I addressed, don't you think they could have waited another week?"

This was Adlai's response to the conflict that turned almost certain defeat into a humiliating one. Polls indicated that the Suez crisis had cost him three to five million votes. The personal nature of the rejection was emphasized by the fact that although the voters chose Eisenhower by a margin of nearly ten million votes, they also made him the first President since 1848 to whom they refused a majority for his party in in both houses of Congress. The Democrats even picked up an additional governorship.

Any personal hurt, he joked with friends, was assuaged by the memory of a pregnant woman at one of the campaign rallies joyfully waving a big sign proclaiming, ADLAI'S THE MAN! He also recounted with delight the cartoon in a French newspaper in which a policeman sternly admonished a man on a park bench displaying a hole in the sole of his shoe, "Pas de politique ici!" But to Marietta Tree and a few others he admitted the defeat hurt far worse than it did in 1952.

John Oakes of The New York Times found Adlai in his office a few days after the election working at the thousands of letters that had flooded in. At the top of one pile was a handwritten letter from one of Asia's leading statesmen regretting the outcome but observing, "The Republic will not crumble." Adlai grinned at Oakes and said, "You know, I think he's right."

"What endures out of all of this," he continued more thoughtfully, "is the extent to which one can penetrate the minds of people and influence our generation. If I can't win, I at least want to impress some ideas on the thinking of our times; and if I succeed in doing that, it's compensation enough. . . . I have no doubt at all that many of the views and ideas I have tried to express will ultimately prevail."

Good humor marks the hundreds of letters he wrote to well-wishers in the weeks after the election, but there was a deeper undercurrent. He expressed his concern at the "euphoria and complacency so vigorously cultivated by the administration and the press," so that when faced with crisis in the Middle East "millions of voters turned to the Eisenhower administration for security from the Eisenhower administration's mistakes." He had long been rankled by a remark attributed to C. D. Jackson, a top man at Time, Inc., who had taken leave to become an influential member of the White House staff, declaring, "We will merchandise the hell out of the Eisenhower program." The election, he felt, was a triumph for this approach, which posed questions far more serious than his personal defeat.

"I am appalled by the ignorance which this last minute voters' panic disclosed about our foreign affairs and the responsibility for the crisis in the Middle East," he wrote his Princeton classmate, Colgate University president Everett Case. ". . . The problem remains of how we can successfully conduct both the popular government system and an effective foreign policy in a state of popular ignorance."

The reluctance of the Rayburn/Johnson leadership in Congress to debate administration policies, his own mistake in not making foreign policy more central to his campaign, the difficulty of getting attention for the issues he had injected into the campaign, all convinced him that something new and different had to be done between elections well in advance of the campaigns. He reminded Oakes that he had written in one of his books, "Sustained and thoughtful criticism and self-examination is the not-so-secret weapon of a successful and functioning democracy." A party out of power, he stressed, should maintain "the posture of opposition . . . and a constant attitude of inquiry and skepticism to keep them on their toes and make them prove they are right." He emerged from the election determined to try to improve the means for doing that.

Within three days after the election, he began writing letters to political leaders, expressing in varying terms the same message set forth in this letter to Senator Paul Douglas: "I am afraid the deluge of votes at the last moment for the administration in view of the Middle East crisis which it precipitated presents very neatly the problem of public communication and enlightenment which underlies our predicament. The readiest answer would seem to be a more active opposition role in the Congress for the Democrats."

Similar expressions went into letters to such people as Eric Sevareid, John Steinbeck, Reinhold Niebuhr, Matthew H. McCloskey, Mr. and Mrs. Dore Schary, and Mr. and Mrs. Alistair Cooke. Mixed in with these letters one finds thoughtful notes to young people who had written him of their disappointment. Tommy Reston, the ten-year-old son of *New York Times* correspondent, James B. Reston, when told by his father it was time to take down his Stevenson placards, buttons, and other campaign mementos, moved them to the attic—and moved up there with them. "I hope you were not too upset by the election," he wrote Tommy. "After all, it was a difficult undertaking at best. But I am sure you will agree that it was worth while keeping up a good, vigorous contest about things we believe in. . . . Some day I hope we can have a good talk about it all."

He mourned the Election Day death of his friend Marshall Field III, after undergoing emergency brain surgery for the removal of a blood clot. At the funeral, Field's widow, Ruth, insisted that Adlai proceed with a long-planned vacation at their twenty-thousand-acre estate in South Carolina. On November 18, Adlai traveled to Chelsea Plantation where Tom Finletter joined him to shoot a few quail and develop Adlai's plan for "an effective and sustained opposition."

They realized that it was difficult for any senator or congressman to speak and act as a *national* Democratic leader. Each member is responsible to his or her direct and often parochial constituency. To expect two Texans like Johnson and Rayburn to assert vigorous leadership contrary to intense local and regional interests and the passions aroused by the civil rights movement and school desegregation was hardly reasonable. The party's congressional members could not be the only spokesmen of national party policy.

The answer—for the first time in the history of national party politics—was in the Finletter Group. On November 27—just three weeks after the election—Democratic National Committee Chairman Paul Butler announced the establishment of a Democratic Advisory Council authorized to issue party policy declarations during the interval between national conventions.

Tense intraparty negotiations preceeded the announcement. The formal motion proposing the DAC had been made by three of Adlai's closest supporters on the committee: Jacob M. Arvey of Illinois, Paul Ziffren of California, and David L. Lawrence of Pennsylvania. The initiative of the northern urban Democrats had been adamantly opposed by rural and conservative southern Democrats. The Democratic congressional leadership declined to join and discouraged others from doing so. Senators Kefauver and Humphrey joined promptly, and Senator Lehman a short time later. As the race for the Democratic presidential nomination got under way in 1959, both Senators Kennedy and Symington joined in recognition of the council's impact on public opinion. Rayburn continued to resent what he regarded as an intrusion on congressional territory. Johnson, according to Reston in *The New York Times,* "tried to gut it."

Twice during the first year attempts were made in the National Committee to strip the Advisory Council of its authority. Both attempts failed. Ultimately, the council had more than thirty members, including the governors of California, Colorado, Michigan, Minnesota, and Massachusetts, as well as Mr. Truman, Harriman, Adlai, and, in effect, Mrs. Roosevelt. She declined her invitation on the ground that it might compromise her work as a newspaper columnist, but she served actively as a "consultant" and later even chaired a subcommittee.

Eventually, some 278 people participated in the work of subcommittees, each of which usually had about 25 members. The National Committee gave the Advisory Council strong backing, with an executive director, a general counsel, a three-man administrative committee, and a five-man steering committee of which Adlai was a member. The work of the committee was financed largely by private contributions. Finletter initially assumed the burden of finance director, until March 1958, when Robert S. Benjamin, New York lawyer, chairman of United Artists, and friend of Adlai's, was officially elected to the post. Thus was laid the foundation for the big Democratic advances in the congressional elections of 1958 and the narrow victory in the 1960 presidential contest.

During the struggle to establish the DAC, the question of how a presidential candidate who had run so far behind his party could be most effective was the subject of intense discussion. Finletter believed that Adlai could not be fully effective as a liberal opposition spokesman so long as he continued, or was perceived, to aspire to the presidency. Marietta Tree, who had joined the two men at the Field estate, and Clayton Fritchey, whose political views Adlai respected, agreed with Finletter, and Adlai was receptive.

"To say to your party that 'I'm the best man to be President' seems to me to be inconsistent with the grandeur of the office; and I've never quite made the reconciliation in my own mind," he had told John Oakes. "But, of course, to say that my party—its philosophy, its record, its program—is better than the other one is a different matter. And about such a contest I have felt strongly."

The statement indicates why he was so ready to give first priority to the work of the DAC; and also why it was so easy, in the aftermath of his defeat, to make a decision that he would regret later. On December 4, through the Democratic National Committee, he issued a statement announcing his intention "to resume the practice of law in Chicago on January 1st with my old friends and associates, W. Willard Wirtz, William McC. Blair, Jr., and Newton M. Minow." He then added, "I will not run again for the Presidency."

The wisdom of this action was evident in January when he went to Washington for the first meeting of the DAC, during which he went to Capitol Hill for the swearing-in ceremonies in the Senate. His presence in the gallery created such a stir that Majority Leader Lyndon Johnson called attention to Adlai from the floor; he rose to acknowledge the hearty applause from both Republicans and Democrats. More significant was his ability to block power grabs in the DAC by both Mr. Truman and Paul Butler and to overcome the Rayburn/Johnson opposition. His withdrawal, and the fact that most of its financing came from Adlai's supporters, enabled him to gain control over the DAC's organization.

Adlai faithfully attended the meetings, held about every three months. Dean Acheson's subcommittee on foreign policy, and John Kenneth Galbraith's on economic policy, had at least one major statement ready for discussion and release at virtually every meeting. In addition, during that first year, the Advisory Council issued statements on civil rights, Alaska-Hawaii statehood, the Senate filibuster, right-to-work laws, immigration, the launching of the first Russian satellite, and defense policy. In its second year, twelve more papers were released; in 1959, twenty; and in 1960, fifteen. The papers covered the most important issues of the period. Ideas launched by the earlier Finletter Group were developed in these papers and became legislation in the Kennedy and Johnson administrations. One, for example, led to the creation by President Kennedy of the Arms Control and Disarmament Agency.

Having announced his intention not to seek the presidency, Adlai entered into a period of happiness in his personal life comparable only to his term as governor and the early days of his marriage. When he returned from Chelsea Plantation, he found nearly forty thousand letters awaiting him. In the hundreds of replies he dictated himself there is ample evidence of a positive, even buoyant, attitude and a zest for continuing debate on the issues he felt important.

He even enjoyed getting back to the law. In a letter to Alicia Patterson reporting the possibility that papers in Connecticut and Texas might be for sale, he nonetheless added, "It is wonderful to be a lawyer again!" He also considered briefly the possibility of joining with others to buy the *Chicago Sun-Times.* He joined the board of the Field Foundation and he accepted William Benton's invitation to become a member of the Board of Editors of the *Encylopaedia Britannica,* a member of the Britannica Board of Directors, chairman of the Executive Committee of the Britannica Film Company and chairman of its Board of Consultants.

He was momentarily intrigued by a report that he was under consideration for president of Princeton, but when that quickly evaporated in the light of a policy that dictated someone younger than he there is no evidence of regret. Moreover, he promptly entered into negotiations with his old friend Lloyd Garrison in New York to unite his firm in Chicago with Paul, Weiss, Rifkind, Wharton, and Garrison. A major satisfaction of the new arrangement for a man as money-conscious as Adlai was an annual income, before taxes, in six figures—much more than he had ever earned before.

Far more satisfying was the time he now could spend with his boys. The strong sense of family was, if anything, intensified by the divorce.

When it was no longer possible to shield the boys from the vagaries of Ellen's behavior, he nonetheless urged them to spend as much time as possible with her. This sometimes led to sad consequences that they tried to shield from him. Once, when Adlai had suggested to Borden that he spend Christmas with his mother, she refused to let him in when he arrived home from boarding school. Late at night, and not wanting to tell his father, Borden sought refuge with friends. While Adlai was at Chelsea Plantation, Ad and Nancy invited Ellen to have Thanksgiving with them. During the toasts, Ellen refused to lift her glass when Nancy was toasted. But incidents of this kind were seldom shared. Each sought to spare the others from the pain of Ellen's illness.

After his graduation from Harvard Law School in June 1957, Adlai III returned to Chicago and became law clerk to Chief Justice Walter V. Schaefer, whom Adlai had appointed to the Illinois Supreme Court. (In a letter commending "my beloved Adlai," Adlai called his son "really a first rate and most conscientious fellow.") Adlai was immensely proud of his son; he adored his vivacious daughter-in-law and the grandson he "won" at election time. The three saw one another during the week in Chicago and spent nearly every weekend together in Libertyville. There was no repetition of the lonely and forsaken feeling that followed the defeat of 1952.

Borden, bearing his mother's family name, often had been the target of her attacks and bore many of the scars. Gregarious, handsome, and full of fun, Borden's "playboy" tendencies had worried Adlai. "I lectured him about cigarette poisoning, about taking more exercise, going to bed earlier and getting up earlier, etc.," he wrote Ad at Harvard on January 2, 1957. "I think it would be wonderful if both you and he could arrange to play squash three times a week. . . . But most of all I think it might be very helpful if Borden could be induced to spend an evening of forthright talk with Carl Binger," the family friend and psychiatrist whom he had asked Ad and Nancy to see when Ellen's behavior was threatening their marriage. Nevertheless, Borden's letters during this period were frequent and Adlai proudly showed them to Buffie, Ernest, and close friends. "Borden," he told them, "is the best writer in the family."

John Fell was doing well at Harvard. His shyness, accompanied by a winning smile, caused him to be regarded generally as the "most lovable" of the boys. He was recovering completely from the physical injuries of the automobile accident. Extremely sensitive to the possible psychic injuries, Adlai had been reluctant to go to court over the accident. He feared that if the driver of the truck were acquitted, John Fell might blame himself for the deaths of his two friends. Newt Minow persuaded Adlai that the trial was necessary to protect John Fell's interests. The trucker, who had been indicted for involuntary manslaughter, was convicted on a lesser charge and given a suspended sentence.

Encouraged by the warmth of his family relationships, Adlai's ideas about marriage took on new life during 1957. The mutual interest aroused by attractive, intelligent, public-spirited women is evident in hundreds of letters from the final years of his marriage until his death. Whether to men or women, his letters nearly always were marked by warmth and wit, but those to women had an extra sparkle. His diligence in writing them was awesome; often dashed off while waiting at an airport, on a plane or train, in a car or, exhausted, late at night. Most of the women were socially prominent, rich—and married. The most notable exception was Dorothy Fosdick, with whom a close relationship faded away after the 1952 campaign, undoubtedly pushed along by the overt antagonism of Buffie. Indeed, Buffie maintained a jealous watch over her brother's relationships, and of the few angry letters he wrote, most are injunctions to Buffie to desist. Often they are matched by notes to the objects of her ire asking for understanding.

Foremost in this fascinating, and puzzling, record is the decades-long correspondence with Jane Dick and Alicia Patterson. It is difficult to imagine a more consistently devoted friendship than Jane Dick's, supported by the interest of her husband, Edison. In the difficult years before and after Adlai's divorce, she was a sensitive intermediary with Ellen. She was one of the earliest and most dedicated "volunteers." She was a steady source of counsel on both private and public matters.

A more passionate tone marks the sometimes tempestuous correspondence with Alicia Patterson. She was brilliant, strong-willed, erratic, and profoundly fascinating to Adlai. From the time they resumed their friendship in 1946, after a lapse of twenty years, until her death in 1963, the relationship persisted on an uneven path. His cable from Paris to her husband, Harry Guggenheim, saying "She was my oldest dearest friend," was a massive understatement. She and Ellen were the loves of his life.

Carol Evans recalls that during the years in Springfield she always put on his desk unopened the letters from Alicia, Dorothy, and Jane. In the later years, she added other correspondents, including Ruth Field, Mary Lasker, Agnes Meyer, Nan Tucker McEvoy, Marietta Tree, Barbara Ward, and Suzie Zurcher. Of all of them, Agnes Meyer was the most uninhibited in pushing him into consideration of his emotional life—a subject he usually avoided or diverted by humor. An especially pointed letter in May 1957 elicited an unusual and revealing protest:

> *I think you are right that I've been so busy most of my life with impersonal things, and still am, that I'm not a very fit candidate for marriage and probably never was. But isn't there something to be said for the proposition that until I am married to the right sort of person I won't get what you call my "ego-ambitions" (I say, if any!) into balance and behave, and love, etc. as you have suggested I must? All of which is by saying that perhaps it is*

*a vicious circle?? I hope not. But it's not easy to wholly dismiss
the idea of marriage as you enjoin me because I would make a
bad husband when my best chance of being a proper person & of
fulfillment is by love and marriage. . . . But, madam! I protest
again that "mother's boy has in self-defense never loved anyone
but himself." He has, he does, love, really love, many people and
very especially a great tutor, benefactor and comrade on this exciting, fearful, beautiful journey we call life—*

Meyer wrote in reply, "Of course, you must marry. Eleanor
[Roosevelt] and I only wanted it postponed until you were rested. . . .
Your dear heart is more than ever set on marriage but your head is in
union with your drive for loving companionship. Fear not—you will find
the mate you deserve." (In an earlier letter he had told her that "Eleanor
admonished me to do nothing impetuous romantically, and I guess there
is no likelihood anyway.")

Adlai clearly loved the thought of being married, but he pulled back
from committing himself to one person. Perhaps the pain from the commitment he made to Ellen and memories of his parents' unhappy marriage were too strong to enable him to move from the thought of
marriage to the reality.

In addition to the zest and gaiety he brought into every social gathering, women responded to him because they felt he took their ideas seriously. Except for a commencement address at Smith College that
assumed the graduates' horizons would be restricted to home and children, his writings and attitudes regarded gender with the same lack of
prejudice that marked his approach to race. Some of the women in his
life felt that the dominance of his mother caused him to seek a mother
figure rather than a wife, but most of them felt enriched by the association. Even after their hopes of marriage were frustrated, some of them
referred to him as a "life enhancer."

Chicago society was intrigued by Adlai's frequent appearances at important social occasions for over two years with Suzie Morton Zurcher,
heiress of the Morton salt fortune. Her beauty, wealth, and social position were offset by an indifference to politics and a staunchly Republican
family background. Gossip columns during this period also speculated
about marriage with Ruth Field; Mary Lasker, widow of advertising executive, Albert Lasker; and even Mrs. Roosevelt. Dr. Karl Menninger,
the noted psychiatrist, wrote to express his pleasure that Adlai might be
marrying Mrs. Lasker, and he replied: "The news about Mary Lasker to
which you refer is flattering in the extreme but highly exaggerated."
Asked at another time if he were going to marry Mrs. Roosevelt, he said
of the lady sixteen years his senior, "Oh, she is much too young to consider me!" In at least two public speeches where she was present, he
humorously proposed marriage with such grace and obviously sincere af-

fection that her delight shone through her laughter. It is an injustice to describe their friendship as a mother/son relationship; the dimensions of their love and respect for each other were infinite.

An honorary degree from Oxford University provided the climax to this happy spring. En route to Europe, Adlai stopped in New York for dinner and theater with Borden, John Fell, and Mary Lasker. In addition to clients and friends in Paris, Brussels, and London, he saw the president of France, the king and queen of Belgium, the prime minister and foreign secretary of Great Britain. Then he went on to Oxford, now accompanied by Buffie and Ernest Ives, Adlai III and Nancy, Bill Blair and Barbara Ward (Lady Jackson), for the unusual tribute to an American of a degree as Doctor of Civil Law, *honoris causa*. Excerpts from Barbara Ward's long letters to Jane Dick and Carol Evans best describe the extraordinary event.

The citation, she said, was "one of the warmest and most flattering I have ever read in a University not over given to enthusiasm." It called Adlai "the champion of humanism in word and deed, and himself the source." After its reading,

> *a really very surprising thing happened—for Oxford at least. The assembled audience raised the roof. They clapped, they stamped, they banged the benches and the hurricane went on for at least two minutes. Many of the dons were visibly surprised—and as visibly delighted. I am told that all over the upper tier, where the undergraduates were thickest, there appeared a rash of Stevenson buttons. . . . It was a wonderful demonstration of affection and respect and, I believe, unique in Oxford, at least in these last cynical, unemotional decades.*
>
> *The Governor then lectured for nearly an hour and was listened to with deep attention. . . . He won all the hearts at the beginning by referring to the saying that Oxford is reputed the home of Lost Causes. Whom, then, could they more fitly distinguish than the man who was probably the world's greatest living exponent of the lost cause? . . . At the end, the ovation was as warm as at the start. . . . And the demonstration was all the more remarkable in that 1957 is not, alas, a year in which America is much loved in Britain. The Oxford occasion turned into a reaffirmation of our deeper links and only the Governor could have achieved this.*

The speech, which he felt was one of his most important, dealt first with strains in the Anglo-American relationship. "As long as an American wears braces on his teeth and an Englishman on his pants, how shall they ever agree?" he began.

Reviewing events in the Suez that had given the Russians a foothold in the Middle East and weakened the Western alliance, he said:

> I hope we Americans have learned a lesson about the hazards of subordinating foreign policy to domestic politics . . . just as I hope our French and English friends have learned some lessons about the conditions of successful coalition. . . . Everywhere one looks it is apparent that the combination of British and American power, prestige and ideals can benefit the free world. So I do not like what I hear in Europe about our crumbling alliance when it seems more imperative than ever.

Neutralist sentiment, then described as a "Third Force," he called foolish. "There is no such margin of strength on our side of the Iron Curtain that we can afford to split up."

The core of his message was his continuing concern for the future of the new nations of Asia and Africa.

> The new nations of Asia and Africa are not less, but more than ever, in need of administrative stability, economic growth and international security. They are all under steadily mounting popular pressure to show results in terms of economic expansion and human welfare. The whole postwar world is caught up in what I have called "the revolution of rising expectations" [the phrase that would mark international dialogue for decades].

After a series of proposals emphasizing joint action and United Nations involvement, he exhorted Britain and the United States to work "patiently with other nations in pursuit of joint solutions. . . . In a few decades we of the West—the guardians of that divine fellow I talk so much about—the individual—will not even be heeded unless we lift our tired minds to originality, invention, daring."

Adlai's own reaction was capsuled in a letter to Carol Evans: "Oxford was beyond description." He couldn't resist pointing out that he had dined "with the Warden of Saint Anthony, the Principal of All Souls and the Master of Jesus!" Also, he was sending her his "incredible scarlet gown and huge Tudor hat . . . the paraphanalia [sic] of my new estate," which he would thereafter wear proudly at every academic occasion where it was conceivably appropriate.

He remained in England for another ten thoroughly enjoyable days, seeing a wide range of people, and then flew to Africa, stopping first in Ghana as the guest of Prime Minister Kwame Nkrumah and guided by Sir Robert Jackson, Barbara Ward's husband, soon to become head of the Development Commission of Ghana. In Ghana, in the Belgian Congo, and in French West Africa, Adlai discussed the interest of his clients, the

Reynolds Metals Company, in huge development projects then under consideration. He also prepared a report on development prospects for the J. Henry Schroder Banking Corporation. Clearly, although he used his political reputation to advance his clients' interests, his letters and reports also stress an enlightened approach. To Richard Reynolds, for example, he expressed the hope that foreign aluminum companies would make "a substantial contribution to political and economic stability" in Africa.

In South Africa, in addition to government officials, including the prime minister, Adlai again persisted in seeing Negro leaders who nonetheless had to slip through a back door. Bill Blair recalls "the Governor's quiet fury" when the concierge at their Johannesburg hotel refused entry to a young African who had an appointment. Adlai came down to the lobby and then walked around the block with the young man "who wanted nothing more than some help in persuading his government to let him accept a medical scholarship in the United States." A few days later at a press conference he remarked, "Honesty compels me to say that the policy of total racial separation does not seem to me either practical or realistic in a modern state where white and nonwhite are interdependent." He added that "repression, fear and indignity will only increase racial consciousness and solidarity and hasten the day of reckoning and reconsideration."

Business and public affairs were secondary to enjoying himself with an enlarged party that now included Bill Blair, Adlai III and Nancy, Alicia Patterson, Marietta and Ronald Tree, and Marietta's daughter, Frances FitzGerald. The latter's recollections are filled with both awe and laughter. The awe arises from Adlai's energy in escaping from official functions to visit native markets, walk streets, and talk to people; and from his recklessness as illustrated by an incident on a later trip to Spain when a helicopter dropped them into a huge hunting preserve where Adlai mounted a horse and charged after a combative wild boar armed only with a spear. The laughter accompanies memories of running jokes, "impish wit," a sense of "never knowing what was going to happen next" that made it "incredible fun" and "the most amusing trip I have ever been on."

This time, Adlai fulfilled his ambition to visit Dr. Albert Schweitzer at his hospital in Lambaréné, where he filled twelve pages with notes on Schweitzer's observations on theology and philosophy, nuclear weapons, a definition of culture, and the politics of the cold war. After his visit to the Belgian Congo, he wrote his friend Geoffrey Crowther at *The Economist* in London that few of the "thoughtful" Belgians "think they can hold out indefinitely." The question is "whether they can guide the evolution to independence and some sort of African rule which will preserve order, responsibility, and their investments." A few years later at the

UN, he would be confronted with the bloody consequences of the failed effort.

As Adlai was leaving Africa, he wrote Buffie and Ernest, thanking them for being with him at Oxford, and added, "That experience and having Adlai and Nancy along this time have reminded me more poignantly than ever how much of my life and travels have been alone, without kith or kin."

Alone? Without kin, perhaps. But few public men have had so many good and constant friends standing out among the casual acquaintances, the opportunists, and hangers-on. Adlai's tendency toward self-pity, especially in correspondence with women, was one of his less attractive characteristics.

On August 21, two weeks after Adlai's return, and ten months after the election, President Eisenhower offered to suspend the testing of nuclear weapons for two years if the Soviet Union would agree to begin a permanent end to production of fissionable materials for military purposes. In at least a limited form, Adlai's "theatrical gesture" had become United States policy. Even the *Chicago Tribune* wrote, "Adlai is entitled, at least, to a good, broad smile."

He had held tenaciously to the issue after the election, in spite of the almost contemptuous opposition from Eisenhower and Nixon and from most of the press as well. He had gained front-page attention for a restatement of his case in an article in *Look* in which he asserted that he had "reason to believe that the National Security Council itself between September 5 and September 19 had voted unanimously" for a similar proposal. The President's response to the inevitable press conference questions was equivocal. While Adlai was abroad, hearings on the question of radioactive fallout dangers from testing had been held by the Joint Congressional Committee on Atomic Energy and its report sustained his position. The debate continued until, on August 22, 1958, the day after announcing the decision to suspend nuclear testing, President Eisenhower also announced the "successful conclusion" of a Geneva meeting in which American, Soviet, and other experts agreed that if an agreement to stop nuclear testing were in effect "its effective supervision and enforcement would be technically possible." On October 31, both sides suspended testing while a treaty was being negotiated.

Negotiations dragged on. Tests were resumed by the Soviets in 1961 and by the United States in 1962. Then, on August 5, 1963, in Moscow, with Adlai in attendance, the Limited Nuclear Test Ban Treaty was signed outlawing nuclear tests in the atmosphere, in outer space and under water, and outlawing also underground tests if they resulted in spreading radioactive debris outside the territory of the testing state. By the end of the year, 133 countries, but not France or China, had acceded to the treaty.

* * *

Action on Adlai's military draft proposal would begin even more quickly, although it was—of all people—Richard Nixon who became its advocate and signed it into law. Soon after the election, a special Defense Department committee headed by Ralph J. Cordiner, president of General Electric, had been appointed to study armed forces manpower requirements. In May, the committee recommended an armed forces "pay for merit" program in place of the draft to "gain the skill and experience levels we need."

Stuart Gerry Brown, in *Conscience in Politics,* states that the Cordiner report, "A Modern Concept of Manpower Management and Compensation," read "from beginning to end . . . like a documented elaboration of Stevenson's proposals" that the President had described as "incredible folly" that would "lead down the road to surrender." The draft was extended in 1959 when the Soviet Union was making new threats over Berlin, but in 1968, in his successful campaign for the presidency, Mr. Nixon cited the report in advocating the end of the draft, largely for the reasons Adlai, and Cordiner, had argued. As President, he signed into law the policy Adlai had advocated.

Another major echo of the 1956 campaign resounded soon after his return. On September 3, Arkansas governor Orval Faubus called out the National Guard to prevent nine black children from attending Little Rock's Central High School. He thus "interposed" state authority against an order of the federal district court to proceed with integration. On September 8, on the television program *Face the Nation,* Adlai applauded President Eisenhower's statement that he would do everything in his power to see that the Constitution was upheld. He then recalled that just a year earlier, in Little Rock, he had urged the President to exercise "the great moral influence and great prestige" of his office by calling together white and Negro leaders from the areas concerned in the South "to explore ways and means of allaying these rising tensions." Later in that month, the President federalized the National Guard, ordered paratroops to Little Rock to reopen the schools to the Negro students and disperse the mobs. It was then that he announced a White House conference of southern governors to discuss the Little Rock situation and school integration. Arguably, if such a conference had been called earlier to "strengthen the hands of the thoughtful and responsible leaders of both races," as Adlai had advocated, "before the situation gets any more serious," this enduringly sad event in American history might have been averted.

Soon after the Little Rock crisis, through Sherman Adams, the President invited Adlai to become a member of the presidential Commission on Civil Rights. Adlai's advisers were divided. On October 28, he declined, expressing the belief that "I can be of more service to improve race relations if I am free to do and say what I think not restricted by the proprieties of an official position on this Commission."

Part of his reluctance arose from having before him at the same time what he described to Buffie as "a plaintive plea" from Secretary Dulles to help prepare for a crucial meeting of NATO in Paris in December, the first since Suez. He recognized an exceptional situation created by the disarray among the Allies that had followed the Soviet Union's success in orbiting Sputnik I a few weeks earlier. Prime Minister Harold MacMillan had flown to Washington for hurried conferences that resulted in agreement to convert the December NATO meeting into a conference of Allied Heads of State. Secretary Dulles persuaded the President, despite his dislike of Adlai, that a dramatic step was needed to demonstrate American unity.

Quietly, Adlai flew to Washington on October 30 to meet with Secretary Dulles and was presented with a six-page "Secret" memorandum setting forth the duties he would be expected to perform as "Special Assistant to the President." He would receive political guidance from the secretary of state, be provided with offices and staff support from the Departments of State and Defense and the Atomic Energy Commission, and undertake the following specific tasks: "(a) To develop the U.S. Government position" on the points covered in the communiqué from the Eisenhower/MacMillan meeting . . . "(b) To coordinate this position" with the United Kingdom, France, Germany, and Italy; "(c) To assist in developing public understanding and support for the U.S. position," and "(d) To participate in the presentation of this position to the North Atlantic Council in December."

Such a sweeping mandate from the source of so much he disagreed with troubled him. Although Adlai had been asked to prepare the American position, the President and secretary of state were free to use it as they saw fit. It would be difficult for Adlai to escape responsibility for final policies, whether or not he agreed with them. He sought the advice of members of the Democratic Advisory Council, Speaker Rayburn, Senator Johnson, Tom Finletter, George Ball, and a few other close friends.

Consequently, on November 3 he wrote Secretary Dulles expressing his desire to help but concluded that

> it would be a mistake for me to attempt to formulate policies
> for presentation by the President. . . . I would be glad to review
> and discuss your proposals from time to time before they are put
> into final form. And, where we are in agreement, I will do such
> "missionary" work as I can and give such policies all the support,
> private, public and political, as I can both here and abroad. In-
> deed, if advance consultation with our Allies would be helpful or
> contribute to greater solidarity and confidence, I would undertake
> to make such a journey as a special envoy of the President. What

> *I am trying to say is that in this situation, I don't believe I care to assume the responsibility for formulating United States policy and position. I believe that is for the President to do. But I have both a duty and desire to do what I can to strengthen the Atlantic Community and to be as helpful to the President and to you as I can.*

The next day, he followed with an extended "preliminary memorandum" calling attention to the "almost exclusively military" nature of the Eisenhower/MacMillan communiqué and suggesting economic and political measures that might be taken, citing as an example, "I have found *no one* who agrees with our rigid China policy and *many* who credit it with much of our lost confidence." He also told Dulles his "familiar thesis that Russia is in disorder and if we hold fast the Communist system will break down or be modified . . . is a premise that few leaders I know accept, with the exception of Chancellor Adenauer, and therefore should not be constantly repeated as a reassurance."

When news of the administration's overtures to Adlai began to leak, the President's grudging acceptance of the arrangement was clearly reflected in the clumsy handling of the announcement by the usually adroit press secretary, James Hagerty. After first saying that Adlai had turned down the administration's request for help, he then announced that Adlai would be a "consultant." Even more indicative was a remark by Sherman Adams that Adlai had been called in because the nation wanted bipartisanship, but he doubted the services of Democrats would be worth much. Adlai was sworn in at the State Department on November 20 in a private ceremony without press or photographers. The President pointedly had left town the day before for a golf-and-work vacation in Augusta, Georgia.

Adlai did work hard on the substantive issues, calling on help from his usual advisers and a number of journalists. His intensive activity on both the substantive and public relations fronts prompted a famous Herblock cartoon showing a cherubic Ike on golf links outside an office building in which a sweating, shirt-sleeved Adlai was toiling over a high stack of papers. In a hovering flying saucer one Martian asked another, "How did you say their election came out?"

Nine days after his swearing in, Adlai delivered to Dulles a lengthy "Personal and Confidential" memo. "I am troubled by the lack of a sense of urgency," it stated bluntly. "The response to Sputnik, etc. does not seem to meet the measure of the emergency." In this, and in further communications, he argued strongly against what he regarded as excessive reliance on "massive retaliation" with nuclear weapons, urged greater attention to building "the conventional strength of NATO to resist a limited Soviet aggression," and pressed for a much larger economic component in our whole approach to NATO. "Just now the hottest war is the cold war. I think the United States should take a strong affirmative lead to organize and enlarge the financial and technical resources of the capital countries to accelerate the economic development of the under-developed areas."

George Ball has written critically of Adlai's performance. He did not agree with the emphasis on economic development and third world prob-lems; he felt that "Adlai's interest was in grand concepts and uplifting sentiments, and he was impatient with the practical issues then seriously troubling the Western alliance."

In any event, none of Adlai's ideas made appreciable impact on ad-ministration policy at the NATO meeting. The President returned to Washington as Adlai was preparing to leave. Their first meeting in four years was a chilly one. An invitation to Paris was couched in terms sug-gesting that if Adlai wanted to go, the President would welcome his pres-ence. Adlai declined.

Adlai returned to Chicago feeling that his labors had been futile but that he had escaped undamaged. Press comment suggested he had done better than that; and, in 1960, he had the satisfaction of recognizing his recommendations in the articles setting up the Organization for Eco-nomic Cooperation and Development (OECD). As Professor Stuart Gerry Brown has observed, "Another Stevenson proposal was adopted by its detractors."

STEVENSON BACK IN THE LIMELIGHT was the headline on an article in the Sunday *New York Times Magazine* of December 22, 1957, written by John B. Oakes. "Mr. Stevenson has no political organization and very little direct political impact," Oakes wrote. "Yet today his voice is heard and heeded both here and abroad."

With greater prescience than he—or Adlai—probably realized, Oakes then commented:

Whether Mr. Stevenson still has any political ambitions is anybody's guess. He gazes at you with amazement if you put the question; and it is hard to imagine so sensitive a man who went through what he went through twice wanting to do it a third time. However, any experienced politician will tell you that the Presidential virus is harder to get rid of than the Asian flu. No matter with what reluctance a candidate may originally have been drawn into the prison of Presidential aspirations, he usu-ally is even more reluctant to leave it.

In his critical biography of Eisenhower, the British scholar and jour-nalist, Piers Brandon, covers 1958 in a chapter titled "The Worst Year." On November 25, 1957, the President had suffered a slight stroke, and the third illness in two years of a sixty-seven-year-old man filled the

White House with concern. There was widespread speculation that he would not be able to complete the remaining three years of his second term. Stephen E. Ambrose has written:

> Although few Democrats were ready to go after General Ike personally, many columnists were, especially on such specific issues as the Middle East crisis, Hungary, Little Rock, and most of all, Sputnik. Critics were questioning his leadership abilities, and pointing to the botched "Battle of the Budget" of 1957, the inept attempt to put through a civil-rights bill with some meaning, and the recession as examples of his failures. The charge that hurt most was that he had "lost" the space race and had neglected the nation's defenses. Implicit in all the criticism was the idea that he was too old, too tired, too sick, to run the country.

In this atmosphere, talk of how to fill in for an incapacitated President and of succession filled the air. The spotlight focused on Nixon and Adlai. The door set ajar in the Oakes article kept receiving increasingly urgent nudges throughout 1958. On March 30, Adlai was asked on a television program if he were a candidate for the 1960 nomination. He replied: "Let me just say once more what I have said repeatedly, and that is that I haven't been a candidate, I am not a candidate and I will not be a candidate." Asked if he still "recoiled" at the prospect that Nixon might become President, he said he did.

That same day, Agnes Meyer wrote him that Roscoe Drummond, the *New York Tribune*'s Washington columnist, was predicting that Adlai would be the nominee and that he need know nothing about the efforts she was going to make to fulfill the prediction. Indeed, on April 15, she wrote again reporting a long conversation with Mr. Truman in which the latter had explained his changing attitude toward Adlai. He now felt Adlai's strength had grown greatly in the postelection period and while he could not be an avowed candidate for 1960 it would be wise for him to begin cultivating "friends."

Adlai was not inclined to respond to Truman's advice. To those who were writing to urge him to consider a third race he responded with a usually jocular, sometimes earnest, appeal to desist. To Congressman Stewart L. Udall, who had written an article in *The New Republic* encouraging a Stevenson candidacy, he wrote that such talk "leaves me a little uneasy and uncomfortable," but it definitely did not leave him uninterested or displeased.

Foremost among the many things engaging Adlai's interest that spring, however, was the prospect of a trip to the Soviet Union. A commission from the Authors' League of America to seek royalty payments for American authors on books published in the Soviet Union was promptly and enthusiastically accepted. As early as April 3, he began producing memoranda detailing conversations with State Department experts on the Soviet Union and cultural exchange, the librarian of Congress and his colleagues, and a variety of experts on copyright law. He also arranged for Robert Tucker, who had worked at the United States embassy in Moscow for six years to accompany him as interpreter, and began making appointments with Soviet scholars and journalists, such as Harrison Salisbury of *The New York Times* and Thomas Whitney of the Associated Press.

Adlai's travel preparations went forward in the midst of shocking events accompanying Mr. Nixon's "goodwill" tour of Latin America in early May. It had begun well in Uruguay, Paraguay, Bolivia, and Argentina. In Lima, Peru, however, Nixon and his party had been stoned and spat upon by mobs. Stops in Ecuador and Colombia were without incident. Then, in Caracas, Venezuela, the attacks by the mobs were so vicious and organized, the foreign minister and at least one member of Nixon's party were injured by flying glass as the mobs sought, in a clearly life-threatening situation, to break limousine windows and reach the Vice President. The reports reaching Washington were so alarming that the President ordered airborne troops to Puerto Rico and marines to Guantanamo, Cuba, within quick flying time of Caracas, and he sent an aircraft carrier to the Venezuelan coast. Adlai's intense dislike of Nixon did not diminish his horror at such treatment of the nation's Vice President. His conviction that greater attention had to be given to problems of the third world became stronger than ever.

On June 15 he flew to London with Borden and two days later was joined there by John Fell and Bill Blair. He took the boys to Stratford to see *Romeo and Juliet,* and tour the Cotswolds with them; he lunched and dined with a wide variety of friends, did some legal business for clients interested in Africa and with the directors of *Encyclopaedia Britannica,* and gave a press conference in which he once again denied he would seek the presidential nomination.

With the boys and Bill he flew to Brussels where they were joined by Mrs. Marshall Field and her daughter Fiona. There, he met with his client, Maurice Tempelsman, attended the World's Fair, saw the Bolshoi Ballet perform *Romeo and Juliet,* and again, was entertained by the royal family. In Copenhagen, he interrupted a round of sightseeing to take a call from Chicago thinking it might be news of the arrival of a second grandchild, and discovering it was Lauren Bacall calling from "the Pump Room at 3 A.M.!"

Former UN secretary general Trygve Lie met them on their arrival in Oslo and mixed Adlai's insatiable appetite for sightseeing with visits to the prime minister, foreign minister, and other officials. In his diary on July 3, Adlai wrote: "Cable with breakfast—Lucy Wallace Stevenson has arrived 8 lbs 1 ounce—Hooray. Woke up boys. Sent cable.'' In a letter to Marietta Tree, he commented that Lie calls the foreign minister "a little contemptuously, an 'intellectual,'" and then added, "Why do I always get along best with the wrong people—intellectual men and married women!"

Stockholm was next for a similar round and then on to Helsinki where Alicia, her niece, Alice Albright, and Robert C. Tucker were waiting to join the party of eight that arrived in Leningrad on July 13.

This trip was to be the best documented of all of Adlai's travels. For once, he succeeded in keeping a diary that missed very few days; he wrote twelve articles for the North American Newspaper Alliance. With some slight editing, they were published as a book in 1959 under the title *Friends and Enemies; What I Learned in Russia*.

Adlai's identity did not become known in Leningrad until the second day. Before that, John Fell and his cameras excited interest. Russians crowded around asking questions about "every aspect of life in America"; their questions were "searching and always accompanied by politeness and dignity." Soon, though, the curious focused on Adlai, wanting to know about his plans, and laughing when he told them, "I am going to Siberia—and hope to return."

A different atmosphere took over on their arrival in Moscow. A military coup d'état in Iraq had seen the young King Faisal assassinated and removal of the pro-Western leaders. Almost simultaneously, U.S. Marines had landed in Lebanon in response to an appeal from President Camille Chamoun.

An air of tension was palpable in the Soviet capital as a big propaganda campaign against "American and British aggression against the Arab peoples" gathered steam. Worry that there would be war was evident on all sides, fueled by the government's willingness to let a mob attack the American embassy.

This setting makes all the more remarkable the outpouring of hospitality and goodwill Adlai's party encountered wherever they went. On their first stop after Moscow, in Tashkent, Uzbekistan, they rode from the airport between big road signs declaring THE WORKING PEOPLE OF UZBEKISTAN ARE WRATHFULLY PROTESTING THE IMPERIALIST AGGRESSION. Beneath the signs, however, crowds of working people were smiling broadly and clapping their hands as Adlai waved to them. A few days later, in Alma-Ata, Kazakhstan, near the Chinese border, he noted that what was proclaimed as a "Day of Wrath Against Imperialist Aggressors" was in reality, a Day of Warmth for the capitalist invaders. In Novosibirsk, the largest city in Siberia, they ended another "Day of Wrathful Indignation" attending a performance in the largest theater in the country. After applauding the performers, the entire audience turned and applauded the Stevenson party in the center box.

Many of the places they visited, such as Novosibirsk, were closed to foreigners. Nonetheless, the group was permitted to visit wherever they wished, and even John Fell's and Borden's nonstop shutter-clicking was unhindered. Many of the interviews were surprisingly frank; one official adding to his presentation of the party line an invalidating injunction from the Koran to "believe not what you hear, but only that which you see." The hosts also were alert to what they regarded as the American "party line." In the Ukraine, discussing farm problems with a provincial official, Adlai mentioned that some farmers in the United States were paid not to produce. "He gave me the sly, amused wink of a politician not unfamiliar with gullible audiences," Adlai reported.

The month in the Soviet Union extended into areas of that vast empire rarely, if ever, visited by Americans and brought Adlai into contact with a broader spectrum of Soviet society than only a handful of foreigners can claim, even now.

Interviews with Khrushchev, Deputy Premier Anastas Mikoyan, Foreign Minister Andrey Gromyko, and Minister of Culture N. A. Mikhailov were cordial, but tough. Khrushchev had just returned from a four-day secret visit to China the day before Adlai was summoned. The premier's apparent fatigue vanished in the vigor of the two-and-one-half-hour conversation.

Lebanon was the opening subject, with the Soviet leader taking a very hard line, rejecting proposals that had just come in from President Eisenhower. Adlai sensed that Khrushchev welcomed the opportunity to take the offensive to avoid discussing the recent execution of Hungary's Imre Nagy. The talk ranged over trade between the two countries, economic aid for underdeveloped countries, and Western anxiety about Soviet objectives. Khrushchev favored nonintervention in the affairs of other countries until Adlai mentioned Soviet actions in Eastern Europe. Then he exploded, "Americans poke their noses where they shouldn't." When the premier complained about American bases, Adlai told him "what he knows full well—that the bases represent only a response to our fear of postwar Soviet ambitions."

"Mr. Premier, there should be no conflicts between us," Adlai concluded. "We each have enough territory and resources. Our troubles arise from the outside. Maybe we Americans have made mistakes, but this is the way we see things, and I'm sure my countrymen are very eager to find a way to settle the conflicts that divide us."

"This I believe," Khrushchev replied. "I have read your speeches. Some things in them are wrong and even offensive, but on the whole I think you stand for improving relations, and we welcome it."

"I felt quite proud of my firm defense of the Republican administration," Adlai wrote later, "and assured him that, while there are many differences between us, on some things we Americans were united, including our anxieties about the dangers of war and our desire, regardless of domestic politics, to reduce the tensions and reach agreements."

After a laughing agreement that there should be a summit meeting in an Illinois cornfield, Khrushchev summoned a photographer and sent for Borden and John Fell, who were exploring the Kremlin. "While the pictures were being taken, he talked gaily to the boys," Adlai reported.

>His youngest son, Borden's age, was working in the field of rocket launching, he said proudly. When I mumbled something banal about launching doves of peace, he nodded a solemn, "yes, yes," and said that his older son, a flier, was first wounded and then killed in the war. Then, jovial again, he suggested that my sons come back and marry Russian girls—"that would be a contribution to Russian-American relations!" The boys were noncommittal.

As the meeting was ending, Adlai said he had a personal favor to ask; it involved permission for the Russian mother of Mr. Tucker's wife to join them in the United States. Khrushchev accepted a memorandum on the subject and said he would look into it. The following January, she arrived.

On the question of royalty payments, Adlai received little encouragement from the minister of culture beyond a promise to study the matter. Adlai was so irked he issued a public statement that concluded: "When compared with the major questions that divide our two great countries, this is a small matter indeed. But the recognition of the rights of creative writers and artists would be a significant forward step on the highway to mutual understanding."

His annoyance was more than a reflection of his client's interest; it was part of his deep concern over the barriers to communication between the two countries. He commented repeatedly on the ignorance of the Russian people about the United States and wondered at the friendship and eagerness for contact despite the lack of information and hostile propaganda. When he complained to Mikoyan about the jamming of the Voice of America, the deputy premier's response was that he would congratulate the minister of communications on his effectiveness—a comment typical of the aggressive nature of the interview.

Many of the observations Adlai made during his visit remain relevant, except for one notable exception—China. The Soviet Union and China, he wrote, "may fight like cats and dogs with each other, but as far as the outside world is concerned their unity is formidable. They will stick together." He was also overly impressed by the industrialization that had taken place since his earlier visit and overly optimistic about the success of the recently launched effort to decentralize industrial organization. In other respects his analyses were more durable.

>The present massive stability of the U.S.S.R. obscures the insidious instability of a big, modern, industrial state ruled auto-

cratically. When a system, like the Soviet, lacks a legalized opposition, it is inherently unstable. And I suspect the reason they have not solved the problem of orderly transfer of power is that it is insoluble in a dictatorial framework. . . .

One is amused by the spectacle of a whole nation damning "capitalists" and the United States, while at the same time busily trying to "catch-up" with the United States and the hated capitalists. . . . On the assumption that well-to-do people are more passive and peaceful than the envious and poor, the liberalizing tendencies in Russia should increase as prosperity increases. So why not trade with them? Why not help them improve living standards? Why not encourage the growth of material abundance? . . . Why not help the Soviet leaders subvert their own system of fear with the confidence bred of plenty?

He was impressed with the emphasis on education, and called particular attention to instruction in languages. Young people, he said, were getting five years of foreign languages and four more at the university level, and warned that "it won't be long before the Russians will have a great advantage in every exchange—cultural, political and propaganda." There was one big reservation: "The Soviets have a passion for black and white, for a single solution for every problem—the official solution. They do not understand choice. Hence the curriculum is rigid and does not encourage individual creative thinking and originality."

In his conclusion, he stressed that "we have been badly informed and are badly mistaken" about the Soviet Union. It was

a stable power system and is not on the brink of internal collapse. The reasonable hope is not that it will disintegrate but that it may evolve into something less aggressive and menacing to peace and freedom. . . .

The economic goal is to catch up with America in per capita production. . . . The political goal is to displace the United States as the foremost world power, and, as it has always been, to make the whole world Communist. . . . The Soviet challenge is formidable, and it will be with us for a long time to come. . . . The greatest danger is not in Europe but in Asia and Africa.

I think we must plug patiently away at stopping the arms race, with international supervision, and forgo any lingering ideas of military superiority. . . . It would be most realistic and helpful if we recognized the principle of equality with the Soviet Union. And we should always be ready to talk with them at all levels, but with little hope of quick success. . . . They are tough, fearful, and going places. But they are also very human and friendly. Their hopes and desires are for peace—and an apartment. The leaders are scornful of "capitalism," yet even Khrushchev wants to attain the American standard of living more than anything else. And we still have the supreme advantage of living under the system most people want if they can get it and afford it. This should give us calm and final confidence.

From Moscow, the party scattered, some of them to join up with him later as he moved on to Warsaw, Praque, Zurich, Bern, Florence, Paris, for interviews with de Gaulle, Mendès-France, Guy Mollet, Couve de Murville, and others, and a press conference at which he gave a somewhat softer answer to the inevitable question about 1960: "I will not again seek nomination by the Democratic party."

CHAPTER EIGHTEEN
Courting the Lightning

THE STEEPEST AND DEEPEST economic decline since World War II eased
during the summer, as did the tension over Lebanon; but a new crisis was
building up. Once again it was focused on the tiny islands of Quemoy and
Matsu.

Chiang Kai-shek, taking advantage of the friendly disposition of the
Eisenhower administration, early in 1958 began building his garrisons on
these islands. By summer, they were crowded with some 100,000 troops,
fully a third of all Nationalist ground forces. Since the Nationalist regime
repeatedly proclaimed its intention to reconquer the mainland, and since
the capacity to wage even a defensive war depended entirely on United
States support, the Chinese Communists understandably assumed that an
American-supported attack was being prepared. They built up their
strength in the area opposite the islands and on August 23 began a massive artillery bombardment that continued for weeks, accompanied by
strafing from the air and a sea blockade. Strident broadcasts also declared
a determination to "liberate" not only the islands, but also Taiwan.

Under the terms of the resolution he had obtained from Congress
during the 1955 crisis, the President was required to intervene if the Communists attempted to occupy the two islands. This is unquestionably what
Chiang Kai-shek desired. He asserted he could not defend the islands
unless permitted to attack the mainland; he demanded a pledge that the
United States would support the action. As in 1955, the nation again
appeared to be on the brink of war.

Adlai watched these developments in dismay and anger. He felt the earlier crisis had provided an opportunity to open communications with the Communists and perhaps to initiate negotiations for renunciation of the use of force in seeking stability in the region. Indeed, he later told Theodore H. White that he regarded the opportunity lost in 1955 "one of the greatest political crimes of our times." This suggests the strength of his reaction when the "crime" was repeated in 1958. He began sending copies of his speech of April 11, 1955, to key people all over the country. The *Atlanta Constitution* printed excerpts and a number of papers commented in editorials. Walter Lippmann wrote, "I did not realize until I reread it this morning how perfectly clear the problem was to you away back in 1955." It left Lippmann wondering "whether Democratic leaders in Congress have done their full duty as an opposition party."

Adlai's major answer to the wonderment had been the Democratic Advisory Council, but his personal answer came in increasingly direct and sharp attacks on the President and his leadership—or what Adlai saw as lack of leadership. He said Eisenhower's comparison of Quemoy with Munich "was hardly worthy of him," and that his branding as "appeasers" those who opposed war with China over Quemoy was "below him."

"We should make it absolutely clear that the United States is not helplessly entangled with nationalist China," he declared in an October 2 speech in California. ". . . The fight for these islands which have always belonged to China is a continuation of the Chinese Civil War in which we should not intervene."

Although American policy and passivity had helped create the crisis, the President acted with prudence that avoided confrontation and finally produced a stalemate. Communist shelling and threats dwindled away, Nationalist forces on the islands were reduced, and the truce was restored.

Quemoy and Matsu were not the only objects of Adlai's attacks on the Eisenhower administration in the final months before the 1958 elections. His campaigning was not as sustained as it had been in the races for Congress and governorships in 1954, but it was far more pointed. In an October 18 speech in Milwaukee he compressed many of his thrusts into one paragraph:

> If this crisis in the Formosa straits is a needless crisis, so too is the crisis of our educational system. So too is the school desegregation crisis. All of these things could have been avoided if we had an Administration which took thought in advance—instead of waiting placidly on the fairways until mortal danger is upon us and then angrily calling out the Marines. The tragedy of the Eisenhower administration is that its only weapons seem to be platitudes or paratroops. And this seems to be true whether

the situation is Little Rock or Lebanon, South America or Quemoy.

The President's "worst year" culminated in the biggest victory for the Democrats in an off-year election since the Roosevelt landslide of 1936. The Democrats gained 15 seats in the Senate, giving the party a majority of 64 to 34. In the House, a gain of 48 seats gave them the biggest majority since 1936, 282 Democrats to 154 for Republicans. In addition, the Democrats gained 6 governorships. The biggest Republican victory was Nelson Rockefeller's defeat of Averell Harriman in New York.

It is likely the waning recession was the most important factor in the sweeping Republican reversal. Nevertheless, it is reasonable to claim some credit for Adlai. The acquiescence in administration policies by Democrats in Congress under the Johnson leadership, Adlai characterized as "a disposition for meeting adequacy half-way." Johnson made little effort to conceal his annoyance at the Democratic Advisory Council's papers and statements that had helped to focus the issues much more sharply. Together with the "New America" papers from 1956, they provided the substance for the campaigns of many of the party's candidates. Many of the new faces in Congress were Democrats whose entry into politics had been stimulated by Adlai's example and who welcomed the policy thinking he had initiated. Adlai's own persistent and generally thoughtful, informed, and responsible criticism of the administration in speeches, articles, and in the media certainly helped turn the country toward the possibility of a Democratic victory in 1960.

Presidential ambitions and speculations inevitably were aroused by the sweeping nature of the Democratic victory. Formal declarations would not be made until late 1959 and early 1960, but it was evident very early that there would be at least four Democratic candidates. Senator Hubert Humphrey was identified with the liberal wing of the party. Whether or not Senator John F. Kennedy was liberal or conservative was overshadowed by the question of religion. Similarly, the chief identification of Senator Stuart Symington was with his fellow Missourian, former President Truman. Senator Lyndon Johnson was placed with the southern conservatives. And then there was Adlai's ambiguous position.

Despite worries during earlier campaigns about his conservatism, Adlai was now clearly identified with the liberal wing of the party, thanks to his writings and the work of the Democratic Advisory Council. More important, there was a hard core of enthusiastic supporters scattered around the country whose dedication approached the intensity of a cult. They were determined that their hero should have the opportunity to run against someone other than Eisenhower.

As questions about Adlai's intentions repeatedly arose, they examined his answers for changes in nuance, and found enough to keep alive their hopes. He did not repeat the flat phrase of May 1957 again. On his return from his African trip later in 1957, for example, he simply said he could "conceive of no circumstances" that would induce him "to seek the Presidency again." (The emphasis was on "seek.") Occasionally, in answer to questions, he would speak well of Humphrey, Kennedy, and Johnson—but not Symington. He generally avoided answers that dealt with his intentions and focused instead on what he thought would happen. "I will not be the nominee," was a typical answer.

Nineteen fifty-nine and 1960 represent the most puzzling period of his life. Even now, it is not possible to write of his conduct with assurance. It was a period of uncertainty and mixed emotions for him. A variety of political forces were at work to which he was exceptionally sensitive. And the record is confused by his lifelong tendency to throw out observations that sounded like set opinions or conclusions but were really intended to stimulate reactions. Even such intimate associates as Bill Blair and Willard Wirtz are uncertain or differ on key details, even though there emerges a clear consensus on his basic strategy. "Deep down," a very close friend said, "he wants it. But he wants the Convention to come to him, he doesn't want to go to the Convention."

No one has analyzed Adlai's state of mind toward the 1960 nomination more perceptively than Theodore H. White in his Pultizer Prize-winning *The Making of the President—1960*:

> With half his mind Stevenson shrank from memory of the sordid brutality of pre-Convention politics; nothing so exhausted his vitality or good spirits as the murderous continental string of primaries he had fought to defeat Estes Kefauver in 1956. . . . Stevenson knew and hated the intraparty warfare of domestic politics that, in the American system, creates and commands internal power.
>
> On the other hand, there was the other aspect of the Presidency, the outer disposition of American power: that which lies at the disposal of a President once he arrives at the White House, the immense and majestic forces and influence that belong to any President. These fascinated Stevenson. His chief concern lay with America's position and role in the changing outer world; his journeys abroad for eight full years had made him intimately aware of the pressures in the world about us, of its dangers and promises. This concern . . . had communicated itself across the country. . . . To dispose of the power of America in the outer world was a task that Stevenson, as a good citizen, could not shrink from if called on; but he would not act, or deal, or connive, or strike a blow to seize the Presidential nomination if his party did not offer it to him. Nor could any man

shake him from this simple stand until the last twenty-four hours before the nomination at Los Angeles.

His defeats at the hands of Eisenhower obscure the fact that Adlai was an exceptionally shrewd politician. Also, our preoccupation with personalities obscures the fact that his goals were different from those of most politicians. He liked to win as much as anyone, but winning and personal power were not, as White suggests, an end in themselves. Long-term influence on policy was more important to him than present and personal gain. This motivation in a politician is so rare that while some see it as a desirable model, it has prompted many to regard him as politically naïve. The record suggests otherwise.

He ran for governor against the odds in 1948 because he was convinced he could and should win. And he did. He did not want to run in 1952 because he knew it would take four more years to give a lasting quality to the reforms he had initiated in Illinois. He was right. Moreover, he did not believe he could win, and, at the outset, he even doubted whether he should win. In 1956, he doubted he could win, but his disappointment in Eisenhower and especially in Dulles's leadership in foreign policy made him determined to sharpen the issues and then to ignore advice to wait until 1960. To a large but, to him, inadequate extent, he succeeded. He also learned that dialogue on difficult issues could not be conducted effectively in the heat of a campaign; so, with consummate skill, he managed to create the Democratic Advisory Council against the powerful opposition of Democratic power centers in Congress. In doing so, he paved the way for a party, if not a personal, victory in 1960, and he set much of the agenda of the Kennedy and Johnson administrations. However summary, this is not a record of political naïveté. Nor, however uncertain, is the record of his approach to the 1960 presidential nomination.

Just as he realized that concern over his possible candidacy might block the creation of the Democratic Advisory Council, he also knew that the surest way to destroy whatever chance he might have of being nominated would be to declare his interest. It would focus on him the opposing ambitions of all the other Democrats. This involved more than the personal aversion to the primaries perceived by White, but also a determination not to sow division in the party. He saw strict neutrality as the best hope for his own unexpressed ambitions, and the best course for the party as a whole. It kept the track clear for attacks on Eisenhower administration policies and on the evident Republican choice for the nomination—Richard M. Nixon—for whom Adlai's antagonism approached revulsion.

In conversations with Kenneth Davis who was working on a biography of him, he used unaccustomed words such as "sly," "slippery," and "ruthless," as well as "thoroughly unprincipled," in describing Nixon. To another friend he wrote, "It seems to me unthinkable that a man with his background of slander, abuse, innuendo, expediency and resort to all the most devious political devices should ever occupy an office which we have tried for generations to exalt in the esteem of young people and the world." He not only loathed and despised Nixon but truly feared the possibility of his becoming President. As long as the polls showed him having the best chance of defeating Nixon—which they did repeatedly throughout 1959—he could not help thinking about running again.

One of his favorite methods of deflecting inquiries about his willingness to accept a draft was to declare that lightning never strikes in the same place twice. However true, he also knew that lightning repeatedly strikes an object that stands high on the landscape. He made sure throughout 1959 and into 1960 that he did just that.

The major lightning rods were a series of notable news-making speeches that culminated in an article in the January 1960 *Foreign Affairs,* that was reprinted with other 1959 writings in a successful book published by Random House early in the election year of 1960 under the title of the magazine article, *Putting First Things First.* It was his sixth book in seven busy years.

Characteristically, he put first "The Political Relevance of Moral Principle." It was the first annual lecture given in memory of the well-known Unitarian minister A. Powell Davies, delivered to an audience of four thousand people in Washington's Constitution Hall. Davies had used his Washington pulpit for many years to argue that politics without moral idealism is a sham and a betrayal of American civilization; that compromise between just and honorable men is necessary; but compromise with evil is intolerable. Adlai had known and admired Davies, welcomed the opportunity to pay tribute to him, and took as his text a theme of Davies's: "The world is now too dangerous for anything but the truth, too small for anything but brotherhood."

Adlai began his lecture by asserting that the capacity of modern weapons for mass destruction had created "a desperate physical solidarity," but that

> the moral and social solidarity in the family of man is still to be found. . . . No country on earth owes the sense of community more explicitly to the fact that it is united not by race or nationality but by fidelity to an idea. We were born "dedicated to a proposition" and our greatest leaders [were great] because they were able to speak for humanity at large and extend their vision to the whole family of man. . . .
>
> All our talk . . . in all the intricacies of our worldwide relations—has been to a depressing degree purely defensive. We have offered aid not to help others but to shield ourselves. We

have reacted to countless Soviet initiatives; acted on our own initiative barely at all. . . .

There is no more urgent duty than to discover why we have failed and to get back into the arena, aspiring, striving, fighting once more for what we believe. An examination of what you might call our collective conscience is to my mind far more important than particular projects or programs. . . .

In recent years we were stifled with complacent self-confidence. We believed ourselves dominant in every field. . . . We talked of "the American Century." . . . We have confused the free with the free and easy. If freedom had been the happy, simple relaxed state of ordinary humanity, man would have everywhere been free—whereas through most of time and space he has been in chains. Do not let us make any mistake about this. The natural government of man is servitude. Tyranny is the normal pattern of government. It is only by intense thought, by great effort, by burning idealism and unlimited sacrifice that freedom has prevailed as a system of government. . . .

I doubt if any society in history has faced so great a moral challenge as ours, or needed more desperately to draw on the deepest sources of courage and responsibility. Ours is the first human community in which resources are so abundant that almost no policies lie beyond our capacity for purely physical reasons. What we decide to do, we can do. Thus, perhaps for the first time in the world, choice, not means, ends, not instruments, are decisive.

He then offered three specific areas in which to test "the quality of our moral response," since "most of the major problems of our day present themselves in moral terms." The first was what he called "remedial poverty." The minority living in squalid conditions "depend, for remedies, on the alert conscience of the majority."

The second test dealt with "the rights and status of our colored citizens." He pointed out that "four hundred years of dominance by men of white skins is ending."

The third test arose from the fact that the Atlantic world, with 16 percent of the globe's population, consumed 70 percent of its wealth.

We can not be indifferent to the moral implications of this gap. . . .

You may argue that these qualities—of dedication and selflessness—are pretty remote from the realities of politics. . . . And yet, I wonder. It has been the view of great philosophers and statesmen that our system of free government depends in the first instance on the virtue of its citizens. . . . For no democratic system can survive without at least a large and active leaven of citizens in whom dedication and selflessness are not confined to private life but are the fundamental principles of their activity in the public sphere. . . .

It is more difficult, they say, to give time to public affairs when private life is so urgent and absorbing. Yet is it, I wonder, more urgent and absorbing than a hundred years ago when young men not only married young, had large families and built up careers, but also opened up new frontiers, created new cities from the wilderness and gave to new states and communities the framework of active political life? . . .

In a century in which so many of the mentors of the public mind—from psychiatrists to ad-men—speak to us in terms of "what we owe ourselves" may there not indeed have been a slackening of devotion compared with those days, not so long distant, when what man owes to God and his neighbor was a common theme of public discourse? If so, this is a dangerous hour for our politics and for government by consent of the governed. For at no time have so many of the great issues of the day demanded clear, real moral vision to bring them into focus.

The speech gave few answers to the questions it raised, but the editorial response was so favorable and widespread that he was encouraged in turning, just eight days later, to what he regarded as one of the most basic answers—education.

As governor, education had been an important priority. As candidate, it had been a favorite though not crowd-stirring subject. In the penny-pinched 1956 campaign, a national telecast was devoted to schools to call attention to a program paper to be issued a few days later—and both went largely unnoticed. He welcomed, and was ready to respond to, an invitation from the National School Boards Association to speak at their convention in San Francisco on January 26, because, as he said earlier, "for me, the dream of the New America begins in the classroom."

He drew on his Russian experience and quoted a Russian saying that "with good schools and hard work we will earn our place on the earth—and on the moon, too!" The Russian zeal for education, and its extension throughout a huge, backward, agrarian land in little more than a generation was, he said, "a spectacular achievement."

"Now that we have been jolted into a realization of our inadequacy, why do we find it so difficult to cope with the problem?" he asked; and answered, "The political fact is that education is a national problem which, alone among our national problems, is not handled on a national basis."

He touched on specific needs being met in various studies and reports then current: more classrooms; more counseling and guidance; better instruction in mathematics, science, and languages; improvement in compensation, working conditions, and training for teachers; less emphasis on teaching methods and more on subject content; and, especially, "a breakthrough in educational financing." "The truth is," he stressed, "that compared to all other public expenditures, the ratio of what we are spending on education is not more but very much less than was the case fifty years ago." This brought him to his main point.

I conclude that it is we the people, we the parents, we the community, that are most to blame for the failure of our education. . . . If the community wants driver education and bachelor cooking instead of Latin and mathematics, it will get it. . . . If our freedom means ease alone, if it means shirking the hard disciplines of learning . . . we may keep for a time the forms of free society, but its spirit will be dead.

He had endorsed specific recommendations of the experts, but his closing was a warning that their recommendations were meaningless in the absence of a widespread sense of individual responsibility.

From the West Coast and education, he moved to the East Coast and the problems of the cities. In Newark, New Jersey, on May 5, he spoke to the American Council to Improve Our Neighborhoods in terms that sound as if they had been uttered yesterday:

We are not concerned just with the low-income and minority ghettos in some cities, nor just the real estate values in the downtown central business districts, nor the bedeviled commuter, nor the costly, growing traffic congestion, nor the general offensiveness of the urban sprawl. The deficiencies in our schools and communal services, like parks, playgrounds, hospitals, and the ugly outcroppings of juvenile violence, are all pleading for attention and are all part of the broader task of revitalization and reinvigoration of the city as a way of life.

He spoke of the pressing need for housing he found wherever he had traveled and the necessity of cooperative effort by private enterprise and government to make progress on urban problems. "The plain fact is that those who oppose federal aid for urban renewal are actually against urban renewal," he told the predominantly business audience. "I hope we are ready to stop the demagogic political debate which assumes that government and private enterprise are inherently antagonistic." He spoke with equal bluntness about the administrative shortcomings of various federal programs and stressed the need for "developing new machinery of decision" that could bring together the variety of political jurisdictions involved in urban planning. In an early recognition of pollution problems, he warned that land, water, and "breathable air are getting scarcer." He called for care to prevent subsidized housing from becoming segregated housing. The sweep of his assessment of needs, and his suggestions for meeting them are underscored by their relevance to conditions that still prevail.

The next week Adlai was at the University of Illinois at Urbana with a speech on foreign policy that was to be the take-off point for the *Foreign Affairs* article. The two aims of the United States for the future, he said, should be the development of a "world under law" and a satisfactory relationship "with the vast revolution sweeping our planet." The immediate "hard political realities" centered on the division of the world into three blocs—free, Communist, and neutral—and how best to handle relations with them. In a passage of political courage in the existing climate, he recalled that "years ago" he had proposed discussing the independence of Formosa (Taiwan) and the admission of China to the United Nations. "I believe we should not veto the admission of China to the United Nations," he declared, pointing out that in China's absence, the Soviet Union inevitably became its spokesman in the UN.

The United States and the Soviet Union, he maintained, should forgo the race for superiority and seek equality of power. Both needed to work toward "a fully integrated system of controlled disarmament" in persistent negotiations that probably would have to go on "for the next two decades." He spoke at length of the UN's capabilities, and its value in helping to fill the vacuums created by the collapse of colonialism. He stressed the importance of the European Common Market and third world economic development; themes he would repeat in receiving an honorary degree at McGill University in Montreal on May 29.

Next, Adlai courted liberal business leadership with a speech at the Harvard Business School on June 6 to the concluding session of the National Business Conference, aimed at "Businessmen Who Think Greatly." He dealt bluntly with past business opposition to many of the major innovations of recent years such as the graduated income tax, social security, and minimum wages. He then sketched current economic challenges such as the worldwide disparity in living standards, the Soviet economic offensive, huge social capital requirements at home, and inflation control without recession.

"You bear a heavy responsibility for the Republic's well-being and democracy's survival," he told the business leaders.

The immediate means by which this is achieved—and the arena of decision-making is government, and the machinery of choosing government is politics. The health of both is the first business of every businessman, like every other citizen. . . . What we need, and better have a good deal more of, quickly, is a concern for the *national* interest, and not the selfish interest of business, labor, farmers or any single economic, racial or religious group. . . . Evolve a vision of the America you would like to see that must take account of considerations above and beyond the success of any business.

While staking out positions on high ground, Adlai was not neglecting the more mundane aspects of politics. Before leaving for a long summer vacation in Europe he gave public support to Mayor Richard Daley's campaign for reelection in Chicago, spoke at a fund-raising dinner in Boston for Endicott Peabody, a brother of Marietta Tree's who was to become governor of Massachusetts, and maintained a voluminous correspondence with journalists and political leaders, most of whom were urging him to run again.

The European summer lasted from June 18 until August 21. There were some meetings with clients and with *Encyclopaedia Britannica* people, but it was mainly a summer of "sun and sea, crumbling castles and iced wine, laughter, reading, sleeping—and eating," as he wrote to Agnes Meyer.

The highlight was a long cruise in the Mediterranean on William Benton's luxurious yacht, the *Flying Clipper,* a two-hundred-foot-long Scandinavian vessel. Various people would arrive and depart at ports of call, but the core group consisted, in addition to the Bentons, of Adlai III and Nancy; the Dutch Smiths; the Francis Plimptons; Marietta Tree and her daughter, as well as the chairman of the Book of the Month Club, Harry Scherman, and his wife; Mr. and Mrs. Bruce Gould, the editors of the *Ladies Home Journal;* and *Economist* editor Sir Geoffrey Crowther and Lady Crowther. Adlai wrote Buffie that there had been "a little too much society & people for my taste," but he had enjoyed it thoroughly.

The political winds, George Ball had written Adlai, were "blowing your way again." And, indeed, they were.

A July 22 Gallup poll reported 53 percent for a Stevenson-Kennedy ticket as compared to 42 percent for Nixon-Rockefeller, with only 5 percent undecided. He admitted in a letter to Chester Bowles, who had written about the poll, that "the continued talk about me is rewarding and a great satisfaction"; it was also, "very disquieting." In Madison, Wisconsin, James Doyle, former chairman of the state Democratic party who had been an effective supporter in 1956, had announced publicly he was for Stevenson and had begun privately to explore the organization of a

Draft Stevenson movement. Adlai was not only aware of these activities; his letters, while replete with mild protests, reveal a lively interest in them. So he arrived at the airport in New York prepared to deal with the political questions. He told the waiting newspapermen:

> I am flattered that so many people still want me to run for President again. Such continued confidence is the greatest possible reward in public life and I am deeply flattered. But—as I have said since 1956—I will not seek the nomination in 1960. And I hope all my friends will work for the avowed candidates of their choice . . . I have never thought for a moment it was possible for me to be drafted and I have no reason to think it now.

The record of what he said always has to be measured during this period against what he was doing. He was holding firmly to his conviction that his only hope of being nominated again was to avoid any semblance of seeking it. This led not only to public disavowals but private messages to close friends and associates affirming that they should, if they wished, work for other candidates. To Arthur Schlesinger, for example, he wrote on November 2: "I have told all my friends—who have asked—to go to work for 'the candidate of their choice.' That includes my partners and Marietta, who is active for Hubert Humphrey, I gather. And I think I told *you* that sometime ago. If I didn't, I do herewith!"

Even to Schlesinger, he was dissembling. If the party was to turn to him, it would be only if none of the alternative candidates emerged as clear leaders. Although he would, with damaging determination, avoid overt support for any of the contenders, at that point encouragement of the Humphrey candidacy helped to balance the strength of the Kennedy drive. And, despite his explicit authorizations, the later active role in the Kennedy campaign of Schlesinger and other colleagues would evoke unmistakable notes of sadness.

Meanwhile, the encouragement of his own candidacy went forward. On November 22, *The New York Times* reported that along with a Draft Stevenson organization in Wisconsin, there were loosely coordinated groups in Ohio, Oregon, Washington, California, Missouri, Texas, and Washington D.C. Shortly thereafter, James Doyle was given national press coverage for an interview in which, while denying there was a "formal organization," he stated there was an "informal drive" for a Stevenson draft because so many felt it was the country, and not Stevenson, that deserved "another chance in 1960."

At the same time, a polling and planning organization was being set up secretly in New York under the name of Russel D. Hemenway and Associates at 745 Fifth Avenue. Mr. Hemenway, an advertising executive who had been active in Democratic reform politics, set out to identify areas of Stevenson strength. Leaders in the group included Tom Finletter, Roger Stevens, the film executives Robert Benjamin and Arthur Krim, Ruth Field, Adele Levy, Agnes Meyer, and Mary Lasker. In Washington, George Ball and his young law partner, John Sharon, together with Senator A. S. Mike Monroney of Oklahoma, were developing what became in effect the strategic center for the various operations. And in Los Angeles, film executive Dore Schary headed another loosely organized group that would be very effective in fund raising.

Many of these elements came together at a Democratic Advisory Council dinner in New York in honor of Mrs. Roosevelt on December 7. Adlai prefaced his moving and eloquent tribute to her with a story designed to divert personal political speculation. He identified himself with an alleged guest at the hotel who had placed an early morning call to the manager to ask when the bar would open. When the manager asked why he would want to get into the bar at such an early hour, the caller replied, "I don't want to get in; I want to get out!"

Despite all the protestations, Adlai continued to keep closely informed on all the activity on his behalf. "I always told him exactly what we were up to," Finletter later told Kenneth Davis. "He made no objections." Generally, he remained more remote, receiving letters and reports with silence or diverting comment, while he went forward erecting lightning rods of his own; the most important being the article for *Foreign Affairs* and a trip to Latin America. Two other international incidents intervened, however; one out of comic opera, the other with potential for high drama.

Sekou Touré, the president of Guinea, was on an official visit and Adlai, as a consequence of his earlier personal contacts and his representation of Reynolds Metals, invited the president and his party to dinner at Libertyville. He called Viola, his cook, to tell her only that eighteen guests would arrive for dinner at six-thirty. Later he called back to say there would be twenty-eight and she should get more food. She was making beef Stroganoff and decided it could be expanded by adding ham that she had on hand. Adlai was delayed at the office and the guests arrived before he did. When Viola answered the doorbell, she was confronted by a group of people in flowing robes. It was the night before Halloween, and thinking they were trick-or-treaters, she passed around fruit, candy, and peanuts, and shut the door. The doorbell rang again; this time a State Department escort explained that these were the expected guests. With embarrassed warmth, Viola invited them in and asked for their hats, which, as Muslims, they were not prepared to part with. Shortly thereafter, Adlai rushed in with Bill Blair and Newt Minow, who has given this account of what happened next:

Touré said, "What a quaint American custom to serve guests nuts and apples at the door before dinner. . . . The next thing that went wrong was Mrs. Touré. I heard a scream—I looked around—her dress had fallen off. It was held up by one strap and the strap broke. She was naked to the waist. . . . She rushed to the bathroom. The Governor was trying to jolly everyone along. We went into dinner. There was a lot of excited conversation in French—I can't speak French. I heard somebody say something about pork. The question was: Is there any ham in the stew? The Gov (knowing Muslims can not eat pork) said, "Oh, no—this is beef stroganoff." Just then the girl from the State Department said, "Governor Stevenson, this ham is absolutely delicious."

At that point the doorbell rang. It was more trick-or-treat, real this time—Marshall Field and his kids came in flowing robes. Viola invited them in, thinking they were more guests. They joined the party. I tried to save the evening. There was a very good looking Negro who spoke English. I said to him, "You speak English beautifully." He looked at me and said, "Why not? I'm the United States Ambassador to Guinea."

The other incident was more portentous.

In Moscow, Adlai had joked with Khrushchev about having a summit meeting in an Illinois cornfield. When Khrushchev's first trip to the United States was arranged in the autumn of 1959, Adlai wrote an article for the July 5 *New York Times Magazine,* titled "Tour for Khrushchev: The Real America," emphasizing the importance of seeing the country's heartland. Thus it was not surprising that when Khrushchev visited the Coon Rapids, Iowa, farm of Roswell Garst, a specialist in hybrid corn seed, Adlai should be invited to meet him there.

He took John Fell with him to the banquet the night before and to the morning appointment and lunch at the Garst farm, during which he and Khrushchev had a long discussion on disarmament and other topics. A few days later, at the United Nations General Assembly in New York, Khrushchev proposed that in four years all nations abolish their weapons and armed forces, except for internal peace units, and turn to competition in the art of peace. His proposal generally was dismissed as a propaganda gesture, but Adlai issued a statement that contrasted sharply with the official reaction:

Mr. Khrushchev's total disarmament proposal must be taken seriously. The only way to eliminate the scourge of war is to eliminate the means of war. . . . Whether he means what he says is a question now. We have reason to be skeptical, but we have better reason to study his proposal with an open mind and high hope for progress at last toward arms control and security. . . . I have often said that a danger greater to us [than unlimited war] is Soviet economic and political penetration around the world. So I do not dismiss Mr. Khrushchev's speech as propaganda only.

All of this, however, was preliminary to one of the most extraordinary incidents in Soviet-American relations.

The following January, Soviet Ambassador Mikhail A. Menshikov called Adlai to say that he wished to come to Chicago to deliver some presents and messages from Mr. Khrushchev. Adlai was going to Washington and arranged, instead, to call at the Soviet embassy at 4:00 P.M. on January 16. Adlai III reports that on arrival, his father was greeted warmly and "invited to sit in the middle of the room to indicate it was a very private conversation and that he did not need to worry about being bugged." What happened next, Adlai recorded himself in a memorandum he wrote afterward for his personal confidential file.

> After the usual pleasantries about health, family, and the usual caviar, delicacies, fruits and drinks, Menshikov removed from his pocket a carefully folded sheaf of notes written in ink on small paper and spoke to me something as follows: (I hesitated a week before making any record of this curious conversation.)
>
> Before returning last week from Moscow, he had spent a considerable time alone with Premier Khrushchev. He wishes me to convey the following: When you met in Moscow in August, 1958, he said to you that he had voted for you in his heart in 1956. He says now that he will vote for you in his heart again in 1960. We have made a beginning with President Eisenhower and Khrushchev's visit to America toward better relations, but it is only a beginning. We are concerned with the future, and that America has the right President. . . .
>
> In Russia we know well Mr. Stevenson and his views regarding disarmament, nuclear testing, peaceful coexistence, and the conditions of a peaceful world. He has said many sober and correct things during his visit to Moscow and in his writings and speeches. When we compare all the possible candidates in the United States we feel that Mr. Stevenson is best for mutual understanding and progress toward peace. These are the views not only of myself—Khrushchev—but of the Presidium. We believe that Mr. Stevenson is more of a realist than others and is likely to understand Soviet anxieties and purposes. Friendly relations and cooperation between our countries are imperative for all. Sober realism and sensible talks are necessary to the settlement of international problems. Only on the basis of coex-

istence can we hope to really find proper solutions to our many problems.

The Soviet Union wishes to develop relations with the United States on a basis which will forever exclude the possibility of conflict. We believe our system is best and will prevail. You, Mr. Stevenson, think the same about yours. So we both say, let competition proceed, but excluding any possibility of conflict.

Because we know the ideas of Mr. Stevenson, we in our hearts all favor him. And you (Ambassador Menshikov) must ask him which way we could be of assistance to those forces in the United States which favor friendly relations. We don't know how we can help to make relations better and help those to succeed in political life who wish for better relations and more confidence. Could the Soviet press assist Mr. Stevenson's personal success? How? Should the press praise him, and, if so, for what? Should it criticize him, and, if so, for what? (We can always find many things to criticize Mr. Stevenson because he has said many harsh and critical things about the Soviet Union and Communism!) Mr. Stevenson will know best what would help him. . . .

The presentation concluded with questions about "Mr. Stevenson's rival," meaning Vice President Nixon, and repeated declarations of desire not "to interfere in an American election" together with many sober statements about the profound "interest" of the Soviet Union, and of all countries, in the American election. The protestations about non-interference were interspersed throughout the presentation, which I did not interrupt. The distaste and distrust of Nixon was expressed cautiously but clearly. . . .

Mr. Menshikov concluded by saying that this interview was the best evidence of the confidence reposed in me by the Premier and his colleagues and that he had no misgivings about my keeping it in confidence.

At the conclusion, I made the following points:

1. My thanks for this expression of Khrushchev's confidence.

2. My thanks for his proffer of aid.

3. However I was not a candidate for the nomination and did not expect to be a candidate for the Presidency in 1960.

4. My grave misgivings about the propriety or wisdom of any interference, direct or indirect, in the American election. . . .

5. Finally, I said to him that even if I was a candidate I

could not accept the assistance proffered. I believe I made it clear to him that I considered the offer of such assistance highly improper, indiscreet and dangerous to all concerned. . . .

His manner was extremely amiable but very serious throughout his presentation of Khrushchev's message, which was done in a low voice, in a parlor adjoining the family dining room on the third floor. On two occasions when a waitress appeared with food, etc., he interrupted the conversation.

On January 22, 1960, I wrote Mr. Menshikov the attached letter.

"My dear, Mr. Ambassador:

"I am most grateful to you and Premier Khrushchev for the splendid gift you delivered to me at the Embassy in Washington last week. So much delicious Russian caviar and wine may not be good for me—but I like it! I hope you will extend my very warm thanks to Premier Khrushchev and also my best wishes for his health and happiness in the New Year and the New Decade. That the year and decade will see ever closer and constantly improving relations between our great countries is my highest hope, and I am sure you and Mr. Khrushchev have similar sentiments about our common future.

"The confidence expressed in me during our conversation and Premier Khrushchev's interest in my views were flattering, and I wish I could thank him in person. But I must repeat that I will not seek the nomination for President again and I do not expect to be the candidate of the Democratic party this year. Even if I was, however, I would have to decline to take advantage in any way of the confidence and goodwill I am happy to enjoy among your compatriots. I am sure you and Premier Khrushchev will understand, and I hope respect, my feelings about the proprieties in the circumstances we discussed, and I trust my reaction will not be misconstrued as discourteous or ungrateful.

"With renewed thanks to you and the Premier, together with my hope that we may have further talks from time to time, I am

"Cordially yours."

The profound political dangers inherent in the meeting troubled Adlai deeply. Any report to the White House or the State Department he was sure would be leaked under the most damaging possible circumstances. He realized he also was vulnerable to leaks from Soviet or perhaps other sources. His solution was to confide in Scotty Reston, the head of the *New York Times* Washington bureau, who, in turn, wrote a generalized article saying that the Russians were showing "both a keen interest in the United States election and an appalling ignorance of the dangers in commenting on it." This provided the basis for a more specific story should one become necessary. Adlai's other protective measures were the memo he wrote for his own file and the January 22 letter.

This extraordinary effort to influence the 1960 election never leaked, so the possible consequences are incalculable. It must have entered his mind many times during the Cuban missile crisis. The fact that the choice of candidates had been a subject of such serious consideration not only by Khrushchev but by the entire Presidium, and that the theme of Khrushchev's message is apparent in the later approaches of General Secretary Mikhail Gorbachev, merit continuing thought in our developing relations with the Soviet Union.

The article for *Foreign Affairs* was one of the most calculated and carefully planned that Adlai ever wrote. Early in the year, he had sent a copy of the University of Illinois speech to Hamilton Fish Armstrong, the magazine's noted editor, and asked if he thought it was worth expanding into an article. Armstrong's answer was encouraging, though he cautioned about too much emphasis on economic development. During the summer cruise, Adlai had discussed with Harry Scherman the plans of the Book of the Month Club to send the January issue he was aiming for as a special dividend to all the club's members, thus ensuring exceptionally wide distribution to an educated audience. In September he sent copies of the speech and his correspondence to Barbara Ward in Ghana with a long letter outlining his thoughts on what the article should cover and asking if she "could put together anything thoughtful and considered by the end of October which I could rework in early November to meet his deadline for the January issue."

He fully intended the article to be a preconvention manifesto to draw the lines at issue with the Eisenhower administration and, most especially, Nixon. It became more than that. It became a major keynote of the 1960 presidential campaign, echoed in the speeches of both Humphrey and Kennedy, and its theme runs through much of the Kennedy-Rusk foreign policy. Its publication was greeted by an extensive front-page story in *The New York Times* and by editorial comment all over the country and abroad. Its reception prompted Random House to build a book around it despite the unprecedented circulation it had already received thanks to the Book of the Month Club.

The article presented a program for peace, "the most imperative business in the world today." Adlai asked, "Why haven't we really led the postwar world since the Korean war?" and then gave the answer to his own question: "The root of the trouble lies in this: the nation faces a series of massive changes in the world scene; they call for new ways of looking at the world, for new policies, for increased efforts. But since

Korea our political leadership has not clearly and insistently acknowledged this fact." He charged that "Messrs. Eisenhower and Dulles" had "denounced 'containment' as 'immoral'" but followed the policy in reality; and that Vice President Nixon "saw something disloyal in my warnings about the Soviet rate of economic growth." He charged that the "Eisenhower-Dulles era" failed to face the realities posed by four major revolutions: the political revolution posed by vanishing colonialism and the rise of new nations; an economic revolution; the biological revolution of population growth; and the scientific revolution.

"New centers of power are rising from old ashes in Asia," he stressed.

> As Europe becomes more unified, it too will reemerge as a great center of power. And who can doubt that regional unification is going to take place in Latin America and emerging Africa? So this is not the beginning of the American Century, or anyone else's. . . . But if our tradition does not require us to be the world's boss, it does require us to keep alive and vigorous the great traditions of political freedom and legal order which underlie Western society. . . .
>
> To me, the two most dangerous realities we now face are the multiplication of nuclear weapons and the disparity in living standards between the rich nations and the poor.

He then said that these "statements of high generality" could be turned into policy "only by specific application and negotiation," and proposed concentrating in six areas: economic development, the Atlantic community, arms control, China, Europe and the Middle East, and, finally, a sense of purpose.

He put economic development first because the gap between an average annual income of $2,000 in the United States, and an average income of less than $100 among one third of the world's peoples, was getting wider. This gap, "underlies most, if not all, aspects of the twentieth-century crises."

He then described in detail the steps he thought needed to be taken in a long-term program of "at least forty years," including training of professional staff. He emphasized the necessity for cooperation with other developed nations and their full participation in the effort.

"Failure to develop an organic Atlantic community with common institutions and common purposes," stood in the way of "a joint program for world investment and growth."

Since his participation in planning for the 1957 NATO meeting, he had been convinced the administration's attitude toward the Atlantic community was not sufficiently positive or politically realistic. He urged "systematic" cooperation by the United States and Canada "to enlarge and use our influence vigorously to help solve in common the tough questions of commercial policy." He stressed, in terms that echo today, that "the unfavorable American balance of payments and fears for American reserves are already leading to a new isolationism, to creeping protectionism, to reduced foreign aid and to further divisions in our unity and strength."

In the military field he expressed concern over NATO's diminishing deterrent capacity and observed, "As I have said to Mr. Khrushchev, equality of strength and equality of risk are only the starting point for disarmament discussions."

He advocated the establishment of "an Atlantic Council with real powers" to formulate joint policies "for sharing our responsibilities and bringing about a genuine and equal partnership between the United States and Western Europe." Negotiations with the Russians should be accompanied by "new common policies for defense, disarmament, space exploration, monetary reserves, tariffs and a large economic sphere, and aid to the underdeveloped areas, giving, I hope, new terms of reference to NATO and other organizations."

Turning to arms control, he expressed the belief that "we may be approaching the time when the arms race with Russia can be arrested. Once a revolutionary regime leaves behind its adolescent fanaticism, risk and cost become powerful considerations. I believe they exercise genuine influence in Moscow today and that we should do what we can to encourage this trend."

Adlai approached China in terms of disarmament and reduction of the risks of war in the area. In doing so, he set forth a position that stopped short of recognition but was nonetheless intensely unpopular and invited attack. Terms for a settlement in the Far East would require concessions on the Communist side that would include China's agreement to international inspection of disarmament, the end to the threat of force against Taiwan and subversion in Indochina, a frontier settlement with India, free elections under United Nations supervision in Korea, and the right of the people on Taiwan "to determine their own destiny." On our side, the concessions would include China's admission to the United Nations, the evacuation of Quemoy and Matsu, and the inclusion of Japan and Korea in the atom-free zone and area of controlled disarmament.

In the Middle East, an atom-free zone should be considered along with an embargo on arms shipments into the area. Since neither the Soviet Union nor the West

> have gained much from their recent policies of intervention in the Middle East, I suggest we now give nonintervention a trial. Some international problems are never solved; they just wear out. But meanwhile the United States should call upon the Soviet Union and everyone in the United Nations again and again

to use their influence to harmonize relations between the Arab states and Israel and end this prolonged and useless hostility.

The reunification of Berlin and of Germany, he said, required "a reduction of fear in Russia and the West" that would subside "only when there is progress toward disarmament with adequate controls."

His final section was a frontal assault on the Eisenhower administration.

> The truth is that nations cannot demonstrate a sense of purpose abroad when they have lost it at home. There is an intimate connection between the temper of our domestic leadership and the effectiveness of American influence in the world at large. . . . If we can not recover an aspiring, forward-looking, creative attitude to the problems of our own community, there is little hope of recovering a dynamic leadership in the world at large. . . . I believe the United States is ready for a new awakening and the achievement of greater goals. Within it are the moral and material elements of new purpose and new policy. It is the task of leadership to marshall our will and point the way. We had better start soon for time is wasting.

The trip to Latin America, like the *Foreign Affairs* article, was carefully calculated and planned. It was the only major geographical region he had not visited and he wanted to fill that gap in his education. It was timed to take him out of the country during the early months of 1960 when primary elections would intensify the pressure on him to declare himself one way or another. Yet, he hoped, it would keep him in the news. And he definitely was mindful of the opportunity to create a sharp contrast with the disastrous Nixon trip of 1958. In that, he succeeded beyond all designs.

The ostensible reason for the trip was the promotion of a new Portuguese edition of the *Encyclopaedia Britannica* and an article he had agreed to write for *Look*. He prepared himself intensively. Carlton Sprague Smith of New York University, a leading scholar on Latin America and head of the Brazilian Institute at the university, would travel with him, along with William Benton, Bill Blair, and John Fell.

In nine weeks they visited Mexico, Guatemala, Costa Rica, Panama, Colombia, Ecuador, Peru, Chile, Argentina, Uruguay, Brazil, and Venezuela. "It was in Latin America," Benton wrote later, "that I realized fully the extent, and even the intensity—the depth and sincerity—of the world's admiration for Adlai Stevenson, as the very conscience of the American people." The spirit of receptions in city after city was caught in a column Ralph McGill wrote for the *Atlanta Constitution* on the arrival in Bogotá, Colombia, early in the trip.

> He and his group were whisked, so to speak, from airport to bull ring. A massed group outside, which was in a near state of rebellion because it could not obtain tickets, set up a great cry of acclaim. Inside, the massed benches let loose such a roar on Stevenson's entry he flinched, thinking nothing less than a riot had erupted. . . .
>
> Speeches were made. The great gates of the arena opened for the ritual of the bullfight processional. It brought further salutes to the visiting American. Nor was this the end. The matadors dedicated their bulls to him. And when the long hours of death in the afternoon were done, Stevenson was hoisted to the shoulders of the crowd, along with the three matadors, and carried about the ring to the vast delight of the crowd which kept up a Niagara of shouts. Chief among them was "uno" meaning the first or the best.

Adlai felt it was "good to be a national hero instead of coping with one," and it was even better to note the contrast with Nixon's earlier reception.

Hard work went on beneath the surface of ceremony and official meetings. In nearly every country, he visited universities or had meetings and freewheeling discussions with delegations of students. Also, wherever possible, he had extended sessions with labor union leaders, for many of whom it was their first encounter with a leading American. And, of course, he indulged his insatiable interest in poking and probing his way through markets.

In Bogotá, after receiving an honorary degree, he was asked for an interview by a group of students, during which they told him he should see their slums. He promptly asked them to take him, and asked particularly to see the areas where refugees from the country's recent civil war were huddled. Word of this action spread to other countries, where other students or social activists saw to it that he saw the worst of their slums.

In every country, the range of people and places he saw, as usual, was awesome. Benton, in his book on the trip, *The Voice of Latin America,* wrote:

> Throughout the trip, Governor Stevenson was infinitely patient. The entire two-month-long journey was a great personal triumph for him. . . . He was besieged everywhere by admiring crowds seeking autographs, bows, handshakes and smiles. Though we traveled strictly as private citizens, his appearances became a triumph also for the United States; he symbolizes, in

his learning, his wisdom and wit, his urbanity, oratory and his humane qualities, the characteristics the Latin Americans most value in their intellectuals and political leaders.

In his article for *Look,* Adlai began by noting that President Eisenhower had been visiting the area at the same time. "I traveled through twelve countries in eight weeks. The President went to four countries in ten days. He came back optimistic. I came back deeply concerned." He then proceeded to state why.

> I am concerned because Latin America is in social and political revolution—like most of the evolving regions of the world . . . because, in a region rich in resources, half the people are hungry, half don't sleep in beds, half are illiterate . . . because the population increase is the fastest in the world and is outstripping production . . . because of our ignorance about our Latin neighbors and because of the anti-Americanism I found, in spite of their moving welcome to me. And I am concerned that if they don't achieve their desire for a better economic and political life, we may find enemies, not friends, on our doorstep.

The rest of the long article was an elaboration on these points together with sharp criticism of what he saw as the inadequacy of Eisenhower administration policies toward the region.

Although one gets the impression that Asia, and perhaps Africa, interested him more than Latin America, he was nonetheless quick to perceive its basic problems—schools, housing, land reform, unstable or authoritarian politics, and inequitable distribution of wealth coupled with economic backwardness. John Bartlow Martin has noted that "much of what he said during and after his trip anticipated President Kennedy's Alliance for Progress."

The trip failed to attract the news coverage he had hoped for—they once went for four weeks without encountering a single American newspaper correspondent—and it was only partially successful in keeping him out of the line of fire as the battle for the nomination gained in intensity. While trying to dodge the bullets, some of which ricocheted all the way to Latin America, he was also shaping another rod that might—just might—help attract the lightning.

CHAPTER NINETEEN
Disappointed Hopes

BEFORE LEAVING FOR LATIN America, Adlai accepted an invitation to deliver the Founders' Day address at the University of Virginia and began corresponding with Julian P. Boyd, editor of *The Papers of Thomas Jefferson,* about the relevance of Jefferson to "the forthcoming Presidential campaign," because "I suspect you will agree that we have little to look forward to from Nixon but a continuation of the sedatives and half truths which satisfy the majority of people." Also, it had been arranged, with financial help from Agnes Meyer and Mary Lasker, for William Attwood to take a leave of absence from *Look,* beginning February 15, to assist on anticipated speeches and articles—"not," as he wrote Adlai, "to help you get the nomination but to help defeat Nixon."

Both the nomination and the election surely were in Adlai's mind as he sketched out a University of Virginia speech that was to be as politically hard-hitting as the occasion allowed. Boyd had sent him a first draft, which he worked on along the way in Latin America. Attwood was also working on a draft with more "political punch" and flew with it to Barbados, where Arthur Schlesinger also was waiting at the home of Sir Ronald and Marietta Tree. The three of them, Attwood later wrote, "used up a couple of yellow pads producing a version that would satisfy Stevenson and the scholars without sparing Nixon." (His comments on his role would shortly lead to a crisis in his relationship with Adlai.) The other preoccupation was how best to handle the press conference set for his arrival in New York.

Much had been happening on the political front. The day Adlai arrived in Barbados, John F. Kennedy won the Wisconsin primary race against Hubert Humphrey. But because the victory fell far short of predictions and was based significantly on the state's large Catholic vote, it was not decisive. Moreover, it gave renewed impetus to the interest in Adlai that had continued to develop during his months away. In March, Mary McGrory, in her syndicated column, reported the growth of Draft Stevenson clubs and their collection of signatures to present to convention delegates. Doris Fleeson, in her syndicated column, had discussed a California opinion poll showing that either Stevenson or Kennedy could carry the state against Nixon. At the end of the month, a national opinion survey conducted by Louis Bean was released showing Adlai receiving 54 percent of the vote to Nixon's 46 percent. Hemenway, who had arranged the poll, admitted that its central purpose was "to jar [Adlai] loose from the consistently passive and discouraging role he had elected to follow."

The April 11 press conference in New York was packed. The Stevenson for President Committee of New York, headed by David Garth, then a television producer and later a specialist in political polling, had chosen that day to open officially its New York headquarters; the Democratic convention was exactly thirteen weeks away. Adlai started by reading a statement written in Barbados repeating that he was "not a candidate" for the Democratic nomination. "While I have never said that I would refuse the nomination," he continued,

> another draft at the convention has seemed to me out of the question. I do intend, however, to keep on speaking as clearly as I can on public questions and in support of the Democratic party. I think its victory in November is imperative to the country's welfare. . . . If what I do is misinterpeted by some as political self-promotion, the alternative of keeping completely still is too much for me.

Then, because Attwood's employment had become known and stimulated speculation, he added, "As for recent newspaper stories about hiring ghost writers, I have suffered from the do-it-yourself habit too long to look or hope for relief now."

He then spoke about Latin America, but the minute he invited questions the subject was back to the nomination. Would he accept the nomination of a deadlocked convention? "If I said I'd accept a draft I'd be courting it; if I said I would not, I'd be a 'draft evader.'" He did not regard the Humphrey candidacy as a "holding operation" for him; he did regard Kennedy as a liberal; he did not have a favorite candidate; he could not predict whether a Kennedy victory in the West Virginia primary would assure Kennedy the nomination. Would he like to be President? "I have trifled with that thought so long, and so often in past years, that I think I have reached the point where I can view the possibility that I will never be President with the utmost equanimity."

Asked about religion as a campaign issue, he said, "It seems to me that the issues of this campaign are far too grave for the voters to be distracted by such questions as in what church the candidates pray. I think it would debase the campaign, for example, if so fine an American as Jack Kennedy were to be forced to defend himself against bigots." Would he remain neutral to the end or could he foresee circumstances where he would endorse a candidate? "Yes, I don't exclude the possibility that before the nominating convention is over that I might want to express a view and a very positive position on the selection. But I can't at the moment foresee under what circumstances that possibility would arise." Asked for his preference as a running mate if he were nominated, he replied, "Why did I come home anyway? I was getting along so well down there!" Amid laughter, he moved on to Charlottesville where, as Bill Blair had cabled him in Barbados, "Washington press converging on Charlottesville to cover speech. Expecting something great."

The scholars in the audience gave him an ovation, and the press gave it national political impact with such headlines as: STEVENSON BLASTS REPUBLICANS and ADLAI FLAYS IKE ADMINISTRATION. Among its distinctions was probably the longest sentence in modern American political oratory—216 words—which nonetheless succinctly summarized the failures of the Eisenhower administration as liberals saw them:

> The people have a right to know why we have lost our once unquestioned military superiority; why we have repeatedly allowed the Soviets to seize the diplomatic initiative; why we have faltered in the fight for disarmament; why we are not providing our children with education to which they are entitled; why— nearly a century after the Fourteenth and Fifteenth Amendments—all of our citizens have still not been guaranteed the right to vote; why we spend billions of dollars storing surplus food when one-third of humanity goes to bed hungry; why we have not formulated an economic development program geared to the world-wide passion for economic growth; why we have failed to win the confidence and respect of the billions of impatient people in Asia, Africa, and Latin America; why millions of Americans live blighted lives in our spreading urban slums; why we have fewer doctors per capita than we did forty years ago and pay more for our medical care than ever before; why we spent more money last year on tranquillizers than on space exploration, and more on leisure than on learning; why the richest nation in the history of the world cannot support the public services and facilities we must have not only for world power but for national growth and opportunity.

The speech was broadcast nationally by the American Broadcasting Company and was played on front pages of newspapers all over the country. More significant, two days later newspapers throughout the country reported the launching in New York of a campaign by local groups to obtain more than a million signatures on petitions urging that he be drafted.

The success of the speech produced one unhappy reaction—a crisis in his relations with William Attwood. A letter to "Dear Bill" on April 16 began, "I write this with distress because of my affection and respect for you—but I am afraid I no longer have any choice but to sever any 'editorial' relationship." It then explained:

> You know, I am sure, how badly I felt about the original announcement that you were going "to write speeches" or something for me. I assume you must have felt that I didn't want you to come to Barbados or Charlottesville after that. And now I have two reports from the latter place of audible remarks "I (Attwood) wrote half the speech; (Julian) Boyd the other half"—or to that effect—and "Lawrence (or some news man) is angry because Stevenson changed my speech." Frankly I've never had any experience of this kind before. If these reliably reported statements were true, they grossly violate the conventions I assumed you knew. SO PLEASE DON'T WRITE OR DRAFT ANYTHING MORE FOR ME. I'll be in N.Y. April 25–26 and perhaps we can talk then about what you can do—along lines I originally suggested to Mrs. Meyer—that would be useful to the party, whoever its nominee.

The rift subsequently was patched over but the incident does illustrate Adlai's sensitivity about "ghost writers." Many people submitted drafts to him, usually at his request, and he constantly sought material like an insatiable vacuum machine; but even the best of the writers testify that the final product nearly always was distinctively his own. He might lose his campaigns for the presidency, but he was determined not to lose his identity as a writer.

A different problem arose in his relations with Schlesinger, who was a personal friend not only to him but also to Humphrey and Kennedy. The mounting bitterness of the battle for the nomination between the latter two was painful to Schlesinger, but even more difficult was the conflict in his loyalties to both Kennedy and Adlai. He knew the latter well enough to suspect strongly that, despite the disavowals, Adlai's strategy was aimed at the possibility of a draft at a deadlocked convention. In Barbados, acting on a Kennedy suggestion, he had told Adlai that Kennedy would feel "under certain obligations" to any major Democratic leader who came out for him prior to the West Virginia primary. He knew his man too well to be more specific than that. Adlai had replied that he was pledged to neutrality during the preconvention campaigning and intended to keep his pledge, adding that his great concern was to prevent a split in the party.

Having the trust of both men, Schlesinger was able to act as a discreet intermediary in the midst of surging and emotional cross-currents. Thanks to his skill, relations between Adlai and Kennedy, though never comfortable, were not marked by the intense animosity that persisted into the years of the Kennedy presidency on the part of some of those close to the President, including his brother, Robert. Kennedy saw Adlai's support as the quickest way to win the nomination and was disappointed not to have it. Later, though he never saw Adlai as personally involved in a Stop Kennedy effort, he accurately assessed the Draft Stevenson movement as having that effect, and, inevitably, Adlai became his main, though unannounced, rival.

Emotions intensified in the ferocious and pivotal primary battle in West Virginia. Humphrey had started out with a wide margin in the polls. Despite his repudiation of religious bigotry, it was a major factor in the opposition to Kennedy. These factors, and the crucial importance of the result, justified to Kennedy's supporters a ruthlessness and an expenditure of money and man-hours without parallel in the history of primaries. For Adlai, it was dramatic evidence of the wisdom of his decision not to become a candidate. On May 10, Kennedy won nearly 60 percent of the vote and a few days later Humphrey withdrew from the race.

Prevailing wisdom regarded West Virginia as the decisive contest. Events often frustrate political forecasts, however, and this was especially the case in the spring and summer of 1960.

When Adlai spoke at Charlottesville, the country was basking in the "spirit of Camp David," which was proclaimed at the end of Khrushchev's visit to the United States the previous autumn. A mild thaw in the cold war had set in as conversations between Eisenhower and Khrushchev resulted in removal of a deadline Khrushchev had set for the signing of a treaty with East Germany, agreement on a summit meeting in the spring of 1960, to be followed by an Eisenhower visit to the Soviet Union. Then, on May 5, disaster struck.

Amid a long speech to the Supreme Soviet, Khrushchev announced in outraged and belligerent terms that an American reconnaissance plane had just been shot down deep inside Soviet territory. In Washington, with the President's approval, the National Aeronautics and Space Administration gave out a CIA cover story of a lost weather research plane and a State Department spokesman said that "there was no deliberate attempt to violate Soviet air space and there never has been."

Thereupon, Khrushchev sprung the trap he had baited. Again before the Supreme Soviet, he announced the pilot of the plane, Francis Gary Powers, was in Soviet hands and had confessed that he was engaged in aerial photographic espionage. Pictures were released of Powers, his wrecked plane, and some of the equipment he had used.

Yet, again with the President's approval, the State Department repeated the original falsehood that the U-2 had been engaged in weather research and had accidentally strayed, but it tacked on a sentence saying that intelligence-collection activities were a necessity. It was not until the following day that the decision was made to tell the truth since it was already known to everyone. The statement, edited by Eisenhower in order, as he later wrote in his memoirs, "to eliminate any phrase that seemed to me defensive in tone," gave the public for the first time information about the development of the U-2 plane that had been making flights over Soviet territory since 1956.

In this setting, on May 12, Adlai spoke at a Conference on World Tensions at the University of Chicago; his central theme was that American foreign policy should be based on a recognition of the worldwide human community and aimed toward the development of effective world law. He prefaced his argument, however, with a reference to the U-2 affair.

"In spite of all the rhetoric of the past few days," he said,

no one questions the necessity of gathering intelligence for our security. The Russians, of course, do the same, and they have a great advantage because of their addiction to secrecy, while our countries are virtually wide open to all the world's spies. But our timing, our words, our management must and will be sharply questioned. Could it serve the purpose of peace and mutual trust to send intelligence missions over the heart of the Soviet Union on the very eve of the long awaited Summit Conference? Can the President be embarrassed and national policies endangered at such a critical time by an unknown government official?

This last was an inference drawn from a sentence in the State Department statement that prior presidential approval had not been required for each U-2 overflight. Khrushchev also hit upon this statement to offer the President an out by suggesting that the President might not have been directly responsible for the violation of Soviet territory. But the implication that he was not being kept informed of important government activities struck the President as personally insulting and he publicly insisted not only that he was responsible but that the flights would continue. In fact, he issued orders that the flights were not to be resumed but made no public announcement of his action.

In this atmosphere, President Eisenhower left on May 14 for the summit meeting in Paris. Upon arrival he was confronted with messages

Khrushchev had sent to President Charles de Gaulle and Prime Minister Harold MacMillan demanding that the President denounce the flights and punish those responsible for them. The President told both leaders that the demands were unacceptable and on Sunday night, May 15, on the eve of what had been heralded as a "peace summit," he ordered a worldwide alert of United States combat forces.

The next morning at the first scheduled session of the conference, Khrushchev demanded the floor and delivered a bitter indictment of the United States, during which he withdrew the invitation to the President to visit the Soviet Union. Eisenhower made a moderate, conciliatory response. "I have come to Paris," he said, "to seek agreements with the Soviet Union which eliminate the necessity for all forms of espionage," and expressed a willingness "to undertake bilateral conversations . . . while the main conference proceeds." Khrushchev's answer was to stalk from the room. The Paris summit had collapsed even before negotiations had begun.

Serious as these events were, they were not the only ones that troubled the political setting in May and June. Rioting in Turkey shook and nearly wiped out a friendly government. Student riots in Korea reached a violence so great that the government of Syngman Rhee was overthrown. In Cuba, Fidel Castro made military alliance with Khrushchev, who threatened war if the United States invaded the island. More personally humiliating for the President was the Japanese government's withdrawal of its invitation to visit, fearing it could not guarantee his personal safety. And finally, in the Congo, Belgium suddenly withdrew its rule and the newly independent Congo descended into an anarchy and savagery that not only made a Communist takeover seem imminent but also threatened to tear apart the United Nations.

The collapse of the Paris summit had clouded the West Virginia results; moreover, it threw an unexpected spotlight on Adlai. Theodore H. White, the "sage" of the 1960 election, reported the impact of events abroad on Adlai in these words:

> Over the previous eight years, Adlai Stevenson had become the most clear and eloquent voice on foreign policy in the Democratic Party. By his travels, his writings, by his speeches, by the simple seepage of his ideas, he had, in good season and bad, outlined a picture of the world and the direction of American movement that, though frequently abused on first enunciation, had become so accepted as to have become a cliché of everyone's thinking by the spring of 1960. The strengthening of the UN, the cessation of bomb testing, the reorganization of the Atlantic Alliance, the search for a modus vivendi with the Soviet Union in Europe—all these positions—first pioneered by Ste-

venson, were now the common utterance of all Democratic speakers.

Thus, when in May of 1960 American policy in the outer world crumbled and a new architecture seemed necessary, Democrats high and low, who had been neutral and indifferent before, suddenly took note of Stevenson again. . . . Across the country, the leaderless troops of the 1952 and 1956 campaign began to stir. If he would lead, they would march. But would he lead?

Adlai avoided the "unauthorized" headquarters at 100 Indiana Avenue, N.W., when he went to Washington on May 16. He was there to testify before a Senate committee on a proposal he had made in a widely discussed article recently published in *This Week* magazine proposing compulsory free equal time during presidential campaigns for both parties. But he could not avoid the intensified interest in him as a possible candidate.

Because the proposal has had continuing impact on presidential elections ever since, it is worth pausing a moment to take note of it. Its origins were in the 1956 election. Early in the campaign, President Eisenhower had been asked to make an appeal for the Community Chest on *The Ed Sullivan Show*. Shortly thereafter, Adlai was surprised to be asked by NBC if he wanted equal time to make *his* appeal to the Community Chest. Much to NBC's relief, he said that the President was not acting as a candidate or a politician and that for him to take advantage of the equal-time provision would tend to politicize the Community Chest, which he did not think desirable. In the midst of the Hungarian and Middle East crises near the end of the campaign, however, his request for equal time to present the Democratic view in response to the President's broadcast met with resistance. The Federal Communications Commision refused to rule, and finally the networks, on their own, decided to give him time. This experience convinced him of the inadequacy and inequity of Section 315 of the Federal Communications Act dealing with equal time in political campaigning. The two-part article in *This Week* was the result, followed by the introduction of legislation on which he had been invited to testify.

"I would like to propose that we transform our stumbling, fumbling presidential campaign into a great debate, conducted in full view of all the people," he said to the committee.

Suppose that every Monday evening at peak viewing time, for an hour and a half, from Labor Day until election eve, the two candidates aired their views. They might on each evening take up a single issue. Each in turn might discuss it for half an hour, followed by rebuttal of one another for the third half hour. There are other possibilities, including face-to-face debate. But the central idea is that, in some manner, the principal figures, the candidates for president, appear together at the same prime time for a serious presentation of views on public questions. The time should not cost them or their parties anything.

He argued that television had become "almost prohibitively" expensive, so that the party with the most money could purchase the most time, and that the complexities of scheduling obliged candidates to employ advertising agencies who turned to "the jingle, spot announcement and animated cartoon" so successful in "selling soap, cereal and deodorants." Occasional television appearances, helped little to enlighten the public.

Presidential campaign ritual requires that the candidate be shuttled from coast to coast as many times as possible, assuring maximum physical exhaustion, and minimum opportunity to prepare his statements. The result is ever greater use of the ghost writer and the ever greater difficulty of knowing the candidate himself. . . . It would end the tendency to reduce everything to assertions and slogans. It would diminish the temptation of politicians to entertain, to please and to evade the unpleasant realities.

The time, he stressed, would have to be used personally by the candidate and not for, say, a musical extravaganza. "The purpose is not to entertain but to enlighten." Vice presidential candidates, however, could use some portion of the time.

Buying even brief segments from favorite prime-time programs had its risks. He told the committee that in 1956 the purchase of time for a brief speech that shortened Lucille Ball's popular program by five minutes had been rewarded with a telegram saying: "I like Ike and I love Lucy. Drop dead."

Prophetically, he told the senators that "it may turn out that the direction we give to political television is one of the great decisions of the decisive decade of the 1960's."

The bill, understandably, encountered strong opposition from the networks and from those who wanted to preserve the advantage arising from access to larger amounts of money. Under pressure, the Congress compromised and voted suspension of the "equal time" provision of the Federal Communications Act for the 1960 election. This made possible the famous Kennedy-Nixon debates—the first face-to-face nationwide television confrontation of presidential candidates in history—that many analysts believe gave Kennedy his narrow margin of victory. The access to free time through "debates" and "forums" and other devices that was initiated by Adlai's article continues to evolve as one of the most notable features on the political landscape.

In the midst of Adlai's testimony, the proceedings were interrupted for a brief announcement of the collapse of the summit meeting in Paris. Senator Mike A. S. Monroney, a sponsor of the bill, has written of what then happened:

> Adlai Stevenson spoke to a room packed to capacity. These were no visionary intellectuals, but political pros—Senators and Congressmen, members of their staffs, White House and Capitol reporters—and they had come to hail and hear the man to whom they naturally turned in times of crisis. Most of the crowd followed Stevenson from the hearing room, and as he entered the hall outside, he confronted a mob of hundreds more pressing forward to ask a question or shake his hand. Slowly he made his way down the hall toward my office. As he reached the door his faithful favorite, Mary McGrory, caught him for a final question: "Governor, are you going to the convention?" Stevenson answered with a couplet,
> "I'm growing too old for the kind of affairs
> "Where the people outnumber the comfortable chairs."
> He finally escaped into my office, visibly shaken by his experience. When the crowd finally drifted away, we guided him to a room where he met with Lyndon Johnson and received a stern warning that he might yet be the nominee of the Democratic party. It was a sober Adlai Stevenson who returned to meet with some of his advocates, understanding, I think for the first time, the extent of his responsibility. And in this atmosphere, we levied our demands: that he provide the voice of leadership for the Democratic party, that he do nothing to handicap our effort to secure his nomination. We asked more, but to these two he agreed.

Within three days he acted on the first promise and created an uproar. On May 16 he joined with Speaker Sam Rayburn, Majority Leader Lyndon Johnson and Foreign Relations Committee Chairman William Fulbright in sending a cable to the President in Paris asking him to convey to Khrushchev that leaders of the opposition were behind the President's efforts to continue the meeting. But by May 19, when a Democratic fund-raising dinner was scheduled in Chicago, Adlai had become increasingly disgusted with Republican demands for uncritical national unity behind the President. Chester Bowles was scheduled to be the speaker and Adlai was slated only to be on the dais. That afternoon, however, he called Mayor Richard Daley, who was hosting the dinner, to say he was "damned sore" and had something he wanted to say on foreign policy. Daley said he could have five minutes. He spoke for seven, and aroused a storm. It was one of the toughest speeches he ever made.

> It appears that this year's campaign will be waged under the darkest shadows that ever hovered over the world—the mushroom clouds of a nuclear war no one wants. This terrible danger—and how to avert it—will and should overshadow every other issue. For the chances of a more stable world, which seemed to be brightening, have been rudely reversed by the breakdown of the summit conference in this historic week.
>
> Premier Khrushchev wrecked this conference. Let there be no mistake about that. When he demanded that President Eisenhower apologize and punish those responsible for the spy plane flight, he was in effect asking the President to punish himself. This was an impossible request, and he knew it. But we handed Khrushchev the crowbar and the sledgehammer to wreck the meeting. Without our series of blunders, Mr. Khrushchev would not have had a pretext for making his impossible demand and wild charges. Let there be no mistake about that either.

He then recounted the events which, he said, made Khrushchev's anger "predictable, if not his violence"; and added, "How would we feel if Soviet spy planes based in Cuba were flying over Cape Canaveral and Oak Ridge?"

"We resent deeply and bitterly the gross affront to the President and his office," he continued. "There is no question about national unity in a time of crisis. But . . . it is the duty of responsible opposition in a democracy to expose and criticize carelessness and mistakes, especially in a case of such national and world importance as this. . . . We cannot sweep this whole sorry mess under the rug in the name of national unity."

The Chicago politicians listened in silence and then erupted in the loudest cheers Adlai had heard in years. Headlines all over the country drew attention to the bluntness of the attack. Thunder as well as lightning crashed around his head. He was accused of a disruption in national unity akin to treason. Lyndon Johnson thought the indictment was too harsh and too sweeping. Of the three declared Democratic candidates, only one publicly approved of what he had said—John F. Kennedy.

Ironically, it was Kennedy's political campaign that was hurt the most by the terrors of the U-2 incident. Was such a young man equal to handling the threat of nuclear war? That question was in the minds of many and would not be resolved until the confrontation with Khrushchev over missiles in Cuba after he was President. Now, however, it was to Adlai and his background in foreign affairs that many Democratic leaders appeared to turn. Certainly, the Kennedy bandwagon faltered. After West Virginia, every week had registered gains for the Kennedy campaign, until, at the end of May, as Arthur Schlesinger has written, there was "a convulsive movement" toward Stevenson.

Kennedy won the Oregon primary that all observers thought Adlai would have won had he not insisted on withdrawing his name. Blair had arranged for Kennedy to stop in Libertyville en route back to Boston, and he and Minow met him at the airport. Both of them had been telling Adlai for some time that his best course was to support Kennedy. Together with Schlesinger, they thought that if the two men came to know each other better they would become natural allies. Driving to Libertyville, Kennedy asked, "Do you think I ought to offer him the State Department?" There was an extended silence in the car until finally Minow replied, "No, It would be a great mistake. For one thing, he would resent it. For another, you don't want to tie your own hands."

There are varying assessments of this fateful meeting. Blair and Minow agree that the breakfast did not go well, that Adlai was unusually stiff and hesitant. Then, just Kennedy and Adlai moved into the study where they were alone for nearly forty-five minutes. When they emerged, Blair and Minow suggested they have a statement ready in case newspapermen learned of the meeting. Adlai's insistence on maintaining a neutral position stood in the way of a joint statement and they drafted separate statements.

On the way back to the airport, Minow asked, "Did you offer him the State Department?" Somewhat surprised, Kennedy said, "No, certainly not. You told me not to bring it up." Minow then began to wonder if he had done the right thing and the next morning, somewhat guiltily, told Adlai what he had done. The latter at once assured him he had been right. Arriving at the airport, Kennedy said to Blair, "Guess who the next person I see will be—the person who will say about Adlai, 'I told you that son-of-a-bitch has been running for President every moment since 1956'?" Blair answered correctly, "Daddy."

Adlai thought the meeting had gone well. In a longhand letter written to Schlesinger on board an airplane that same afternoon he reported:

> As to the campaign, Jack reviewed all the states and said he will still be short 80–100 votes probably; that I was strong especially in Oregon, Wash., Calif., Colo., Pa., etc.—that I could help him and he wanted the help without specifying when. I explained that I wanted to be consistent and didn't feel therefore that I could come out for him now, but that he could be sure that I would not be a party—overtly, covertly, etc.—to any "stop Kennedy" movements; that I had been approached—and have I— with that proposal and had emphatically and unequivocally rejected the overtures; that, further, I would as in the past do

nothing to encourage "Draft Stevenson" movements which could embarrass or weaken him. . . . The meeting was entirely satisfactory from my point of view and I can not say he seemed disappointed or surprised about my attitude and certainly not elated! . . . And I think—and hope—*that I left him with a feeling of great good will, determination not to* hinder, *and no doubt about my preference and anxiety to* help *in any way if he is nominated.*

The following day, Schlesinger's journal recorded a telephone call from Kennedy to report on the talk. "He said it had been wholly pleasant, but that obviously AES did not intend to do anything for the moment. Jack said he was not much impressed by AES's account of why he did not wish to act; but supposed this to be because he did not wish to disclose his real reason—that, if he said nothing, there might still be a possibility that he would emerge out of the scramble as the candidate."

Robert Kennedy, to whom his brother reported the meeting, has left a harsher account: "He just never felt that Stevenson was being frank or candid. He was shocked or surprised that Stevenson would be addressing himself to these matters in this way. President Kennedy felt that he and Stevenson could understandably be guarded when talking to the press but when they sat down together they ought to be able to speak frankly, as man to man."

Theodore C. Sorensen's recollections come close to those of the younger brother.

> It was clear to Kennedy that if the Stevenson process would deadlock the convention, it would not benefit Stevenson—it would benefit Symington or possibly Johnson. We used Johnson as a scare-word to the liberals, but we really thought it would be Symington if we didn't make it on the first ballot. Kennedy thought Stevenson was being unrealistic about it and he also thought Stevenson was not being as candid with him in private conversation as he should have been.

Schlesinger, a confidant of both Adlai and Kennedy, has best summarized the situation in *A Thousand Days.*

> Each felt the other did not understand his problems. Each doubted that the other appreciated what had been done for him—Stevenson by giving Kennedy his opportunities in the 1956 convention, Kennedy by campaigning in twenty-six states for Stevenson in the election. And rivalry now made the differences in temperament and age emotionally more important than the affinities. Certainly the contrast between Stevenson's diffidence

and Kennedy's determination in the spring of 1960 heightened for each his misgivings about the other. And Stevenson, like all the political leaders of his generation, thought that Kennedy was a young man pushing too hard who should await his turn. Yet every day made Stevenson more crucial to Kennedy's hopes. . . . "He is the essential ingredient in my combination," he told me in mid-May. "I don't want to have to go hat in hand to all those southerners, but I'll have to do it if I can't get the votes from the north. . . . I want to be nominated by the liberals."

Despite his annoyance, a few days later at Hyannis Port, Kennedy said to Schlesinger:

"One reason I admire him [Stevenson] is that he is not a political whore like most of the others. Too many politicians will say anything which they think will bring them votes or money. I remember in 1956 when Adlai met Judge Dewey Stone and some other big contributors in Boston a few days after Suez. They wanted him to say certain things about Israel and Egypt. If he had said them, he could have had a lot of money out of that room; but he refused to say them. I admired that."

Tension gripped all the camps as the struggle for the nomination moved into June. Beginning in late May and lasting all through June, Senator Monroney and John Sharon traveled incessantly to every part of the country to develop support for Adlai. Theodore White summarized their efforts saying, "If there was a stop-Kennedy movement rolling, it rolled wherever Sharon and Monroney moved."

The calculations of the Kennedy and the Draft Stevenson planners were remarkably close. The Kennedy camp estimated a shortfall of about 100 in the 761 votes needed to nominate. At Indiana Avenue the estimate was about 150. The Stevensonians estimated that Johnson had between 400 and 450 votes, nearly all from the South and West with a scattering over the Midwest, while Symington was believed to have between 100 and 150. Adlai, they believed, was assured of at least 45 first-ballot votes. The votes of five states—Iowa, Kansas, Minnesota, New Jersey, and California—were pledged to favorite sons. In addition, Illinois and Pennsylvania were uncommitted. The thinking was that if all the favorite-son states refused to release their delegates on the first ballot and if a substantial portion of the delegates from Illinois and Pennsylvania held back from Kennedy, a deadlock was almost certain. Everyone agreed that if Kennedy were to win he had to win on the first ballot or come very close to it. Failing that, he was not likely to gain on the second ballot and surely would start losing on the subsequent ballots. Then, they reasoned,

Adlai's popularity, demonstrated statesmanship, and high prestige would exert rising pressure on the convention floor and the stampede to their candidate would be on.

Jim Doyle had moved from Wisconsin to the Indiana Avenue headquarters in Washington and officially announced an organized Draft Stevenson movement. By the end of June there were forty-two state organizations. News releases poured out of the headquarters, paid spot announcements began to be made on local radio and TV stations, and full-page advertisements calling for a Stevenson draft, signed by influential citizens, began appearing in leading newspapers. To pay for the first one in the Sunday *New York Times* on May 21, a member of the New York committee mortgaged his house, but the response to its appeal for funds had brought in over seven times the cost of the ad.

The troubling news from abroad placed Adlai in the spotlight he had hoped to occupy. What he had not anticipated, though, was the effectiveness of the carefully calculated, lavishly financed Kennedy campaign. In this circumstance of enhanced popularity but diminishing likelihood of a deadlock, he came under increasing pressure, if not to declare himself, then to seek support quietly from key leaders in key delegations. Pressed by Finletter to make a direct bid, with uncharacteristic petulance he replied, "*You* made me put out that damned statement," referring to his 1956 announcement that he would not run again. "And now you want me to break my word."

During June, also, Attwood, who had restored his relationship with Adlai, was living at Libertyville and drafting speech material and position papers for which he sought help from Walter Johnson and his colleagues at the University of Chicago. Johnson has recounted to Kenneth Davis how, in mid-June, he responded to a plea from Attwood to come to Libertyville to help persuade Adlai he had to assume a more active role. Their conversation lasted for many hours that afternoon and evening and provides the best picture we have of Adlai's preconvention thinking.

Adlai thought Kennedy, though bright and able, was too young, too unseasoned to be President; he pushed too hard, was in too much of a hurry; he lacked the wisdom of humility, and that wisdom, so necessary in the judicious exercise of executive power, would not be encouraged by success in the current campaign. Both Kennedy and the nation would profit from a postponement of his ambition. He believed this feeling to be widespread and would weaken Kennedy as a candidate against Nixon.

Symington, he thought, was simply not qualified for the White House, nor could he be counted upon to wage a sufficiently vigorous campaign against Nixon. He was too easy, too safe. He seemed blandly indifferent to many of the most crucial national and world issues while vastly exaggerating the importance of national defense, and especially the technical details of air and missile strength, in the total scheme of things.

Johnson seemed to Adlai too regional a candidate to be a strong contender against Nixon; he had great abilities but they were those of a skilled political tactician rather than of a top policy-making statesman and he certainly could not, on the record, be deemed a dedicated liberal. He had bitterly (if covertly) opposed the Democratic Advisory Council and his candidacy was strongly opposed by Walter Reuther and, in general, by the liberal wing of the party.

"Look, Governor," Johnson told him, "since you feel the way you do about the other candidates, it seems to me beholden upon you to lift up the telephone, call Dave Lawrence, call Mike Monroney, invite them to fly to O'Hare and bring them here secretly. Tell them you really want to do this thing, that you're not going to campaign for it but you do want it. Let them take it from there."

Adlai insisted that his analysis was not an argument for decisive action on his part, and Johnson soon realized it was, instead, an argument in favor of a draft. Johnson argued a repeat of the 1952 draft simply was not possible in 1960. The Kennedy bandwagon, stalled at the end of May, was rolling again. There would now be no convention deadlock and thus no nomination for Adlai *unless* he did more than merely indicate he would serve if called. It was necessary for him to say he *wanted* to be called to make it possible for the Stevensonians to rally and organize the support they needed to prevent Kennedy's nomination, probably on the first ballot. It was not too late, but a forthright indication of Adlai's real opinions and wishes was absolutely essential.

Johnson said Adlai simply shook his head and said, "No, I can't do that. . . . Why can't these people understand my position? I said when I got back from Latin America I wasn't a draft evader. I said in 1952 that the office should seek the man. I wrote in the introduction to my 1952 speeches the same thing." Despite a few hours of inconsistent behavior at Los Angeles, it was the most succinct and definitive statement of his position he was to make.

On Saturday, July 9, Adlai flew to Los Angeles, accompanied by Ad and Nancy, Buffie and Ernest Ives, their son Timothy and his wife, the Edison Dicks, and Marietta Tree. The flight was delayed at Las Vegas in stifling heat and they arrived three hours late at Los Angeles International Airport, where more than heat was raising the temperature. The largest crowd in the history of the airport—some seven to ten thousand people—had assembled to greet him. He told the sweating, tumultuous crowd, "I see you like your egg-heads hardboiled!"

More seriously, he told them their greeting recalled for him something Woodrow Wilson had said "when greeted as you have greeted me" that was "something along these lines: 'Great outpourings like this are not in compliment to an individual; they are demonstrations of a purpose. And all I have to say is that, whoever may be the Democratic candidate for the Presidency, I pray God he may be shown the way not to disappoint the expectations of such people.'" Then he continued:

We believe together that politics is important business—worth giving up a Saturday afternoon for, and a lot more besides. Partly, I suppose this is because we want to be part of something bigger than we are—to give ourselves meaning. We see Democracy as a restless, demanding, animate ideal. We want to do our part to make it work—for us as individuals, and for the country and for the whole world.

It's partly, too, I guess, because we realize—especially today—that the whole future depends on political decisions here in the United States. We want to make these decisions, and not have them made for us. We don't want to see this society of ours drifting. We don't want to be shipwrecked on other people's reefs. We know this is the 20th century; that we need the world, but that the world needs us, too, and our way of finding the right answers together—as a people.

If Adlai had been as eloquent at the convention as he was at the airport, the result might—just might—have been different. Other "ifs" hang over the history of this fateful convention, even though it was shaped fundamentally by the effectively organized strength and ruthless determination of the Kennedy forces. The contrast between the tight control of the Kennedy campaign and the sprawling, occasionally coordinated, enthusiasm-driven Draft Stevenson movement could hardly have been more extreme.

The airport arrival had been a media event (all three television networks had been alerted to be there) that excited conversation among the delegates. Such events were central to the strategy of the Draft Stevenson people. David Garth has said: "I think his no-campaign strategy was right. Adlai would otherwise have been subject to criticism that he had no right to run a third time. That meant that others had to make a movement to prepare a climate of momentum around the country for him and we did it." They really did do it.

With money raised from previous supporters and a nationwide fundraising campaign among small contributors, Senator Monroney and Jim Doyle, together with Senator John Carroll of Colorado, Tom Finney from Monroney's staff, John Sharon from Ball's office, Hemenway, Garth, and Tedson Meyers had set up headquarters in Los Angeles in late June. National Committee chairman Paul Butler had ruled that since Adlai was an avowed noncandidate, they were not entitled to offices at the party's Biltmore Hotel convention headquarters or to tickets for the Sports Arena convention-hall activities. Under pressure, he later assigned the Stevensonians two small rooms on the hotel's mezzanine, far from the spacious offices and delegates' lounges assigned to the Kennedy, Johnson, and Symington committees. It happened to be adjacent to a banquet kitchen and the press quickly dubbed the space "Butler's pantry." Butler also allocated from among the more than five thousand seats he had available for each session, seventy-five for Stevenson spectators.

Undaunted, Meyers rented the condemned and abandoned-for-demolition six-story Paramount Building on the sleazy side of Pershing Square Park. Soon a 107-foot banner proclaiming STEVENSON FOR PRESIDENT faced across the park toward the Biltmore inviting the attention of delegates and the 4,750 media representatives attending the convention. Moreover, outside the hotel, delegates, reporters, and television crews began having to push through a steadily growing crowd of demonstrators arriving from all over the country, some of them hitchhiking, or packed into old jalopies getting there on their last gasps.

Thomas B. Morgan, who had been brought in by Attwood to serve as press secretary, described the setup in a 1984 article in *American Heritage.*

> There was a Stevenson campaign office staffed by two dozen experienced political operators and about one hundred and fifty amateurs, doing everything from delegate contacts, intelligence gathering, and public relations to sign painting, running the headquarters elevator, and driving the campaign bus. The organization functioned on a low budget and devotion; for penniless volunteers it provided a dormitory and sleeping bags on the top floor of the Paramount Building. It manufactured and distributed thousands of buttons and fliers . . . installed about two hundred phone lines, and rounded up demonstrators to greet Stevenson at every public appearance. More important, led by Doyle and Monroney, it had opened discussions with delegates from many states, including California, Iowa, Kansas and New Jersey.
>
> We argued that our man had made a wise decision and was sticking to it; willing to run if nominated, unwilling to block his competitors. Yes, we expected an active candidacy; no, we could not say when. That settled, the numbers would tell the truth: neither Kennedy nor anybody else could say he had 761 votes sewn up. And this led to a repeated litany, one I also used with any reporter who came by my office for a chat: "If Stevenson were to receive the vote of every delegate who really prefers him but is voting for Johnson to stop Kennedy, or for Kennedy to stop Johnson, it would be Stevenson on the first ballot." Until the airport reception for Stevenson and its replay on television, the argument was debatable at best; afterward it was credible.

On Sunday, Monroney, Sharon, and Finney came to Adlai's Beverly Hills Hotel cottage with their delegate count to persuade him the nomination could be won if he would now abandon his noncandidacy and fight for it. When they arrived, he was in his bedroom with Walter Reuther, who was telling him Kennedy had the nomination won. Their analysis hinged on favorite sons holding firm through the first ballot and a few states where the votes were demonstrably fluid. Newt Minow interrupted their presentation, took Adlai into the bathroom, and told him his contacts with the Kennedy people had convinced him Reuther was right, that what he now was hearing was wrong. The Illinois delegation was about to declare for Kennedy, Minow told him and advised him to go to the meeting and declare for Kennedy.

Adlai's intelligence told him Minow was right, his emotions told him to accept the Monroney analysis, but, more basically, his deep desire to be President caused him to cling to the hope that lightning could strike again. So his answer was to visit the Stevenson headquarters where, an observer said, he seemed "overwhelmed" by what he saw there.

A few hours later, his inner turmoil led him to his closest declaration of his candidacy on the CBS network program *Face the Nation*. Asked if there was "any way" his supporters could make him say he was a candidate, he replied:

> While I am personally not a candidate, and I don't believe you can persuade me to be a candidate, and I do insist on being consistent about it, I think these supporters of mine have converted me into a candidate. That is, I am their candidate, the candidate, I dare say, of a great many people around the country who signed these petitions. They have moved me very deeply. . . . If they want me to lead them, I shall lead them. I have indicated that many times. I don't see why it is so complicated . . . for one to say he will not seek the nomination, who has enjoyed the greatest honors that his party can accord to anyone, not once but twice, to step aside and say, "Now it is time for someone else," and likewise to say that if called upon of course I will serve.

That afternoon, as Minow had predicted, the Illinois caucus had voted to give 59½ of its 69 votes to Kennedy, 6½ to Symington, and only 2 to Adlai. One was uncommitted. During the spring, Mayor Daley had said to Adlai, "Tell me if you are a candidate—I've had trouble with the delegates before but I'll try if you are a candidate." Adlai had told him he was not. In the meantime, Joseph Kennedy, John's father and owner of Chicago's Merchandise Mart, had exerted great pressure on Daley to obtain support for his son, which Daley had finally pledged. That afternoon, too, Governors Docking of Kansas and Loveless of Iowa, both with favorite-son delegations, had declared for Kennedy, and Governor Pat Brown had announced that California also would be for Kennedy.

That meant that everything depended on Pennsylvania and its 81 votes, controlled by Governor David L. Lawrence.

Lawrence had come to Los Angeles hoping for a Stevenson-Kennedy ticket. Theodore White has written, "The respect and affection that David Lawrence had paid Adlai E. Stevenson over the previous eight years had come close to public adoration; this affection still remained and all who dealt in national politics recognized it." Late Saturday night he had made his preference known to Adlai, and now at 2:00 A.M. on Monday, with the Pennsylvania caucus scheduled for later that morning, he drove the eight miles to Adlai's hotel for one more meeting.

"Lawrence met with Adlai and half a dozen of us late Sunday night," Russell Hemenway reported to Tom Morgan.

> Lawrence wanted a Stevenson-Kennedy ticket even though his delegation belonged to Kennedy. We had a Louis Bean poll showing that Stevenson now was actually a better bet to beat Nixon than Kennedy, because of the Catholic issue. So Lawrence said he would hold Pennsylvania if Adlai would tell him then and there he was running. If not, in the morning, he was appearing on the *Today Show* with Dave Garroway to tell the world Pennsylvania was going for Jack Kennedy.
>
> And Adlai said to Lawrence, "Do what you have to do, Dave."
>
> And Bill Wirtz who was there, asked Adlai, "Governor, are you sure that's the message you want to give Governor Lawrence?"
>
> And Adlai said it was.
>
> Christ, Adlai could've said anything but that and he would've stopped Pennsylvania from going to Kennedy. David Lawrence was the ace in the hole and we let him go. You know something? That might have been a watershed in American history. Think of it! No Vietnam War!

The next morning the Pennsylvania delegation caucused and voted to give 64 of its 81 votes to Kennedy, 8 to Stevenson, and the remainder scattered. It was reported that Lawrence wept at the decision.

Kennedy's first-ballot strength now seemed sufficient to nominate him and Adlai was being urged not merely to withdraw but to place Kennedy in nomination. Some of Adlai's closest friends, including Blair and Minow, were urging him to follow this course. But the leaders of the draft movement were not yet ready to give up. Not only did they doubt that Kennedy's strength was as great as the delegate counts suggested, but they sensed a rising resentment among the delegates of the unremitting pressures put on them by the Kennedy organization, and particularly of the often intimidating tactics of the campaign manager, the candidate's brother, Robert.

Reports of numerous promises involving the vice presidential nomination began to circulate. "If they called a meeting of all the people to whom they've promised the Vice-Presidency, they couldn't find a room in Los Angeles big enough to hold it in," Monroney reported with disgust. The delegations of two of the favorite-son states on which such reports had focused, Iowa and Kansas, with their fifty-two votes, were reported to be in revolt against their governors' declarations for Kennedy. The unit vote in the Iowa delegation had gone to Kennedy by a mere half-vote. Brown was reported in difficulty holding his California delegation in line. Monroney believed that other revolts and defections would be encouraged by the massive demonstrations that were being planned and that the whole trend could be reversed.

"Stand firm," he advised Adlai. "If you can't declare your candidacy, at least maintain your present position."

Mrs. Roosevelt was more insistent. At a luncheon in her honor at noon on Monday, the audience that packed the large dining room of the Beverly Hills Hotel listened raptly as she seemed to address her speech to an audience of one—Adlai. She barely took her eyes off him as she fervently declared that the country needed "maturity, judgment, and the goodwill of the uncommitted peoples of the world," and twice repeated her belief that the best ticket the Democrats could offer the nation was Stevenson and Kennedy. In the flush of the event, Monroney suggested that Adlai hold a press conference Tuesday afternoon, and Mrs. Roosevelt quickly volunteered to introduce him. Adlai agreed.

On the way back to his hotel he wondered aloud to the associates who packed the limousine whether he would have a chance to go to the convention. "I'm a delegate, I should go," he said, "but perhaps an appearance would be misunderstood." Tradition proscribed candidates from attending the convention until after the balloting. But his status was unique; he was still a noncandidate. He decided to go. Morgan states: "The discussion had been very casual. No plans were made. No hour of arrival set, no talk of a demonstration." Nonetheless, a newspaper described what followed as a "deliberate attempt to stampede the convention."

"That night, as the delegates convened for the first time, they found the Sports Arena unexpectedly surrounded by a large, well-behaved, noisy crowd of perhaps a thousand Stevenson demonstrators," Morgan wrote. "Not only had there been no such demonstration outside a political convention in recent memory but none in history had ever been seen 'live' [on T.V.]. It was bigger news than the keynote address. It was sensational!"

When the meeting adjourned, no matter what exit the delegates and spectators used, they had to push their way through lines of pickets, some in jeans, some in business suits, some women pushing baby carriages or leading their children by the hand, rhythmically chanting "We want Stevenson" and waving Stevenson placards. "It was more than a demonstration," Theodore White wrote. "It was an explosion."

On Tuesday morning, demonstrators cheered again as Adlai left his hotel with Monroney for a day on which, Monroney wrote later, "they 'thrice presented him a kingly crown, which he did thrice refuse.'" He had agreed to appear before the delegates of one of the two undecided states—Minnesota.

"Minnesota had only 31 votes—but Minnesota's influence in the Convention was nationwide," White reported in his Pulitzer Prize-winning book.

> Still floating through Los Angeles, still drifting and questioning, were perhaps several hundred delegates and alternates, heavy of conscience and burdened with citizen responsibility. For such people as these, the Minnesota delegation, conscience-heavy itself, could set an example. Hubert Humphrey had freed his state's delegates of all personal loyalty to him and urged them to vote their conscience. But what did conscience dictate? Was it Stevenson, whose international experience seemed best to meet the challenge of the headlines? Or was it Kennedy, who had taken his cause directly to the people and won in seven primaries across the country? Who was the best man? . . . The Minnesotans caucused on Sunday and on Monday (twice) and on Tuesday (twice) and still they could not make up their minds. Symbolically, the high command of their hitherto united party split—Governor Orville Freeman would nominate Kennedy, Junior Senator Eugene McCarthy would nominate Stevenson; and their leader, Hubert Humphrey, would make no decision at all.

Monroney went into the caucus room first. There was standing room only. Not only delegates and alternates, but their spouses, friends, reporters, and observers from all the contending camps had squeezed inside before the doors were closed. Humphrey planned to introduce him and announce his support of Adlai, but the ovation he received when he rose to speak made him burst into tears, and he sat down. His endorsement came the next morning. Monroney gave a fighting speech filled with gambling images all aimed at telling the delegates they must "take the long chance." In the midst of a standing ovation, he brought Adlai in from a side door to a great rush of cheers. They were ready—eager—to respond to his appeal. He would not make it. He avoided any word that could so easily have ignited their enthusiasm. Instead, he spoke of the administration's foreign policy errors and was wholly noncommittal about himself.

Schlesinger, who had remained behind after making an appeal on Kennedy's behalf, torn by conflicting loyalties and emotions, stood in the back and he, too, wept. The applause at the end lacked the warmth of the welcome. That was his first refusal of the kingly crown.

A revolt in the delegation of the other uncertain state, California, kept hope alive. Brown had promised Kennedy the state's 81 votes on the first ballot even though he had admitted to Monroney earlier that he thought Adlai was best qualified to be President, and clearly there were people in the delegation who preferred Adlai. Then, Mrs. Roosevelt had come to a secret caucus and pled with them not to "desert what your heart tells you to accept" but to "fight to the bitter end." Just before the evening session opened, news swept the Sports Arena that California had split wide open: 31½ would go to Stevenson on the first ballot, and only 30 would go to Kennedy. The rest were scattered.

The press conference Adlai had agreed to the day before took on the atmosphere of a rally in anticipation of a ringing declaration that he was at long last an avowed candidate. They did not know he had decided to go to the convention that evening and thus was precluded from announcing his candidacy. The mass of microphones transmitted mainly an impassioned endorsement addressed *at* him by Mrs. Roosevelt. He spoke only briefly, thanking his supporters, and left an enormously disappointed audience that sought to suggest the meeting with the press was clear evidence he was a candidate.

Tuesday night was scheduled as a dull night of window-dressing and party-platform speeches. "So hundreds (but not thousands) of Stevenson demonstrators, many of them simply tired of marching all Tuesday afternoon, filled an empty section upstairs to watch the show," Morgan wrote. ". . . only in that sense did they 'pack' the galleries, which were not full in any case. I underscore this to foreshadow the momentous greeting waiting for Stevenson at the hall."

Adlai arrived with Marietta Tree. Garth and Sharon met them at the VIP entrance. Marietta borrowed a delegate's badge and went inside. A crush of latecomers briefly blocked the way, and then "without plan, prior announcement, or prepared remarks Adlai walked on to the floor with Garth and Sharon." Morgan continues the extraordinary story:

> The closest delegations discovered him almost at once and broke into a cannon roar of delight. Then the delegations across the entire convention floor seemed to rise as one to begin a splendid, spontaneous, spectacular adoration. They filled the aisles, laughing, yelling, crying, crazily counterpointed by the orchestra playing an Illinois fight song. They stopped Stevenson dead in his track far from his seat. The galleries exploded in the next instant, exaltation following astonishment following recognition of what was going on down below.

Surrounded by swirling marchers, Stevenson seized Garth's arm and turned to him in disbelief. "What's happening, Dave? What's happening?"

"It's the people, Governor," Garth said. "They love you! They want you!"

The demonstration consumed the floor and the galleries for seventeen minutes. It subsided only after Garth and Sharon managed to guide Stevenson through the melee to the rostrum where [Governor] Collins [the evening's chairman] awaited him. With twenty or so volunteers, I had been watching on television from the press office at Stevenson headquarters down town. My eyes were filled with tears, and many of the volunteers were weeping and cheering at the same time. Now, we knew, Stevenson had only to speak out! The prize was within his grasp. His strategy had been perfect. Just say you want it, I was thinking. We saw Stevenson pause, taking another resounding blast of affection.

Then, after a few shaky words of greeting, he said: "I am grateful for this tumultuous and moving welcome. After going back and forth through the Biltmore today, I know who's going to be the nominee for this convention—the last man to survive."

Stevenson added a bit more, but nothing could recapture the crowd after such a lame joke. Stevenson's greatest of opportunities, the hope of our campaign, seemed all but wasted. He had missed it. Who can say why?

Thus, his second refusal of the kingly crown. The third came only a few hours later.

About midnight, Senator Herbert Lehman and former deputy New York City mayor Stanley H. Lowell gathered a group of the state's delegates in Bill Benton's hotel suite in the hope of galvanizing them into a reconsideration of New York's votes. Adlai not only said nothing new but insisted that he would not be "so immodest as to ask for [the nomination] again." He then went on to a larger, even more important gathering— some 250 delegates and alternates assembled by the draft movement leaders. They were excited, expectant; they had been encouraged to believe that Adlai, persuaded by popular demand, would now say, as Monroney had urged him to do, "I seek your nomination. I need your help." This time, his words were warm, eloquent, moving; but instead of the anticipated clarion call, he closed with the enigmatic message of Robert Frost's poem:

"The woods are lovely, dark and deep
"But I have promises to keep,
"And miles to go before I sleep,
"And miles to go before I sleep."

Eager listeners assumed this meant he had finally decided to fight for the nomination and would, as Attwood has written, "spend the night rallying support for his cause." So he was wildly cheered as he left the room. "But when I went up to his suite a few minutes later," Attwood added, "he was already in his pajamas."

Who can tell what might have happened if he had spent the night in a personal campaign for votes. North Dakota, another unit state, had split in a late Tuesday night caucus, going to Kennedy by only half a vote. Idaho, where the governor was a vice presidential hopeful, was shaky. There were unexploited opportunities in the large New York and California delegations. Lawrence would surely welcome an opportunity to return to Adlai in a later ballot. The speculation could go on. But not until the next morning, when it was too late, did he make a direct move to secure the nomination.

He sought to reach Mayor Daley, who, suspecting the purpose of the call, avoided it. Not until late in the afternoon, under pressure from Arvey claiming that he owed it to Adlai, did he return the call. Adlai said that while he had not sought the nomination, his name was nevertheless going to be placed before the convention. In that circumstance he wanted to know from Daley if the meager 2 votes out of 69 that the Illinois delegation had given him on Sunday was the full measure of his home base support. Daley replied curtly that it was. Daley slammed down the phone. Adlai's last chance was gone. He must have been bemused by the headlines in the afternoon newspapers: KENNEDY TIDE EBBS; KENNEDY'S BANDWAGON FALTERS.

Reality prevailed in his suite and in Kennedy's. Robert Kennedy called to ask Adlai directly to make one of the nominating speeches for his brother that evening. There are those who believe his refusal ended his chance to be secretary of state. Bill Blair and Willard Wirtz, who were with him throughout, doubt that is the case; that the animosities by then aroused in the Kennedy entourage would have blocked his selection in any event. "His declining reflected a characteristically level-headed, carefully considered, deliberate decision," Wirtz commented long after the event. "As I saw it then, and recall it now, his course all the way through was controlled and deliberate, reflecting so strong a desire to be President that he would take any honorable, even last ditch risk. Beneath that idealism was a toughness that few people knew."

The kingly crown was all but gone, but there was still one act of the drama to be played.

During the night, more than twenty-five thousand telegrams flooded into Western Union. Long-distance calls jammed the switchboard at the Paramount Building, with callers asking how to get messages to their state's delegations. All day Wednesday, volunteers carried the phone messages to delegates' hotels all over Los Angeles County.

In the Sports Arena, the nominating speeches began. Sam Rayburn's nomination of Lyndon Johnson had been followed by a large but rather mechanical demonstration. Orville Freeman's nomination of John Kennedy had been followed by a larger, more enthusiastic demonstration. The demonstration for Stuart Symington was almost perfunctory. Then, at 7:56, Chairman Collins recognized Wilson Wyatt of Kentucky, who promptly yielded to Senator Eugene McCarthy of Minnesota. There was an audible, visible stir as McCarthy strode to the platform for what White has called "the high point of drama" in the convention and, certainly, one of the finest nominating speeches ever made.

In a voice throbbing with emotion he reviewed Adlai's eight-year record of prophecy. "And so I say to you Democrats here assembled: Do not turn away from this man. Do not reject this man. He has fought gallantly. He has fought courageously. He has fought honorably. . . . He has made us all proud to be Democrats," he said, reminding them of the "calls to greatness."

> He did not say he possessed it. He did not even say he was destined for it. He did say the heritage of America is one of greatness and he described that heritage for us. . . . Do not reject this man who, his enemies said, spoke above the heads of the people, but they said it only because they did not want the people to listen. He spoke to the people. He moved their minds and stirred their hearts, and this was what was objected to. Do not leave this prophet without honor in his own party. . . . I submit to you a man who is not a favorite son of any one state. I submit to you a man who is the favorite son of fifty states . . . Adlai E. Stevenson of Illinois.

With that, a demonstration unprecedented in the memory of the Democratic party erupted. The only precedent that could be recalled was the uprising in the galleries of the 1940 Republican convention that helped Wendell Willkie win the nomination. Now, with the added excitement of live television, might it not happen again?

Suddenly, at least two thousand of the placard-waving supporters who had been marching outside poured into the hall. A guard at one of the main entrances had been lured away and replaced by a Stevensonian wearing a duplicate uniform that Dore Schary had made at a movie studio, and the imposter opened wide the gates. Awaiting them in the balcony were another two thousand or so. They had swelled their numbers by rotating over and over again the few tickets allotted to them to those waiting outside, by gathering unused tickets from friendly delegates, and by many who had put on Kennedy buttons and stood in line to get tickets allotted to Kennedy supporters.

On the floor, first dismay, and then pandemonium. Ten minutes into the demonstration, an all-girl brass band in handsome star-spangled uniforms appeared at the back of the hall and stepped smartly into the fray. Ted Meyers had hired them with the last small amount remaining in the treasury of the Associated Stevenson Clubs of California. Then, as band and banners snaked through the aisles, a giant papier-mâché "snowball"—made of petitions bearing more than a million signatures calling on the convention to "Draft Stevenson"—rolled out from behind the rostrum and floated above the crowd as though lifted on an invisible wave of enthusiasm. It had been driven all across the country by Harold Humes, a New York writer, gathering petitions all the way. Tom Morgan completes the description of the scene:

> Madly for Adlai, individual delegates, and then whole delegations, joined in the demonstration. In the New York section, the elder statesman Herbert Lehman fought a younger and opposing delegate for their state's stanchion, tore it free, and proudly flung himself into the maelstrom. Snake-dancing Californians undulated through neighboring delegations, hoping to attract the uncommitted like filings to a magnet. Before long, the stanchion of every state had been moved into the aisles and could be seen bobbing above the swirling human traffic.
>
> By my watch, the demonstration lasted twenty-seven minutes. It might have gone on that much longer had not the convention chairman, Gov. LeRoy Collins of Florida, dimmed the lights and silenced the band to restore order. Even when it was over, it was not really over. Eleanor Roosevelt came on to second the Stevenson nomination and started another stampede that convulsed the convention for fifteen minutes more!

It was, in reality, the last hurrah.

The roll call of the states began. By the time Washington was reached, Kennedy had 710 of the necessary 761. Wisconsin made it 748. The TV cameras focused on the Wyoming delegation where the candidate's youngest brother, Teddy, could be seen in its midst talking earnestly. All 15 of Wyoming's votes went to Kennedy, giving him 763. It was over on the first ballot.

Adlai had been watching the proceedings with friends in his hotel suite. Those with him say he gave not the slightest sign of hurt or disappointment. Grinning, he remarked that the time had again come for "some purple prose" and, with George Ball, went into another room to compose a statement. In his informal acceptance speech to the convention a short time later, Kennedy referred by name to Johnson, Symington, and the favorite sons, but pointedly made no mention at all of Adlai. On Friday evening, before a crowd of eighty thousand in the Los Angeles Coliseum, Adlai introduced the candidate for his formal acceptance speech, saying, "He will lead our people into a new and spacious era, not for us alone, but for our troubled, trembling world."

Saturday morning, mournful supporters swarmed around him as he prepared to leave the hotel. "I don't know why you are all so sorry," he told them. "I had no expectation of being a candidate again. You made me one, and it was a very happy, happy experience. The important thing now is to win in November." Somebody thrust into his hand a miniature golf club and an oversize golf ball, telling him it was a "do-it-yourself politician's kit." Laughing, he took it. "In Teddy Roosevelt's day it was 'Speak softly and carry a big stick.' Nowadays it's become, 'Don't talk, I'm putting.'" The crowd roared. Adlai smiled broadly, and climbed into the waiting limousine.

Some of his supporters left Los Angeles not only in sorrow, but in bitterness. "Yet, neither sorrow nor bitterness was warranted," Theodore H. White wrote. "Stevenson as an agent of American politics had left behind him such an infection as no other defeated candidate for President had ever left. He had left behind the virus of morality in the bloodstream of both parties; there was a permanent monument to him in the behavior and attitude of the victorious candidate; and also of his antagonists, the Republicans."

Tom Morgan, writing more than two decades later, saw in the young demonstrators "the vanguard of a new political style for America.

"The very essence of the Stevenson movement was about something new in participatory politics, the television audience and televised citizen action," he wrote.

> The struggle of media masses against the system was moving center stage in our political culture. The Stevenson phenomenon of 1960 would play back into the civil rights movement that was to peak in a few years. It would echo in the coming antiwar movement. . . . And perhaps most significantly, it would be reprised at the future's quadrennial Democratic national conventions as other outsiders struggled to become insiders through the powerful combination of mass and media. Not only did the Stevensonians give a hopeful start to the sixties in Los Angeles, but they also influenced a long, slow reformation of the Democratic party by blacks (1964), youth (1969), peaceniks (1972), women (1976), Kennedyites (1980), and by blacks again, and Hispanics and gays as well (1984).

Across the park from the Biltmore, the old Paramount Building, teeming with purposeful frenzy barely hours before, now in echoing emptiness awaited the wrecker's ball and bulldozer. Outside on the street, a young bearded, shirtless man in tattered jeans was loading his creaking car. He was recognized as one of those who had become that week one of the most creative and prolific of the placard painters. Along the backpack-encrusted body of his rusty wreck was emblazoned one last, heartfelt banner: IT'S BETTER TO HAVE LOVED AND LOST THAN NEVER TO HAVE LOVED AT ALL!

CHAPTER TWENTY
The Biggest Disappointment

FROM THE DAY OF Kennedy's nomination, Adlai focused his hopes on becoming secretary of state. So overt and sustained was his ambition that many have said he wanted to be secretary of state more than he wanted to be President. That is not the case. He was simply open and direct about being secretary of state. He could not know it, but from the very beginning he was doomed to disappointment.

Theodore Sorensen, in his superb biography of *Kennedy,* states that after the nomination, Adlai was never even seriously considered for the post. Nevertheless, both Kennedy and Adlai, in their separate ways and for their separate reasons, kept the question very much alive throughout the hard-fought battle with Mr. Nixon.

The issue was on the top of Adlai's agenda when he arrived back in his Chicago office on Monday, July 25, after vacationing with California friends in Santa Barbara, San Francisco, and Lake Tahoe. To an invitation from William Benton to cruise the Baltic aboard the *Flying Clipper,* Adlai immediately responded, "Baltic [beckons] but so does Kennedy. Deep regrets." More seriously, he turned to reports already surfacing that he would be passed over for secretary of state and offered the ambassadorship to the United Nations instead. Robert Hutchins was the source of one such report, which added that Kennedy preferred Chester Bowles because of his experience in Africa and Asia. In reply, Adlai pointed out that he had spent far more time than Bowles, not only in Africa and, except for India, Asia, but also in South America, the Middle East, and the Soviet Union.

The important report that would effect the launching of the new administration was from George Ball. He warned Adlai that if Kennedy won and offered the UN assignment, there would be acute embarrassment on all sides if he rejected it.

"You and I know that the function of the United States Ambassador to the United Nations is largely ritualistic and ministerial but the public does not know this. Your refusal to undertake the responsibility could easily be interpreted by a none-too-friendly press as sour grapes on your part. I think, therefore, that you might be well advised to clarify your position with Jack [now]." While a firm commitment at this time would be inappropriate and perhaps even illegal, Ball continued, Adlai should let Kennedy know he was interested "solely" in being secretary of state. Since the addition of Henry Cabot Lodge to the Nixon ticket would give it strong foreign policy credentials, Kennedy would "need desperately to associate you as closely as possible" with the campaign, and "this means that your bargaining position will probably never be higher than it is at the moment."

Ball suggested that Adlai not only indicate his willingness to campaign but propose "the desirability of your setting up an ad hoc group to formulate a specific foreign affairs program for execution during the first months of next year." The continuing deterioration of the administration's grip on foreign policy, he stressed, meant that the new administration must give evidence of its ability "to regain the diplomatic initiative." In the opening days of a Kennedy administration, foreign policy would present a situation akin to the domestic crisis in the first hundred days of Roosevelt in 1933. Therefore, Adlai should offer to prepare a program that Kennedy could take into office with him, which would have two objectives: specific actions to be undertaken the first six months to restore American leadership, and fresh formulation of long-term policy goals.

"Whatever you have to say to Jack, I am sure this is the time to say it." From this advice would arise the well-known Stevenson task force report to Kennedy that would influence policy, but not, as Adlai hoped, his objective of becoming the secretary of state who would implement the recommendations.

A trip to Hyannis Port to see Kennedy was arranged for the next weekend. "I am content," he wrote to Martha Matthews. "I thought it impertinent to seek a third nomination, and I did not. But the outpouring of love and loyalty across the country and in the streets of Los Angeles and at the convention surprised and moved me. . . . Of course I will campaign for the ticket. . . . Beyond the campaign I have no assurances of any kind nor can I ask any."

"The Kennedy operation was, as you know, powerfully financed and organized and prolonged and the consequences were virtually inevitable," he wrote Lady Spears. "But Kennedy is an able man and there should be no possible question in your mind about his superiority to

Nixon—one of the few people in my life I really deeply distrust and dislike."

He told Barbara Ward he would agree to "eight major speeches" in California, New York, Philadelphia, St. Louis, Denver, and "doubtless more will be added later." The "several million" Stevenson people "who are a little disaffected at present for a variety of reasons," would be needed "badly." Kennedy "will, of course, try to delay an indication about the Secretary of State and may not want me at all, also for a variety of reasons. But in any event I must and want to help as best I can even without assurances on that score." He asked all three of them to send him ideas for campaign speeches.

Arriving at Cape Cod on Friday afternoon, Adlai was met by Mr. and Mrs. David Bruce, Eunice Kennedy Shriver, and "200–300 Adlai addicts." The Bruces, at whose home he spent the night, would later go to London after Mr. Bruce accepted the ambassadorship, one of the three alternatives that would be offered to Adlai. The next day, the Schlesingers drove him to Chatham where he was to be the overnight guest of one of his college friends, Lorna Underwood, and her husband, George Sagendorph. Schlesinger's notes of the conversation en route observed:

> He said he had no expectation of being appointed Secretary of State, that he wasn't even sure that he wanted it or could serve with Kennedy. He felt Kennedy to be cold and ruthless, although he readily differentiated Jack from his brother in this respect and in certain contexts (especially foreign policy) expressed a high opinion of Jack. His mood was one of essential relaxation and composure, tinctured by a fairly mild streak of suspicion and resentment.

On Sunday morning, the Sagendorphs drove him "to Jack's at Hyannisport [sic]," he wrote to Marietta Tree,

> *and there followed five hours in the bosom—or the shark's teeth—of the Kennedy family ashore and afloat. Even the Black Prince [Robert] and wife were there. Jack talked of the campaign, the Jews, the Negroes, the farmers, and the N.Y. situation. He wants me to campaign extensively but details were deferred until his and Johnson's schedules are worked out. I promised him a memo on how to meet the Rep. attack on his youth and inexperience. And he also eagerly accepted my suggestion that he put someone to work on a post election and inauguration program of legislation and pronouncements to immediately take firm and resolute hold of foreign policy. And guess who got the job? There*

was no hint of post election plans re Sec. State etc. and I said nothing. So that remains where it was.

After recounting some of the problems they anticipated Kennedy would have with some of the ardent Stevensonians in New York, he included "one final morsel." "Jackie—soto [*sic*] voce 'I can't bear all those people peering over the fence. Eunice loves the whole horrible business. I may abdicate.' Adlai—likewise soto [*sic*] voce, 'Steady kid, you ain't seen nothin' yet.'" Then he added a poignant sentence reflecting the greatest missing ingredient in his life: "But what a fortunate fellow he is to have that large team of competent dedicated family around him—all knowing what to do!"

At the end of their meeting, they held a press conference at which Kennedy issued a statement that Adlai had drafted:

> Governor Stevenson will be advising me on foreign policy and on campaign strategy generally. I want to take advantage of his presidential and foreign experience. I expect to see him periodically and will talk with him by telephone from time to time. Because of his recent experience in Latin America and extensive travels in Africa I have sought his views on the current crises in those areas. I have also asked him for a review of the principal problems that will confront a new President.

During the questioning, Adlai did most of the talking. He would never be able to conceal a sense that the sixty-year-old veteran had more and better answers than the young and relatively inexperienced senator.

Kennedy told Schlesinger following the visit that not only was it satisfactory but, somewhat to his surprise, he found Adlai's political advice shrewd and realistic. Rather sadly, he said he wished he had better rapport with Adlai. He had it with Blair, and his wife had it with Adlai. He said he would not be asking for Adlai's help if he did not think of him "as playing a role" in his administration, and asked, "If you were me, would you appoint Stevenson Secretary of State?" Schlesinger said he would, and gave reasons. Kennedy listened without revealing a reaction.

The campaign, as Adlai had predicted, was "tough, rough and dirty." He had begun hoping that Kennedy would not have to respond to those attacking him on religious grounds, that others would do that for him, and that the bigots would create a backlash. He thought the latter was happening in the aftermath of a statement issued by a group of prominent Protestant clergymen who had formed a National Conference for Religious Freedom. Their statement, issued after a daylong closed meeting, opposed Kennedy on the ground that he would be unable to free himself from the "determined efforts" of the Catholic Church "to breach the wall of separation of church and state." Norman Vincent Peale, a friend of Nixon's, was chairman and spokesman of the conference, but in the uproar that followed the statement, he announced he was withdrawing. Adlai, contrasting Peale with Saint Paul, declared that while Saint Paul was appealing, Peale was appalling. The main result of the whole incident was to set the stage for Kennedy's later courageous and effective confrontation with the Protestant ministers at Houston.

The biggest challenge to Adlai in the campaign was to persuade his disappointed and disaffected supporters to campaign and vote for Kennedy. There were many who agreed with Eric Sevareid's column written soon after the Republican convention describing both candidates as junior business executive types with little to choose between them. All over the country, chapters of the Americans for Democratic Action that had campaigned for Adlai now were "sitting it out" or deciding reluctantly to endorse Kennedy; often making it clear it was their aversion to Nixon rather than their affection for Kennedy that motivated them. These were the voters Adlai most persistently and most effectively pursued. Some of them, he wrote Barbara Ward, are recommending "vote No on November 8 and keep the White House empty another four years." In the end, he wound up making not the eight addresses he had promised, but eighty-four in what were believed to be among the most crucial states.

Adlai's greatest contribution, however, had been made before the campaign began—that was the change in the equal-time requirement that made possible the Kennedy-Nixon debates. Without them, there is no doubt that the better-known Nixon would have won. Even so, the margin of victory was razor-thin.

In the national popular vote, Kennedy-Johnson led Nixon-Lodge by just 112,803 votes out of more than 68 million cast. A switch of fewer than 25,000 votes in five closely contested states lost by Nixon would have reversed the results. In eleven states, a shift of less than 1 percent of the votes would have switched the state's electoral votes. By carrying certain big states, Kennedy's margin in the Electoral College was more substantial—303 to 219.

This included Adlai's home state of Illinois, which Kennedy carried by fewer than 9,000 votes out of 4,757,000; votes, it was quickly alleged, that had been provided in questionable circumstances by Daley's machine. Significantly, Daley's planners had not invited Adlai to appear at the huge final-week rally for Kennedy in Chicago. Wry comments were made later that an invitation would have saved them a lot of late election-night juggling of votes.

New York, Pennsylvania, and New Jersey in the East, Illinois, Michigan, and Minnesota in the Midwest, strong Stevenson states where Adlai had campaigned extensively, went to Kennedy. California, where Adlai had campaigned with greater vigor than in any state except New York, was lost by a narrow margin—36,000 out of a total of more than 6.5

million, only after the counting of 260,000 absentee ballots. Victories in Texas and in other southern states could properly be credited to the margin provided by Johnson.

Theodore White, in his summation of Kennedy's victory, commented that "Stevenson changed the Democratic party almost as much as did Franklin D. Roosevelt, by trumpeting to its service scores of thousands of emancipated middle-class Americans who fit no neat category of occupations, traditions or pressure blocs."

Election Day, and the day before, Adlai had spent working on the foreign policy task force report for Kennedy with George Ball, Tom Finletter, and J. R. Schaetzel. What was in the hearts of many that day was expressed in a letter from his faithful friend, Jane Dick:

"It hurts me more than I can ever express to anyone—even perhaps to you—that circumstances and timing have been such as to deny America its potentially greatest president—and to deny to my most beloved friend the opportunity to serve—and lead!"

Adlai had not been deeply engaged in the work of the task force until the end of the campaign. After attending one group meeting at Mary Lasker's apartment in New York, his enlarged role in the campaign got in the way and he had turned the main responsibility over to George Ball. They had kept in touch by phone and by letter, especially during a brief flurry caused by Kennedy's appointment of another task force, to be headed by Paul Nitze, dealing with "national security." It was explained (to Adlai and Ball, but not publicly) that the involvement of Nitze, a Republican, was to bring bipartisanship into the picture and that the group would concentrate on security issues as distinguished from the broader issues of foreign policy and that there would be no overlap.

Adlai's communications with George Ball also included a letter he forwarded from Peter Grothe, a foreign relations consultant to Hubert Humphrey, proposing "a Peace Corps of 5,000 dedicated young men . . . to work in development projects in Asia, Africa, and Latin America." Adlai's comment was, "Perhaps this should go in your lesser ideas file."

Three days after the election, Adlai wrote two letters to Kennedy. The first, addressed to "Dear Jack," was appended to a more formal "Dear Mr. President" letter transmitting the task force report. Its main purpose was to provide a light touch to the heavier tome: "Do you remember the story about Lincoln when the White House corridors were crowded with job seekers, even the family living quarters, and the doctor told him he had a light case of smallpox. 'Open the door,' he said, 'and let 'em all in. At last I've got something I can give every one.'"

John Sharon, George Ball's able associate, had stayed behind to wait for Adlai to finish writing, and finally, in the late afternoon left for Palm Beach, Florida, where Kennedy was resting, with the letter and finished report. Adlai's letter, which emphasized the confidential nature of the report, said it had been reviewed "with general approval," by Senator William Fulbright, Chester Bowles, and David Bruce, and suggested "two broad *new* lines of policy in foreign economic policy and in nuclear cooperation within NATO." It also suggested "a new emphasis on disarmament." He felt that the report, for which Ball was largely responsible, was deficient in providing enough details on disarmament, East-West negotiation, and on ways to shift emphasis on aid programs from military assistance to economic development. More work needed to be done also on personnel. Finally, he called attention to the recent creation of the Organization for Economic Coordination and Development (OECD) along lines he had advocated three years earlier, and enclosed his *Look* articles on Africa and Latin America. It was a not-so-subtle reminder of the breadth of his foreign experience.

When Sharon presented the 150-page report to Kennedy at breakfast on Monday, November 14, he suggested that Kennedy might want to read the first seventeen pages. Kennedy said he wanted to read it "right now," and did. As he read, he asked Sharon questions about points made. When he got to the recommendation that he appoint a secretary of state promptly, he asked how many jobs in the State Department he would have to fill. Sharon volunteered that Adlai could provide a list with job descriptions, and Kennedy replied that that would be "most helpful," especially since his brother-in-law, Sargent Shriver, was already at work preparing lists of qualified people for top government jobs. He also asked for more information relating to OECD, and more facts on the effects of the economic blockade of Cuba. As he finished, he said, "Very good. Terrific. Just what I needed," and asked for the names of all those who had worked on the report.

An undated memo in Adlai's files, but written at this same time, outlined points to be made in talking to Kennedy about his qualifications for secretary of state. Point number one was "Decisiveness." It pointed out that as governor he had been "so decisive and effective (with a Rep. legislature) that he was drafted for Pres." Point number two was "Competance [*sic*]"; he briefly summarized not only his "lifetime interest in foreign affairs," but his seven years' experience in the Agriculture, Navy, and State departments. Point number three immodestly dealt with "Influence, respect, popularity," describing it "unequaled abroad by any American, including Ike!" Point number four, "Position at home," set forth "Twice nominee virtually without opposition. Respect evidenced by draft movement culminating in Los Angeles ovations—after keeping out of politics completely, except for DAC for four years and out of the country much of the time." Finally, he listed his efforts on Kennedy's behalf. "Between 60–75 speeches in 12 states during campaign. Host and speaker at fund raising affairs. Gave JK first national prominence by invitation to nominate AES in 1956 and throwing Vice Pres open to give him chance without offending Kefauver followers. Keeping out of the contest and strictly neutral for 4 years; doing *nothing* to encourage draft."

So very rarely did he ever engage in such explicit self-promotion, there could hardly be more dramatic evidence of how much he wanted to be secretary of state. In letters, however, he was insisting that he did not want the job unless Kennedy wanted him, "and badly."

Prompt action on the appointment of the secretary of state was one recommendation in the report on which Kennedy pointedly was not acting. Shriver's energetic efforts to fit people to jobs were moving ahead and appointment after appointment was announced or became known. Kennedy was subjected to a persistent bombardment on Adlai's behalf from many of his own supporters as well as Adlai partisans such as Mrs. Roosevelt. Adlai, too, was gently prodding with memos of further conversations with Ambassador Menshikov bearing messages from Khrushchev, a memo from an American industrialist with business interests in Guinea about threatened Soviet penetration, and correspondence with a leading Chilean about the "explosive" situation in Latin America.

Kennedy had added to his note of thanks for the task force report urgent requests for further reports on Latin America, Africa, and the U.S. Information Agency (USIA). He was considering a hemispheric meeting that turned out to be the Punta del Este conference held in Uruguay in the summer of 1961, at which the Alliance for Progress was established. In the exchange of notes on these additional activities, he told Adlai he would be returning to Washington about December 1 and hoped to see him shortly thereafter.

Bill Blair went to Washington and on Tuesday, December 6, saw the President-elect. His telephone call reporting the meeting was not what Adlai wanted to hear. Adlai's notes of the conversation record that Kennedy was "not prepared" to appoint him secretary of state. The appointment would be too "controversial" and Kennedy did not want to start his administration on a note of controversy. The closeness of the election and the "belligerence" of the Republicans would make relations with Congress difficult. His decision was no reflection on Adlai's "qualities or capabilities" and he repeated that the decision was based on his conviction that the appointment would be "too controversial." (Adlai wrote after that, "Poppycock".)

Kennedy was considering Senator Fulbright, David Bruce, and Dean Rusk for the post. He had a high opinion of Fulbright but he had joined with the southerners on civil rights issues. Bruce was good but had "no fire in his belly." Kennedy did not know Rusk. Bowles also was "too controversial" but might be appointed undersecretary. Adlai could have his choice of three posts, attorney general, ambassador to Britain, or ambassador to the United Nations. Kennedy hoped very much it would be the latter. He then proceeded to try to persuade Adlai to accept the appointment.

He regarded State, Treasury, Defense, and the UN ambassadorship as the four most important posts in his administration. G. Mennen Williams, as assistant secretary of state for African affairs, would be more important than Secretary of Health, Education, and Welfare Abraham Ribicoff. Adlai would have Cabinet rank. It was absurd to suggest, as he had heard, that the UN post would have nothing to do with policy; Adlai would make policy in whatever job he held, and he would always have the President's ear. With Khrushchev scheduled to come in the spring, it would be important to have Adlai at the UN. He laughed off a Joseph Alsop column saying that Stevenson, at Hyannis Port, had urged the "kind of a compromise at Berlin which would have left freedom of the city quite largely dependent on the reliability and good faith of Soviet guarantees." He then appealed to Adlai's patriotic spirit and asked him to come to Washington on Thursday afternoon to see him and make it possible for him to announce the appointment.

At the end of Blair's report, Adlai blurted, "How many times do I have to tell you I won't be Ambassador to the UN?"

All day Tuesday and until he left for Washington late on Wednesday, there was a flurry of meetings, including a deskside sandwich lunch with Arvey, and telephone conversations with Senators Humphrey and Monroney, Congressman Sid Yates, Lloyd Garrison, Marietta Tree, members of his family, and others; virtually all of them urging him to accept. His argument was that he had served at the UN, he knew the job to be one of advocacy rather than one of policy-making and direction. The latter was his real interest; he was not interested in being an advocate for the policies of an administration whose foreign policy aims were still so unclear.

He spent Wednesday night at the George Balls', where they argued until two in the morning, with Adlai insisting that he should not accept. Ball, as he did so often, laid out the hard realities. As secretary of state, Adlai would be opposed by conservative Catholics, Nixon, and McCarthyites. More important, all of the key figures in Truman's White House—Dean Acheson, Charles Murphy, and Paul Nitze—were opposed to him. Still more important, Kennedy's closest associates, led by his brother, were bitter over Adlai's conduct in Los Angeles and in the primaries. He had a great role to play in the UN. He was in a position to attach conditions to his acceptance. If he refused simply because he wanted to be secretary of state, he would be considered a bad sport. If he accepted and it did not work out, he could resign, having been a good soldier. Basically, without an active role he would be miserable. There was no way of predicting how things would develop and he would find far more satisfaction inside than out. Ball has said he was convinced that Adlai's negative arguments were merely his way of evoking the positive reasons for taking the appointment.

On Thursday afternoon, Adlai went to Kennedy's Georgetown

home. It is not clear whether his notes on the conversation were written before or after the meeting, but they begin, "I'll be Frank—Expected Sec. State." It went on to stress that administration and policy-making, not representation, were his interests. His notes indicate that Kennedy stressed the importance of the assignment and underscored, "Save UN! Will depend on US." Questions about his role in policy-making were raised along with inquiry as to who would be secretary of state. Adlai said bluntly that he would not accept if there was truth in the rumor that McGeorge Bundy would be secretary of state. "I won't work for that young Republican," he declared. Kennedy said he was leaning toward Dean Rusk, whom he had met, for the first time, that morning, but he assured Adlai that "I'll be your boss. You can have a direct line to me."

This exchange resulted in misunderstanding that would leave a long-term scar. Adlai thought he had made it clear he would not decide until he knew who was to be secretary of state. Kennedy thought his assurance of direct access answered that concern.

When they emerged from the meeting, they encountered a crowd of Stevensonians, largely Georgetown University students, waving placards urging Adlai's appointment as secretary of state. From the steps of his red-brick house, Kennedy announced the offer he had made and added: "I can think of no American who would fill this responsibility with greater distinction. . . . I regard this as one of the three or four most important jobs in the entire Administration. . . . The job is part of the Cabinet and it is my hope, if Governor Stevenson accepts the position, that he will attend Cabinet meetings and will serve as a strong voice in foreign policy over its entire range. He has always answered the call of duty on every other occasion in his life, and I am hopeful that he will find it possible to serve the United States in this most vital position."

In response, Adlai told the crowd and the reporters among them: "I appreciate Senator Kennedy's confidence, and I share his view about the difficulty and the importance of this assignment. The United Nations is the very center of our foreign policy, and its effectiveness is indispensable to the peace and security of the world. While I have not sought this assignment, I want to be helpful. I have some matters both of the organization of the work and of ways and means of strengthening that I want to consider and discuss with him further. I hope to do this in the very near future."

"Are we to understand you have not accepted it?" a reporter asked.

"I have not accepted it, pending a further talk," Adlai replied, ". . . which I hope will be very soon."

"I hope it will be before the middle of next week," Kennedy said, and went inside. Adlai left immediately for Chicago.

Although Bill Blair had warned Kennedy that Adlai would not accept until he knew who was going to be secretary of state, Robert Kennedy wrote later: "The President was shocked. Of all the conversations he ever had with major figures over a period of five years, one of the most unsatisfactory was when he invited Stevenson to become Ambassador to the UN. He was absolutely furious." Theodore Sorensen's more measured account says that Adlai's inquiring about the job and who would be secretary of state was "different from the reaction from everyone else. . . . Everyone else was accepting with pride and pleasure. So this naturally also impaired their relationship. All this is essential to understand their relationship later."

Hard bargaining, not normally associated with Adlai, then ensued. More experienced in the ways of the bureaucracy than Kennedy was at that point, Adlai was not beguiled by the promise that he would always have the President's ear. He knew that, with the best of intentions, layers of bureaucracy inevitably would intervene between the White House and an ambassador in New York receiving his instructions through the State Department. Those familiar with the operations of the U.S. Mission in New York and its relations with Washington officialdom are impressed by the sophistication and extent of the conditions Adlai attached to his acceptance. His longhand memo—"Notes on Negotiations with Senator Kennedy—Regarding UN Post"—used for a joint telephone conference with Kennedy and Rusk on December 11 are not clear on the agreements reached. There would later be discussion as to whether it was agreed the UN should be *the* center of foreign policy, or *a* center of foreign policy. The evidence is clear that he got what he wanted in organizing the U.S. Mission to the United Nations; on policy questions, the evidence is mixed; and the personal relations, complex at the outset, would become more so.

I have something to say about *job* before I could accept it.

1. My tastes & experience—executive, administrative & creative—not legislative or representational. Don't know whether I can do this job or will care for it, but willing to try if JK and Sec. want me to—*and* are sympathetic to following suggestions.

1. Member of Cabinet.

2. Option to attend NSC [National Security Council] when foreign policy matters considered.

3. Should be in mainstream of policy making. No important decisions without opportunity to express views. How? (a) Restore traditional position of "counsellor" to Sec'y level—Amb. to UN is "senior advisory" to Secy extending beyond UN.

4. Free hand with staff in Wash. and N.Y.—or at least a veto. . . .

5. Assign 3 deputies to Ambassadorial rank to N.Y.

6. Chief of Mission & senior members of staff-adequate

quarters and representation allowance. Congress (Have to appropriate funds?).

7. Better coordination between State & Defense on UN matters.

8. Clear definition of attitude toward UN and conceptual idea of mission. UN center of our foreign policy. Will use it more—not just occasionally in desperation as Dulles did.

a. To preserve UN as center of our foreign policy ag. Soviet attacks.

b. Create feeling that we want to end the cold war as soon as poss. To win support of less developed countries.

(1) Channel more of our aid through UN. Point when UN can't absorb.

(2) Hold more conferences at all levels under UN auspices.

c. Our aid not just anti Comist but pro improvement of std of living literacy, health, etc.

9. I'll be consulted about organization and direction of disarmament. Negotiations should be resp. to *Sec. State*. [He then listed the names of Arthur Dean and Bill Foster. Kennedy appointed Foster to head the Arms Control and Disarmament Agency.]

10. U.S. should get on offensive not just defensive: for example—we should press USSR to speed econ. dev. [of underdeveloped nations].

a. Join [World] Bank & [International Monetary] Fund & DLF [Development Loan Fund].

Whatever the uncertainties about the agreement reached, enough of the points were answered to his satisfaction so that the next day Kennedy announced the appointments of Dean Rusk as secretary of state and Adlai E. Stevenson as United States ambassador to the United Nations.

The same day, Adlai held a press conference in Chicago and began discussions with his partners about the future of the law firm, and that night went to a University of Chicago theater and dinner party, taking the recently widowed Mrs. Walter Paepcke, sister of Paul Nitze, who now seemed increasingly to be favored over Suzie Zurcher. The next morning he flew to New York to see people he knew at the U.S. Mission to the UN, lunch with Secretary General Dag Hammarskjöld, meet again with Ambassador Menshikov, Krishna Menon of India, and George Kennan. At a meeting with his New York law partners it was decided that he should resign from the firm. Then, at the law office, he and Dean Rusk held a joint press conference in which Rusk emphasized Kennedy's intention that Adlai would "play a key role" in the formulation of foreign policy. Rusk, who had been assistant secretary of state for international organizations in the Truman administration and had headed the Draft Stevenson group in his hometown of Scarsdale, described himself and Adlai as "friends and future colleagues," adding that Adlai probably knew more about the UN than any other American.

Back in Chicago the next day, Adlai began work on organizing his new office. A note from Senator Wayne Morse, who had just served on a delegation to the UN General Assembly, recommended a "housecleaning." Adlai's notes indicate he was already considering Francis Plimpton; Charles Yost, then ambassador to Morocco; Philip Klutznick, a leading Chicago businessman prominent in many Jewish organizations; and Marietta Tree, who later would be joining him; Dorothy Fosdick, Barry Bingham, and Ellsworth Bunker, who would not. Also, he promptly proposed a visit to Chicago to Harlan Cleveland, dean of the Maxwell Graduate School of Citizenship and Public Affairs at Syracuse University, and former editor of *The Reporter* magazine, whom he had come to know earlier when a possible relationship with the magazine was discussed.

Cleveland recalls that during their day-long conversation, it became apparent that Adlai had read almost everything he had ever written—and that was a great deal. Unlike Rusk, who had been for Adlai, Cleveland had been head of Citizens for Kennedy in upstate central New York, although he barely knew Kennedy. A few days later, Cleveland was offered the key spot of assistant secretary of state for international organizations—Adlai's principal connection to the foreign policy apparatus— and he accepted. Although the position was a presidential appointment, the record indicates the decision was Adlai's.

A note on a telephone conversation with the President-elect, in which Adlai informed him that Cleveland had been "signed up," reported he was going to make offers to Klutznick; Jonathan Bingham, who had been recommended by Averell Harriman; and Charles P. Noyes, with whom he had worked in London and San Francisco. Clearly, the agreement to give him a free hand in organizing the United States Mission was being honored. His notes on the same conversation show that his recommendation of Tom Finletter as ambassador to NATO had been accepted, and that the President would ask Mrs. Roosevelt to serve on the UN General Assembly session meeting in March.

They discussed several possibilities for appointment to the UN Human Rights Commission that had achieved such prestige during Mrs. Roosevelt's incumbency and her leadership in drafting the Universal Declaration of Human Rights; most notably, Marietta Tree and Gladys Tillett, Democratic national committeewoman from North Carolina. Kennedy leaned in favor of Mrs. Tillett. In the end, she was appointed the United States representative to the UN Commission on the Status of Women and Marietta received the Human Rights Commission assignment.

He was busy, too, on other personnel fronts. Adlai wrote Chester

Bowles that a letter from Jo Forrestal, the widow of James Forrestal, who had blocked his Navy Department promotion, revealed a strong interest in becoming ambassador to Ireland. He recommended Harold Taylor, president of Sarah Lawrence College, "if anything comes of the Peace Corps idea." He wrote Mayor Daley suggesting that Jane Dick be made Democratic national committeewoman for Illinois. He had better luck with Kennedy than he did with Daley.

In celebration of Adlai's appointment, Buffie opened the old house in Bloomington and gave a Christmas Eve party for about two hundred people. Adlai drove back to Chicago on Christmas Day for dinner with Ad, Nancy, and his grandchildren, and found a family utterly distraught. The story that follows is taken from the 1964 court proceedings in which the three boys joined with Ellen's mother, Mrs. Carpenter, to have Ellen declared incapable of handling her financial affairs by reason of "mental and emotional disturbances," and to obtain the appointment of a conservator.

Ad had invited his mother to have Christmas Day lunch with the family. The mental illness afflicting her had continued its insidious progression. The once lovely, tastefully dressed belle now was frequently seen on Chicago's streets in a baggy pullover sweater and sneakers. As often happens in such cases, she behaved most vindictively toward those most earnestly seeking to help. The club and center for artists that she had set up in her mother's house at 1020 Lake Shore Drive had been, in financial terms at least, a dubious undertaking from the start. She would tell the children she was making a fortune with it while at the same time asking them for money to keep it open. Finally, it had to be closed and the furnishings auctioned off. A set of two candlesticks had not been sold and Mrs. Carpenter had given them to Nancy.

There was a happy exchange of presents and everyone then went into the dining room for lunch. Ellen noticed the candlesticks on the sideboard. She turned on Nancy, declaring, "You are a thief. You have stolen my candlesticks." While Nancy tried to explain that they were a gift from Ellen's mother, she kept calling Nancy a thief; Ad and the children sat stunned. Weeping, Nancy retreated to the kitchen to pull herself together. As she brought in the soup course, she said, "I'm sorry. There's been a misunderstanding, and I don't care that much about the candlesticks, of course, and please won't you take them?" Ellen now called her not only a thief but also a son of a bitch and a liar. Finally, Nancy said, "Please, this is Christmas and the children are here. Let's sit down and have lunch and please let's not mention this again during Christmas." With that, the lunch proceeded in quiet. When Ellen left, Nancy gave her the candlesticks. A few days later Nancy found them on the doorstep.

At the office the next morning, Adlai found a telegram from Sorensen requesting suggestions for the Inaugural Address by December 31.

He went to work immediately and on December 30 mailed an extended memo, purposely dealing only with foreign policy, and setting forth eleven points for consideration. It placed heavy stress on disarmament, called for recognition of a special responsibility for Latin America, "*perhaps* a conditioned hint of re-examination of our China policy," and wondered, "What about a proposal to put all space exploration under UN control?" He appended an even longer memo containing "Some Miscellaneous Paragraphs."

Several of his ideas, with the language more carefully honed by Sorensen and the President, appeared in the memorable Inaugural Address.

Friday the thirteenth was to be the last day Adlai would spend in his Chicago law office. The packing, the visitors, and the calls were interrupted by a long telephone conversation with Kennedy. His notes report his saying that "the most important thing that this administration has to do . . . is to discover what is on K[hrushchev]'s mind." The "only way I know of" to do this "would be by direct talks in Moscow without formality by somebody who is not the diplomatic agent but someone who corresponds to Khrushchev's concept of power. That is a political figure rather than a diplomatic one." After a discussion of the subjects of such a mission, Adlai was asked, "Who would be the best one to talk to K?" and responded, "The unhappy thing is the best one is me." Even though "it would come at an awkward time, I would do this if it were deemed wise and helpful." A possible alternative was Averell Harriman. Kennedy said he would be seeing him at the Inauguration and they would talk about it again.

Nothing ever happened. In view of the stridently unsuccessful meeting between the new President and Khrushchev in Vienna a few months later, and the possible link of the impressions gained there to the later Cuban missile crisis, it is tempting to speculate how history might have been different if the way to Vienna had been paved as Adlai suggested.

The last day in the office, marking the end of a remarkably happy and prosperous relationship, was not a joyous one. A picture of Adlai and his partners captured the mood. He sat behind his desk, piled high as always with papers and standing behind him in a semicircle were Blair, Ed McDougal, Wirtz, and John Hunt towering over the shorter Newt Minow. Adlai's sad eyes stared straight into the camera; his set jaw and straight mouth showed no hint of the usual smile. Melancholy was reflected also on the faces of his partners.

There was an extra dimension of sadness in the knowledge that Carol Evans, his discreet and indefatigable secretary of thirteen years, would not be going to New York with him. Her reluctance to move to New York, added to Adlai's frank acknowledgment that the knowledge of languages and other cultures possessed by her skilled associate, Roxanne Eberlein, would give Roxanne a senior classification, decided her in favor of a parting. It was painful for both of them. "The Guv" helped in finding her another position. Her fidelity to him was manifested again years later when she joined Walter Johnson, editor of *The Papers of Adlai E. Stevenson,* as his assistant editor.

The law firm quickly dissolved. Bill Blair was named ambassador to Denmark and then later to the more difficult embassy in the Philippines. Willard Wirtz was made undersecretary of labor, and after Arthur Goldberg's resignation to go to the Supreme Court, he became secretary of labor in the Johnson administration. Newton Minow was to become chairman of the Federal Communications Commission and became famous for his characterization of television as a "vast wasteland." Adlai joked, "I regret that I have but one law firm to give to my country."

On Wednesday, January 18, he appeared before the Senate Foreign Relations Committee for his confirmation hearing. It was a generally friendly encounter; only once did Chairman Fulbright intervene to divert a slightly hostile inquiry from Iowa Republican Senator Bourke Hickenlooper. The committee's favorable recommendation was quickly approved by the Senate.

As the round of Inauguration parties began, Adlai was pleased at the numbers that crowded about him in the midst of the electric enthusiasm for the new First Family. On the cold, snowy day that clogged the streets of the capital, Adlai, along with other members of the Cabinet, sat on the platform behind the President as he was sworn into office. After the ceremony, as the procession of limousines started down Capitol Hill toward the reviewing stand at the White House, Adlai discovered that he, alone among those of Cabinet rank, had not been assigned a limousine. In the biting wind he walked the long distance to the White House. His feet were cold, but his heart was warmed by the cheers of people recognizing him walking among them. This lapse in the otherwise meticulous and efficient arrangements was not the last slight he would receive from the unforgiving "Irish Mafia" surrounding the President.

CHAPTER TWENTY-ONE

From Crisis to Crisis with Kennedy

ON SUNDAY, JANUARY 22, 1961, Adlai flew to New York to begin his career as United States ambassador to the United Nations. It was the job he least wanted; it was also the one that most established his reputation; much of it based on two events that erupted on the fringes of his main efforts.

Crises are frequent visitors to the UN; it is usually their port of last resort. As Adlai arrived to present his credentials to Secretary General Dag Hammarskjöld, many crises were waiting on the doorstep. One already had crashed through, bringing into the corridors and Security Council chambers the chaos that had bathed the Congo in blood since it had gained its independence six months earlier. The agonized death throes of a colony important to European economic interests would kill Hammarskjöld, nearly kill the UN, and would cover Adlai with scars of battle in Washington as well as New York.

The Congo occupied an area about the size of the United States east of the Mississippi. The boundaries had been drawn to fit the reach of the European colonists rather then the loyalties of the inhabitants. Internally, it was shredded into fragments, led by dozens of tribal chieftains whose rivalries generally had been contained by the ruling Belgian authorities. Within days of its independence on June 30, 1960, utter chaos took over. At the request of the first premier, Patrice Lumumba, a former postal clerk, the UN sent troops assembled from member states other than the great powers. It was hoped this formula would avert the confrontation inherent in the only other assemblage of UN forces, Korea.

Vastly oversimplified, this is the situation that confronted Adlai and the new administration: The mineral-rich Katanga Province had seceded; Lumumba and Hammarskjöld had clashed over the latter's refusal to use UN forces to end Katanga's secession. Hammarskjöld at the same time was in increasing disrepute with Britain, France, and Belgium because they wanted to maintain their hold on the Congo's vast mineral resources and wanted to limit the role of the UN. Lumumba had turned to the Soviet Union for help in putting down the Katanga secession and the latter had seized the opportunity to establish a foothold in Africa. This brought it into conflict with Hammarskjöld and the UN.

The United States' role had been equivocal: Public support for independence in Africa was accompanied by practical support for the measures desired by the colonial powers; mainly in terms of advocating a go-slow policy in the UN, while also supporting Hammarskjöld in his opposition to Russian support of Lumumba's anti-Katanga drive. While the country had been preoccupied with the 1956 election, Hungary, and the Middle East, Lumumba had been taken into custody by the military leader of the central government, Colonel Joseph Mobutu. Finally, the UN learned with dismay that he had been turned over to his archenemy, Moise Tshombe, the leader of the Katanga secession, who, it was widely assumed, would not hesitate at assassination.

During Khrushchev's visit to the UN in September 1959, the support of Lumumba had been converted into an assault on the UN itself. He called on Hammarskjöld to resign and demanded that he be replaced by a "troika," a three-man secretariat, one from a Communist country, one from the West, and one from a neutral country, with each one possessing a veto. By the time Adlai arrived, the attacks on Hammarskjöld were growing in intensity, there was a pro-Western government in Leopoldville, the Tshombe secessionist group held Elizabethville and much of Katanga, another secessionist group was in Stanleyville, the pro-Soviet Lumumba was in jail, and anarchy was everywhere.

Concern over Lumumba's fate permeated nearly every UN discussion. Usually unspoken was the realization that far more than the life of Lumumba, or even of the Congo was at stake. During the eight years of the Eisenhower administration, the number of UN member states had grown from sixty to ninety-nine. Nearly all the new states were arriving at the UN from Asia and Africa to assert their hard-won nationhood. Katanga's secession and Lumumba's resistance to it posed in dramatic terms the question of whether the former colonial masters were, in fact, prepared to tolerate independence or would resort to various devices to continue their control.

The European-African struggle was waged with almost equal intensity and quiet animosity at both ends of Pennsylvania Avenue. The Europeans, and especially the Belgian mining interests, had determined supporters on Capitol Hill. In the State Department the lines had long been drawn between those oriented toward Europe and the importance of Europe's power and position in the cold war, and the so-called "woolheads" who emphasized coming to terms with the aspirations of the new nations. In the struggle over the Congo, the previously polite debate escalated into bitterness, with the Pentagon and significant elements in the Central Intelligence Agency siding with the State Department's hitherto dominant Europeanists. Being linked with the "wool-heads" was only part of the price Adlai would pay for winning many of his battles with the Europeanists; the poison of their animosity would be injected into other issues and into his relations with Kennedy and Rusk.

Adlai's prestige in the diplomatic world was demonstrated persuasively at his first appearance in the Security Council on February 1. The outpouring of tributes included lavish praise from the Soviet Union and China, as well as Britain and France, the United Arab Republic, and the African and Latin American states. After using his old joke about flattery being fine as long as it wasn't inhaled, he put his prestige to work promptly. Against the opposition of Britain and France and their State Department supporters, the President accepted Adlai's argument that the United States should support Hammarskjöld's initiatives (some of which Adlai had helped devise). At one of the most tense moments in one of the numerous crises, the President, after a telephone conversation with Adlai, expressed to one of his associates his surprise at Adlai's toughness. "Adlai's got an iron ass and, my God, in this job, the nerve of a burglar."

By February 7, Nigeria and India, to the dismay of Ambassador Valerian Zorin of the Soviet Union, switched their support, bringing other votes with them. The long, intricate negotiations, marked by Lumumba's murder, Hammarskjöld's death in a still-unexplained airplane crash in Africa, and other recurring crises need not be recorded here. The remarkable—historic is not too strong a word—achievement was the ultimate success of the efforts to keep the Congo united and return control to its own central government. The martyred Hammarskjöld was the central hero, but Adlai's success in rallying his own government behind Hammarskjöld and winning the support of the significant African, Asian, and Latin American states was critical to the outcome.

The murder of Lumumba by Katanga forces became known on February 13 and killed Adlai's hopes for more constructive relations with the Soviet Union. Zorin, who had been invited to lunch that day at Adlai's Waldorf-Astoria residence, canceled at the last minute, and announced that the Soviet Union would no longer recognize Hammarskjöld, the "organizer" of Lumumba's murder, as the Secretary General of the UN. The United States, he charged, was a leader in the "hypocritical maneuvers" in the Security Council. The rhetoric became even more shrill when Foreign Minister Andrey Gromyko arrived in March for the resumed session of the General Assembly. To Adlai, who had hoped dialogue with the Soviet Union could continue on a reasonable basis, Gromyko's speech "was in the worst and most destructive traditions of the cold war." Replying to Gromyko the same day he told the Assembly that the Soviet Union was demanding surrender to anarchy, and that its "wild and irresponsible and absurd attacks" were evidence that "the Soviet Union does not regard our Organization as a means of international cooperation but simply as an instrument of international discord."

Thus was signaled the launching of a campaign that threatened to kill the UN as well. The plan to replace the Secretary General with a troika was, in the American view, an effort to make the office an instrument of Soviet policy and, in the end, destroy the UN. Although that effort finally was thwarted, the refusal of the Russians and the French to pay their shares of the expenses of the UN forces in the Congo would lead to another major crisis during Adlai's life and leave a legacy that haunts the UN to this day.

Other issues plagued those hectic opening months.

In the eyes of the Africans, another major test already was on the table when Adlai arrived—Angola, then ruled by Portugal. Like Belgium, Portugal was a NATO ally, and had the backing of the Pentagon, the State Department's Europeanists, and such sharply unrelenting advocates as former Secretary of State Dean Acheson. Portugal also was an ally that adamantly refused to recognize Angola's right to independence, maintaining that it was not a colony but an overseas province of Portugal itself. In the final months of the Eisenhower administration, in an effort to head off a Soviet initiative, the United States had joined with Afro-Asian delegations to draft a resolution endorsing the "granting independence to all colonial countries and principles." At the last minute, President Eisenhower had acceded to pressure from British Prime Minister Harold MacMillan and instructed the United States delegation to abstain. Dismay and feelings of betrayal were left behind among the Africans, who felt they had modified their stands to meet United States wishes.

On February 4, the simmering unrest in Angola broke into violence. As killing spread from the capital city of Luanda into the countryside, the Soviet Union, the United Arab Republic, and Ceylon joined to bring the issue before the UN. Battle lines already drawn in Washington over the Congo quickly stretched to Angola while the African states and their supporters watched to see if the Kennedy administration would reverse the Eisenhower stand. It did. Kennedy's interest in Africa, growing out of his advocacy of Algerian independence while a senator, put him behind Adlai, Bowles, Assistant Secretary G. Mennen Williams, and his able deputy Wayne Fredericks, in what was seen as a pivotal internal struggle to shift away from almost automatic support of NATO interests as against those of the third world. The Afro-Asian resolution calling for the establishment of a subcommittee to look into the situation in Angola was defeated in the Security Council by British and French vetoes, but this seemed far less important than the fact that the United States had voted with the three Afro-Asian sponsors and the Soviet Union in support. The perceived shift in United States policy was enhanced by continuing support for the resolution in the General Assembly, where, after the Portuguese delegation angrily walked out, it was finally adopted.

The American position on Angola unquestionably strengthened American efforts in the far more explosive situation in the Congo, but it intensified the antagonisms of the Europeanists. They regarded continuation of landing rights in Portugal's Azores as more important than Angola or the reactions of the weak African states. Such security issues would increasingly cause them to regard Adlai as "soft" and embitter later struggles over larger issues. Former Undersecretary of State Robert D. Murphy, leader in the American Council of NATO, for example, promptly told Adlai that the Soviet attack on colonialism was simply a smokescreen for its attack on Europe itself, and that "the spectacle" of the United States voting with the Soviet Union against her own NATO allies was "a matter of deep concern." Adlai wrote in response: "I hope that neither you nor your colleagues have any doubts about my own or the Administration's recognition of the fundamental importance of NATO. . . . At the same time I am sure you will agree that the age of colonialism in Africa is coming rapidly to an end." Events would demonstrate he was much too sanguine.

The alignment of forces spotlighted by Africa extended into the complex and technical debates over disarmament that also began in those early months. The Geneva Conference on the Discontinuance of Nuclear Weapons Tests was scheduled to resume work in March with Ambassador Arthur H. Dean representing the United States. General disarmament negotiations were scheduled to begin soon thereafter under the leadership of John J. McCloy. Adlai's efforts to participate in the policy reviews leading up to these sessions provide the first example of the difficulty of trying to influence policy in Washington while under severe pressure from immediate events in New York.

To Adlai, "general and complete disarmament" was central to developing world community under world law; any retreat from such emphasis damaged not only the UN but the place of the U.S. in world opinion. The UN and world opinion were not major concerns of McCloy, Robert Lovett, and Dean Acheson, nor was disarmament high on the President's agenda in those early months of his administration. "His initial interest in disarmament," Sorensen has written, "was largely for propaganda reasons—a desire to influence neutral and 'world opinion.'" Although he later "underwent a degree of redemption on this subject," it would be an important element in the tensions that built up between the

President and Adlai. Meanwhile, it made Adlai vulnerable to charges by such sharp and knowledgeable critics as Dean Acheson that sentimentalism over the end of colonialism and vague hopes for disarmament endangered the security of Europe.

Communist China's admission to the UN was another issue that came early and stayed into the Nixon administration. Nationalist China's ambassador, T. F. Tsiang, sought an appointment almost immediately to protest mildly but pointedly that Adlai's testimony before the Senate Foreign Relations Committee struck his government as being "defeatist" on preventing the admission of Communist China. If anything, Adlai's statement had been a more cautious expression of views he had expressed during the campaign; it was also one of the particulars in Kennedy's argument that Adlai was too "controversial" to be secretary of state. It was necessary to face the fact, Adlai told the ambassador, that the votes for refusing admission were declining each year and the present policy was headed toward failure. When Tsiang asked if he supported a two-China approach, Adlai replied it was "a possibility worth exploring." His government could not accept such a policy, Tsiang said. Did he have any alternatives to suggest? Adlai inquired. He had none.

In reporting the conversation to the State Department, Adlai urged that the issue be given high priority. It was on the agenda of meetings with the prime ministers of Britain, Australia, and New Zealand in March and April, augmented by an intransigent letter to the President from Chiang Kai-shek. White House, State Department, and U.S. Mission all recognized the inevitable, but the President's narrow margin of victory and his still-uncertain relations with Congress made him want to postpone a decision on such a controversial issue as long as possible.

These were only the major issues crowding into those early months. Events moved so swiftly and Adlai received so much publicity that the President began to wonder if his UN ambassador might be operating independently. He had not really regarded the UN as the central instrument of foreign policy and suddenly Adlai was making it seem so. His inquiries satisfied him that Rusk and Cleveland were in control, but he insisted that he wanted to know what was happening at the UN without having to read it first in *The New York Times*. Finally, Cleveland worked out with McGeorge Bundy and Arthur Schlesinger, Jr., at the White House a system of ensuring that the President would have available for reading before going to bed a memo that would inform him about any UN development that might be on the front pages the next day.

All this activity and more were shoved into the background in early April by the Bay of Pigs.

The plan, or rather, alternative plans, for the invasion of Cuba by Cuban refugees trained and equipped by the United States had originated in the CIA during the Eisenhower administration. Kennedy had been informed of it as President-elect and, after his inauguration, the various proposals had become the center of intense planning and debate—among a strictly limited number of people in the top reaches of the White House, CIA, and State and Defense departments. Adlai was not among them, although Senator William Fulbright, chairman of the Senate Foreign Relations Committee, was. As the operation got under way, the President, aware that Adlai was facing a debate in the General Assembly over a Cuban charge of aggressive intentions by the United States, decided Adlai should be informed. On April 7, in directing Arthur Schlesinger to go to New York to brief Adlai, the President told him: "The integrity and credibility of Adlai Stevenson constitute one of our great national assets. I don't want anything to be done which might jeopardize that."

The briefing the next morning conducted by Schlesinger and Tracy Barnes of the CIA, Schlesinger concedes in *A Thousand Days,* "was probably unduly vague," and "left Stevenson with the impression that no action would take place during the UN discussion of the Cuban item." He recounts that, when Assistant Secretary Cleveland and Clayton Fritchey of the Mission staff, joined them for lunch, Adlai "made clear he wholly disapproved of the plan, regretted that he had been given no opportunity to comment on it and believed that it would cause infinite trouble. But if it was national policy, he was prepared to make out the best possible case."

An opening air strike against Cuba on Saturday, April 15, prompted an emergency meeting of the General Assembly's Political Committee. Cleveland and his deputy, Joseph Sisco, both sought to verify the facts about the strike and, based on what they were told, drafted and sent to New York a speech for Adlai with the caution that not one word was to be changed.

Charges made by Cuba's foreign minister, Dr. Raoul Roa, were rejected "categorically" as being "without foundation." Adlai repeated the President's earlier press conference statement that "there will not be under any conditions—and I repeat, any conditions—any intervention in Cuba by the United States armed forces," and that "the United States will do everything it possibly can to make sure that no Americans participate in any actions against Cuba. Then he presented as fact the CIA cover story.

> Regarding the two aircraft which landed in Florida today, they were piloted by Cuban Air Force pilots. These pilots and certain other crew members have apparently defected from Castro's tyranny. No United States personnel participated. No United States Government aircraft of any kind participated. These two planes, to the best of our knowledge, were Castro's

own Air Force planes, and according to the pilots, they took off from Castro's own fields.

To prove his statement, Adlai had a blow-up of a photograph of one of the planes. He pointed to the Cuban star, the Revolutionary Air Force initials, on the tail. He ended by declaring that the United States was far too honorable to engage in such sneaky deceptions as Dr. Roa had charged.

Not until late that afternoon did Secretary of State Rusk learn that even he, along with Adlai and Cleveland, had been misled by a CIA cover story and that the planes had been provided by the United States and flown by exiles trained by the United States. Moreover, despite an explicit order from President Kennedy against direct involvement of Americans, the first frogmen to walk on each of the invasion beaches on Monday were Americans. It was not until Sunday, as the CIA cover story began to break down, that Adlai and his colleagues began to realize the statements he was making to the UN were false.

At 7:00 A.M. on Monday, Adlai's aide, Richard Pedersen, called with the news that Cuban exiles were going ashore at the Bay of Pigs. "Yes, I know," Adlai replied. "Bundy is here." The President had sent McGeorge Bundy to tell him the whole story, including the CIA cover story. "I told him all about it," Bundy said later. "We should have done that a week earlier. It was most difficult for him. He was very decent about it. He did *not* fuss about the box he was in. All he wanted was more information so he would not dig deeper holes." It was another example of Adlai's calm in adverse situations, and of the fact that his grumbling usually was directed at small personal situations, not important public matters.

That afternoon, while the Cuban exile brigade was landing on the beach, Adlai was having to deal with charges by Dr. Roa that the invasion was coming from Florida. "These charges are totally false," he told the Political Committee in a carefully hedged statement claiming that "no offensive has been launched from Florida or from any other part of the United States."

Jane Dick recalls that after the meeting adjourned, she encountered Adlai entering the elevator at the Waldorf as she was leaving for a reception. He walked past her without recognizing her, trancelike, his face drawn, pale, tense. She turned around and took the next elevator back up to the embassy residence on the forty-second floor. He opened the door to her ring. He still looked ghastly.

"Adlai, what in heaven's name has happened?" she asked.

"You heard my speech today?" he replied. "I did not tell the whole truth; I did not know the whole truth. I took this job at the President's request on the understanding that I would be consulted and kept fully informed on everything. I spoke in the United Nations in good faith on that understanding. Now my credibility has been compromised, and therefore my usefulness." She says, "He kept repeating, 'I've got to resign—there's nothing I can do but resign.' Then he'd say, 'But I can't resign—can't—the young President and the country are in enough trouble.'"

The broader peril was evident the next day as Ambassador Zorin read the text of a message to President Kennedy from Premier Khrushchev warning that the Soviet Union would give the Cuban government all necessary assistance in repelling attack. Adlai responded by reading the President's reply telling Khrushchev he was "under a serious misapprehension," and that the United States "intends no military intervention in Cuba," and that if outside force intervened, "we will immediately honor our obligations under the inter-American system to protect this hemisphere from external aggression." He referred to Khrushchev's statement that events in Cuba might affect peace in all parts of the world, and added, "I trust this does not mean that the Soviet government, using the situation in Cuba as a pretext, is planning to inflame other areas of the world."

The torrent of abuse poured on the United States during the day prompted Adlai to return to the Political Committee that night, after speaking at a college banquet, for another defense of American policy toward Cuba. There were resolutions of censure pending, ranging from a mild reprimand, sponsored by seven friendly Latin American countries, to extreme condemnations sponsored by the Soviet Union and by Rumania. The most troublesome, however, was a sharply critical resolution proposed by Mexico. It threatened to split apart whatever support the United States had among the Latin Americans. Adlai was fighting a difficult and intricate battle to limit the damage.

Meanwhile, a final vote on the Angola issue was nearing in the General Assembly where Charles Yost was sitting in for the United States; various delegates were seeking meetings on the Congo, on the admission of Mauritania, and on Israel; Phil Klutznick was pleading for help in the Fifth Committee where he was short of votes needed to put pressure on the Russians to pay their assessment for the Congo operation. Adlai told him to lose gracefully in the committee; they would try to win later when the issue came before the full Assembly. Effort had to be focused on defeating the Mexican, Russian, and Rumanian resolutions.

When the vote came, the Latin American resolution, with United States support, was passed by a vote of 61 to 27 with 10 abstentions. But so was the Mexican resolution, over American opposition, by a vote of 42 to 31, with 25 abstentions. The battle moved promptly into the plenary session of the full Assembly. The session did not end until 6:00 A.M., but in the end the Latin American resolution was adopted. The Soviet Union and Rumania withdrew their resolutions and threw their support behind the Mexican resolution in the hope of gaining the necessary two-thirds vote. But the vote of 41 to 35 with 20 abstentions meant not only that it had lost, but also that votes had been brought over to the United States position. Adlai slept for two hours, and then at 8:30 telephoned to report to the President.

Despite the congratulations at the outcome, there was little pride or satisfaction in the victory. On Wednesday, the men on the beach had sent a final message, destroyed their radio, and fled into the swamp. Adlai was appalled at the tragic fiasco. He was exhausted; he felt humiliated. Charles Yost has said, "He thought his credibility and usefulness had been destroyed." He underestimated his standing. "We got amazingly little flack under the circumstances," Yost added. Undersecretary General Ralph Bunche observed that any other American ambassador at the UN would have been destroyed, but such was the respect for Adlai that the UN delegates directed their criticism at Washington rather than at him.

Lasting damage had been inflicted, however, on the Kennedy-Stevenson relationship. Perhaps, for reasons beyond personalities, it was doomed from the beginning. Unlike other ambassadors who represent the United States in only one country, the ambassador at the UN and his staff of about a hundred deal on an almost daily basis with virtually the same number of countries as the entire apparatus of the State Department with a staff of thousands. Moreover, as Schlesinger wrote, "Washington had an ineradicable tendency to think of foreign policy as a matter between the United States and another country." Yet, whatever happens in the bilateral relationship is more often than not reflected in the UN setting—which is fundamentally different from that prevailing in Washington.

Country-to-country diplomacy bears little resemblance to the scramble for votes that dominates the parliamentary structure of the UN. In New York the more crass skills of a vote-seeking politician need to be part of the diplomat's baggage. The untidy requirements of the vote-seeking legislative process often repel the foreign service officer. In the scheme of career advancement, Schlesinger asserts, it was more important to be a third secretary in Stockholm or Pretoria than to serve at the U.S. Mission. Yost once explained, "The Africans were a nuisance to the State Department, but they meant votes to us." Even with frequent interchanges of personnel and agreement on objectives, inevitable differences in methods and perceptions produce tensions.

Far from helping bridge the gap, making the UN ambassador a member of the Cabinet increases the difficulties. It creates the illusion that he or she is a part of the policy-making process when, in fact, that rarely happens or is possible. To this day, manifold difficulties in the relationship between the State Department, the UN ambassador, and the U.S. Mission to the UN remain unresolved. Thus, the Kennedy-Stevenson relationship was built from the beginning on erroneous assumptions.

Moreover, it was built on tenuous personal grounds less tangible than the resentment of the President's brother and close associates over Adlai's refusal to support his candidacy in the primaries or at Los Angeles. President Kennedy not only refrained from manifesting their vindictiveness, he was known to express disapproval if criticism became too overt. "Let's not talk that way about Stevenson," he once chastised Bundy. "He is indispensable." He told Schlesinger he wished he had "more rapport" with Adlai. Schlesinger also commented in *A Thousand Days* that the President, "who had an essential respect and liking for Stevenson, tried, when he thought of it, to make their relationship effective." He understood Adlai's prestige in the world and his influence on a large following in the United States, Schlesinger wrote. In addition, he admired Adlai's "public presence and wit, valued his skills as a diplomat and orator, and considered him . . . capable of original thought."

Nevertheless, there was an inescapable incompatibility in their personal styles. Adlai enjoyed playing intellectual games with a problem. At best, this was irritating to Kennedy, who was direct, practical, operational, and preferred crisp, concise statements. It caused him to feel that Adlai could not make up his mind. "It was his manner, deliberately self-deprecatory, that conveyed an appearance of indecision which did not really exist," Schlesinger has written. The consequence, however, was that Adlai "never seemed wholly at ease on visits to the White House . . . instead of the pungent, astute and beguiling man he characteristically was, he would seem stiff, even at times solemn and pedantic."

There were even deeper irritations in the complex relationship, beginning with the difference in their ages. Adlai's long-standing concern about Kennedy's youth and lack of experience in foreign policy seemed to be confirmed by the Bay of Pigs. He saw "the bright young men" around Kennedy as "brash and arrogant" and capable of bumbling the nation into nuclear war. "I believe in on-the-job training," he commented after the Bay of Pigs, "but not for Presidents." His habit of making such uninhibited personal comments to friends was indulged in with damaging indiscretion. Many of these derogatory comments inevitably got back to the President. Kennedy liked to deal with facts, while Adlai preferred ideas. Kennedy focused on the present while Adlai liked to consider the future. Even their sense of humor clashed. Kennedy's was dry, sharp, sometimes caustic. Adlai's was more discursive, and its self-derogatory quality contributed to Kennedy's perception that he was uncertain and indecisive.

John Steele, the head of the Time-Life bureau in Washington, and a good personal friend, wrote after Adlai's death:

Stevenson was miscast on the New Frontier. The men of John F. Kennedy were flat-stomached; Stevenson was paunchy. They talked in cryptic, often barely understandable phrases; Ste-

venson talked in long sentences, comma-struck with paren-
thetical, often qualifying phrases. He was epigrammatic,
enjoyed discourse for discourse's sake. The New Frontiersmen
were grim, passionate men with their own brand of acidic
humor. Stevenson's eyes lit up with his own wry wit, often directed at himself and never cruelly at others.

Added to all this was the fact that the man senior in years and experience now was receiving his instructions from one whom he sometimes
referred to as "that young man." Beyond the humiliation of engaging in
falsehood, the Bay of Pigs was a dramatic demonstration that he was not
genuinely a part of the administration's foreign policy making.

There were mitigating reactions on both sides. Adlai came to realize
that the President, too, had been misled by his advisers. He had inherited
from the Eisenhower administration an operation that was wrong in con-
ception and incompetent in execution. It would have been difficult to
undo what had been done by the time he came into office—but he could
have. So, Adlai respected the way in which the President acknowledged
and shouldered responsibility while seeing to it that those directly responsible quietly left the administration. Kennedy, on his side, developed new
respect for Adlai's calm under fire, and willingness, "like a good soldier,"
to carry out orders he might not agree with. He was more understanding
and forgiving of Adlai's private grumbling than his associates. He and the
secretary of state both resolved, and so made clear to Adlai, that the
latter would never again be kept in the dark about any development regarding the UN. Nevertheless, the assertion of greater White House control inevitably meant that, though better informed, Adlai's freedom of
action was still further restricted.

As a healing gesture after the Bay of Pigs, the President quickly
asked Adlai to make a fence-mending tour of Latin America. Initially, he
resisted; if it were simply to be a "goodwill" trip he would not go, but if
there were a United States policy toward Latin America for him to sell—
which he agreed with—he would go. He complained he had never seen
National Security Council papers on the countries of the region. That was
remedied, and he quickly began making appointments, reading, and
seeing diplomats and scholars knowledgeable about Latin America.

At the same time, Kennedy brought him into the preparations for his
first trip to Europe as President during which he would see both Khrushchev and de Gaulle. At a long meeting with the President and Secretary Rusk on May 24, he handed Kennedy a memo that took a tough
stand in regard to the Russian premier. While specific questions such as
disarmament, nuclear tests, Berlin, Laos, and Cuba would surely arise,
he urged the President to concentrate on the "basic question which gov-
erns all these—the Soviet interpretation of 'peaceful coexistence.'" The

Russians maintained an "absolute taboo" on any Western intervention inside the Communist bloc and yet insisted on a free hand in aiding "wars of liberation," or any Communist-supported activity elsewhere. Khrushchev should be told that "the West could not conceivably accept such a policy or that 'peaceful coexistence' could long exist under it." He urged the President to "lay bare the fundamentals of the problem as you see it and make it clear that we propose to deal in the future much more vigorously with those fundamentals." The memo might have given pause to those bent on labeling Adlai as "soft on Communism."

As for de Gaulle, Adlai counseled support for de Gaulle's effort in Algeria, and then concentrated on UN matters: the admission of Mauritania supported by "the French Africans (12 votes)"; the refusal of France to contribute to Congo expenses, "which puts her in the same category as the USSR"; and, most of all, the effort "to persuade him that, irresponsible and inconvenient as the United Nations appears to be, it is perhaps the central point at which the great body of uncommitted Afro-Asian States can be influenced and where their ultimate commitment to either European civilization or to Communist economic and political forms is likely to be determined."

At Kennedy's request, he returned two days later to discuss growing concern over the status of Berlin and to present an even longer memorandum the President had requested on "the way Soviet leaders see things." He traced in some detail the sources of Soviet suspicion and concluded that agreement on "significant disarmament" depended on resolving issues of inspection, military equality between the two parties, Chinese cooperation, Communist support of "wars of liberation," and "international policing after disarmament." He was skeptical of short-term progress but felt it was important for the United States to maintain the initiative.

Before leaving for South America on June 4, Adlai found time to register an unsuccessful protest against reports that the United States was planning to sell arms to South Africa and establish a missile tracking station there. He also wrote a memo urging the appointment of Carl McGowan, who would be named to the U.S. Circuit Court of Appeals in Washington, regarded as the court closest to the Supreme Court. On the day of his departure he wrote the wife of Nixon's recent running mate and his predecessor at the UN, Mrs. Henry Cabot Lodge, saying he would be away and "if you and Cabot can use the place [his apartment in New York] I hope very much that you will. It would please me, and it is where you belong!"

In seventeen days, his visited ten countries, accompanied by Borden; three members of his Mission staff; Ellis O. Briggs, a Latin American expert then serving as ambassador to Greece; Professor Lincoln Gorden, soon to become ambassador to Brazil and then assistant secretary of state for Latin American affairs; as well as two other Washington experts and eight newspapermen. This time there was less sightseeing and far more talk about specific issues.

His report to the President on his return was unsparing in its criticism of the Bay of Pigs, reporting "governments are unanimous in condemning unilateral United States action." He quoted President Jânio Quadros of Brazil as saying that not only was it "disastrous," but any further unilateral intervention would be "fatal" to "support for or cooperation with the United States." This was especially pointed since, other than Cuba, the main point of discussion was the Alliance for Progress, proposed by the President on March 13 and the main topic for the meeting scheduled a few months later at Punta del Este. Special importance attached to the President's initiative because "political stability . . . is under severe strain and attack almost everywhere. Communist and other extreme left wing forces have generally gained in strength and aggressiveness in the last year, and the danger of right wing coups d'état in several countries is still evident."

As Adlai returned from Latin America, Kennedy returned from the Vienna meeting with Khrushchev to face a test of wills over Berlin. Although Adlai and the UN were not directly involved, the Berlin crisis would cast its shadow over nearly every other issue in the Kennedy/Stevenson relationship.

It is now evident that throughout 1961 Khrushchev operated on a conviction, supported by event after event, that the victory of communism was inevitable. Success in developing the hydrogen bomb and surpassing the United States in long-range missiles gave Soviet leaders confidence in their technological prowess and ability to withstand foreign attack. The Soviet rate of industrial growth then exceeded that of the United States. Soviet disagreements with China appeared to have been resolved. From Laos and Vietnam to Cuba, ferment in underdeveloped countries promised the movement of the third world into communism. Khrushchev had boasted in a January speech that the world situation "greatly exceeded the boldest and most optimistic predictions and expectations," and that "there is no longer any force in the world capable of barring the road to socialism." In this context he declared his intention to sign a separate peace treaty with East Germany and to end the rights of the three Western powers in Berlin.

Khrushchev's first test of the young President had been in Laos and Vietnam where Communist guerrillas were conducting savage campaigns. Eisenhower's last meeting with Kennedy before the Inauguration had been devoted mainly to Laos; strangely, no mention was made of Vietnam. In February, Soviet air shipments of arms to Laos had increased alarmingly. In March, the President had quietly moved the Seventh Fleet into the South China Sea, alerted combat troops in Okinawa, strengthened garrisons in Thailand, and launched a diplomatic offensive to assure backing from Britain and, hopefully, France, as well as countries in the region. Confronted with all these moves, Khrushchev told our ambassador, Llewellyn Thompson, "Why take risks over Laos? It will fall into our laps like a ripe apple."

This little-known crisis in 1961 "seems in some ways a dress rehearsal for the Cuban missile crisis of 1962," Arthur Schlesinger, who was involved in both, has written. This time the tension subsided only to be revived on the European front.

Kennedy's May requests to Adlai for memos on Khrushchev and other Russian leaders was designed in part to offset bellicose advice on Berlin he was receiving from Dean Acheson. Adlai's disagreements with Acheson had their roots in the work of the Democratic Advisory Council. As early as 1958, he had written Chester Bowles expressing anxiety over the "military emphasis" in Acheson's leadership of the foreign policy committee. Adlai and Bowles had found themselves aligned against Acheson over issues of colonialism, and now Adlai found himself aligned with Harriman opposing Acheson on Berlin. Acheson's proposals tended to pose policy in terms of a choice between a military showdown and negotiations, which he thought suggested weakness. Adlai believed that the position argued by Acheson "should be the conclusion of a process of investigation, not the beginning." It was a basic difference that would erupt again and again and hurt the reputations of both.

By July 25, the President had announced plans to call up Reserve and National Guard units, seek an additional $3.25 billion for the defense budget, and, in a key section of the announcement that was largely ignored by the press, to press an active diplomatic offensive. It was a skillful adaptation of both viewpoints. On August 13, the crisis deepened as East German troops moved to the dividing line to stop the hemorrhage of people fleeing to the west; in July alone the total was thirty thousand. On August 17, construction of the infamous Berlin Wall began. The Berlin crisis clouded events for months to come, and left abiding tensions, not only with Khrushchev but within our own country. This remained true even after Khrushchev, in October, indicated a willingness to negotiate. Khrushchev was aware of these divisions, as he indicated to Harriman in 1963, in saying that he fully intended from time to time to stamp on the corns of the exposed Western foot.

Kennedy's dissatisfactions with the State Department reached a peak during these weeks and gave him some understanding of the difficulties that Adlai had been having. "The State Department is a bowl of jelly," he had exploded to Hugh Sidey of *Time* during this tense summer.

If Adlai's relations with Kennedy were difficult, they were more so with Secretary of State Rusk. Adlai, in his foreign policy report to Kennedy after the election, had warned of the "tremendous institutional inertia" of the State Department, "which, unless manipulated forcefully from the outset, will overwhelm and dictate to the new regime." During the Berlin crisis, Kennedy had found, it was an accurate warning. Perhaps it should have been addressed to Rusk as well because it was he who, at critical times, was overwhelmed.

Kennedy once remarked that Rusk was the only Cabinet member he did not call by his first name. When this was reported to Rusk, he replied simply that he preferred it that way. His profound reserve was concealed by an attractive personality, a remarkable capacity for lucid analysis, and an exceptional intelligence. The hidden difficulty was that he had trained himself all of his life to be an ideal chief of staff rather than a leader—a Rhodes Scholar who had become a college dean, an intelligence officer on General Stilwell's staff in New Delhi, on Marshall's staff in the Defense Department, assistant secretary of state for United Nations and also for Far Eastern affairs, and president of the Rockefeller Foundation. He was a proud, self-made man, sensitive of his humble origins, and now surrounded by prominent public figures such as Adlai, whom he unfailingly treated with great deference in public. Never once while Adlai was ambassador did Rusk make a General Assembly speech as other foreign ministers did. He insisted the spokesmen there should be either the President or Adlai.

Rusk could analyze differing views brilliantly, but what he himself thought would remain a mystery. As the clashes with the Europeanists escalated from being a battle between the "hard-liners" and the "softies," to one between "hawks" and "doves," Rusk's ambiguous position became increasingly frustrating to Adlai. The situation would have been far worse and more intractable except for the skill of Harlan Cleveland and his able colleagues.

Adlai escaped most of the tensions rising in the State Department during the summer by going to Geneva at the urgent request of Philip Klutznick to attend the session of the Economic and Social Council. His speech there on July 10 was the first to be given by the chief American ambassador to the UN and the delegates besieged Klutznick for appointments.

He spoke of his trip to Latin America, and the misery he had seen there, as indicative of the urgency of addressing the needs of the poor everywhere, he spoke of the importance of disarmament and derided fears that disarmament would harm capitalist economies, and he ended by declaring that stagnant, status-quo systems must yield to peaceful change. The new decade, he said, should be remembered "not as a period of power struggle, but as the decade of great triumphs in the age-old struggle to provide a better life for men everywhere."

Buffie and Ernest Ives had a villa in Florence for the summer, and when Adlai arrived there on July 15, there was a call awaiting him from Chester Bowles announcing that he was about to be fired or forced to resign as undersecretary of state. Bowles and Adlai shared many of the same views. Bowles, too, had been right on the Bay of Pigs. They both placed high priority on relations with the third world. But they also shared some of the same weaknesses. His style, like Adlai's, was unduly discursive for the New Frontiersmen, and thus, he seemed to them to be indecisive. Actually, he had done a brilliant job in bringing fresh blood and viewpoints into top positions in the State Department; but, in doing so, he had made implacable enemies of the career men whose careers he had derailed. As Kennedy's dissatisfaction with the State Department mounted, the blame increasingly was directed at the hapless Bowles. Adlai immediately sent a telegram of protest to Kennedy. Support for Bowles gained him a brief reprieve, but Adlai was aware that the people and forces opposing Bowles were his enemies also.

On July 27, Adlai received a summons to see de Gaulle the next afternoon, and he flew to Paris from Florence. They spoke of Algeria, of the fighting between French and Tunisian forces in Bizerte, and of Berlin. As Adlai was leaving, de Gaulle said, "We supported you in Cuba. Our situation in Bizerte is like yours in Cuba. We are not in Bizerte for our pleasure. You were not in Cuba for your pleasure." Then, more warmly, he told Adlai it was always a pleasure to see him—"always so full of life, spirit, ideas, and hope. Notice," he added, "I did not say, full of illusions."

On Saturday, August 5, his first weekend home, he went to Hyannis Port with Cleveland to meet with Kennedy and Schlesinger who, thereafter, would be Adlai's contact man at the White House. Adlai had been urging the President to speak at the opening of the UN General Assembly in September and they were to discuss the issues that might be covered.

"I can think of no better position for the United States in the forthcoming General Assembly than the earnest advocacy of disarmament as our top priority national interest," Adlai had written the President, adding that the United States must "seize the initiative in disarmament which the Russians have held too long. . . . The United States must appear second to none in its desire for disarmament."

Both Cleveland and Schlesinger have vividly described the encounter. Despite "sullen" weather, Kennedy was determined to take his guests out on the sound for luncheon in his boat. While a chilly wind kept his wife and two of his sisters huddled forward, discussion of the UN went on in the stern. Kennedy promptly acknowledged Adlai's interest in the disarmament issue, but noted that its popularity in the UN did not seem to be duplicated in the United States. However, he recognized it as an issue on which we could score points against the Soviet Union. Stevenson agreed and then added earnestly:

> We can't do this effectively if we ourselves equivocate. Your first decision, Mr. President, must be to make sure you yourself

are genuinely for general and complete disarmament. . . . Only total disarmament will save the world from the horror of nuclear war as well as from the mounting expenses of the arms race. Your basic decision must be to identify yourself with a new approach to disarmament. This must be our principal initiative in the United Nations.

Both the observers report that Kennedy listened with interest but also with some skepticism. With tension mounting in Berlin and the beginning of the Berlin Wall barely two weeks in the future, progress seemed highly unlikely and he saw the issue primarily in terms of political warfare. Thus his first response to Adlai's plea was that he well understood the "propaganda" importance of disarmament. Adlai, stung, made the absolutely wrong response. To the man who liked facts he said, "Jack, you've got to have faith." It was one of the few times he called the President by his first name.

"I never felt so keenly the way these two men, so united in their objectives, could so inadvertently arrive at cross purposes," Schlesinger has written.

"I thought Adlai Stevenson was going through the floor," Cleveland has said. "You could almost see what was going through his mind—'Oh, my God, I've been devoting my life to this, I built my 1956 campaign around it, and here I've got to educate this kid all over.'"

Cleveland's intervention saved the day. The Soviet Union, he said, had always talked in the UN about general and complete disarmament while we talked about "next steps." This left the world thinking the Russians were more devoted to disarmament than we were. If we now accepted general and complete disarmament as the goal, this would cast all subsequent debate in terms of "next steps," and then our specific proposals could expose or test the real Soviet desire for arms reduction. This argument was far more persuasive than Adlai's plea for faith and Kennedy quickly agreed to the proposal they had brought. Moreover, by the time he made his American University speech in 1963, he had arrived at the priority Adlai had pled for.

The conversation turned to Communist China. To the prickly issue of its presence in the UN had been added the admission of Outer Mongolia, proposed by the Soviet Union and threatened with a veto by Nationalist China backed by its Republican supporters in Congress and major elements of the press. Various parliamentary maneuvers were discussed, and when Adlai protested that one was "too transparent," Kennedy replied, "If we can buy twelve months, it will be more than worth it. We may be preparing the way for admission of Peking in another year; but in another year things will be different." Then, turning to Adlai, he said, "What do you think we ought to do? If you are not for this policy, we should not try and do it." Somewhat embarrassed by this gesture, Adlai responded, "I will be for it if you decide it's the policy."

They talked about India, Pakistan, Berlin, and Kennedy handed him a paper written by Acheson outlining a strategy for the Berlin issue and asked Adlai to give him his reactions. In his response some ten days later, Adlai congratulated the President for the way he had "damped down the fires in the Berlin military planning," and closed with a statement that summarized the deep division in government ranks:

> It would be extremely dangerous for us to allow our attention to be so absorbed by Berlin that we overlook attitudes in Asia, Africa and Latin America, or take decisions or public positions based on the exigencies of our NATO allies rather than the exigencies of those areas. To do so would, in my view, play into the Soviet-Chicom [State Department jargon for Communist China] hands by sacrificing ground in what they consider to be the decisive areas of struggle in order to hold the line in Europe.

Four weeks later, with the Berlin Wall in its second week of construction, the Soviets resumed the testing of nuclear weapons and touched off another tense debate between the same groupings within the United States government. Adlai promptly sent a memorandum to Kennedy and Rusk proposing the United States call for a meeting of the Security Council to deal with the "threat to peace and security," and a series of follow-up actions centered on a speech by the President in the General Assembly. Only then, if the Soviets had not suspended testing, would the United States announce it would resume testing.

Cleveland joined in pressing Adlai's proposal with John J. McCloy and Arthur Dean, who opposed going to the Security Council on the ground that it would gain nothing and might restrict freedom of action. When Cleveland mentioned the effect on world opinion, McCloy exploded: "World opinion? I don't believe in world opinion. The only thing that matters is power. What we have to do now is to show that we are a powerful nation and not spend our time trailing after the phantom of world opinion." This statement, put together with Adlai's response to Acheson's Berlin memorandum, highlights the sharp internal conflict. It surfaced in a meeting with the President on September 5.

Two days before, the Russians had exploded a huge nuclear device in the atmosphere over central Asia, giving additional strength to the powerful proponents of testing above and below ground. Kennedy accepted the McCloy-Dean position opposing a call of the Security Council but rejected the proposed tests in the atmosphere with their danger of radioactive fallout, and joined with British Prime Minister Harold MacMillan in proposing to Khrushchev that the three governments agree now to ban atmospheric tests. He had accepted Adlai's argument for a major disarmament initiative in a speech to the UN General Assembly. But he had also decided to resume testing underground, and he called in Adlai, Rusk, and Cleveland, to join with Bundy, Sorenson, and Schlesinger to discuss what his speech and the announcement might say.

Adlai urged the President to hold a special press conference to emphasize his interest in negotiations over Berlin and to unveil the new American disarmament plan. This was to guard against the possibility that Khrushchev, in answering the Kennedy-MacMillan message, would call again for general and complete disarmament and take the edge off the President's disarmament initiative. It is likely he was also trying to head off the opposition to the disarmament plan. Then, he expressed his personal regret over the decision to resume nuclear testing.

"What choice did we have?" the President replied tartly. "They had spit in our eye three times. We couldn't possibly sit back and do nothing at all. We had to do this."

"But we were ahead in the propaganda battle," Adlai persisted.

"What does that mean?" came back the President's sharp reply. "I don't hear of any windows broken because of the Soviet decision. The neutrals have been terrible. The Russians made two tests *after* our note calling for a ban on atmospheric testing. Maybe they couldn't have stopped the first, but they could have stopped the second. . . . All this makes Khrushchev look pretty tough. He has had a succession of apparent victories—space, Cuba, the thirteenth of August [the Berlin Wall], though I don't myself regard this as a victory. He wants to give out the feeling that he has us on the run. The third test was a contemptuous response to our note. . . . Anyway, the decision has been made." He abruptly turned to the question of China and the UN. It had been one of their sharpest encounters.

To ease the tension, he told Adlai: "You have the hardest thing in the world to sell. It really doesn't make any sense—the idea that Taiwan represents China. But if we lost this fight, if Red China comes into the UN during our first year in town, your first year and mine, they'll run us both out. We have to lick them this year. We'll take our chances next year. It will be an election year, but we can delay the admission of Red China till after the election."

Although a canvass at the beginning of the session found tie votes at best in support of the United States position, the victory that was finally won prompted the President to wire Adlai: "Today's votes . . . are further evidence of your outstanding skill and leadership in the UN. I am grateful for your eloquent and active support on this issue. With esteem and warm regards."

Adlai needed all the support he could muster in view of the harmful event that had occurred in Belgrade, Yugoslavia, where Nehru, Tito, Nasser, and Sukarno convened the first meeting of twenty-eight of the self-styled neutral, nonaligned nations. Adlai, and Galbraith from his ambassadorship in India, had warned the President that he could expect no support from the meeting on Berlin or other cold war issues. The Europeanists in the State Department sought to prevent the President from even sending a message to the opening of the conference. Despite the warnings, the President was deeply and profanely annoyed at what he saw as the one-sided attitudes displayed at Belgrade. As it turned out, the Russians had at least equal reason for disappointment in failing to win support for their positions on Berlin, on the troika in the UN, or on disarmament. Nonetheless, Washington corridors soon rang with the President's irritated comment to Bundy: "Do you know who the real losers were at Belgrade? Stevenson and Bowles." The third world leaders had, indeed, struck a heavy blow at their friends in the United States government.

Belgrade also gave new impetus to the continuing effort to persuade the President not to go to the UN General Assembly, and if he did go, not to emphasize disarmament. The debate was ended abruptly on September 18 by the tragic news that Dag Hammarskjöld had been killed in a plane crash in Africa. The President knew instinctively that this was a time for a dramatic demonstration of support.

The President's speech on September 25 was a triumph of draftsmanship on the part of Sorenson and, in its substance, a triumph for Adlai's long battle for a new initiative on disarmament. Moreover, with the help of the President's speech, and relentless negotiating, the Assembly ended as a triumph for the United States.

After paying tribute to Hammarskjöld and urging the Assembly to reject the Russian proposal for a troika because it would weaken the UN, the President asserted that in the nuclear age the world needed the UN more than ever before. For "a nuclear disaster, spread by wind and water and fear, could well engulf the great and small, the rich and the poor, the committed and the uncommitted alike. Mankind must put an end to war—or war will put an end to mankind. . . . Let us call a truce to terror." The goal of disarmament, he continued, "is no longer a dream—it is a practical matter of life or death." He described in general terms an American program for disarmament and asked that negotiations continue "without interruption until an entire program for general and complete disarmament has not only been agreed but has been actually achieved." The logical place to begin, he said, was a test ban treaty. He also called for further contributions to a United Nations peacekeeping force, the improvement of UN machinery for the peaceful settlement of disputes, the extension of world law to outer space and support of the UN Decade of Development.

"Never have the nations of the world had so much to lose, or so much to gain," the President concluded. "Together we shall save our planet, or together we shall perish in its flames. Save it we can—and save it we must—and then we shall earn the eternal thanks of mankind and, as peacemakers, the eternal blessings of God."

The reception gave Kennedy a new appreciation of the United Nations and of Adlai's role there. He had reason to be gratified at the results that were achieved by the time the Assembly adjourned in December. The groundwork was laid for new negotiations on disarmament. The Assembly called for a treaty to ban nuclear tests under effective international measures of verification and control and asked the Soviet Union to refrain from exploding its 50-megaton bomb. The troika was defeated and U Thant of Burma was made the new secretary general with undiminished authority. The application of Communist China for admission was defeated by a decisive vote and it was agreed that any proposal to make a change in the representation of China was an "important question" requiring a two-thirds majority. Nationalist China was persuaded to refrain from vetoing Outer Mongolia and it was admitted to membership along with Mauritania. To deal with the financial problems caused by the UN operations in the Congo, the Assembly authorized a $200-million bond issue to be taken up by the member nations.

U Thant's election was a particular success for Adlai. By skillfully pushing Frederick Boland of Ireland, Mongi Slim of Tunisia, and U Thant of Burma into leadership in opposing the troika idea, he soon saw that the Russians were isolated on their proposal but that an acceptable candidate was necessary to kill it. He realized that the quiet U Thant from neutral Burma was someone whom the Russians would find it difficult to oppose. He had learned in talks with U Thant that his definition of a neutral posed no problem for the West. In an encounter before U Thant was aware he was under consideration, he had observed to Adlai that it would be difficult for a UN official to be neutral "on the burning issues of the day."

"Do you mean," Adlai asked him, "that there can be no moral neutrality?"

"That is true," the devout Buddhist responded. "Whoever occupies the office of Secretary General must be impartial, but not necessarily neutral. . . . I think the judges of the . . . Supreme Court must be impartial. . . . But they are not neutral as regards who is the criminal and who is the person on whom the crime has been committed."

Adlai carried the proposal of U Thant directly to the Russians. Realizing that they were defeated on the troika proposal and could not stand in the way of a popular Asian from a small neutral country, the Russians demanded only that the election be for Hammarskjöld's unexpired term and that U Thant be designated acting secretary general. That was accepted. Two years later, he was elected to a full term and "acting" disappeared. Behind the victory so critical to the UN's future were two months of unremitting effort.

"Life at the U.S. Mission is a mad house," Adlai wrote Barbara

Ward (Lady Jackson), midway during the session, and it was hardly an overstatement. He had tried unsuccessfully to negotiate a compromise in the French-Tunisian struggle over Bizerte. His frustration, he said, was "boundless." On this one, the Europeanists won and the United States abstained on the resolution that Adlai had succeeded in getting watered down substantially.

He also lost the running battle against tests in the atmosphere over the Eniwetok proving grounds, and on October 19 was obliged to announce the official United States position in the Political Committee. The continuing Soviet tests, he said, had created an "emergency," and demonstrated that the Russians were not negotiating in good faith in Geneva. Therefore, the United States reserved the right to test above as well as below the ground, while it stood ready to negotiate a test ban treaty. Then, he added, "I have claimed the privilege of making this declaration because few delegates, I dare say, feel more deeply about this matter than I do, in part, perhaps, because I proposed that nuclear tests be stopped almost six years ago—and lost a great many votes in the 1956 presidential election as a result." Thus he not only publicly announced a policy he privately opposed, but he put his personal prestige behind it. Even Bundy, who was not an admirer, praised him for being a good soldier.

Between November 13 and 24, the Security Council met eight times on the Congo and, to head off extremist demands on the UN forces there, Adlai spoke at nearly all of them. To this was added a series of meetings, beginning on November 22, at which Cuba accused the United States of threatening the sovereignty of the Dominican Republic by moving warships into the area after the assassination of General Rafael Trujillo, even though the show of force was designed to encourage democratic forces seeking to displace the dictator's family.

In mid-December, India had launched its invasion of the Portuguese colonies of Goa, Damao, and Diu. Adlai's outrage at the use of force was enhanced by the long lectures he had endured from the Indian delegate on the necessity for American restraint in dealings with the Soviet Union. Adlai's unsuccessful efforts to obtain a ceasefire and a resort to negotiations led him to some of his most bitter utterances. Nehru lodged an official protest and even Adlai admitted he may have gone too far.

In the midst of it all, came the "Thanksgiving Day Massacre." Adlai had flown to Trinidad to meet President Arturo Frondizi of Argentina, who was beginning a tour of Europe and had requested the meeting. While there, he received a cable from President Kennedy saying he was trying to reach him by telephone. It was to inform him that Bowles had been removed as undersecretary as part of a far-reaching shuffle of top positions. While Adlai's good friend, George Ball, had become undersecretary, the perceived significance of the changes at the time was that the hard-liners and Europeanists had won out in a pivotal struggle for control over the Bowles-Stevenson third world advocates.

Into this setting came another of those events cited as evidence of indecisiveness that actually was the calculated use of uncertainty to serve a different goal. A statement by Senator Paul Douglas that Adlai headed his list to run for the Illinois seat held by Senate Minority Leader Everett Dirksen was handled with sufficient ambiguity to encourage a flow of letters, telegrams, and newspaper comment urging him to run. Soon thereafter, he received a call from Mayor Daley asking if he would run. Arvey made clear he would support him. Adlai's response was that he would "have to think it over" and "talk it over with the President."

The evidence is now persuasive that he did not really give it serious consideration, but used it to test his situation in the aftermath of the Thanksgiving Day Massacre. Two days later, he saw the President on UN matters and mentioned the possibility of the Senate race. Without particular emphasis, Kennedy said he hoped Adlai would stay but that the decision was up to him. This was not the response Adlai had been hoping for. On returning to New York, he told his friend Max Frankel at *The New York Times* that he had told the President he would decide before the end of the year about resigning. Frankel reported that Kennedy "had made no strenuous effort to hold Stevenson in a position of cabinet rank," adding that "Mr. Stevenson's status on the New Frontier has always been somewhat ambiguous and, for him, uncomfortable."

The anticipated uproar ensued and when Adlai returned for Sunday lunch at the Kennedys' Virginia retreat, Glen Ora, he was greeted with unusual warmth. After lunch, he and the President were closeted alone for four hours. "I told Adlai that he would be even more frustrated as a junior Senator than he is at the UN," Kennedy said later. "I reminded him about Alben Barkley, who came back to the Senate [after being Vice President] with much fanfare, and a week later was just another junior Senator at the bottom of the list. I told him we needed him at the UN and that I counted on him to stay on."

While Daley and Arvey waited for Adlai's decision, he and Kennedy engaged in a shadow dance over how Adlai's decision would be announced. With Clayton Fritchey's help, it was finally agreed that Adlai would issue a statement saying the President had "greatly reinforced my view" that he could best serve the country "in the field of foreign policy." Whereupon, the President issued a statement saying: "I am delighted with Governor Stevenson's decision. I expressed to him this weekend my emphatic hope that he will continue at the United Nations and play an expanding role in the making and execution of our foreign policy. I believe his work is vital to the cause of peace and of top importance to the country."

Adlai had won a public relations victory, but he paid a price. Daley and Arvey suspected, rightly, that they had been used. The President recognized and was not amused by the purpose behind Adlai's ploy. The purpose became still more evident as papers flew back and forth among Mission, State Department, and White House to establish new lines of liaison.

In addition to all this, Adlai agreed to host an ABC network television program every other Sunday beginning in October entitled *Adlai Stevenson Reports*. Dean Rusk was his first guest, followed by U Thant and Prime Minister Nehru.

To ensure that Adlai didn't escape the mundane, the Waldorf-Astoria sought an increase in rent on the ambassadorial apartment from $30,000 to $45,000 a year. With the help of his Republican friend in Chicago, Henry Crown, a member of the Hilton Corporation Board, the rent increase was dropped.

Adlai's frenetic social life had altered only slightly in the move from Libertyville to the Waldorf-Astoria. His letters are full of constant entreaties to the Dicks, the McGowans, the Lou Kohns, and Harriet Welling in Chicago; the Fulbrights and the Paul Douglases in Washington; the Joseph Bohrers in Bloomington; Sir Robert and Lady Barbara Jackson in Ghana; the John Steinbecks; and the Archibald MacLeishes to come and stay with him. Widows such as Pussy Paepcke and Evelyn Huston were especially welcome.

The apartment, as well as his company, was an experience to share. Its location, high in the towers of the Waldorf-Astoria, gave it a spectacular view of the city. Ambassador and Mrs. Lodge had decorated it beautifully and left it furnished with fine eighteenth-century French, English, and American pieces. Adlai changed only the curtains in the dining room, and the color of his bedroom was changed from pink, which he disliked, to his favorite color, blue. Visitors were most impressed, though, by the personal memorabilia that soon was scattered about the apartment, including framed letters of Washington, Lincoln, and Albert Schweitzer. Mary Lasker's friendship with James Rorimer, the director of the Metropolitan Museum, led to the loan of magnificent paintings by John Singer Sargent, Whistler, Monet, and Utrillo. Ruth Field was the source of other priceless works. Her presence was most evident in a profusion of flowers that Adlai loved, sent almost daily from her Long Island gardens and greenhouses for attractive arrangements in every room.

Viola Reardy, having survived her encounter with the president of Guinea in Libertyville, presided over the household. There were frequent houseguests, nearly always guests at breakfast, lunch, and dinner. During the days Adlai spent in New York during 1961, there was only one vacant luncheon date on his calendar, and he had put a big question mark on that.

Whenever he went to Washington, Adlai had almost another home in the Georgetown residence of Dr. and Mrs. Paul B. Magnuson. Another convenience was the residence of the Schlesingers just across the street.

In both Washington and New York his social life was dizzying. It was not unusual for him to get to several parties in the course of an evening. He liked diplomatic receptions less than gatherings that included old friends. He was also an incessant collector of interesting people.

"His life was intensely social and active," Archibald MacLeish has said.

> He used to get fed up with it. Every now and then we'd get an appeal to come in [from their home in the Berkshires]. Sometimes he'd have a party for us, sometimes we'd see him alone. Once he urged us to come on a Sunday afternoon for supper that night. . . . We found his secretary had invited [Richard] Burton and Liz [Taylor]. . . . Adlai came in, so tired he could hardly sit up. He immediately took the center of the stage and talked until eleven-thirty, completely relaxed, lying back, laughing his head off. He rejoiced in the company of pretty women.

During the first year at the UN, the actress Joan Fontaine was a frequent companion. Adlai took particular delight in escorting Jacqueline Kennedy to dinners, concerts, and the theater; they clearly enjoyed each other's company immensely. And, whenever they could be persuaded, his sons would join him. When Borden turned the tables and invited him to spend a weekend with his young friends on Long Island, Adlai reveled in it.

He and young people always found instant rapport. This was especially the case with the daughters of his good friends: Dutch Smith's daughter, Adele; Marietta's daughter, Frankie; Kay Graham's daughter, Lally; the Plimptons' daughter, Sarah; and Ruthie Field's daughter, Fiona. Mrs. Field, in turn, became virtually a second mother to Borden.

He made young people feel he was genuinely interested in them. And he was. He listened intently, he asked questions, he engaged in serious conversation, examining, arguing, sometimes even agreeing. Agreement was not the important thing; being taken seriously was.

An example of this capacity is told by Carl McGowan in relation to his daughter, Mary, then a student at Wellesley.

> She was singing with the Glee Club at the World's Fair and called Adlai's secretary to see if she and a friend could stay in the apartment Friday night and leave early Saturday morning without disturbing anybody. They came to the empty apartment about 10 and went to bed. At 11:30 there was a pounding on their door. "Girls, girls, get up. You have to help me entertain. I have people here, including the 18-year-old Crown Princess of

Denmark. You have to get up and help me." That made them feel really great. That was the kind of thing he was always doing.

It was noted that Adlai paid special attention to young staff members in the delegations of the smaller nations, particularly the new African states, many of whom lacked training in either diplomatic or parliamentary practice. One young Latin American diplomat, expressing appreciation to a colleague for help Adlai had given him, commented that when an epitaph was written for Adlai it should read, "Once upon a time there was an American diplomat." When this was reported back to Adlai he was deeply touched.

It was the Lake Forest friends who were feeling neglected, and he tried to make up for that at Christmastime. Amid the round of gay parties there was a sharp reminder of his continuing family sorrow. John Fell took his grandmother, Mrs. Carpenter, to visit his mother. What occurred was described in later court testimony. As they arrived, Mrs. Carpenter presented Ellen a purse for a Christmas gift. Ellen's response was that it was the only thing her mother had ever given her. They then proceeded into the living room. John Fell stood at the fireplace as the two women sat in sofas facing each other. Suddenly, Ellen picked up a silver cigarette box and drew back her arm as if to throw it at her mother. John Fell stepped between them and took the cigarette box out of her hand. Ellen then jumped to her feet and began screaming curses at her mother. Frightened, Mrs. Carpenter tried to leave the room, but Ellen followed her into the hall, struck at her head, and tried to choke her. John Fell managed to get between them and hold his mother's wrists. Thinking she was calmed, he let her go, and she hit him. This time he forced her into a nearby chair and asked her to calm down. But when he let her go, she jumped up and attacked her mother. He had to subdue her again, and they then escaped. For weeks, she tried to tell almost anyone who would listen that her son had tried to break her arms.

The incident lends particular poignancy to the year-end letter Adlai wrote Marietta Tree: "The person who can face both life and love with confidence and courage—and give himself for the sheer joy of giving—is sure to find joy and contentment. For loving *is* living. It sounds well—and is, no doubt, but my trouble seems to be that 'life' is so dependent on love."

CHAPTER TWENTY-TWO
More Crises—and Tragedy

"TALKING ABOUT THE UNITED Nations is a little like being the fan in relation to the fan dancer," Adlai often said during his last years. "You can't possibly cover the subject; all you can do is call attention to it."

His was an energetic fan throughout his UN years, but never was it waved more urgently than during 1962.

The accelerating dissolution of European colonialism had brought many new states into the United Nations, and along with them a number of bitter conflicts. The founding 51 were outnumbered at the beginning of 1962 in a membership that totaled 104. The fact that many nations had been born and become United Nations members peacefully, or with little conflict, was lost in the intensity of the current flare-ups in Tunisia and Algeria, the Congo and Angola, between Israel and Syria, between India and Pakistan over Kashmir, between India and China over their border, and the overarching struggle between the United States and the Soviet Union. Following the Berlin crisis, that struggle focused first on nuclear testing and then, in October with the discovery of missile sites in Cuba, on the horrifying possibility of nuclear war.

These events and the trends they reflected had caused a tightening of battle lines within our own society that, though often barely tangible, were intense, emotional, and, as was to be seen, sometimes ruthless. Often the United States was faced with choices seen as damaging to important European allies, such as Britain and France in the Suez; France in Algeria, Tunis and Laos; the Netherlands in Indonesia; Belgium in the Congo; Portugal in Angola. It did not help that, as a consequence of their long struggles to end European domination, the new nations were either insensitive to or even hospitable to a new imperialism emanating from the Soviet Union. They demonstrated these tendencies in voting on resolutions in the UN General Assembly that, while usually more moderate than the Soviets sought, were discomfiting to the Europeans and to many Americans.

The swing from Eisenhower's European-oriented policy to Kennedy administration support for third world aspirations in the United Nations gradually began to focus opposition on the United Nations itself. Senator Henry M. Jackson, respected chairman of the Senate Subcommittee on National Security, gave a major speech reflecting this position to the National Press Club on March 20. It was a significant watershed in the history of American support for the UN and made a deep impact on the remaining years of Adlai's life.

Jackson's basic theme was that while the United Nations was an important instrument of American foreign policy, the alliance with NATO was paramount. But he did not stop there. He asserted that

> practices have developed which, I believe, lead to an undue influence of UN considerations in our national decision-making. Indeed it is necessary to ask whether the involvement of the UN in our policy-making has not at times hampered the wise definition of our national interests and the development of sound policies for their advancement. . . . The truth is . . . that the best hope for peace with justice does not lie in the United Nations. . . . The best hope for the United Nations lies in the maintenance of peace. In our deeply divided world, peace depends on the power and unity of the Atlantic Community and on the skill on our direct diplomacy.

It was a cogent statement of the view that had been at the heart of most of Adlai's foreign policy battles, beginning with Dean Acheson in the Democratic Advisory Council. On the margin of the copy he obtained after the speech hit the front pages, Adlai penciled in:

> Peace depends on many things—the power of the West and effectiveness of UN in many places—New Guinea, Middle East, Congo, Cuba, Laos. In long run it will depend on the friendly relations of the non-aligned and the West—and the UN is the principal forum in which those political relations are developed so US is not isolated. Will depend on economic development of those countries with help of West.

Jackson went on to say that the United States should "take a more restricted view" of the UN and not ask it "to shoulder responsibilities it can not meet." Adlai wrote: "Congo? Suez?" Jackson criticized the volume of speeches, the numerous votes, and then asked if the United States delegation should play a larger role in policy-making than its representatives to NATO and major world capitals. Adlai wrote in, "Of course!" Jackson's answer was that the "embassy in New York" should play the same role as any other major embassy—but no more. He thought it was unfortunate that both Eisenhower and Kennedy had given the UN ambassador Cabinet rank, stressed he was not "a second Secretary of State," and wondered if the U.S. Mission was "properly manned." He ended by emphasizing: "We need to take another look at our role in the United Nations. . . . We should have a top-level review conducted under the authority of the President and the Secretary of State."

The speech, pulling together as it did many misgivings, started an uproar. At the President's press conference the next day a statement prepared by Adlai and Cleveland, strongly endorsing both Adlai personally and the role of the UN, went unused. Instead, without referring to Adlai, Kennedy reaffirmed his support for both the UN and NATO. The President, knowing he would soon need Jackson's vote on the UN bond issue, tried to play down the quarrel in his own ranks. In a March 29 letter, he wrote Adlai:

> *I hope that Senator Jackson's speech has not given you serious concern. I have felt it better not to take it seriously, but you ought to know that when I commented on it in my press conference last week, I was not aware of Jackson's direct criticism of the position of the US Ambassador at the UN. I disagree with him on that and on other points, but I don't want to build up his criticism by too much notice—and I also have to bear in mind that he has been a strong and consistent supporter of our whole program in Congress. Now we are watching to see how he votes on the [UN] bond issue; my bet is that his voice is worse than his vote.*

But Adlai was seriously concerned. His apprehensions heightened when, on April 2, the Democratic leader in the Senate, Mike Mansfield, rose in the Senate to make a thoughtful statement on the "crisis" in the UN. The one-state, one-vote formula in the General Assembly, he said, gave small new countries the power to vote decisions without responsibility for enforcing them. The General Assembly had "little relevance to the great and fundamental questions," and had become simply "a marketplace for the trading of votes." A quick letter from Adlai was rewarded with a reply stating, "I fully appreciate the difficulties of your job and I want to assure you of my confidence and support."

Communication with Jackson, however, was more difficult; partly for personal reasons. It was widely reported that the speech had been drafted by Dorothy Fosdick, now on Jackson's staff, and Bob Tufts, who had left the State Department to teach at Oberlin but was serving Jackson as a consultant. While they almost certainly had major roles in drafting the speech, it is a serious mistake to assume, as was done, that the speech was motivated and shaped by personal feelings. The speech was consistent with Jackson's convictions and those of key elements in his constituency. Most of all, his subcommittee was the logical place for the views of the pro-NATO elements to center. It was the expression of strong convictions of powerful forces and, as such, needed to be taken seriously. The unfortunate impact of personal feelings occurred in the inability to establish effective communications in the aftermath of the speech.

Letters to Jackson on March 22 and April 13 were unavailing in the effort to make the point that American interests in NATO and the UN were not in conflict. Bob Tufts replied that he was mystified by Adlai's unhappiness with the speech, and repeated that the role of the UN in American foreign policy merited serious discussion.

Dorothy Fosdick's response was more abrupt. On April 20, she suggested that

> *you people take seriously the concern of the internationally minded Senators about the relation of our operations in the UN to the making and executing of our national security policies. You may not agree with particular criticisms, but the warning signals are up. . . . What Senator Jackson had to say was considered by him to be serious and constructive. . . . A strategy of distorting this concern and retaliating with assorted brickbats is no answer.*

Adlai's answer on May 1 said he was "surprised and grieved" by the tone of her letter.

> *I had always assumed that we could discuss such concerns as Senator Jackson recited, which have caused me such difficulty,* before *rather than* after. *But* after *is better than not at all, and I hope we will have an early opportunity to discuss your misgivings and his. P.S. I shall refrain from any talk of "brickbats" and "retaliation" which have never had a part in my dialogue with Democrats—let alone you!*

His letter was signed "Affectionately." Hers ended simply with "Regards."

The incident had taken place in, and may even have been sparked by, an atmosphere charged by the debate over the UN bond issue, which was in trouble on Capitol Hill. The United States originated the idea of the $200-million bond issue, to be sold to member states to cover the unpaid expenses of the Congo operations, because of Soviet and French refusals to pay their assessments. President Kennedy had included support for it in his State of the Union message. Adlai and Rusk had testified for it in early February, but had made statements conflicting with each other's testimony and, in some respects, with the President's.

The poor presentations did little to rescue a proposal that was unpopular from the beginning; many saw it as an act to bail out the Russians—the French failure to pay its share of the assessment for the Congo operation was rarely, if ever, mentioned. Strong White House lobbying was necessary before the bond issue measure finally passed, with help from both Jackson and Mansfield. Adlai had underestimated the difficulties the legislation would face and it resulted in one of his most unhappy periods.

Like all of Adlai's unhappy periods, this one contained cases of happiness and satisfaction. Foremost in 1962 had been John Fell's February marriage in California to Natalie Owings, daughter of the well-known architect. It was a happy time barely marred by a few outbursts from Ellen. The dinner Adlai and Ellen gave jointly for the bridal party was without incident, to the joy and relief of all. Another happy wedding that spring was that of Ruth Field's daughter, Fiona. The bittersweet nature of these family events was underscored by Adlai's being named the 1961 National Father of the Year. There was probably less satisfaction in being ranked fourth in the Gallup poll's rating of the Most Admired Men, even though he was one rank above his first appearance on the list in 1952.

Part of his difficulty arose from the large portion of his time he had been devoting to public opinion. As a result of his speaking activities, he was becoming known as the UN ambassador to the United States as well as the United States ambassador to the UN. His speeches defended the UN's role in the ending of colonialism, justified its weaknesses, and projected his vision for its future.

"This is about all the law and order our anarchic world will swallow today," he told the students at Colgate University.

> . . . What we have is man's first sketch of the world society he has to create. He can build better than this. . . . But will he go on building at all if we are forever tearing up the foundations? The experiment of living together as a single human family—and we aim at no less—is more likely to grow from precedent to precedent, by experience and daily work and setbacks and partial successes, than to spring, utopian and fully formed, from the unimaginable collective agreement of world minds. Let us go on with what we have. Let us improve it whenever we can. Let us give it the imaginative and creative support which will allow its authority to grow and its peacekeeping capacities to be more fully realized.

He wrote numerous letters to critics, including the Reverend Billy Graham, who had asserted in his broadcasts that the United States was characterized as "pagan" in a United Nations listing of countries by religion. Adlai told him there was no such list and urged him to join with other religious leaders in supporting the United Nations. Graham accepted the correction and praised Adlai for the "magnificent" job he was doing at the UN.

After the Jackson speech, Adlai asked Clayton Fritchey, who was in charge of public relations at the Mission, to take a new look at his speaking schedule and see if he could not be doing even more in the months ahead. On his ABC television program, *Adlai Stevenson Reports,* he gave particular attention to the UN-NATO relationship and sought guests who could deal with the Jackson arguments. He encouraged others to speak out and wrote expansive letters of thanks to people, such as Senators Wayne Morse and William Proxmire, who did.

A National Security Council review of foreign policy was scheduled by President Kennedy for June 26 and Adlai was asked to make a one-hour presentation of the UN aspects. In preparation, a long paper had been drafted in the State Department Policy Planning Council by Walt Rostow and a copy had been sent to Adlai for comment. His long response, which Charles Yost helped draft, was sharply critical. He felt the paper was too narrowly focused on the struggle with communism and that "disproportionate emphasis is laid on the military factor." While "a very strong" military deterrent was essential, "other equally important elements are passed over very cursorily." The paper "touched on the UN only in the most sketchy fashion." Even if the concentration were on the contest with communism, the orientation of the Afro-Asians and the Latin Americans could be "most significant" in a hot war and "decisive" in a long cold war, and the UN offered many opportunities to influence their stands. He also felt that the paper dealt inadequately with nuclear arms control.

His own paper, also long, was entitled "U.S. Foreign Policy as Seen from New York." He saw two basic objectives in our foreign policy: the security of the United States, and "peaceful evolution in freedom and diversity." The first could be promoted by maintaining our nuclear deterrent, by balanced NATO forces in Europe, by improving antiguerrilla and antisubversion capabilities, by the earliest possible control, reduction and elimination of nuclear weapons, and by improving international peacekeeping machinery. He pointed out that only these last two involved the UN. The second objective should be to concentrate on strengthening international institutions until it was politically unacceptable to use force in international relations, on strengthening the solidarity of the Atlantic community, and on helping Asia, Africa, and Latin America throw off colonialism, develop, and mature.

He dealt directly with criticism of the UN. Isolationists opposed it on principle, but they were not as important as the larger group who feared that the Russians had somehow seized control of the UN as a result of the influx of new members and colonial issues. The problems, including the strains imposed on relations with European allies, would exist without the UN, and he detailed how the UN had helped ameliorate many of them. In the defense of Europe, he said, the UN was largely irrelevant, but in relating to Asia, Africa, and Latin America, NATO was irrelevant and the UN essential.

"Perhaps the most important single impression I want to leave with you," he wrote,

> is that we should think of the UN not just as a convenient repository for insoluble problems, but rather as an instrument of United States policy which we should use to further our objectives. . . . Building the UN is the world's toughest, most complex, most delicate, most advanced task of institution-building in the world. . . . And the stake is no less than a future system of world order in which the United States can find long-term security in the postcolonial age of atoms and outer space.

Opinions differ on the impact of Adlai's presentation. Schlesinger thought he "flopped." Sorensen was more charitable. "I was impressed with his paper and so, I think, was the President. It had a slightly academic air—and that's not derogatory—and gave us a good picture of the UN's role." Since there was nothing in the paper that required action, no conclusion is possible. Two days later he wrote the President to say he was leaving for Geneva to attend the Economic and Social Council meeting there and take a vacation.

"As I see it, the moment is not very propitious even for minimal progress," he said.

> The general international atmosphere is not good, despite the precarious agreement on Laos. Any one of a half dozen smouldering crises could flare up during the next few months. Internal difficulties in the Soviet bloc are more likely to lead to heightened cold war tensions than the reverse. There are already signs of a tougher line in Soviet propaganda pronouncements. In such a period it seems to me all the more important for us to go to great lengths to keep disarmament discussions alive.

There was then a long analysis of options, including a prophetic passage on the role that overseas bases might assume in any disarmament agreement. It was part of a running battle that he would be waging until the day he died.

It had been a difficult six months, and for the first time Adlai's re-markably healthy and vigorous body sent out warning signals. It began with insomnia and unsuccessful efforts to read himself to sleep. Early in the year, he had gone to see Dr. Henry Lax, who found him suffering from arteriosclerotic heart disease with hypertension. He was also very overweight. Adlai had long been a compulsive eater. He would consume large helpings and then invade the plates of his companions. Frequent tennis combined with extraordinary activity generally had kept his weight under control until he encountered the more restrictive life of New York and the UN. Dr. Lax prescribed a diet to reduce the weight and medica-tion to lower the blood pressure, and at the beginning Adlai heeded his injunctions.

His friend, John Steele, who saw him just before his departure for Europe, reported in *Time:* "Adlai Stevenson looks much older these days. The pudginess is still there. But the eyes are a tired, baleful blue; the eyebrows whitening perceptibly; the hair no less, but amply streaked with silver. He talks in a hoarse semi-whisper. The tone bespeaks age and a sort of I've-been-through-it-once-too-often attitude." Adlai told him he had few regrets other than insufficient time to participate in broad policy decisions in Washington. Kennedy had met the commitments given when he was appointed but "I just don't feel I am in the center of things."

The trip to Geneva was largely a cover for the vacation to follow, but he also wanted to appear with Philip Klutznick, who was about to leave as the United States representative on the Economic and Social Council and was to speak to the council on the UN's World Development De-cade.

The highlight of the summer was a ten-day cruise through the Greek islands on Agnes Meyer's chartered yacht, the *Lisboa,* with Chief Justice and Mrs. Earl Warren, Alicia Patterson, the Drew Pearsons, the Bill Att-woods, Clayton Fritchey, and Kay Graham's daughter, Lally. At one point they discovered with horror that Adlai and the Chief Justice had been swimming in shark-infested waters. In addition there was a trip through northern Italy with John Fell and Natalie to see Ernest and Buf-fie Ives at Villa Capponi in Florence, visits with Italian prime minister Fanfani, the Greek president and foreign minister, the foreign minister of Spain, and Marshal Tito on his island of Brioni.

Along the way, Adlai wrote a memo to himself to

take up with the President and the Secretary the necessity for a United Nations man in the major embassies. No one with any substantive knowledge or interest in the embassies in Paris and London. . . . Foreign service officers with a view to advance-ment bypass it if they can. This *must* be corrected and promotion granted on the same basis or better in view of the importance of the work and the quality of the workers.

Personal affairs crowded the return home in early August. An infected jaw sent him to the hospital almost immediately. A visit from Ad and Nancy was clouded by their "sad sadder saddest tale," as he put it in a note to Jane Dick, of Ellen's deteriorating condition and finances. "She is destitute and getting more neurotic and difficult," he wrote Mary Lasker. The good news was Francis Plimpton's recovery from a near fatal illness contracted in the Congo and Carl McGowan's appointment to the U.S. Court of Appeals for the District of Columbia.

Most depressing of all was the serious illness of Eleanor Roosevelt. Through August and early September she resisted Dr. David Gurewitsch's urgent advice to enter the hospital. Doggedly, she kept on doing the things she had always done, even going to a meeting to discuss the problems of merging several UN-related private organizations into the present United Nations Association of the United States—the UNA-USA. Feverish and weak from chronic bleeding, she finally relented and entered the hospital on September 26.

She told Dr. Gurewitsch that she did not want people to see her in an invalid condition and he, not realizing that Adlai occupied a special place in her heart, turned him away when he came to call. The letter he then wrote her departed from the customary "Dear Mrs. R." and addressed her as "Dearest Eleanor": "Every *day* people ask tenderly about you—and every *night I pray* that your recovery will be swift. I love you dearly—and so does the whole world! But they can't *all* come to see you and perhaps I can when David gives me permission." It was signed, "Devotedly." He was one of the very, very few people not members of her immediate family who would see her again.

A joint Soviet-Cuban communiqué issued on September 2 announced that the Soviet Union had agreed to furnish arms and send specialists to train Cuban military personnel. Actually, the technicians and the arms, including missiles, had begun arriving secretly in late July. President Kennedy, on September 4, issued a statement saying that while there was no evidence of "significant offensive capability" being installed in Cuba, if that should develop, "the gravest issues would arise." A Soviet response on September 11 maintained that the military equipment sent to Cuba was "exclusively for defensive purposes" and warned that United States action against Cuba would be met by "a crushing retaliatory blow." Two days later, the President repeated at his press conference that if the Soviets establish "an offensive military base of significant capacity," the United States would "do whatever must be done to protect its own security and that of its allies."

As a result of these public exchanges, the Congress gave the President standby authority to call up military reserves. Meanwhile, Kennedy had increased the photo reconnaissance flights of U-2's over Cuba. On the morning of October 16, he was given clear evidence that the Soviets had begun construction of a base for medium-range ballistic missiles capable of reaching Washington, St. Louis, Dallas, and all Strategic Air Command bases south and east of that arc. The rate of construction suggested operational capability inside of two weeks.

The Cuban missile crisis, in George Ball's words, "has been minutely described and endlessly dissected," and will not be repeated here. The focus here is on the distortion of Adlai's role that sought to drive him from office; distortion that continues to this day in the ongoing struggle between those who see conflict with the Soviet Union primarily in military terms and those who emphasize patient but firm political negotiation.

That same day, October 16, Adlai was in Washington to make a speech and attend a White House luncheon in honor of the crown prince of Libya. As the luncheon ended, the President asked Adlai to stay behind, and took him up to his second-floor study. There he told him what he learned that morning and asked if he could postpone his return to the UN, where the question of Communist China's admission was about to come up. A small group of carefully selected advisers were beginning to meet to consider possible courses of action and he hoped Adlai could join them for as long as he could remain away from New York. This detail is important in view of the later charge that Kennedy reluctantly brought Adlai into the discussions only toward their conclusion.

In describing the missile sites revealed in the photographs, Kennedy remarked that time was of the essence and he "supposed" that an air strike might be necessary to "wipe them out" before they became fully operational, or perhaps some other forceful action that would make the weapons inoperable. This reaction disturbed Adlai, who said he hoped there would be no air strike until every possibility of a peaceful solution was explored. He emphasized that sooner or later the United States would have to go to the UN to explain its action and it was "vitally important we go there with a reasonable case." Since secrecy gave time to consider various options, Adlai urged the President to maintain his speaking schedule for the midterm election campaign as cancellations would arouse speculation. Kennedy had already decided to do so and left Wednesday morning to campaign in Connecticut.

Before leaving, he received a handwritten memo from Adlai that, according to Theodore Sorenson, annoyed Kennedy because of its "somewhat ambivalent" contents. Eventually, every conceivable alternative, from surprise attack to living with the missiles was discussed, but Adlai's memorandum was written sometime Tuesday when air strikes and/or invasion were the center of discussion. The idea of a naval blockade would not be suggested until Wednesday afternoon by Defense Secretary Robert McNamara. In that context, Adlai wrote the memo that began by urging the President to send personal emissaries to Castro and Khrushchev to underscore the gravity of the situation. While the disadvantages of this course were quickly recognized in the discussions that afternoon, the memo was basically an argument for mobilizing international political support.

"Because an attack would very likely result in Soviet reprisals somewhere—Turkey, Berlin, etc.—it is most important that we have as much of the world with us as possible," Adlai wrote.

> To start or risk starting a nuclear war is bound to be divisive at best and the judgments of history seldom coincide with the tempers of the moment. If war comes, in the long run our case must rest on stopping while there was still time the Soviet drive to world domination, our obligations under the Inter-American system, etc. We must be prepared for the widespread reaction that if we have a missile base in Turkey and other places around the Soviet Union surely they have a right to one in Cuba. If we attack Cuba, an ally of the Soviet Union, isn't an attack on NATO bases equally justified. One could go on and on. While the explanation of our action may be clear to us it won't be clear to many others. Moreover, if war is the consequence, the Latin American republics may well divide and some say the U.S. is not acting with their approval and consent. Likewise unless the issue is very clear there may be sharp differences with our Western allies who have lived so long under the same threat of Soviet attack from bases in the satellite countries by the same IRBMs.

And, toward the end of the memo, he stated that "I confess I have many misgivings about the proposed course of action."

Sorenson indicates that the President contrasted those statements with lines in the closing section of the memo:

> I know your dilemma is to strike before the Cuban sites are operational or to risk waiting until a proper groundwork of justification can be prepared. The national security must come first. But the means adopted have such incalculable consequences that I feel you should have made it clear that the existence of nuclear bases anywhere is *negotiable* before we start anything. Our position, then, is that we can't negotiate with a gun at our head, a gun that imperils the innocent, helpless Cuban people as much as it does the U.S., and that if they won't remove the missiles and restore the status quo ante we will have to do it ourselves—and then we will be ready to discuss bases in the context of a disarmament treaty or anything else with them. In short, it is they, not the U.S. that have upset the balance and

created this situation of such peril to the whole world . . . . we
have no choice except to restore that balance, i.e. blackmail and
intimidation *never,* negotiation and sanity *always.*

As the Executive Committee, or ExComm, continued its intensive
discussions there was a swing away from the air strike and invasion options,
although one or the other or both would continue to have ardent advocates
in such people as Dean Acheson, Paul Nitze, Douglas Dillon, and CIA
Director John McCone. Acheson, particularly, maintaining that the President's previous statements constituted adequate warning, argued insistently for an immediate attack. His chief adversary, to the surprise of
many, became Robert Kennedy, who was sitting in for his brother. By
Friday afternoon, Robert Kennedy, supported by Robert McNamara,
Roswell Gilpatric, and others, had pushed the naval blockade to the
forefront. It was now being referred to as the quarantine, in recognition of
the fact that in international law a blockade is regarded as an act of war.

Adlai returned from the UN to the discussions on Saturday. While
he had been gone, tension had been heightened by photographic reconnaissance disclosing more missile sites that could become operational
within a few days. Sorenson had worked most of the night on the draft of
a speech for the President based on the naval blockade option and took it
to an ExComm meeting that began at 9:00 A.M. Adlai joined the meeting
after it had been in progress for several hours. He spoke in favor of a
quarantine as against an air strike, which apparently annoyed some members who felt they had already gone over that ground.

President Kennedy arrived back from Chicago and at 2:30 Saturday
afternoon presided over a formal meeting of the National Security Council, thus enlarging the group that had been meeting as ExComm. After
indicating his agreement with the naval blockade option, the President
raised the question of possible impact on Berlin. This opened the discussion to possible diplomatic moves that needed to be taken. Adlai had
brought with him a memo addressed to the President, presumably written
in New York the day before, entitled "Political Program to be Announced by the President," and he quickly pointed out that little had
been done to work out the political-diplomatic side of the program to
ensure the support of NATO allies and the Organization of American
States.

He proposed that simultaneously with the President's speech, the
United States should call for an emergency meeting of the UN Security
Council and have ready an acceptable resolution supporting the action to
forestall any initiative the Russians might take. He did not anticipate any
quick UN support, but approval by the Organization of American States,
he stressed, was vital. With that in mind he recommended that the action
be presented in terms of what would be done rather than in terms of a *fait
accompli.* He suggested that the President propose, in exchange for the

removal of all Soviet missiles, the demilitarization, neutralization, and guaranteed territorial integrity of Cuba. This would mean giving up the base at Guantanamo, which he said was of little use to us. He then repeated what someone had said earlier, that we might want to consider giving up Jupiter missile bases in Turkey and Italy. Adlai next spoke of the possibility of sending UN inspection teams to all the foreign bases maintained by both sides to prevent their use in a surprise attack, and of a summit meeting.

"There was not a hint of 'appeasing the aggressor' in these plans, as some would charge," Sorenson wrote in his *Kennedy* biography,

> only an effort to propose a negotiating position preferable to war and acceptable to the world. Even the synopsis prepared by the air-strike "hard-liners" earlier in the week had included not only a call for a summit but a pledge that the United States was prepared to promptly withdraw all nuclear forces based in Turkey, including aircraft as well as missiles. The Joint Congressional Committee on Atomic Energy had also recommended the Jupiter's withdrawal the previous year.

Sorenson noted earlier that at the meeting "an adviser who had served in the preceding administration agreed . . . that the Jupiter missiles in Turkey and Italy were obsolescent and of little military value."

George Ball has written, that "there was nothing new in any of Stevenson's proposals"; that removal of the missiles had been discussed from the very beginning; that McNamara had earlier conceded it might be necessary to give up Guantanamo; and that both McNamara and Robert Kennedy had expressed the view that some such trade might be necessary before the Soviets would accept our demand for the removal of the missiles.

Nonetheless, Adlai had no opportunity to discuss the sequence or timing of the possible moves he suggested. He was promptly, bitterly, and, some say, insultingly attacked by Dillon, McCone, and Robert Lovett. These three, according to Ball, who was present, "violated the calm and objectivity we had tried to maintain in our ExComm meetings when they intemperately upbraided Stevenson," in the course of a discussion Ball characterized as "outraged and shrill."

The President accepted Adlai's suggestion that the speech be postponed from Sunday until Monday night to give time for diplomatic groundwork, and he agreed to the recommendations regarding the UN and the OAS, including reference to the proposed action in the future tense rather than the present. He agreed that the political passages in his speech needed to be strengthened. He rejected the idea of a summit meeting and did not want to relate to this crisis, at least at the outset of possible negotiations, any reference to the missiles or bases. Nor did he want to risk an adverse reaction from NATO allies, especially de Gaulle, who might think the United States was too ready to sacrifice its allies' interests. Adlai scored a high batting average with his recommendations.

Immediately after the meeting, in a contemplative conversation with his brother and Sorenson, the President commented, "You have to admire Adlai, he sticks to his position even when everyone is jumping on him." Robert Kennedy, in his account of the crisis, *Thirteen Days,* which was published after his death, although never an admirer of Adlai's, wrote:

> Stevenson has since been criticized publicly for the position he took at the meeting. I think it should be emphasized that he was presenting a point of view from a different perspective than the others, one that was therefore important for the President to consider. Although I disagreed strongly with his recommendations, I thought he was courageous to make them, and I might add they made as much sense as some others considered during that period of time.

Certainly, there is nothing to support the later charge that "Adlai wanted a Munich."

The next day, Sunday, Adlai set down his thoughts on strategy in the UN. He saw no hope of winning, in advance, votes needed to authorize action against Cuba. The OAS, however, offered the possibility of multilateral support and its approval could provide some protection in law and a great deal in public opinion. It was important to seize the initiative in the UN. To prevent resolutions against the quarantine, the United States had to propose a political path out of the military crisis. His negotiating program, following those expressed in the ExComm meeting, focused on removing from Cuba, under UN supervision, missiles, installations, and Soviet personnel. As evidence of our restraint and goodwill, he would throw a noninvasion guarantee and Guantanamo into the bargain. But he now wrote that the Jupiter bases in Turkey and Italy should not be included because that would divert attention from the Cuban threat to the general issue of foreign bases. This broader question might be considered later apart from Cuba as part of general disarmament negotiations.

President Kennedy continued to regard any political program as premature. He felt attention should be concentrated on the single issue of the introduction of the missiles and the necessity for their removal. Arthur Schlesinger reports that Adlai took the decision "realistically; he felt he had done his job as custodian of our UN interests in making the recommendation, and the decision was the President's."

But the ExComm debate had aroused abiding concerns about Adlai among some of the participants, most notably, Robert Kennedy. John J. McCloy was summoned back from Europe to join Adlai at the UN.

Schlesinger, who was already at work with Harlan Cleveland and Thomas W. Wilson at the State Department on Adlai's speech in the Security Council, was directed to go to New York. "We're counting on you to watch things in New York," the attorney general told him. "That fellow is ready to give everything away. We will have to make a deal at the end, but we must stand absolutely firm now. Concessions must come at the end of the negotiation, not at the beginning."

The assignment of McCloy was to block any tendency toward "softness" that Adlai might display. "As a Republican," Robert Kennedy wrote in *Thirteen Days,* "he made our efforts there bipartisan, and as a counter balance to Stevenson's point of view, he had initially favored a military attack and an invasion of Cuba." What no one other than Ball knew was that Adlai welcomed working with McCloy. In his presidential campaigns, Adlai had scrupulously avoided any discussion of Cabinet choices in the event of his election—with one exception: McCloy. In 1952, he confided to Ball that he would like to have McCloy as his secretary of state. Years later, McCloy wrote Walter Johnson, the editor of the Stevenson papers, saying:

> *In some respects this was a rather awkward relationship because I am sure that President Kennedy's motive in asking me to come to New York was to counteract what he thought might be a too soft attitude on the part of Adlai. When I got to New York . . . I even found him tougher than I was prepared to be. . . . I thought the way he presented the case of the United States once it was disclosed that the missiles were there was most effective.*

Following President Kennedy's Monday night speech, which sent a chill of apprehension around the world, the spotlight swung to New York. While the President was speaking, Adlai had delivered to the president of the Security Council a formal request for an emergency meeting of the council. Attached was a proposed resolution calling for the immediate dismantling and removal of Soviet missiles and bombers from Cuba under UN supervision, for an end to the quarantine once the missiles were gone, and for negotiations between the United States and the Soviet Union "on measures to remove the existing threat." The president of the Security Council for the month of October happened to be Ambassador Valerian Zorin of the Soviet Union. Zorin, along with his colleague, Platon Morozov, Adlai described to John Steele as "two of the nastiest bastards I ever dealt with."

Zorin, opening the meeting at 4:00 P.M. on Tuesday, used the presentation of the agenda as an excuse to say, "The Soviet Union considers the question raised by the United States . . . to be made up out of whole cloth." He described the Security Council proceedings as a "clumsy attempt to cover up the unprecedented aggressive acts carried out by the United States against Cuba—the arbitrary and illegal naval blockade of the Republic of Cuba. In actual fact, the substance of the matter is that the United States—"

Adlai interrupted, "Point of order, please. Are you speaking on the adoption of the agenda or are you making a speech?" Zorin responded that he was speaking only on the agenda, and after a few more brief comments in similar vein, went through the motions of adopting the agenda that included the United States resolution and two counterresolutions submitted by the USSR and Cuba. Adlai's speech, based on the draft Schlesinger had cleared with the President and brought from Washington, was eloquent, and long, some eight thousand words.

Since nine o'clock that morning, the Organization of American States had been meeting in Washington, unable to vote until some ambassadors received instructions. As Adlai was speaking, the vote was taken and adopted; the vote was 19 to 0. Uruguay had abstained in the absence of instructions, but the next day registered an affirmative vote to make the result unanimous. Cleveland telephoned the result to his deputy, Joe Sisco, in New York. On their television sets, he and the President saw Sisco leave the Security Council chamber and then return shortly placing news of the OAS action on the desk in front of Adlai. Absorbed in his speech, Adlai did not seem to notice it. Kennedy called Cleveland and asked if Adlai knew of the OAS action. Just then, Adlai reached for the paper Sisco had placed before him, and the President said, "I guess he has it now."

The OAS resolution, Adlai told the council, called for the immediate dismantling and withdrawal from Cuba of all missiles and other offensive weapons, and recommended that the member states

> take all measures, individually and collectively, including the use of armed force, which they may deem necessary to ensure that the Government of Cuba cannot continue to receive from the Sino-Soviet Power military material and related supplies which may threaten the peace and security of the Continent, and to prevent the missiles in Cuba with offensive capability from ever becoming an active threat to the peace and security of the Continent.

It resolved to report to the UN Security Council and asked it to send UN observers to Cuba. By this action, the naval blockade that was scheduled to take effect the next morning at 10:00 A.M. became legitimate in international law.

"The hopes of mankind are concentrated in this room," Adlai concluded. ". . . This is, I believe, a solemn and significant day for the life of the United Nations and the hope of the world community. Let it be remembered not as the day when the world came to the edge of nuclear war, but as the day when men resolved to let nothing thereafter stop them in their quest for peace."

President Kennedy promptly sent Adlai a telegram saying: "Dear Adlai: I watched your speech this afternoon with great satisfaction. It has given our cause a great start. . . . The United States is fortunate to have your advocacy. You have my warm and personal thanks."

Even more promptly, the Cuban delegate denounced the "blockade" as an "act of war," and asked the Security Council to call for the immediate withdrawal of all troops, ships, and planes deployed on the approaches to Cuba and for an end to all "interventionist" measures. Ambassador Zorin followed, charging that the quarantine was a "new and extremely dangerous act of aggression," was "undisguised piracy," and branding as false the claims that his country had set up offensive armaments in Cuba. The resolution he submitted condemned the United States for violating the UN Charter and "increasing the threat of war," and called for an end to the quarantine and for negotiations among the three countries.

By the time the council adjourned at 8:30 P.M., the U.S. Mission had taken on the attributes of a wartime command center. Mission officers were fanning out to rove corridors and call on other delegations to win support. Their work was needed. Some African states wanted proof that the missiles really threatened the United States. A large number of neutral states, thought to be as many as forty, met for two hours and tentatively decided to ask the three countries to do nothing pending further UN action; the signs were that pressure would be put on the United States to lift the quarantine.

Early on Wednesday, Adlai heard that U Thant was about to take an initiative responsive to the feelings of the neutrals. Adlai was not able to reach U Thant until 2:30 P.M., and was told that an appeal was being sent at six o'clock to Kennedy and to Khrushchev proposing a two-week voluntary suspension of all arms shipments to Cuba, the lifting of the quarantine, and immediate negotiations; in effect, a standstill agreement. He declined Adlai's request to hold off for twenty-four hours but agreed to see Adlai and Yost at 5:00. When they arrived, they found the telegrams had already been sent. At Adlai's urging, U Thant agreed to include in the statement he was going to make to the Security Council that evening a sentence about stopping military construction inside Cuba, but he refused to say anything about missiles already in place.

Adlai made his statement at the end of a long Security Council meeting in which France, Nationalist China, and Chile supported the United States, while Ghana and the United Arab Republic spoke in support of a resolution they submitted calling for an end to the quarantine.

Early the next morning, Adlai received instructions to tell U Thant that the United States hoped Khrushchev would keep his ships out of the quarantine interception area for a limited time in order to permit discussion and, in the interim, avoid dangerous incidents. Adlai was told the administration was ready to discuss U Thant's proposals but to avoid giving U Thant any idea that we would accept a voluntary suspension of the quarantine without UN observation of the sites in Cuba.

Adlai saw U Thant immediately, and he agreed to transmit the United States views to Khrushchev confidentially. Adlai learned that Zorin had been incensed by U Thant's remarks to the Security Council, contending that the quarantine should have been condemned as illegal. U Thant reported he replied that he was not concerned about the legalities when he was trying to prevent an explosion. He also told Adlai that the Afro-Asians were putting pressure on Zorin to accept his standstill proposal. In transmitting Kennedy's message, U Thant added his own request that the Soviet ships be told to stay away from the quarantine area. He suggested to Adlai that if Kennedy now instructed American ships to do everything possible to avoid a confrontation, U Thant would report to Khrushchev that he had Kennedy's assurance of cooperation in avoiding a confrontation.

Adlai, Cleveland, and others were making suggestions about Kennedy's reply to U Thant to avoid any appearance of a rejection of the appeal. That afternoon, Adlai delivered the President's reply, which said:

> I deeply appreciate the spirit which prompted your message of yesterday. As we made clear in the Security Council, the existing threat was created by the secret introduction of offensive weapons into Cuba, and the answer lies in the removal of such weapons. . . . You have made certain suggestions and have invited preliminary talks. . . . Ambassador Stevenson is ready to discuss promptly these arrangements with you. I can assure you of our desire to reach a satisfactory and peaceful solution of this matter.

From Khrushchev, U Thant received a reply saying: ". . . I welcome your initiative. I understand your anxiety over the situation obtaining in the Caribbean, since the Soviet Government also regards the situation as highly dangerous and calling for immediate intervention by the United Nations. I declare that I agree with your proposal, which accords with the interests of peace." Khrushchev had not bothered to inform his ambassador who was calling on U Thant to protest and reject the standstill proposal.

By Thursday, the results of all these activities seemed promising although nothing had really changed and nuclear war still threatened. During the day, the Mission's officers were reporting increasing evidence that the Soviet Union and its supporters were surprised and impressed by the firmness of the United States stand, and that support was gaining among the neutrals. In Washington, meanwhile, Secretary Dillon and others in ExComm were meeting to discuss an air strike on Cuba in the event the Soviets vetoed the United States resolution in the Security Council and the buildup in Cuba continued.

When the Security Council reconvened on Thursday, all members had spoken and Adlai took the floor to respond to the various views. At the outset, his tone was conciliatory, but he then proceeded to rebut the statements by Khrushchev, Zorin, and others that it was the United States that was threatening the peace. "This is the first time, I confess, that I have ever heard it said that the crime is not the burglary but the discovery of the burglary." There had been complaints that the quarantine was "an inappropriate and extreme remedy. . . . Were we to do nothing until the knife was sharpened? Were we to stand idly by until it was at our throats?" He ended by reading Kennedy's response to U Thant's appeal.

Zorin's sharp and lengthy reply charged that the United States had no proof of its contentions. He quoted Kennedy's speech saying that the United States had "unmistakable evidence" of the missiles by October 16, but when he had seen Foreign Minister Gromyko two days later had said nothing about it "because there is no such evidence." Whatever evidence the United States might claim was "fake."

Adlai immediately asked for the floor and made, with the possible exception of his welcoming address to the 1952 Democratic convention, his most memorable speech.

I want to say to you, Mr. Zorin, that I do not have your talent for obfuscation, for distortion, for confusing language, and for double-talk—and I must confess to you that I am glad I do not. But, if I understood what you said, you said that my position had changed; that today I was defensive because we do not have the evidence. . . . Well, let me say something to you, Mr. Ambassador: We do have the evidence. We have it and it is clear and incontrovertible. And let me say something else: Those weapons must be taken out of Cuba.

Next, let me say to you that, if I understood you, you said—with a trespass on credulity that excels your best—that our position had changed since I spoke here the other day because of the pressures of world opinion and a majority of the United Nations. Well, let me say to you, sir: You are wrong again. We have had no pressure from anyone whatsoever. We came here today to indicate our willingness to discuss U Thant's proposals—and that is the only change that has taken place.

But let me say to you, sir, that there has been a change. You, the Soviet Union, have sent these weapons to Cuba. You, the Soviet Union, have upset the balance of power in the world.

You, the Soviet Union, have created this danger—not the United States. . . .

Finally, Mr. Zorin, I remind you that the other day you did not deny the existence of these weapons. Instead, we heard that they suddenly had become defensive weapons. But today—again, if I heard you correctly—you say that they do not exist, or that we have not proved they exist—and you say this with another fine flood of rhetorical scorn. All right, sir, let me ask you one simple question: Do you, Ambassador Zorin, deny that the USSR has placed and is placing medium and intermediate range missiles and site in Cuba? Yes or no? Do not wait for the interpretation. Yes or no?

Zorin's response: "I am not in an American court of law, and therefore do not answer a question put to me in the manner of a prosecuting counsel. You will receive the answer in due course in my capacity as representative of the Soviet Union."

Adlai: "You are in the court room of world opinion right now, and you can answer 'Yes' or 'No.' You have denied that they exist—and I want to know whether I understood you correctly."

Zorin: "Please continue your statement, Mr. Stevenson. You will receive my answer in due course."

Adlai: "I am prepared to wait for my answer until Hell freezes over, if that is your decision. I am also prepared to present evidence in this room."

Zorin, as president, pointedly called on the Chilean ambassador who had asked to speak. However, Ambassador Schweitzer said he would prefer to speak after Zorin had replied to Adlai's question, whereupon Adlai interjected:

I had not finished my statement. I asked you a question, Mr. President, and I have had no reply to that question. I will now proceed, if I may, to finish my statement. . . . I doubt whether anyone in this room, except possibly the representative of the Soviet Union, has any doubt about the facts, but in view of his statements and the statements of the Soviet government up until last Thursday, when Mr. Gromyko denied the existence or any intention of installing such weapons in Cuba, I am going to make a portion of the evidence available right now. If you will indulge me for a moment, we will set up an easel here in the back of the room where I hope it will be visible to everyone [and, not so incidentally, the television audience].

Adlai then proceeded with a detailed explanation of a collection of photographs, many of them showing the progressive construction on the various sites that he located with precision. He described the type and range of the missiles that could be launched from each site. The photos showed missiles on trailers waiting for installation. He showed a large reinforced concrete building under construction that "may well be intended as the storage area for nuclear warheads," although none "are yet visible." He next showed photos of twenty-two crates designed to transport Ilyushin bombers, with four uncrated bombers and one partially assembled. The weapons, the launching pads, the planes, he said, were but part of a total weapons system. "To support this build-up, to operate these advanced weapons systems, the Soviet Union has sent a large number of military personnel to Cuba, a force now amounting to several thousand men." The photographs, he added, were available for detailed examination.

Zorin denied again that there were "offensive weapons" in Cuba. As for the photographic evidence, "Similar methods were used by Mr. Stevenson, though without success, in April, 1961," at the time of the Bay of Pigs when he introduced photographs of a "Cuban aircraft" with the "markings of the Castro air force" as evidence that Cuban defectors had strafed Havana. Since those photographs were faked by the Central Intelligence Agency, what was the value of the present photographs? "He who lies once is not believed a second time," Zorin declared.

Adlai replied:

> I have not had a direct answer to my question. . . . The question is: has the USSR missiles in Cuba? And that question remains unanswered. I knew it would remain unanswered. As to the authenticity of the photographs, about which Mr. Zorin has spoken with such scorn, I wonder if the Soviet Union would ask their Cuban colleagues to permit a United Nations team to go to these sites. If so, Mr. Zorin, I can assure you we can direct them to the proper places very quickly. And now I hope we can get down to business, that we can stop this sparring. We know the facts, Mr. Zorin, and so do you, and we are ready to talk about them. Our job here is not to score debating points; our job, Mr. Zorin, is to save the peace. If you are ready to try, we are.

"The Stevenson speech," Arthur Schlesinger, Jr., has written, "dealt a final blow to the Soviet case before world opinion." Uncertainty and foreboding intensified on Friday and Saturday. The Joint Chiefs recommended an air strike on Monday followed by an invasion. The State Department was instructed to be ready to conduct civil government in Cuba after the invasion. A U-2 was shot down over Cuba and the pilot killed. The FBI reported that the Soviet Mission in New York was apparently preparing to destroy all sensitive documents. The atmosphere in Washington and at the UN was grim. Then, on Sunday, with the two superpowers eyeball to eyeball, as Dean Rusk commented, "the other fellow blinked"; Cuba-bound ships stopped and turned back, and the crisis swiftly eased.

U Thant went to Cuba on October 31, Deputy Premier Anastas Mikoyan arrived in Cuba on November 2, Zorin was replaced at the UN by First Deputy Foreign Minister V. V. Kuznetsov, with whom Adlai had met for lengthy discussions during his 1958 trip to the Soviet Union. This latter move Adlai regarded as especially helpful, since he and McCloy now were responsible for the greater part of the mopping-up operations; they would be busy negotiating with Soviet representatives over Cuba until January 1963. But, meanwhile, on November 20, President Kennedy announced that all known offensive missile sites had been dismantled and removed from Cuba and that the United States would end its quarantine. It is also worth noting that the American bases in Turkey and Italy that aroused such passionate debate were quietly dismantled the following year.

Over much of the world, and especially in Washington and New York, there was relief and rejoicing that, with crucial political backing from the United Nations and the Organization of American States, nuclear war had been averted. Success in averting war has clouded the fact that the United States came very close to choosing the military option. The arguments of those who fought for time and political negotiation are therefore worth recalling. For Adlai, though, the sweet taste of success soon turned sour. First, there was the death of Eleanor Roosevelt, and then there was a vicious personal attack from which he never fully recovered.

When Mrs. Roosevelt reluctantly entered the hospital, it was thought she was suffering from aplastic anemia, but on October 25 her condition had been diagnosed as a rare and incurable bone-marrow tuberculosis. She was prepared to die; indeed, she was determined to die rather than be a useless invalid. The children decided that Adlai should be allowed to make a last visit to his old friend. "I don't think she will recognize you," Anna Roosevelt warned him. He came immediately. He bent over her and whispered lovingly into her ear. When he asked if she had heard him, she replied, "Yes, my dearest." Tears filled his eyes as he quietly withdrew from the room.

On November 9, two days after her death, the General Assembly put aside other business and delegate after delegate expressed their personal grief and their country's sorrow. It was the first time any private citizen had been so honored. Adlai told friends that his speech to the General Assembly and the one he gave on November 17 at a memorial service at the Cathedral of St. John the Divine, were the most difficult and certainly the saddest of any tasks he had ever been called upon to perform.

"Yesterday I said I had lost more than a friend," he told the delegates.

I had lost an inspiration. For she would rather light candles than curse the darkness, and her glow had warmed the world. . . . The sadness we share is enlivened by the faith in her fellow man and his future which filled the heart of this strong and gentle woman. She imparted this faith, not only to those who shared the privilege of knowing her and of working by her side, but to countless men, women and children in every part of the world who loved her even as she loved them. For she embodied the vision and the will to achieve a world in which all men can walk in peace and dignity. And to this goal of a better life she dedicated her tireless energy, the strange strength of her extraordinary personality. . . . While she lived, Mrs. Roosevelt rekindled faith in ourselves. Now that she is gone, the legacy of her lifetime will do no less.

And at the cathedral, he closed his long eulogy: "We pray that she has found peace, and a glimpse of sunset. But today we weep for ourselves. We are lonelier; someone has gone from one's own life who was like the certainty of refuge; and someone has gone from the world who was like a certainty of honor."

Soon after her death, Adlai joined with others of her friends to establish the Eleanor Roosevelt Foundation to promote causes to which she had devoted her life. In the remaining years of his life he devoted much of his time and energy to the foundation.

A harbinger of the brewing storm came in an attack from Senator Barry Goldwater.

On November 13, papers quoted him as saying, "I am more concerned over a civilian like Adlai Stevenson telling the United Nations we are prepared to take 'risks' to lessen the chance of an intensified arms race with Russia than I am about military men who regard the Soviets as an implacable foe which will never deal in honor." That same day, in a sharp letter, Adlai pointed out that the statement was based on only a portion of a paragraph which "as you must know, reads as follows:

We have demonstrated again and again during long negotiations that we are prepared to take certain risks to lessen the chance of an intensified arms race. *But we are not prepared to risk our survival.* If other nations permit—as we have agreed to do—the degree of international inspection technically required for mutual security, we can end the arms race. *But we can not stake our national existence on blind trust—especially on blind trust in a great and powerful nation which repeatedly declares its fundamental hostility to the basic values of a free society.*

He expressed the hope that the senator would "feel some obligation to be accurate and responsible in your public statements."

The senator would later repeat the charge.

On Saturday, December 1, President Kennedy summoned Arthur Schlesinger and said, "You know that Charlie Bartlett and Stewart Alsop have been writing a piece on Cuba for the *Saturday Evening Post.* I understand that Chalmers Roberts is planning to do a story on the Alsop-Bartlett piece for the *Washington Post* and that he is going to present it as an attack on Adlai Stevenson. You had better warn Adlai that it is coming."

Schlesinger asked what the article said. The President understood that it accused Adlai of advocating a "Caribbean Munich," and added, "Everyone will suppose that it came out of the White House because of Charlie [one of Kennedy's closest personal friends]. Will you tell Adlai that I never talked to Charlie or any other reporter about the Cuban crisis, and that this piece does not represent my views."

A short while later, Clayton Fritchey called from New York. He had obtained an advance copy of the article. It featured a large photograph of Adlai with an agonized expression and a large caption declaring: "An opponent charges 'Adlai wanted a Munich.' He wanted to trade U.S. bases for Cuban bases." Thus was highlighted two short passages that appeared only toward the end of the article.

The first quoted "one of the actors in the drama" saying that "at first we divided into hawks and doves, but by the end a rolling consensus had developed, and except for Adlai, we had all ended up as dawks and hoves." The second asserted:

> Only Adlai Stevenson, who flew down from New York on Saturday, dissented from the ExComm consensus. There is disagreement in retrospect about what Stevenson really wanted. "Adlai wanted a Munich," says a non-admiring official who learned of his proposal. "He wanted to trade the Turkish, Italian and British bases for the Cuban bases." The Stevenson camp maintains that Stevenson was only willing to discuss Guantanamo and the European bases with the Communists after a neutralization of the Cuban missiles. But there seems no doubt that he preferred political negotiation to the alternative of military action.

Why this preference was considered so horrible, it is now difficult to understand.

A huge furor erupted. It was almost universally assumed that such an intimate glimpse into White House decision-making in a crisis could only have been written with the approval of the President, especially since one of the two writers was his close friend. Moreover, it was recalled that a Bartlett column had preceded the departure of Chester Bowles from the administration, and it was assumed that the pattern was being repeated, that Bartlett was helping the President force Adlai out.

Much mystery still remains. The weight of evidence suggests, however, that the President was implicated in the writing of the article, but never imagined that an effort to cut Adlai down to ambassadorial size would be regarded as a drive to force him out. The aim of focusing attention on the administration's success was frustrated by the reaction to the attack on Adlai.

On Sunday, Schlesinger and Fritchey drafted a statement to be released by a "Stevenson spokesman." Schlesinger sent it to the President, who made a few minor changes and suggested checking the minutes of the climactic October 20 ExComm meeting to ensure accuracy. Schlesinger planned to do so the next morning, but that night Fritchey learned from Roberts that his story would break in the Monday morning *Washington Post* and he gave Roberts the statement so that the rebuttal would appear with the original charge.

Greatly upset, Adlai broke an appointment with Kuznetsov, who was coming to the apartment for lunch, and flew to Washington to attend an ExComm meeting in order to cast some doubt on the *Post* charges. He and Fritchey then talked to the President and they agreed on a statement that Pierre Salinger would read at his regular noon briefing of White House reporters. Adlai left, satisfied with the statement, but the reporters were far more critical. They pointed out that the statement did not really deny the *Post* article; it spoke of Adlai's support of the quarantine policy without stating whether he favored or opposed it before it was adopted. Back in New York, Adlai was being persuaded by one or more of his newspaper friends that Bartlett would never have written the article unless he was confident he was writing what the President wanted. When Schlesinger called Adlai that afternoon, Adlai told him "grimly" that if the President wanted him to go he did not have to go about it in such a roundabout fashion.

Deeply disturbed, Schlesinger went to Kennedy; in *A Thousand Days,* he reports their conversation: "Mr. President, everyone in town thinks that the Bartlett article is a signal from the White House that you want to get rid of Stevenson. You know that, if you really want Stevenson's resignation, you have only to say a word now and he will resign immediately without any fuss or controversy."

Schlesinger writes that the President swore briefly and said, "Of course I don't want Stevenson to resign. I would regard his resignation as a disaster. . . . In the first place, where could I possibly find anyone who could do half as good a job at the UN? . . . In the second place, from a realistic political viewpoint, it is better for me to have Adlai in the government than out. In the third place, if I were trying to get him out, Charlie Bartlett is a good friend, but he's the last medium I would use."

Schlesinger later said he had the impression that the President was slightly more sympathetic with Bartlett's predicament than Adlai's, but he left that impression out of his report that evening to a "profoundly depressed" Adlai. After listening to Schlesinger's account of what the President had said, Adlai replied abruptly, "That's fine, but will he say it publicly?" The next morning the New York *Daily News* proclaimed, ADLAI ON SKIDS OVER PACIFIST STAND ON CUBA.

When Schlesinger sent the *Daily News* clipping to Kennedy with a suggestion that he consider doing something further, the President discounted it and tried to play down the entire affair. He had asked Sorenson to draft a personal letter to Adlai, but he would go no further. If everyone sat tight, it would all subside. The President was much too optimistic. That afternoon, Fritchey reported that Adlai might well resign. Harlan Cleveland, who was in New York, also told Schlesinger that public action by the President was absolutely essential not only to restore Adlai's morale but also his position at the UN. He added that Adlai was convinced that the article was part of a deliberate plan to get rid of him and that the President must have known about it.

On Wednesday morning, Adlai appeared on the NBC *Today* show and his anger was barely repressed. He called the article "wrong in literally every detail." He pointed out that he supported the quarantine proposal days before the decision was made. "What the article doesn't say is that I opposed . . . an invasion of Cuba at the risk of nuclear war until the peace keeping machinery of the UN had been used." On the bases, "I said that, if the United States started a negotiation about the elimination of the bases with Mr. Khrushchev, we would have to develop well in advance the context, the political context, of whatever our position would be. Among these would inevitably be the subject of bases which Mr. Khrushchev would raise." As, indeed, he did.

Kennedy was furious. Profanely, he asserted that Adlai's television statement changed the story "from a local New York-Washington story, of interest to a few politicians and newspaperman, into a great national scandal. Millions of people who never heard of the attack on Adlai now know he is in trouble. Why the hell couldn't he have kept quiet?"

He was wrong. Papers all over the world were assuming the premise behind the *Daily News* headline was correct. Even as far away as Melbourne, Australia, stories the two previous days lamented Adlai's anticipated departure. Kennedy insisted to Schlesinger he did not want to issue a statement that would give the newspapers more to write about, but he gave Schlesinger a letter drafted by Sorenson and asked him to deliver it personally to Adlai in New York.

The letter, which now appears not to have been entirely truthful, stated:

> *This is just a note to tell you again how deeply I regret the unfortunate fuss which has arisen over the statements contained in the* Saturday Evening Post *article. I think you know how greatly we have all admired your performance at the United Nations in general and during the Security Council debate and private negotiations connected with the Cuban crisis in particular. Both of us are accustomed to receiving the slings and arrows of those in the press or elsewhere who delight in stirring needless controversy— and I know you share my confidence that this furor will pass as have all the others.*
>
> *The fact that Charlie Bartlett was a co-author of this piece has made this particularly difficult for me—perhaps you have had the same problem with personal friends in the newspaper profession. In this particular case, I did not discuss the Cuban crisis or any of the events surrounding it with* any *newspapermen—and I am certain that the quotations in the* Saturday Evening Post *article with respect to your role did not come from the White House, as is clear from its obvious inaccuracies alone. While I realized when Bartlett started this piece that everything controversial in his article would be laid at my door, whether I talked to him or not, I did not feel I could tell him or any other friend in the press what subject to write or* not *write about.*
>
> *However, both of us have much more important matters to concern us and the continued success and significance of your role at the UN will soon wash out any doubts others may be trying to plant.*

By the time Schlesinger arrived in New York, Salinger had called to say that it was now felt that word of the letter should be leaked to the press. As the two of them looked at it in that light, they both thought it would not be possible to leak excerpts and that therefore the references to Bartlett would have to be deleted. In their redraft they added a sentence expressing "my fullest confidence and best wishes." When they showed it to Adlai, he added a sentence saying that the elimination of "the nuclear menace from Cuba is the best evidence of the wisdom of our policy and its execution, in which you have played such an active part." They then telephoned the President who added the strongest statement himself, that "your continued work at the UN will be of inestimable value."

With the release of the letter the public furor did begin to die down, but not before *Life* magazine published a huge double-page spread on THE ADLAI STEVENSON AFFAIR—HARD FACTS SUPPORT THE AMBASSADOR

AGAINST IRRESPONSIBLE CHARGES. It was written by Adlai's good friend, John Steele, the chief of the Time-Life bureau in Washington.

A quarter of a century later, the incident was still reverberating. The Sunday *New York Times Magazine,* on August 30, 1987, published as its main article an account of a reunion of the ExComm participants. It reported a letter Rusk had sent to the gathering in which he revealed that the President had authorized him to telephone U Thant's American deputy, Andrew Cordier, and tell him we would remove the Jupiter missiles from our bases if that would obtain the removal of the Cuban missiles. McGeorge Bundy was quoted as saying that Rusk's revelation showed that Kennedy "was prepared to go the extra mile to avoid the conflict and absorb whatever political costs that may have entailed." No one mentioned the hit-and-run tactics aimed at Adlai to hurt him politically as he tried to map out that extra mile. Yesterday's sin became today's virtue.

Hawks can be hardy birds. As another example, there continued to pop up in conservative journals, into the 1980s, the myth that Adlai had persuaded Kennedy to cancel an air strike that could have averted disaster in the Bay of Pigs.

For months, Washington continued to buzz over what everyone saw as an effort to force Adlai's resignation. It now appears that the primary source was the one who, after Adlai, was most troubled by it: the President himself. Attorney General Robert Kennedy once said:

> I think it came from a conversation between President Kennedy and Bartlett. But the article was misinterpreted and out of context. What developed was not what was intended by President Kennedy. He was aghast at what developed. I'm sure he did talk to Bartlett—that he told him Stevenson didn't behave very well—he might have said something that Bartlett talked to others about and put together. So he does bear some responsibility for this.

In a book published in 1968, Otto Friedrich quoted a *Saturday Evening Post* editor as saying that Kennedy read the article twice before it was published and that he wanted the Munich phrase left in. Kennedy's involvement was corroborated by Stewart Alsop in a 1973 letter to Walter Johnson. Kennedy did not inspire the article. He was not the "nonadmirer" who said "Adlai wanted a Munich," Alsop wrote, and then added:

> But it is true that Kennedy read the piece for accuracy and proposed a couple of minor changes. . . . One of the changes was in the section dealing with Adlai Stevenson and Cuba. It was his clear intention to give this section a tone less critical of Mr. Stevenson. The actual result was precisely the opposite

since the President cut out two or three sentences which reflected Clayton's [Fritchey] explication and justification for Stevenson's position on the bases. Stevenson's position was thus
made to seem less rational than in fact it was. One moral seems
to be that overworked Presidents are lousy editors. Another
moral that I have since abided by is not to submit any article to
anybody in advance, including Presidents.

Perhaps another sad moral is that people can do petty and hurtful
things even while acting greatly.

On December 9, Adlai went to Washington with McCloy and
Schlesinger and that night performed brilliantly as toastmaster at a dinner
of the Joseph P. Kennedy, Jr., Foundation. He introduced the President's
mother as the head of the "world's greatest employment agency." When
he had been introduced by Sargent Shriver, the President led a standing
ovation.

The confrontation with Zorin was the most popular thing that Adlai
had ever done. He could not avoid noting the irony of this adulation in
the light of his years of effort to develop better relations with the Soviet
Union. "What a helluva thing to be remembered for," he commented
wryly to a friend.

More important, the injury inflicted by the magazine article lingered
on, and on. "After the Cuban missile crisis," George Ball has said,
"Adlai was only going through the motions. . . . From then on he knew
he was not going to have an impact on foreign policy—which was what
was most important to him."

His custom was to send a card to those who sent him Christmas
greetings containing a quotation, usually a prayer. This year, he found in
Robert Louis Stevenson's writings the message that reflected his reaction
to the trials of the year:

> Give us grace and strength to persevere. Give us courage
> and gaiety and the quiet mind. Spare to us our friends and
> soften us to our enemies. Give us strength to encounter that
> which is to come, that we may be brave in peril, constant in
> tribulation, temperate in wrath and in all changes of fortune,
> and down to the gates of death loyal and loving to one another.

Constant, almost compulsive travel and increasing self-indulgence
marked the months following the Cuban encounter. Much of it was devoted to "waving the fan dancer's fan" to call attention to the UN, but
two trips to Europe mixed business and pleasure, with the latter getting
more than usual attention. The immediate reason was an invitation to
speak at the NATO War College in Paris on March 25, and before leaving

he left a long memo for Kennedy and Rusk arguing again for giving NATO a larger political dimension.

In barely three weeks, Adlai visited Paris, London, Brussels, Bonn, Berlin, Madrid, Rabat, Marrakech, Fez, and Seville. Everywhere he met political and diplomatic leaders, held press conferences, met with correspondents and editors; he addressed the Berlin House of Representatives, visited the Berlin Wall, and kept an unrelenting schedule of lunches and dinners, not all, by any means, for official business. He spent time with Marietta's daughter, Frankie FitzGerald; the Plimptons' daughter, Sarah; and saw actress Ava Gardner. In Fez he was entertained by the minister of tourism who provided, according to Marietta, who was with him, "three terrifying belly dancers. I was so embarrassed. Adlai thought it was funny. He was not nearly as shocked as I'd hoped he'd be."

Africa dominated life at the UN. Fighting in the Congo climaxed in the early months of 1963, but not before there was another State Department struggle between the European and NATO group on one side and the African and UN sections, and Adlai, on the other. The latter carried to the President and the ExComm their argument in favor of providing an air squadron and combat supplies to help the UN end the Katanga secession. After sharp fighting, UN forces entered Jadotville, and war in the Congo quickly ended.

The infighting continued, however, over apartheid in South Africa and self-determination for Angola. Adlai planned to return to Europe on June 30, and, again before leaving, he left a memo for Kennedy. This one reviewed the debate over the choice "between Africa and the European colonial powers," and urged the President to "favor our future relations with the people of Africa."

In Paris, on July 3, he received phone calls from Jane Dick and Ruth Field telling him Alicia Patterson had died the night before. Apparently he could not face the strain of saying good-bye to the one who for years had been closest to him and he did not return for the funeral. Jane Dick sent flowers in his name and then wrote him a moving description of the service. Thanking her, he said, "It seems unthinkable that she is gone and I, for one, will have a hard time reconciling myself to life without the comforting assurance that she would always be there when needed."

On July 15, Adlai was summoned back to Washington to meet with Kennedy and Rusk on South Africa and Angola. They had already virtually decided the position on South Africa. The decision sounds much like the policy that prevails to this day. We would express our opposition to apartheid and call on member states to refrain from supplying arms that could be used to enforce it. We would oppose "extremist" African resolutions that called for economic sanctions, an immediate arms embargo, and expulsion from the UN. We would announce that the United States unilaterally would end all arms shipments to South Africa after the end of 1963. During the week-long debate, he persuaded the Afro-Asians to remove the call for an economic boycott and an arms embargo, and the amended resolution was adopted 9 to 0.

Concerning Angola, the President wanted to avoid trouble that could jeopardize our bases in the Azores; among other considerations was the unfavorable impact that could have on the pending Senate ratification of the test ban treaty. Adlai said we must do our best to preserve the presently favorable position the United States enjoyed in Africa without losing the Azores. He favored taking the initiative in gaining support for a resolution that had been hammered out under Harlan Cleveland's guidance that would call on Portuguese and African nationalist leaders to discuss how self-determination could be achieved and refrain from sending arms the Portuguese could use in its African territories. The President ruled against taking the lead and urged Adlai to try to moderate extremist African moves.

The Security Council met on Angola from July 22 through July 31. Adlai felt he made progress in obtaining amendments to the Afro-Asian resolution that he hoped would make it acceptable to Portugal, the Afro-Asians, and the United States. He was also working hard to bring Britain and France along with him. But at the last minute, when the amended resolution came to a vote on July 31, the President instructed Adlai to abstain. It was adopted with the United States, the United Kingdom, and France abstaining. Adlai was reported to be "disgusted."

Satisfactions centered on the arrival of another grandson born to John Fell and Natalie, and the signing of the nuclear test ban treaty in Moscow on August 5. His inclusion on the delegation to Moscow, however, had required Arthur Schlesinger's intervention. A note to the President on July 29 said he had "underestimated" Adlai's "feeling about going to Moscow. . . . He feels that this is an issue on which he was prematurely right, that he has been vindicated, and that no one could be a more appropriate participant in the final ceremony."

His approach to the September session of the UN General Assembly was halfhearted. There were no initiatives, none of the excitement that marked earlier sessions and the succession of crises. He looked forward mainly to a trip to the West Coast that would begin in Dallas with a speech on UN Day, October 24.

The day before his arrival, the National Indignation Convention held a "United States Day" with retired General Edwin A. Walker as the principal speaker. The morning Adlai arrived, Dallas was flooded with handbills bearing a photograph of President Kennedy and captioned WANTED FOR TREASON. Adlai spoke to a UN Day luncheon at the Sheraton-Dallas, held a press conference, and then went on to an Eleanor Roosevelt Foundation reception and dinner prior to the big evening rally. An enthusiastic audience of some five thousand people filled the hall, but it was the presence of a handful that is remembered.

While he was speaking, Walker's supporters began heckling loudly, and some fistfights broke out in the audience. As the police removed one of the hecklers, Adlai said, "I believe in the forgiveness of sin and the redemption of ignorance." When he finished speaking, he left the hall to go to his waiting car. He had to pass through a crowd of pickets that started shoving him about. He stopped to try to reason with a screaming woman, and the crowd closed in. Another woman hit him on the head with the sign she was carrying. Two men spat in his face. Wiping his face, he said, "Are these human beings or are these animals?" The police moved to rescue him. As they started to arrest the woman who had hit him, he asked them to let her go. "I don't want to send her to jail, I want to send her to school."

After reading press accounts of the incident the next morning, President Kennedy asked Schlesinger to telephone Adlai on his behalf, express concern at his treatment, and congratulate him on how he had handled the attack on him. At first Adlai joked with Schlesinger about the affair, then added: "You know, there was something very ugly and frightening about the atmosphere. Later I talked with some of the leading people out there. They wondered whether the President should go to Dallas [as planned for a month later] and so do I."

Schlesinger was reluctant to convey Adlai's concern to the President, fearing that Adlai's apprehensions would feed criticisms of Adlai voiced around the White House. A few days later when Adlai asked Schlesinger if the warning had been passed on, he expressed relief when told it had not been—it would be out of character for Kennedy to fear physical danger. Adlai also felt reassured by reaction in Dallas. The *Times Herald* had published an editorial headlined DALLAS DISGRACED. The City Council voted an official apology. The mayor called on the city to redeem itself next month when President Kennedy visited Dallas.

On November 22, at a luncheon given by the Chilean ambassador, Adlai received a whispered message from Frank Carpenter, the U.S. Mission press relations officer. He excused himself and rushed across the street to the Mission offices. He sat in front of the television screen, watching the reports from Dallas, and every now and then said, "That Dallas! Why, why, didn't I *insist* that he not go there?"

CHAPTER TWENTY-THREE

"Blinded by the Sunset and Groping for the Path Down"

PRESIDENT LYNDON JOHNSON FOCUSED his formidable persuasive powers on maintaining continuity in the new administration. Adlai was one of those on whom he lavished his blandishments, beginning the day of President Kennedy's funeral.

"You should be sitting here," Johnson told him. "You carried the banner when the going was hard." Arthur Schlesinger, Jr., to whose office Adlai went following the meeting, adds that Johnson said further, "You kept your word to me that you would stay out of the campaign of 1960, and that is why I am sitting here instead of you—and you know more about foreign policy than anyone in the party—you will be my man on foreign relations." Adlai told Schlesinger he thought he would play a much larger role in foreign policy than he had been permitted to play under Kennedy.

"I think," Schlesinger said,

he felt his own generation was coming back to power and that those bright, hard, definite young men who made him vaguely uneasy would fade out of the picture. In a way he appreciated Kennedy—his eulogy of Kennedy at the UN was marvelous—but he was not given to generous remarks about him. I suppose he never overcame a certain resentment about Kennedy being years younger and denying him first the Presidency and then the

Secretary of State. . . . Now his ambition revived . . . Stevenson was laboring under a delusion. It turned out he was in worse shape with Johnson than he had been with Kennedy because Rusk quickly got more power. . . . Johnson had been stringing him along.

Schlesinger's observation is corroborated by others, including Adlai. "Having known Lyndon Johnson for more than 30 years," he wrote Barbara Ward, "I feel that the relationship will be even better than with Kennedy." Newton Minow recalls: "Johnson told Stevenson, 'Anything you want—anything you want—tell me—you deal directly with me. I want your advice. You and I have been friends for thirty years and we are going to show these young people how to do things.'" (Adlai was eight years older than Johnson.) Harlan Cleveland reports that Adlai told him, "I've known Johnson for years, it'll be quite a different relationship." But, Cleveland adds, "the relationship, in the end, was not as good with Johnson as with Kennedy." McGeorge Bundy puts it most bluntly. "After Johnson came in Stevenson was deceived. He thought he was going to be heard at last. He wasn't."

The alienation process was a gradual one. As the war in Vietnam intensified and United States involvement expanded, Johnson came to rely most heavily on McNamara, Rusk, and Bundy. Adlai, after all, was in New York, and, as Charles Yost observed, "the man from out of town is always wrong." Moreover, Adlai was concentrating on finding a way through the political minefields toward a negotiated settlement, in opposition to increasing reliance at the center of decision making on military action behind a smokescreen of talk about negotiation. In Washington, the UN's peacemaking and peacekeeping machinery increasingly came to be seen as irrelevant, or worse, annoying. After Johnson's landslide victory over Goldwater in 1964, even the smokescreen began to dissipate, along with whatever little influence Adlai had left. Adlai himself was slow to see the truth, causing lingering disappointment, disillusion, and, in some cases, anger among many admirers.

At the beginning, though, hope was high and the energy that had oozed away after the *Saturday Evening Post* article rushed back. President Johnson readily accepted Adlai's suggestion that he speak to the UN General Assembly on December 17, prior to its adjournment. The President and his wife both accepted honorary chairmanships of the Eleanor Roosevelt Foundation, and Lady Bird rearranged her schedule to appear at a foundation fund-raising luncheon in New York. Effusive letters were exchanged.

Christmas at Libertyville and Bloomington was one of his happiest. With him were Adlai III, Nancy, and their four children; John Fell and Natalie and their son, Borden; and, of course, Viola Reardy. On his schedule, he wrote, "What a day!" The next day, he took Borden and

John Fell to Bloomington and the old house on Washington Street for a happy round of reunions with Buffie, her son Tim and his wife, and other old Bloomington friends.

A foretaste of the year to come was an abrupt summons back to New York for a meeting over the dispute between the Greek and Turkish communities on Cyprus. A few days later, at Kennedy airport en route to visit the Dicks in Jamaica, Adlai was called back because nationalist elements protesting American policy on the canal had created a crisis in Panama. He spoke that evening in the Security Council and then left for the shortened week in Jamaica. On his return, he hoped to spend a few days in Chicago and Libertyville, but again he was called back—this time because of Cyprus and Kashmir.

Less immediate, but more persistent and important, were the negotiations that began with the Soviet Union in March over the nonpayment of assessments—what would become known as the Article 19 dispute. By now, the Soviet Union and the Eastern European countries except Yugoslavia were nearly two years in arrears on the payment of assessments for peacekeeping operations in the Middle East and the Congo. When the General Assembly opened in the fall, they would be subject to the provisions of Article 19, depriving the right to vote to those more than two years in arrears. The following year, the same would apply to France. This posed a constitutional crisis for the UN and a serious policy dilemma for the United States.

Insistence that Article 19 applied to the special assessments voted by the General Assembly, rather than by the Security Council where the Russians had a veto, could drive the Soviet bloc and France out of the UN. Not to insist on it would undermine the ability to finance future peacekeeping operations that might be authorized by the General Assembly when blocked by a veto in the Security Council. Moreover, in persuading the Congress to vote for the UN bond issue, assurances had been given that the United States would stand behind the application of Article 19. At the Senate hearings, Adlai had said, "We shall be extremely stubborn about this." No one then thought that the issue would go unresolved for so long, but now it posed the possible destruction of the UN—a possibility that found a hearty advocate in the prospective Republican candidate for President, Senator Barry Goldwater.

As the negotiations that Adlai began in March dragged on through the summer, both the House and Senate unanimously passed a joint resolution calling on Adlai to see that the debts were paid. Representative Gerald Ford of Michigan reflected sentiment in both parties and in both bodies when he said: "There is no room for compromise. Our U.N. delegates should demand that these other nations make their payments as they are required to do. . . . This is not a negotiable issue in the U.N. Payment is to be made, or else."

Despite the earlier assurances to Congress, no one in the administration wanted to force the issue to the point of driving the Russians out. After long discussions in Washington involving both Johnson and Rusk, Adlai suggested to Soviet Ambassador Nikolai Fedorenko that a partial "voluntary" contribution could avoid the application of Article 19 without having to confront questions of legality or principle. In return, countries would not be required in the future to help pay for UN peacekeeping operations they objected to. It seemed like an adroit way out with no one losing face. But in late March, the suggestion was rejected. The negotiations went on, and on, as varying formulae and devices were put forward in the effort to avoid breaking up the organization. Adlai and his colleagues not only had to be persistent in the negotiations with the Russians, but diligent in their canvassing of other delegations to make sure that there would be majority support for whatever was proposed to the General Assembly. By fall, when nothing had worked, the American elections were used as an excuse to postpone the Assembly session from September to December.

The early months of 1964 were full of activities outside the UN's corridors. *The New Yorker,* in an article describing in detail Adlai's working days and nights, marveled at his "fantastic energy." Almost as intense as his activity at the UN were his efforts to help build the Eleanor Roosevelt Foundation. In February alone he gave speeches at five fund-raising events in New York and Florida in addition to letters and personal calls on potential donors. Ironically, he found himself competing with the Kennedy Foundation for funds, and sent a check of his own to the Kennedys.

Others were calling on him to explore the possibility of his becoming a candidate either for Vice President, or for the Senate in New York in opposition to Senator Kenneth Keating. Johnson's statement that he did not want a running mate chosen from members of his Cabinet was aimed at Robert Kennedy, who was still serving as attorney general, but it hit Adlai as well. There is little evidence that Adlai took either possibility very seriously. It appears he did toy briefly with the vice presidential idea, but, as in the earlier case involving the Illinois Senate seat, it is likely that he sought to use the possibilities either to strengthen his UN position, or as part of his search for a graceful way out of the UN role. In any event, on April 30, he announced he would not seek the Senate seat, and in August he declared his support of Robert F. Kennedy. And he genuinely rejoiced in Johnson's choice of his good friend, Hubert Humphrey, as Vice President.

Most commentaries place Adlai's desire to leave the UN in the context of his growing doubts about American involvement in Vietnam. What this ignores is that early in 1964, Adlai had begun discussions with Lloyd Garrison and Simon H. Rifkind about returning to the law firm.

On March 5, he had been informed that the partners of Paul, Weiss, Rifkind, Wharton, and Garrison were agreed on the arrangements for his return. Only the date remained uncertain, but Adlai had written on March 27 that January 1965 appeared feasible. What only a very few intimates knew was that Adlai had a health problem requiring a change of life-style from one he felt was inescapable in the UN job. During 1963, he had turned his back on Dr. Lax's stern injunctions. He began ignoring his diet and his weight, forgetting to take the medicine, and breaking appointments with the doctor. He also resumed smoking, which he had not done since 1954.

After a June television appearance, he sent Clayton Fritchey a note saying people were commenting on "how deathly sick and tired I always look on television," and then suggesting what he had resisted vehemently during the presidential campaigns: "Is there some way we could experiment with make-up to improve this gargoyle?"

Others noticed evidences of extreme fatigue. Now, the life of the party would sometimes fall asleep in the midst of one. Adlai III reports seeing him "literally staggering with fatigue late in the evening, clutching at walls and tables." The grumbling he often indulged in when surrounded by sympathetic friends, especially women, became progressively more somber. Most of them dismissed his occasional talk about resignation as a response to temporary frustration, but in 1964 his obvious strain and exhaustion caused some of them to urge resignation on him. He told friends he had promised Johnson he would remain through the election, and that would oblige him to stay on through the General Assembly because a new man wouldn't be ready to handle the range of upcoming issues. Also, even if reasons of health were given, a resignation would be seen as a repudiation of Johnson and his policies. He told a few he felt trapped.

The haunting problem of Ellen also clouded his morale. He had been forced long ago to withdraw from any direct dealings with her, as a reference to him would aggravate her behavior. A heavy burden had fallen on his sons. He spent many hours discussing the problem with the boys and he helped them meet the financial demands she was making on them. Adlai III says his father was "exceedingly generous." Ellen was calling Adlai III as many as ten times a day and at all hours of the night. Borden had his telephone unlisted to avoid his mother's calls. Her complaints, though erratic, centered mainly on financial matters as her imprudence caused more and more of her assets to evaporate. Ad discovered that she was selling her furniture to a dealer, and thereafter the family bought whatever she did not want. On one occasion she called him pleading hunger and the exhaustion of her credit at all the grocery stores. He sent her the eight hundred dollars she said she needed to cover her food bills for a month, only to discover the next day that she had spent the entire sum on flowers and still had no food.

He learned that she was calling the wife of a Libertyville farmer to say that he was "insane," that he and his brothers, together with her mother, were trying to murder her. Once when five-year-old Adlai answered the phone she told him she had ordered a cobra for him and it would arrive soon; that it was "a real, live snake . . . that would grow to be bigger and bigger and when he opened the cage and let it out . . . it was going to eat his mommy and daddy." One night in Libertyville during a family discussion of his mother's condition, Ad took down a volume of the *Encyclopaedia Britannica* to see what it said about paranoia. What his father had just been saying was almost a verbatim repetition of the encyclopedia's entry.

Early in 1964, a decision had been reached that legal action would have to be taken to protect what few assets Ellen had left. On May 15, the three boys and Ellen's mother joined in petitioning Cook County Probate Court for appointment of the Continental Illinois National Bank and Trust Company as the "conservator" of Ellen's financial affairs. The action was taken, they told the court, "after years of painful deliberation and fruitless attempts to help." More years ensued of painful depositions, of testimony describing increasingly bizarre and occasionally violent behavior, of court proceedings and of other legal maneuvers, as Ellen resorted to various devices to delay or overturn court action. When she could no longer avoid the court's ruling in favor of the conservatorship, she fled to Indiana to escape the court's jurisdiction. Ellen settled, in the company of her "financial manager," James Ingram, on her Indiana farm until her death from cancer in an Indiana hospital on July 28, 1972, refusing to see any member of her family, including Adlai III who was waiting outside her hospital room door.

On May 19, 1964, Vietnam came to the UN. Cambodia requested a meeting of the Security Council to consider "acts of aggression" by the armed forces of South Vietnam and the United States—"terrorist raids" into Cambodia on May 7, and other violations.

The tragedy of Vietnam had long antecedents, beginning for the United States with President Roosevelt's unsuccessful opposition to the return of French rule after the Japanese occupation. In the postwar years, more aid had gone to Vietnam than to all of France under the Marshall Plan. Fighting in Laos had been a concern of Eisenhower's. Under Kennedy, the scale of military aid rose rapidly and several thousand troops were sent to help train the South Vietnamese Army. The new Johnson administration expanded the military assistance and by May there were sixteen thousand American troops in South Vietnam with the dispatch of another five thousand approved and consideration being given to air strikes on North Vietnam.

The uninformed U.S. Mission to the UN could only pass on to the State Department a request from U Thant for a confidential account of what had actually happened on the border. It developed that, in pursuit of Vietcong forces, South Vietnamese forces had crossed into Cambodia, killing seven Cambodians and wounding three. No United States personnel was involved. South Vietnam expressed regrets, offered indemnity, and suggested bilateral talks with Cambodia about the use of its territory as a Vietcong sanctuary.

Summoned back from London, Adlai joined the Security Council debate on May 21. His speech, prepared by the State Department and approved by the President, was a full-dress defense of the United States position in the area. He admitted that "mistakes" had been made in trying to repel "aggression" against South Vietnam, and declared that there were two major elements of United States policy. First, the United States had "no national military objective anywhere in Southeast Asia"; and second, the United States was involved "only because the Republic of Vietnam requested the help of the United States and of other governments to defend itself against armed attack fomented, equipped and directed from the outside." The speech suggested that Cambodia and Vietnam might establish a military force to patrol the frontier and report to the UN secretary general—a force that could be augmented by UN observers, or placed under UN command. The proposal was made despite the fact that our ambassadors in the area, whose opinions had been sought, pointed out the difficulties of patrolling 350 miles of jungle border.

The lasting strain in Washington's relations with U Thant began a few days later. U Thant told reporters that he had personal doubts about the UN's ability to direct effectively the suggested UN peacekeeping force; moreover, the problem was primarily political, not military. His questioning of American policy was regarded as "naïve" and "unrealistic." History gives him far higher marks. Adlai, while faithfully seeking to carry out instructions from Washington, found himself increasingly in sympathy with U Thant.

On this occasion, Adlai was told that U Thant's statement was "outrageously offside" and could be "damaging." He was instructed to speak strongly to U Thant and point out that it was not for U Thant to decide what was the UN's capacity for peacekeeping. When Adlai and Yost talked to him on May 27, U Thant held his ground and maintained that solutions should be found in the fourteen-power conference on Southeast Asia that had been set up in Geneva. He was told the United States opposed this because such action would involve Vietnam and Laos as well as Cambodia and thus would damage morale in Vietnam, Thailand, and other countries. In a statement that was more significant than he knew, Adlai told U Thant that if the Communists continued their pressure the United States would have no alternative but to step up its military effort.

What may be regarded as Adlai's definitive view at the outset of the Vietnam War is set forth in a memorandum he gave to President Johnson the next evening at a political fund-raising party. His deputy, Charles Yost, an exceptionally able career officer who had served as ambassador in Laos, had joined in its preparation. It began with a heavily underlined sentence: "We must demonstrate to the world that all peaceful remedies through the United Nations have been exhausted before resorting to an escalation of United States military action." The next sentence was a reminder that "in fact, we have an obligation to report to the Security Council before taking such action."

Section I dealt with Cambodia, and asserted, "As of today, there is no possibility of a large and effective UN force to *protect* the border." A commission of inquiry might be possible, and this "very meager" action "would at least get a UN foot in the door." Section II dealt with Laos and described several options depending on whether or not support from France could be obtained. "In either approach our main aim should be to introduce the United Nations into Laos with sufficient physical presence and political will that it would make any further Pathet Lao military action politically costly and build the basis for a political settlement."

Vietnam itself was the subject of Section III and had disturbing elements of prophecy.

> Regardless of how serious the situation in Vietnam seems to us, world opinion is simply not sufficiently prepared for either U.S. military action in North Vietnam or a U.S. appeal to the United Nations. The first would be widely considered an irresponsible escalation of the war likely to bring in Communist China. The second would not produce a useful Security Council resolution because most members of the Council still believe the war is essentially a civil war and Hanoi assistance only of secondary importance. So, at present, before or after military action on our part, we would be more likely to get a UN resolution against us than one for us.
>
> There is grave question in my mind whether U.S. armed intervention in North Vietnam, consisting of more than sabotage and harassment, makes military sense. However, if the situation in South Vietnam is so grave that military reaction against North Vietnam is the only way out, much more political preparation is necessary. . . . If over a period of time at the UN or in Geneva we can demonstrate clearly that it is Hanoi which keeps the Vietnam War going, we can perhaps build up the necessary support for UN action or justification for U.S. action.

If Adlai had any illusions about his role in shaping Vietnam policy, they were sunk in the engagement in the Tonkin Gulf on August 4. His information was restricted largely to the speech he was sent to deliver in the Security Council. Uneasy, he protested to Cleveland: "But are our hands clean? What the hell were our ships doing there in the first place?" His main comfort was in the fact that the administration's program of "limited, measured" responses in Southeast Asia was in sharp contrast to the more belligerent actions being advocated by presidential candidate Goldwater.

Little would be served by recounting the intricate maneuvers at the UN that accompanied the tragic struggles in Vietnam. In retrospect, it is clear that despite the barrage of proposals and counterproposals, debates and internal battles, the advocates of a military solution became dominant early in the Johnson presidency. The hope of a political settlement was kept alive more as deception than as reality. Even the brilliant Arthur Goldberg was beguiled by Johnson into resigning from the Supreme Court after Adlai's death to accept the UN ambassadorship with the prospect of becoming the Vietnam peacemaker. With commitment in Washington commensurate with Goldberg's own, and a willingness to accept losses far less grievous than those ultimately suffered, a political settlement might have been possible. It certainly could not have been more costly.

A ceasefire in Cyprus was the UN's major achievement that summer. Adlai filled speaking engagements on college campuses, which he enjoyed, and participated in the Democratic convention and presidential campaign, which were not so enjoyable. For the first time, he began using the same speech with only slight variations in several places. One, however—the Dag Hammarskjöld Memorial Lecture at Princeton on March 23—was one of the most notable he would give in the final years of his life. He worked on it with Thomas W. Wilson in Harlan Cleveland's office to project a blueprint for policies "beyond containment" that had been the guiding concept of the cold war period.

> The only sane policy for America—in its own interests and in the wider interests of humanity—lies in the patient, unspectacular, and if need be lonely search for the interests which unite the nations, for the policies which draw them together, for institutions which transcend rival national interests, for the international instruments of law and security, for the strengthening of what we have already built inside and outside the United Nations, for the elaboration of further needs and institutions of a changing world for a stable, working society.

He appeared before the Platform Committee of the Democratic National Convention and delivered a tribute to Mrs. Roosevelt to the full convention. In urging his paper to print the full text of the eulogy, Alfred Friendly of *The Washington Post* said, "We are not likely to get anything better than this until they resurrect Lincoln."

In general, though, Adlai found himself on the periphery of events. His enthusiasm for the campaign was fired mainly by the opportunity to respond to Goldwater's attacks on the United Nations.

As the campaign ended, he flew to Santiago, Chile, to lead the United States delegation to the inauguration of President Eduardo Frei Montalvo, stopping first in Mexico and Panama. His mission was more than ceremonial. He had been asked to dissuade the new president from establishing diplomatic relations with the Soviet Union. The interview went badly and was ended abruptly by Frei, who resented the interference and declared his intention to renew relations as planned.

Good Democrat that he was, Adlai was delighted by the election returns that he listened to in Santiago. He cabled President Johnson, "If I drink any more toasts to El Presidente Johnson, I may disgrace you. Coming Home." He cabled Dick Daley in Chicago to thank him "for all you did for Adlai," who had been elected to the state legislature. But to his son, he telephoned. His pride in Ad was too great to be confined to a cable.

The election removed the necessity of countering Goldwater's belligerence with restraint. The Pentagon Papers later revealed that in the weeks following the election detailed planning for bombing the North and escalating the war began. Not only was Adlai not involved in any of the planning, on his return from Chile he went to work with Yost on a memo advocating a wholly different course. The memo President Johnson had requested was entitled "A Reassessment of United States Foreign Policy—1965–70." Adlai regarded it as a major effort and sent copies to Humphrey, Rusk, and Cleveland. It was one of the fullest statements of his foreign policy views he ever made during his government service.

He extended the "beyond containment" analysis of his Princeton speech and set forth five "serious encroachments on the stability of the current 'balance of terror.'" These were: (1) proliferation of nuclear weapons; (2) Communist "wars of liberation" through tactics that cannot be overcome solely by outside military forces; (3) impatience with the growing economic burden of armaments; (4) impatience with the failure to reduce armaments and dangers to nuclear war; and (5) the existence of obstacles to effective UN peacekeeping. Instability and radicalism in the third world and changes in the Communist world driven by increasing concentration on domestic needs, he claimed, tended "to recreate an international anarchy which no single Great Power, such as the United States, can dominate, and no regional or international organization, such as the United Nations, is yet strong enough to control."

This situation could not be met "simply by more of the same old prescriptions: more United States and Western armament, more NATO unity, more alliances with small states in the Far East, more bilateral military and economic aid to underdeveloped states in Asia and Africa.

Most of these measures continue to be desirable, but they are increasingly inadequate and unreliable."

The threat of the Soviet Union continued, but the "principal threat to world peace and Western security in the foreseeable future will almost certainly be Communist China." It was "aggressive, resourceful and resolute," militarily stronger than all other Asian countries except the Soviet Union, and its ability to "create maximum disorder in Asia and Africa" would increase. This suggested the need to mobilize far stronger forces in Asia to contain China, including seeking the cooperation of India, Japan, Britain, Australia, and New Zealand. He called for "more vigorous efforts to develop a meaningful continuous dialogue with Peking" and relaxation of opposition to participation in the UN and other international agencies.

In essence, Adlai was arguing for a basic shift in emphasis from Europe to Asia—a concept that would not be fashionable until a quarter of a century later.

Stopping the spread of nuclear weapons was an "obvious" need, but the greatest dangers arose from wars between medium and small powers and from "wars of liberation." As examples of the former, Adlai cited "Israel-Arab, India-Pakistan, Malaysia-Indonesia, Ethiopia-Somalia, Greece-Turkey," all of which held dangers of Great Power confrontation. "Wars of liberation" were often conducted as guerrilla wars and Westerners, "no matter how excellent their training and equipment," were not "well fitted to fight among and against colored populations." Therefore, "Western Powers should exhaust all other possibilities of checking this type of war before becoming directly involved themselves."

The weak regional organizations in Latin America and Africa and the absence of regional organization in Asia "emphasizes the vital importance of rapidly developing United Nations peacekeeping capabilities." He described various obstacles standing in the way and suggested approaches to their removal.

Two extended sections of the memo emphasized the importance of attacking the "enlarging gap between developed and underdeveloped countries." He urged that "means must be found promptly to convince public opinion" in the developed world that "despite its growing cynicism and weariness, the world which will result from the aggravation of this development gap will be an extremely dangerous one for their children to live in." Rapid population growth "can seriously upset even the most modern guided economy," he warned, calling for a "forthright campaign of public education" and government aid. Unless "the crazy automaticity of death control without birth control" was checked, it would "before many decades escalate all the problems of the world into intractability, intolerability, war and catastrophe."

Asked what happened to the memo, McGeorge Bundy replied that "its fate was like all after the election. . . . Everybody assumed that there was a mandate for Johnson to do as he pleased." Although the view of China has changed, it is amazing—and distressing—to observe how much of the memorandum remains relevant.

A casualty of the election campaign was U Thant's already strained relations with Johnson, Rusk, and to a much lesser extent, Adlai, over the "lost peace initiative."

A charge by U Thant during a February 24 press conference that the United States government was withholding from the American people the truth about the possibility of peace talks jolted the country, and especially Washington. "I am sure," he said,

> that the great American people, if only they knew the true facts and background to the developments in South Vietnam, will agree with me that further bloodshed is unnecessary. The political and diplomatic method of discussions and negotiations alone can create conditions which will enable the United States to withdraw gracefully from that part of the world. As you know, in times of war and of hostilities, the first casualty is truth.

Adlai, in Jamaica, received an urgent phone call from Harlan Cleveland to check on the somewhat fragmentary background he had available. The background remains somewhat incomplete as not all documents have been declassified, but an exceptionally diligent effort by Walter Johnson in editing the Stevenson papers has provided the essential elements of the story.

During a visit to Washington on August 6, 1964, arranged by Adlai, U Thant talked with him, Rusk, Yost, Harriman, and William Bundy and suggested that leaders from Hanoi and Washington should talk face to face to end the fighting in Vietnam. Thinking his views had been welcomed, U Thant, on his return to New York, asked the Soviet government, through the highest-ranking Soviet citizen in the UN Secretariat, to sound out the North Vietnamese about the idea. On September 23, U Thant told Adlai there had been a favorable response from Hanoi, and Adlai reported this to Washington. On October 15, Adlai told U Thant that Johnson was too preoccupied with the election and advised U Thant to shelve the initiative for the time being.

After the elections, Adlai told U Thant that Washington had checked through its own channels and received the impression that Hanoi did not want a conference. On December 1, meeting with Soviet Foreign Minister Gromyko and Ambassador Fedorenko, U Thant had discussed with them North Vietnamese willingness to enter into bilateral discussions. Then, early in January 1965, he pressed Adlai for an answer from Washington. On his own initiative, Adlai asked U Thant where such a meeting might take place and U Thant suggested Rangoon. Adlai then asked him to ascertain whether the Burmese government would provide facilities for secret talks. On January 18, the Burmese government agreed. Adlai returned to U Thant on January 30 with word that Washington was opposed to holding the conversations because it would be difficult to keep them quiet and any publicity might bring about the downfall of the South Vietnamese government.

Two weeks later, on February 16, Adlai asked U Thant if he had received any reaction from Hanoi on Washington's decision. U Thant later told Walter Johnson that at this meeting Adlai "appeared distressed" at the massive bombing of North Vietnam that had occurred on February 7 while Soviet Premier Alexei Kosygin was on an official visit in Hanoi. He suggested to Adlai that a way to proceed would be to issue a statement that would be short of a ceasefire proposal but would contain "some form of words regarding a more congenial climate for negotiations." If bilateral talks were not possible, a seven-nation meeting could be held (perhaps in Rangoon), consisting of the two Vietnams, the People's Republic of China, the Soviet Union, France, the United Kingdom, and the United States.

Later, Washington would argue that U Thant had not made a "proposal," that he had merely made a procedural suggestion. When Adlai reported the conversation to Rusk, the latter made it clear that the bilateral meeting had never been seriously considered because the United States could not possibly meet secretly behind the back of our ally. Adlai argued that the United States should say it was ready to negotiate and propose a meeting of the seven nations. If an agreement was reached, the United Nations should be involved in implementing it.

Following this conversation with Rusk, perhaps because of its unsatisfactory nature, Adlai sent a memorandum of his conversation with U Thant to the President on February 16, and, on February 17, followed it with a longer personal letter to the President outlining a detailed course of action that could be taken to follow up on U Thant's suggestion, including a draft statement for the President to issue to the press. Copies were sent to Rusk. After Adlai's death, Johnson would tell U Thant that he never heard of his peace initiative. This is simply not credible.

Adlai sent his letter and memorandum of conversation to the President through Bill Moyers who, in 1972, wrote Adlai III:

> Your father sent his original memo to the President through me, feeling, as he later told me, that it would be assured of getting to Mr. Johnson. It did go immediately to the President and he called Secretary Rusk. . . . My wife and I subsequently had lunch with your father in New York and he lamented the murky ending to which the initiative and his memo came. He never understood why no one at any high level gave U Thant the benefit of any doubt.

Adlai left for Jamaica on February 19, where his vacation was broken into by the anxious call from Cleveland who correctly assessed the uproar that was to follow. White House Press Secretary George Reedy strongly denied that any proposal had been received or that negotiations were in progress.

That night, February 24, at ten o'clock, Rusk telephoned U Thant and the conversation that ensued, even from the denatured State Department memo that exists, can only be described as harsh. Rusk evinced little interest in U Thant's proposals, contending they were "just procedural." What concerned him was the statement that the truth was being withheld from the American people. U Thant insisted he had made proposals and had been patient throughout the discussions that had begun seven months earlier in August. Rusk asked him to correct the impression that he was aiming his comments at the American people over the heads of their government. U Thant rejected that interpretation of his remarks and repeated his belief that most Americans did not know the true facts about the war in Vietnam. Rusk closed the conversation saying that he was instructing Yost to call on him the next morning to convey the government's adverse reaction to U Thant's press conference comments.

Relations between Rusk and U Thant, rarely more than polite, never recovered from the recriminations and attitudes that flowed from that day. When he accompanied Johnson to the meeting with U Thant in September, after Adlai's death, Rusk told the secretary general, "Stevenson was not authorized to reject the approach and he should have kept the channels open." Neither is this credible.

A declassified document released by the State Department reports:

> Stevenson later told Cleveland that the answer from Washington was always: "There may be a time . . . but not now." Secretary Rusk's recollection was that it was one of those things he talked over with Stevenson along with others and because [at the time they were getting messages from various intermediaries] it did not have the mark of seriousness, he was very much afraid it was a move to embarrass us with Saigon and there was doubt of anything substantive. We did not reject it—we simply did not indicate that we wanted to go ahead at that time but put it on the shelf for consideration for future.

Cleveland made this assessment years later: "The basic problem (I think) was that Stevenson did not like the answer he got from Secretary Rusk, hoped it would be moderated in time, and therefore did not pass it along to U Thant in a timely manner. This produced a growing resentment in U Thant, which finally boiled over in his February 24 press conference."

Adlai not only had failed to "pass it along to U Thant in a timely manner," he had not confided to his associates, Plimpton, Yost, or Pedersen, the content of his discussions with U Thant or Rusk. When the bombshell of U Thant's press conference burst, they were unable to explain his action. If Adlai had been present, or if Rusk had ever regarded the conversations as offering an opportunity for political negotiation, the immediate turmoil and the lasting tension might have been avoided.

Afterward, in the passionate debate over the Vietnam War, charges of dark conspiracies would be made. The essence of what happened seems much more simple. By this time, virtually the entire weight of the governmental machinery was behind a military solution. The sustained bombing of the north that was supposed to break Hanoi's will already was scheduled to start within a week of U Thant's press conference. George Ball's was almost the only voice in favor of a negotiated political solution that was being heard in the higher reaches of policy-making. The UN, U Thant, and Adlai had been shoved to the sidelines, tolerated because of possible usefulness in the future, but by no means major players. U Thant's "peace initiative" was never "lost"; in terms of serious consideration, it was not even "received."

Adlai can be faulted for not pushing more vigorously for U Thant's initiative or for his own follow-up suggestions in the February 17 letter to the President. But the sad truth is, by this time he had lost hope of exerting any decisive influence. He held on to, but did not really believe, Johnson's renewed blandishments. Johnson asked Adlai to come see him the day after his Inauguration and heaped praises on him for his "brilliant" job at the UN. He said Adlai could never be replaced at the UN and he hoped Adlai would stay throughout his administration. He wanted to issue a public statement saying so and expressing admiration and gratitude. Adlai expressed appreciation but said he really wished to resign after the forthcoming General Assembly. He also commented that he had little participation in foreign policy discussions.

He was tired, disillusioned about his role in general rather than in relation to any particular policy, and he was looking for a graceful and noncontroversial way to exit. He was also worried about his health although his overt response was to ignore his doctor's advice and to enjoy himself.

His social calendar became even more packed, and the list of ladies he was seeing became longer and more varied. Around the UN there were many smiling references to "Adlai's harem," and "Adlai's dowagers." In addition to Marietta, there were Jane Dick, Ruth Field, Mary Lasker, Barbara Ward, Mrs. Vincent Astor, Mrs. John Gunther, Evelyn Houston, Beth Currie, and Mrs. Walter Paepcke. His warm friendship with Jacqueline Kennedy continued unabated after the President's death and they were often seen at public events. In Washington, Nan McEvoy, Betty Beale of the *Washington Star*, and columnist Mary

McGrory, as well as Agnes Meyer and her daughter Mrs. Kay Graham, were special favorites. There were also Ava Gardner and Mercedes Mc-Cambridge. Gossip columns noted both of these, and Buffie was heard admonishing him about his relationship with Gardner. In a letter to Marietta, he referred to her as "this lovely, lush, strange girl."

Nor did he neglect the daughters of his good friends. Marietta's daughter, Frankie; the Plimptons' daughter, Sarah; the Smiths' daughter, Adele; Kay Graham's daughter, Lally, make frequent appearances on his appointment calendar and in his correspondence in his final months.

Marriage figured in many of his discussions with his sons and close friends during this period. After Alicia, his sons felt that Marietta was the one that interested him most. Borden held a strong preference for Ruth Field, who had become a second mother to him. Adlai's enjoyment of the fantasy of a happy marriage became a substitute for the reality. At sixty-five, he was not prepared to make the personal adjustments that marriage would entail. He radiated in the company of attractive, intelligent women, and enjoyed the amenities provided by the wealth of some. But the prospect of having to deal with servants and other aspects of the deeply entrenched life-styles of women with strong personalities as well as wealth appalled him. He had always traveled light, traveled fast, pursuing his insatiable curiosity, and he was not prepared to risk losing that freedom. This is far more plausible than the charge of a few of the disappointed that what he wanted was a mother, not a wife.

In his enjoyment of the company of beautiful women—some of them married, most of them rich—proposals of marriage would sometimes be made. They were impulses of the moment, and those who knew him were aware they were not intended to be taken seriously. But in at least a few cases, they were, and feelings were hurt. A lady in England, while in the process of assembling her trousseau, reluctantly accepted advice from mutual friends that she had misunderstood Adlai. It is exceedingly curious that a man who, throughout his life, was so sensitive to others, especially women, and who had never been known to inflict pain knowingly, could have been so unthinking.

Curious, also, was his response to warnings about his health. Time after time, he broke appointments with Dr. Lax, one of them just before leaving on his last trip to London. In May, during one of his increasingly rare visits to the doctor, he admitted that he was going to parties almost every night, and had not been taking the medicine or adhering to the diet prescribed.

"Governor, it cannot go on like this," Dr. Lax told him sternly. "You have to stop this way of living, even if it means to resign as an Ambassador. You are on a suicidal course."

After looking at him for a moment, Adlai smiled and replied, "How do you know I want to live long? My father died at the age of sixty; my mother at sixty-five. I am now sixty-five; that will be enough for me." He agreed to return later in the month. When he did, the doctor found he had gained an additional five pounds. Dr. Lax told him he was dissatisfied with his condition, but Adlai merely looked at him and shrugged his shoulders.

Despite this behavior, he was concerned. He confided in Adlai III and Borden, as well as Marietta and Carl McGowan, rarely saying more than he had "a heart problem," or "heart flutters." Their pleas for him to resign or cut down went unheeded. His calendar from March through June was even more crowded, with numerous engagements around the country added to a heavy burden at the UN.

In March, Adlai was sent to Vienna to represent the United States at the funeral of the Austrian president, made three speeches in Washington, narrated Dore Schary's reenactment of Abraham Lincoln's second Inaugural Address on the steps of the Capitol, recorded it with Eugene Ormandy and the Philadelphia Orchestra, and spoke at the convention of the United Federation of Teachers.

In April, he spoke at the Eleanor Roosevelt Memorial Award Dinner and the American Newspaper Publishers' Association Bureau of Advertising meeting in New York, the dedication of the Prudential Center in Boston, and the Massachusetts Legislature.

In May, he spoke and received an honorary degree at the University of Toronto. At a Memorial Day concert in Washington he narrated the *Lincoln Portrait* by composer Aaron Copland "so eloquently," according to *The Washington Post,* "that even fidgeting school boys sensed a moment to remember."

In June, he spoke at the convention of Rotary International in Atlantic City, the Arkansas Bar Association at Hot Springs National Park, gave the commencement address and received an honorary degree from Williams College, spoke at the Harvard commencement and received an honorary degree he had long wanted, spoke at the dedication of the Equitable Life Assurance Building in Chicago, and appeared on NBC's *Meet the Press.*

While all this was going on, there were active negotiations at the UN on the Article 19 financing issue, a humiliating "flap" over Johnson's appearance at the twentieth anniversary gathering of the UN in San Francisco, a major and profoundly unsettling crisis over the sending of troops to the Dominican Republic, more efforts to find a peacemaking role for the UN in Vietnam, and mounting pressure on him to resign in protest to the war.

Such a schedule would have strained a young and sturdy heart. Not all of it was necessary, and one cannot help but wonder if Adlai was imposing the strain deliberately.

The General Assembly that began in mid-January met under rules of procedure that Adlai had suggested without authorization. It shocked those in the State Department who had been working to devise a policy that would be sustained in Washington as well as successful at the UN. In seeking to avoid paralysis over the voting issue, Adlai had suggested during a conversation with Fedorenko that the Assembly might meet to discuss pending questions but act only "by consensus." He then persuaded Rusk to go along with the no-voting proposal and the plan was presented to the public as representing no change in policy but simply a tactic to allow time for negotiations. Elections to Assembly offices were handled by informal ballots in the office of the president of the Assembly.

Under this arrangement, the Assembly debated Cyprus for nearly a month and complex negotiations proceeded on Article 19, guided largely by Cleveland's exceptionally skillful and imaginative deputy, Richard N. Gardner. Much of the negotiating that went on inside the United States government focused on the speech that President Johnson was to make at the UN's anniversary meeting in San Francisco. The idea was for the President to state that the United States considered its position on Article 19 to be sound, but it would no longer insist on its being invoked if the UN did not wish to do so. Instead, the United States would reserve the same option to withhold payments for UN expenses to which it had strong political objections.

Johnson agreed to the change in policy and approved the speech that, with suggestions from Adlai and Yost, was prepared to announce it. Someone leaked the speech to James Reston. When the plan appeared in *The New York Times,* Johnson refused to deliver the speech and ordered the writing of a new draft with no policy proposal in regard to Article 19. When an officer of the Mission called the State Department to inquire about the new speech, he was told that the President had issued specific instructions that no one at the Mission, including Adlai, was to be given any information about it whatsoever.

The anticipation aroused by the fact of the President's coming to San Francisco, enhanced by the Reston story, built up to a terrific letdown. Not only was the speech devoid of substance but even the rhetoric was pedestrian. In the disappointment that settled over the entire event, Adlai's humiliation was evident to all. Two months later, after Adlai's death, his successor, Arthur Goldberg, would announce the policy that had been written into the President's undelivered speech. (Twenty-three years later, the United States would be the UN's biggest debtor.)

On Wednesday, April 28, Adlai was attending a late-afternoon meeting at the White House with Rusk, McNamara, and Bundy on Vietnam. As they were meeting, an urgent message arrived from the United States ambassador in the Dominican Republic reporting that the rebellion begun four days earlier by followers of Juan Bosch was creating anarchy and endangering American lives. He asked the President to send Marines.

They were sent at once, and the President announced his action on nationwide radio and television that night.

Adlai had no part in the decision, though it took much of his time in the remaining months. His UN colleagues have said that the Dominican crisis troubled him more than anything that happened during his time at the UN. He told a newspaper correspondent that the Dominican intervention had taken years off his life. Arthur Schlesinger declined a request from Johnson to explain the policy to Latin America because he thought it was wrong, and he sent Adlai a copy of his letter criticizing the action. In response, Adlai wrote him, "Nothing has caused me as much trouble since the Bay of Pigs and it goes on and on." Encountering Schlesinger in Washington a few weeks later, he said, "If we did so badly in the Dominican Republic, I now wonder about our policy in Vietnam."

Sending troops, as it was done, could only have disturbed him deeply since it struck at the principle of peaceful settlement of disputes, ignored both the UN and the OAS, and in the process alienated Latin American opinion. On April 29, as twenty-three thousand marines began landing in the Dominican Republic, he informed the Security Council that the action had been taken to protect and evacuate American citizens and that the United States had asked for a meeting of the OAS. The next day, Cuba lodged a protest, and the following day the Soviet Union requested an urgent meeting of the Security Council to consider "the armed interference by the United States in the internal affairs of the Dominican Republic."

Adlai and his colleagues at the Mission were called on to defend a highly unpopular action. His main help came from the violence of the Soviet and Cuban attacks. The Soviet resolution condemning the United States and demanding immediate withdrawal was defeated. Lacking strong Latin American support, the United States accepted a resolution expressing concern "at the grave events in the Dominican Republic," called for a ceasefire, and asked the secretary general to send a representative to observe and report on the "present situation." In May, Adlai spoke in the Security Council on twelve different days, and in June, twice. Charges against the United States would continue, and Adlai would be wearily and unenthusiastically involved until the end.

"I'm getting so sick of this place & this job and 'public life.' I don't like watersheds; I've had too many in life and now I'm on another one— blinded by the sunset and groping for the path down."

This note, written during a late-night meeting of the Security Council, and added to a letter to Marietta Tree on August 8, 1964, expressed the dominant theme in the last year of his life. Following the March decision to return to the law firm, he was approached about the presidency of George Washington University, and of the Motion Picture Producers Association. Of far greater interest to him were offers from New York University and Columbia University opening the possibility of combining with law practice the opportunity to write, lecture, and maintain a continuing association with young people. The latter was important to him; so was the possibility that the law firm affiliaton would permit the reopening of a base in Chicago as well as New York.

At the time of his death, the only definite agreement was with the law firm. Though he had promised Andrew Cordier, who was acting on behalf of Columbia, not to make any university decision without further discussion, New York University's offer appeared to be the most appealing. Date and details had yet to be worked out but the law firm-university base was almost certainly the center of his post-UN planning. The irony that marked so much of his life was present in the fact that the Vietnam War, which made him want to leave "public life," was what prevented him from doing so, frustrating him as he was "groping for the path down."

The "sunset" blinding him was not so much fatigue, with its reminder of an overworked heart, and a sense of déjà vu, but the continuing search, led by the persistent U Thant, to find some way to open political negotiations over Vietnam. Any doubt about Adlai's own position was removed at a meeting with the President, Rusk, and Cleveland on March 12. For the first time signaling an open break with Rusk, he gave the President a memorandum stating, "I think the conditions that Sec Rusk has attached to any talk about peaceful settlement is [sic] unrealistic and unsupported by the illustrations he uses."

Some two weeks later, on April 1, a new opening was presented by a call issued by seventeen nonaligned nations for negotiations without preconditions. On April 7, in a speech at Johns Hopkins University, President Johnson responded that the United States was ready for such "unconditional discussions," and went on to describe a gigantic Southeast Asian development program for which he would ask Congress for a billion dollars and in which North Vietnam could participate.

Undaunted by the diplomatic tonguelashing he had received in February, U Thant either ignored or did not see the "catch" in Johnson's statement. Johnson had spoken of negotiations with "governments," and that did not include the Vietcong, without whom North Vietnam would not negotiate. U Thant, instead, hailed the speech as a "turning point" and praised the "positive, forward-looking and generous" proposal for a development program. The next day Premier Pham Van Dong of North Vietnam indicated to the press that talks might be possible, and U Thant drafted an appeal for a ceasefire. He gave the draft to Adlai, saying he would be willing to consider any changes the United States might suggest.

Once again, delay set in. Adlai's presence in the White House on April 28, when the intervention in the Dominican Republic began, was for the purpose of trying to get a reply to U Thant's ceasefire proposal. It was then that the unacceptable exclusion of the Vietcong became apparent, and the hope that flared so brightly after the Johnson speech slowly dimmed. During this period, Adlai repeatedly found himself trying to mollify U Thant in New York while defending him in Washington. The role depressed him, particularly as he found himself having to justify escalating military action he opposed, and rejections of political discussions that he favored. But he knew that whatever hope there was of pushing the administration toward political negotiations required a public defense of the overall policy.

In the running internal battle over the response to U Thant's ceasefire proposal, Adlai had allies in Harlan Cleveland and his designated successor, Joseph Sisco. But he was reduced to writing memos to himself, the thread of which would appear later in the draft letter released after his death that the administration would claim supported its Vietnam policy: "Military track runs into dead end. . . . How get on parallel track . . . should attack on political side. . . . Could change entire climate of world opinion. Ready to discuss means of settlement that will protect all sides—reestablish elements of Geneva accords."

His effort to define a two-track policy, with emphasis shifting from the military to the political track, emerged most clearly in the speech he gave on May 28 at the University of Toronto, where he had gone to receive an honorary degree. On his arrival, students were picketing in protest to United States Vietnam policy and the award of an honorary degree to its spokesman in the UN. Toward the end of his speech, he said, "It seems to me—and I speak for myself only—that the only solution to Southeast Asia compatible with the postcolonial world we are trying to build is to give these states between the Chinese and Indian colossi international security guarantees, impartially policed frontiers, long-term development and broad framework of social and economic cooperation." The audience gave him a standing ovation.

The success of the speech left him more torn than ever. He saw confirmation that the energy of youth could be mobilized behind the goals he mentioned if only the fighting could be stopped.

The treasured rapport with young people was put under increasing strain with each passing day as the protests grew. Educators at some twenty-five New England colleges urged negotiations in an advertisement in *The New York Times*. Oberlin College held a hunger strike. Over 2,000 students attended a teach-in at Columbia University. Then a total of 100,000 students and faculty at one hundred colleges watched a television teach-in. At Berkeley, 10,000 attended a teach-in. Old friends like Archibald MacLeish and John Kenneth Galbraith joined the protesters. The UN and the U.S. Mission were ringed with student pickets.

Adlai was intensely unhappy at having to carry on a fight marked by few victories within the administration, but he was appalled at the alternative presented to him by those to whom he always felt close: that was to get out and find himself leading a public crusade against the war and the administration. As he had suggested months earlier, this was one "watershed" too many.

About this time he flew out to Chicago to see Phil Klutznick.

"Phil," he said abruptly, "I have to resign."

"Adlai, you can't do that," Klutznick replied.

"Why not? You did."

"Adlai, I'm not you. If you resign now, all the opposition to Vietnam will coalesce around you, and you will find yourself, whether you want it or not, leading a crusade against the Johnson administration. Is that what you want?"

"Oh, God! You're right!"

Klutznick later commented that "Adlai knew this was the situation without my saying it, and even before he asked me. He just wanted to hear it from somebody who knew him, knew the UN, and knew something about public life."

After his June 27 appearance on *Meet the Press*, his good friend James Wechsler wrote in the *New York Post:* "What Stevenson seemed to be saying . . . was that a man does not lightly walk out on a major government mission unless convinced that conflicts over strategy have become irreconcilable issues of principle. The obscure twilight zone lies between 'detail' and doctrine." He then added that Adlai was being reduced too often to the role of debater rather than a creator of policy. Adlai thanked him for understanding "with such clarity what is obscure to others." Referring to his role as "debater" rather than "creator," he said, "There you touch the nerve with precision!"

The long Fourth of July weekend he spent at Libertyville, thoroughly enjoying chaotic romps with his grandchildren and a concert at Ravinia, where he was surrounded by admirers. Barbara Ward arrived and they worked together on a speech he was to give in Geneva and the draft of a reply to a widely circulated "Declaration" expressing "dismay" at American policy in Vietnam and the Dominican Republic. It urged Adlai to resign, and "having done that, to become the spokesman again for that which is humane and in the traditions and in the people of America."

The "Declaration" had been prepared by a group called Artists and Writers Dissent, and on June 21, he had met with eight of the signers: Kay Boyle, Paul Goodman, Nat Hentoff, Dwight McDonald, former Congressman William S. Mayer, A. J. Muste, David McReynolds, and Harvey Swados. The meeting lasted over an hour as they pressed their case. Writing of the meeting in *The Village Voice,* Hentoff said, "Leaving, I was depressed. I had the sense of his impotence—and the sense of his knowing and caring deeply, hopelessly about the impotence. He could not resign. That was not the way he played the game. And because he could not—would not—change the rules, he had been trapped by them."

Adlai also had brought with him to Libertyville another printed letter headed "Volunteers for Stevenson—1965," by a self-described organization dedicated to the ideals Adlai had represented in his presidential campaigns. The letter stated: "The nation and the world desperately need a strong and eloquent voice to oppose the policy which is leading mankind towards the final confrontation. We implore you to be that voice. With full knowledge of the sacrifice we ask, we who have loved you, plead with you now to resign." These documents, together with the draft reply that would become the center of controversy, were in his briefcase when he fell dead on a London street.

From Libertyville, he flew to Washington, and then on to New York, where, after repacking, walking through picket lines, and working with his secretary, Roxane Eberlein, he took a night flight to Geneva. Although he arrived exhausted, he met with U Thant to discuss Vietnam and then lunched with the Australian ambassador. He telephoned Rusk to report the U Thant conversation, worked on the speech he was to give in the Economic and Social Council, went to a reception in his honor given by Ambassador Roger Tubby and his wife, had dinner with William Benton, then took a walk in the rain before going to bed "at last" at eleven-thirty. A similar schedule filled the next day, and on Friday, he gave the speech dealing with growing problems of urbanization in the world. The next morning, at breakfast with the Tubbys, before leaving for London, he suddenly stopped talking, put both hands on the table, and said, "I'm a bit dizzy." After a moment, the conversation resumed.

In London, he met Benton and they drove together to Chequers, the official residence of the British prime minister and spent the afternoon talking with Harold Wilson. Back at the American embassy that night he talked to Ambassador and Mrs. Bruce about playing tennis on each of the five days he would be there. He and Benton drove to the country for lunch with Ellen's aunt, Lady Spears, and then went on to Oxford for dinner with Lord Franks, the former British ambassador in Washington, who was now provost of Worcester College.

On the way back to London that night, Adlai told Benton he planned to resign after the General Asembly that fall. Benton advised him that controversy might be alleviated if a good replacement were available, and they discussed Senators Eugene McCarthy and John Sherman Cooper as well as Chester Bowles. Benton told him he was foolish to return to the law firm when he could make much more money working for *Britannica,* and mentioned a $100,000-a-year salary and a similar amount in expenses. They agreed to discuss it further, although it is doubtful that being, in effect, Benton's employee would have been his choice.

On Sunday, he appeared on a television program where he was quizzed about Vietnam, and attended a buffet supper in his honor by the British Broadcasting Corporation. Afterward, he asked his old and trusted friend, CBS correspondent Eric Sevareid, to come back to the embassy residence and talk. That conversation, too, became an object of controversy.

On Wednesday, July 14, he and Robert Hutchins, both directors of the *Encyclopaedia Britannica*, were guests of honor at a *Britannica* luncheon given by Benton. At four, he held a small press conference at the embassy, and then, with a few hours to spare before his evening engagements, asked Marietta to go for a walk with him. He wanted to show Marietta the house at 2 Mount Row, not far from Grosvenor Square, where he and Ellen, with Adlai III and Borden, had lived in the early days of the UN. Alas, it was gone and a new building was in its place.

"It makes me feel old," Adlai said sadly.

As they walked along, he lamented that he hadn't been able to play more tennis, he talked of his hope to resign after the General Assembly and of the job offers he had received. Suddenly, he said, "Keep your head high!" Marietta had no idea what he meant. Next she heard him say, "You are walking much too fast for me." Always a fast walker, she slowed down but was still ahead of him as they walked along the picket fence surrounding the Sportsman's Club. In a voice she barely recognized, she heard him say, "I feel faint." She turned around and saw that his face was a ghastly gray. She also saw through the picket fence a box or stool, and her first thought was to get that for him to sit on. As she turned to get it, she heard his head hit the concrete with a horrible thud.

He lay on the sidewalk, his face ashen, his eyes wide open. Marietta ran into the club and asked that the American minister, Phil Kaiser, and a doctor be called immediately. When she returned, she found a passerby lifting Adlai's head to put a coat under it. Fearing Adlai had cracked his skull in the fall, she asked him not to move the head further and knelt helplessly beside him. Someone handed her a glass of water, and she tried to pour a little through his lips and over his brow. At that point, another man arrived who identified himself as a doctor and, diagnosing a heart attack, began to massage Adlai's heart. He asked if there was anyone in the gathering group who could give mouth-to-mouth resuscitation. Marietta said she would if the doctor would show her how. In a moment or two, Adlai began to breathe again in long, shuddering sobs. The doctor who had been summoned by phone arrived and immediately administered injections. The great, shuddering breaths continued as an ambulance came, and, with an oxygen mask over his face, Adlai was lifted into it.

As Marietta was about to climb in beside him, she saw scattered on the sidewalk from the manila folder Adlai had been carrying, a number of papers whose pink color identified them as classified documents. She quickly gathered them up, and got back into the ambulance as it speeded toward St. George's Hospital. There, a few minutes later, she was told that he was dead. She was haunted by the thought that the fall had killed him; that if she had only held him up instead of starting for the box he might be alive. Only days later would she learn that he had died almost instantly of a massive hemorrhage and that the awful breathing probably was a reflex action.

* * *

Broadcasts from London by Eric Sevareid and by David Schoenbrun reporting Adlai's doubts about the administration's Vietnam policy and his intention to resign immediately sparked into action a huge propaganda counteroffensive by the administration. Both correspondents were attacked either for violating Adlai's confidence or being misled by his chronic grumbling, or both. The administration was determined not to allow Adlai, after his death, to become the antiwar focus he had consciously avoided becoming during his life.

To strengthen its rebuttal, the administration zeroed in on the draft letter to Paul Goodman of the Artists and Writers Dissent, a copy of which Adlai had given to Phil Kaiser at the embassy with a request for his comments. On his way through Washington he had given a copy to Joseph Sisco to review and then send to Clayton Fritchey in New York with his comments. In New York, he left a memo for Fritchey saying, "Perhaps you could then look it over and see that it is mailed . . . and also consider whether it should be published in view of the extensive publication of the appeal to me to resign." Both Sisco and Fritchey doubted that the draft accurately reflected Adlai's thinking. Fritchey, particularly, thought the defense of administration policy was stronger than Adlai intended and, knowing Adlai's habit of revising a draft up to the last minute, held the letter.

The long letter asserted that "whatever criticisms may be made over detail and emphasis of American foreign policy, its purpose and direction are sound. Our over-riding purpose must be to avoid war." He argued that two lines of policy had to be pursued at once; the first to stop the extension of Communist power and influence, and the second to build an international system that would "turn our small vulnerable planet into a genuine economic and social community." The draft seemed to be probing for a formula that would make it possible for the intellectual community to accept his refusal to resign:

> My hope in Vietnam is that relatively small-scale resistance now may establish the fact that changes in Asia are not to be precipitated by outside force. This was the point in the Korean war. This is the point of conflict in Vietnam. . . . I believe we must seek a negotiated peace in Vietnam based upon the internationalization of the whole area's security, on a big effort to develop, under the UN, the resources of the Mekong River and guarantees that Vietnam, North and South, can choose, again under international supervision, the kinds of governments, the form of association and, if so decreed, the type of reunification of the two states they genuinely want to establish.

The letter was something less than the all-out support that the administration claimed it to be. Yet, the administration could not afford even a posthumous split with Adlai. The week of Adlai's funeral, Johnson ordered 100,000 Americans to Vietnam in the first huge expansion of the American commitment. It was an interesting coincidence. Within two years, the number would reach nearly half a million.

The draft came to light in the aftermath of Eric Sevareid's article in the November issue of *Look,* giving an extended account of his last evening with Adlai. Its persuasive report of Adlai's unhappiness over Vietnam and his intention of resigning renewed attacks on Sevareid as being inaccurate, disrespectful of the dead, gullible, excessively sentimental, or all four. This prompted Fritchey, by now a columnist for *Newsday,* to refer to the unsent letter, after which Adlai III, who had received the copy his father had given to Phil Kaiser in London, released it to the press. He regarded it as a reaffirmation of support for administration policy, but pointed out that the draft contained a number of handwritten corrections, indicating it might not have been finished. Although at the time he felt he was carrying out his father's wishes, he now wonders if the letter sufficiently reflected his father's beliefs to have warranted its release. One must remember that the awesome toll of death and destruction was mostly still to come.

Many of Sevareid's critics, who preferred not to analyze the whole article too closely, instead ridiculed the sentimentality of Adlai's response to the question of what he intended to do.

"For a while," Sevareid quoted him as saying, "I'd really just like to sit in the shade with a glass of wine in my hand and watch the dancers."

Many of those who knew Adlai recognized the quote as a thought Adlai had been expressing in similar terms in recent months. Those who knew of his relationship with Sevareid, and read the whole article, saw it as authentic Adlai, talking to someone who understood him and was perceptive about him. Fred W. Friendly, in the *Columbia Journalism Review* described the article as the most distinguished piece of journalism done outside of Vietnam by a broadcast journalist in 1965. Sevareid deserves the last word:

> Governor Stevenson died of exhaustion; he just wore himself out. I don't know how else to put it. Of course, the gathering frustration was part of this, but he did not die of a broken heart. If others regarded him as a "tragic" figure, I don't think he thought of himself that way. Let others call his life a failure; I think it was a wonderful success. When he was 50 years old, almost nobody but his private friends knew his rare quality; when he died 15 years later, a million people cried.

CHAPTER TWENTY-FOUR
"A Strange Animal"

"MAN IS A STRANGE animal. He doesn't like to read the handwriting on the wall until his back is up against it."

Adlai made this comment with increasing frequency in the final months of his life. Its uncharacteristic pessimism could hardly have been prompted by developments in domestic policy; so much of what he had advocated in 1956 and earlier had been implemented by Kennedy and even expanded by Johnson's Great Society program.

Federal aid to education, almost a heresy when proposed in 1956, had been ushered in tentatively by the National Defense Education Act in 1958 in reaction to the Soviet Union's successful launching of Sputnik. Federal financing of housing for the elderly, which Adlai proposed in 1956, was passed by Congress in 1962. The hospital insurance proposed in 1956 became Medicare in 1965. McCarthyism had been removed as a national scourge and become an object of scorn. Racism and its evils received heavy emphasis in his speeches, especially to college audiences, in the final months of his life, but he also pointed out that historic progress had been made in civil rights.

He had to be aware, too, that he had profoundly affected the character of American politics. Wherever he went, he encountered in town halls, in statehouses, the courts, and the Congress new young faces demonstrating he was right when, way back in 1935, he told the Legal Club of Chicago that he looked forward "to the time when government service will be one of the highest aspirations of educated men." They had responded to the theme expressed then and repeated persistently that "bad government is bad politics and good government means good men."

"A generation of younger Americans, brought up to feel that politics were sordid or dirty or corrupt or boss-manipulated, learned from him that American politics were the mirror of American life, and could be made to reflect the best in that life as well as the worst." This comment was by Theodore H. White, written after Adlai's death. White added that "his call brought thousands of new men into arenas they had hitherto despised or feared." To this White added "the tone he gave the dialogue of American politics. He brought to it a quality of ideas, of thinking, of excitement as if, somehow, one could have a reasonable discourse with people about the future." The result, White concluded, was that "no man left a larger legacy."

The New York Times concluded that Adlai "had a more profound and lasting effect on his party as an opposition leader out of power than his successful Republican opponent had on his party in power." Whatever wry satisfaction this tribute might have given him is suggested by an earlier response to an audience wildly cheering his late arrival at a rally. He explained that his plane had been delayed at the airport by ceremonies welcoming President de Gaulle of France. "It is curious," he said, "how often some national hero seems to be in my way."

This self-denigrating sense of humor repeatedly minimized his impact, as indicated by his response to an admirer in the 1956 campaign who told him "every thinking person was on his side." He replied, "That's wonderful! But I need a majority." Nevertheless, a survey of the domestic scene warranted much cause for satisfaction.

Overshadowing it all for him was his profound concern with developments, or lack of them, in international affairs. There, he saw a turning away from handwriting that to him was so clear, and so very portentous.

His increasing discomfort was graphically, if somewhat crudely, revealed in a telephone conversation with Jonathan Daniels just before he left on his last trip to Europe. He asked the respected editor and friend for his sense of public reaction to the mounting commitment in Vietnam.

"To tell you the truth," Daniels told him, "they think you and Lyndon Johnson both have firecrackers up your tails."

"Yes," Adlai shot back, "and his is lit."

Vietnam and the abrupt intervention in the Dominican Republic dramatically underscored the ascendancy of military considerations in the conduct of foreign policy. But his concerns ran even deeper. In May 1961, he had built a speech at the Jewish Theological Seminary in New York around a quotation from Plato, "The creation of a world order is the victory of persuasion over force." He pointed to the United Nations as the "symbol" of progress, but its successes he usually cast in terms of reasons for hope and faith. He saw the UN as only the first step in a long process of building world community with broadly accepted international institutions and rules of conduct. He described it as the "first sketch of the world society" that had to be created.

Faced with criticism of the UN, he would tell the complainers that when Adam first proposed to Eve in the Garden of Eden she also hesitated. Whereupon Adam asked, "Is there someone else?"

The beginning that had been made must not be obscured by the obstacles standing in the way. Violence had been restrained by the UN as the colonial system crumbled, but intense nationalism had accompanied the birth of numerous new states and essential cooperation was being blocked; nuclear weapons, missiles, outer space, and other aspects of modern technology posed incalculable new threats to the existence of the human race itself; and beneath this potential universal holocaust the smoldering fire of the growing gap between rich and poor within and among nations.

Paradoxically, what was perhaps the UN's greatest achievement was the primary source of the attacks on him: the transition from pre-World War II colonialism to independence that more than doubled the membership of the United Nations in barely two decades. It had also made nationalism a dominant element in international life. Adlai described it as "belligerent and even chauvinistic, unrealistic and unthinking." Yet he felt that Western imperialism "might have been expected to leave deeper scars of resentment than has in fact proved to be the case."

The ending of empires in the past, he kept stressing, often had been the beginning of wars. "It is precisely the fact that so much violence and so many quarrels have not led to war that puts a special mark on our times," he told students at Princeton in 1964. He pointed to the Congo operation as "precisely the type of operation which the United Nations should dare to undertake."

But he went further. He defended the principle of one nation and one vote that was and remains an object of attack. He saw this as a necessary effort to apply to nations the principle we try to apply to individual citizens: the principle of equality before the law—one man, one vote; one nation, one vote.

"The effects of this system can be very strange," he conceded. "No one supposes that in spite of equality of voting rights, the head of United States Steel has no more influence on American society than an unskilled laborer in one of his plants. There is an element of fiction in the equality."

Nepal, he said, could not pretend to be carrying the same weight in the world community as its neighbor, India, but its equal vote in the UN "is a first step toward covenanted political recognition, by international society, of its right to separate statehood and its right not to be handed over to the political control of more powerful neighbors." These rights, he declared, were "as astonishing as the right of commoners to protection and due process of law in a post-feudal age."

It was in this context that he saw the need for expanding the peace-keeping functions of the United Nations and improving the capabilities of UN peacekeeping forces.

"There is, after all, something grotesque, unreal and nightmarish about a world with 20 million men under arms and a military budget of 120 billion dollars when we can't seem to find 20 thousand men and 120 million dollars for international peace-keeping by the United Nations." This statement, made to the American Newspaper Publishers in April 1965, could be repeated today, except that the military expenditures have climbed steeply upward while the investment in UN peacekeeping functions virtually has stood still. The creation of a United Nations International Police Force, trained specifically for peacekeeping functions, so earnestly advocated by the United States in the early 1960s, has been forgotten, despite repeated demonstrations that, as Adlai said, "a UN soldier in his blue beret is like no other soldier in the world—he has no mission but peace and no enemy but war."

The truth of this statement, as well as of the unrealized potential, is underscored by the award of the 1988 Nobel Peace Prize to the makeshift UN Peace Forces made up on a largely ad hoc basis of volunteered contingents from national armies.

Although he saw disarmament as an even greater imperative, he saw little hope for advance beyond the nuclear test ban he had advocated in 1956. He had urged Kennedy, with some success, to make disarmament a major policy commitment, but in June 1962, with the realism that tempered his idealism, he had written Kennedy that "the general international atmosphere" in regard to disarmament "is not propitious even for minimal progress." With Kennedy's death and Johnson's preoccupation with Vietnam, whatever hope remained withered.

Adlai's concerns focused increasingly on the fear that people would become accustomed to the threat of nuclear war and lose incentive to deal with the possibility of global annihilation. An increasing tone or urgency, and perhaps of frustration, is evident in the speeches of the last few years.

"The pursuit of peace—the pioneering work of peacekeeping and peacemaking—the control of armaments—the construction of world order and community—has become the most important business of the human race," he had stressed to the American Bar Association in 1964. As progress on the first two appeared to be blocked for the time being, he spoke increasingly of the third, longer-range vision, which he saw as the essential goal. "Do we perceive," he asked at Princeton, "perhaps dimly, the world groping for, reaching out to the fuller vision of a society based upon human brotherhood, to an order in which men's burdens are lifted, to a peace which is secure in justice and ruled by law?"

Increasingly he spoke of the scientific and technological revolutions that for the first time in human history, he said, made it possible for the human race to rise above the poverty, misery, and degradation of past ages. The fight against poverty, he declared repeatedly, not only could be won but had to be won as it was the "seed-bed of world disorder." In our interdependent world, he maintained, "there is no longer any line of demarcation between social problems and political problems."

Although economic assistance programs were regarded with "growing cynicism and weariness" in developed countries, the increasing gap between the rich countries of the Northern Hemisphere and the poor countries below the equator was creating a world that would be "an extremely dangerous one for their children to live in," he told President Johnson in his postelection memo of 1964. The trend, he warned, could result in "a general North-South confrontation, more uncontrollable and more bloody than East-West confrontation." He urged the President to expand "substantially international instruments and resources for accelerating economic development, international trade and investment, and balanced, progressive and complementary economic growth throughout the world."

In his last speech to the United Nations, at the Economic and Social Council in Geneva, five days before he died, he told the delegates:

Already science and technology are integrating our world into an open workshop where each new invention defines a new task, and reveals a shared interest, and invites yet another common venture. In our sprawling workshop of world community, nations are joined in cooperative endeavor: improving soils, purifying water, harnessing rivers, eradicating disease, feeding children, diffusing knowledge, spreading technology, surveying resources, lending capital, probing the seas, forecasting the weather, setting standards, developing law, and working away at a near infinitude of down-to-earth tasks—tasks for which science has given us the knowledge, and technology has given us the tools, and common sense has given us the wit to perceive that common interest impels us to common enterprise. Common enterprise is the pulse of the world community—the heartbeat of a working peace.

Then, in a final expression of faith, he declared, "Just as Europe could never again be the old, closed-in community after the voyages of Columbus, we can never again be a squabbling band of nations before the awful majesty of outer space."

The roots of his vision, like so much of his character, were sunk deep in American soil.

"Now, as in the days of the Founding Fathers, even the faintest possibility of achieving such an order depends upon our steadfast faith," he told one of his favorite audiences, students at Princeton gathered for a lecture in honor of Dag Hammarskjöld.

In their day, too, democracy in an age of monarchs and freedom in an age of empire seemed the most remote of pipedreams. Today, too, the dream of a world which repeats at the international level the solid achievements—of law and welfare—of our domestic society must seem audacious to the point of insanity, save for the grim fact that survival itself is inconceivable on any other terms. . . .

I believe, therefore, that at this time the only sane policy for America—in its own interests and in the wider interests of humanity—lies in the patient, unspectacular, and if need be lonely search for the interests which unite nations, for the policies which draw them together, for institutions which transcend rival national interests, for the international instruments of law and security, for the strengthening of what we have already built inside and outside the United Nations, for the elaboration of a changing world for a stable, workable society.

This vision remains a long way from realization; but no one has yet offered a better one. And, certainly, he was pursuing his own injunction to statesmen to "seek to improve the state of the world as well as the state of the nation."

The historian, Henry Steele Commager, wrote in the *London Observer* after Adlai's death:

Adlai Stevenson presents us with a spectacle rare in American, and probably in modern, history—a man whose public career was crowded into a few short years, whose every foray into large politics was marked by defeat, and who exercised immense authority wholly without power, an authority whose sanctions were entirely intellectual and moral. . . . [He] managed, by sheer force of intelligence and moral distinction, to lift the whole level of public life and discourse, and to infuse American politics with a dignity, a vitality, an excitement it had not known since the early days of the New Deal.

Professor Commager's assertion received strong support in the titles of books written about Adlai following his death: *The Politics of Honor,* by Kenneth S. Davis; *Conscience in Politics,* by Stuart Gerry Brown; and *Adlai Stevenson: A Study in Values,* by Herbert Muller.

Walter Lippmann, after Adlai's death, saw America's future hanging on questions raised by Adlai's career. After asserting that Adlai was "a living specimen of the kind of American that Americans themselves, and the great mass of mankind, would like to think Americans are," Lippmann stated, "there is abroad in this land a very different spirit contending for the soul of our people.

"On one course we shall plunge ourselves into the making of a ramshackle empire in an era when no empire can long survive, and we shall wave the flag to cover our spiritual nakedness," Lippmann wrote. "Or we shall, as Adlai Stevenson would have done, remain true to our original loyalty, and transcending assertiveness, vulgar ambition and the seductions of power, make this country not only great and free but at peace with its own conscience."

Reflecting this struggle, perhaps, in June 1964, Adlai told the students graduating from Colby College in Waterville, Maine, that "every age needs men who will redeem the time by living with a vision of things that are to be." He redeemed his time and he may yet help us to redeem ours.

Bibliography

ACHESON, DEAN. *Present at the Creation.* New York: W. W. Norton, 1969.

AMBROSE, STEPHEN E. *Eisenhower: Soldier, General of the Army, President-elect. 1890–1952.* New York: Simon & Schuster, 1983.

———. *Eisenhower: The President.* New York: Simon & Schuster, 1984.

———. *Nixon: The Education of a Politician, 1913–1962.* New York: Simon & Schuster, 1987.

ATTWOOD, WILLIAM. *The Twilight Struggle: Tales of the Cold War.* New York: Harper & Row, 1987.

BACALL, LAUREN. *By Myself.* New York: Alfred A. Knopf, 1979.

BALL, GEORGE W. *The Past Has Another Pattern.* New York: W. W. Norton, 1982.

BINGHAM, JUNE. *U Thant: The Search for Peace.* New York: Alfred A. Knopf, 1966.

BLUM, JOHN MORTON, ed. *Public Philosopher: Selected Letters of Walter Lippmann.* New York: Ticknor & Fields, 1983.

BOWLES, CHESTER. *Promises to Keep: My Years in Public Life, 1941–1969.* New York: Harper & Row, 1971.

BRENDON, PIERS. *Ike, His Life and Times.* New York: Harper & Row, 1986.

BROWN, STUART GERRY. *Conscience in Politics.* Syracuse, N.Y.: Syracuse University Press, 1961.

BUSCH, NOEL F. *Adlai Stevenson of Illinois: A Portrait.* New York: Farrar, Straus & Young, 1952.

CAPA, CORNELL; INGE MORATH; and JOHN FELL STEVENSON. *Adlai Stevenson's Public Years*. Preface by Walter Lippmann. New York: Grossman, 1966.

COCHRAN, BERT. *Adlai Stevenson, Patrician Among the Politicians*. New York: Funk & Wagnalls, 1969.

COOKE, ALISTAIR. *Six Men*. New York: Alfred A. Knopf/Berkley, 1978.

COOPER, CHESTER L. *The Lost Crusade*. New York: Dodd, Mead, 1970.

DAVIS, KENNETH S. *The Politics of Honor*. New York: Putnam, 1967.

———. *A Prophet in His Own Country*. Garden City, N.Y.: Doubleday, 1957.

DICK, JANE. *Whistle-stopping with Adlai*. Chicago: October House, 1952.

DONOVAN, HEDLEY. *Roosevelt to Reagan*. New York: Harper & Row, 1987.

DOYLE, EDWARD P., ed. *As We Knew Adlai: The Stevenson Story by 22 Friends*. New York: Harper & Row, 1966.

EISENHOWER, DWIGHT D. *Crusade in Europe*. Garden City, N.Y.: Doubleday, 1948.

———. *Mandate for Change*. Garden City, N.Y.: Doubleday, 1963.

FOSDICK, DOROTHY, ed. *Staying the Course: Henry M. Jackson and National Security*. Seattle: University of Washington Press, 1987.

GALBRAITH, JOHN KENNETH. *A Life in Our Times*. Boston: Houghton Mifflin, 1981.

———. *Annals of an Abiding Liberal*. Boston: Houghton Mifflin, 1979.

GORE-BOOTH, LORD PAUL. *With Great Truth and Respect*. London: Constable, 1974.

GREENSTEIN, FRED I. *The Hidden Hand Presidency*. New York: Basic Books, 1982.

HOOPES, TOWNSEND. *The Devil and John Foster Dulles*. Boston: Little, Brown, 1973.

HUGHES, EMMET JOHN. *The Ordeal of Power*. New York: Atheneum, 1963.

HUMPHREY, HUBERT H. *The Education of a Public Man*. Garden City, N.Y.: Doubleday, 1976.

HYMAN, SYDNEY. *The Lives of William Benton*. Chicago: University of Chicago Press, 1969.

ISAACSON, WALTER, and EVAN THOMAS. *The Wise Men*. New York: Simon & Schuster, 1986.

IVES, ELIZABETH STEVENSON, and HILDEGARD DOLSON. *My Brother Adlai*. New York: William Morrow, 1956.

——— and SAM RAGAN. *Back to Beginnings: Adlai Stevenson and North Carolina*. Charlotte, N.C.: Heritage Printers, 1969.

JOHNSON, WALTER, and CAROL EVANS, eds. *The Papers of Adlai E. Stevenson*, 8 vols. Boston: Little, Brown, 1972.

JOHNSON, WALTER. *How We Drafted Adlai Stevenson*. New York: Alfred A. Knopf, 1955.

KENNEDY, ROBERT F. *Thirteen Days: A Memoir of the Cuban Missile Crisis.* New York: W. W. Norton, 1969.

LARABEE, ERIC. *Commander in Chief: Franklin Delano Roosevelt, His Lieutenants and Their War.* New York: Harper & Row, 1987.

LASH, JOSEPH P. *Eleanor: The Years Alone.* New York: W. W. Norton, 1972.

MACLEISH, ARCHIBALD. *Reflections.* Amherst: University of Massachusetts Press, 1986.

MARTIN, JOHN BARTLOW. *Adlai Stevenson of Illinois.* Garden City, N.Y.: Doubleday, 1976.

———. *Adlai Stevenson and the World.* Garden City, N.Y.: Doubleday, 1977.

———. *It Seems Like Only Yesterday.* New York: William Morrow, 1986.

MATHEWS, T. S. *Angels Unawares: Twentieth-Century Portraits.* New York: Ticknor & Fields, 1985.

MCCARTHY, EUGENE. *Up 'Til Now.* New York: Harcourt Brace Jovanovich, 1987.

MILLER, MERLE. *Plain Speaking: An Oral Biography of Harry S. Truman.* New York: Berkley Medallion Books, 1973.

MOSLEY, LEONARD. *Marshall: Hero For Our Times.* New York: Hearst Books, 1982.

MULLER, HERBERT. *Adlai Stevenson: A Study in Values.* New York: Harper & Row, 1967.

NEFF, DONALD. *Warriors at Suez.* New York: Simon & Schuster, 1981.

NIXON, RICHARD. *Memoirs.* New York: Grossett & Dunlap, 1978.

POGUE, FORREST C. *George C. Marshall: Statesman 1945–59.* New York: Viking, 1987.

POWERS, RICHARD GID. *Secrecy and Power: The Life of J. Edgar Hoover.* New York: Macmillan, 1987.

ROSS, LILLIAN. *Adlai Stevenson.* New York and Philadelphia: J. B. Lippincott, 1966.

ROVERE, RICHARD H. *Affairs of State: The Eisenhower Years.* New York: Farrar, Straus & Cudahy, 1956.

———. *Senator Joe McCarthy.* New York: Harcourt Brace Jovanovich, 1959.

SCHLESINGER, ARTHUR M., JR. *A Thousand Days.* Boston: Houghton Mifflin, 1965.

———. *Robert Kennedy and His Times.* Boston: Houghton Mifflin, 1978.

———. *The Cycles of American History.* Boston: Houghton Mifflin, 1986.

SEVAREID, ERIC. *Small Sounds in the Night.* New York: Alfred A. Knopf, 1956.

SORENSON, THEODORE C. *Kennedy.* New York: Harper & Row, 1965.

SPENDER, A. M. *Murrow: His Life and Times.* New York: Freuchlich, 1986.

STEVENSON, ADLAI E. *Speeches*. Foreword by John Steinbeck; biography by Debs Myers and Ralph Martin. New York: Random House, 1952.

———. *Major Campaign Speeches, 1952*. New York: Random House, 1953.

———. *Call to Greatness*. New York: Harper & Brothers, 1954.

———. *What I Think*. New York: Harper & Brothers, 1956.

———. *The New America*. New York: Harper & Brothers, 1957.

———. *Friends and Enemies: What I Learned in Russia*. New York: Harper & Brothers, 1958.

———. *Putting First Things First*. New York: Random House, 1960.

———. *Looking Outward*. New York: Harper & Row, 1961.

———. *An Ethic for Survival*. Edited by Michael H. Prosser. New York: William Morrow, 1969.

SULZBERGER, C. L. *A Long Row of Candles*. New York: Macmillan, 1969.

TRUMAN, HARRY S. *Memoirs*, Vol. 2, *Years of Hope and Trial, 1946–1952*. Garden City, N.Y.: Doubleday, 1956.

URQUHART, BRIAN. *Hammarskjöld*. New York: Alfred A. Knopf, 1972.

WALTON, RICHARD J. *The Remnants of Power*. New York: Coward-McCann, 1968.

WHITE, THEODORE H. *In Search of History*. New York: Harper & Row, 1978.

———. *The Making of the President, 1960*. New York: Atheneum, 1961.

WHITMAN, ALDEN, and THE NEW YORK TIMES. *Portrait: Adlai E. Stevenson*. New York: Harper & Row, 1965.

WYATT, WILSON. *Whistle Stops: Adventures in Public Life*. Lexington, Ky.: University Press of Kentucky, 1985.

YOST, CHARLES. *The Insecurity of Nations*. New York: Praeger, 1968.

———. *The Conduct and Misconduct of Foreign Affairs*. New York: Random House, 1972.

Index

Abdullah, king of Jordan, 299
Abdullah, Mohammed, 294
Acheson, Dean, 92, 349, 395
   Kennedy years and, 484, 485, 486, 495, 499, 509, 519
   as secretary of state, 174, 214, 230, 231, 243, 252
Adams, Sherman, 226, 234, 403, 405
Adenauer, Konrad, 405
Adlai Stevenson: A Study in Values (Muller), 251
Adlai Stevenson Reports, 505, 513
Africa, 343–345, 400
Agar, Herbert, 208, 309
Agriculture Department, U.S., 384–385
Akers, Milburn P., 110
Albright, Alice, 409
Aldrich, Winthrop, 310
Alexander, Archibald, 193, 357
Alexander the Great, 296, 300
Allen, George, 294
Allen, Terry, 92
Alliance for Progress, 494
Allsworthy, Joseph, 203
Alsop, Joseph, 176, 191, 194, 247–248, 252, 473
Alsop, Stewart, 191, 194, 247–248, 531, 535–536
Altgeld, John Peter, 22, 195
Altschul, Frank, 370
Ambrose, Stephen E.:
   on Eisenhower, 262–263, 319, 378, 381, 383, 386, 407
   on McCarthyism, 235–236, 319
   on Nixon, 228–230, 378

America First, 73–74, 90
American Legion, 151, 159, 160, 214–215
American Voter, The, 206
Anderson, Robert B., 378
Anderson, Warwick, 345–347
Andrus, Bob, 361
Angola, 484–485, 538
Annunzio, Frank, 117
anti-Semitism, 46, 62, 63, 222
apartheid, 344, 537
Appleby, Paul, 316
Aquino, Corazón, 286
Armstrong, Hamilton Fish, 431
Army-McCarthy hearings, 321–322, 325
Arnall, Ellis, 326
Artists and Writers Dissent, 561, 564
Arvey, Jacob M., 120, 140
   appointments sought by, 129
   background of, 105, 107–108
   on Jewish voters, 363, 364
   lobbying efforts of, 135, 136
   party organization and, 205, 393
   on patronage curtailment, 134–135
   Stevenson's gubernatorial campaign and, 110, 111–117, 126
   Stevenson's presidential campaigns and, 185, 188, 190, 191, 193, 196, 212–213, 220, 237, 244, 253, 356, 363, 376, 461, 504
Ashmore, Harry, 354–355, 357, 368, 373
Asia, 296, 297, 334, 336, 400
   see also specific countries
Atkinson, Brooks, 267
Atlanta Constitution, 415, 435
Atlantic Charter, 77

Attwood, William, 516
  1960 election and, 451, 454, 461
  Stevenson's speeches and, 437, 438, 440, 451
  on world tour, 273, 278, 280, 282, 283, 288,
    291, 294, 295, 297, 299, 301, 303, 306,
    308–310
Auriol, Vincent, 307
Austin, Ed, 61
Austin, Warren R., 103, 106

Bacall, Lauren, 249, 277, 331, 408
Backer, George, 356
Bailey, Lady Mary, 308
Baker, Newton D., 47
Balch, Richard H., 311
Baldwin, Charles F., 292
Ball, George W., 64, 71, 76, 88, 91–92, 349,
    406
  Kennedy presidency and, 466, 470, 471, 473,
    503, 517, 520, 536
  law practice of, 70, 267, 316
  Stevenson's nominations and, 176, 177–182,
    185, 186, 198, 424, 426
  Stevenson's presidential campaigns and,
    206, 209, 230, 236, 243, 248, 253,
    261–262, 264, 368, 374
Ball, Lucille, 445
Bao Dai, 287
Barkley, Alben, 120, 212, 374, 504
  as presidential candidate, 186, 190, 193,
    196–197, 204
Barnes, Tracy, 487
Bartlett, Charlie, 531–535
"Baruch" proposals, 370
Battistini, Lawrence, 280
Battle, John S., 222
Battle of the Bulge (1944), 91–92
Baw U, 292
Bay of Pigs invasion, 486–490, 497
Bean, Louis, 438, 456
Bell, Daniel W., 285
Bell, David, 208, 213, 314
Bell, Laird, 90, 96, 110
Ben-Gurion, David, 302
Benjamin, Robert S., 394, 426
Bennett, Arthur A., 133
Bentley, Elizabeth T., 320
Bentley, Richard, 140
Benton, William, 105, 126, 347, 460
  Britannica groups and, 395, 562
  as host, 331, 365, 424, 465
  travels of, 434, 435–436, 562
Beria, Lavrenti, 306
Berlin, Germany, 306–307, 494, 495, 496, 498,
    499
Berlin, Isaiah, 252
Biffle, Leslie, 109
Binder, Carroll, 65, 89
Binger, Carl, 347, 396
Bingham, Barry, 80, 181, 204, 278, 280, 282,
    287–288, 291, 293–294, 295, 297, 329,
    330, 357, 477
Bingham, Jonathan, 477
Birge, Claire, 50
Bissell, Richard, 316
Blaine, James G., 173

Blair, William McCormick, Jr., 73, 147, 273,
    312, 331, 343, 426
  on governor's staff, 133, 134, 164, 188, 203,
    268, 276
  Kennedy administration and, 118, 468,
    472–473, 474, 480
  law practice of, 342, 394, 479
  in presidential campaigns, 203, 206, 259,
    266, 342, 356, 365, 417, 448, 456, 461
  travels of, 278, 280, 282, 291, 294, 295, 297,
    303, 304, 307, 343, 344, 399, 401, 408,
    434
Bloom, Sol, 94, 103
Bloomington, Ill., 33–34
Blough, Roy, 316
Bogart, Humphrey, 249, 277
Boggs, Hale, 357
Bohlen, Charles E. "Chip," 97, 317–318
Boland, Frederick, 502
Book of the Month Club, 424, 431
Booth, John Wilkes, 20
Borden, Ellen, see Stevenson, Ellen Borden
Borden, Ellen Waller, see Carpenter, Ellen
    Waller Borden
Borden, John, 56–57, 58, 70
Bosch, Juan, 557
Bowles, Chester, 349, 424, 446, 471, 478, 484,
    495, 532, 562
  as ambassador, 289, 295, 314
  Finletter Group and, 314, 315, 316
  as undersecretary of state, 465, 472,
    496–497, 503–504
Boyd, Julian P., 437, 440
Boyden, William C., 140
Boyle, John, 170
Brademas, John, 328, 355, 357, 372, 380
Bradley, Omar, 92
Brandon, Piers, 406
Breasted, James, 300
Brevard, Hugh, 15
Brewton, Charles, 207
Bricker amendment, 327
Briggs, Ellis O., 493
Brooks, C. Wayland "Curly," 108, 110, 125,
    126
Brown, Edmund, 357–358, 455, 457, 459
Brown, Edward Eagle, 126
Brown, Jack O., 121
Brown, Stuart Gerry, 87, 223, 351, 403, 406,
    571
Brownell, Herbert, 320
Broyles, Paul, 159, 214, 231
Bruce, David K. E., 309, 467, 471, 472, 562
Bryan, William Jennings, 17, 23, 29, 49
Bryant, William Cullen, 26
Bulganin, Nikolay A., 382, 383, 387
Bulletin, 48, 49
Bunche, Ralph, 97, 163, 168, 319, 490
Bundy, McGeorge, 541, 550–551
  in Kennedy cabinet, 474, 486, 488, 491, 500,
    501, 503, 535
Bundy, William, 551
Bunker, Ellsworth, 477
Burgess, Kenneth F., 116, 131
Burma, 292–293
Butcher, Harry, 232, 240

Butler, Paul, 376, 378, 393, 395, 453–454
By Myself (Bacall), 277
Byrd, Harry F., 222, 276
Byrnes, James F., 94, 96, 97, 100, 101, 204, 232, 320

Calkins, Hugh, 86
Cambodia, 286, 287–288, 545–547
Campbell, Eliza, 54
capital punishment, 166–167
Capone, Al, 119, 123, 148, 150
Carnegie Endowment for International Peace, 102, 144, 228, 239
Carpenter, Ellen Waller Borden, 56, 57, 141, 360
    daughter's illness and, 123, 190, 329, 347, 478, 507
Carpenter, Frank, 539
Carpenter, John Alden, 57
Carroll, John, 453
Carvel, Elbert N., 194, 197
Cary, William, 210
Case, Everett, 349, 392
Castro, Fidel, 443, 487–488, 518
Catholic Church, 456, 468–469
cats, legislation on, 134
Centralia, Ill., mine explosion in, 120, 169
Centre College, 16
Cerf, Bennett, 210
Cermak, Anton, 107
Chamberlain, Henry, 53
Chambers, Whittaker, 144, 320
Chamoun, Camille, 300, 409
Chandler, Kent, 227
Chapman, Oscar, 177, 180, 207
Chaucer, Geoffrey, 304
Checkers, 226, 229
Chiang Kai-shek, 273, 282–284, 291, 294, 350, 414, 486
Chicago, University of, 65
Chicago Daily News, 50, 65, 70, 72, 74, 89–91, 97, 119, 237
Chicago Downs, 147–148
Chicago Herald-American, 51, 125, 141
Chicago Sun, 89, 110, 118
Chicago Sun Times, 118, 119, 148, 180, 395
Chicago Tribune, 37, 43, 56, 57, 64, 72–74, 89, 97, 99, 108, 119, 125, 133, 141, 154, 155, 175, 402
Chicherin, Georgi Vasilievich, 52, 53
Childs, Marquis, 176, 178, 191, 245
China, "loss" of, 231, 241, 246
China, Nationalist, 348, 349
    see also Chiang Kai-shek; Taiwan China, People's Republic of, 281, 318, 334–335, 405, 411, 423
    Korean War and, 241–246, 318
    offshore islands and, 348–352, 381, 414–415, 433
    UN admission of, 309, 423, 433, 486, 498, 500, 502, 517
Choate School, 36, 37, 38, 39, 41
Christian Science Monitor, 185, 197
Churchill, Sir Winston, 77, 86, 94, 267, 273, 310
CIA (Central Intelligence Agency), 293, 348, 386, 441, 483, 486–490, 528

Cicero, Ill., racial tension in, 168, 170, 177, 221
cigarette stamps, 154–155
civil liberties, 20, 49–50, 171
civil rights, 120, 167–168, 221–223, 364, 374, 403
Civil War, 21, 23, 26, 250
Clark, Harvey, 168
Clark, Mark, 280
Clark, Tom, 320
Clay, Lucius, 229
Cleveland, Grover, 16, 17, 68, 179
Cleveland, Harlan, 477
    in Johnson administration, 541, 547, 548, 553, 557, 559, 560
    in Kennedy administration, 486, 487, 496, 497–499, 522, 523, 533, 538
Cohan, George M., 36
Cohen, Benjamin V., 349, 370, 380
Cohn, David, 208
Cohn, Roy M., 304, 306, 311
Collins, LeRoy, 460, 462, 463
Coming of the New Deal, The (Schlesinger), 63
Commager, Henry Steele, 267, 571
Communism, 54, 159–160, 186, 228–240, 281, 294, 334–335
    Korean War and, 241–246
    "softness on," 239–240, 244
    see also McCarthyism
Conant, James Bryant, 307, 317
Con-Con (constitutional convention bill), 135–137
Congo, 401–402, 443, 481–484, 503, 537
Connally, Tom, 94, 103
Conners, William "Botchy," 61
Connolly, Marc, 139
Conscience in Politics (Brown), 228, 351
Cooke, Alistair, 198, 392
Coolidge, Betty, 28, 34
Coolidge, Calvin, 179
Cooper, John Sherman, 562
Copland, Aaron, 556
Cordier, Andrew, 535, 559
Cordiner, Ralph J., 403
Council on Foreign Relations, 55, 64–65, 70, 72, 75, 83, 89, 104, 106, 110, 175
Courtney, Thomas J., 80
Cousins, Norman, 267
Cowan, Louis G., 207, 250, 383
Cowles, Gardner, Jr., 66, 273
Cowles, Harriet, 45–46
Cowles, John, 66, 90
Cox, James M., 43
Craig, Mae, 185
Crowe, Dorsey R., 61
Crowley, Leo T., 85–86, 89
Crown, Henry, 84, 116, 505
Crowther, Geoffrey, 310, 401, 424
C(2)K(1), 237, 241
Cuba:
    Bay of Pigs invasion of, 486–492, 497, 535
    missile crisis and, 431, 479, 495, 516–536
Curie, Eve, 267
Curtis, Charles, 58
Cutler, Lloyd, 235
Cutting, Moore and Sidley, 54, 58

Daley, Richard J., 105, 129, 424
  national politics and, 376, 446–447, 455, 461, 469
  state politics and, 129, 135, 478, 504, 549
Dallman, V. Y., 119
Daniel, Price, 213, 276
Daniels, Jonathan, 331, 367
Daniels, Josephus, 37, 38
Darrow, Clarence, 49
Daughters of the American Revolution, 18
Davies, A. Powell, 419
Davies, John Paton, 317
Davis, Bert, 48
Davis, Eliza Fell, 21
Davis, Jefferson, 15
Davis, John W., 47, 144, 207
Davis, Kenneth, 28, 52, 53–54, 59–60, 71, 74, 88, 571
  on Stevenson's campaigns, 378–379, 418, 426, 451
Davis, Lewis E., 39
Davis, Norman P., 46
Davis, Saville R., 101
Davis, William Osborne, 21–22, 24, 28, 30, 48
Dawson, William L., 237
Day, J. Edward, 131, 133, 134, 147, 208, 227, 341
Dean, Arthur H., 476, 485, 499
de Gasperi, Alcide, 306
de Gaulle, Charles, 443, 492, 493, 497, 521, 567
Delroy, Irene (Josephine Sanders), 36, 38
Democratic Advisory Council (DAC), 393–395, 415, 416, 418, 452, 495
Democratic national conventions, 42, 46–47, 62, 70, 73
  of 1948, 120–127, 173
  of 1952, 173, 190–202
  of 1956, 375–377
  of 1960, 452–464
Democratic party, 195, 198, 470
  leadership of, 204–206, 267, 268–270, 313–314, 326, 393
  policy papers for, 314–317, 393–395
  Stevenson family and, 16, 17, 22, 23, 29, 46–47
  see also elections
Denby, Charles, 45, 50
Depression, Great, 55, 60
desegregation, 85, 167–168, 221, 327, 366, 369, 376, 384, 403
Dever, Paul, 197
De Voto, Bernard, 163, 208, 316
Dewey, Thomas E., 120, 154, 250, 322, 328, 382
Dick, Edison, 55, 132–133, 397, 452, 505
Dick, Jane Warner, 59, 118, 124, 132–133, 140, 163, 166–167, 209, 210, 238, 357, 374, 488–489
  Stevenson's correspondence with, 105, 121, 124, 269, 286–287, 295, 397, 470, 516
  Stevenson's friendship with, 55, 56, 165, 272, 273, 397, 478, 505, 537, 542, 555
Dietrich, Marlene, 249, 331
Dillon, Douglas, 519, 520, 526
Dirksen, Everett, 504

Dixon, Sherwood, 138, 202, 203, 254–255, 256
Dominican Republic, 557–558
domino theory, 288
Douglas, Helen Gahagan, 103, 228
Douglas, James, 62
Douglas, Paul H., 89, 180, 197, 207, 392, 504, 505
  campaign of, 112–113, 115, 119
  foreign policy and, 72, 349
  party leadership and, 268–269
  senatorial campaigns of, 80, 82–83, 110, 119, 125, 126, 311, 327, 328
  in World War II, 83, 108
Douglas, Stephen, 19
Douglas, William O., 287
Doyle, James, 204, 424–425, 451, 453, 454
draft, military, 379, 380–383, 403
Draft Stevenson Committee, 186, 191–192, 193–194, 196
Dreiske, John, 119
Drummond, Roscoe, 185, 197, 407
Duff, Alverta, 35–36
Duff, Jim, 308
Duffy, LaVern, 318
Dulles, John Foster, 94, 97, 102, 103, 180, 351
  foreign policy and, 214, 218, 245, 274–276, 293, 327, 349, 386, 387, 404–405, 432
  McCarthyism and, 144, 145–146, 239, 304, 319
Dunne, Edward Fitzgerald, 30, 33, 195
Duranty, Walter, 53

Eadie, Walter, 169
Eastern Europe, Soviet Union and, 214, 218, 304–305, 385–387, 410
Eaton, Charles A., 94, 103
Eberlein, Roxanne, 479, 562
Eden, Anthony, 387
Edson, Peter, 225
Education of a Public Man, The (Humphrey), 264
education programs, 384, 421–422
"egghead," origin of term, 247–248, 270–271
Egypt, 297, 298–299, 386–387
Eichelberger, Clark, 72
Eighteenth Amendment, repeal of, 63
Einstein, Albert, 267
Eisenhower, Dwight D., 178, 226, 313, 327, 328, 338, 362–363, 365, 367, 377–378, 379, 444
  criticism of, 341, 407, 432, 434, 436, 439
  Democratic nomination and, 115–116, 120, 174
  domestic policies of, 364, 366, 384, 403
  in election of 1952, 170, 180, 181, 184, 186, 187, 190, 198, 202, 203, 211–215, 217–218, 220, 224–239, 241–246, 248–253, 259, 260, 262–264, 277
  in election of 1956, 340–341, 353, 354, 355, 383–385, 389, 391, 392
  foreign policy of, 217–218, 245–246, 276, 286, 288, 289, 292, 311–312, 348–351, 358, 404–405, 410, 432, 441–443, 447, 484, 486, 492, 509, 545
  health of, 352, 355–356, 358, 362–363, 365, 375, 376, 388, 406–407

Korean War and, 241–246, 281, 282, 286
McCarthyism and, 230–237, 238–239, 251,
    306, 313, 317–325
Marshall and, 106, 230–236, 321
1948 draft refused by, 187, 193
Nixon and, 225, 226, 229–230, 378
on nuclear testing, 370, 372, 381–383, 402
private life of, 237, 240
World War II and, 86, 87
Eisenhower, Milton, 104
elderly, federal programs for, 385
elections:
    of 1912, 173
    of 1920, 42, 43
    of 1932, 61–62
    of 1940, 70, 73
    of 1944, 89
    of 1948, 108, 111–127, 187, 193, 218
    of 1952, 170, 173–264, 277, 340, 418
    of 1954, 269, 311–313, 327–334, 340, 352,
        355–357, 364, 374–376
    of 1956, 340–390, 391, 392, 418
    of 1958, 415–416
    of 1960, 406–408, 416–419, 424–426,
        428–430, 437–470
    of 1964, 541, 548
    primary, 356, 358, 359, 366–374
Eliot, George Fielding, 232
Elliott, Ivan, 151
Ellis, Charles, 20
Emmerson, John, 296
Encyclopaedia Britannica, 395, 562, 563
Ervin, Sam, 349
Evans, Carol, 117–118, 400
    campaigns and, 206, 260, 365
    as secretary, 131, 133, 268, 276–277, 312,
        342, 343, 397, 479–480
    on Stevenson's decisiveness, 254
Ewing, James, 16, 17, 54

Face the Nation, 362, 403, 455
Fair Employment Practices Commission
    (FEPC), 122, 132, 134, 136, 137, 157,
    221, 222
Faisal, Prince, 297
farm marketing agreements, 63–64
farm policy, 219–220, 356–357
Farrin, Michael, 254
Fasi, Frank, 279
Faubus, Orval, 403
Fawzi, Mahmoud, 298
Federal Alcohol Control Administration, 63
Fedorenko, Nikolai, 543, 551, 557
Fell, Jesse, 18–21, 35, 45
Field, Ellen, 273
Field, Marshall I, 99, 273
Field, Marshall III, 89, 90, 118, 393, 427
Field, Ruth, 408, 426, 506, 512
    Stevenson's friendship with, 393, 397, 398,
        408, 505, 537, 534, 555
Fine, Alvin I., 363
Finletter, Thomas K., 95, 314–317, 393, 394,
    470, 477
    background of, 314–315
    elections and, 368, 370, 426, 451
    opposition tactics and, 393, 394

Finletter Group, 314–317, 326, 341, 355, 370,
    393, 395
Finley, Robert, 46
Finnegan, James A., 193, 356–358, 363, 368,
    378–380, 389
Finnerud, Clark, 212
Finney, Tom, 453, 454–455
Fischer, John, 208
Fisher, Walter T., 130
FitzGerald, Frances, 401, 537
Fitzpatrick, Paul, 188
Flanagan, William I., 133, 185, 190
    in public relations, 131, 147, 206–207, 268
    in Stevenson's campaigns, 118, 206–207, 209
    Stevenson's presidential nomination and,
        176, 178, 188, 189, 194
Flanders, Ralph, 325
Fleeson, Doris, 438
Fontaine, Joan, 506
Ford, Gerald R., 542
Foreign Affairs, 419, 431–434
Foreign Economic Administration, 85
Formosa, see Taiwan
Forrestal, James, 75, 79, 83, 88, 478
Forrestal, Jo, 478
Forsyth, Don, 156
Fosdick, Dorothy, 164–166, 175, 188–189,
    199, 208, 272, 397
Fosdick, Harry Emerson, 164, 166
Foster, Bill, 476
France, 307–309, 386–387
Francis of Assisi, Saint, 195
Franco, Francisco, 214, 300
Frank, Jerome, 62, 63
Frankel, Max, 504
Fredericks, Wayne, 484
Freeman, Orville, 198, 365, 367, 458, 461–462
Frei Montalvo, Eduardo, 549
Friedrich, Otto, 535
Friendly, Fred W., 565
Friends and Enemies: What I Learned in
    Russia (Stevenson), 409
Fritchey, Clayton, 207, 316, 349, 394, 487,
    513, 544
    Bartlett article and, 531–533, 536
    editorial aid from, 349, 504, 564
Frondizi, Arturo, 503
Frost, Robert, 460
Fry, Joshua, 16
Fulbright, William, 208, 268–269, 309, 321,
    359, 472
    foreign policy and, 349, 446, 471, 480, 487

Galbraith, John Kenneth, 208, 218, 314–316,
    395, 501, 560
Galitzine, Countess Anastasia, 53
Galitzine, Prince Nicholas, 53
gambling network, 150–152
Gardner, Ava, 249, 537, 555
Gardner, Richard N., 557
Garfield, James A., 173
Garrison, Lloyd, 268, 273, 342, 344, 395,
    543–544
Garst, Roswell, 427
Garth, David, 438, 453, 459–460
Gateway Amendment, 136

Geological Survey, U.S., 23
George, Walter, 349
Germano, Joe, 116–117, 125
Germany, 306–307, 434
Gilpatric, Roswell, 316, 519
Glasgow, William, 31
Glubb, John Bagot, 301
Goldberg, Arthur, 80, 480, 548, 557
Goldwater, Barry, 530–531, 541, 542, 548, 549
Gomulka, Wladslaw, 386
Goodman, Paul, 561, 564
Goodwin, Ralph, 38, 40, 45
Goodwin, Richard N., 263–264
Gorbachev, Mikhail, 431
Gorden, Lincoln, 493
Graebel, Richard Paul, 25, 360
Graham, Billy, 513
Graham, Kay, 506, 516, 555
Granata, William John, 122–123
Grant, Ulysses S., 17, 173
Great Britain, 298, 309–310, 386–387,
    399–400
Green, Dwight, 89, 110, 116, 119–123, 125,
    130–133, 169
Gromyko, Andrey, 97, 98, 410, 483–484, 526,
    527, 551
Grothe, Peter, 470
Gruenther, Alfred, 309, 348
Guggenheim, Harry F., 124, 142, 165, 397
Gunther, Mrs. John, 554
Gurewitsch, David, 516
Gustafson, Phyllis, 268, 342
Gutnecht, John, 170

Hagerty, James, 320, 381, 405
Halifax, Lord, 95
Hammarskjöld, Dag, 326, 476, 481–484, 501,
    502, 570
Hammett, Dashiell, 304
Hancock, Winfield Scott, 179
Hansen, Alvin, 316
Hardin, Julia, 31, 60
Harding, Warren, 84, 262
Hare, Raymond, 297–298
Harlan, John, 39–40, 41, 44
Harper, Samuel, 65
Harriman, Averell, 188, 207, 274, 275, 311,
    315, 328, 394, 477, 479, 495, 551
    in election of 1952, 180, 185, 186, 190, 192,
        193, 196, 197, 201
    in election of 1956, 355–357, 364, 374–376
    in election of 1958, 416
    Finletter group and, 315, 316
Harris, Seymour, 384
Harvard University, 45, 46, 317, 332–336
Hauge, Gabriel, 235, 328
Hay, John, 35
Hay, Logan, 35
Hay, Mary Douglas, 35
Hearst, George R., 18
Hearst, Phoebe Apperson, 18, 23
Hearst, William Randolph, 18, 23–24, 29
Hechler, Ken, 357, 372
Heineman, Ben W., 154–155, 238, 267
Hemenway, Russel D., 425–426, 438, 453, 456
Hennessey, Spike, 108, 114

Hentoff, Nat, 561
Herblock, 405
Hersey, John, 210
Hertz, John, 57
Hewitt, Robert, 291
Hickenlooper, Bourke, 480
highway program, 132, 156–157, 266
Hill, Lister, 207, 349
Hiss, Alger, 63
    campaign rhetoric on, 170, 211, 228–230,
        237, 239, 252
    peace work of, 94, 102, 144, 228
    Stevenson's association with, 144–146, 161,
        170, 185–186
Hitler, Adolf, 72, 74, 77, 79, 307
Ho Chi Minh, 287
Hodes, Barney, 80, 89
Hodgins, Eric, 208, 355
Hoehler, Fred, 129, 131, 135
Hoffman, Paul, 229
Holmes, Julius, 104
Holmes, Oliver Wendell, 50
Hong Kong, 284–285
Hoover, Herbert, 58, 62, 122, 262, 269
Hopkins, Harry, 78, 207
Horner, Henry, 62, 108, 195
horsemeat scandal, 153–154, 155
Houston, David F., 47
Hughes, Charles Evans, 200
Hughes, Emmet John, 234, 244, 245, 317, 379,
    381
Humes, Harold, 463
Humphrey, Hubert, 120, 264, 325, 393, 470,
    543
    as candidate, 184, 186, 416, 417, 425, 431,
        438, 440, 441, 458
    Stevenson candidacy and, 267, 356, 367,
        376, 377
Hungary, uprising in, 386, 387
Hunt, John, 479
Hussein I, king of Jordan, 301
Huston, Evelyn, 505
Hutchins, Robert M., 65, 70–71, 74, 142, 465,
    563
Hyman, Sydney, 208
Hyndman, T. Don, 131, 147, 207

Ibn Saud, king of Saudi Arabia, 297
Ickes, Harold L., 62, 168
Illinois, 469
    civil-rights issues in, 167–168
    constitution of, 122, 132, 134, 138
    Democratic organization in, 61, 266
    legislature of, 33, 132, 134–138, 156–158,
        159–161
    Lincoln and history of, 15, 34, 162, 163, 164,
        203
    mental-health system in, 122, 132, 171, 266
    organized crime in, 150–151
    state police of, 132, 134–135, 137, 151
    Stevenson as governor of, 128–172
    Stevenson as senatorial contender in,
        108–111, 112, 116
    Stevenson's gubernatorial campaign in,
        107–127
    Stevenson's victory in, 126–127

Welfare Department of, 129, 266
Independent Voters of Illinois, 180–181, 186
India, 289, 293–296, 503
Indochina, 288, 291, 308
Indonesia, 289–290
Information Service, U.S., 304, 318
Ingersoll, Robert, 25
Iraq, military coup in, 409
Irvin, Lawrence, 131, 133
"I See America" (Stevenson), 256–257
isolationism, 72–74, 99, 174
Israel, 297–303, 358, 362–364, 366, 369, 386, 387
Italy, 51–52, 85–87, 305–306
Ives, Elizabeth Ewing Stevenson "Buffie":
    on campaign promises, 38
    childhood of, 24–31, 37
    correspondence of, 36, 402, 424
    education of, 32, 33, 35, 43
    father's gift to, 59
    homes of, 16, 24, 125, 236
    as hostess, 140, 162, 163, 478, 496
    intrusiveness of, 397, 555
    marriage of, 51, 58
    romantic advice from, 165–166
    on sister-in-law, 81, 132
    social life of, 39, 41, 55
    Stevenson's career and, 89, 452
    theater and, 32, 34, 51
    travels of, 43, 44, 61, 399, 515, 542
Ives, Ernest, 51, 61, 81, 123–124
    homes of, 162, 163, 236
    travels of, 306, 308, 452, 515
Ives, Timothy Read, 58, 81, 121, 164, 452, 542

Jackson, Andrew, 179
Jackson, C. D., 392
Jackson, Henry, 207, 349, 509–513
Jackson, Sir Robert, 400, 505
Japan, 279–281, 283, 286, 433
Jefferson, Peter, 16
Jefferson, Thomas, 15, 16, 88, 215, 437
Jenner, William E., 214, 215, 231, 234, 263
Jerusalem, 300, 301
Jessup, Philip, 229, 252
Johnson, Gerald R., 375
Johnson, Lady Bird, 541
Johnson, Lyndon B., 84
    in election of 1960, 416, 417, 446–454, 461, 467, 469
    in election of 1964, 541, 549, 551
    as president, 314, 316–317, 384, 395, 480, 540, 556–558, 566
    in Senate, 268–269, 274, 275, 276, 313, 314, 325, 327, 349, 357, 392, 393, 394, 416
    staff of, 130, 263, 315, 480
    Stevenson candidacy and, 213, 268, 356, 358, 376
    Vietnam policy of, 92, 288, 541, 545–554, 559–560, 565
Johnson, Samuel, 215
Johnson, Walter, 45, 100–101, 191–192, 193, 214, 480, 522, 551, 552
    on world tour, 278, 280, 282, 287, 291, 294, 295, 296, 297, 299, 300, 331
Jones, G. Lewis, 298

Jones, Jesse, 90, 91
Jordan, 297, 299, 300, 301
Judson, Clay, 65, 74
Jung, Carl, 43

Kádár, János, 387
Kaghan, Theodore, 307
Kaiser, Phil, 563, 564, 565
Keating, Kenneth, 543
Kefauver, Estes, 201, 202, 393
    Crime Committee of, 148, 152, 153, 170
    presidential candidacy of, 180, 181, 184, 186, 192, 193, 197–198, 355, 358, 359, 364, 366, 367–369, 373–375, 417
    as running mate, 354, 357, 376, 377, 389
Keller, Helen, 267
Kelly, Ed, 80, 107, 108
Kennan, George F., 174, 314, 315–316, 327, 370
Kennedy, Edward M., 463
Kennedy, Jacqueline, 468, 506, 554
Kennedy, John F.:
    appointments of, 118, 130, 208, 263, 315, 448, 461, 465, 471–474, 476, 477, 503–504
    assassination of, 539, 540
    Cuba and, 486–489, 516–526, 529, 531
    disarmament and, 395, 485, 497, 498, 500, 569
    foreign policy of, 288, 431, 464, 494–495, 499, 537–538
    nuclear testing and, 499–500, 538
    presidency of, 314, 316, 384, 478–479, 480, 509–511, 566
    presidential campaign of, 264, 274, 393, 416, 417, 424, 425, 431, 438–441, 445, 447–470
    Stevenson candidacy and, 196, 264, 357, 359, 376, 377
    Stevenson's relationship with, 405, 449–450, 463, 480, 483, 487, 490–492, 498, 504–505, 532–533, 539, 541–542
Kennedy, Joseph, 318, 448, 455
Kennedy, Robert F., 318, 474–475, 519–522, 535, 543
    1960 campaign and, 441, 449, 457, 461
Kennelly, Martin H., 105, 108, 109, 112, 113, 137, 310
Kent, Carlton, 177–178
Kerr, Robert S., 180, 186, 192, 193, 197, 275
Khan, Sir Zafrullah, 296
Khrushchev, Nikita, 386, 413, 479, 494, 495, 518
    Cuba and, 489, 518, 524–526, 533
    J. F. Kennedy and, 492–493, 494
    nuclear tests and, 499–500
    Stalin condemned by, 386
    Stevenson's visits with, 410–411, 427, 479
    U.S. politics and, 428–431, 472
    U.S. visits by, 427, 473, 482
    U-2 incident and, 441–443, 446, 447
Kingsley, Donald, 281
Kintner, Robert, 97
Kissinger, Henry, 253
Klutznick, Philip, 477, 489, 496, 516, 561
Knickerbocker, H. R., 53

Knight, John, 90
Knowland, William, 349
Knowlson, James, 111
Knox, Annie Reid, 90, 91
Knox, Frank, 72
  death of, 88, 89–90
  as Navy Secretary, 73, 75–79, 80, 83, 84,
    85–86, 215, 236
Kohler, Walter, 234
Kohn, Louis A., 108–109, 110, 118–119, 122,
    128, 131, 281–283
Korea, 281–283, 433, 443
Korean War, 158, 166, 229, 241–246, 281, 282,
    286, 291, 318
Korn, Edward, 287
Kosygin, Alexei, 552
Kresl, Carl, 130
Krishna Menon, V. K., 476
Krock, Arthur, 83, 95, 127, 174, 190
Kuznetsov, V. V., 529, 532

labor movement, 218–219
Ladejinsky, Wolf, 280, 283
La Guardia, Fiorello H., 103
Lahey, Edwin A., 94, 185
Lambert, W. H., 291
Landon, Alfred M., 72
Lane, Roger, 152–153
Lanigan, James, 207
Laos, 287, 494–495, 514, 547
Larabee, Eric, 232
Lasker, Albert, 398
Lasker, Mary, 426, 437, 470
  correspondence of, 397, 516
  Stevenson's friendship with, 398, 399, 500,
    555
Latin America, 408, 434–436, 492, 493–494,
    558
Lawrence, David L., 185, 193, 205, 376, 393,
    452, 456, 461
Lax, Henry, 515, 544, 555–556
League of Nations, 43, 47, 96, 98, 102
Lebanon, 299–300, 409, 410
Lehman, Herbert, 274, 357, 366, 367, 393,
    460, 463
Lend-Lease agreement, 73, 84
Lewis, J. Hamilton, 61
Lewis, John L., 177, 180
Lewis, Kathryn, 114
Lewis, Lloyd, 50, 65, 68, 80, 89, 114, 118, 139
Lie, Trygve, 104, 267, 408, 409
Life, 194, 252
Life in Our Times (Galbraith), 218
Limited Nuclear Test Ban Treaty, 402
Lincoln, Abraham, 556
  anecdotes about, 250, 260, 470
  assassination of, 20
  celebrations of, 556
  Civil War and, 21, 250
  Illinois history and, 15, 34, 162, 163, 164,
    203
  political career of, 18, 19–20
  Republican party and, 250, 323
  scholarship on, 35, 62, 68, 163
Lindsay, Vachel, 34, 195
Link, Theodore C., 121

Lippmann, Walter, 83, 163, 186, 264, 415,
    571–572
Little Rock, Ark., racial issues in, 403
Lloyd, David D., 86, 176, 180
Lodge, Henry Cabot, 387, 466, 469, 493, 505
Loeb, James, Jr., 176, 178, 182
Lohman, Joseph D., 131, 254
Long Island Newsday, 124, 142
Look, 273, 278–310, 331, 363, 434, 436
Lopez, Pedro, 99
Los Angeles Examiner, 23–24
Louisville Courier Journal, 51, 181, 204, 208,
    251, 278
Lovett, Robert A., 80, 485, 520
Lowell, Stanley H., 460
loyalty oaths, 159, 160–161, 230
Lucas, Scott W., 109, 110
Lumumba, Patrice, 481, 482, 483
Lyon, Cecil B., 307

Maass, Arthur, 316
McAdoo, William G., 47
MacArthur, Douglas, 241, 242
McCambridge, Mercedes, 249, 555
McCarran, Pat, 186, 276
McCarthy, Eugene, 458, 462, 562
McCarthy, Joseph:
  Catholic vote and, 220
  downfall of, 325, 328
  Marshall denounced by, 230–236
  "pansies" speech and, 238, 240
  on Stevenson, 54, 87, 144, 159
  support for, 214
  targets of, 317–318, 321–322, 323
McCarthyism, 145, 224, 229–230, 253, 328
  campaign endorsements and, 251–252
  Dulles on, 144, 145–146, 239, 304, 319
  Eisenhower and, 230–237, 238–239, 251,
    306, 313, 317–325
  foreign reactions to, 293, 295, 304, 306–307,
    308
  impact of, 230, 320, 323–324
  legislation inspired by, 159–161
  Stevenson on, 151, 228, 275, 319, 320–324
McClatchy, C. K., 357
McClelland, Margery, 30, 31
McCloskey, Matthew H., 392
McCloy, John J., 79, 325, 484, 498, 521, 522,
    529, 536
McCone, John, 519, 520
McCormick, Robert R., 56, 65, 175
MacDonald, Malcolm, 290
McDougal, Edward, Jr., 65, 96, 101, 479
McEvoy, Nan Tucker, 397, 554
McGill, Ralph, 326, 435
McGowan, Carl, 88, 161, 169
  background of, 146, 370
  career of, 171, 268, 370, 493, 516
  at Navy Department, 75–76, 84
  on nomination, 183, 187–188
  in presidential campaigns, 203, 204, 206,
    207, 208, 214, 217, 218, 220, 243, 248,
    249, 253, 254, 259, 264, 266, 369
  prison riot and, 254–256
  on Stevenson's effectiveness, 150, 158–159
  as Stevenson's friend, 505, 506–507, 556

in Stevenson's governorship, 130, 133, 147, 150, 152, 153–154, 155, 158–159, 162, 163, 171–172
on Stevenson's marriage, 139, 141
McGrory, Mary, 264, 438, 446, 555
McIlvaine, William, 45
McInerary, John, 107
McIntyre, Marvin, 78
McKinney, Frank, 194, 201, 204–205, 254
MacLeish, Archibald, 75, 560
campaign assistance from, 210, 214
job offered by, 92, 93
as Stevenson's friend, 505, 506
on Stevenson's marriage, 161–162
United Nations and, 89, 94
wartime posts of, 80, 83, 92, 93
MacMillan, Harold, 404, 405, 443, 484, 499–500
McNamara, Robert, 517, 519, 520, 541, 557
Magnuson, Paul B., 505
Magsaysay, Ramón, 285, 286
Major Campaign Speeches of Adlai E. Stevenson, 1952, 274, 305
Making of the President–1960, The (White), 417–418
Malaya, 290–292
Manly, Chesley, 175
Manning, Robert, 210
Mansfield, Mike, 349, 510, 512
Mao Tse-tung, 284, 295
Marshall, George C., 105–107, 207, 240, 267, 270, 284, 285, 321
McCarthyism and, 215, 230–236
Martin, John Bartlow, 108, 120, 255
on Finletter Group, 316–317
on Kennedy administration, 436
presidential campaigns and, 208, 217, 218, 366, 368, 373, 384
on Stevenson governorship, 159, 171, 172
on Stevenson's family life, 61, 68–69
Martin, Joseph, 276
Martin, Ralph, 210
Matthews, Martha, 466
Matthews, T. S., 40, 42, 176, 310
Maverick, Maury, Jr., 373
Meadow, Florence, 342
Meany, George, 367
Medicare, 372, 385
Meet the Press, 184, 185–186, 561
Menard Prison, 254–256
Mendelssohn, Jack, 361
Menninger, Karl, 398–399
Menshikov, Mikhail A., 428–430, 472, 476
Merwin, David, 48, 49, 50
Merwin, Davis, 28, 31, 36, 49, 62, 66–67, 75
Merwin, Jessie Davis, 22, 48–49
Merwin, Loring "Bud," 66–67, 91, 109, 190, 252
Merwin, Mrs. Clarence, 31
Merwin, Ruth, accidental death of, 30–31
Meyer, Agnes, 353–354, 360, 361, 366, 407, 424, 426, 437, 440
Stevenson's friendship with, 331, 397–398, 515, 555
Meyer, Eugene, 95
Meyers, Maude, 131

Meyers, Tedson, 453, 454, 462–463
Middle East, 358, 363, 387, 433–434
see also specific countries
Mikhailov, N. A., 410
Mikoyan, Anastas, 410, 411, 529
Mikva, Abner, 171
Miller, Edward, 95
Miller, Juanda, 342
Miller, Merle, 240
Miller, Mrs. John S., 132
Milota, William, 129
mine safety, 120, 132, 137, 169, 177
Minor, Harold B., 299
Minow, Newton, 180, 203, 219, 426–427, 480, 541
law career of, 171, 342–343, 394, 396, 479
presidential races and, 209, 254, 255, 266, 355–356, 368, 448, 456
Minton, Sherman, 171
Mitchell, George, 129
Mitchell, Stephen A., 96, 109, 110, 118, 128, 156, 205, 220, 221, 226, 227, 259, 352
as party chairman, 205, 269, 304, 311, 312
Mobutu, Joseph, 482
Molotov, V. M., 97, 106
Monaghan, Jay, 164
Monnet, Jean, 309
Monroney, Mike, 327, 357, 426, 446, 450, 452–455, 457–460
Montero, Frank, 177
Montgomery, Robert, 379
Moretti, Mike, 170
Morgan, Thomas B., 454, 456, 457, 459–460, 463, 464
Morozov, Platon, 522
Morris, Joe Alex, 87–88
Morse, Wayne, 235, 477, 513
Mowrer, Paul Scott, 89
Moyers, Bill, 552
Muller, Herbert, 251, 571
Mulroy, Helen, 227
Mulroy, James, 118, 122, 131, 133, 147–148, 155
Mundt, Karl, 237
Munn, Margaret, 131, 133, 206
Murphy, Charles, 176, 180, 182, 184, 315
Murphy, Robert D., 279, 485
Murray, James, 328
Murray, Thomas E., 370, 371
Murrow, Edward R., 163, 235, 383
Musgrave, Richard, 316
Muskie, Edmund, 357
Mussolini, Benito, 52, 85
Myers, Francis J., 193, 194, 204
Myers, Maude, 265

Nagy, Imre, 386, 387, 410
Nash, Pat, 107
Nasser, Gamal Abdel, 386–387, 500
National Geographic Society, 23
National Industrial Recovery Act, 64
NATO (North Atlantic Treaty Organization), 404–406, 432–433, 471, 484–485, 519, 521, 537
UN vs., 509–514
Navy Department, U.S., 75–81, 83–86, 88, 96, 97, 215

Nehru, Jawaharlal, 294, 295, 500–501, 503, 505
Nelson, Richard J., 146, 147, 207, 209
Neuberger, Richard L., 102–103, 327, 357
"New America" program, 379, 383
New Deal, 62, 88
Newsweek, 121, 126, 253
New York *Daily News*, 56, 238, 533
New York Herald Tribune, 90, 174, 225, 407
New York Times, 90, 95–96, 126, 197, 234, 236, 251, 257, 294, 295, 391, 393, 408, 425, 427, 430–431, 451, 486
Nicolson, Sir Harold, 309
Niebuhr, Reinhold, 174, 267, 392
Nimitz, Chester, 77, 79, 84, 85
Nitti, Frank, 123
Nitze, Paul, 327, 349, 470, 476, 519
Nixon, Richard M., 261, 270, 272
    in election of 1952, 211, 217, 222, 224–230, 237, 243, 262
    in election of 1956, 377–378, 383, 388
    in election of 1960, 407, 418–419, 424, 429, 437, 438, 445, 451–452, 456, 465–467, 469
    foreign policy and, 350, 431
    McCarthyism and, 54, 144, 145, 159, 224, 229–230, 237, 317, 319, 325, 328
    presidency of, 388, 486
    slush fund of, 222, 224–226, 242
    as vice-president, 317, 319, 382, 402, 403, 408, 432
Nkrumah, Kwame, 400
Nobile, Umberto, 51
Norman, John, 87
Northwestern University, 50, 174
Norton, George, 51, 52
Notti, Robert W., 227–228
Noyes, Charles P., 477
nuclear test ban, 312, 380–381, 382, 402, 485, 503
nuclear weapons, 312, 348, 349, 370–372, 379–383, 402, 499–500, 538

Oakes, John B., 391, 392, 394, 406, 407
Oates, James, 61, 96, 97, 259
O'Dwyer, William, 116
oil industry, 84, 212–213, 276, 297
O'Mahoney, Joseph, 328, 349
Ordeal of Power, The (Hughes), 244, 317, 381
Organization of American States (OAS), 519, 520, 521, 523
Ormandy, Eugene, 556

Paepcke, Mrs. Walter, 476, 505, 554
Page, Bob, 51, 52
Pakistan, 294, 296
Palestine refugees, 299, 301, 302
Palmer, Mrs. Potter, 56
Pantagraph, 19, 21, 30
    articles in, 31, 43, 50, 51–52
    family involvement with, 29, 33, 41, 45, 47–50, 60, 66–67
    politics and, 62, 190, 252
Papers of Adlai Stevenson, The (Johnson), 100–101
Pares, Sir Bernard, 52
Pargellis, Mrs. Stanley, 131

Patterson, Alicia:
    death of, 397, 537
    marriage of, 124, 165
    Stevenson's correspondence with, 124–125, 138, 142–144, 148, 162, 166, 170, 182, 189, 190, 272, 397
    Stevenson's friendship with, 56, 164, 165, 272, 331, 397, 401, 409, 515
Patterson, Joe, 56
Patterson, Robert P., 79, 177
Patton, George S., 92
Peabody, Endicott, 272, 424
Peace Corps, 470, 478
Peale, Norman Vincent, 469
Pearson, Drew, 166, 225, 515
Pederson, Richard, 488
Pepper, Claude, 78
Peress, Irving, 321
Perkins, Frances, 70
Persons, S. Gordon, 326
Persons, Wilton B., 317
Pettibone, Holman D., 90
Philippines, 285–286, 289
Pirie, Betty Borden, 57, 70, 100
Pirie, Robert S., 100
Plimpton, Francis T. P., 45, 46, 146, 342, 424, 477, 506, 516, 537, 555
Pogue, Forrest C., 106, 233
Pois, Joseph, 129, 171
Poland, 386
Poole, William, 238
Powell, Adam Clayton, 366
Powell, John Wesley, 23
Powell, Paul, 132, 138, 147, 148, 157
Powers, Francis Gary, 442
Princetonian, 41, 43–44
Princeton University, 36, 39–41, 43–45, 123
Progressive Mine Workers, 167
Proxmire, William, 513

Quadros, Jânio, 494
Quemoy and Matsu, 348–352, 381, 414–415, 433
Quirino, Elpidio, 285, 286

Rabb, Maxwell, 319
Rabi, Isidor, 381
Radford, Arthur W., 279, 349
Randolph, Ross, 153, 154
Raskin, Henry, 357
Ravenholt, Albert, 284, 285
Rayburn, Sam, 274, 275, 276, 349, 312, 357
    Democratic party leadership and, 268, 313, 314, 327, 392, 393, 446
    presidential races and, 197–198, 201–202, 356, 358, 376, 461
Reardy, Viola, 426–427, 505, 541
Reedy, George, 553
Republican national conventions:
    of 1940, 73
    of 1952, 193
    of 1956, 377–378
Republican party:
    business interests in, 274
    congressional leadership of, 268
    Illinois establishment of, 19
    Lincoln and, 250, 323

McCarthyism and, 323–324, 325
see also elections
Reston, James "Scotty," 95, 96, 163, 192, 295, 393, 557
  on elections, 180, 196, 236, 393, 430–431
Reuter, Ernst, 306–307
Reuther, Walter, 209, 218, 268, 452, 455
Reynolds, Richard, 401
Rhee, Syngman, 282, 283, 443
Ribicoff, Abraham, 376, 473
Rifkind, Simon H., 543–544
Riggs, Austen, 66
Ringling, Henry, 234
rising expectations, revolution of, 87, 333–334, 336
Risse, Anne, 131
Rivkin, William R., 118
Roa, Raoul, 487, 488
Roache, Neale, 207
Roberts, Chalmers, 531, 532
Robinson, Joseph T., 58
Robinson, William, 225, 229
Rockefeller, John D., Jr., 164
Rockefeller, Nelson, 416, 424
Ronan, Jim, 311
Roosevelt, Anna, 529
Roosevelt, Eleanor, 78
  Advisory Council and, 394, 426
  death of, 516, 529–530, 548
  McCarthyism and, 252, 293, 306
  political support from, 367, 374, 375, 457, 459, 463, 472
  Stevenson's friendship with, 104, 367, 398–399
  travels of, 283, 287, 295, 305
  UN and, 100, 103, 477, 516, 529
Roosevelt, Franklin D., 47, 88, 89, 94, 107, 144
  domestic policies of, 75, 122, 245
  presidential campaigns of, 62, 90, 179, 195, 262, 341, 416
  World War II and, 72, 73, 76–79, 85, 86, 91, 94, 232, 243
Roosevelt, Franklin D., Jr., 116
Roosevelt, Theodore, 75, 464
Roper, Elmo, 206, 263
Rorimer, James, 505
Rosenwald, Lessing, 90
Ross, Lillian, 253
Rostenkowski, Daniel, 118
Rostow, Walt, 513
Rovere, Richard, 247, 352
Rusk, Dean, 496
  in Johnson administration, 541, 543, 551–554, 557, 559, 562
  in Kennedy administration, 472, 474–477, 486, 492, 495–496, 500, 512, 529, 535, 537, 559
Russell, Richard B., 180, 192, 276, 325, 326
  candidacy of, 186, 193, 197, 198
Russian Revolution, 51, 52
Ryan, C. J., 283

Sagendorph, George, 467
St. John, George, 38
St. Louis Post-Dispatch, 121, 251
Salinger, Pierre, 532

Salisbury, Harrison, 408
Salisbury, Lord, 309
Sandburg, Carl, 132–133, 163, 267
Sanders, Josephine (Irene Delroy), 36, 38
San Francisco United Nations Conference, 94–96, 144
Saud, Crown Prince, 297–298
Saudi Arabia, 297–298
Schaefer, Walter V., 118, 146
  judicial career of, 169, 396
  in Stevenson administration, 128, 131, 133, 134, 138, 154, 158
Schaetzel, J. R., 470
Schary, Dore, 249, 392, 426, 462, 556
Scherman, Harry, 424, 431
Schine, G. David, 304, 306, 311
Schlesinger, Arthur, Jr., 63, 163, 312, 314, 316, 349, 558
  Kennedy administration and, 467, 468, 487, 491, 495, 498, 521–523, 528, 531, 532–533, 538, 539, 541–542
  in presidential campaigns, 207–208, 214, 238, 253, 261, 362, 368, 370, 384
  Stevenson candidacy and, 185, 425, 437, 440–441, 448–450, 459
  UN and, 486, 490, 514
Schoenbrum, David, 564
schools, desegregation of, 20, 223, 327, 366, 369, 376, 384, 403
Schricker, Henry, 194, 197
Schweitzer, Albert, 344, 401
Scopes "Monkey" trial, 49
Scott, Julia Green, 16, 24
Scott, Matthew, 16
Scott, Sir Walter, 29
Sevareid, Eric, 152, 249, 367, 392, 469, 562, 564, 565
Seyfrit, Michael, 254, 256
Shakespeare, William, 19
Sharett, Moshe, 302
Sharon, John, 316, 426, 450, 453–455, 459, 470–472
Sherman, John, 173
Sherwood, Robert, 310
Shishikli, Adib, 300–301
Shivers, Allan, 212–213, 268
Shriver, Eunice Kennedy, 467, 468
Shriver, Sargent, 471, 472, 536
Sidey, Hugh, 495
Sidley, William, 96, 116
Simon, Paul, 152
Sisco, Joseph, 487, 523, 560, 564
slot machines, 151–152
Smith, Alfred E., 47, 58, 223
Smith, Carlton Sprague, 434
Smith, Dana, 225
Smith, Ellen, 80, 81, 135, 258, 354
Smith, Herman Dunlop "Dutch," 55, 124, 128, 227, 555, 596
  Stevenson's campaigns and, 109–113, 118, 126, 204, 209, 227, 258
  Stevenson's friendship with, 38, 55, 80, 258, 354, 424
Smith, Sidney, 28, 33
Smith, Walter Bedell, 86, 317
Sorensen, Theodore C., 449, 465, 475, 485, 514

Sorensen, Theodore C. (*cont.*)
  draftsmanship of, 478, 479, 500, 501, 519,
    533–534
  on missile crisis, 517–521
South Africa, 344, 401, 537–538
Soviet Union, 303, 384
  Chinese alliance with, 411, 423
  Cuba and, 489, 516–529
  Eastern Europe and, 214, 218, 304–305,
    385–387, 410
  Egyptian alliance with, 386, 387
  expansionism of, 332–333
  nuclear weapons and, 382, 383, 402
  Stevenson's visits to, 51–54, 407–413
  UN and, 97–98, 104, 106, 483–484, 501,
    502, 542–543
  U.S. elections and, 428–431
  U-2 incident and, 441–443
Sparkman, John, 201–202, 205, 221, 317, 326,
    349
Spears, Sir Edward Louis, 56
Spears, Lady Mary Borden, 56, 347, 467, 562
Spellman, Francis Cardinal, 220–221
Spivak, Lawrence, 185–186
Sprague, A. A., 61
Springfield, Ill., 34
Spruance, Raymond, 285, 286
Sputnik, 384
Stalin, Joseph, 53, 94, 175, 302, 305, 386
  World War II and, 77, 79, 86, 245
Standard Oil, 84
Stanton, Edwin F., 292
Stassen, Harold E., 94, 95, 180, 235, 318–319
State Department, U.S., 92–96, 105–106, 110,
    229, 322, 323, 441–442, 483, 484, 490,
    495–496, 501
  Stevenson's hopes for secretary post at,
    465–468, 470–475
Stearns, Harry, 37
Steele, John, 491–492, 515, 522, 535
Steinbeck, John, 210, 267, 392, 505
Stern, Phil, 207, 316, 349
Stettinius, Edward R., Jr., 80, 92–97, 100, 103
Stevens, Robert, 321–322, 426
Stevens, Roger, 209, 365, 366
Stevenson, Adlai Ewing I (grandfather), 33,
    45, 54, 68
  family life and, 16–17, 18, 24, 25
  political career of, 16, 17–18, 22, 23, 29, 30,
    62, 185
Stevenson, Adlai Ewing II:
  appearance of, 40, 55, 122
  articles by, 153, 273, 355, 363, 402, 419,
    431–434, 436, 444
  birth of, 25
  books written by, 267–268, 273, 274, 295,
    305, 309, 313, 408, 409, 419
  campaign style of, 372–373, 379–380
  childhood of, 24, 25–31, 32, 35–36
  church membership of, 360–361
  death of, 563–565
  divorce of, 140–143, 161–162, 166, 204, 220,
    237, 329, 395, 397
  education of, 28, 32, 33, 35, 36–37, 38,
    39–41, 43–45, 46, 50
  family background of, 15–24

  as father, 68, 69, 81–82, 101, 112, 123, 162,
    181, 183, 184, 248, 345–348, 360,
    395–396, 549
  foreign travels of, 29, 42–44, 50–54, 83–87,
    91–92, 268, 276, 278–310, 343–345,
    400–402, 407–413, 434–436, 493–494,
    515, 536–537, 549
  Hamlet image of, 178, 352–354
  health of, 35, 189–190, 331–332, 327, 515,
    544, 554, 555–556
  homes of, 66, 67–68, 505
  honors given to, 96, 102, 326, 358, 399, 423,
    512, 556, 560
  humor of, 138–139, 176, 203, 242, 250–251,
    446, 469, 491, 508
  income of, 54, 58, 60, 67, 97, 128, 395
  indecisiveness attributed to, 114, 169, 183,
    205, 253–254, 491
  as lawyer, 54, 60, 65, 66, 67, 70–71, 75, 96,
    101, 116, 185, 342–343, 394, 395,
    543–544, 558–559
  marriage of, 50, 56–60, 62–63, 65, 81–82,
    101, 124, 140, 353
  name of, 25
  nicknames of, 40, 43
  personal attacks on, 530–536, 537
  political defeat and, 259–262, 272, 389–392
  press and, 203–204, 249–250, 251–252, 272,
    362
  on public affairs, 71, 88
  racial issues and, 85, 167–168, 177, 221–223,
    327, 364, 369, 374, 384, 403–404
  radio talks by, 135, 136–137, 149
  romantic life of, 28, 34–35, 36, 40, 45–46,
    50, 124–125, 164–166, 397–399,
    554–555
  shooting accident and, 30–31, 353, 360
  social life of, 39, 45, 46, 54–56, 60–61, 65,
    162–163, 273–274, 277, 343, 505–506,
    554–555
  social service commitments of, 55, 60, 70
  as speaker, 65–66, 83, 102, 105, 114–115,
    121–123, 139, 174–175, 194–196, 207,
    248–249, 312–313, 332, 368–369, 372,
    441–442, 512, 526, 530, 648, 560
  thoughtfulness of, 117, 162
  thriftiness of, 21, 60, 261
  as titular head of Democrats, 311–339
  young people and, 118, 152, 169, 171–172,
    506–507, 560
  see also specific individuals and topics
Stevenson, Adlai Ewing III (son):
  birth of, 60
  career of, 396, 549
  childhood of, 68–69, 97, 100, 101
  children of, 367, 389, 541
  education of, 123
  father's campaigns and, 112, 121, 131–132,
    375, 452
  father's visits with, 112, 181, 354, 516, 541,
    565
  in Marine Corps, 190, 222, 310
  marriage of, 329–331, 342, 345–348, 352
  mother's illness and, 478, 516, 544–545
  on parents' marriage, 81–82, 141
  travels of, 355, 399, 401, 402, 424

Stevenson, Adlai Ewing IV (grandson), 389, 545
Stevenson, Borden (son), 555, 556
  childhood of, 60, 68, 69, 97, 99, 123, 131–132, 141, 174, 396
  family visits and, 181, 326, 389, 399, 506, 541–542
  father's campaigns and, 121, 192, 260, 390
  mother's illness and, 331, 347–348, 544
  travels of, 298, 408, 410, 411, 493
Stevenson, Elizabeth Ewing "Buffie," see Ives, Elizabeth Ewing Stevenson "Buffie"
Stevenson, Ellen Borden (wife):
  appearance of, 56, 61
  artistic interests of, 57–58, 61, 81, 101, 114
  background of, 56–57
  damaging behavior of, 189, 190, 192, 198, 353
  daughter-in-law opposed by, 329–331, 345–348
  death of, 545
  divorce of, 140–142, 143, 161–162, 237, 397
  finances of, 60, 70, 141, 516, 544
  husband's career and, 89, 92, 93, 102, 105, 111–114, 121, 123–124, 126, 131–132, 139–140, 247
  marriage of, 50, 56–60, 62–63, 65, 67–68, 81–82, 101, 124, 140
  mental illness of, 57–58, 66–67, 69–70, 124, 140, 164, 184, 237, 329–331, 345–348, 362, 396, 478, 507, 544–545
  as mother, 60, 69, 81–82, 100, 360
  social life of, 60–61, 70, 99, 102
  on Stevenson family, 15
  travels of, 96, 97, 99, 100, 563
  Washington life and, 63, 80–81, 89, 92, 93
Stevenson, E. M. (cousin), 59
Stevenson, Helen Davis (mother):
  daughter-in-law vs., 61
  death of, 66
  health of, 24–25, 27, 39, 66
  marriage of, 22, 26–27, 59, 60, 61
  as mother, 24–28, 30–32, 35, 37, 39, 41, 43, 44
  musical interests of, 25–26, 33
  Pantagraph and, 48–49
  travel by, 29, 32, 44, 51, 59
Stevenson, James (great-great-grandfather), 15
Stevenson, John Fell (son), 45, 538
  in auto accident, 359–360, 362, 396
  campaigns and, 191–192, 260, 375
  childhood of, 60, 68, 97, 100, 102, 114, 139, 141, 181–182
  family visits and, 181, 326, 345, 389, 399, 541–542
  at inauguration, 131–133
  marriage of, 512
  mother's illness and, 331, 362, 507
  travels of, 298, 308, 326, 408–411, 427, 434, 515
Stevenson, John Turner (ancestor), 16
Stevenson, Letitia Green (grandmother), 16–17, 18, 33

Stevenson, Lewis (father):
  death of, 59–60
  family life of, 17, 30–37, 39, 43, 45, 50, 51, 60–61
  health of, 23, 26
  jobs of, 18, 23–24, 27, 39, 42
  marriage of, 22, 26–27, 60
  political career of, 29, 30, 33, 34, 37–38, 42, 46–47, 58, 61, 62
  temper of, 26, 27, 36
Stevenson, Lucy Wallace (granddaughter), 408–409
Stevenson, Mary (aunt), 26
Stevenson, Nancy Anderson (daughter-in-law):
  campaign and, 375, 452
  children of, 367, 389, 541
  marriage of, 329–331, 345–348, 352, 396
  Stevenson's visits and, 354, 399, 401, 402, 424
  travels of, 355, 399, 401, 402, 424
Stevenson, Nancy Brevard (great-great-grandmother), 15
Stevenson, Natalie Owings (daughter-in-law), 512, 515, 538, 541
Stevenson, Robert Louis, 536
Stevenson, William (ancestor), 15
Stevenson for President Committee, 180, 203, 357, 369, 438
Stilwell, Joseph, 284, 496
Stimson, Henry L., 73, 75
Stokes, Thomas L., 268
Stone, Dewey, 450
Stone, John Timothy, 58
Stoneman, William H., 100–101
Stratton, William G., 186
Strauss, Lewis, 381
Stuart, Jeb, 69
Stuart, John T., 18
Suez Canal, 298, 299, 386–388, 391
Sukarno, Achmed, 289, 500–501
Sullivan, Roger, 37
Sullivan, T. P., 133
Sulzberger, Arthur Hays, 234
Summersby, Kay, 237
Sun Li-jen, 283–284
Sun Yat-sen, 284
Swing, Raymond Gram, 89, 163
Symington, Stuart, 393, 450
  as presidential candidate, 416, 417, 449, 451, 453, 455, 462
Syria, 297, 299, 300–301

Taft, Robert A., 94, 174, 241, 268, 309–310, 317–318
  candidacy of, 170, 178, 180, 181, 190, 192, 198, 211, 242, 271
Taft, William Howard, 17, 179
Taft-Hartley Act, 218–219
Taiwan (Formosa), 276, 283–285, 348–352, 414, 423, 433
Talmadge, Herman, 326
Taylor, Harold, 478
Taylor, Maxwell, 282–283
Taylor, Myron, 78
television, political campaigns and, 185, 250, 374, 383–384, 444–446

Tempelsman, Maurice, 408
Templar, Sir Gerald, 290, 291
Thailand, 292
Thanksgiving Day Massacre, 503–504
Thant, U, 292, 502
   Cuban missile crisis and, 524–526, 529
   Vietnam and, 545–546, 551–554, 559–565,
      567
third world, 423, 484–485, 504, 509–514
Tholand, Nils K., 86
Thompson, "Big Bill," 107
Thompson, Llewellyn, 306, 495
Thompson, Walter, 138
Thousand Days, A (Schlesinger), 449–450,
   491, 532–533
Till, Emmett, 364
Tillett, Gladys, 477
Time, 31, 119, 171, 176, 177, 180, 495, 515
Tito (Josip Broz), 304, 305, 386, 515
Tocqueville, Alexis de, 332
Tolstoy, Countess Sophia, 53
Tonkin Gulf incident, 547
Touré, Sekou, 426–427
Toynbee, Arnold, 310
Treaty of Versailles (1919), 42
Tree, Marietta, 343, 477, 563
   background of, 99, 272–273, 424
   daughters of, 374, 401, 506, 537
   Stevenson's correspondence with, 288, 331,
      409, 467–468, 507, 555, 558
   Stevenson's friendship with, 272–274, 391,
      394, 397, 555, 556
   Stevenson's political campaigns and,
      369–370, 425, 437, 452, 459
   travels of, 401, 424, 452, 537
Tree, Sir Ronald, 99, 272, 273, 401, 437
Trotsky, Leon, 53
Trujillo, Rafael, 503
Truman, Harry S, 140, 275, 312, 416
   anti-Communism and, 229, 230, 320
   appointments of, 94, 96, 204, 207, 229, 231,
      315, 320, 473, 477
   campaigns of, 105, 115–116, 120, 126, 173,
      250, 380
   criticism of, 214, 229, 230, 252, 322
   Democratic party and, 195, 198, 267–270,
      313–314, 394
   domestic policies of, 212, 213, 245
   on Eisenhower, 240
   foreign policy of, 189, 241–245, 276,
      285–286, 327
   Kefauver disliked by, 186, 202
   party leadership and, 204–206
   reelection question and, 170, 174, 184–185
   Stevenson's nominations and, 176, 177–183,
      187, 190, 196–197, 199, 201–202, 254,
      352, 357, 375–376, 407
   United Nations and, 100, 102, 174
Truman, Margaret, 274
Truman Doctrine, 303, 305
Trumbull, Robert, 294
Tshombe, Moise, 482
Tubby, Roger, 269, 357, 360, 368
Tucker, Robert, 408, 409, 411
Tufts, Bob, 208, 214, 314, 349, 370, 510–511
Tully, Grace, 78

Turkey, 303–304, 443
Tydings, Millard, 326

Udall, Stewart L., 407
Underwood, Lorna, 45, 46, 467
United Auto Workers, 209, 218
United Mine Workers, 167, 177
United Nations, 165, 516
   administrative structure of, 97–98, 483–484,
      501, 502
   armed troops of, 481–482, 537, 546
   assessments by, 542–543, 557
   China's membership in, 309, 423, 433, 486,
      498, 500, 502, 517
   criticism of, 119, 175, 513–514
   Cuban missile crisis and, 517, 519–536
   delegates to, 477
   establishment of, 94–101, 127
   first General Assembly sessions of, 99–101,
      102, 103–105, 106
   headquarters of, 98–99, 174
   Korean War and, 241, 242, 281
   member states of, 482, 498, 508, 537
   Middle East and, 358, 363, 387
   politics within, 489–490
   procedural rules of, 556–557
   public education on, 89, 94, 102
   relief agency of, 103
   Stevenson as alternate delegate to, 102–103
   Stevenson as ambassador to, 472–477,
      481–565
   Stevenson as head of U.S. delegation at,
      97–101
   third world vs. European orientation in,
      484–485, 504, 509–514
   U.S. racial issues and, 177
   U.S. support of, 509–514
   Vietnam and, 548–554, 557, 559–565
Utley, Clifton, 64, 72–73, 74
Utley, Frayn, 124
U-2 incident, 441–443, 446, 447

Van Buren, Martin, 179
Vandenberg, Arthur, 94, 95, 103, 105, 243
Velde, Harold, 320
Vietnam, 92, 245, 287, 288, 541, 543, 545–554,
   557, 559–565, 567
Viner, Jacob, 65
Vinson, Fred M., 171, 174, 176, 180, 186, 270
Voice of America, 318, 386, 411
Voice of Latin America, The (Benton),
   435–436
Volunteers for Stevenson, 202, 209, 258, 262,
   264
Voorhis, Jerry, 228

Walker, Edwin A., 538–539
Walker, Harold, 169
Walker, Kenneth, 360–361
Walker, Thomas, 16
Wallace, Henry A., 79, 116
Wallner, Woodruff, 304
Warburg, James P., 349
Ward, Barbara (Lady Jackson), 331, 397, 399,
   400, 505, 555, 561

correspondence with, 431, 467, 469, 502–503, 541
Warren, Earl, 225
Washington, George, 16, 34, 46
Washington Post, 90, 174, 225, 407
Waters, Ethel, 57
Wechsler, James, 561
Weinstein, Jacob, 363–364
Weisman, Al, 196
Welling, Harriet, 55, 56, 64, 81, 505
Welling, John Paul, 55
What I Think (Stevenson), 313
Whig party, 19
White, Harry Dexter, 320
White, Theodore H., 415, 417–418, 443–444, 456, 458, 459
 on Stevenson's influence, 464, 470, 567
White, William Allen, 72, 73
White Committee, 72–73, 74, 75, 118
Whitmer, Bob, 30
Whitney, Thomas, 408
"Who Runs the Gambling Machines?" (Stevenson), 153
Wickenden, Elizabeth, 314
Wiesner, Jerome, 370
Wigmore, John Henry, 50
Williams, G. Mennen, 473, 484
Willkie, Wendell, 73, 341, 462
Wilson, Charles E., 274
Wilson, Harold, 562
Wilson, Richard, 185
Wilson, Thomas W., 522, 548
Wilson, Woodrow, 36, 37, 40, 44–45, 46, 47, 179, 452

presidential campaigns of, 29, 30, 173
Stevenson's meeting with, 29
Winter, Ruth, 56, 61, 81
Wirtz, Willard, 130, 172, 360, 480
 law practice of, 342, 394, 479
 1960 election and, 417, 456, 461
 in Stevenson's 1952 campaign, 218, 356, 368, 380–381, 389
Wood, Robert E., 73, 74, 130
World War II, 72–89, 91, 94, 108, 232, 243
Wray, Charles W., 153–154
Wright, Louise, 95, 139, 175
Wright, Quincy, 65, 72
Wyatt, Wilson, 104, 330, 341, 462
 as campaign manager, 204–214, 220, 222, 248, 261, 368

Yates, Richard, 138
Yates, Sid, 196
Yoshida, Shigeru, 279
Yost, Charles, 477, 489, 490, 513, 549, 557
 Vietnam policy and, 541, 546, 547, 551, 553
Young, Roy E., 153
Young, Stephen, 234
Youngman, Lucy, 29
Yugoslavia, 304–305

Ziegler, Martha, 131
Ziffren, Paul, 393
Zorin, Valerian, 483, 489, 522–529, 536
Zurcher, Suzie Morton, 397, 398, 476
Zwicker, Ralph W., 321–322, 323